TENTH EDITION

KOVELS'

BOTTLES

PRICE LIST

ILLUSTRATED

W9-BZB-015

Ralph and Terry Kovel

Crown Trade Paperbacks
New York

BOOKS BY RALPH AND TERRY KOVEL

Published by Crown Trade Paperbacks, 201 East 50th Street, New York,
New York 10022. Member of the Crown Publishing Group.

Random House, Inc.   New York, Toronto, London, Sydney, Auckland

CROWN TRADE PAPERBACKS and colophon are trademarks of Crown Publishers, Inc.

Printed in the United States of America

Library of Congress Cataloging-in-Publication Data
Kovel, Ralph M.

Kovels' bottles price list / by Ralph and Terry Kovel.—9th ed.
p. cm.
Includes bibliographical references and index.
1. Bottles—United States—Catalogs. I. Kovel, Terry H.
II. Title
NK5440.B6K6   1992
748.8'2'   0973075—dc20   92-5192

ISBN 0-517-88435-6

10 9 8 7 6 5 4 3 2 1

First Edition

Keep Up On Prices All Year Long

Have you kept up with prices? They change! Last year a collector-dealer discovered a rare fire grenade at a sale in Europe. He bought it for more than $200. A few months later more of these "rarities" were found and the price of the fire grenades fell $100. When a barrel of them was found, the news came out that there were now many mint examples available and the price fell to $20. Prices change with discoveries, auction records, even historic events. Every entry and every picture in this book is new and current, thanks to modern computer technology. This book is a handy overall price guide, but you also need news.

Books on your shelf get older each month, and prices do change. Important sales produce new record prices. Rarities are discovered. Fakes appear. You will want to keep up with developments from month to month rather than from year to year. *Kovels on Antiques and Collectibles,* a nationally distributed, illustrated newsletter, includes up-to-date information on bottles and other collectibles. This monthly newsletter reports current prices, collecting trends, and landmark auction results for all types of antiques and collectibles, including bottles, and also contains tax, estate, security, and other pertinent news for collectors.

Additional information and a free sample newsletter are available from the authors at P.O. Box 22200-B, Beachwood, Ohio 44122.

Clues to the Contents of This Book

Some product slogans brag, "We did it right the first time." But we know that anything can be improved; and, with this new edition, we have put in a few extra features. This is the all new, better-than-ever, tenth edition of *Kovels' Bottles Price List.* We wrote the first bottle price guide twenty-five years ago. This year, the book's format has been updated to reflect the changing interests of the 1990s. Paragraphs have been expanded. The histories of companies and their products have been researched, and we have tried to note any important changes in ownership of modern brands. A new color-picture section provides a look back at the prices and trends of the past years.

All of the prices in the book are new. They are compiled from sales and offerings of the past year. You will find that many modern bottles are no longer listed by brand because collector interest has lagged. We still have extensive listings of the more popular modern bottles like Jim Beam and Ezra Brooks. The pictures of old bottles are all new and were taken with special equipment so that they will be clearer and more informative.

"Go-withs," the bottle-related items that are bought and sold at all the bottle shows, are listed in their own section at the end of the book. Jar openers, advertisements, corkscrews, bottle caps, and other items that picture or are used with bottles have been classified as bottle go-withs. There is a bibliography and a listing of publications included in this book to aid you in further research. This list was checked and is accurate as of January 1996. The national and state club lists are accurate as of January 1996. Unfortunately, addresses do change; if you cannot find one of the listed clubs, write us, P.O. Box 22200-B, Beachwood, Ohio 44122.

NOTE: Bottles which contained alcoholic beverages must be sold empty to conform with the law in most states. To sell a filled liquor bottle, you must have a liquor license from the state where you live or where you sell the bottle. It is illegal to ship full bottles across some state lines. The value is the same for full or empty liquor bottles.

DEFINITIONS

Novice collectors may need a few definitions to understand the terms used in this book. *A pontil mark* is a scar on the bottom of a bottle. It was made by the punty rod that held the glass for the glassblower. If the scar is rough, it is called a *pontil*. If it is smoothed out, it is called a *ground pontil*. *Free-blown* or *blown* means that the glass was blown by the glassmaker, using a blowpipe; it was not poured into a mold. *Mold-blown* means it was blown into a mold as part of the forming process. A *kick-up* is the deep indentation on the bottom of a bottle. Kick-ups are very often found on wine bottles. Describing glass as *whittled* or having *whittle marks* means there are irregular marks that look like the rough surface of a piece of whittled wood. Such marks are found on bottles that were made before 1900 and were caused by hot glass being blown into a cold mold. *Embossed* lettering is raised lettering. *Etched* lettering was cut into the bottle with acid or a sharp instrument. *Bubbles, teardrops,* or *seeds* describe types of bubbles that form in glass. A *seam* is the line left on the bottle by the mold. A seam may go up the neck of the bottle. If it goes over the lip, the bottle was machine made. An *applied lip* is handmade and applied to the bottle after the glassmaker has formed the bottle. A *sheared lip* is found on bottles made before 1840. The top of the bottle was cut from the blowpipe with shears and the result is the sheared lip. The *2-piece,* or *BIMAL, mold* was used from about 1860 to 1900. The *3-piece mold* was used from 1820 to 1880. The automatic bottle machine was invented in 1903, and *machine-made* bottles were the norm after that date. *Black glass* is not really black. It is very dark olive green or olive amber that appears black unless seen in a bright light. *Milk glass* is an opaque glass made by using tin or zinc in the mixture. Although most milk glass is white, it is correct to call colored glass of this type "blue" or "green" milk glass. If glass that was made from 1880 to 1914 is left in strong sunlight, it often turns colors. This is because of the chemical content of the old glass. Bottles can turn purple, pale lavender, or shades of green or brown. These bottles are called *sun-colored*. Bottles can also be *iridized* and colored by a radiation process similar to that used for preserving vegetables. There are a few other terms that relate to only one type of bottle, and these terms have been identified in the proper paragraphs.

Bottle clubs and bottle shows have set the rules for this edition of *Kovels' Bottles Price List*. We have used the terms preferred by the collectors and have tried to organize the thousands of listings in an easy-to-use format. Many abbreviations have been included that are part of the bottle collectors' language. The abbreviations are listed below and appear throughout the book.

ABM means automatic bottle machine.

ACL means applied color label, a pyroglaze or enameled lettering.

BIMAL means blown in mold, applied lip, open pontil.

DUG means literally dug from the ground.

FB means free blown.

IP means iron pontil.

ISP means inserted slug plate. Special names were sometimes embossed on a bottle, especially a milk bottle, with a special plate inserted in the mold.

OP means open pontil.

Pyro means pyroglaze or enamel lettering often found on milk bottles and soda bottles.

SC means sun-colored.

SCA means sun-colored amethyst.

To make the descriptions of the bottles as complete as possible, an identification number has been added to the description in some categories. The serious collector knows the important books about a specialty, and these books have numbered lists of styles of bottles. Included in this book are identification numbers for flasks from McKearin, bitters from Ring, and fruit jars from Creswick. The full titles of the books used are included in the Bibliography and listed in the introductory paragraph for each category.

Medicine bottles include all medicine bottles except those under the more specific headings such as "Bitters" or "Sarsaparilla." Modern bottles of major interest are listed under the brand name.

If you are not a regular at bottle shows, it may take a few tries to become accustomed to the method of listing used in this book. If you cannot find a bottle, try several related headings. For instance, hair products are found under "Cosmetic" and "Cure."

Many named bottles are found under "Medicine," "Food," "Fruit Jar," etc. If your fruit jar has several names, such as "Ball Mason," look under "Fruit Jar, Ball" or "Fruit Jar, Mason." If no color is listed, the bottle is clear.

The prices shown for bottles are the *actual* prices asked for or bid for bottles during the past year. We know collectors try to get discounts, so some of these bottles may have sold for a little less than the listed price. Prices vary in different parts of the country and, if more than one price for a bottle has been recorded, a range is given. Because of the idiosyncrasies of the computer, it was impossible to place a range on prices of bottles that are illustrated. The prices listed for the bottles illustrated in the book are actual prices or an average of several actual prices.

Spelling is meant to help the collector. If the original bottle spelled "Catsup" as "Ketchup," that is the spelling that appears. The abbreviation "Dr." for "doctor" may appear on bottles as "Dr" (no period) or "Dr." (period). However, we have included a period each time to keep the computer alphabetizing more consistent, except in the case of bottles of Dr Pepper. The period was omitted in Dr Pepper by the company in 1950, and we use whatever appeared on the bottle. Also, if a word is written, for example, "Kennedy's," "Kennedys'," or "Kennedys," we have placed the apostrophe or omitted it as it appeared on the bottle. A few bottles are included that had errors in the original spelling in the bottle mold. In these cases the error is explained. Medicine, bitters, and other bottle types sometimes use the term "Dr." and sometimes use just the last name of the doctor. We have used the wording as it appears on the bottle. The one exception is "Whiskey," which is used even if the bottle held scotch or Canadian or was spelled "Whisky."

Every bottle or go-with illustrated in black and white is indicated by the abbreviation "Illus" in the text. Bottles shown in color pictures are priced in the center section where they appear.

We have tried to be accurate but cannot be responsible for any errors in pricing or information that may appear. Any information about clubs, prices, or content for future books will be considered for the next book. Please send it to Kovels, P.O. Box 22200-B, Beachwood, Ohio 44122.

Ralph M. Kovel, Life Member, Federation of Historical Bottle Clubs
Accredited Senior Appraiser, American Society of Appraisers

Terry H. Kovel, Life Member, Federation of Historical Bottle Clubs
Accredited Senior Appraiser, American Society of Appraisers

ACKNOWLEDGMENTS

We want to give special thanks to Ronald Binek and the Metropolitan Detroit Antique Bottle Clubs for allowing us to take photographs at their 22nd Annual Show and Sale in Livonia, Michigan. Exhibitors and visitors were gracious and helped us find the best bottles to picture. Thanks to this very enthusiastic group of bottle collectors. More thanks to Dale Mooney of Western Glass Auctions, who helped us with photographs and information based on his sales.

Pictured items and information were furnished to us by Jeff Anders; Alvin J. Anderson; David Argentati; John C. Barclay; Charlie Barnette; BBR Auctions; Harold Beard; Bruce Bearman of Austin Nichols; Cyril Bish; Bill Borchert; Ralph Bowman; Doris Brooks; William E. Brown; Michael Brozik; Donald Burkett; Rodney Buroughs; Tom & Deena Caniff; Richard Coppler; Jim & Beth Daniels; Robert Dashek; Robert Davison; Steve Deboode; Doug Dezso; Howard Diffenbacher; Don Eager; William Edmondson; Tom Feltman; Ralph D. Finch; Fink's Off the Wall Auction; Brad Fortier; William Fry; Michael Garrett; Rob & Kath Goodacre; Ned Gowing; Kitty Grandstaff; Ernest Griffin; Jim & Jodi Hall; Bruce Hickman; Frank Hill; Gordon & Sharon Hubenet; Engvard Johnson; Robert Karle; Susan Kekete of Austin Nichols; Harold Kilgore; C. D. Knibbe; Knobby Pine Antique Market; Adam Koch; Bob & Linda Koimig; Sharon Kotlarsk; Shaun M. Kotarsky; Doris Ladd; Tim Landry; Lance Lewis; O.B. Lund; Keith Lunt; Shirlee MacDonald; Don McCall; Mark McNee; James Meehan; Nick Merten; Dale Mlasko; Monsen & Baer; Chris Morris, archivist for United Distillers; Nola Murdock; Joe R. Myhand; George Neneth; Mike Neuendorf; Wade Nicholson; Digger (John) Odell; Patrick Parish; Greg Price; Tom Quinn; Tom Ramsey; Steve & Cindy Reddin; Gene Rice; Stephanie Roberts; Dick & Darren Romitti; John Ronald; Richard Roosen; Joe Rubio; Lorraine Saucier; Harold Sauer; Jeff Scharnowske; Jerry Schmidt; Paul & Janet Schofield; Faye & John Shaw; Mark Slepak, one of the founders of Lionstone; Dave Stivers, archivist for Nabisco; Frank Sherman; Stuckey's Auction Co.; M. Elaine Sullivan; T.B.R. Bottle Consignments Auction; Jerry Tebbano; Michael Vande; George Waddy; Marian Walthorn; Robert & Kim Waterman; and Margaret Wunderlich. Thank you to all.

Each edition of this book about bottles seems to be better. That is because of the careful work of many of the staff. For doing so much of the price information plus the difficult problems of proofreading, special thanks to Edie Smrekar. And to the coordinator and "boss" of the project we say, "Thank you, Gay Hunter." Sharon Squibb, our editor, Pam Stinson-Bell, Merri Ann Morrell, and Karen Minster at Crown Publishing made the book look great. Benjamin Margalit took many of the black-and-white and color pictures, making even the common bottles look like gems.

PUBLICATIONS OF INTEREST TO BOTTLE COLLECTORS

-see the club list for other publications-

NEWSPAPERS

These are general newspapers with some articles and ads for bottles.

Antique Trader Weekly
P.O. Box 1050
Dubuque, Iowa 52004-1050
Collector's News

P.O. Box 156
Grundy Center, Iowa 50638

NEWSLETTERS

Advertising Collectors Express
P.O. Box 221
Mayview, Missouri 64071

Bitters Report
P.O. Box 1253
Bunnell, Florida 32110

Creamers
P.O. Box 11
Lake Villa, Illinois 60046-0011

Fruit Jar Newsletter
364 Gregory Avenue
West Orange, New Jersey
07052-3743
Just For Openers

3172 Sunningdale Way
Durham, North Carolina 27707

Kovels on Antiques and Collectibles
P.O. Box 22200-B
Beachwood, Ohio 44122

Mini-Scents
28227 Paseo El Siena
Laguna Niguel, California 92677
(miniature perfume bottles)

Root Beer Float
P.O. Box 571
Geneva, Wisconsin 53147

MAGAZINES

Antique Bottle & Glass Collector
P.O. Box 180
East Greenville,
Pennsylvania 18041

Bottles & Bygones
30 Brabant Road
Cheadle Hulme
Cheadle, Cheshire
SK8 7AU, England

British Bottle Review
5 Ironworks Row
Elsecar Project, Wath Road
Elsecar, Barnsley, S. Yorkshire S74
8HJ, England

Canadian Bottle
& Stoneware Collector
179 D Woodridge Crescent
Nepean, Canada ON K2B 7T2

The Miniature Bottle Collector
P.O. Box 2161
Palos Verdes Peninsula,
California 90274

BOTTLE CLUBS

There are hundreds of bottle clubs that welcome new members. The list of local clubs is arranged by state and city so that you can find the club nearest your home. If no local club listed is nearby, we suggest you contact the national organizations, which follow. Any active bottle club that is not listed and wishes to be included in future editions of *Kovels' Bottles Price List* should send the necessary information to the authors, P.O. Box 22200-B, Beachwood, Ohio 44122. The information in this list has been compiled with the help of the Federation of Historical Bottle Collectors, The Miniature Bottle Collector, and the National Bottle Museum.

NATIONAL CLUBS

Many of these clubs have local chapters and shows.
Write to them for more information.

AMERICAN
BREWERIANA
ASSOCIATION, INC.
P.O. Box 11157
Pueblo, CO 81001

AMERICAN
COLLECTORS OF
INFANT FEEDERS
1849 Ebony Drive
York, PA 17402-4706

ANTIQUE ADVERTIS-
ING ASSOCIATION
OF AMERICA
P.O. Box 1121
Morton Grove, IL 60053

AVON TIMES
P.O. Box 9868
Kansas City, MO 64134

CANDY CONTAINER
COLLECTORS OF
AMERICA
PO Box 352
Chelmsford,
MA 01824-0352

COCA-COLA
COLLECTORS CLUB
INTERNATIONAL
P.O. Box 49166
Atlanta, GA 30359-1166

CREAM SEPARATOR
COLLECTORS
ASSOCIATION
W20772 State Road 95
Arcadia, WI 54612

CROWN COLLECTORS
SOCIETY INTERNA-
TIONAL
4300 San Juan Drive
Fairfax, VA 22030

DR PEPPER
COLLECTORS CLUB
P.O. Box 153221
Irving, TX 75015

EASTERN COAST
BREWERIANA
ASSOCIATION
P.O. Box 349
West Point, PA 19486

FEDERATION OF
HISTORICAL BOTTLE
COLLECTORS
c/o Barbara Harms
P.O. Box 224
Dolton, IL 60419

FIGURAL
BOTTLE OPENER
COLLECTORS
117 Basin Hill Road
Duncannon, PA 17020

INTERNATIONAL
ASSOCIATION OF JIM
BEAM BOTTLE AND
SPECIALTIES CLUBS
2015 Burlington Avenue
Kewanee, IL 61443

INTERNATIONAL
CHINESE SNUFF
BOTTLE SOCIETY
2601 North Charles
Street
Baltimore, MD 21218

INTERNATIONAL
PERFUME BOTTLE
ASSOCIATION
3519 Wycliffe Drive
Modesto, CA 95355

INTERNATIONAL
SWIZZLE STICK
COLLECTORS
ASSOCIATION
P.O. Box 1117
Bellingham, WA
98227-1117

JELLY JAMMERS
(jelly jars)
6086 West Boggstown
Road
Boggstown, IN 46110

LILLIPUTIAN BOTTLE CLUB
5626 Corning Avenue
Los Angeles, CA 90056

NATIONAL ASSOCIATION OF AVON COLLECTORS CLUB
P.O. Box 7006
Kansas City, MO 64113

NATIONAL ASSOCIATION OF BREWERIANA ADVERTISING
2343 Met-To-Wee Lane
Wauwatosa, WI 53226

NATIONAL ASSOCIATION OF MILK BOTTLE COLLECTORS, INC.
4 Ox Bow Road
Westport, CT
06880-2602

NATIONAL ASSOCIATION OF PAPER AND ADVERTISING COLLECTORS
P.O. Box 500
Mount Joy,
PA 17552-9984

NATIONAL SKI COUNTRY BOTTLE CLUB
1224 Washington Avenue
Golden, CO 80401

PAINTED SODA BOTTLE COLLECTOR'S ASSOCIATION
9418 Hilmer Drive
LaMesa, CA 91942

PEPSI-COLA COLLECTORS CLUB
P.O. Box 817
Claremont, CA 91711

SOCIETY OF INKWELL COLLECTORS
5136 Thomas Avenue South
Minneapolis, MN 55410

TOPS & BOTTOMS CLUB
(for Renee Lalique bottles only)
P.O. Box 15555
Plantation, FL 33317

VIOLIN BOTTLE COLLECTORS ASSOCIATION OF AMERICA
21815 106th Street East
Buckley, WA 98321

WHISKY PITCHER COLLECTORS ASSOCIATION OF AMERICA
19341 West Tahoe Drive
Mundelein,
IL 60060-40612

STATE CLUBS

ALABAMA

Mobile Bottle
 Collectors Club
8844 Lee Circle
IRVINGTON, AL 36544

Montgomery Bottle &
 Insulator Club
2021 Merrily Drive
MONTGOMERY,
AL 36111

ARIZONA

Phoenix Antique Bottle
 & Collectors Club
1939 West Waltann Lane
PHOENIX, AZ 85023

ARKANSAS

Indian Country Antique
 Bottle & Relic Society
3818 Hilltop Drive
JONESBORO,
AR 72401

Little Rock Antique
 Bottle Collectors Club
16201 Highway 300
ROLAND, AR 72135

CALIFORNIA

California Miniature
 Bottle Club
1911 Willow Street
ALAMEDA, CA 94501

Bakersfield Bottle &
 Insulator Collectors
1023 Baldwin Road
BAKERSFIELD,
CA 93304

Miniature Bottle Club
 of Southern California
836 Carob
BREA, CA 92621

Fresno Antique Bottle
 & Collectors Club
281 West Magill Avenue
CLOVIS, CA 93612

Mother Lode Antique
 Bottle Club
P.O. Box 165
DOWNIEVILLE,
CA 95936

San Luis Obispo
 Bottle Society
124-21st Street
PASO ROBLES,
CA 93446

'49er Historical Bottle
 Association
P.O. Box 561
PENRYN, CA 95663

Superior California
 Bottle Club
3220 Stratford Avenue
REDDING, CA 96001

Golden Gate Historical
 Bottle Society
P.O. Box 5331
RICHMOND, CA 94805

Mission Trail Historical
Bottle Club
1475 Teton Avenue
SALINAS, CA 93906

San Bernardino County
Historical Bottle &
Collectors Club
P.O. Box 6759
SAN BERNARDINO,
CA 92412

San Diego Antique
Bottle Club
P.O. Box 5137
SAN DIEGO, CA 92165

San Jose Historical
Bottle Collectors
Association
P.O. Box 5432
SAN JOSE, CA 95150

Los Angeles Historical
Bottle Club
1030 West MacArthur
Boulevard, #154
SANTA ANA,
CA 92707

Northwestern Bottle
Collectors Association
P.O. Box 1121
SANTA ROSA,
CA 95402

Sequoia Antique Bottle
& Collectable Society
P.O. Box 3695
VISALIA, CA 93278

COLORADO

Southern Colorado
Antique Bottle
Collectors
843 Ussie Avenue
CANON CITY,
CO 81212

Peaks & Plains
Antique Bottle &
Collectors Club, Inc.
308 Maplewood Drive
COLORADO SPRINGS,
CO 80907-4326

Antique Bottles &
Collectables of
Colorado
P.O. Box 245
LITTLETON, CO 80160

Western Slope
Bottle Club
P.O. Box 354
PALISADE, CO 81526

CONNECTICUT

Somers Antique
Bottle Club
27 Plank Lane
GLASTONBURY,
CT 06033-2523

Southern Connecticut
Antique Bottle
Collectors
Association, Inc.
34 Dartmouth Drive
HUNTINGTON,
CT 06484

DELAWARE

Delmarva Antique
Bottle Collectors
57 Lakewood Drive
LEWES, DE 19958

Tri-State Bottle
Collectors &
Diggers Club
2510 Cratchett Road
WILMINGTON,
DE 19808

FLORIDA

M-T Bottle Collectors
Association Inc.
P.O. Box 1581
DELAND, FL 32720

Treasure Coast Bottle
Collectors
6301 Lilyan Parkway
FT. PIERCE, FL 34951

Sun Coast Antique
Bottle Collectors
Association, Inc.
5305 8th Avenue South
GULFPORT, FL33707

Antique Bottle Collectors
of North Florida
P.O. Box 14796
JACKSONVILLE,
FL 32238

Central Florida Insulator
Collectors Club
707 N.E. 113th Street
MIAMI, FL 33161

Mid-State Antique
Bottle Collectors, Inc.
3400 East Grant Avenue
ORLANDO, FL 32806

Association of Florida
Antique Bottle Clubs
P.O. Box 3105
SARASOTA, FL 34230

GEORGIA

Southeastern Antique
Bottle Club
1546 Summerford Court
DUNWOODY, GA
30338

HAWAII

Hawaii Historical
Bottle Collectors Club
P.O. Box 90456
HONOLULU, HI 96835

Hilo Bottle Club
287 Kanoelani Street
HILO, HI 96720

ILLINOIS

Metro-East Bottle
& Jar Association
309 Bellevue Drive
BELLEVILLE, IL 62223

First Chicago Bottle
Club
P.O. Box A3382
CHICAGO, IL 60690

Pekin Bottle
Collectors Association
1511 Norwood Avenue
PEKIN, IL 61554

Antique Bottle Collectors
of Northern Illinois
436 Center
WOODSTOCK,
IL 60098

INDIANA

Midwest Antique
Fruit Jar & Bottle Club
P.O. Box 38
FLAT ROCK, IN 47234

Fort Wayne
Historical Bottle Club
P.O. Box 475
HUNTERTOWN,
IN 46748

IOWA

Iowa Antique Bottleers
Route 1, Box 145
MILTON, IA 52570

KANSAS

Southeast Kansas
Bottle & Relic Club
Route 2, Box 107
HUMBOLDT,
KS 66748

North Central
Kansas Antique Bottle
& Collectors Club
336 East Wisconsin
RUSSELL, KS 67665

KENTUCKY

Kentuckiana
Antique Bottle &
Outhouse Society
4017 Shady Villa Drive
LOUISVILLE,
KY 40219

MAINE

New England
Antique Bottle Club
RFD 1, Box 408
NORTH BERWICK,
ME 03906

MARYLAND

Baltimore Antique
Bottle Collectors, Inc.
P.O. Box 36061
TOWSON, MD 21286

MASSACHUSETTS

Berkshire Antique
Bottle Association
Box 415
MONTEREY,
MA 01245

MICHIGAN

Great Lakes
Miniature Bottle Club
P.O. Box 230460
FAIR HAVEN,
MI 48023

Metropolitan Detroit
Antique Bottle Club
410 Lothrop Road
GROSSE POINT
FARMS, MI 48236

Kalamazoo Antique
Bottle Club
1121 Maywood
KALAMAZOO,
MI 49001

Flint Antique Bottle
& Collectable Club
6349 Silver Lake Road
LINDEN, MI 48451

Grand Rapids
Antique Bottle Club
1368 Kinney N.W.
WALKER, MI 49504

Huron Valley Bottle
& Insulators Club
2475 West Walton
WATERFORD,
MI 48329-4435

MINNESOTA

Minnesota First
Antique Bottle Club
5001 Queen Avenue
North
MINNEAPOLIS,
MN 55430

North Star Historical
Bottle Association
3308 32nd Avenue South
MINNEAPOLIS,
MN 55406

MISSOURI

St. Louis Antique Bottle
Collectors Association
71 Outlook Drive
HILLSBORO, MO
63050

NEBRASKA

Nebraska Antique Bottle
& Collectors Club
14835 Drexel Street
OMAHA, NE 68137

NEVADA

Las Vegas Bottle Club
3901 East Stewart, #16
LAS VEGAS, NV
89110

Antique Bottle Club
of Reno & Sparks
P.O. Box 1061
VERDI, NV 89439

NEW HAMPSHIRE

Yankee Bottle Club
382 Court Street
KEENE,
NH 03431-2534

Merrimack Valley
Antique Bottle
Collectors
776 Harvey Road,
Route 10
MANCHESTER,
NH 03103

New England
Antique Bottle Club
4 Francove Drive
SOMERSWORTH,
NH 03878

Central New Hampshire
Antique Bottle Club
RFD 2, Box 1A
Winter Street
TILTON, NH 03276

NEW JERSEY

South Jersey's
  Heritage Bottle
  & Glass Collectors
P.O. Box 122
GLASSBORO, NJ
08028

North Jersey
  Antique Bottle
  Collectors Association
36 Williams Street
LINCOLN PARK,
  NJ 07035

Central Jersey
  Bottle Club
93 North Main Street
NEW EGYPT, NJ 08533

Jersey Shore Bottle Club
P.O. Box 995
TOMS RIVER,
  NJ 08754

NEW YORK

Lions Club
  of Ballston Spa
37 Grove Street
BALLSTON SPA,
  NY 12020

Western New York
  Miniature Liquor Club
P.O. Box 182
CHEEKTOWAGA,
  NY 14225

Mohawk Valley
  Antique Bottle Club
1735 State Route 173
CHITTENANGO,
  NY 13037

Hudson Valley
  Bottle Club
6 Columbus Avenue
CORNWALL ON
  HUSDON, NY 12520

Finger Lakes Bottle
  Collectors Association
3250 Dubois Road
ITHACA, NY 14850

Long Island Antique
  Bottle Association
46 Evergreen Avenue
PATCHOGUE,
  NY 11772

Genesee Valley Bottle
  Collectors Association
Box 15528
West Ridge Station
ROCHESTER, NY
  14615

Ball Metal
  Container Group
One Adams Road
SARATOGA SPRINGS,
  NY 12866-9036

Empire State Bottle
  Collectors Association
P.O. Box 3421
SYRACUSE, NY 13220

NORTH CAROLINA

Western North Carolina
  Antique Bottle Club
P.O. Box 18481
ASHEVILLE, NC 28814

The Johnnyhouse
  Inspector's Bottle Club
1972 East
  US 74 Highway
HAMLET, NC 28345

OHIO

Ohio Bottle Club, Inc.
P.O. Box 585
BARBERTON,
  OH 44203

Southwestern Ohio
  Antique Bottle
  & Jar Club
273 Hilltop Drive
DAYTON, OH 45415

Findlay Antique
  Bottle Club
407 Cimarron Court
FINDLAY, OH 45840

Superior Bottle Club
22000 Shaker Boulevard
SHAKER HEIGHTS,
  OH 44122

OKLAHOMA

Midwest Miniature
  Bottle Collector
3108 Meadowood Drive
MIDWEST CITY,
  OK 73110-1407

Oklahoma Territory
  Bottle & Relic Club
1300 South
  Blue Haven Drive
MUSTANG, OK 73064

Tulsa Antique
  Bottle and Relic Club
P.O. Box 4278
TULSA, OK 74519

OREGON

Oregon Bottle Collectors
3565 Dee Highway
HOOD RIVER,
  OR 97031

Siskiyou Antique
  Bottle Collectors
2715 East McAndrews
MEDFORD, OR 97504

Empire City
  Old Bottle Society
1991 Sherman Avenue,
  Suite #206
NORTH BEND,
  OR 97459

Northwest Mini Club
  of Portland
P.O. Box 6551
PORTLAND, OR 97228

PENNSYLVANIA

Washington County
  Antique Bottle Club
RD 2, Box 342
CARMICHAELS,
  PA 15320

Laurel Valley Bottle
  Club
P.O. Box 201
HOSTETTER,
  PA 15638

Ligonier Historical
  Bottle Collectors
P.O. Box 188
LIGONIER, PA 15658

Bedford County
  Bottle Club
P.O. Box 116
LOYSBURG, PA 16659

Kiski Mini Beam
  & Specialties Club
816 Cranberry Drive
MONROEVILLE,
  PA 15146

Forks of the
  Delaware Bottle
  Collectors Association
164 Farmview Road
NAZARETH,
  PA 18064-2500

Pittsburgh Antique
  Bottle Club
235 Main Entrance Drive
PITTSBURGH,
  PA 15228

Del-Val Miniature
  Bottle Club
57-104 Delaire
  Landing Road
PHILADELPHIA,
  PA 19114

Jefferson County
  Antique Bottle Club
6 Valley View Drive
WASHINGTON,
  PA 15301

Pennsylvania Bottle
  Collectors Association
251 Eastland Avenue
YORK, PA 17402

RHODE ISLAND

Little Rhody Bottle Club
210 South Pier Road
NARRAGANSETT,
  RI 02882

TENNESSEE

Memphis Bottle
  Collectors Club
3706 Deerfield Cove
BARTLETT, TN 38135

Middle Tennessee
  Bottle Collectors Club
1221 Nichol Lane
NASHVILLE,
  TN 37205

East Tennessee
  Bottle Society
220 Carter School Road
STRAWBERRY
  PLAINS, TN 37871

TEXAS

Gulf Coast Bottle
  & Jar Club
P.O. Box 1754
PASADENA, TX 77501

North Texas
  Longhorn Bottle Club
4205 Donnington Drive
PLANO, TX 75092

Austin Bottle
  & Insulator Collectors
1300 Sunrise, #269
ROUND ROCK,
  TX 78664

UTAH

Utah Antique Bottle
  & Relic Club
517 South Hayes
MIDVALE, UT 84047

VIRGINIA

Potomac Bottle
  Collectors
8411 Porter Lane
ALEXANDRIA,
  VA 22308

Historical Bottle
  Diggers of Virginia
242 East Grattar Street
HARRISONBURG,
  VA 22801

Richmond Area
  Bottle Collectors
  Association Inc.
7024 Pointer Ridge Road
MIDLOTHIAN,
  VA 23112

Apple Valley
  Bottle Collectors Club
P.O. Box 2201
WINCHESTER,
  VA 22601

WASHINGTON

Washington Bottle
  Collectors Association
5492 Hannegan Road
BELLINGHAM,
  WA 98226

WISCONSIN

Antique Bottle Club
  of Northern Illinois
P.O. Box 571
GENEVA, WI 53147

Milwaukee Antique
  Bottle Club
2343 Met-To-Wee Lane
WAUWATOSA,
  WI 53226
e-mail: MTTRILLY@
  eWORLD.COM

CANADA

Bytown Bottle Seekers'
  Club
7 Queenston Drive
RICHMOND,
  ONTARIO, CANADA
  K0A 2Z0
e-mail: af262@
  freenet.carleton.ca

Four Seasons Bottle
  Collectors Club
8 Stillbrook Court
WEST HILL,
  ONTARIO,
  CANADA M1E 3N7

OTHER SOURCES

National Bottle Museum
76 Milton Avenue
Ballston Spa, NY 12020
518-885-7589

Rakow Library
Corning Museum of Glass
One Museum Way
Corning, NY 14830-2253
607-937-5371

AUCTION GALLERIES

Some of the prices and pictures in this book were furnished by these auction houses and dealers and we thank them. If you are interested in buying or selling bottles, you may want to contact these firms.

BBR AUCTIONS
5 Ironworks Row
Elsecar Project,
Wath Road
Elsecar, Barnsley
S. Yorkshire,
S74 8HJ, England

CHARLES G. MOORE AMERICANA LTD.
(formerly Harmer
Rooke Galleries—
Americana Division)
32 East 57th Street
New York, NY 10022

COLLECTORS AUCTION SERVICES
R.R. 2, Box 431
Oil City, PA 16301

DUMOUCHELLE'S ART GALLERIES, INC.
409 East
Jefferson Avenue
Detroit, MI 48226
(Royal Doulton)

EARLY AUCTION CO.
123 Main Street
Milford, OH 45150

FINK'S OFF THE WALL AUCTIONS
108 East Seventh Street
Lansdale,
PA 19446-2622

GARTH'S AUCTIONS, INC.
P.O. Box 369
Delaware, OH 43015

GARY METZ'S MUDDY RIVER TRADING CO.
4803 Lange Lane SW
Roanoke, VA 24018

GLASS-WORKS AUCTIONS
P.O. Box 180
East Greenville,
PA 18041

GORE ENTERPRISES
P.O. Box 158
Huntington, VT 05462

HOWARD PARZOW
5 Bostwick Court
Gaithersburg,
MD 20878

MONSON AND BAER
P.O. Box 529
Vienna, VA 22183
(perfume bottles)

NORMAN C. HECKLER & COMPANY
79 Bradford Corner Road
Woodstock Valley,
CT 06282

NOSTALGIA PUBLICATIONS, INC.
21 South Lake Drive
Hackensack, NJ 07601

PACIFIC GLASS AUCTIONS
1507 21st Street,
Suite 203
Sacramento, CA 95814

POP SHOPPE
Jim Millar
2180 Ellery Avenue
Clovis, CA 93611-0652
(specializing in
ACL soda bottles)

RICHARD OPFER AUCTIONEERING, INC.
1919 Greenspring Drive
Timonium, MD 21093

ROCKY MOUNTAIN BREWERY COLLECTIBLES
P.O. Box 242
Winter Park,
CO 80482-0242

SHOT GLASS EXCHANGE
Box 219
Western Springs,
IL 60558

SKINNER, INC.
The Heritage
on the Garden
63 Park Plaza
Boston, MA 02116

STUCKEY'S AUCTION CO.
315 West Broad Street
Richmond, VA 23220

WESTERN GLASS AUCTIONS
The Bottle Mine
P.O. Box 28
New Brighton,
PA 15066

RICHARD W. WITHINGTON, INC.
Hillsboro, NH 03244

BIBLIOGRAPHY

We've found these books to be useful. Some may be out of print, but your local library should be able to get them for you through interlibrary loan.

GENERAL

Antique Bottles Collectors Encyclopedia with Price Guide. South Yorkshire, England: B.B.R. Publishing, 1986.

Blakeman, Alan. *Antique Bottles Collectors Encyclopaedia with Price Guide,* 2 volumes. Elsecar, Barnsley, England: B.B.R. Publishing, 1995.

Feldhaus, Ron. *The Bottles, Breweriana and Advertising Jugs of Minnesota: 1850–1920,* 2 volumes. Privately printed, 1986 and 1987 (6724 Xerxes Avenue South, Edina, Minnesota 55423).

Fletcher, Johnnie W. *Kansas Bottles: 1854 to 1915.* Privately printed, 1994 (1300 South Blue Haven Drive, Mustang, Oklahoma 73064).

Fred's Price Guide to Modern Bottles. Issued quarterly (P.O. Box 1423, Cheyenne, Wyoming 82003). (Price lists for modern bottles.)

Kovel, Ralph and Terry. *Kovels' Antiques & Collectibles Price List* (annual). New York: Crown Publishers.

McKearin, George L. and Helen. *Two Hundred Years of American Blown Glass.* New York: Crown Publishers, 1950.

Megura, Jim. *Official Price Guide Bottles.* New York: House of Collectibles, 1996.

Ohio Bottles, 20th Anniversary Edition. Barberton, Ohio: Ohio Bottle Club, 1989.

Polak, Michael. *Bottles Identification and Price Guide.* New York: Avon Books, 1994.

Toulouse, Julian Harrison. *Bottle Makers and Their Marks.* Camden, New Jersey: Thomas Nelson, Inc., 1971.

AVON

Avon 8 (1985) and *Avon 8: Supplement 1 (1987).* Pleasant Hill, California: Western World Publishing.

Hastin, Bud. *Bud Hastin's Avon Products & California Perfume Co. Collector's Encyclopedia,* 14th edition. Privately printed, 1995 (P.O. Box 9868, Kansas City, Missouri 64134).

BARBER

Holiner, Richard. *Collecting Barber Bottles.* Paducah, KY: Collector Books, 1987.

Odell, John. *Digger Odell's Official Antique Bottle and Glass Collector Magazine Price Guide, Volume 1: Barber Bottles.* Privately printed, 1995 (1910 Shawhan Road, Morrow, Ohio 45152).

BEAM

Cembura, Al, and Constance Avery. *A Guide to Jim Beam Bottles,* 12th edition. Privately printed, 1984 (139 Arlington Avenue, Berkeley, California 94707).

Honeyman, Betty, ed. *Jim Beam Bottles: A Pictorial Guide.* Downers Grove, Illinois: International Association of Jim Beam Bottle and Specialties Clubs, 1982. (2015 Burlington Avenue, Kewanee, Illinois 61443). Price guide updated 1993.

Jim Beam Bottles 1993 Price Guide. Downers Grove, Illinois: International Association of Jim Beam Bottle and Specialties Clubs.

BEER

Van Wieren, Dale P. *American Breweries II.* Privately printed, 1995 (Eastern Coast Breweriana Association, P.O. Box 1354, North Wales, Pennsylvania 19454).

Yenne, Bill. *The Field Guide to North America's Breweries and Microbreweries.* New York: Crescent Books, 1994.

BITTERS

Brown, William E. *The Auction Price Report 1995 Edition: Bitters, Historical Flasks, Medicines, Whiskeys, Sodas & Mineral Waters.* Privately printed, 1995 (8251 N.W. 49th Court, Coral Springs, Florida 33067).

Odell, John. *Digger Odell's Official Antique Bottle and Glass Collector Magazine Price Guide, Volume 2: Bitters Bottles.* Privately printed, 1995 (1910 Shawhan Road, Morrow, Ohio 45152).

Ring, Carlyn. *For Bitters Only.* Privately printed, 1980 (P.O. Box 357, Sun Valley, Idaho 83383).

Ring, Carlyn, and Sheldon Ray. *For Bitters Only: Update & Price Guide.* Privately printed, 1984 (P.O. Box 357, Sun Valley, Idaho 83383).

Watson, Richard. *Bitters Bottles.* Fort Davis, Texas: Thomas Nelson & Sons, 1965.

_____. *Supplement to Bitters Bottles.* Camden, New Jersey: Thomas Nelson & Sons, 1968.

CANDY CONTAINERS

Eikelberner, George, Serge Agadjanian, and Adele L. Bowden. *The Compleat American Glass Candy Containers Handbook.* Privately printed, 1986 (6252 Cedarwood Road, Mentor, Ohio 44060).

COCA-COLA

Goldstein, Shelley and Helen. *Coca-Cola Collectibles with Current Prices and Photographs in Full Color,* 4 volumes and Index. Privately printed, 1971–1980 (P.O. Box 301, Woodland Hills, California 91364).

Hill, Deborah Goldstein. *Price Guide to Coca-Cola Collectibles.* Radnor, Pennsylvania: Wallace-Homestead Book Co., 1991.

Mix, Richard. *The Mix Guide to Commemorative Coca-Cola Bottles.* Privately printed, 1990 (P.O. Box 558, Marietta, Georgia 30061-0558).

Petretti, Allan. *Petretti's Coca-Cola Collectibles Price Guide,* 9th Edition. Radnor, Pennsylvania: Wallace-Homestead Book Co., 1994.

Schaeffer, Randy and Bill Bateman. *Coca-Cola: A Collector's Guide to New and Vintage Coca-Cola Memorabilia.* London: Courage Books, 1995.

Wilson, Al. *Collectors Guide to Coca-Cola Items.* Gas City, Indiana: L-W Book Sales, 1985.

COLOGNE, SEE PERFUME

COSMETIC

Fadely, Don. *Hair Raising Stories: A Comprehensive Look at 19th & Early 20th Century Hair Preparations and the Bottles They Came In.* Privately printed, 1992 (P.O. Box 273, USAF Academy, Colorado 80840).

CURES, SEE MEDICINE; SARSAPARILLA

DECANTER

Davis, Derek Co. *English Bottles & Decanters 1650-1900.* New York: World Publishing Co., 1972.

DRUG, SEE MEDICINE

FIGURAL, SEE ALSO BITTERS

Christensen, Don and Doris. *Violin Bottles: Banjos, Guitars & Other Novelty Glass.* Privately printed, 1995. (21815 106th Street East, Buckley, Washington 98321).

Revi, Albert Christian. *American Pressed Glass and Figure Bottles.* New York: Thomas Nelson & Sons, 1964.

FIRE GRENADE

Odell, John. *Digger Odell's Official Antique Bottle and Glass Collector Magazine Price Guide, Volume 6: Colognes, Poisons, Foods, Pattern Mold, Label Under Glass, Target Balls & Fire Extinguishers.* Privately printed, 1995 (1910 Shawhan Road, Morrow, Ohio 45152).

FLASKS

Brown, William E. *The Auction Price Report 1995 Edition: Bitters, Historical Flasks, Medicines, Whiskeys, Sodas & Mineral Waters.* Privately printed, 1995 (8251 N.W. 49th Court, Coral Springs, Florida 33067).

McKearin, Helen, and Kenneth M. Wilson. *American Bottles & Flasks and Their Ancestry.* New York: Crown Publishers, 1978.

Odell, John. *Digger Odell's Official Antique Bottle and Glass Collector Magazine Price Guide, Volume 3: Flasks.* Privately printed, 1995 (1910 Shawhan Road, Morrow, Ohio 45152).

Roberts, Mike. *Price Guide to All the Flasks.* Privately printed, 1980 (840 Elm Court, Newark, Ohio 43055).

FOOD, SEE ALSO FRUIT JARS; VINEGAR

Odell, John. *Digger Odell's Official Antique Bottle and Glass Collector Magazine Price Guide, Volume 6: Colognes, Poisons, Foods, Pattern Mold, Label Under Glass, Target Balls & Fire Extinguishers.* Privately printed, 1995 (1910 Shawhan Road, Morrow, Ohio 45152).

FRUIT JARS

Bowditch, Barbara. *American Jelly Glasses: A Collector's Notebook.* Privately printed, 1986 (400 Dorchester Road, Rochester, New York 14610).

Creswick, Alice. *The Fruit Jar Works,* 2 volumes. Privately printed, 1987 (Doug Leybourne, P.O. Box 5417, North Musketgon, Michigan 49445).

Leybourne, Douglas M., Jr. *Red Book: The Collector's Guide to Old Fruit Jars,* No. 7. Privately printed, 1993 (P.O. Box 5417, North Muskegon, Michigan 49445).

McCann, Jerry. *Fruit Jar Annual.* Privately printed, 1996 (5003 West Berwyn Avenue, Chicago, Illinois 60630).

Roller, Dick. *The Standard Fruit Jar Reference.* Privately printed, 1983 (607 Driskell, Paris, Illinois 61944).

Toulouse, Julian Harrison. *Fruit Jars: A Collector's Manual.* Jointly published by Camden, New Jersey: Thomas Nelson & Sons, and Hanover, Pennsylvania: Everybody's Press, 1969.

INK

Covill, William E., Jr. *Ink Bottles and Inkwells.* Taunton, Massachusetts: William S. Sullwold Publishing, 1971.

Odell, John. *Digger Odell's Official Antique Bottle and Glass Collector Magazine Price Guide, Volume 4: Ink Bottles.* Privately printed, 1995 (1910 Shawhan Road, Morrow, Ohio 45152).

Rivera, Betty and Ted. *Inkstands and Inkwells.* New York: Crown Publishers, 1973.

JAR, SEE FRUIT JAR

MEDICINE

Brown, William E. *The Auction Price Report 1995 Edition: Bitters, Historical Flasks, Medicines, Whiskeys, Sodas & Mineral Waters.* Privately printed, 1995 (8251 N.W. 49th Court, Coral Springs, Florida 33067).

Odell, John. *Digger Odell's Official Antique Bottle and Glass Collector Magazine Price Guide, Volume 5: Medicines.* Privately printed, 1995 (1910 Shawhan Road, Morrow, Ohio 45152).

MILK

Edmondson, Bill. *The Milk Bottle Book of Michigan.* Privately printed, 1995 (317 Harvest Lane, Lansing, Michigan 48917).

Giarde, Jeffrey L. *Glass Milk Bottles: Their Makers and Marks.* Bryn Mawr, California: The Time Travelers Press, 1980.

MILK GLASS, SEE ALSO FIGURAL

Belknap, E. M. *Milk Glass.* New York: Crown Publishers, 1959.

Ferson, Regis F. and Mary F. *Yesterday's Milk Glass Today.* Privately printed, 1981 (122 Arden Road, Pittsburgh, Pennsylvania 15216).

MINERAL WATER, SEE SODA

NURSING

Ostrander, Diane Rouse. *A Guide to American Nursing Bottles.* Privately printed, 1984, revised 1992 (Will-O-Graf, P.O. Box 24, Willoughby, Ohio 44094).

PEPPER SAUCE, SEE PICKLE

PEPSI-COLA

Ayers, James C. *Pepsi-Cola Bottles Collectors Guide.* Privately printed, 1995. (RJM Enterprises, P.O. Box 1377, Mount Airy, North Carolina 27030).

Lloyd, Everette and Mary. *Pepsi-Cola Collectibles with Price Guide.* Atglen, Pennsylvania: Schiffer, 1993.

Rawlingson, Fred. *Brad's Drink: A Primer for Pepsi-Cola Collectors.* Privately printed, 1976 (FAR Publications, Box 5456, Newport News, Virginia 23605).

Stoddard, Bob. *Introduction to Pepsi Collecting.* Privately printed, 1991 (Double Dot Enterprises, P.O. Box 1548, Pomona, California 91769).

Vehling, Bill, and Michael Hunt. *Pepsi-Cola Collectibles (with prices),* 3 volumes. Gas City, Indiana: L-W Book Sales, 1988, 1990, 1993.

PERFUME, COLOGNE, AND SCENT

Baccarat: The Perfume Bottles. Privately printed, 1986 (Addor Associates, Inc., P.O. Box 2128, Westport, Connecticut 06880).

Gaborit, Jean-Yves. *Perfumes: The Essences and Their Bottles.* New York: Rizzoli International Publications, Inc., 1985.

Latimer, Tirza True. *The Perfume Atomizer: An Object with Atmosphere.* Atglen, Pennsylvania: Schiffer, 1991.

Lefkowith, Christie Mayer. *The Art of Perfume: Discovering and Collecting Perfume Bottles.* New York: Thames and Hudson, 1994.

Martin, Hazel. *A Collection of Figural Perfume & Scent Bottles.* Privately printed, 1982 (P.O. Box 110, Lancaster, California 93535).

North, Jacquelyn Y. Jones. *Commercial Perfume Bottles.* Atglen, Pennsylvania: Schiffer Publishing, Ltd., 1986.

_____. *Perfume, Cologne and Scent Bottles.* Atglen, Pennsylvania: Schiffer Publishing, Ltd., 1986.

Odell, John. *Digger Odell's Official Antique Bottle and Glass Collector Magazine Price Guide, Volume 6: Colognes, Poisons, Foods, Pattern Mold, Label Under Glass, Target Balls & Fire Extinguishers.* Privately printed, 1995 (1910 Shawhan Road, Morrow, Ohio 45152).

Sloan, Jean. *Perfume and Scent Bottle Collecting with Prices.* Radnor, Pennsylvania: Wallace-Homestead Book Co., 1989.

Utt, Mary Lou and Glen, and Patricia Bayer. *Lalique Perfume Bottles.* New York: Crown Publishers, 1985.

PICKLE

Zumwalt, Betty. *Ketchup Pickles Sauces.* Privately printed, 1980 (P.O. Box 413, Fulton, California 95439).

POISON

Odell, John. *Digger Odell's Official Antique Bottle and Glass Collector Magazine Price Guide, Volume 6: Colognes, Poisons, Foods, Pattern Mold, Label Under Glass, Target Balls & Fire Extinguishers.* Privately printed, 1995 (1910 Shawhan Road, Morrow, Ohio 45152).

ROYAL DOULTON

Dale, Jean. *The Charlton Standard Catalog of Royal Doulton Jugs.* Privately printed, 1991 (Charlton Press, 2010 Yonge Street, Toronto, Ontario M4S 1Z9, Canada).

SARSAPARILLA

DeGrafft, Joan. *American Sarsaparilla Bottles.* Privately printed, 1980 (47 Ash Street, North Attleboro, Massachusetts 92760).

Shimko, Phyllis. *Sarsaparilla Bottle Encyclopedia.* Privately printed, 1969 (Box 117, Aurora, Oregon 97002).

SCENT, SEE PERFUME

SODA, SEE ALSO COCA-COLA; PEPSI-COLA

Bowers, Q. David. *The Moxie Encyclopedia.* Vestal, New York: The Vestal Press Ltd., 1984.

Brown, William E. *The Auction Price Report 1995 Edition: Bitters, Historical Flasks, Medicines, Whiskeys, Sodas & Mineral Waters.* Privately printed, 1995 (8251 N.W. 49th Court, Coral Springs, Florida 33067).

Ferguson, Joel. *New Orleans Soda Water Manufacturers History.* Privately printed, 1995 (106 Dixie Circle, Slidell, Louisiana 70458).

Fowler, Ron. *Washington Sodas: The Illustrated History of Washington's Soft Drink Industry.* Privately printed, 1986. (Dolphin Point Writing Works, P.O. Box 45251, Seattle, Washington 98145).

Odell, John. *Digger Odell's Official Antique Bottle and Glass Collector Magazine Price Guide, Volume 7: Sodas and Mineral Waters.* Privately printed, 1995 (1910 Shawhan Road, Morrow, Ohio 45152).

Tucker, Donald. *Collector's Guide to the Saratoga Type Mineral Water Bottles.* Privately printed, 1986 (Box 429, North Berwick, Maine 03906).

TARGET BALL

Odell, John. *Digger Odell's Official Antique Bottle and Glass Collector Magazine Price Guide, Volume 6: Colognes, Poisons, Foods, Pattern Mold, Label Under Glass, Target Balls & Fire Extinguishers.* Privately printed, 1995 (1910 Shawhan Road, Morrow, Ohio 45152).

TONIC, SEE MEDICINE

WHISKEY

Brown, William E. *The Auction Price Report 1995 Edition: Bitters, Historical Flasks, Medicines, Whiskeys, Sodas & Mineral Waters.* Privately printed, 1995 (8251 N.W. 49th Court, Coral Springs, Florida 33067).

Odell, John. *Digger Odell's Official Antique Bottle and Glass Collector Magazine Price Guide, Volume 8: Whiskeys.* Privately printed, 1995 (1910 Shawhan Road, Morrow, Ohio 45152).

Spaid, David, and Henry Ford. *The One Hundred and One Rare Whiskeys.* Privately printed, 1989 (P.O. Box 2161, Palos Verdes, California 90274).

Westcott, David. *Westcott Price Guide to Advertising Water Jugs.* Privately printed, 1991 (P.O. Box 245, Deniliquin, NSW, 2710 Australia).

GO-WITHS

Congdon-Martin, Douglas. *America For Sale.* Atglen, Pennsylvania: Schiffer Publishing Ltd., 1991.

Hake, Ted, and Russ King. *Price Guide to Collectible Pin-Back Buttons 1896-1986.* Privately printed, 1986 (Hake's Americana & Collectible Press, P.O. Box 1444, York, Pennsylvania 17405).

Huxford, Sharon and Bob. *Huxford's Collectible Advertising: An Illustrated Value Guide, Second Edition.* Paducah, Kentucky: Collector Books, 1995.

Klug, Ray. *Antique Advertising Encyclopedia,* 2 volumes. Gas City, Indiana: L-W Book Sales, 1978, 1985.

Morrison, Tom. *Root Beer Advertising: A Collector's Guide.* Privately printed, 1990 (2930 Squaw Valley Drive, Colorado Springs, Colorado 80918).

────────────────────────── **AESTHETIC SPECIALTIES** ──────────────────────────

In 1979 the first bottle was released by ASI, or Aesthetic Specialties, Inc., of San Mateo, California. It was a ceramic vodka bottle that was made to honor the 1979 Crosby 38th National Pro-Am Golf Tournament. According to the company president, Charles Wittwer, 400 cases of the bottle were made. The company continued making bottles: the 1979 Kentucky Derby bottle (600 cases); 1909 Stanley Steamer (5,000 cases in three different colors made in 1979); 1903 Cadillac (2 colors made in 1979, gold version, with and without trim, made in 1980); World's Greatest Golfer (400 cases in 1979); World's Greatest Hunter (1979); 38th and 39th Crosby Golf Tournaments (1979 and 1980); 1981 Crosby 40th Golf Tournament (reworked version of World's Greatest Golfer, 100 cases); Crosby Golf Tournaments (1982, 1983, and 1984); Telephone Service Truck (1980); Ice Cream Truck (1980); 1910 Oldsmobile (1980, made in three colors); Packard (1980); 1911 Stanley Steamer (1981, 1,200 cases); 1937 Packard (1981, produced with McCormick); 1914 Chevrolet (1981); and Fire engine (1981).

AESTHETIC SPECIALTIES, Bing Crosby, 38th, 1979	14.00
Bing Crosby, 39th, 1980	25.00
Bing Crosby, 40th, 1981	36.00
Bing Crosby, 41st, Otter, 1982	32.00
Bing Crosby, 42nd, Seal, 1983	40.00
Bing Crosby, 43rd, Clam, 1984	45.00
Bing Crosby, 44th, 1985	51.00
Cadillac, 1903 Model, Blue, White, 1979	47.00
Cadillac, 1980 Model, Gold	124.00
Chevrolet, 1914 Model, 1979	46.00
Chevrolet, 1980 Model, Gold	170.00
Kentucky Derby, 1979	26.00
Model T Ice Cream Truck, Ford, 1980	65.00
Model T Telephone Truck, Ford, 1980	60.00
Oldsmobile, 1910 Model, Black, Green, 1980	80.00
Oldsmobile, Gold, 1980	205.00
Oldsmobile, Platinum, 1980	307.00
Stanley Steamer, 1909 Model, Black, 1981	50.00
Stanley Steamer, 1911 Model, Black, 1981	50.00
Stanley Steamer, Gold, 1981	113.00
Stanley Steamer, Green, 1981	42.00
World's Greatest Golfer, 1979	35.00
World's Greatest Hunter, 1979	29.00
ALPHA, see Lewis & Clark	
AUSTIN NICHOLS, see Wild Turkey	

────────────────────────────── **AVON** ──────────────────────────────

David H. McConnell started a door-to-door selling company in 1886. He recruited women as independent sales representatives to sell his perfume. The company was named the California Perfume Company even though it was located in New York City. The first product was a set of five perfumes called Little Dot. In 1928 it was decided that CPC was too limiting a name so a new line called Avon was introduced. By 1936, the Avon name was on all of the company's products, including perfumes, toothbrushes, and baking items. Avon became a public company in 1946. Collectors want the bottles, jewelry, and sales awards, but there is also interest in the early advertising and pamphlets. For information on national and local clubs, books, and other publications, contact the National Association of Avon Collector Clubs, P.O. Box 9868, Kansas City, MO 64113.

AVON, After Shave On Tap, 1974-1975	6.00
Airplane, see Avon, Spirit of St. Louis	
Albee, 1979	90.00
Albee, 1980	90.00
Albee, 1981	50.00
Albee, 1982	50.00
American Buffalo, Box	5.00
Angel, see Avon, Heavenly Angel	
Angler, 1970	12.00
Anniversary Keepsake, Eau De Toilette, Special Edition, 1979	8.00

Avon, Avon Lady, Club Bottle,   *Avon, Boot, Amber,*   *Avon, California Perfume Co.,*
1936 Lady, 1980, 7 1/2 In.   *Gold Top*   *Face Lotion, Box*

Arctic King, 1976-1979	4.00
Army Jeep, 1974-1975	10.00
Atlantic, 4-4-2, 1973	8.00
Auto Lantern, 1973	10.00
Avon Calling, 1905, Phone 1973	12.00
Avon Lady, Club Bottle, 1936 Lady, 1980, 7 1/2 In. ....*Illus*	25.00
Baby Bassett, 1978	2.00
Baby Grand Piano, 1971	10.00
Barrel, see Avon, After Shave On Tap	
Bay Rum Keg, 1965-1967	8.00
Bell, Birthday, March	13.00
Bell, Butterfly, Crystal, 1990	25.00
Bell, Christmas, 1985	15.00
Bell, Christmas, 1986	8.00 to 15.00
Bell, Christmas, 1987	8.00 to 15.00
Bell, Christmas, 1988	15.00
Bell, Christmas, 1989, Under The Mistletoe	8.00 to 15.00
Bell, Christmas, 1990, Waiting For Santa	12.50
Bell, Christmas, Garlands Of Greetings, 1991	12.00
Bell, Floral Bouquet, Crystal, 1989	12.00
Bell, Giving Thanks, 1990	10.00 to 15.00
Bell, Heart Song, 1988	15.00
Bell, Hudson Manor, Hostess	19.00
Bell, Love, 1991	15.00
Bell, Moonlight Glow, 1981-1982, Topaz Cologne	9.00
Bell, Mother's Love, 1988	8.00
Bell, Spring Chimes, 1991	25.00
Bell, Tapestry, 1981	15.00
Benjamin Franklin, 1974-1976	8.00
Betsy Ross, 1976	5.00
Big Whistle, 1972	5.00 to 7.00
Bird Of Paradise, Decanter, 1970-1972	8.00
Blue Blazer After Shave, 1964	10.00
Bold Eagle, 1976	8.00
Bon Bon, White, 1972-1973	5.00
Boot, Amber, Gold Top ....*Illus*	5.00
Boot, Cologne, 1967	4.00
Bucking Bronco, 1971	5.00
Buffalo Nickel, 1971	6.00
Bunny Bright Candle, 1980	10.00 to 12.00
California Perfume Co., Daphne Perfume, Gold Label, Small, 1926	45.00
California Perfume Co., Face Lotion, Box ....*Illus*	50.00
California Perfume Co., Fruit Flavors, 1923	55.00
California Perfume Co., Perfection Almond Extract, ABM, Label, 1934	15.00

California Perfume Co., Rose Water & Glycerin, ABM, Label, Sample, 1925 .... 58.00
California Perfume Co., Tooth Tablets, Embossed Metal Top, 1895 .... 65.00 to 75.00
Canada Goose, 1973 .... 8.00
Candle, Catnip, 1975 .... 8.00
Candle Caroling Trio, 1981 .... 2.00
Candleholder, Birds, Terra-Cotta, Pair 6.00
Candleholder, Cape Cod, Tall 10.00
Candleholder, Gingerbread House, 1986 .... 16.00
Candleholder, Goblet, Cape Cod, 1978 .... 4.00
Candleholder, Lotus, Black, 1974-1975 .... 8.00
Candleholder, Milk Glass, 1964-1966 .... 10.00
Candleholder, Snuggly Mouse, 1983 .... 5.00 to 10.00
Candleholder, Spring Hostess, 1987 .... 7.00
Candleholder, Teddy Bear, 1980 .... 10.00
Candlestick, Enchanted Mushroom, 1975 .... 4.00
Candlestick, Ho Ho Glow, 1982 .... 5.00
Candlestick, Hurricane, Cape Cod, 1985 .... 12.00
Candlestick, Mrs. Snowlight, Bayberry, 1979 .... 7.00
Candlestick, Plum Pudding, 1978 .... 3.00
Cannon, see also Avon, Defender Cannon
Capital, White, 1976 .... 6.00
Captain's Lantern, 1964-1976 .... 5.00
Car, Auburn, Bobtail Speedster, 1983-1984 .... 25.00
Car, Camper, 1972 .... 3.50
Car, Chrysler, Model 1948, 1976 .... 10.00
Car, Classic, 1990 .... 10.00 to 25.00
Car, Silver Duesenberg, 1970 .... 10.00
Car, Stanley Steamer, Silver, 1978 .... 12.75
Car, Station Wagon, 1971 .... 9.00
Car, Sterling Six, Silver, 1978 .... 9.00
Car, Stock Car Racer, 1974 .... 8.00
Car, Straight Eight, 1973 .... 8.00
Car, Sure Winner Race, 1972-1975 .... 5.00
Car, Touring T, 1969 .... 12.75
Car, Volkswagen, Black, 1970 .... 7.00
Casey's Lantern, Amber, 1966-1967 .... 25.00
Cat, see Avon, Ming Cat
Catch-A-Fish, 1976 .... 5.00
Chess Piece, Bishop, 1974-1978 .... 2.00
Chess Piece, King, 1973 .... 3.00
Chess Piece, Queen, 1975-1978 .... 5.00
Chess Piece, Rook, 1974 .... 2.50
Chess Set, 32 Piece 103.00
Chimney Lamp, 1973-1974 .... 5.00
Christmas Ornament, Melvin P. Merrymouse, 1982 .... 8.00
Christmas Ornament, Remembrance Angel, White Ceramic, 1982 .... 4.50
Christmas Ornament, Remembrance Dove, 1981 .... 5.00
Christmas Ornament, Remembrance Wreath, White Ceramic, 1980 .... 4.50
Christmas Ornament, Snowflake, White Ceramic, 1983 .... 4.50
Christmas Surprise, 1976 .... 2.00
Christmas Tree, Crystal, 1975 .... 6.00
Clock, Smile, 1978 .... 25.00
Cluck A Doo, 1971 .... 5.00
Coffee Mill, see Avon, Country Store Coffee Mill
Coleman Lantern, 1977-1979 .... 5.00
Colt Revolver, 1851, 1975 .... 9.00
Country Store Coffee Mill, 1972 .... 3.50
Courting Carriage, 1973 .... 3.00
Covered Wagon, 1970 .... 7.00
Dachshund, 1973 .... 5.00
Dear Friends, 1974 .... 10.00
Decanter, Cape Cod, 1977 .... 14.00 to 20.00
Decanter, Eiffel Tower, 1970 .... 3.50

Decanter, Emerald Accent, 1982	6.00
Decanter, Speed Boat, 1989	8.00
Decanter, Town Pump, 1968	8.00
Decanter Set, Tray, Emerald Green, 8 Piece, 1982	25.00
Decisions, 1965	10.00
Defender Cannon, 1966	12.00
Dog, see Avon, Bon Bon; Avon, Dachshund; Avon, Snoopy Surprise	
Dollars 'n' Scents, 1966	7.50 to 15.00
Dolphin, Large, 1968	5.00
Dolphin, Miniature, 1973	2.50
Door Bell, Golden Door Knocker, 1979	15.00
Duck, see Avon, Mallard-In-Flight	
Dueling Pistol, 1960, 1973	8.00
Dueling Pistol II, 1975	9.00
Dutch Girl, 1973	8.00
Egg, Autumns, 1987	7.50
Egg, Summers, 1977	7.50
Egg, Winters, 1977	7.50
Elizabethan, 1972	16.00
Fairy Tale Frog, 1976	4.00
Fish, see Avon, Dolphin; Avon, Sea Spirit	
Flower Maiden, 1973	7.00
Fly-A-Balloon, 1975-1977	7.00 to 20.00
French Telephone, Box, 1971	10.00 to 20.00
Gallery Ginger Jar, 1983	65.00
Garden Girl, 1978	3.00
Gay Nineties, 1974	10.00
Glass Set, Cape Cod, Footed, 1988	15.00
Goblet, Cape Cod, 1977-1980	5.00
Goblet, Convention, Las Vegas	12.00
Goblet, Convention, Queen Mary	12.00
Goblet, Convention, Spokane	12.00
Goblet, Convention, St. Louis	12.00
Goblet, Hummingbird	4.50 to 10.00
Golf, see Avon, Swinger	
Goodyear Blimp, 1978	7.00
Heavenly Angel, 1974	3.00
Humpty Dumpty, 1963	10.00
Hurricane Lamp, 1973	15.00
Indian Tepee, 1974	5.00
Jolly Santa Cologne, 1978	1.50
Just A Twist, 1977	6.00
La Belle Telephone, 1974	5.00
Lamp, see Avon, Hurricane Lamp; Avon, Tiffany Lamp	
Lantern, see also Avon, Casey's Lantern	
Lantern, Whale Oil, 1974	7.00
Lemonade Set, Avon 100, 1986, 5 Piece	10.00
Liberty Bell, 1971	7.00
Linus Shampoo, 1970	5.25
Little Brown Jug, 1978	3.00
Little Girl Blue, 1972	7.00
Little Kate, 1973	8.00
Mallard-In-Flight, 1974	6.00
Mandolin, 1971	10.00
McConnells, General Store, 1982	25.00
Ming Cat, 1971	8.00
Monkey Shines, 1979	6.00
Moonwind Cologne, Stockholder Gift	25.00
Mother's Touch, 1984	25.00
Mr. Avon, NAAC, 1985	5.00
Mrs. Quackles, 1979	4.00
Mug, 12 Days Of Christmas, 4 Piece, 1985	16.00

Mug, Freddy Frog, 1970	6.00
Mug, Some Bunny, 1990	9.00
Mug, Sweet Sentiments, 1986	5.00
Mug, Wild Rest, 1988	6.00
NAAC, 1st Annual Club, 1972	150.00 to 250.00
NAAC, 1st Convention, 1980	33.00
NAAC, 2nd Annual Club, 1973	30.00
NAAC, 2nd Convention, 1981	30.00
NAAC, 3rd Annual Club, 1974	10.00 to 15.00
NAAC, 3rd Convention, 1982	3.00 to 10.00
NAAC, 4th Annual Club, 1975	10.00 to 20.00
NAAC, 4th Convention, 1983	3.00 to 10.00
NAAC, 5th Annual Club, 1976	10.00
NAAC, 5th Convention, 1984	3.00 to 10.00
NAAC, 6th Annual Club, 1977	10.00 to 15.00
NAAC, 7th Annual Club, 1978	10.00
NAAC, 9th Convention, 1988	4.00
NAAC, 10th Annual Club, 1981	10.00
NAAC, 10th Convention, 1989	4.00
NAAC, 12th Annual Club, 1983	12.00
NAAC, Bell, Miss Nashville	15.00
NAAC, Bell, San Diego, 1988	15.00
Ornament, see Avon, Christmas Ornament	
Peanuts Pals Shampoo, 1971	4.50
Pineapple Petite, 1972	3.00
Pipe, American Eagle, 1973	5.00
Pipe, Blood Hound, 1976	10.00
Pipe, Bulldog, 1972	10.00
Pipe, Corn Cob, 1974	5.00
Pipe, Pony Express Rider, 1975	5.00
Pipe, Uncle Sam, 1975	7.00
Pipe Dream, 1967	15.00
Pitcher, Water, Currier & Ives, 1977, 6 1/2 In.	18.00
Planter, Bunny, 1979	10.00
Plate, Betsy Ross, 1973	15.00
Pluto Shampoo, 1970	6.00
Pot Belly Stove, 1970	3.50
President Washington, 1974	8.00
Princess Of Yorkshire, 1976	4.00
Radio, Red, Award, 1980	25.00 to 40.00
Rainbow Trout, 1973	10.00
Roaring Twenties, 1972	8.00
Salt & Pepper, Cape Cod, 1978	5.00
Sauce Boat, Cape Cod, Footed, 1988	5.00 to 10.00
Scimitar, 1968	15.00
Scottish Lass, 1975	6.00
Sea Spirit, 1973	3.50
Sea Treasure, 1971	6.00
Sea Trophy, 1972	12.00
Seashell, see Avon, Sea Treasure	
Short Pony, 1968	7.00
Small Wonder, 1972	7.00
Smart Move, see Avon, Chess Piece	
Snail, Box, 2 In.	*Illus* 15.00
Snoopy & Doghouse, 1969	4.50
Snoopy Surprise, 1969	9.00
Snoopy's Ski Team, 1974-1975	5.00
Snoopy's Snow Flier, 1973	4.50
Soap Dish, Hearts & Diamond, Fostoria, 1977	15.00
Spanish Senorita, 1975	5.00
Spirit Of St. Louis, 1986	12.00
Splash 'n' Spray Set, 1968	15.00

Avon, Snail, Box, 2 In.

Stein, American Armed Forces, 1990	35.00
Stein, Bald Eagle, Box, 1990, Miniature	8.00
Stein, Blacksmith, 1985	35.00
Stein, Car Classic, 1979	30.00
Stein, Fire Fighter, 1989	35.00
Stein, Fishing, 1990	35.00
Stein, Gold Rush, 1987	35.00
Stein, Great American Football, 1982	30.00
Stein, Great Dogs, 1991	50.00
Stein, Hunters, 1972	8.00
Stein, Indians Of American Frontier, 1988	30.00
Stein, Iron Horse, 1985, Miniature	25.00
Stein, Racing Car, 1989	35.00
Stein, Ship Builder, 1986	40.00
Stein, Sperm Whale, Box, 1992, Miniature	10.00
Stein, Sporting, 1978	30.00
Stein, Tall Ships, 1978, Miniature	25.00 to 40.00
Stein, Western Roundup, Box, 1980	30.00
Stein, Wild West, 1993	18.00 to 30.00
Summer Bride, 1986	20.00
Sweet Dreams, 1974	13.00
Sweet Treats, 1975	5.00
Swinger, Golf Bag, 1969	11.00
Sword, see Avon, Scimitar	
Tankard, Casey At The Bat, 1980	12.00
Telephone, see Avon, Avon Calling; Avon, French Telephone; Avon, La Belle Telephone	
Ten Point Buck, Box	5.00
Tepee, see Avon, Indian Tepee	
Tiffany Lamp, 1972	8.00 to 12.00
To A Wild Rose Cream Lotion, 1950	2.00
Touch Of Christmas, 1975	1.00 to 3.00
Treasure Chest, 1973	30.00
Treasure Turtle, 1977	3.00
Tub Talk, Telephone, 1969	8.00
Turtle, see Avon, Treasure Turtle	
Twenty Dollar Gold Piece, 1971	3.50
Vase, Bud, Here's My Heart	3.50
Vase, Bud, Imperial Garden, Awards, 1973	8.00
Vase, Cape Cod, 1985	10.00
Vase, Hummingbird, Crystal, 1986	27.00
Vase, Spring Bouquet, 1981	6.00
Victorian Lady, 1972	3.50
Vigorate After Shave, Black Tube Box, 1959	40.00
Viking Horn, 1966	10.00
Western Saddle, 1971	6.00 to 8.00
Wild West, Bullet, 1977	1.00
World Wide, Jo Olsen, 1975	25.00

BALLANTINE

Ballantine's Scotch was sold in figural bottles in 1969. The five bottles were shaped like a golf bag, knight, mallard, zebra, or fisherman. Ballantine also made some flasks and jugs with special designs.

BALLANTINE, Fisherman, 1969 .... 15.00
Jug, Miniature.. 15.00
Scotch Whiskey Jug, Tan & Cobalt, Miniature... 19.00

BARBER

The nineteenth-century barber either made his own hair tonic or purchased it in large containers. Barber bottles were used at the barbershop or in the home. The barber filled the bottles each day with hair oil, bay rum, tonic, shampoo, witch hazel, rosewater, or some other cosmetic. He knew what was inside each bottle because of its distinctive shape and color. Most of the important types of glass were used for barber bottles. Spatter glass, milk glass, cranberry, cobalt, cut, hobnail, vaseline, and opalescent glass were used alone or in attractive combinations. Some were made with enamel-painted decorations. Most of the bottles were blown. A pontil mark can be found on the bottom of many bottles. These special fancy bottles were popular during the last half of the nineteenth-century. In 1906 the Pure Food and Drug Act made it illegal to use refillable, nonlabeled bottles in a barbershop and the bottles were no longer used.

BARBER, Amethyst, Cut Glass, Enameled Design, 9 1/4 In. 120.00
Amethyst, Enameled Floral, Ribbed, Bulbous, OP.. 90.00
Amethyst, Enameled Flowers, Corset Waist, Pontil.. 125.00
Amethyst, Floral Sprig Design, Pontil, Bulbous, 8 1/8 In. 88.00
Amethyst, Mary Gregory Type, Boy Pointing, Flying Birds, Pontil, Bulbous, 7 In. 231.00
Amethyst, White, Orange, Yellow, Gold Enameled Design, Barrel Shape, 7 1/4 In. 195.00
Barbasol, Pat. No. 81737, 3 In..*Illus* 2.00
Bay Rum, Amber, Woman, Hat, Label Under Glass, 10 1/2 In. 412.50
Bay Rum, Iridized, Scene, 8 In...*Illus* 345.00
Black Amethyst, Silver Overlay, Frosted, 7 5/8 In. 160.00
Blown, Cut Front, Star Pattern Base, 6 In. 40.00
Cobalt Blue, Enameled Dot & Flower Design 160.00
Cobalt Blue, Gold Design, 7 In..*Illus* 200.00
Cobalt Blue, Mary Gregory Type, White Enameled Design, 7 1/2 In........................... 125.00
Cobalt Blue, White & Orange Enamel Design, Pontil, Modified Bell Form, 7 1/2 In..... 110.00
Cobalt Blue, White & Orange Flowers, Gold Trim, 11 In. 250.00
Cobalt Blue, White, Green, Pink, Enameled Design, Ribbed, 7 3/4 In. 120.00
Coin Spot, Cranberry Opalescent, 1870-1920, 6 7/8 In... 100.00
Coin Spot, Teal Blue, Segmented Body, 8 3/8 In. 77.00
Cranberry Opalescent, Spanish Lace Design, White, 8 1/4 In...................................... 120.00

Barber, Barbasol,
Pat. No. 81737, 3 In.

Barber, Light
Green, Pear
Shape, 5 3/4 In.

Cranberry Opalescent Swirl, Rolled Lip, Square 210.00
Daisy & Fern, Cranberry Opalescent, Melon Form, Pontil, 7 3/8 In. 100.00
Emerald Green, Mary Gregory Type, White Boy, Garden, Metal Stopper, Pontil, 7 3/4 In.. 210.00
Frosted Brown, Flowers & Leaves, White Enameled, Stopper, 9 In. 125.00
Good Luck, Horseshoe, 11 1/2 In...*Illus* 20.00
Light Green, Pear Shape, 5 3/4 In...*Illus* 50.00
Milk Glass, 3 Cherubs, Hand Painted, 7 5/8 In. 375.00
Milk Glass, Art Deco, 6 3/4 In. 35.00
Milk Glass, Basket Weave Gold Trim... 25.00
Milk Glass, Fox Hunting Scene, Gold Design, 7 1/2 In. ....*Illus* 250.00
Milk Glass, Girl's Head Picture, 12 In. ....*Illus* 125.00
Milk Glass, Hair Tonic, Enameled Tulips, Light Blue Ground, Cylinder....................... 160.00
Milk Glass, Koken Style 40.00
Milk Glass, Koken Type, 7 3/4 In. 40.00
Milk Glass, Water, Art Deco, 6 3/4 In. 35.00
Opalescent, Enameled Gold Leaf Design, Pontil 75.00
Opaline, Art Deco, 6 3/4 In. 30.00
Pink Cranberry, Hobnail, Pontil, 1880-1900.. 129.00
Pressed Glass, Zipper Pattern Neck, 6 1/2 In. 40.00
Red Cased Glass, 8 1/2 In..*Illus* 80.00
Toilet Water, 3-Piece Mold, Purple Amethyst, Vertical Rib, Pontil, 5 3/4 In., Type 4.... 253.00
Toilet Water, Rib Pattern, Swirled Left, 3-Piece Mold, Cobalt Blue, Pontil, 5 1/2 In. ... 275.00
Toilet Water, Sapphire Blue, Stopper, 2-Piece Mold, 6 In... 176.00
Toilet Water, Vertical Rib, 3-Piece Mold, Cobalt Blue, Pontil, 6 In............................... 302.00
Turquoise Blue, White, Pink, Red & Yellow, Enameled Design, Ribbed, 7 5/8 In........ 160.00
Turquoise Opalescent, Blue, Tooled Lip, Melon Sides, 7 1/8 In.................................. 80.00
U.S.Q.M.C., 4-Piece Mold, Paneled, Pontil.. 35.00
Vegederma, Amethyst, Bust Of Women, White Enamel, Pontil, Bulbous, 8 In............. 385.00
Venetian, Clear, Red & White Bands, Tooled Mouth, 8 1/2 In. 125.00
Venetian, Gold, Blue & White Vertical Stripes, Pontil, 7 1/2 In.................................... 195.00
White, Turquoise Overlay, Lady's Leg Neck, Melon Body, 1880, 8 1/2 In. 121.00
Witch Hazel, Amethyst, Rib Pattern, Enameled, White Cottages, 8 In. 300.00
Witch Hazel, Label, Shaker Stopper, 4 1/2 In. 45.00
Witch Hazel, Milk Glass, Koken Style, 6 Sides, 7 3/4 In.. 40.00
Yellow, Ribbed, Swirled Right, Sheared 6 1/2 In. 45.00
Yellow, Ribs Swirled Right, Tool Sheared Lip, 6 1/2 In.. 55.00

Barber, Bay Rum, Iridized, Scene, 8 In.

Barber, Cobalt Blue, Gold Design, 7 In.

Barber, Good Luck, Horseshoe, 11 1/2 In.

Barber, Milk Glass, Girl's Head Picture, 12 In.

Barber, Milk Glass, Fox Hunting Scene, Gold Design, 7 1/2 In.

Barber, Red Cased Glass, 8 1/2 In.

Yellow-Green, Enameled Design, OP.. 80.00
BATTERY JAR, see Oil

BEAM

The history of the Jim Beam company is confusing because the progeny of the founder, Jacob Beam, favored the names David and James. Jacob Beam had been a whiskey distiller in Virginia and Maryland before moving to Kentucky in 1788. He was selling Kentucky Straight Bourbon in bottles labeled *Beam* by 1795. His son David continued to market Beam bourbon. His grandson, David M. Beam, was the next to inherit the business. One of David M.'s brands was Old Tub, started in 1882 at Beam's Clear Springs Distillery No. 230. The company was called David M. Beam. The next Beam family member in the business was Col. James B. Beam, son of David M., who started working at the distillery in 1880 at the age of 16. By 1914 he owned the Early Times Distillery No. 7 in Louisville, Kentucky. J.B. Beam and B.H. Hurt were partners in the distillery from 1892 to 1899. In 1915, when the colonel died, the distillery was acquired by S.L. Guthrie and some partners. Then T. Jeremiah Beam, son of James B. Beam, inherited the James Beam Company, and with his cousin, Carl Beam, continued to make the famous bourbon. Booker Noe, Baker Beam, and David Beam, sixth-generation descendants of Jacob Beam, continued in the business. Today, Jim Beam Brands is a wholly-owned subsidiary of American Brands, Inc.

Beam bottles favored by today's collectors were made as containers for Kentucky Straight Bourbon. In 1953, the company began selling some Christmas season whiskey in special decanters shaped like cocktail shakers instead of the usual whiskey bottles. The decanters were so popular that by 1955 the company was making Regal China bottles in special shapes. Executive series bottles started in 1955 and political figures in 1956. Customer specialties were first made in 1956, decanters (called *trophy series* by collectors) in 1957, and the state series in 1958. Other bottles are classed by collectors as Regal China or Glass Specialty bottles. A small number of special bottles were made by Royal Doulton in England from 1983 to 1985. These are not often found in the books about Beam. The rarest Beam bottle is the First National Bank of Chicago bottle; 117 were issued in 1964. The Salute to Spiro Agnew bottle made in 1970 was limited to 196. Six men making counterfeits of the very rare Beam bottles were arrested in 1970. Jim Beam stopped making decanters for the commercial trade in 1992.

The Foss Company made a limited number of decanters exclusively for the International Association of Jim Beam Bottle and Specialties Club (IJBBSC). Cinnamon Teal was issued in 1994 and Harlequin Duck in 1995 with the Ducks Unlimited label.

The Jim Beam company has also made many other advertising items or *go-withs* such as ashtrays and openers. The International Association of Jim Beam Bottle & Specialties Clubs (2015 Burlington Avenue, Kewanee, IL 61433) has regional and sectional meetings. They sell a book, *Jim Beam Bottles: A Pictorial Guide,* and a price list is also available. Bottles are listed here alphabetically by name or as Convention, Executive, Political, or other general headings. This is because beginning collectors find it difficult to locate bottles by type. Miniature bottles are listed here also. Go-withs are in the special section at the end of the book.

BEAM, 101st Airborne Division, Armed Forces, 1977 .... 10.00
A-C Spark Plug, 1977 .... 29.00 to 30.00
A.H. Steve Stephenson, Past Presidents, 1982 .... 5000.00
ABC Florida, 1973 .... 7.00 to 10.00
AHEPA, 1972 .... 6.00
Aida, Opera, 1978 .... 125.00
Alaska, State, 1958 .... 52.00
Alaska Purchase, Centennial, 1966 .... 5.00
Alaska Star, State, 1958 .... 45.00
Amaretto, Crystal, 1975 .... 3.00
Amber, Crystal, 1973 .... 5.00
Ambulance, Emergency, White, 1985 .... 40.00
American Brands, 1989 .... 275.00
American Cowboy, 1981 .... 15.00 to 25.00
AMVETS, 25th Anniversary Of American Wars, 11 3/4 In. 5.00
Angelo's Delivery Truck, 1984 .... 85.00
Antioch, 1967 .... 5.00 to 8.00
Antique Trader, 1968 .... 5.00
Appaloosa, 1974 .... 10.00 to 12.00
Arizona, State, 1968 .... 5.00
Armadillo, 1981 .... 12.00
Armanetti, Award Winner, 1969 .... 5.00 to 7.00
Armanetti, Bacchus, 1970 .... 10.00
Armanetti, Fun Shopper, 1971 .... 5.00
Armanetti, Vase, 1968 .... 5.00 to 6.00
Army Jeep, Regal China, 1987 .... 35.00
Azur-Glo, Crystal, 1975 .... 2.00 to 4.00
Barney's Slot Machine, 1978 .... 15.00 to 25.00
Barry Berish, Presidential, 1984 .... 90.00
Barry Berish, Presidential, 1985 .... 90.00
Bartender's Guild, Crystal, 1973 .... 7.00 to 25.00
Baseball, 1969 .... 25.00
Bass Boat, 1988 .... 32.00
Beam Pot, 1980 .... 12.00
Beatty Burro, Glass, 1970 .... 18.00
Beaver Valley Club, 1977 .... 10.00 to 13.00
Bell Ringer, A Fore Ye Go, 1970 .... 7.00
Bell Ringer, Plaid Apron, 1970 .... *Illus* 7.00 to 8.00
Bell Scotch, Miniature, 1969 .... 17.00
Bell Scotch, Qt., 1969 .... 23.00
Benjamin Franklin, Saturday Evening Post Cover, 1975 .... 5.00
Big Apple, 1979 .... 10.00
Bing Crosby, 29th National Pro-AM, 1970, 12 In. 5.00
Bing Crosby, 30th, 1971 .... 5.00 to 8.00
Bing Crosby, 31st, 1972 .... 20.00 to 22.00
Bing Crosby, 32nd, 1973 .... 20.00 to 25.00
Bing Crosby, 33rd, 1974 .... 20.00 to 25.00
Bing Crosby, 34th, 1975 .... 57.00 to 65.00
Bing Crosby, 35th, 1976 .... 25.00
Bing Crosby, 36th, 1977 .... 20.00 to 22.00
Bing Crosby, 37th, 1978 .... 18.00
Binion's Horseshoe Casino, Las Vegas, 1970 .... *Illus* 7.00
Black Katz, 1968 .... 15.00
Blue Crystal, 1971 .... 5.00 to 10.00

Beam, Bell Ringer, Plaid
Apron, 1970

Beam, Binion's Horseshoe
Casino, Las Vegas, 1970

Beam, Churchill Downs,
Kentucky Derby, 96th,
Double Roses, 1970

Front   Back

Blue Daisy, 1967 .... 5.00
Blue Fox, 1967 .... 77.00 to 92.00
Blue Goose, 1971 .... 5.00
Blue Goose, 1979 .... 10.00 to 12.00
Blue Hen, 1982 .... 18.00 to 20.00
Blue Jay, 1969 .... 10.00
Blue Slot Machine, 1967 .... 10.00
Bluegill, 1974, 9 3/4 In. 20.00
Bob Hope Desert Classic, 14th, 1973 .... 10.00
Bob Hope Desert Classic, 15th, 1974 .... 10.00 to 14.00
Bohemian Girl, 1974 .... 15.00
Bonded Gold, 1975 .... 5.00
Bonded Mystic, 1979 .... 8.00
Bonded Silver, Regal, 1975 .... 5.00
Boothill, 1972 .... 8.00
Boris Godunov, Opera, 1982 .... 200.00
Box Car, 1983 .... 55.00
Boy's Town, 1973 .... 10.00
BPAA, Bowling Proprietors, 1974 .... 5.00
BPO Does, 1971 .... 6.00
Broadmoor Hotel, 1968 .... 5.00 to 7.00
Buccaneer, Multicolored, 1982 .... 50.00
Buccaneer, Solid Gold, 1982 .... 50.00
Buffalo Bill, 1971 .... 6.00
Bulldog, Armed Forces, 1979 .... 25.00
Cable Car, 1968 .... 5.00
Cable Car, 1983 .... 48.00
Cal Neva, 1969 .... 7.00
California Derby, With Glasses, 1971 .... 35.00
California Mission, 1970 .... 10.00 to 15.00
Camellia City Club, 1979 .... 18.00 to 20.00
Cameo, Blue, 1965 .... 5.00

Cannon With Chain, 1970 .... 3.00
Canteen, 1979 .... 15.00
Captain & Mate, 1980 .... 10.00
Cardinal, Female, 1973 .... 10.00
Cardinal, Male, 1968 .... 25.00
Carmen, Opera, 1978 .... 20.00
Carmen, Opera, Paperweight, 1978 .... 30.00
Carolers, Holiday, 1988 .... 35.00
Carolers, Presidential, 1988 .... 80.00
Cat, Burmese, 1967 .... 10.00
Cat, Siamese, 1967 ....9.00 to 10.00
Cat, Tabby, 1967 .... 10.00
Catfish, 1981 ....20.00 to 35.00
Cathedral, Radio, 1979 .... 10.00
Cedars Of Lebanon, 1971 .... 6.00
Charisma, Decanter, 1970 ....10.00 to 11.00
Charlie McCarthy, 1976 .... 25.00
Chateaux, 1953 .... 28.00
Chateaux Classic Cherry, 1976 .... 2.00
Cherry Hills Country Club, 1973 ....5.00 to 6.00
Chevrolet, Bel Air, 1957 Model, Black, 1988 .... 90.00
Chevrolet, Bel Air, 1957 Model, Dark Blue, 1987 .... 75.00
Chevrolet, Bel Air, 1957 Model, Gold, 1988 .... 125.00
Chevrolet, Bel Air, 1957 Model, Red, 1987 .... 75.00
Chevrolet, Bel Air, 1957 Model, Turquoise, 1987 .... 65.00
Chevrolet, Camaro, 1969 Model, Blue, 1989 .... 65.00
Chevrolet, Camaro, 1969 Model, Green, 1989 .... 125.00
Chevrolet, Camaro, 1969 Model, Pace Car, 1989 .... 70.00
Chevrolet, Camaro, 1969 Model, Silver, 1989 .... 95.00
Chevrolet, Convertible, 1957 Model, Black 75.00
Chevrolet, Convertible, 1957 Model, Cream 95.00
Chevrolet, Convertible, 1957 Model, Red 79.00
Chevrolet, Corvette Stingray, 1963 Model, Black, 1987 .... 90.00
Chevrolet, Corvette, 1953 Model, White, 1989 .... 150.00
Chevrolet, Corvette, 1954 Model, Blue, 1989 .... 85.00
Chevrolet, Corvette, 1955 Model, Black, 1990 .... 125.00
Chevrolet, Corvette, 1955 Model, Copper, 1989 .... 80.00
Chevrolet, Corvette, 1955 Model, Red, 1990 .... 125.00
Chevrolet, Corvette, 1957 Model, Black, 1990 .... 75.00
Chevrolet, Corvette, 1957 Model, Blue, 1990 .... 75.00
Chevrolet, Corvette, 1957 Model, Copper, 1991 .... 125.00
Chevrolet, Corvette, 1957 Model, White, 1990 .... 125.00
Chevrolet, Corvette, 1963 Model, Blue, 1987 .... 100.00
Chevrolet, Corvette, 1963 Model, Red, 1988 .... 65.00
Chevrolet, Corvette, 1963 Model, Silver, 1988 .... 65.00
Chevrolet, Corvette, 1978 Model, Black, 1984 .... 150.00
Chevrolet, Corvette, 1978 Model, Pace Car, 1987 .... 195.00
Chevrolet, Corvette, 1978 Model, Red, 1988 .... 55.00
Chevrolet, Corvette, 1978 Model, White, 1985 .... 70.00
Chevrolet, Corvette, 1978 Model, Yellow, 1985 .... 60.00
Chevrolet, Corvette, 1984 Model, Bronze, 1989 .... 95.00
Chevrolet, Corvette, 1984 Model, Gold, 1989 .... 95.00
Chevrolet, Corvette, 1984 Model, Red, 1988 .... 80.00
Chevrolet, Corvette, 1985 Model, White 55.00
Chevrolet, Corvette, 1985 Model, Yellow 45.00
Chevrolet, Corvette, 1986 Model, Bronze 89.00
Chevrolet, Corvette, 1986 Model, Pace Car, Yellow 95.00
Chevrolet, Corvette, 1986 Model, Red 89.00
Chevrolet, Hot Red, 1957 Model, Yellow, 1988 .... 100.00
Cheyenne, 1967 .... 5.00
Chicago Art Museum, 1972 ....10.00 to 12.00
Chicago Club Loving Cup, 1978 ....14.00 to 15.00
Chicago Cub, 1985 .... 35.00

Chicago Fire, 1971 .... 15.00
Chicago Show, 1977 .... 10.00
Chocolomi, 1976.. 2.00
Christmas, 1973... 15.00
Christmas Tree, 1986...100.00 to 135.00
Christmas Tree, Paperweight, 1986 .... 35.00
Churchill Downs, Kentucky Derby, 95th, Pink Roses, 1969............................. 6.00
Churchill Downs, Kentucky Derby, 95th, Red Roses, 1969.............................. 6.00
Churchill Downs, Kentucky Derby, 96th, Double Roses, 1970 ....*Illus* 24.00
Churchill Downs, Kentucky Derby, 97th, Horse & Rider, 1971 .... 7.00
Churchill Downs, Kentucky Derby, 98th, Horse & Rider In Wreath, 1972 .... 6.00
Churchill Downs, Kentucky Derby, 100th, 1974 .... 10.00
Circus Wagon, 1979 ....23.00 to 25.00
Civil War, North, 1961 .... 20.00
Civil War, South, 1961 .... 30.00
Clear Crystal, Bourbon, 1967 .... 10.00
Clear Crystal, Vodka, 1967 .... 10.00
Cleopatra, Rust, 1962 .... 5.00
Cleopatra, Yellow, 1962...10.00 to 15.00
Clint Eastwood, 1973 ....*Illus* 12.00
Clock, Antique, 1985.. 40.00
Coach Devaney, Nebraska, 1972 .... 10.00
Cocktail Shaker, 1953.. 6.00
Coffee Grinder, Antique, 1979 ....8.00 to 12.00
Coffee Warmer, Pyrex, Gold Metal Band, 1956.. 5.00
Coffee Warmer, Pyrex, Gold, 1954 .... 10.00
Coho Salmon, 1976 .... 15.00
Colin Mead, 1984... 150.00
Collectors Edition, Vol. 1, Aristide Braunt, 1966 .... 2.00
Collectors Edition, Vol. 1, Artist, 1966... 2.00
Collectors Edition, Vol. 1, Blue Boy, 1966 .... 9.00
Collectors Edition, Vol. 1, Laughing Cavalier, 1966 .... 2.00
Collectors Edition, Vol. 1, Mardi Gras, 1966...2.00 to 3.00
Collectors Edition, Vol. 1, On The Terrace, 1966... 7.00
Collectors Edition, Vol. 2, George Gisze, 1967.. 2.00
Collectors Edition, Vol. 2, Man On A Horse, 1967... 2.00
Collectors Edition, Vol. 2, Night Watch, 1967 .... 2.00
Collectors Edition, Vol. 2, Nurse & Child, 1967.. 3.00
Collectors Edition, Vol. 2, Soldier & Girl, 1967.. 3.00
Collectors Edition, Vol. 2, The Jester, 1967.. 2.00
Collectors Edition, Vol. 3, American Gothic, 1968.................................2.00 to 4.00

Beam, Clint Eastwood, 1973

Beam, Collectors Edition, Vol. 12, Labrador Retriever, 1977

Beam, Ducks Unlimited, No. 1, Mallard, 1974

Collectors Edition, Vol. 3, Buffalo Hunt, 1968 ....2.00 to 4.00
Collectors Edition, Vol. 3, Indian Maiden, 1968 ....2.00 to 5.00
Collectors Edition, Vol. 3, The Kentuckian, 1968 .... 2.00
Collectors Edition, Vol. 3, The Scout, 1968 .... 4.00
Collectors Edition, Vol. 3, Whistler's Mother, 1968 .... 2.00
Collectors Edition, Vol. 4, Balcony, 1969 .... 2.00
Collectors Edition, Vol. 4, Boy With Cherries, 1969 .... 5.00
Collectors Edition, Vol. 4, Emile Zola, 1969 ....2.00 to 5.00
Collectors Edition, Vol. 4, Fruit Basket, 1969 .... 5.00
Collectors Edition, Vol. 4, Sunflowers, 1969 ....2.00 to 5.00
Collectors Edition, Vol. 4, The Judge, 1969 .... 5.00
Collectors Edition, Vol. 4, Zouave, 1969 .... 2.00
Collectors Edition, Vol. 5, Au Cafe, 1970 .... 2.00
Collectors Edition, Vol. 5, Gare Saint Lazare, 1970 .... 2.00
Collectors Edition, Vol. 5, Old Peasant, 1970 .... 2.00
Collectors Edition, Vol. 5, The Jewish Bride, 1970 .... 2.00
Collectors Edition, Vol. 5, Titus At Writing Desk, 1970 .... 5.00
Collectors Edition, Vol. 6, Boy Holding Flute, 1971 .... 2.00
Collectors Edition, Vol. 6, Charles I, 1971 .... 4.00
Collectors Edition, Vol. 6, The Merry Lute Player, 1971 .... 2.00
Collectors Edition, Vol. 7, Maidservant, 1972 ....2.00 to 4.00
Collectors Edition, Vol. 7, Prince Baltasor, 1972 .... 2.00
Collectors Edition, Vol. 7, The Bag Piper, 1972 .... 2.00
Collectors Edition, Vol. 8, Frederic F. Chopin, 1973 .... 2.00
Collectors Edition, Vol. 8, Ludwig Van Beethoven, 1973 .... 2.00
Collectors Edition, Vol. 8, Wolfgang Mozart, 1973 .... 2.00
Collectors Edition, Vol. 9, Cardinal, 1974 ....3.00 to 4.00
Collectors Edition, Vol. 9, Woodcock, 1974 .... 3.00
Collectors Edition, Vol. 10, Largemouth Bass, 1975 .... 3.00
Collectors Edition, Vol. 10, Sailfish, 1975 .... 3.00
Collectors Edition, Vol. 11, Bighorn Sheep, 1976 .... 5.00
Collectors Edition, Vol. 11, Chipmunk, 1976 .... 3.00
Collectors Edition, Vol. 12, Irish Setter, 1977 .... 3.00
Collectors Edition, Vol. 12, Labrador Retriever, 1977 ....*Illus* 3.00
Collectors Edition, Vol. 12, Springer Spaniel, 1977 .... 3.00
Collectors Edition, Vol. 14, Cottontail Rabbit, 1978 .... 3.00
Collectors Edition, Vol. 14, Mule Deer, 1978 .... 3.00
Collectors Edition, Vol. 14, Red Fox, 1978 .... 3.00
Collectors Edition, Vol. 15, Cowboy 1902, 1979 ....2.00 to 3.00
Collectors Edition, Vol. 15, Indian Trapper 1908, 1979 .... 2.00
Collectors Edition, Vol. 15, Lt. S.C. Robertson 1890, 1979 .... 5.00
Collectors Edition, Vol. 16, Canvas Back, 1980 .... 3.00
Collectors Edition, Vol. 16, Mallard, 1980 .... 3.00
Collectors Edition, Vol. 17, Great Elk, 1981 .... 3.00
Collectors Edition, Vol. 17, Pintail Duck, 1981 .... 3.00
Collectors Edition, Vol. 18, Cardinal, 1982 .... 4.00
Collectors Edition, Vol. 18, Whitetail Deer, 1982 .... 4.00
Collectors Edition, Vol. 19, Scarlet Tanager, 1983 .... 4.00
Colorado, State, 1959 .... 25.00
Colorado Centennial, 1976 ....10.00 to 15.00
Colorado Springs, 1972 .... 10.00
Convention, No. 1, Denver, 1971 .... 10.00
Convention, No. 2, Anaheim, June 19-25, 1972 ....35.00 to 37.00
Convention, No. 3, Detroit, 1973 ....16.00 to 19.00
Convention, No. 4, Lancaster, 1974 ....7.00 to 70.00
Convention, No. 5, Sacramento, 1975 ....11.00 to 12.00
Convention, No. 6, Hartford, 1976 ....5.00 to 9.00
Convention, No. 7, Louisville, 1977 ....5.00 to 9.00
Convention, No. 8, Chicago, 1978 ....5.00 to 10.00
Convention, No. 9, Houston, 1979, Cowboy 58.00
Convention, No. 9, Houston, 1979, Tiffany On Rocket 49.00
Convention, No. 10, Norfolk, 1980 ....6.00 to 25.00
Convention, No. 11, Las Vegas, 1981 ....20.00 to 25.00

Convention, No. 12, New Orleans, 1982 .... 7.00 to 29.00
Convention, No. 13, St. Louis, 1983 .... 50.00 to 151.00
Convention, No. 14, Hollywood, Florida, 1984 .... 20.00 to 24.00
Convention, No. 15, Las Vegas, 1985 .... 40.00 to 45.00
Convention, No. 16, Boston, Mass., 1986 .... 37.00 to 55.00
Convention, No. 17, Louisville, 1987 .... 65.00 to 66.00
Convention, No. 18, Portland, 1988 .... 29.00 to 35.00
Convention, No. 19, Kansas City, 1989 .... 45.00
Convention, No. 20, Kissimmee, 1990 .... 37.00
Convention, No. 21, Reno, 1991 .... 64.00
CPO, 1974 .... 12.00
Crappie, 1979 .... 15.00
Crispus Attucks, 1976 .... 5.00
CRLDA, 1973 .... 7.00
Dancing Scot, Short, 1963 .... 75.00
Dancing Scot, Tall, 1964 .... 25.00
Dancing Scot, Tall, Couple, 1964 .... 195.00
Dark Eyes Vodka, Jug, 1978 .... 6.00
Delaware, State, 1972 .... 6.00
Delco Battery, 1978 .... 25.00
Delft Blue, 1963 .... 5.00
Delft Rose, 1963 .... 6.00
Denver Rush To Rockies, 1970 .... 10.00
Dining Car, 1982 .... 80.00
Distillery, Red Fox, 1973 .... 800.00
District Executive Urn, 1986 .... 36.00
Due, 1963 .... 25.00 to 30.00
Don Giovanni, Opera, 1980 .... 150.00 to 165.00
Duck, 1957 .... 25.00
Duck Decoy, 1988, 375 Ml. 30.00
Ducks & Geese, 1955 .... 8.00
Ducks Unlimited, No. 1, Mallard, 1974 .... *Illus* 43.00 to 50.00
Ducks Unlimited, No. 2, Wood Duck, 1975 .... 45.00
Ducks Unlimited, No. 3, 40th Anniversary, 1977 .... 50.00
Ducks Unlimited, No. 4, Mallard, 1978 .... 39.00 to 45.00
Ducks Unlimited, No. 5, Canvasback, Drake, 1979 .... 40.00
Ducks Unlimited, No. 6, Blue-Winged Teal, 1980 .... 50.00
Ducks Unlimited, No. 7, Green-Winged Teal, 1981 .... 45.00
Ducks Unlimited, No. 8, Woody & His Brood, 1982 .... 45.00
Ducks Unlimited, No. 9, American Widgeons, 1983 .... 40.00 to 45.00
Ducks Unlimited, No. 10, Mallard, 1984 .... 65.00
Ducks Unlimited, No. 11, Pintail, Pair, 1985 .... 35.00
Ducks Unlimited, No. 12, Redhead, 1986 .... 30.00
Ducks Unlimited, No. 13, Bluebill, 1987 .... 50.00
Ducks Unlimited, No. 14, Gadwall Family, 1988 .... 39.00
Ducks Unlimited, No. 15, Black Duck, 1989 .... 85.00
Ducks Unlimited, No. 16, Canada Goose, 1989 .... 75.00
Ducks Unlimited, No. 17, Tundra Swan, 1991 .... 54.00
Duesenberg, 1934 Model J, Dark Blue, 1981 .... 125.00
Duesenberg, 1935, Convertible, Coupe, Gray, 1983 .... 245.00
Duesenberg, Light Blue, 1982 .... 110.00
Eagle, 1966 .... 10.00 to 12.00
Elks Club, 1968 .... 5.00 to 6.00
Emerald Crystal, Bourbon, 1968 .... 10.00
Emmett Kelly, Native Son Of Kansas, 1973 .... 60.00 to 65.00
Emmett Kelly, Willie The Clown, 1973 .... 25.00
Ernie's Flower Cart, 1976 .... 25.00
Evergreen State Club, 1974 .... 11.00 to 12.00
Executive, 1955, Royal Porcelain 300.00
Executive, 1956, Royal Gold Round 75.00
Executive, 1957, Royal Di Monte .... 45.00 to 50.00
Executive, 1958, Gray Cherub .... 200.00 to 250.00
Executive, 1959, Tavern Scene .... 49.00 to 54.00

Executive, 1960, Blue Cherub...75.00 to 85.00
Executive, 1961, Golden Chalice 40.00
Executive, 1962, Flower Basket.. 36.00
Executive, 1963, Royal Rose 30.00
Executive, 1964, Royal Gold Diamond.. 30.00
Executive, 1965, Marbled Fantasy 40.00
Executive, 1966, Majestic..22.00 to 25.00
Executive, 1967, Prestige.. 10.00
Executive, 1968, Presidential..7.00 to 10.00
Executive, 1969, Sovereign... 10.00
Executive, 1970, Charisma.. 10.00
Executive, 1971, Fantasia 10.00
Executive, 1972, Regency.. 12.00
Executive, 1973, Phoenician.. 10.00
Executive, 1974, Twin Cherubs 12.00
Executive, 1975, Reflections In Gold 12.00
Executive, 1976, Floro De Oro ....*Illus* 12.00
Executive, 1977, Golden Jubilee.. 12.00
Executive, 1978, Yellow Rose Of Texas... 15.00
Executive, 1979, Mother Of Pearl Vase 15.00
Executive, 1980, Titian.. 14.00
Executive, 1981, Royal Filigree, Cobalt Deluxe 18.00
Executive, 1982, Americana Pitcher.. 26.00
Executive, 1983, Musical Bell 20.00
Executive, 1984, Musical Bell, Noel.. 25.00
Executive, 1985, Italian Marble Vase 16.00
Executive, 1986, Bowl, Italian Marble... 32.00
Expo 74, 1974... 9.00
Falstaff, Opera, 1979 .... 125.00
Father's Day, 1988 .... 19.00
Fiesta Bowl, 1973.. 10.00
Figaro, Opera, 1977 .... 174.00 to 190.00
Fighting Bull, 1981... 15.00
Fiji Islands, 1971 .... 5.00
Fire Chief's Car, 1981 .... 125.00
Fire Engine, Ford, 1930 Model A, 1983 .... 165.00
Fire Engine, Mississippi, 1978...*Illus* 115.00
Fire Pumper Truck, Ford, 1934 Model, 1988 .... 50.00
Fire Truck, Mack, 1917 Model, 1982 .... 125.00
First National Bank Of Chicago, 1964... 2000.00 to 2200.00
Five Seasons Club, 1980... 10.00
Fleet Reserve, 1974... 7.00
Florida Shell, 1968 .... 5.00
Football, 1989.. 55.00
Football Hall Of Fame, 1972.. 14.00
Ford, Delivery Truck, Angelo's, Black, 1900 Model, 1984 .... 695.00
Ford, Fire Chief, 1928 Model, 1988... 110.00
Ford, Fire Chief, 1934 Model, 1988... 50.00
Ford, International Delivery Wagon, Black, 1984... 95.00
Ford, International Delivery Wagon, Green, 1984 .... 95.00
Ford, Model A, 1903 Model, Red, 1978.. 35.00
Ford, Model A, 1928 Model, 1980.. 70.00
Ford, Model A, Model 1903, Red, Black Trim, 1978... 55.00
Ford, Model T, Black, 1913 Model, 1974 .... 58.00
Ford, Mustang, 1964 Model, Black.. 110.00
Ford, Mustang, 1964 Model, Red... 60.00
Ford, Mustang, 1964 Model, White 60.00
Ford, Phaeton, 1929 Model, 1982 .... 55.00
Ford, Pickup Truck, 1935 Model, 1988... 59.00
Ford, Pickup Truck, Angelo's, 1935 Model, 1990 .... 80.00
Ford, Police Car, 1929 Model, Blue, 1982 .... 79.00
Ford, Police Car, 1929 Model, Yellow, 1983 .... 395.00
Ford, Police Tow Truck, 1935 Model, 1988... 24.00

Ford, Roadster, 1934 Model, Cream, 1990 .... 80.00
Ford, Salesman's, 1928 Model, Black, 1981 .... 1200.00
Ford, Salesman's, 1928 Model, Yellow, 1981 .... 800.00
Ford, Thunderbird, 1956 Model, Black, 1986 .... 75.00
Ford, Thunderbird, 1956 Model, Blue, 1986 .... 85.00
Ford, Thunderbird, 1956 Model, Gray, 1986 .... 65.00
Ford, Thunderbird, 1956 Model, Green, 1986 .... 65.00
Ford, Thunderbird, 1956 Model, Yellow, 1986 .... 55.00
Ford, Woodie Wagon, 1929 Model, 1983 .... 70.00
Foremost, Black & Gold, 1956 .... 100.00
Foremost, Gray & Gold, 1956 .... 100.00
Foremost, Pink Speckled Beauty, 1956 .... 100.00
Fox, Gold, 1969 .... 65.00
Fox, Green, 1965 .... 20.00

Beam, Executive, 1976,
Floro De Oro

Beam, Fire Engine,
Mississippi, 1978

Beam, Koala Bear, 1973

Beam, Maine, State, 1970

Fox, On Dolphin, 1980 ....15.00 to 21.00
Fox, Rennie The Runner, 1974 .... 14.00
Fox, Rennie The Surfer, 1975 .... 16.00
Franklin Mint, 1970 .... 6.00
Gem City Club, 1983 ....30.00 to 44.00
General Stark, 1972 .... 15.00
George Washington, 1976 ....14.00 to 15.00
Germany, Armed Forces, 1970 .... 5.00
Germany, Hansel & Gretel, 1971 ....5.00 to 6.00
Germany, Pied Piper, 1974 .... 6.00
Germany, Wiesbaden, 1973 .... 7.00
Gibson Girl, 1983 ....75.00 to 90.00
Gladiolas Festival, 1974 .... 7.00
Glen Campbell, 1976 ....11.00 to 15.00
Globe, Antique, 1980 .... 10.00
Golden Gate Casino, 1969 .... 79.00
Golden Nugget Casino, 1969 ....48.00 to 50.00
Golf Cart, Regal China, 1986 .... 30.00
Goose, Blue, 1979 .... 14.00
Grand Canyon, 1969 ....5.00 to 10.00
Gray Poodle, 1970 .... 10.00
Great Dane, 1976 .... 10.00
Great Expectations, Dickens, Holiday, 1988, 750 Ml. 50.00
Grecian, 1961 .... 5.00
Green China Jug, Pussy Willow, 1965 ....5.00 to 6.00
Hannah Dustin, 1973 .... 15.00
Harley-Davidson, 1988 .... 170.00
Harolds Club, Covered Wagon, Reno Or Bust, 1974 .... 25.00
Harolds Club, Covered Wagon, 1969 ....5.00 to 15.00
Harolds Club, Man In Barrel, No. 1, 1957 .... 400.00
Harolds Club, Man In Barrel, No. 2, 1958 .... 150.00
Harolds Club, Nevada, Gray, 1963 .... 100.00
Harolds Club, Nevada, Silver, 1964 ....100.00 to 150.00
Harolds Club, Pinwheel, 1965 ....40.00 to 50.00
Harolds Club, Silver Opal, 1957 .... 20.00
Harolds Club, Slot Machine, Blue, 1967 .... 12.00
Harolds Club, Slot Machine, Gray, 1968 .... 5.00
Harolds Club, VIP, 1967 ....40.00 to 55.00
Harolds Club, VIP, 1968 .... 57.00
Harolds Club, VIP, 1969 .... 250.00
Harolds Club, VIP, 1970 .... 47.00
Harolds Club, VIP, 1971 .... 60.00
Harolds Club, VIP, 1972 .... 20.00
Harolds Club, VIP, 1973 .... 25.00
Harolds Club, VIP, 1974 .... 15.00
Harolds Club, VIP, 1975 .... 20.00
Harolds Club, VIP, 1976 .... 20.00
Harolds Club, VIP, 1977 .... 20.00
Harolds Club, VIP, 1978 .... 25.00
Harolds Club, VIP, 1979 .... 30.00
Harolds Club, VIP, 1980 .... 30.00
Harolds Club, VIP, 1981 .... 95.00
Harolds Club, VIP, 1982 .... 95.00
Harrah's Club, Nevada, Gray, 1963 .... 650.00
Harrah's Club, Nevada, Silver, 1963 .... 500.00
Harvey's, 1969 .... 14.00
Hatfield, 1973 .... 20.00
Hawaii, State, 1959 ....32.00 to 35.00
Hawaii, State, 1967 .... 40.00
Hawaii Aloha Club, 1971 ....6.00 to 15.00
Hawaii Paradise, 1978 .... 15.00
Hawaiian Open, 7th, Pineapple, 1972 .... 7.00
Hawaiian Open, 8th, Golf Ball, 1973 .... 8.00

Hawaiian Open, 9th, Tiki God, 1974 ....7.00 to 10.00
Hawaiian Open, 10th, Menehune, 1975 .... 14.00
Hawaiian Open, 11th Outrigger, 1976 .... 13.00
Hawaiian Open, 11th, US Emblem, 1976 .... 14.00
Helmet & Boots, Short Timer, 1984 .... 29.00
Hemisfair, San Antonio, 1968... 10.00
Herre Bros., 1972 .... 40.00
Hoffman, 1969 .... 6.00
Home Builders, 1978.. 25.00
Hone Heke, 1981 ....195.00 to 200.00
Hongi Hika, 1980 ....195.00 to 200.00
Horse, Black, 1962...20.00 to 25.00
Horse, Brown, 1962 .... 15.00
Horseshoe Club, Reno, 1969... 8.00
Hyatt House, Chicago, 1971 .... 10.00
Hyatt Regency, New Orleans, 1976...10.00 to 12.00
Idaho, State, 1963 .... 50.00
Illinois, State, 1968..5.00 to 6.00
Indian Chief, 1979 ....10.00 to 12.00
Indianapolis Sesquicentennial, 1971 ....8.00 to 10.00
Indianapolis Speed Race, 1970.. 6.00
International Chili Society, 1976 .... 10.00
International Petroleum, 1971 ....5.00 to 7.00
Jackelope, 1971 .... 10.00
Jaguar, 1981.. 30.00
Jewel Tea, 50th Anniversary, 1982 .... 50.00
Jewel Tea Wagon, 1974... 75.00
Jim Beam Jug, Black, 1982... 35.00
Jim Beam Jug, Dark Blue, 1982 ....25.00 to 35.00
Jim Beam Jug, Dark Green, 1982 .... 35.00
Jim Beam Jug, Light Blue, 1982... 35.00
John Arthur, Past Presidents, 1977 .... 5000.00
John Henry, 1972 .... 15.00
Kaiser International, 1971.. 5.00
Kangaroo, 1977 .... 15.00
Kansas, State, 1960.. 40.00
Kentucky, Black Horse Head Stopper, State, 1967 .... 12.00
Kentucky, White Horse Head Stopper, State, 1967................................. 30.00
Kentucky Colonel, 1970 .... 5.00
Key West, Florida, 1972..5.00 to 6.00
King Kamehameha, 1972.. 9.00
King Kong, 1976 .... 8.00
Kiwi Bird, 1974 ....5.00 to 10.00
Koala Bear, 1973.. *Illus* 15.00 to 16.00
Laramie, Centennial Jubilee 1868-1968, 1968 .... 6.00
Largemouth Bass, 1973 .... 15.00
Las Vegas, 1969... 6.00
Las Vegas Show Girl, Blond, 1981.. 50.00
Legion Music, Joliet Legion Band, 1978 .... 15.00
Light Bulb, 1979 .... 14.00
Lombard, Lilac, 1969.. 5.00
London Bridge, 1971..5.00 to 8.00
London Bridge With Medallion, 1969.. 175.00
Louisville Downs, 1978...5.00 to 10.00
Madame Butterfly, Opera, 1977.. 225.00
Madame Butterfly, Opera, Paperweight, 1977 .... 35.00
Magpies, 1977.. 18.00
Maine, State, 1970..*Illus* 6.00
Mallard Duck, 1957.. 20.00
Marbled Fantasy, 1965 .... 37.00
Mare & Foal, For The Love Of A Foal, 1982 .... 50.00
Marina City, 1962.. 20.00
Marine Corps, 1975..30.00 to 35.00

Beam, Martha Washington, 1975

Beam, Mortimer Snerd, 1976

Beam, Muskie, National Freshwater
Fishing Hall Of Fame, 1983

Mark Anthony, 1962		20.00
Martha Washington, 1975	*Illus*	10.00
McCoy, 1973		15.00
Mephistopheles, Opera, 1979		150.00
Mercedes Benz, 1974 Model, Blue, 1987		35.00
Mercedes Benz, 1974 Model, Gold, 1988		75.00
Mercedes Benz, 1974 Model, Green, 1987		45.00
Mercedes Benz, 1974 Model, Mocha, 1987		40.00
Mercedes Benz, 1974 Model, Sand Beige, Pa., 1987		35.00
Mercedes Benz, 1974 Model, Silver, Australia, 1987		130.00
Mercedes Benz, 1974 Model, White, 1986		45.00
Michigan, State, 1972		5.00 to 6.00
Milwaukee Stein, 1972		28.00 to 45.00
Mint 400, 3rd, China Stopper, 1970		90.00
Mint 400, 4th, Metal Stopper, 1971		8.00
Mint 400, 5th, 1972		8.00
Mint 400, 6th, 1973		8.00 to 9.00
Mint 400, 7th, 1975		9.00 to 10.00
Mint 400, 8th, 1976		10.00
Montana, State, 1963		60.00 to 65.00
Monterey Bay Club, 1977		9.00 to 10.00
Mortimer Snerd, 1976	*Illus*	25.00
Mr. Goodwrench, 1978		30.00
Mt. St. Helens, 1980		25.00
Multi-Glo, 1975		6.00
Musicians On Wine Cask, 1964		5.00
Muskie, 1971		15.00 to 20.00
Muskie, National Freshwater Fishing Hall Of Fame, 1983	*Illus*	30.00
National Licensed Beverage Assoc., 1975		5.00
Nevada, State, 1963		35.00
New Hampshire, State, 1967		5.00 to 6.00
New Hampshire Eagle, 1971		20.00
New Jersey, Blue Gray, State, 1963		45.00 to 52.00
New Jersey, Yellow, State, 1963		50.00

New Mexico, Bicentennial, 1976... 10.00
New Mexico, State, 1972 .... 5.00
New Mexico, Wedding Vase, 1972 .... 10.00
New York, The Big Apple, 1979 .... 12.00
New York World's Fair, 1964 .... 10.00
Noel, Executive Bell, 29th, 1983 .... 30.00
Noel, Executive Bell, 30th, 1984 .... 25.00
North Dakota, State, 1964 ....55.00 to 60.00
Northern Pike, 1978.. 15.00
Nutcracker, 1978...18.00 to 100.00
Nutcracker, Holiday, 1989 .... 50.00
Nutcracker, Holiday, 1990 .... 49.00
Nutcracker, Presidential, 1989 .... 50.00
Oatmeal Jug, 1966.. 45.00
Oh Kentucky, 1981 .... 75.00
Ohio, State, 1966 .... 5.00
Ohio State Fair, 1973 ....Illus 5.00 to 6.00
Oldsmobile, 1904 Model, 1972...45.00 to 65.00
Olsonite Eagle Race Car, No. 48, 1975 .... 65.00
Opaline Crystal, 1969.. 10.00
Oregon, State, 1959.. 22.00
Oregon Liquor Control, 1984... 32.00
Osco Drug, 1987 .... 40.00
Owl, L.V.N.H., 1982.. 45.00
Paddy Wagon, 1983.. 140.00
Panda Bears, 1980 .... 20.00
Passenger Car, 1981 .... 45.00
Paul Bunyan, 1970 .... 9.00
Paul Saroff, Past Presidents, 1976.. 5000.00
Pearl Harbor, 1972..17.00 to 18.00
Pearl Harbor Survivors, 1976.. 10.00
Pennsylvania, State, 1967.. 6.00
Pennsylvania Dutch Club, 1974 ....11.00 to 12.00
Perch Pretty, 1980 .... 15.00
Permian Basin Oil Show, 1972 .... 5.00
PGA 53rd Golf Tournament, 1971.. 5.00
Pheasant, 1960..10.00 to 12.00
Phi Sigma Kappa, 1973.. 5.00
Phoenician, 1973... 10.00
Police Car, 1929 Model, 1982 .... 100.00
Police Car, 1929 Model, Yellow, 1983... 450.00
Police Patrol Car, 1934 Model, Black & White, 1989 .... 72.00
Police Patrol Car, 1934 Model, Yellow, 1989 .... 130.00
Political, Democrat, Convention, 1988 .... 35.00
Political, Donkey & Elephant, 1980, Superman, Pair 24.00
Political, Donkey, 1960, Campaigner 16.00
Political, Donkey, 1968, Clown ....6.00 to 22.00
Political, Donkey, 1972, Football ....6.00 to 7.00
Political, Donkey, 1976, Drum 6.00
Political, Donkey, 1980, Superman...10.00 to 12.00
Political, Elephant, 1960, Campaigner... 16.00
Political, Elephant, 1964, Boxer 20.00
Political, Elephant, 1968, Clown.. 6.00
Political, Elephant, 1970, Spiro Agnew.................................Illus 1000.00
Political, Elephant, 1972, Miami Beach........................400.00 to 550.00
Political, Elephant, 1972, San Diego 20.00
Political, Elephant, 1972, Washington, D.C., Feb. 10 Dinner 350.00
Political, Elephant, 1976, Drum... 8.00
Political, Elephant, 1976, Kansas City.. 15.00
Political, Elephant, 1980, Superman... 10.00
Political, Republican Convention, 1988.. 35.00
Ponderosa, 1969.. 6.00
Pony Express, 1968.. 8.00

Portland Bottle & Rose, Convention, Red, 1988.. 35.00
Portland Bottle & Rose, Convention, Yellow, 1988... 35.00
Portland Rose Festival, 1972 ....3.00 to 5.00
Poulan Chain Saw, 1979 .... 25.00
Powell Expedition, 1969 .... 6.00
Preakness, 100th, Pimlico, 1975.. 8.00
Pretty Perch, 1980 .... 15.00
Prima Donna, 1969... 8.00
Pyrex Coffee Warmer, Black, 1954 .... 10.00
Queensland, 1978... 20.00
Rabbit, Texas, 1971 .... 8.00
Rainbow Trout, 1975... 15.00
Ralph's Market, 1973.. 14.00
Ram, 1958, Trophy... 80.00
Ramada Inn, 1976 ....8.00 to 10.00

Beam, Ohio State Fair, 1973

Beam, Political, Elephant, 1970, Spiro Agnew

Beam, Rocky Marciano, 1973

Beam, Spenger's Fish Grotto, 1977

Red Mile, 1975 .... 12.00
Redwood Empire, 1967 .... 5.00
Reflection In Gold, 1975 .... 15.00
Reidsville, 1973 .... 5.00
Renee, 1974 .... 14.00
Rennie The Runner, 1974 .... 12.00
Rennie The Surfer, 1975 .... 12.00
Republic Of Texas Club, 1980 ....15.00 to 16.00
Richard's, New Mexico, 1967 .... 7.00
Robin, 1969 .... 8.00
Rocky Marciano, 1973 ....*Illus* 25.00
Rubber Capitol Club, 1973 .... 15.00
Ruidoso Downs, Pointed Ears, 1968 .... 25.00
Sahara Invitational, 1971 .... 7.00
Sailfish, 1957 .... 20.00
Saint Louis Arch, 1964 .... 10.00
Salesman Glass Bottle, Award, 1980 .... 250.00
Samoa, 1973 ....5.00 to 7.00
San Diego, 1968 .... 5.00
San Francisco Cable Car, 1983 ....35.00 to 45.00
Santa Claus, 1983 ....130.00 to 150.00
Santa Fe, 1960 ....125.00 to 150.00
Saturday Evening Post, Benjamin Franklin, 1975 .... 4.00
Saturday Evening Post, Game Called Because Of Rain, 1975 .... 4.00
Saturday Evening Post, Ye Pipe & Bowl, 1975 .... 4.00
Screech Owl, 1979 .... 22.00
Seafair, 1972 .... 30.00
Seattle World's Fair, 1962 ....10.00 to 18.00
Seoul, Korea, 1988 .... 40.00
Setter, 1958 .... 20.00
Sheraton Hotel, 1975 .... 8.00
Short Timer, Armed Forces, 1975 .... 20.00
Showgirl, Blond, Las Vegas Convention Gift, 1981 .... 50.00
Showgirl, Brunette, Las Vegas Convention Gift, 1981 .... 50.00
Shriners, El Kahir Pyramid, 1975 .... 15.00
Shriners, Moila, Camel, 1975 ....10.00 to 15.00
Shriners, Moila, Sword, 1972 .... 25.00
Shriners, Order Of Shriners, 1970 .... 5.00
Shriners, Rajah, 1977 ....20.00 to 25.00
Shriners, Western Shriners Association, 1980 .... 20.00
Siamese Cat, 1967 .... 12.00
Sigma Nu Fraternity, Kentucky, 1977 .... 10.00
Sigma Nu Fraternity, Michigan, 1977 .... 10.00
Slot Machine, Gray, Regal China, 1968 .... 8.00
Smith's North Shore Club, 1972 .... 15.00
Smoke Glo, 1975 .... 4.00
Smoked Geni, 1964 ....9.00 to 20.00
Snow Goose, 1979 .... 40.00
South Carolina, State, 1970 .... 6.00
South Dakota, Mt. Rushmore, 1969 .... 6.00
South Dakota, State, 1969 .... 5.00
Space Shuttle, 1986 .... 30.00
Spenger's Fish Grotto, 1977 ....*Illus* 20.00
Sports Car Club Of America, 1976 .... 15.00
St. Bernard, 1979 .... 30.00
St. Louis Arch, 1964 .... 10.00
St. Louis Club, 1972 ....10.00 to 12.00
Statue Of Liberty, 1975 .... 10.00
Stein, German, 1983 .... 25.00
Stone Mountain, 1974 .... 8.00
Sturgeon, 1980 ....15.00 to 18.00
Stutz Bearcat, 1914, Gray, 1977 .... 55.00
Stutz Bearcat, 1914, Yellow, 1977 .... 58.00

Beam, Tigers,
1977

Beam, Uncle Sam With Eagle,
Royal Doulton, 1984, 5 In.

Beam, White
Poodle, 1970

Submarine Redfin, 1970 ....5.00 to 6.00
Sunburst Crystal, Black, 1974.. 5.00
Sunburst Crystal, Red, 1974... 2.00
Superdome, 1975 .... 5.00
Swagman, 1979 .... 15.00
Sydney Opera House, 1977... 18.00 to 20.00
Te Rauparaha, 1982... 175.00
Telephone, 100 Digit, 1983 ....40.00 to 50.00
Telephone, 1897 Model, 1978 .... 65.00
Telephone, 1919 Dial, 1980... 50.00
Telephone, Battery, 1982..25.00 to 35.00
Telephone, French Cradle, 1979...15.00 to 25.00
Telephone, Wall Set, 1975...42.00 to 55.00
Texas Rabbit, 1971...5.00 to 10.00
Thailand, 1969 .... 5.00
Thomas Flyer, Blue, 1976.. 65.00
Thomas Flyer, White, 1976 .... 65.00
Tiffany Poodle, 1973 ....15.00 to 20.00
Tigers, 1977 ....*Illus* 25.00
Tobacco Festival, 1973 .... 15.00
Tombstone, 1970... 6.00
Train, Caboose, Gray, 1988.. 50.00
Train, Caboose, Orange, 1980.. 75.00
Train, Caboose, Yellow, 1985... 65.00
Train, Casey Jones Accessory Set 60.00
Train, Casey Jones Bumpers.. 12.00
Train, Casey Jones Caboose, 1989 .... 32.00
Train, Casey Jones Tank Car, 1990 .... 40.00
Train, Casey Jones Track 7.00
Train, Casey Jones With Tender, 1989.. 39.00
Train, Combination Car, 1988... 30.00
Train, Flat Car, 1988 .... 35.00
Train, General Locomotive, 1986.. 69.00
Train, Grant Baggage Car, 1981... 45.00
Train, Grant Dining Car, 1982.. 85.00
Train, Grant Locomotive, 1979 .... 80.00
Train, Grant Passenger Car, 1981... 40.00
Train, J. B.Turner Locomotive, 1982 .... 50.00
Train, Log Car, 1984.. 65.00
Train, Lumber Car, 1985 .... 45.00
Train, Tank Car, 1983 ....30.00 to 40.00
Train, Track.. 10.00

Train, Water Tower, 1985 ....25.00 to 30.00
Train, Wood Tender, 1988 .... 50.00
TraveLodge, Sleepy Bear, 1972 ....8.00 to 35.00
Treasure Chest, 1979 .... 10.00
Trout Unlimited, 1977 .... 15.00
Truth Or Consequences, 1974.. 8.00
Turquoise China Jug, 1966 .... 6.00
Turtle, 1975.. 20.00
Twin Bridges Club, 1971 ....22.00 to 40.00
Twin Cherubs, 1974... 10.00
U.S. Open, 1972.. 10.00
Uncle Sam Fox, 1971... 15.00
Uncle Sam With Eagle, Royal Doulton, 1984, 5 In................................*Illus* 70.00
Veterans Of Foreign Wars, 1971 ....5.00 to 10.00
Viking, 1973 .... 12.00
Volkswagen, Blue, 1973 ....49.00 to 50.00
Volkswagen, Red, 1973 ....49.00 to 50.00
Von's 75th Anniversary, 1981 ....25.00 to 35.00
Walleyed Pike, 1977... 15.00
Washington Bicentennial, 1976 .... 12.00
Washington State, State, 1975... 5.00 to 10.00
Waterman, Glazed, 1980 .... 50.00
Waterman, Norfolk Convention Gift, 1980, Pair... 6.00
West Virginia, State, 1963 ....115.00 to 150.00
WGA, 1971... 5.00
White Fox, 1969..35.00 to 65.00
White Poodle, 1970..*Illus* 10.00
Wolverine Club, 1975 ....10.00 to 12.00
Woodpecker, 1969.. 8.00
Wyoming, State, 1965 .... 52.00
Yellow Katz, 1967 ....15.00 to 20.00
Yellowstone, 1972 .... 5.00
Yosemite, Decal Map, 1967 .... 5.00
Yuma Rifle Club, 1968 ....19.00 to 25.00
Zimmerman Liquors, 2-Handled Jug, 1965..55.00 to 65.00
Zimmerman Liquors, 50th Anniversary, 1983 ....40.00 to 50.00
Zimmerman Liquors, Bell, Dark Blue, 1976 .... 5.00
Zimmerman Liquors, Blue Beauty, 1969, 10 In. 10.00
Zimmerman Liquors, Cherubs, Lavender, 1968 .... 5.00
Zimmerman Liquors, Cherubs, Salmon, 1968..5.00 to 7.00
Zimmerman Liquors, Eldorado, Gray Blue, 1978 .... 5.00
Zimmerman Liquors, Peddler, 1971..5.00 to 10.00
Zimmerman Liquors, Vase, Green, 1972 .... 5.00
Zimmerman Liquors, Z, 1970 ....5.00 to 10.00

───────────────── **BEER** ─────────────────

History says that beer was first made in America in the Roanoke Colony of Virginia in 1587. It is also claimed that the Pilgrims brought some over on the already crowded Mayflower. William Penn started a brewery in 1683. By the time of the Civil War, beer was made and bottled in all parts of the United States. In the early years the beer was poured from kegs or sold in ordinary unmarked black glass bottles. English stoneware bottles were in common use in this country from about 1860 to 1890. Excavations in many inner cities still unearth these sturdy containers. A more or less standard bottle was used by about 1870. It held a quart of liquid and measured about 10 inches high. The early ones were plain and had a cork stopper. Later bottles had embossed lettering on the sides. The lightning stopper was invented in 1875 and many bottles had various types of wire and lever-type seals that were replacements for the corks. In the 1900s Crown corks were used. It wasn't long before plain bottles with paper labels appeared, but cans were soon the containers preferred by many. The standard thick-topped glass beer bottle shape of the 1870s, as well as modern beer bottles, are included in this category. The bottles can be found in clear, brown, aqua, or amber glass. A few cobalt blue, milk glass, or red examples are known. Some bottles have turned slightly amethyst in color from the sun. Collectors are

often interested in local breweries and books listing the names and addresses of companies
have been written. (See Bibliography.) Beer bottle collectors often search for advertising
trays, signs, and other *go-withs* collected as *breweriana*. These are listed under Go-Withs
at the end of this book.

BEER, 3-Piece Mold, Red-Puce, Applied Tapered Lip, IP, Dug, 1850, 7 7/8 In. 523.00
A. Berkman & Co., Boston, Mass., Blob Top, Bale.. 12.00
A. Colburn Co., Flask, Embossed Design, Picnic 20.00
A. Marotta, Boston, Mass., A With Leaf Design, Lightning Stopper, Blob Top, Pt. 22.00
A. Scheidt's Brewing Co., Norristown, Pa., Aqua, Squatty Blob................................. 12.00
A.W. Kemison Co., Auburn, Calif., 4-Piece Mold, Amber, Tooled Crown Top 30.00
A.W. Kemison Co., Auburn, Calif., Amber, Blob Top, Qt... 20.00
ABC Co., Cobalt Blue, Embossed.. 22.00
Acme Brewing Co., Los Angeles, Calif., 11 Oz. ....9.00 to 10.00
Acme Brewing Co., San Francisco, Calif., Acme Bock, Green, 12 Oz. 21.00
Adam W. Young, Canton, Ohio, Aqua, Qt.. 29.00
Adam Weiser, Spokane, Wa., Amber, Blob Top, Pt. 50.00
Adam's Ale House, Concord, N.H., Red Amber, Pt. 125.00
Alabama Brewing, San Francisco, Calif., 1/2 Pt.. 30.00
Angel's Brewery, M. Hubler, Chocolate Amber, 4-Piece Mold, Blob Top, Qt. 120.00
Anheuser-Busch, Amber, Applied Crown Top 20.00
Anheuser-Busch, Christmas, Red & White Enameled, Gold Leaf, 1981, 12 Oz. 11.00
Anheuser-Busch, Embossed, A With Eagle, Applied Crown Top................................. 45.00
Anheuser-Busch, Washington, D.C., Large A With Eagle, Pt. 35.00
Anheuser-Busch Brewing Co., Battle Creek, Mi., Embossed..................................... 45.00
Anheuser-Busch Brewing Co., San Francisco, Calif., Medium Amber, 7 3/4 In........... 154.00
Anthracite, Lady's Leg, Amber, Short 80.00
Apache Ale, Arizona Brewing Co., Phoenix, Ariz., 11 Oz... 11.00
August Stoer Milwaukee Lager, Manchester, N.H., Amber, Pt. 30.00
B & J, Oakland, Cal., 1/2 Pt... 15.00
Barbarossa, Red Top Brewing Co., Cincinnati, U.S.A., 12 Oz. 4.00
Bartholomay Brewing, Rochester, Wheel With Wings, Stopper, Amber, Pt................. 40.00
Beisenbach & Co., Boston, Mass., Watermelon Slug On Shoulder, Aqua, Pt............... 15.00
Belmont Brewing Co., Martin's Ferry, Ohio, Amber, Bell, Qt.................................... 20.00
Benckart, Lexington, Ky., Aqua, Qt. 25.00
Berghoff, Fort Wayne, Ind., Script, Amber, Crown Top, Qt.. 7.00
Berghoff Brewing Co., Fort Wayne, Ind., Amber, Blob Top, Qt.................................. 15.00
Blackhawk, Rock River Brewing Co., Rockford, Ill., Painted Label, 8 Oz.................... 11.00
Blatz Old Heidelburg, Label, Case, May, 1935... 195.00
Boca Bob, Golden Yellow Amber, 11 1/2 In. 143.00
Boca Bob, Yellow Amber, Qt.. 15.00
Boefer & Kruse, K.C., Green, Porcelain Stopper, Pt. 15.00
Botanic, Liverpoole, Picture Of Eye, Emerald Green, Applied Top, Pt. 25.00
Brady Birds, Hartford, Ct., Stoneware, Lightning Stopper, Qt. 45.00
Breckenfelder & Jochem, Oakland, Calif., Qt... 18.00
Brilliant Emerald Green, Blob Top, S On Front, 11 1/2 In. 68.00
Budweiser, Amber, 4 1/4 In...*Illus* 3.00
Buffalo Brewing, San Francisco, Medium Yellow Amber, 9 1/8 In. 44.00
Buffalo Brewing Co., Sacramento, Cal., Horseshoe With Buffalo, Amber.............25.00 to 85.00
Bunker Hill Lager, Charlestown, Mass., Amber, Pt. ....20.00 to 65.00
C. Berry, Boston, Watermelon Slug Plate Shoulder, Porcelain Stopper, Pt............35.00 to 55.00
C. Schmidt & Sons, Hoboken, N.J., Clear, Pt. 20.00
C.C. Warren & Co., Toledo, Ohio, Blob Top, 5 1/2 In. 52.00
C.R. Hartson, Cooperstown, N.Y., Golden Amber, Porcelain Stopper, Pt.................... 35.00
Cal. Bottling Works, T Bauth Sons Co., Amber, Blob Top, Tooled Lip, Qt. 30.00
Cal. Bottling Co., John Weiland's Export Beer, Honey Amber, Blob Top, Qt. 100.00
Cal. Bottling Co., John Weiland's Export Beer, Honey Amber, Applied Top, Pt. 25.00
Cal. Bottling Co., John Weiland's Export Beer, Red Amber, Blob Top, Pt.................... 45.00
Cal. Bottling Co., John Wieland's Export Beer, Sac., Applied Top, 1/2 Pt. 55.00
California Pop Beer, Stoneware, Gray Color Glaze, Cobalt Blue, 10 3/8 In. 88.00
Carling's Red Cap Ale, Cleveland, Oh., Green, 12 Oz.. 1.00
Central Bottling Co., A. Wolff, New York, Aqua, Lightning Stopper, Pt...................... 30.00
Central Breweries, Inc., East St. Louis, Ill., 1930s, 12 Oz.. 12.00

Beer, Flecks, Amber, 3 3/4 In.;
Beer, Budweiser, Amber, 4 1/4 In.; Beer, Prager, Amber

Charles Joly, Philadelphia, Emerald Green, Blob Top, Pt....................................34.00 to 45.00
Charles L. Lehnert Brewery, Catasauqua, Pa., Aqua, Crown Top, Contents, 1900s, Qt.   25.00
Charles L. Lehnert Brewery, Catasauqua, Pa., Aqua, Crown Top, Pt. 50.00
Chicago Lager, San Francisco, Burst Bubble Side, Qt. 175.00
Chicago Lager, San Francisco, Script, Applied Top, Qt......................................   70.00
City Brewing Co., Wapokeneta, Ohio, Amber, Blob Top, Qt. 30.00
Clark & Roberts, Boston, Mass., Green Aqua, Bail & Stopper, Pt. 25.00
Clark & Roberts, Boston, Mass., Monogram, Whittled, Honey Amber, Pt. 35.00
Columbia Brewing, Logansport, Ind., Amber, Pt. 10.00
Columbia Weiss Beer Brewery, St. Louis, Mo., Teepee, Emerald Green, Pt. 65.00
Columbia Weiss Beer Brewery, St. Louis, Mo., Teepee, Red Amber, Stopper, Pt.......   65.00
Consumer's Brewing Co., Norfolk, Va., Deer, Green Aqua, Pt., 2 Piece 55.00
Coors, Commemorative, Clown, 1776-1976 ....   9.00
Coors, Commemorative, Fisherman, 1776-1976 ....   29.00
Coors Pilsner, Gold Waterfall 7.00
Corona Familiar, Painted Label, Texas Tax Stamp, 940 Ml...................................   4.00
Cream Ale, A. Templeton, Louisville, Ky., Amber, Mug Base, Qt. 55.00
Creedmore, New York, Aqua, Lightning Stopper, Squatty, Qt...............................   75.00
Cripple Creek Bottling Works, Amethyst, Blob Top, 8 1/4 In. 60.00
D.W. Defreest, Stoneware, Cobalt Blue On Reverse 80.00
Davenport Brewing Co., Davenport, Iowa, Hawkeye Emblem, Picnic 40.00
Delaney & Young, Eureka, Des Moines, Iowa, Qt..   7.50
Des Moines Brewing Co., Des Moines, Iowa, Amber, Picnic..................................35.00 to 40.00
Donaher's On The Square, Worcester, Mass., Porcelain Stopper, Blob Top, Pt. 30.00
Double Diamond Ale, Suffolk Brewing Co., Boston, Mass., Olive Green.....................   30.00
Dukehart & Co., Maryland Brewery, Baltimore, Amber, 8 1/8 In. 198.00
Dukehart &. Co., Baltimore, Md., Amber, Bulbous, Long Neck...................................   80.00
E. Bedker Brewing Co., Lancaster, Oh., Citron, Stopper, Qt. 75.00
E. Ottenville, Aqua, Blob, Qt..   125.00
E. Roussel, Philadelphia, Silver Medal 1847, Green, Embossed Star, IP......................   50.00
E. Shaw, Spencer, Mass., Eagle Picture, Clear, Bold Strike, Stopper, Pt. 45.00
E.L. Kerns, Elk Head, Green Aqua, Pt..   20.00
E.O. Jones Co., Pabst, Youngstown, O., Amber, Pt...   37.00
E.T. Delaney & Co., Bottlers, Plattsburg, N.Y., Aqua, Pt. 15.00
Ebner, Wilmington, Dela., Pt..   2.00
Eckert And Becker Brewing, Michigan, Chocolate, Qt....................................   45.00
Edward Wagner, Aqua, Pt...   35.00
Elkins Brewing Co., W.V., Amber, Crown Top, 12 Oz.......................................   6.00
Empire State Bottling Co., N.Y., Amber, Bowling Pin, Pt...................................   25.00
Enterprise Brewing Co., San Francisco, Deep Red Amber, 8 1/8 In. 198.00
Enterprise Brewing Co., San Francisco, Red Amber, 12 In....................................   60.50
Erie Brewing Co., Erie, Pa., Amber, 12 Oz...   12.00
Ernst Tosetti Brewing Co., Tosetti Means Quality, Chicago, Aqua, Blob Top, Pt. 20.00
Etna Brewery, Etna Mills, Amber, 1/2 Pt. 10.00
Excelsior Bottled Lager, Brooklyn, N.Y., Bold Embossing, Pt. 15.00
Excelsior Bottling Works, Dayton, Ohio, Yellow Amber, Qt..................................   25.00

Excelsior Lager, Blatz, Aqua, Applied Blob Top 15.00
Excelsior Lager, Blatz, Aqua, Unusual Cork & Lead Stopper, Pt. 35.00
F. Hinckel Sparkling Lager Beer, Albany, N.Y., Honey, Pt. 36.00
F. McKinney's Mead, Amber, 10 In. ....*Illus* 35.00
Fairbanks & Beard, Stoneware 50.00
Feigenspan, Newark, N.J., Amber, Whittled, Blob Top, Porcelain Stopper, Pt. 38.00
Flecks, Amber, 3 3/4 In. ....*Illus* 3.50
Florida Brewing Co., Tampa, Fla. 25.00
Foss-Schneider Co., Cincinnati, Ohio, Amber, Crown Top, Qt. 7.00
Francis Scheider Dusch, Richmond, Va., Aqua, Blob Top 297.00
Frank Jones Ale, Smoky Clear, Crown Top, Pt. 25.00
Frederick Miller Brewing, Milwaukee, Pt. 30.00
Fredericksburg Bottling Co., 7 7/8 In. 44.00
Fredericksburg Bottling Co., San Francisco, Ca., Green, Qt. ....40.00 to 45.00
Fredericksburg Bottling Co., San Francisco, Dark Olive Green, Qt. 55.00
Fredericksburg Bottling Co., San Francisco, Medium Amber, 7 3/4 In. 88.00
Fredericksburg Brewery Co., San Jose, Red Amber, Blob Top, Qt. ....35.00 to 45.00
Gambrinus Bottling Co., San Francisco, Qt. 25.00
Geo. F. Hewett, Worcester, Mass., Aqua, Blob Top 5.00
Geo. Schlegel & Co., Columbus, Oh., Deep Olive Amber, Qt. 412.50
George Bechtel Brewing Co., Stapleton, Staten Island, Blob Top, Pt. 25.00
George Frank, Orange, N.J., Citron Green, Blob Top, Pt. 75.00
German Brewing Co., Cumberland, Md., Indian Logo, Amber, Crown Top, 12 Oz. 8.00
Globe Steam Brewing Co., Red Amber, Blob Top, Squatty, Pt. 69.00
Gold Crown, United States Brewing Co., Chicago, Ill., 7 Oz. 7.00
Golden Eagle Brewing Co., Philadelphia, Aqua, Lightning Stopper, Blob Top, Pt. 55.00
Golden Gate Bottling Works, Bear, Standing, Amber, Qt. ....60.00 to 100.00
Golden Gate Brewing, San Francisco, Bear, Amber, Qt. 155.00
Grace Bros. Brewing Co., Santa Rosa, Calif., Amber, Blob Top, Pt. ....10.00 to 15.00
Grafton Brewing Co., Grafton, W.V., Amber, Crown Top, 12 Oz. 6.00
Grasser Brand Brewing Co., Toledo, Oh., Amber, Blob Top, Qt. 15.00
H & H, Dover, Mass., Aqua, Bail Type Stopper, Blob Top, Qt. 55.00
H.E. Scott Cream Beer, Stoneware, Salt Glaze, Gray, Cobalt Blue Glaze, 9 1/2 In. 88.00
Haberle's Black River Ale, Haberle Congress Brewing Co., Inc., Syracuse, 1940s 15.00
Halstead, Stoneware, Gray, Cobalt Blue Glaze, Cone Top, Salt Glaze, 10 In. 176.00
Hamm's, Bartender Bear, 1973 .... 135.00
Hansen & Kahler, Stopper, 1/2 Pt. 10.00
Haverhill, Mass., Aqua, Whittled, Lightning Stopper, Pt. 100.00
Hinckel Brewing Co., Smoky Yellow Amber, Pt. 20.00
Hohmann & Bartlett, Schlitz, Manchester, N.H., 1903, Pt. 17.00
Hohmann & Bartlett, Schlitz, Manchester, N.H., Amethyst, Pt. 27.00
Home Brewing Co., Indianapolis, Ind., Red Amber, Qt. ....26.00 to 35.00
Home Brewing Co., Richmond, Va., Amber, Eagle On Tree Stump, Blob Top 88.00
Home Brewing Co., Richmond, Va., Honey Amber, Converted Mold, Blob Top 143.00

Beer, F. McKinney's Mead,
Amber, 10 In.

Beer, Zywiec Beer, Warszawa, Stanley
Stawski, Chicago, Amber, 9 In.

Honolulu Brewing Co., Honolulu, Aqua, Blob Top, Qt. ....35.00 to 40.00
Hoosier Beer, South Bend Brewing Co., South Bend, Ind., 12 Oz. 16.00
Hoppe & Strub, Toledo, Oh., Citron 45.00
Hoster's Weiner Beer, Eagle & Shield, Blob Top, Amber, Qt. 25.00
Howe & Streeter, Schlitz Milwaukee Lager, Manchester, N.H., Aqua, Stopper, Pt. 19.00
Hoxie Brewing Co., Albany, Ice Blue, Square Shoulders, 1/2 Pt. 45.00
I. Joseph, Pittsburgh, Pa., Amber, Blob Top, Large 25.00
Independent Brewing Assn., Marion, Pa., Amber, Hunter, Dog, Tree, Blob Top 30.00
Indianapolis Brewing Co., Indianapolis, Ind., Amber, Pt. 5.00
J. Hindles, Pottery, Cobalt Blue Top, Star 100.00
J. Lebkuchner, N.Y., Eagle, 2 Flags, Aqua, Whittled, Lightning Stopper, Pt. 30.00
J. Nash, Pittston, Pa., Green Aqua, Pt. 8.00
J. Staab, Xx On Shoulder, Pottery, Chocolate Brown 75.00
J. Stoeckert, New Ulm, Pottery, Tan 50.00
J.E. Gilkinson, Sea Beach Palace, Coney Island, Aqua, Blob Top, Pt. 70.00
J.P. Robinson Bottler Of Fine Home Beer, Manchester, Va., Aqua, Blob Top 517.00
Jacob Rupert's New York Lager, Aqua, Stopper, Pt. 20.00
Jacobus Bros., Turner's Falls, Mass., Deep Aqua, Lightning Stopper, Blob Top, Pt. 35.00
John F. McGinty's Brewery, Tamaqua, Pa., Light Yellow 20.00
John Fauser, US Bottling, Deep Red Amber, Whittled, Blob Top, Qt. 50.00
John Haub, Sacramento, Ca., Orange Amber, Blob Top, Qt. 50.00
John Hauck Brewing Co., Cincinnati, Oh., Amber, Blob Top, Qt. 15.00
John Hauck Brewing Co., Golden Eagle, Embossed Label, Original Cap 40.00
John Lannon, Fall River, Mass., Lightning Stopper, Blob Top, Pt. 12.00
John M. Krug, Philadelphia, Blue Green 39.00
John Stanton, Troy, N.Y., Lime Green, Blob Top 50.00
John Walsh, Boston, Mass., Stoneware, Handle, Embossed, 1/2 Gal. 26.00
Jung, Cincinnati, Oh., Amber, Pt. 4.00
K.R. Alpert, Syracuse, Amber, Blob Top, Porcelain Stopper, Pony 10.00
Keep Cool & Keep Coolidge With Near Beer, White Pottery, 1/2 Pt. 35.00
Kessler Brewing Co., Helena, Mont., Amber, Tooled Crown Top 35.00
Lemp, St.Louis, Clear, Embossed, 12 Oz. 23.00
Lexington Brewing Co., Lexington, Mo., Aqua, ABM 12.00
Lion Brewery Inc., Cincinnati, Ohio, Aqua, Qt. 15.00
Louis Ohlman, East Orange, N.J., Blob Top, Pt. 8.00
Louis Ohlman, East Orange, N.J., Bold Embossing, Flint, Pt. 20.00
Louis Trey, South Boston, Embossed, Stopper, Pt. 25.00
Luke Beard, Boston, Smoky Green, Pontil 75.00
M. Benekart, Aqua, Qt. 35.00
Mathie Brewing Co., Los Angeles, California, Aqua, Qt. ....25.00 to 30.00
Milwaukee Lager Beer, J. Gahm & Son, Boston, Yellow, Blob Top, Pontil 110.00
Miniature, see Miniature, Beer
Moerlein Gerst Brewing Co., Old Jug Lager, Krug Bier, Nashville, Stoneware, Pt. 65.00
Molson Golden, Display Bottle 40.00
Muskegon Brewing, Crown Top 20.00
N.W. Burleigh, Franklin Falls, N.H., Aqua, Lightning, Stopper, Blob Top, Pt. 65.00
National Bottling Works, San Francisco, Amber, Qt. ....38.50 to 50.00
National Bottling Works, San Francisco, Eagle & Star, Golden Amber, Qt. 65.00
National Bottling Works, San Francisco, Eagle & Star, Qt. 24.00
National Bottling Works, San Francisco, Eagle, Chocolate Amber, Pt. 150.00
National Brewing Co., Baltimore, Md., Blob Top, 12 Oz. 20.00
National Lager Beer, Stockton, Calif., Amber, Blob Top, Qt. 20.00
Nicholas Talone Brewing Co., Conshohocken, Pa., Embossed 15.00
Northern Brewing Co., Superior, Wis., 1930s, 12 Oz. 18.00
Northwestern Brewery, Chicago, Embossed, Blob Top, 1890s, 12 In. 4.00
Oertel's Ale, Little Brown Jug 22.00
Old Crown Ale, Presentation, With Letter Dated Dec. 12, 1939 .... 50.00
Old Tavern, Warsaw Brewing Co., Warsaw, Ill., 1950s, 7 Oz. 3.00
Olympia Brewing Co., San Francisco, Calif., Amber, Qt. 20.00
Otis Neale, Boston, Aqua, Slug Plate, Lightning Stopper, Blob Top, Pt. 18.00
Otis Neale, Boston, Aqua, Slug Plate, Stopper, Pt. ....16.00 to 35.00
Otto & Layer, Philadelphia, Berlin White Beer, Aqua, Squatty 30.00
Our Pride, White Eagle Brewing Co., Chicago, Il., Painted Label 45.00

P. Ballantine & Sons, Newark, N.J., 1950s, 12 Oz. 3.00
P. Harrington Milwaukee Lager, Manchester, N.H., Yellow Olive, Pt. 12.00
P. Herringbone Bottler Of Milwaukee Lagers, Porcelain Stopper, Pt. 125.00
P. Stumpf's Brewing Co., Richmond, Va., Amber, Eagle Stump, Blob Top ..... 100.00 to 385.00
Pabst, Blue Ribbon, Metal 7.00
Palmetto Brewing Co., Charleston, S.C., Aqua, Blob Top, Dug 5.50
Pearl Brewing Co., San Antonio, Tex., 1960s, 12 Oz. 2.00
Peerless, La Crosse Breweries, Inc., La Crosse, Wis., 12 Oz. 18.00
Peter Mugler Brewery, Sisson, Calif., Yellow Amber, 4-Piece Mold, 1/2 Pt. 45.00
Philadelphia Bottling Co., Lager Beer, Eagle On Nest, Applied Top, Bail, Qt. 950.00
Philip Scheuermann, Union Brewery, Hancock, Mich., Dark Amber, Blob Top, Qt. ... 60.00
Phoenix Brewing Co., Buffalo, Phoenix Picture, Pt. 5.00
Phoenix Brewing Co., N.Y., Blob Top, Pt. 10.00
Portsmouth Brewing & Ice Co., Portsmouth, Oh., Amber, Pt. 25.00
Prager, Amber ....*Illus*   4.00
Queen City Brewing Co., Cumberland, Md., Painted Label, 1950s, 7 Oz. 6.00
Rainer Beer Bottling Works, Reno, Nev., Crown Top, 1905-1918, 11 In. 115.00
Rainier Brewery, Seattle, Light Amber, Pt. ....55.00 to 70.00
Rapp, Honey Amber, Qt. 3.00
Reymann Brewing Co., Wheeling, W.V., Amber, Blob Top, Qt. 25.00
Reymann Brewing Co., Wheeling, W.V., Olive Amber, Blob Top, Qt. 30.00
Richmond Brewery, Kersten & Von N. Roseneck, Amber, Blob Top, Star & Circle 154.00
Robert Dawson, Pontiac, Mich., Amber 45.00
Robichaue & Gauthier, Fall River, Mass., Pt. 35.00
Robinson, Wilson & LeGalles, Dark Green 40.00
Rochester Brewing Co., Boston Branch, Amber, Blob Top 15.00
Rock Island Brewing Co., Rock Island, Ill., Amber, Picnic 35.00
Rosenegk Brewing Co., Richmond, Va., Yellow Amber, Crown Top 126.00
Ruhstallers Gilt Edge, Crown Top, Qt. 6.00
Sabastopol Bottling Works, Stopper, Qt. 30.00
Samuel B. Doty Bottler, Morrisville, Vt., Aqua, Embossed, Lightning Stopper, Pt. 65.00
Samuel Bach Brewing Co., Wheeling.W.V., Amber, Qt. 35.00
San Jose Bottling Co., Golden Honey Amber, Whittled, Lightning Stopper, Qt. 100.00
Scheidt's Valley Forge, Norristown, Pa., Colonial Men Picture, 1940, Qt. 12.00
Schlitz, Anchor Glass, Royal Ruby, 1949, Qt. 45.00
Schlitz, Pale Green Aqua, 7 3/4 In. 49.50
Schlitz, Pilsner Distributing Co., Cedar Rapids, Iowa, 1941, Picnic, 64 Oz. 17.00
Schlitz Milwaukee Lager, Mug Picture, Golden, Stopper, Pt. 35.00
Schlitz W.F. & S.M.F., Amber, Blob Top, Qt. 29.00
Schmulbach Brewing Co., Golden Brew, Wheeling, Amber, Crown Top, 12 Oz. 8.00
Schmulbach Brewing Co., Wheeling, W.V., Amber, Blob Top, Qt. 25.00
Schmulbach Brewing Co., Wheeling, W.V., Amber, Eagle, Blob Top, Qt. 15.00
Schoenhofen Edelweiss Co., Chicago, Pt. 4.00
Smith & Bovee, Troy, N.Y., Star, Blue Aqua, Glob Top, Qt. 65.00
Springfield Breweries Ltd., Springfield, Oh., Amber, Blob Top, Qt. 15.00
Springfield Breweries Ltd., Springfield, Oh., Amber, Pt. 10.00
Springfield Breweries Ltd., Springfield, Oh., Closure, Pt. 17.00
St. Louis Bottling Co., McC & B, Vallejo, Calif., Amber, Blob Top, Tooled Lip, Pt. 15.00
St. Mary's Brewing Co., St. Mary's, Pa., Vaseline Yellow, Pt. 65.00
Staten Island Lager Bier, Adolph Anthes, Aqua, Lightning Stopper, Blob Top, Pt. 22.00
Sterling, Painted Label, 100th Anniversary, 1863-1963, 12 Oz. 11.00
Stoddard, Olive Amber, IP, 1/2 Pt. 60.00
Stoneware, Light Brown, Cylindrical, 9 1/2 In. 66.00
Storz Brewing Co., Omaha, 12 Oz. 10.00
Sunset Bottling Co., San Francisco, Light Amber, Pt. 35.00
Sunset Bottling Co., San Francisco, Red Amber, 4-Piece Mold, Qt. ....44.00 to 55.00
Swan Brewery Co., Deep Root Beer Amber, 1/2 Pt. 685.00
Swan Brewery Co., Yellow Olive Amber, 6 7/8 In. 960.00
Swan Brewery Co., Yellow Olive Green, 1/2 Pt. 770.00
T. Glyn, Newburryport, Light Green Aqua, Blob Top 11.00
T. Mulcare, No. Adams, Mass., Embossing, Sun-Colored, Amethyst, Stopper, Pt. 45.00
T.J. Baker, Oneonta, N.Y., Aqua, Blob Top 25.00
Terre Haute Brewing Co., Terre Haute, Ind., Amber, Pt. 10.00

Tiffany & Allen, Patterson N.J., Orange Amber, Blob Top, Squatty	80.00
Titus Greenwood England, Early 1900s, 8 1/2 In.	4.00
U.S. Bottling, John Fauser & Co., Red Amber, Whittled, Applied Top, Qt.	65.00
Union Brewing & Malting Co., San Francisco, Calif., Amber, 1/2 Pt.	25.00
Van Merritt, Burlington Brewing Co., Burlington, Wis., 7 Oz.	3.00
Vath, San Jose, Calif., Honey Amber, Qt.	4.00
Vic's Special, Northern Brewing Co., Superior, Wis., Painted Label, 7 Oz.	9.00
Walter-Raupfer Brewing Co., Columbia City, Ind., Amber, Eagle, Qt.	20.00
Weiss Bier, Phillip Elbert, Harrisburg, Penna., Aqua, Star Of David, E Center	295.00
West Virginia Brewing Co., Huntington, W.V., Amber, Small Lip, 12 Oz.	10.00
West Virginia Brewing Co., Montgomery & Thurmond, W.V., Amber, 12 Oz.	15.00
Western Beer, Peter Mugler Brewer, Sisson, Calif., Amber, 4-Piece Mold, Blob Top	60.00
Western Brew, Sioux City Brewing Co., Sioux City, Iowa, 1930s, 64 Oz.	26.00
William Gerst Brewing Co., Nashville, Tenn., Light Amber, Qt.	150.00
Willow Springs Brewing Co., Stars & Stripes Special Brew, Blown Crown, Round	20.00
Wm. Best, Philadelphia, Stopper, Pt.	20.00
Wm. Pond, Xx Philadelphia Ale & Porter, N.Y., Emerald Green, 1/2 Pt.	100.00
Wm. White, Manchester, N.H., Lightning Stopper, Blob Top, Pt.	15.00
Wunder Bottling Co., San Francisco, Calif., Amber, Blob Top, 1/2 Pt.	20.00
Wunder Bottling Co., San Francisco, Calif., Stopper, Pt.	15.00
Yoerg Brewing Co., St. Paul, Minn., Qt.	28.00
Zywiec Beer, Warszawa, Stanley Stawski, Chicago, Amber, 9 In. .... *Illus*	1.00

BENNINGTON, see Pottery

--------------------------------- **BININGER** ---------------------------------

Bininger and Company of New York City was a family-owned grocery and dry goods store. It was founded by the 1820s and remained in business into the 1880s. The store sold whiskey, wine, and other liquors. After a while they began bottling their products in their own specially designed bottles. The first bottles were ordered from England but it wasn't long before the local glass factories made the Bininger's special figural containers. Barrels, clocks, cannons, jugs, and flasks were made. Colors were usually shades of amber, green, or puce.

BININGER, A.M. & Co., Barrel, Amber, Pontil, c.1864, 8 In.	110.00
A.M. & Co., Cannon Shape, Amber, c.1870, 12 1/2 In.	3850.00
A.M. & Co., Cannon Shape, Light Golden Amber, 12 1/2 In.	550.00
A.M. & Co., Cannon, Light Amber, 12 1/2 In.	400.00
A.M. & Co., Cylindrical, Handle, Forest Green, 7 3/4 In.	1430.00
A.M. & Co., Jug, Yellow Amber, Applied Handle, Cylindrical, 1870, 8 In.	413.00
A.M. & Co., Old Dominion Wheat Tonic, Olive Green, Applied Mouth, 9 7/8in.	165.00
A.M. & Co., Old Kentucky Bourbon Distilled In 1848, Barrel, OP	250.00
A.M. & Co., Old Kentucky Bourbon, 1849 Reserve, Olive Green, Square, 9 3/4 In.	77.00
A.M. & Co., Old Kentucky Bourbon, Amber, Squared Lip, 8 In.	185.00
A.M. & Co., Old Kentucky Bourbon, Barrel, Amber, Pontil.	250.00
A.M. & Co., Old Kentucky Bourbon, Yellow Olive, Applied Mouth, 1865, 9 3/4 In.	187.00
A.M. & Co., Old London Dock, Emerald Green, 9 3/4 In.	160.00
A.M. & Co., Traveler's Guide, Tear Drop, Yellow Amber, 6 1/2 In.	264.00
Clock Face, Light Amber, 6 In.	185.00
Cluster Of Grapes, Olive Amber Seal, Cylindrical, 11 1/8 In.	990.00
Jug, Amber, Handle	390.00
Knickerbocker, Amber, Handle, Pontil, 6 1/2 In.	880.00
Knickerbocker, Jug, Yellow Amber, Pontil, Bulbous, 6 1/2 In. .... *Illus*	605.00
Knickerbocker, N.Y., Amber, 9 7/8 In.	88.00
Knickerbocker, N.Y., Applied Seal Whiskey, Deep Olive Amber, 11 In.	1485.00
Knickerbocker, N.Y., Clock, Amber, 6 In.	357.50
Knickerbocker, N.Y., Clock, Aqua, 6 In.	687.50
Knickerbocker, N.Y., Deep Olive, 7 7/8 In.	1485.00
Knickerbocker, N.Y., Medium Golden Amber, 6 1/2 In.	1430.00
Knickerbocker, N.Y., Old London Dock, Yellow Olive Amber, 9 5/8 In.	154.00
Knickerbocker, N.Y., Olive Green, 9 3/4 In.	907.50
Old Dominion Wheat Tonic, Yellow Amber, 9 7/8 In.	110.00
Old Kentucky Bourbon, Barrel, Light Amber, OP, Double Collar, 8 1/2 In. .... *Illus*	270.00
Old Kentucky Bourbon, N.Y., 1849, Medium Amber, 9 5/8 In.	93.50

Bininger, Knickerbocker, Jug, Yellow Amber,
Pontil, Bulbous, 6 1/2 In.

Bininger, Old Kentucky Bourbon, Barrel,
Light Amber, OP, Double Collar, 8 1/2 In.

Peep-O-Day, N.Y., Medium Amber, Yellow Amber, 7 3/4 In., Pt. 385.00
Traveler's Guide, N.Y., Yellow Amber, 6 5/8 In. 258.50

--------------------------------------- **BISCHOFF** ---------------------------------------

Bischoff Company has made fancy decanters since it was founded in 1777 in Trieste, Italy.
The modern collectible Bischoff bottles have been imported into the United States since
about 1950. Glass, porcelain, and stoneware decanters and figurals were made.

BISCHOFF, African Head, 1962 .... 14.00
  Alpine Pitcher, 1969 .... 27.00
  Amber Flower, 1952 .... 35.00
  Amber Leaf, 1952 .... 35.00
  Amphora, 2 Handles, 1950 .... 25.00
  Ashtray, Green Striped, 1958 .... 14.00
  Bell House, 1960 .... 39.00
  Bell Tower, 1959 .... 21.00
  Black Cat, 1969 .... 23.00
  Blue Gold, 1956 .... 50.00
  Candlestick, 1958 .... 25.00
  Chariot Urn, 1966, 2 Sections 25.00
  Floral, Canteen, 1969 .... 18.00
  Fruit, Canteen, 1969 .... 20.00
  Porcelain Cameo, 1962 .... 21.00

--------------------------------------- **BITTERS** ---------------------------------------

Bitters seems to have been an idea that started in Germany during the seventeenth century.
A tax was levied against gin in the mid-1700s and the clever salesmen simply added some
herbs to the gin and sold the mixture as medicine. Later, the medicine was made in Italy
and England. Bitters is the name of this mixture. By the nineteenth century, bitters became
a popular local product in America. One brand had over 59% alcohol (about 118 proof). It
was usually of such a high alcoholic content that the claim that one using the product felt
healthier with each sip was almost true. Although alcoholism had become a problem and
social drinking was frowned upon by most proper Victorians, the soothing bitters medicine
found wide acceptance. At that time there was no tax on the medicine and no laws con-
cerning ingredients or advertising claims.

The word *bitters* must be embossed on the glass or a paper label must be affixed to the bottle for the collector to call the bottle a bitters bottle. Most date from 1862, the year of the
Revenue Act tax on liquor, until 1906, the year the Food and Drug Act placed restrictions
on the sale of bitters as a medicinal cure. Over 1,000 types are known. Bitters were sometimes packaged in figural bottles shaped like cabins, human figures, fish, pigs, barrels, ears

of corn, drums, clocks, horses, or cannons. The bottles came in a variety of colors. They ranged from clear to milk glass, pale to deep amethyst, light aqua to cobalt blue, pale yellow to amber, and pale to dark green. A bottle found in an unusual color commands a much higher price than a clear bottle of the same shape. The numbers used in the entries in the form R-00 refer to the book *For Bitters Only* by Carlyn Ring. Each bottle is pictured and described in detail in the book. There is a newsletter for collectors, *The Bitters Report*, P.O. Box 1253, Bunnell, FL 32110.

BITTERS, A. Lambert, Philadelphia, Pa., Olive Green, Cylinder, 11 In. 3135.00
African Stomach, Amber, Cylinder, 9 5/8 In., R-A15 .... 78.50
Amazon, New York, Medium Amber, 9 1/8 In., R-A44 .... 143.00
American Life, Modified Log Cabin, Golden Amber, 9 In., R-A49 .... 2200.00
American Stomach, Rochester, N.Y., Amber, Tooled Lip, 8 7/8 In., R-A54 .... 154.00
Army Bitters, Milk Glass, Wheaton, Reproduction, 8 In. 5.00
Atwood's Quinine Tonic, Emerald Green, 6 Flutes, 11 In., R-A129 .... 220.00
Atwood's Vegetable Dyspeptic, Early Hinged Mold, R-A130 .... 95.00
Baker's Orange Grove, Amber, 9 1/2, 8 In., R-B9 .... 264.00
Baker's Orange Grove, Gasoline Puce, Applied Mouth, 9 1/2 In., R-B9 .... 1320.00
Baker's Orange Grove, Medium Yellow Amber, 9 5/8 In., R-B9 .... *Illus* 303.00
Baker's Orange Grove, Yellow Olive Tone, 9 5/8 In., R-B9 .... 1320.00
Barrel, Claret, Square Mouth, 9 5/8 In. 242.00
Barrel, Deep Olive Green, 9 1/4 In. .... 165.00 to 198.00
Barrel, Deep Olive Green, Applied Square Lip, Smooth Base, 9 3/8 In. 220.00
Barto's Great Gun, Reading, Pa., Cannon, Yellow Olive, 11 In., R-B32 .... 6380.00
Beggs Dandelion, Strap Flask, Amber, R-B53 .... 100.00 to 135.00
Bell's Cocktail, Jas. M. Bell & Co., Lady's Leg, Amber, 10 1/2 In., R-B58 ...... 242.00 to 523.00
Benders, Cincinnati, Yellow Amber, 10 1/4 In., R-B67 .... 5500.00
Bennet's Celebrated Stomach, San Francisco, Amber, 9 In., R-B73 .... 330.00
Berkshire, Amann & Co., Pig, Amber, 9 1/2 In., R-B81.2 .... 1870.00
Berkshire, Amann & Co., Pig, Cincinnati, Amber, 10 1/4 In., R-B81.4 .... 1430.00
Berliner Magen, Medium Amber, 9 In., R-B86 .... 50.00
Big Bill Best, Amber, 12 1/8 In., R-B95 .... 104.50 to 231.00
Big Bill Best Bitters, Amber, Contents, 12 1/8 In., R-B95 .... 120.00 to 300.00
Bismarck, W.H. Muller, N.Y., Amber, 6 1/8 In., R-B107 .... 71.50 to 94.00
Boerhaves Holland, B. Page Jr. & Co., Pittsburgh, Pa., Aqua, 7 1/2 In., R-B134 .... 80.00
Bourbon Whiskey, Barrel, Cherry Puce, Applied Mouth, 9 1/8 In., R-B171 .... 450.00
Bourbon Whiskey, Barrel, Deep Claret, 9 In., R-B171 .... 325.00
Bourbon Whiskey, Barrel, Gray Puce, 9 1/8 In., R-B171 .... 220.00
Bourbon Whiskey, Barrel, Light Pink Puce, 9 3/8 In., R-B171 .... 4730.00
Bourbon Whiskey, Barrel, Medium Apricot Puce, 9 In., R-B171 .... 341.00
Bourbon Whiskey, Barrel, Medium Pink Puce, Applied Mouth, 9 1/4 In., R-B171 .... 242.00
Bourbon Whiskey, Barrel, Puce Amethyst, 9 In., R-B171 .... 495.00
Bourbon Whiskey, Barrel, Red Puce, Applied Mouth, 9 1/4 In., R-B171 .... 413.00

Bitters, Baker's Orange Grove, Medium Yellow Amber, 9 5/8 In., R-B9

Bitters, Dr. Caldwell's Herb, The Great Tonic, Amber, IP, 1865-1875, 12 1/2 In., R-C9

Bitters, Brown's Celebrated Indian Herb, Amber, Pat. 1867, 12 1/4 In., R-B224

Bourbon Whiskey, Barrel, Smoky Pink Puce, 9 1/4 In., R-B171.................................... 385.00
Brady's Family, Amber, 9 1/2 In., R-B193 .... 176.00
Brady's Family, Amber, 9 3/8 In., R-B193 .... 132.00
Brand Bros. Co., Amber, 4 7/8 In., R-B2011... 88.00
Brillanteen, Ruby Red Paneled Design, Stopper, 3 7/8 In. 350.00
Brown & Lyon's Blood, Binghampton, N.Y., Yellow Amber, 9 7/8 In., R-B218 .... 148.50
Brown's Celebrated Indian Herb, Amber, 12 In., R-B225 .... 440.00 to 1870.00
Brown's Celebrated Indian Herb, Amber, 1868, 12 1/8 In., R-B223........................... 413.00
Brown's Celebrated Indian Herb, Amber, Pat. 1867, 12 1/4 In., R-B224............*Illus* 468.00
Brown's Celebrated Indian Herb, Chocolate, 12 1/4 In., R-B223 .... 1075.00
Brown's Celebrated Indian Herb, Lime Green, 1868, 12 1/8 In., R-B225.................. 7810.00
Brown's Celebrated Indian Herb, Patented 1867, Amber, 12 1/4 In., R-B223 . 687.50 to 880.00
Brown's Celebrated Indian Herb, Yellow Green, 12 1/8 In.R-B223 .... 3300.00
Brown's Iron, Amber, Square, 8 1/2 In., R-B231 .... 34.00
Bryant's Stomach, 8-Sided, Lady's Leg, Emerald Green, 12 In., R-B243.................... 5170.00
Buhrer's Gentian, Light Stain, 8 1/2 In., R-B251 .... 210.00
Burdock Blood, Toronto, Ontario, Sun Colored Amethyst, 8 1/2 In., R-B263 .... 50.00
Burdock Blood, Toronto, Sample, 4 In., R-B265 .... 75.00
Byrne, see Bitters, Professor Geo. J. Byrne
C. Gates & Cos., Life Of Man, Aqua, 8 In., R-G7.. 65.00
C.A. Richards & Co, Boston, Mass., Yellow Amber, 9 3/4 In., R-R53......................... 93.50
C.H. Swain's Bourbon, Medium Amber, Whittled, c.1875, 9 1/8 In., R-S228... 148.00 to 165.00
C.W. Roback's, see Bitters, Dr. C.W. Roback's
Cabin, see Bitters, Drake's Plantation; Bitters, Golden; Bitters, Kelly's Old Cabin;
Bitters, Old Homestead Wild Cherry
Caldwell's Herb, Great Tonic, Amber, IP, c.1875, 12 1/2 In., R-C8........................... 121.00
Caldwell's Herb, Great Tonic, Golden Amber, IP, 12 1/4 In., R-C9............................ 330.00
California Fig, San Francisco, Amber, 9 3/4 In., R-C15... 50.00
California Wine, M.Keller, Los Angeles, Apple Green, 12 1/8 In., R-C24................ 12870.00
Canton, Lady's Leg, Amber, 12 1/8 In., R-C35.. 176.00 to 300.00
Carmeliter, Deep Yellow Olive Green, 10 In., R-C54.. 275.00
Carmeliter Stomach, New York, Yellow Olive, 9 7/8 In., R-C54 .... 330.00
Carney's Tonic, Red Amber, Rectangular, 10 1/2 In., R-C56...................................... 55.00
Cassin's Grape Brandy, Yellow Green, 9 3/4 In., R-C79.. 20020.00
Catawba Wine, Bunches Of Grapes, Square, Olive Green, 9 1/4 In., R-C85.................. 1320.00
Celebrated Crown, Amber, 8 3/4 In., R-C93.. 258.50
Clarke's Compound Mandrake, Aqua, Oval, Label, 7 1/2 In., R-C151 .... 65.00 to 85.00
Clarke's Sherry Wine, Aqua, 7 7/8 In., R-C165 .... 143.00 to 150.00
Clarke's Sherry Wine, Only 75 Cents, OP, 1/2 Gal., R-C159 .... 350.00
Clarke's Vegetable Sherry Wine, Aqua, 14 In., R-C155.. 357.00
Clarke's Vegetable Sherry Wine, Aqua, Applied Mouth, 12 3/8 In., R-C156 .... 357.00
Clarke's Vegetable Sherry Wine, Sharon, Mass, Aqua, 14 In., R-C155 .... 385.00 to 467.50
Clarke's Vegetable Sherry Wine, Sharon, Mass, Aqua, 3 Qt., R-C156 .... 400.00
Clarke's Vegetable Sherry Wine, Sharon, Mass., Aqua, 11 3/4 In., R-C160 .... 198.00
Cliff's Aromatic Bitters, Jos. Clifford, Proprietor, Ohio, Amber, 10 In., R-C173.9 ...... 220.00
Cocamoke, Hartford, Conn., Amber, 9 5/8 In., R-C182... 242.00
Congress, Semi-Cabin, Aqua, 10 3/8 In., R-C217 .... 303.00
Constitution, Seward & Bentley, Buffalo, N.Y., Amber, 1864, 9 3/8 In., R-C222 .... 1210.00
Curtis & Perkins Wild Cherry, Aqua, OP, 6 3/4 In., R-C262 .... 66.00 to 80.00
Damiana Bitters, Baja, Calif., Applied Top, Label, 11 1/2 In., R-C4........................... 176.00
David Andrews Vegetable Jaundice, Aqua, OP, 8 In., R-A57..................................... 600.00
Demuth's Stomach, Philada, Square, Pa., Amber, 9 3/8 In., R-D46............. 165.00 to 176.00
Devil-Cert Stomach, Fluted Base, Cylindrical, 1880-1900, 9 1/4 In., R-D58................. 44.00
Dingens Napoleon Cocktail, Banjo Form, Gray Tint, IP, 10 1/4 In., R-N3 .... 6050.00
Doyles Hop, Amber, 1872, R-D93 .... 46.00
Dr. A.H. Smith's Old Style Bitters, Sunken Panels, Amber, 8 3/4 In., R-S127............. 125.00
Dr. A.W. Coleman's Anti Dyspeptic & Tonic, Yellow Green, 9 1/4 In., R-C194 .... 3080.00
Dr. Ball's Vegetable Stomachic, Northboro, Mass., Aqua, OP, 7 In., R-B14... 160.00 to 220.00
Dr. Baxter's Mandrake, Aqua, R-B36... 15.00
Dr. Birmingham's Antibillious Blood Purifying, Green, 8 1/4 In., R-B101.................. 1155.00
Dr. Bishop's Wahoo, New Haven, Conn., Semi-Cabin, Amber, 10 1/8 In., R-B103...... 825.00
Dr. Blake's Aromatic, New York, Aqua, OP, 7 In., R-B120............................88.00 to 225.00
Dr. Bull's Superior Stomach, St. Louis, Amber, 9 In., R-B258 .... 180.00

Dr. C.D. Warner's German Hop, 9 1/2 In., R-W32 .... 275.00
Dr. C.W. Roback's Stomach, Cincinnati, O., Barrel, Amber, 9 In., R-R75 .... 225.00 to 242.00
Dr. C.W. Roback's Stomach, Cincinnati, O., Barrel, Amber, 9 3/8 In., R-R74 .... 143.00
Dr. C.W. Roback's Stomach, Cincinnati, O., Barrel, Olive Green, 10 In., R-R73 .... 1430.00
Dr. C.W. Roback's Stomach, Cincinnati, O., Barrel, Orange Amber, 9 3/8 In., R-R74 ...... 170.00
Dr. C.W. Roback's Stomach, Cincinnati, O., Barrel, Yellow Amber, 10 In., R-R73 .... 495.00
Dr. Caldwell's Herb, The Great Tonic, Amber, IP, 1865-1875, 12 1/2 In., R-C9....*Illus* 204.00
Dr. Carey's Original, Mandrake, Waverly, N.Y., Aqua, 6 3/8 In., R-C48 .... 115.50
Dr. Copp's, Rings Ambrosia Co., Wilton, N.H., Aqua, 8 1/2 In., R-C233 .... 225.00
Dr. De Andries Sarsaparilla, E.M. Rusha, New Orleans, Amber, 9 3/4 In., R-D35 ...... 1370.00
Dr. De Andries Sarsaparilla, New Orleans, Yellow Amber, 10 In., R-D35 .... 1210.00
Dr. E.P. Eastman's, Yellow Dock, Lynn, Mass., Aqua, 7 3/4 In., R-E14 .... 770.00
Dr. F. Fleschhut's Celebrated Stomach, Laporte, Pa., Aqua, 8 3/4 In., R-F54........... 330.00
Dr. Fisch's, Cover, Light Amber, 11 1/2 In., R-F44 .... 180.00
Dr. Fisch's, Light Golden Orange Amber, R-F44 .... 250.00
Dr. Fisch's, W.H. Ware, Pat.1866, Fish, Amber, 11 3/4 In., R-F44.................. 176.00 to 193.00
Dr. Flint's Quaker, Providence, R.I., Aqua, 9 1/2 In., R-F58 .... 825.00
Dr. Forest's Tonic, Bacon & Miller, Harrisburg, Pa., Amber, 9 1/2 In., R-F68 .... 385.00
Dr. Geo. Pierce's Indian Restorative Lowell, Mass., Aqua, 7 1/2 In., R-P96 ......45.00 to 85.00
Dr. Gillmore's Laxative Kidney & Liver, Medium Amber, 10 1/2 In., R G43.....94.00 to 150.00
Dr. Harter's, Orange Amber, Sample, R-H49.. 35.00
Dr. Harter's Wild Cherry, Dayton, Oh., Amber, Contents, 7 3/4 In., R-H46 .... 78.00
Dr. Harter's Wild Cherry, St. Louis, Amber, Design Embossed Base, R-H50.............. 41.25
Dr. Henley's Wild Grape Root, Deep Olive Amber, 9 3/8 In., R-H86 .... 2035.00
Dr. Henley's Wild Grape Root, Medium, Deep Root Beer Amber, 12 In., R-H84......... 4730.00
Dr. Henley's Wild Grape Root, Yellow Olive Green, 12 1/4 In., R-H85 .... 1760.00
Dr. Henley's Wild Grape Root IXL, Aqua, Applied Top, 1880s, 12 In., R-H84 .... 135.00
Dr. Herbert John's Indian, Great Indian Discoveries, Amber, 8 7/8 In., R-J43............ 275.00
Dr. Hoofland's German, Aqua, OP, 8 In., R-H168...27.00 to 55.00
Dr. Hoofland's German, Liver Complaint, Dyspepsia & Co., Phila., Aqua, R-H168..... 35.00
Dr. Hopkins' Union Stomach, Panels, Cover, Amber, Square, 9 1/2 In., R-H180 .... 285.00
Dr. J. Hostetter's Stomach, Dark Red Amber, Applied Top, 8 1/2 In., R-H194.......... 65.00
Dr. J. Hostetter's Stomach, Deep Olive Amber, 8 3/8 In., R-H197 .... 143.00
Dr. J. Hostetter's Stomach, Deep Olive Amber, 9 1/2 In., R-H194 ....*Illus* 143.00
Dr. J. Hostetter's Stomach, Deep Olive Yellow, 8 1/2 In., R-H199 .... 495.00
Dr. J. Hostetter's Stomach, Deep Yellow Citron, L & W, Glob Top, 8 1/2 In., R-H195 235.00
Dr. J. Hostetter's Stomach, Medium Green, 8 5/8 In., R-H195..................................... 231.00
Dr. J. Hostetter's Stomach, Olive Green, Applied Mouth, 9 5/8 In., R-H199 .... 110.00
Dr. J. Hostetter's Stomach, Yellow Amber, A On Base, R-H195 .... 55.00
Dr. J. Hostetter's Stomach, Yellow Olive Amber, 9 1/4 In., R-H195.......................... 145.00
Dr. J. Sweet's Strengthening, Square, Aqua, Square, 8 1/2 In., R-S234...............70.00 to 95.00

Bitters, Dr. Soule Hop,
Root Beer Amber,
9 1/4 In., R-S145

Bitters, Dr. J. Hostetter's
Stomach, Deep Olive
Amber, 9 1/2 In., R-H194

Bitters, Drake's Plantation,
6 Log, Peach Puce, 10 In.,
R-D105

Dr. Jacob's, New Haven, Ct., Aqua, 8 1/2 In., R-J11 .... 88.00 to 150.00
Dr. John Bull's Cedron, Louisville, Kentucky, Olive Amber, 9 7/8 In., R-B254 .... 1375.00
Dr. Kaufmann's Sulphur, Label, Contents, Box, R-K15 .... 55.00
Dr. Langley's Root & Herb, Boston, Amber, 8 1/2 In., R-L21 .... 198.00
Dr. Langley's Root & Herb, Boston, Aqua, 6 1/8 In., R-L26 .... 143.00
Dr. Langley's Root & Herb, Boston, Aqua, 7 1/8 In., R-L22 .... 55.00
Dr. Langley's Root & Herb, Boston, Aqua, 8 1/4 In., R-L25 .... 71.50
Dr. Langley's Root & Herb, Boston, Deep Aqua, 6 3/4 In., R-L24 .... 45.00 to 93.50
Dr. Loew's Celebrated Stomach Bitters & Nerve Tonic, Green, 9 1/2 In., R-L111.... 165.00
Dr. Loew's Celebrated Stomach, Green, Ornate, 3 3/4 In., R-L112 .... 60.00
Dr. Loew's Stomach, Christy Co., Yellow Green, 9 1/4 In., R-L116 .... 385.00 to 467.50
Dr. Mampes Herb Stomach, Oshkosh, Wis., 6 3/4 In., R-M26 .... 75.00 to 150.00
Dr. McHenry Stomach, Aqua, 7 3/4 In. 175.00
Dr. Med Koch's Universal Magen, Medium Olive Green, Germany, 8 1/4 In. 357.50
Dr. Mowe's Vegetable, Lowell, Mass., Aqua, Applied Mouth, 10 In., R-M155 .. 94.00 to 176.00
Dr. Owen's European Life, Detroit, Aqua, OP, 7 In., R-O98 .... 165.00 to 176.00
Dr. Petzold's Genuine German, Pat.1884, Golden Amber, 10 1/4 In., R-P75 .... 150.00
Dr. Petzold's Genuine German, Pat. 1884, Medium Amber, 8 In., R-P76 .... 82.50
Dr. Petzold's Genuine German, Pat. 1884, Medium Amber, 10 1/4 In., R-P74 .... 154.00
Dr. Planett's, Aqua, IP, 9 7/8 In., R-P107 .... 522.00
Dr. Ryder's Clover, Light Golden Amber, Rectangular, 8 7/8 In., R-R135 .... 121.00
Dr. S. Beltzhoover's Dyspeptic, Pittsburgh, Pa., Yellow Amber, 9 1/4 In., R-B65.5.... 357.50
Dr. S. Griggs, Aromatic, Detroit, Yellow Amber, 10 7/8 In., R-G117 .... 1485.00
Dr. S.O. Richardson's, Sherry Wine, South Reading, Mass., Aqua, 6 1/2 In., R-R58 ... 25.00
Dr. Shepard's Compound, Wahoo, Amber, Grand Rapids, Mich., 7 1/2 In., R-S99 ..... 93.50
Dr. Skinner's Celebrated, So. Reading Mass, Aqua, 8 1/4 In., R-S115 .... 302.50
Dr. Skinner's Sherry Wine, So. Reading, Mass., Aqua, OP, 8 5/8 In., R-S116 .... 121.00
Dr. Soule Hop, 1872, Amber, 8 7/8 In., R-S145 .... 176.00
Dr. Soule Hop, 1872, Light Golden Amber, 7 3/4 In., R-S147 .... 165.00
Dr. Soule Hop, 1872, Medium Apricot Puce, 9 1/2 In., R-S146 .... 88.00
Dr. Soule Hop, Dark Root Beer Amber, 9 1/2 In., R-S146 .... 200.00 to 215.00
Dr. Soule Hop, Root Beer Amber, 9 1/4 In., R-S145 .... *Illus*   83.00
Dr. Soule Hop, Semi-Cabin, Golden Amber, 7 3/4 In., R-S147 .... 148.00
Dr. Soule Hop, Yellow Topaz, Square, 8 In., R-S147 .... 258.00
Dr. Stanley's South American Indian, Light Amber, R-S174 .... 115.00
Dr. Stephen Jewett's Celebrated Health Restoring, Aqua, OP, 7 1/2 In., R-J37 ...... 99.00 to 175.00
Dr. Stephen Jewett's Health Restoring, Medium Yellow Amber, 7 1/4 In., R-J38 ..... 1595.00
Dr. Stewart's Tonic, Columbus, O., Amber, 7 3/4 In., R-S194 .... 75.00 to 100.00
Dr. Stiebel's Stomach, Pittsburgh, Golden Amber, 8 5/8 In., R-S196.......................... 236.50
Dr. Stoever's, Kryder & Co., Philadelphia, Medium Amber, 9 1/2 In., R-S199.............. 110.00
Dr. Tompkin's Vegetable, Green, 9 In., R-T36................................ 1375.00
Dr. Von Hopf's Curacoa, Amber, Flask, 7 7/8 In., R-V28 .... 50.00 to 80.00
Dr. Wheeler's Sherry Wine, Aqua, 7 7/8 In., R-W86 .... 66.00
Dr. Wheeler's Tonic Sherry Wine, Boston, Mass., Aqua, 9 1/2 In., R-W87 .... 2970.00
Dr. Wonser's U.S.A. Indian Root, Deep Aqua, 10 7/8 In., Rw-146 .... 3080.00
Dr. Wonser's U.S.A. Indian Root, Root Beer, Amber, 11 In., Rw-146 .... 4730.00
Dr. Young's Wild Cherry, Brooklyn N.Y., Amber, 8 1/2 In., R-Y11 .... 115.00
Dr. Hostetter's, see Bitters, Dr. J. Hostetter's
Drake's Plantation, 4 Log, Amber, 10 1/4 In., R-D110 .... 88.00 to 135.00
Drake's Plantation, 4 Log, Bright Yellow, 10 1/4 In., R-D110 .... 650.00
Drake's Plantation, 4 Log, Golden Yellow, 10 1/4 In., R-D110 .... 495.00
Drake's Plantation, 4 Log, Honey Amber, 10 1/4 In., R-D110 .... 110.00
Drake's Plantation, 4 Log, Lemon Yellow, Tapered Collar, 10 In., R-D110 .... 880.00
Drake's Plantation, 4 Log, Medium Amber, 10 1/8 In., R-D110............................. 187.00
Drake's Plantation, 4 Log, Olive Yellow, 10 In., R-D110 .... 357.50
Drake's Plantation, 4 Log, Yellow Amber, Bubble, 10 In., R-D110 .... 95.00
Drake's Plantation, 4 Log, Yellow Olive Green, 10 In., R-D110............................. 3630.00
Drake's Plantation, 5 Log, Golden Yellow Amber, Variant, 9 7/8 In., R-D109 .... 605.00
Drake's Plantation, 5 Log, Golden Amber, 10 In., R-D109................................ 412.00
Drake's Plantation, 5 Log, Honey Amber, 10 In., R-D109 .... 175.00
Drake's Plantation, 5 Log, Medium Yellow Amber, 9 3/4 In., R-D109 .... 308.00
Drake's Plantation, 5 Log, Orange Amber, Tapered Collar, 10 In., R-D109............... 210.00
Drake's Plantation, 5 Log, Red Amber, 10 In., R-D109 .... 175.00

Drake's Plantation, 6 Log, Apricot Puce, Square, 9 7/8 In., R-D105 .... 187.00
Drake's Plantation, 6 Log, Black Amethyst, 9 7/8 In., R-D105 .... 203.00
Drake's Plantation, 6 Log, Burgundy Puce To Amethyst, 9 7/8 In., R-D105 .... 578.00
Drake's Plantation, 6 Log, Dark Burgundy Puce, R-D105 .... 175.00
Drake's Plantation, 6 Log, Deep Cherry Puce, 9 3/4 In., R-D105 .... 148.00
Drake's Plantation, 6 Log, Deep Strawberry Puce, R-D106 .... 85.00
Drake's Plantation, 6 Log, Deep Yellow Olive, R-D105 .... 1100.00
Drake's Plantation, 6 Log, Dense Amber, Black, 9 1/2 In., R-D105 .... 220.00
Drake's Plantation, 6 Log, Emerald Green, 9 3/4 In., R-D105 .... 7370.00
Drake's Plantation, 6 Log, Gasoline Puce, 9 7/8 In., R-D105 .... 440.00
Drake's Plantation, 6 Log, Gray Moss Green, 9 7/8 In., R-D106 .... 11000.00
Drake's Plantation, 6 Log, Light To Medium Yellow, 9 3/4 In., R-D103 .... 346.50
Drake's Plantation, 6 Log, Medium Green, Yellow Tone, 10 In., R-D106 .... 6600.00
Drake's Plantation, 6 Log, Medium Olive Green, 10 In., R-D108 .... 8855.00
Drake's Plantation, 6 Log, Medium Red Puce, 10 In., R-D108 .... 198.00
Drake's Plantation, 6 Log, Medium Red Puce, Applied Mouth, 10 In., R-D105 .... 104.00
Drake's Plantation, 6 Log, Moss Green, 10 In., R-D106 .... 11000.00
Drake's Plantation, 6 Log, Peach Puce, 10 In., R-D105 ....*Illus* 154.00
Drake's Plantation, 6 Log, Pink Puce, 10 In., R-D108 .... 2860.00
Drake's Plantation, 6 Log, Pink Puce, Whittled, Pat. 1862, 10 In., R-D105 .... 852.00
Drake's Plantation, 6 Log, Puce, 10 In., R-D105 .... 187.00
Drake's Plantation, 6 Log, Strawberry Puce, R-D105 .... 85.00
Drake's Plantation, 6 Log, Yellow Amber, 9 7/8 In., R-D103 .... 88.00
Drake's Plantation, 6 Log, Yellow Lime Green, R-D106 .... 6710.00
Drake's Plantation, 6 Log, Yellow Olive Amber, 9 7/8 In., R-D108 .... 357.00
Drake's Plantation, 6 Log, Yellow Topaz, 9 3/4 In., R-D105 .... 303.00
Drs. Lowerre & Lyon's Restorative, Aquamarine, Pontil, 8 5/8 In., R-L129 .... 660.00
E. Baker's, Premium, Richmond, Va., Aqua, 6 1/2 In., R-B10 .... 187.00
E.R. Clarke's, Sarsaparilla, Sharon, Mass., Aqua, 7 3/8 In., R-C154 .... 137.00 to 165.00
Eagle Angostura Bark, Red Amber, 7 In., R-E2 .... 55.00
Ear Of Corn, see Bitters, National, Ear of Corn
Electric Brand, H.E. Buklen & Co., Amber, Label, R-E30 .... 36.00
Excelsior Herb, J.V. Mattison, Washington, N.J., Golden Amber, 10 In., R-E65 .... 660.00
F. Brown Boston, Sarsaparilla & Tomato, Aqua, OP, 9 1/2 In. Label, R-S36 .... 495.00
F. Brown Boston, Sarsaparilla & Tomato, Aqua, OP, 9 1/2 In., R-S36 .... 150.00
Ferro Quina Blood Maker, Lady's Leg Neck, Sample, R-F41 .... 165.00
Fish, Red Amber, Smooth Base, 11 1/2 In., R-F45 .... 154.00
Fish, W.H. Ware, Chocolate Amber, Pat. 1866, 11 1/2 In., R-F45 .... 253.00
Fish, W.H. Ware, Lime Green, Pat. 1866, 11 3/4 In., R-F46 .... 2200.00
Fish, W.H. Ware, Orange Amber, Applied Mouth, Pat. 1866, 11 1/2 In., R-F45 .... 176.00
Fish, W.H. Ware, Shaded Amber, Figural, 11 5/8 In., R-F46 .... 341.00
Fish, W.H. Ware, Yellow Green, Pat. 1866, 11 1/2 In., R-F46 .... 2750.00
Fish, W.H. Ware, Yellow Olive, Open Bubble, Pat. 1866, 11 5/8 In., R-F46 .... 2200.00
Fish, W.H. Ware, Yellow Root Beer Amber, Pat. 1866, 11 3/4 In., R-F46 .... 209.00
Fowler's Stomach, Arched Panels, Golden Yellow, Olive, 10 In., R-F76 .... 2310.00
French Aromatique, The Finest Stomach Bitters, Aqua, 7 1/8 In., R-F85 .... 82.50
Fritz Reuter, Milk Glass, Case Gin Shape, 10 In., R-R40 .... 275.00 to 302.50
Fulton M. McRae, Yazoo Valley, Square, Amber, 8 5/8 In., R-Y2 .... 154.00
G.C. Blake's Anti. Despeptic, Aqua, Pontil, 7 1/4 In., R-B119 .... 330.00
G.C. Segur's Golden Seal, Springfield, Mass., Aqua, 8 1/4 In., R-S84 .... 121.00
G.C. Segur's Golden Seal, Springfield, Mass., Aqua, OP, 8 1/4 In., R-S84 .... 132.00
G.W. Weston, Yellow Olive Amber, Qt. 40.00
Garnett's Compound Vegetable, Richmond, Va., Amber, Oval BIMAL, R-G5 .... 880.00
General Bolivar, Bright Yellow, 6 3/4 In. 605.00
Geo. Benz & Sons Appetine, St. Paul, Minn., Ornate, Amber, 8 In., R-A78 .... 375.00
Geo. Benz & Sons Appetine, St. Paul, Minn., Ornate, Red Amber, 8 In., R-A78 .... 192.00
Gilbert's Sarsaparilla, Enosburgh Falls, Vt., Yellow Amber, 8 7/8 In., R-G42 .... 495.00
Globe, Byrne Bros., N.Y., Bell, Amber, 10 3/4 In., R-G47 .... 154.00
Goff's Herb, Label, Partial Contents, 4 In., R-G59 .... 25.00
Golden, Geo. C. Hubbel & Co., Modified Cabin, Aqua, 10 In., R-G63 .... 110.00
Good Samaritan Stomach, Dr. Hardman's, Amber, Backward S & N's , 9 In. 75.00
Gordon's Kidney & Liver, Medium Amber, 9 3/8 In., R-G77 .... 154.00
Graves & Son, Louisville, Tonic, Modified Cabin Form, Aqua, 9 3/4 In., R-G96 .... 467.00

Greeley's Bourbon, Barrel, Copper, Square Collared Mouth, 9 In., R-G101 .... 154.00
Greeley's Bourbon, Barrel, Dark Red Puce, 9 1/2 In., R-G101 .... 230.00
Greeley's Bourbon, Barrel, Dark Red Puce, 9 1/8 In., R-G101 .... 250.00
Greeley's Bourbon, Barrel, Deep Red Puce, 9 1/4 In., R-G101 .... 275.00
Greeley's Bourbon, Barrel, Gray Apricot, 9 In., R-G101 .... 412.50
Greeley's Bourbon, Barrel, Gray Olive Green, 9 1/4 In., R-G101 .... 1100.00
Greeley's Bourbon, Barrel, Medium Olive Green, 9 1/2 In., R-G101 .... 1500.00
Greeley's Bourbon, Barrel, Medium Pink Puce, 9 1/2 In., R-G101 .... 412.50
Greeley's Bourbon, Barrel, Medium Smoky Olive, 9 1/4 In., R-G101 .... 1045.00
Greeley's Bourbon, Barrel, Olive Green, 9 1/4 In., R-G101 .... 1595.00
Greeley's Bourbon, Barrel, Pink Puce, 9 1/4 In., R-G101 .... 440.00
Greeley's Bourbon, Barrel, Pink Strawberry Puce, 9 1/2 In., R-G101 .... 660.00
Greeley's Bourbon, Barrel, Puce Amber, 9 1/8 In., R-G101 .... 247.50
Greeley's Bourbon, Barrel, Raspberry Puce, 9 1/4 In., R-G101 .... 605.00
Greeley's Bourbon, Barrel, Smoky Gray Puce, 9 1/8 In., R-G101 .... 578.00
Greeley's Bourbon, Barrel, Smoky Peach, 9 1/4 In., R-G101 .... 198.00
Greeley's Bourbon, Barrel, Strawberry Puce, 9 In., R-G101 .... 522.50
Greeley's Bourbon, Barrel, Yellow Topaz, 9 1/8 In., R-G101 .... 3410.00
Greeley's Bourbon Whiskey, Barrel, Aqua, 9 1/4 In., R-G102 .... 5060.00
Greeley's Bourbon Whiskey, Barrel, Olive Green, 9 1/4 In., R-G102 .... 1100.00
Greeley's Bourbon Whiskey, Barrel, Strawberry Puce, 9 1/4 In., R-G102 .... 385.00
Greeley's Bourbon Whiskey, Light Pink Puce, 9 1/2 In., R-G102 .... 1500.00
Greeley's Bourbon Whiskey, Pink Copper, 9 1/2 In., R-G102 .... 225.00
Greeley's Bourbon Whiskey, Pink Copper, 9 1/4 In., R-G101 .... 467.50
Green Mountain Cider, Aqua, Cylinder, 10 1/4 In., R-G103 .... 100.00 to 187.00
Greer's Eclipse, Amber, Square, 8 3/4 In., R-G112 .... 100.00
Greer's Eclipse, Louisville, Ky., Brilliant Golden Amber, Square, 9 In., R-G110 .... 198.00
Gwilym Evans Quinine, Aqua, Rectangular, 8 3/4 In., R-E58 .... 50.00 to 75.00
H.G. Hotchkiss, Lyons, N.Y., Cobalt Blue, Embossed, 8 3/4 In. 55.00
H.P. Herb Wild Cherry, Cabin, Medium Green, 8 3/4 In., R-H94 .... 3410.00
H.P. Herb Wild Cherry, Cabin, Roped Corners, Yellow Amber, 9 7/8 In., R-H93 .... 330.00
H.P. Herb Wild Cherry, Cabin, With Tree, Amber, 10 In., R-H93 .... 242.00
Hall's, Barrel, E.E. Hall New Haven, Yellow Amber, 9 1/8 In., R-H10 .... 198.00
Hall's, Barrel, Olive Yellow, 9 1/8 In., R-H10 .... 357.50
Hall's, Barrel, Red Amber, Square, 9 In., R-H10 .... 121.00
Hall's, Barrel, Yellow, Amber, Established 1842, 9 1/4 In., R-H10 .... 330.00
Hart's Star, Modified Fish Form, Aqua, 9 1/4 In., R-H58 .... 550.00
Hart's Star, Modified Fish Form, Clear, 9 In., R-H58 .... 341.00
Hart's Star, Philadelphia, Pa., Aqua, 9 1/8 In., R-H58 .... 275.00
Hartwig Kantorowicz, 3 Labeled Sides, Milk Glass, Contents, R-L105 .... 80.00
Hartwig Kantorowicz, Berlin, Olive Amber, 9 1/8 In., R-L104 .... 77.00
Hartwig Kantorowicz, Deep Amber, Germany, 10 In. 100.00
Hartwig Kantorowicz, Posen, Hamburg, Milk Glass, Gin Shape, Sample, 4 1/8 In. 77.00
Hartwig Kantorowicz, Stomach, Milk Glass, 9 1/2 In., R-L106 .... 121.00
Haye's Superior Stomach, Penick & Loving Proprietors, Red Amber, Applied Lip..... 200.00
Herkules, AC Monogram, Yellow Green, 7 1/8 In., R-H98 .... 302.50
Herkules, Ball, AC Monogram, Emerald Green, 7 In., R-H98 .... 1870.00
Herter's Gesundheits, Deep Yellow Olive-Green, Bulbous, 11 7/8 In., R-H104 .... 550.00
Highland Bitters & Scotch Tonic, Amber, Apricot, Barrel, IP, 9 1/2 In., R-H117........ 577.50
Highland Bitters & Scotch Tonic, Amber, Barrel, 9 1/2 In., R-H117 .... 605.00
Highland Bitters & Scotch Tonic, Deep Gold Amber, Barrel, IP, 9 1/2 In., R-H117 ... 1100.00
Holtzermann's Patent Stomach, Cabin, Amber To Yellow, 9 3/8 In., R-H155 .... 1705.00
Holtzermann's Patent Stomach, Cabin, Amber, 4 1/8 In., R-H155 .... 1155.00
Holtzermann's Patent Stomach, Cabin, Amber, 9 5/8 In., R-H155 ....*Illus* 1430.00
Holtzermann's Patent Stomach, Cabin, Amber, Applied Tapered Lip, 9 1/4 In., R-H155 1375.00
Holtzermann's Patent Stomach, Cabin, Amber, Rectangular, 9 3/8 In., R-H155 .... 2090.00
Holtzermann's Patent Stomach, Cabin, Amber, Sample, 4 In., R-H153..............*Illus* 1155.00
Holtzermann's Patent Stomach, Cabin, Amber, Tooled Lip, Label, 9 3/4 In., R-H154 ... 550.00
Holtzermann's Patent Stomach, Cabin, Deep Red Amber, R-G154 .... 175.00
Holtzermann's Patent Stomach, Cabin, Medium Amber, R-H154 .... 200.00 to 210.00
Holtzermann's Patent Stomach, Cabin, Medium Red Amber, 9 7/8 In., R-H154........ 192.50
Holtzermann's Patent Stomach, Cabin, Square, Red Amber, 9 In., R-H155.5 .... 121.00
Holtzermann's Patent Stomach, Cabin, Yellow Amber, 9 1/2 In., R-H155................. 1595.00

Bitters, Holtzermann's Patent Stomach,
Cabin, Amber, 9 5/8 In., R-H155

Bitters, Holtzermann's Patent Stomach,
Cabin, Amber, Sample, 4 In., R-H153

Hops & Malt, Semi-Cabin, Amber, Square, 9 7/8 In., R-H186 .... 1100.00
Hops & Malt, Semi-Cabin, Medium Amber, 10 In., R-H186 .... 154.00
Horse Shoe Medicine Co., Collinsville, Ills., Amber, 8 5/8 In., R-H189 .... 2750.00
Hostetter's, see Bitters, Dr. J. Hostetter's
Hubbell Co., see Bitters, Golden
Hunkidori, Golden Amber, Square, 8 7/8 In., R-H211 .... 104.00
Hutching's Dyspepsia, Aqua, OP, 8 1/4 In., R-H218 .... 137.00
Hutching's Dyspepsia, Aqua, Pontil, Rectangular, 8 3/8 In., R-H218 .... 209.00
Indian Queen, see Bitters, Brown's Celebrated Indian Herb
J.T. Higby Tonic, Milford, Ct., Golden Amber, 9 1/2 In., R-T40 .... 100.00
J.T. Higby Tonic, Milford, Ct., Light Amber, 9 1/2 In., R-T40 .... 78.50
Jamaica Ginger Root Bitters, Milk Glass, Wheaton, Reproduction, 8 In. 5.00
John Moffat, Phoenix, Yellow Olive Amber, 7 7/8 In., R-M111 .... 1540.00
John Moffat, Phoenix, Yellow Olive, OP, 5 1/2 In., R-M111 .... 495.00
John Moffat, Price $1, 00, Phoenix, Olive Green, 5 1/2 In., R-M100 .... 385.00
John Moffat, Price $1.00, Phoenix, Olive Green, 5 1/2 In., R-M112 .... 413.00
John Root's, Buffalo, N.Y., Amber, 9 3/4 In., R-R90.8 .... 1265.00 to 1595.00
John Root's, Rectangular, Beveled Corners, Olive Yellow, 10 In., R-R90.4 .... 1760.00
John W. Steele's Niagara Star, Golden Amber, 10 1/8 In., R-S182 .... 275.00
Johnson's Calisaya, Burlington, Vt., Deep Red Puce, 10 In., R-J45 .... 385.00
Johnson's Calisaya, Burlington, Vt., Medium Dark, Square, 10 In., R-J45 .... 68.00
Julien's Imperial Aromatic, Wear Upham & Ostrom, Amber, 12 1/2 In., R-J57 .... 3025.00
Kelly's Old Cabin, Dark Root Beer Amber, 9 3/8 In., R-K22 .... 2420.00
Kelly's Old Cabin, Medium Amber, 9 5/8 In., R-K21 .... *Illus* 1815.00
Keystone, Barrel, Golden Amber, 9 3/4 In., R-K36 .... 412.00
Keystone, Barrel, Yellow Amber, 9 7/8 In., R-K36 .... 550.00
Khoosh, Amber, England, 12 1/2 In., R-K38 .... 231.00
Kimball's Jaundice, Troy, N.H., Olive Amber, Metallic Pontil, 7 In., R-K42 .... *Illus* 413.00
Kimball's Jaundice, Troy, N.H., Yellow Amber, IP, 7 In., R-K42 .... 577.50
Kimball's Jaundice, Troy, N.Y., Amber, OP, R-K42 .... 400.00
King Solomon's, Seattle, Wash., Amber, 7 In., R-K50 .... 88.00
Lacour's Sarsapariphere, Lime Green, 9 1/4 In., R-L3 .... 5060.00
Lacour's Sarsapariphere, Yellow Root Beer Amber, 9 1/4 In., R-L3 .... 1650.00
Lash's, Sample, 4 1/4 In., R-L31 .... 25.00 to 45.00
Lash's, Yellow Amber, Small Label, Cylinder, 11 1/4 In., R-L41 .... 55.00
Lediard's Celebrated Stomach, Deep Emerald, IP, 10 In., R-L60 .... 2090.00
Litthauer Stomach, see also Bitters, Hartwig Kantorowicz
Loftus Peach, Green, Yellow Tone, England, 11 1/2 In. 176.00
Lohengrin, Adolf Marcus, Von Buton, Germany, Milk Glass, 9 In., R-L117 .... 135.00
Lorimer's Juniper Tar, Elmira, N.Y., Yellow Green, 9 3/8 In., R-L121 .... 770.00
Loveridge's Wahoo, Buffalo, N.Y., Flask, Medium Yellow Olive, 7 In., R-L127 .... 330.00

Bitters, Kelly's Old
Cabin, Medium Amber,
9 5/8 In., R-K21

Bitters, Kimball's Jaundice,
Troy, N.H., Olive Amber,
Metallic Pontil, 7 In., R-K42

Bitters, National, Ear
Of Corn, Amber, Pat.1867,
12 5/8 In., R-N8

Lyman's Dandelion Bitters, Bangor, Me., Aqua, Partial Label, 10 1/2 In., R-L138...... 145.00
M.G. Landsberg, Chicago, Corrugated Corners, Light Golden Amber, 11 In., R-L15 ... 687.50
Mack's Sarsaparilla, San Francisco, Medium Amber, 9 1/4 In., R-M4........................ 242.00
Malarion, St. Louis, Mo., Amber, 9 1/4 In., R-M18 .... 154.00
Mampe Medicinal, Label, 6 1/8 In., R-M24... 55.00
Mandrake, see Bitters, Dr. Baxter's
Mansfield's New Style Highland Stomach, Memphis, Amber, 8 7/8 In., R-M33 .... 750.00
Marshall's Best Laxative, Blood Purifier, Amber, 8 5/8 In., R-M40............................ 44.00
McConnon's Stomach Bitters, Square, Red Amber, 8 5/8 In., R-M53 .... 192.00
McKeever's Army, Drum, Cannonballs, Amber, 10 1/4 In., R-M58................. 852.50 to 1210.00
McKelvy's Stomach, Pittsburgh, Pa., Aqua, 8 7/8 In., R-M59 .... 302.50
Mills's, A.M. Gilman, Lady's Leg, Yellow Amber, 11 1/4 In., R-M93........................... 1540.00
Mishler's Herb, Dr. S.B. Hartmann & Co., Peach, 8 3/4 In., R-M100.......................... 1155.00
Mishler's Herb, Dr. S.B. Hartmann & Co., Strawberry Puce, 8 3/4 In., R-M100.......... 330.00
Morning Inceptum, Star, Amber, Applied Tapered Lip, 12 7/8 In., R-M135................. 231.00
Morning Inceptum, Star, Yellow Amber, IP, 12 1/2 In., R-M135 .... 182.00
Moulton's Oloroso, Pineapple Trade Mark, Aqua, 11 3/8 In., R-M146 .... 110.00 to 385.00
National, Ear Of Corn, Amber, Pat. 1867, 12 5/8 In., R-N8 ....*Illus* 303.00
National, Ear Of Corn, Aqua, Pat. 1867, 12 5/8 In., R-N8... 3135.00
National, Ear Of Corn, Deep Burgundy, 12 1/4 In., R-N8 .... 660.00
National, Ear Of Corn, Lemon Yellow, Pat. 1867, 12 5/8 In., R-N8......................*Illus* 990.00
National, Ear Of Corn, Light Puce, Ring Lip, 12 5/8 In., R-N8 .... 1375.00
National, Ear Of Corn, Medium Amber, Pat. 1867, 12 1/2 In., R-N8 .... 242.00
National, Ear Of Corn, Pink Puce, Pat. 1867, 12 1/2 In., R-N8 .... 3410.00
National, Ear Of Corn, Strawberry Puce, 12 1/2 In., R-N8 .... 935.00
National, Ear Of Corn, Yellow Amber, Patent 1867, 11 7/8 In., R-N8........................... 1265.00
National, Ear Of Corn, Yellow, Olive Tones, Pat. 1867, 12 3/8 In., R-N8 .... 1595.00
National Tonic, Pale Blue Green, Arches, Roped Corners, 9 1/2 In., R-N13.................. 605.00
National Tonic, Pale Electric Blue, 9 5/8 In., R-N13.. 825.00
NK Brown Iron & Quinine, Burlington, Vt., Rectangular, 7 1/4 In., R-I28 .... 86.00
O'Hare, Pittsburgh, Pa., Amber, 9 1/4 In., R-O10 .... 115.00
O'Hare Bitters Co., Pittsburgh, Pa., Yellow Amber, 9 1/4 In., R-O10 .... 66.00
OK Plantation, Olive Amber, 7 Ribs, Applied Collar, 11 1/4 In., R-O13....................... 1100.00
Old Continental, Golden Amber, Square Collar, Rectangular, 10 In., R-O25 .... 413.00
Old Dr. Solomon's Indian Wine, Aqua, 8 3/8 In., R-S138 .... 50.00
Old Homestead Wild Cherry, Cabin, Amber, Label, 9 1/2 In, R-O37............................. 4510.00
Old Homestead Wild Cherry, Cabin, Amber, Patent, 9 3/4 In., R-O37.......................... 220.00
Old Homestead Wild Cherry, Cabin, Puce Amber, 9 1/2 In., R-O37............................. 468.00
Old Homestead Wild Cherry, Cabin, Strawberry Puce, 9 3/8, R-O37 .... 3080.00
Old Homestead Wild Cherry, Cabin, Strawberry Puce, 9 7/8 In., R-O37 ....*Illus* 2090.00
Old Homestead Wild Cherry, Cabin, Yellow Amber, 9 5/8 In., R-O37 .... 467.00

Old Man's Stomach, Deep Amber, 9 7/8 In., R-O42 .... 3080.00
Old Sachem & Wigwam Tonic, Amber, Applied Square Collar Lip, 9 1/2 In., R-R046   275.00
Old Sachem & Wigwam Tonic, Barrel, Aqua, 10 1/8 In., R-O45................................... 4620.00
Old Sachem & Wigwam Tonic, Barrel, Golden Amber, Pontil, 9 1/4 In., R-O46 ....   440.00
Old Sachem & Wigwam Tonic, Barrel, Green Aqua, 9 1/2 In., R-O46 .... 4840.00
Old Sachem & Wigwam Tonic, Barrel, Medium Amber, 9 1/2 In., R-O46........ 176.00 to 250.00
Old Sachem & Wigwam Tonic, Barrel, Medium Copper Puce, 9 1/4 In., R-O46..........   770.00
Old Sachem & Wigwam Tonic, Barrel, Medium Ginger Ale, 9 5/8 In., R-O46 .... 2035.00
Old Sachem & Wigwam Tonic, Barrel, Medium Golden Amber, 9 1/4 In., R-O46 ......   176.00
Old Sachem & Wigwam Tonic, Barrel, Medium Pink Puce, 9 1/2 In., R-O46..............   495.00
Old Sachem & Wigwam Tonic, Barrel, Medium Yellow Amber, 9 1/4 In., R-O46 ....   330.00
Old Sachem & Wigwam Tonic, Barrel, Moss Green, 9 1/4 In., R-O46.......................... 4675.00
Old Sachem & Wigwam Tonic, Barrel, Red Puce, 9 3/8 In., R-O46 ....   242.00
Old Sachem & Wigwam Tonic, Barrel, Salmon Puce, c.1870, 9 1/2 In., R-O46............   121.00
Old Sachem & Wigwam Tonic, Barrel, Strawberry Puce, 9 1/4 In., R-O46 ....   495.00
Old Sachem & Wigwam Tonic, Barrel, Strawberry Puce, 9 3/8 In., R-O46 ....   715.00
Old Sachem & Wigwam Tonic, Barrel, Yellow Amber, 9 1/8 In., R-O46.......................   154.00
Old Sachem & Wigwam Tonic, Barrel, Yellow Hint Of Puce, 9 1/2 In., R-O46...........   440.00
Old Sachem & Wigwam Tonic, Barrel, Yellow Olive, Apricot, 9 3/8 In., R-O46.......... 1870.00
Old Sachem & Wigwam Tonic, Barrel, Yellow, R-O46..   550.00
Old Sachem & Wigwam Tonic, Orange Amber, OP, 9 1/4 In., R-O46 ....   742.00
Old Sachem & Wigwam Tonic, San Francisco, Aqua, Bubbles, 9 1/4 In., R-O46 .... 3300.00
Original Pocahontas, Y. Ferguson, Barrel, Aqua, 9 3/8 In., R-O86.............................. 2695.00
Oswego, Star, 25 Cents, Medium Amber, 7 In., R-O93...   83.00
Oxygenated, Aqua, OP, 7 5/8 In., R-O99...   55.00
Panacea, Frank Hayman & Rhine, Amber, 10 In., R-F7g 1485.00
Pawnee, Green Aqua, Part Indian Picture Label, R-P34 ....   500.00
Penn's Bitters For The Liver, Golden Amber, Square, 6 1/2 In., R-P39 ....   99.00
Penn's Pony, Philadelphia, Pa., Root Beer Amber, 9 In., R-P40..................................   577.50
Pepsin, R.W. Davis Drug Co., Chicago, Bright Green, 8 1/8 In., R-P44.......................   70.00
Pepsin, R.W. Davis Drug Co., Chicago, Yellow Green, 8 1/4 In., R-P44 ....   187.00
Pepsin Calisaya, Bright Lime Green, 7 7/8 In., R-P50..   80.00
Pepsin Calisaya, Dr. Russell, Bright Green, R-P50..   85.00
Pepsin Calisaya, Dr. Russell, Lime Green, R-P50 ....   75.00
Peruvian, Medium Amber, 9 1/2 In., R-P60 ....   495.00
Peychaud's American Aromatic Bitter Cordial, L.E. Jung, New Orleans, Amber, R-P81 65.00
Peychaud's American Aromatic Bitter Cordial, New Orleans, R-P81 ....   45.00
Pig, see Bitters, Berkshire; Bitters, Suffolk
Pineapple, Aqua, Pat. Oct.1, 1870, 8 7/8 In., R-P101... 1870.00
Pineapple, Medium Amber, 8 7/8 In., R-P100 ....72.00 to 132.00

Bitters, National, Ear
Of Corn, Lemon
Yellow, Pat. 1867,
12 5/8 In., R-N8

Bitters, Suffolk, Philbrook
& Tucker, Pig, Yellow
Amber, 10 1/8 In., R-S217

Bitters, Old Homestead
Wild Cherry, Cabin,
Strawberry Puce,
9 7/8 In., R-O37

Pineapple, Medium Yellow Amber, 8 7/8 In., R-P100 .... 121.00
Pineapple, W. & Co., N.Y., OP, 8 7/8 In., R-P100 .... 310.00
Pineapple, W. & Co., Yellow Green, 8 1/4 In., R-P100 .... 4510.00
Pineapple, W. & Co., Deep Yellow Olive, Pontil, 8 1/8 In., R-P100 .... 1320.00
Pineapple, W. & Co., N.Y., Olive Green, Pontil, c.1870, 8 3/8 In., R-P100 .... 1430.00
Pineapple, W. & Co., N.Y., Pontil, Blue Green, 8 1/4 In., R-P100 .... 4510.00
Pineapple, Yellow Olive, Double Collar Lip, 9 1/4 In., R-P100 .... 577.00
Poor Man's Family, Pale Aqua, 6 3/8 In., R-P123 .... 50.00
Prickly Ash, Yellow Amber, Panel, Cover, Square, 9 1/4 In., R-P140 .... 125.00
Prof. Leonnard's Celebrated Nectar, Cincinnati, O., Amber, 9 1/4 In., R-L75 .... 264.00
Professor B.E. Mann's Oriental Stomach, Amber, 10 1/4 In., R-M29 .... 880.00
Professor Geo. J. Byrne, Great Universal Compound, Golden Amber, 10 3/4 In., R-B280 . 4290.00
Professor Geo. J. Byrne, Great Universal Compound, Yellow, 10 1/2 In., R-B280 ...... 6160.00
Prune Stomach & Liver, Orange Amber, 9 1/4 In., R-P151 .... 77.00
Prussian, Orange Amber, 9 1/8 In., R-P152 .... 522.50
Prussian, Square, Beveled, Yellow Amber, 9 In., R-P152 .... 165.00
Rattinger's Root & Herb, Golden Amber, 8 5/8 In., R-R12 .... 145.00
Red Jacket, Monheimer & Co., Amber, Square, 9 1/2 In., R-R20 .... 100.00
Red Star Stomach, St. Paul, Minn., Amber, 11 1/4 In., R-R25 .... 165.00
Reed's, Lady's Leg, Amber, 12 3/4 In., R-R27 .... 187.00
Reed's, Lady's Leg, Medium Orange, Amber, 12 3/4 In., R-R28 .... 385.00
Reed's, Lady's Leg, Orange Amber, 12 1/2 In., R-R28 .... 253.00
Reed's Bitters, Lady's Leg, Medium Orange Amber, R-R27 .... 145.00
Remko Tonic, Appetizer And Health, Clear, Tooled Lip, 9 1/2 In., R-R31 .... 77.00
Rising Sun, Golden Amber, 9 3/8 In., R-R66 .... 80.00
Ritz's, Juniper & Wild Lemon, Modified Cabin, Golden Amber, 10 In. 357.00
Rocky Mountain Tonic, 1840 Try Me 1870, Yellow Amber, 9 3/4 In., R-R82 .... 165.00
Royal Italian, A.M.F. Gianelli, Genova, Light Pink Amethyst, 13 1/2 In., R-R111 .... 2640.00
Royal Italian, A.M.F. Gianelli, Genova, Pink Amethyst, 13 3/8 In., R-R111 .... 990.00
Royal Italian, Medium Amethyst, Cylindrical, 13 1/2 In., R-R111 .... 484.00
Royal Italian, Registered, Pink Amethyst, 13 1/2 In., R-R111 .... 577.50
Rush's, A.H. Flanders, Brown, Applied Lip, 9 In., R-R124 .... 40.00
Russ, St. Domingo, N.Y., Yellow Amber, Olive, 10 In., R-R125 .... 440.00
Russian Imperial Tonic, Arched Panels, Aqua, 9 1/2 In., R-R133 .... 1045.00
S.O. Richardson's, Aqua, OP, R-R57 .... 65.00
S.O. Richardson's, IP Variant, R-R57 .... 100.00
S.O. Richardson's, So. Reading, Mass., Pontil, R-R57 .... 69.00
S.O. Richardson's, South Reading, Mass., Aqua, R-R57 .... 25.00
S.T. Drake's, see Bitters, Drake's Plantation
Saint Jacob, K.Y.G.W. Co., Yellow Amber, 8 1/2 In., R-S13 .... 104.00
Sarracenia Life, Tucker, Mobile, Amber, 9 In., R-S34 .... 154.00
Sazerac Aromatic, Lady's Leg, Amber, 12 In., R-S47 .... 1017.50
Sazerac Aromatic, Lady's Leg, Milk Glass, Applied Ring, 12 1/2 In., R-S47 .... 231.00
Schroeder's, Louisville & Cincinnati, Est. 1845, Lady's Leg, Amber, 5 3/16 In., R-S69 ...... 330.00
Schroeder's, Louisville, Ky., Lady's Leg, Amber, SB&G Co., 8 5/8 In., R-S63 .... 88.00
Schroeder's, Louisville, Ky., Lady's Leg, Golden Amber, 12 In., R-S68 .... 825.00
Schroeder's, Louisville, Ky., Lady's Leg, Orange Amber, 9 In., R-S65 .... 468.00
Seaworth Bitters Co., Lighthouse Form, Golden Amber, 6 1/4 In., R-S82 .... 990.00
Smiths Druid, Barrel, Deep Cherry Puce, 9 1/2 In., R-S124 .... 1375.00
Smiths Druid, Barrel, Light To Medium Amber, 9 In., R-S124 .... 715.00
Sol Frank's Panacea, Lighthouse, Amber, 10 In., R-F79 .... 1485.00
Sol Frank's Panacea, Lighthouse, Medium Amber, 9 7/8 In., R-F79 .... 275.00
Solomon's Strengthening & Invigorating, Cobalt Blue, 9 1/2 In., R-S140 .... 1073.00
Solomon's Strengthening & Invigorating, Cobalt Blue, Square, 9 1/2 In., R-S139 ..... 875.00
St. Gotthard Herb, Mette & Kanne Pros., St. Louis, Amber, 9 In., R-S12 .... 50.00
St. Nicholas Stomach, Medium Honey Amber, OP, Dug, 9 1/4 In., R-S16 .... 3300.00
Star Kidney & Liver, Amber, 8 7/8 In., R-S178 .... 55.00
Suffolk, Philbrook & Tucker, Pig, Yellow Amber, 10 1/8 In., R-S217 ....*Illus* 715.00
Suffolk, Pig, Shaded Golden Yellow, R-S217 .... 550.00
Swiss Alpine Herb, Yellow Amber, Applied Mouth, 9 5/8 In., R-S239 .... 220.00
T.J. Dunbar & Co., Lady's Leg, Green, Embossed, R-D116 .... 125.00
Travellers, Yellow Amber, 10 1/2 In., R-T54 .... 2310.00
Turner Bros., Barrel, Copper Amber, Whittled, R-T67 .... 250.00

Bitters, Wahoo & Calisaya,
Jacob Pinkerton,
Semi-Cabin, Puce Amber,
9 5/8 In., R-W3

Bitters, W.R. Tryee's
Chamomile, Semi-Cabin,
Medium Amber, 9 1/2 In.,
R-T75

Black Glass, English
Onion, Deep Olive Green,
Applied String Lip,
1690-1700, 5 3/4 In.

Turner Bros., Olive Amber, Barrel, 9 In., R-T67 .... 350.00
Tyree's Chamomile, Golden Amber, Oval, 6 1/4 In., R-T73............................... 165.00
W.C. Bitters, Brobst & Rentschler, Light Amber, 10 1/2 In., R-W57...................... 750.00
W.R. Tryee's Chamomile, Semi-Cabin, Medium Amber, 9 1/2 In., R-T75.............*Illus* 578.00
Wahoo & Calisaya, Jacob Pinkerton, Bright Yellow Amber, 9 5/8 In., R-W3 .... 565.00
Wahoo & Calisaya, Jacob Pinkerton, Semi-Cabin, Puce Amber, 9 5/8 In., R-W3,..*Illus* 330.00
Wait's Kidney & Liver, California, Amber, 8 7/8 In., R-W6 .... 71.50
Wakefield's Strengthening, Aqua, R-W7 .... 45.00
Walker's Tonic, Lady's Leg Neck, Red Amber, 11 1/2 In., R-W13 .... 275.00
Walton's Bitters, Cincinnati, Oh., Medium Amber, 9 3/8 In., R-W22 .... 198.00
Wampoo, Siegel & Bro, New York, Amber, 9 5/8 In., R-W25 .... 143.00
Warner's German Hop, Reading, Mich., Yellow Amber, 9 3/4 In., R-W32 .... 440.00
Warner's Safe, Rochester, N.Y., Safe Motif, Amber, 9 1/2 In., R-W34...................... 440.00
Warner's Safe Tonic, Amber, 9 3/4 In., R-W36 .... 500.00
Warner's Safe Tonic, Rochester, N.Y., Yellow Amber, 9 In., R-W34........................ 852.50
Weis Bros., Knickerbocker Stomach, Orange Amber, 11 7/8 In., R-W68 .... 2090.00
West India Stomach, St. Louis, Mo., Amber, 8 1/2 In., R-W79 .... 55.00
Wheeler's Berlin, Baltimore, Yellow Olive, 6-Sided, 9 5/8 In., R-W83...................... 7150.00
White's Stomach, Golden Amber, 9 1/2 In., R-W101.. 154.00
William Allen's Congress, Aqua, 10 In., R-A29 ....185.00 to 247.50
William Allen's Congress, Green, Applied Tapered Lip, 10 1/2 In., R-A29 .... 1485.00
Wilson's Herbine, 6 1/2 In., R-W123 .... 22.00
Woods Sarsaparilla & Wild Cherry, OP, 9 In., R-W151.. 250.00
Yerba Buena, Amber, 8 3/8 In., R-Y4 .... 66.00
Yerba Buena, Amber, 9 1/2 In., R-Y3 .... 49.50
Yerba Buena, San Francisco, Yellow Amber, Flask, Strap, 9 1/2 In., R-Y3................. 65.00
Zingari, F. Rahter, Lady's Leg, Amber, 11 3/4 In., R-Z4...................200.00 to 255.00
Zingari, F. Rahter, Lady's Leg, Amber, 12 1/8 In., R-Z4...................275.00 to 345.00

———————————————— **BLACK GLASS** ————————————————

Black glass is not really black. It is dark green or brown. In the seventeenth century, blown
black glass demijohns were used to carry liquor overseas from Europe. They were usually
heavy glass bottles that were made to withstand shipping. The kick-up bottom also helped
deter breakage. Many types of bottles were made of very dark glass that appeared black.
This was one of the most common colors for glass wine bottles of the eighteenth and
early-nineteenth centuries.

BLACK GLASS, 8-Sided, Olive Green, OP, 1830-1840, 10 1/2 In..................................... 1540.00
A.S.C.R., Belly Seal, Deep Olive Amber, Pontil, Cylindrical, 1820, 10 7/8 In............... 100.00
Ch Ch E/R, 1801 On Seal, Olive Green, Applied Ring Lip, Pontil, England, 10 1/8 In. . 467.00
Con Stantia Wyn, Deep Olive Green, OP, 8 1/4 In. 660.00
Cylinder, Deep Olive Amber, OP, 8 5/8 In.. 357.50
Cylinder, Deep Olive Amber, Pontil, 9 1/2 In. 412.50

Dark Olive Amber, 8 3/4 In.. 192.50
Dutch Kidney, Yellow Olive Amber, 7 In. 385.00
Dutch Onion, Admr. Lutt Pieter-Heterszhein, Long Neck, OP, 9 In...................... 688.00
Dutch Onion, Bell Shaped, Medium Olive Amber, OP, 8 In., 5 In. Diam..................... 88.00
Dutch Onion, Creme De Royeaux, Olive Green, Applied Ring Lip, OP, 11 In............... 1815.00
Dutch Onion, Dark Olive Green, Painted French Naval Battle, 12 In....................... 1430.00
Dutch Onion, David Provost 172 In Belly Seal, Olive Green, 7 In. 4400.00
Dutch Onion, H N I In Shoulder Seal, String Lip, Pontil, Europe, 1700...................... 880.00
Dutch Onion, Olive Amber.. 52.00
Dutch Onion, Olive Green, Applied Collar, Pontil, Squatty, 5 3/4 In. 286.00
Dutch Onion, Olive Green, OP, 7 In. 95.00
Dutch Onion, Olive Green, Tavern Genre Scene, Painted Ground, 10 In. 1915.00
Dutch Onion, Wide Mouth, Olive Amber, OP, String Lip, 8 7/8 In............................... 440.00
English Mallet, Dark Olive Green, 1730, 7 3/4... 55.00
English Mallet, Dark Yellow Olive, 8 3/4 x 4 7/8 In... 175.00
English Mallet, Deep Olive Amber, Applied String Lip, 7 In................................... 330.00
English Mallet, Deep Olive Amber, Pontil, 7 1/4 In... 121.00
English Mallet, Deep Olive Amber, Pontil, 7 7/8 In., 5 In. Diam............................. 110.00
English Mallet, J.A. Oakes Bury, Deep Olive Amber, Pontil, 10 1/4 In..................... 412.50
English Mallet, John Andrew, Medium Olive Green, Pontil, 10 3/4 In. 660.00
English Mallet, Medium Deep Olive Green, Pontil, 8 7/8 In. 742.50
English Mallet, Olive Amber, Pontil, 11 In. 110.00
English Mallet, Olive Green, 8 1/2 In.. 99.00
English Mallet, Picton Castle, Deep Olive Green, Pontil, 11 1/8 In. 357.50
English Onion, Applied String Lip, 1690-1700, 5 3/4 In. 242.00
English Onion, Dark Olive Green, 1680-1700, 6 3/4 x 5 5/8 In............................... 85.00
English Onion, Dark Olive Green, 1725, 6 1/4 x 5 7/8 In...................................... 160.00
English Onion, Deep Olive Amber, Pontil, Magnum, 11 1/4 In................................ 743.00
English Onion, Deep Olive Green, Applied String Lip, 1690-1700, 5 3/4 In...........*Illus* 242.00
English Onion, Medium Olive Green, Pontil, 6 5/8 In. 88.00
English Onion, Medium Olive Green, Pontil, String Lip, 6 7/8 In. 93.50
English Onion, Medium Yellow Olive, Pontil, 6 7/8 In. 77.00
English Onion, Olive Amber, Pontil, 7 1/8 In... 165.00
Globular, Short Neck, Olive Amber, Pontil, Double Collar Mouth, 9 1/2 In. 176.00
Globular, William Allan Margret Bevridge, Scotland, 8 3/8 In............................... 220.00
Green Hill On Seal, Applied Tapered Ring Lip, Pontil, England, 1820, 7 7/8 In. 210.00
H. Ricketts Glass & Co., Bristol, 3-Piece Mold, Applied Mouth, 8 3/4 In................ 302.50
Lay Brandy, Gold Painted, Deep Olive Green, Cylindrical, 1870, 9 In....................... 121.00
Long Neck, Olive Green, Continental, 1780-1820, 11 1/2 In..................................... 50.00
Mallet, Dark Olive Green, Continental, 1750-1760, 7 1/2 In. 80.00
Mallet, Dark Olive Green, Pontil, Continental, 7 3/4 In.. 220.00
Mallet, Olive Amber, OP, c.1740, 7 1/8 In. 66.00
Olive Amber, 10 3/4 In... 385.00
Olive Amber, All Soul C R In Belly Seal, String Lip, Pontil, Cylindrical, 11 In. 550.00
Onion, Blue Green, 7 In.. 176.00
Onion, Deep Blue Gray, 5 1/2 In. 357.50
Onion, Deep Olive Green, Applied Ring Lip, 6 In. 2750.00
Onion, Half-Size, Olive Amber, String Lip, 5 1/4 In... 220.00
Onion, Light Yellow Green, 7 1/2 In... 110.00
Onion, Medium Olive Green, 6 3/4 In. 93.50
Onion, Medium, Dark Green, 6 3/4 In... 93.50
Onion, Olive Amber, 6 1/2 In... 2200.00
Onion, Olive Green, Applied Lip, Pontil, 6 In... 770.00
Onion, Straight Sided, Medium Yellow Green, 6 7/8 In... 121.00
Onion, Straight Sided, Olive Green, 7 3/4 In.. 110.00
Onion, Yellow Olive Amber, 7 7/8 In. 110.00
Pancake Onion, Dark Olive Green, England, 1680-1710, 5 7/8 H x 6 In....................... 350.00
Porter, Lady's Leg, Long Neck, Continental, 1760-1800, 11 1/4 In. 90.00
R.T 1789 Seal, Fat Body, Cylinder.. 480.00
Rum, Cylinder, Dip Mold, Dark Olive Green, England, 8 7/8 In. 35.00
Rum, Cylinder, Dip Mold, Dark Olive Green, England, 1800-1820, 9 1/8 In.................. 30.00
Seal, Eman Coll., Olive Amber, Pontil, England, c.1840, 11 3/8 In............................ 115.00
Seal, Rousdon Jubilee, 1887, Deep Olive Amber, Applied Mouth, 11 5/8 In. 110.00

Shaft & Globe, Olive Green, Applied Ring Lip, Pontil, England, 6 3/4 In. 1870.00
Shaft & Globe, Olive Green, Applied Saturn Ring, Pontil, England, 7 3/4 In. 1650.00
Shaft & Globe, Olive Green, Applied String Ring Lip, England, 1685, 6 In. 1265.00
Shaft & Globe, Yellow Olive Green, Applied Mouth, 8 1/8 In. 742.50
Storage, Globular, Deep Forest Green, OP, Bubbly, 10 1/4 In. 357.00
Utility, Wide Mouth, Laid On Ring, 1/2 Pt. 40.00
W. Peters & Co., Deep Olive Amber, Pontil, Cylindrical, 12 1/2 In. 1265.00
BLACKING, see Household, Blacking

──────────────────── **BLOWN** ────────────────────

The American glass industry did not flourish until after the Revolution. Glass for windows
and blown-glass bottles were the most rewarding products. The bottles were blown in large
or small sizes to hold liquor. Many glassworks made blown and pattern-molded bottles.
Midwestern factories favored twisted swirl designs. The colors ranged from green and
aquamarine to dark olive green or amber. Sometimes blue or dark maroon bottles were
blown. Some were made of such dark glass they are known as *black glass* bottles.

BLOWN, Apothecary, Cobalt Blue Bands, Pontil, Knob Top Lid, c.1870, 9 3/4 In. 275.00
Arch & Thumbprint, 3-Piece Mold, Large Blob Lip, Polished Pontil............................ 130.00
Carafe, 3-Piece Mold, Blue Green, Flared Mouth, Pontil, Qt..................................... 2200.00
Carboy, 3-Piece Mold, Yellow Olive, Semibread Loaf Shape, Europe, 16 1/2 In. 231.00
Decanter, 3-Piece Mold, 3 Neck Rings, Stopper, Pontil, Qt. 1210.00
Decanter, 3-Piece Mold, 8-Sided, Medium Green, Pontil, Pt. 550.00
Decanter, 3 Piece Mold, Clear, Flared Mouth, Pontil, Stopper, 1/2 Pt. 253.00
Decanter, 3-Piece Mold, Bulbous, 3 Neck Rings, Stopper, Pontil, Pt............................ 110.00
Decanter, 3-Piece Mold, Clear, Pontil, Neck Rings, Stopper, 8 1/4 In. 148.50
Decanter, 3-Piece Mold, Clear, Pontil, Neck Rings, Stopper, 7 In. 121.00
Decanter, 3-Piece Mold, Clear, Stopper, Pontil, 5 7/8 In.. 550.00
Decanter, 3-Piece Mold, Light Forest Green, Pontil, 7 1/4 In. 6050.00
Decanter, 3-Piece Mold, Olive Amber, OP, 7 In. 522.50
Decanter, 3-Piece Mold, Olive Amber, OP, Qt. 770.00
Decanter, 3-Piece Mold, Pale Green, Flared Lip, Pontil, Stopper, 7 In. 990.00
Decanter, 3-Piece Mold, Pale Green, Pontil, c.1820, Stopper, 7 In. 990.00
Decanter, 3-Piece Mold, Pontil, Qt... 110.00
Decanter, 3-Piece Mold, Rose Bowl Pattern, Pontil, 1 5/8 In. 220.00
Decanter, 3-Piece Mold, Stopper, Pontil, Pt.. 159.50
Decanter, 3-Piece Mold, Stopper, Pontil, Qt. 242.00
Decanter, Amethyst, Pontil, 10 3/4 In. 55.00
Decanter, Clear, Concave Panels, Pontil, 9 In. 440.00
Decanter, Cobalt Blue, White Swirls, Pontil, Rolled Lip, c.1860, 8 3/4 In................... 137.00
Decanter, Cut Glass, Strawberry Diamond & Fan, Clear, c.1845, 8 1/2 In................... 687.50
Decanter, Pillar Mold, Clear, Cobalt Blue Ribs, Polished Pontil, 8 3/8 In................... 522.50
Flask, Chestnut, Yellow Olive, Pontil, New England, 1780-1830, 5 1/4 In. 209.00
Globular, Dark Olive Green, Pontil, 1780-1830, 8 1/4 In. 429.00
Globular, Yellow Green, Applied Mouth, Pontil, 11 3/8 In. 220.00
Rolling Pin, Clear, Red, Blue, Maroon & Brown Splotches, Pontil, 17 In. 187.00
Rolling Pin, Cobalt Blue, Whimsy, 1870-1900, 28 In. 302.00
Rolling Pin, Dark Olive Green, White Flecks, Pontil, 1850-1870, 15 In....................... 137.00
Rolling Pin, Nailsea Type, Cranberry Red White Loopings, England, 1870-1890, 15 In. ... 231.00
Rolling Pin, Opalescent, Gilt Design, Forget-Me-Not, 1870-1890, Pontil, England 121.00
Utility, Amber, Cone, Tapered, Double Collar, Early 1800s, Qt.................................. 120.00
Utility, Yellow Emerald Green, 8-Sided, Applied String Lip, Europe, 3 3/4 In.............. 330.00
BROOKS, see Ezra Brooks
C.P.C., CALIFORNIA PERFUME COMPANY, see Avon
CABIN STILL, see Old Fitzgerald
CALABASH, see Flask

──────────────────── **CANDY CONTAINER** ────────────────────

The first figural glass candy containers date from the nineteenth century. They were made
to hold candy and to be used later as toys for children. These containers were very popular
after World War I. Small glass or papier-mache figural bottles held dime-store candy. Cars,
trains, airplanes, animals, comic figures, telephones, and many other imaginative containers

were made. The fad faded in the Depression years but returned in the 1940s. Today many of the same shapes hold modern candy in plastic bottles. The paper labels on the containers help a little with the dating. In the 1940s the words *Contents* or *Ingredients* were included on the labels. Earlier, this information was not necessary. Screw tops and corks were used. Some of the most popular early shapes have been reproduced in Taiwan and Hong Kong in recent years. A club with a newsletter is Candy Container Collectors of America, 26 Brian Rd., Chelmsford, MA 01824.

CANDY CONTAINER, Airplane, Army Bomber, Closure	3.00
Airplane, Cardboard Wing	3.00
Airplane, P-38 Lightning, No Closure	200.00
Airplane, P-51, Closure	60.00
Airplane, P-51, No Closure	40.00
Airplane, Patent 113053, Wings, Replacement, Closure	40.00
Amos 'n' Andy, Replacement Closure	500.00
Barney Google, Ball, Closure	300.00
Battleship, Closure	25.00
Battleship, On Waves, Closure	200.00
Bear, On Circus Tub, Wheel, Closure, No Tube	275.00
Binoculars, Floral, Amber, 3 In. *Illus*	135.00
Bird, Cage, Closure	100.00
Bird, On Mound, Whistle	395.00
Boat, Queen Mary, Closure	400.00
Boot, Dress, Closure	45.00
Boot, Santa's, Merry Christmas Label, No Closure	15.00
Boot, Santa's, Merry Christmas Label, Closure	45.00
Boston Kettle, Paper Handle	3.00
Bulldog, No. 2, Stough, Closure	3.00
Bulldog, Oblong Base, No Closure	25.00
Bulldog, Round Base, Closure	75.00
Bus, Victory Lines, Special, Closure	3.00
Cannon, Glass Barrel, Metal Wheels, Carriage, Cobalt Blue, 2 In.	1100.00
Car, Electric Coupe, No Closure	25.00
Car, Ford, 1929, Closure	10.00
Car, Hood, Long Coupe, Long, Wheels, Closure	150.00
Car, Racer, No. 12, No Closure	175.00
Carpet Sweeper, Baby	450.00
Carpet Sweeper, Dolly	450.00
Cat, Black, On Top Hat, Germany, 5 In.	295.00
Charlie Chaplin, George Borgfeldt & Co., N.Y., Painted, c.1918	110.00
Chick, Baby, Standing, Closure	80.00
Chick, In Shell Car, Closure	350.00
Chicken, On Nest, Closure	3.00 to 40.00

Candy Container, Binoculars,
Floral, Amber, 3 In.

Candy Container, Santa
Claus, 5 1/4 In.

Candy Container, Telephone,
Candlestick, 7 3/4 In.

Chicken, On Nest, No Closure 15.00
Chicken, On Oblong Basket, Closure 65.00
Chicken, On Round Base, Closure 300.00
Chicken, On Sagging Basket, Closure 75.00
Child, Naked, Closure 60.00
Circus Clown Dogs, Paper Connector 4.00
Clock, Alarm, Gold Trim, Closure 275.00
Clock, Happy Time 20.00
Clock, Mantel, No. 2, Gold Trim, Closure 175.00
Clock, Octagon, Red Trim, Closure 150.00
Devil, Painted, Germany, 5 In. 475.00
Dirigible, Closure 150.00
Dog, Cardboard Brim, Stough 3.00
Dog, Glass Hat, Large, Stough, Closure 2.00
Dog, Glass Hat, Small, Closure 2.00
Dog, Hound Pup, Cobalt Blue, No Closure 20.00
Dog, Poochie, No Closure 2.00
Dog, Scotty, Closure 15.00
Dog, Scotty, Head Turned To Left, Closure 30.00
Dog, Scotty, Head Up, No Closure 10.00
Dog, Scotty, Stough, Closure 3.00
Drum, Milk Glass, Closure 500.00
Electric Iron, No Closure 30.00
Elephant, G.O.P. 200.00
Elephant, In Swallow-Tail Suit 300.00
Fire Engine, Ladder Truck, Closure 3.00
Fire Engine, Little Boiler, No Closure 50.00
Fire Engine, Miniature, Closure 25.00
Fire Engine, Narrow, No Closure 50.00
Fire Engine No. 11, Closure 25.00
Gun, Barrel, 6-Sided, Closure 30.00
Gun, Diamond In Grip, No Closure 20.00
Gun, Fancy Grip, Closure 25.00
Gun, Flintlock, Amber, Closure 30.00
Gun, Kolt, Painted, Closure 95.00
Gun, Large, Closure 25.00
Hat, High, Penny Toy, No Closure .... 5.00 to 20.00
Hat, Military, Red, White Blue Printing, Closure 30.00
Horn, Trumpet, Milk Glass 200.00
House, All Glass 100.00
Independence Hall, Closure .... 60.00 to 200.00
Kettle, Closure 60.00
Kewpie, By Barrel, Closure 150.00
Kiddies, Breakfast Bell, Closure 50.00
Kiddies Drinking Mug, Millstein, Closure 3.00
Lamp, Hurricane, Miniature 250.00
Lamp, Ribbed Base, Shade, Closure 140.00
Lamp, Street, On Post 100.00
Lantern, Barn, Closure 50.00
Lantern, Beaded Trim, Closure 30.00
Lantern, Cap, Brass, Closure 20.00
Lantern, Diamond Marked, Closure 35.00
Lantern, Railroad, Operating Instructions 1.00
Lantern, Ribbed Base, Closure 3.00
Lantern, Squat Six Rib, Closure 20.00
Lantern, Tiny Pear Shape, Closure 10.00
Liberty Bell, Blue, Closure 50.00
Liberty Bell, Clear, Closure 45.00
Locomotive, France, No Closure 40.00
Locomotive, Lithographed Tin Closure, 3 In. ....*Illus* 145.00
Locomotive, Miniature, Closure 3.00
Locomotive, T.H. Stough, No Closure 25.00
Mailbox, Clear, Closure 300.00

Man On Motorcycle, Closure 500.00
Opera Glass, Brass Frame 125.00
Opera Glass, Milk Glass, Gold Gilded, Closure 150.00
Owl, Closure 150.00
Pencil, Baby Jumbo, Candy 45.00
Piano, Clear, Closure 250.00
Pumpkin, Wax Covered, Pull Slide From Bottom, Germany, 2 x 2 1/4 In. 200.00
Pumpkin Head, Witch, Closure 750.00
Rabbit, Basket On Arm, Closure 75.00
Rabbit, Basket On Dome, Closure 475.00
Rabbit, Eating Carrot, No Closure 25.00
Rabbit, Glass Eyes, Pull Off Head, Germany, 11 In. 150.00
Rabbit, Molded Cardboard, Plaster, Glass Eyes, Germany, 1920s, 11 In. 200.00
Rabbit, Peter, Closure 25.00
Rabbit, Wheelbarrow, Closure 110.00
Rabbit In Egg Shell, Closure 90.00
Radio, Closure 175.00
Rolling Pin, Closure 250.00
Safe, Milk Glass, Penny Trust Co., Closure 85.00
Santa Claus, 5 1/4 In. ....*Illus* 245.00
Santa Claus, Banded Coat 250.00
Santa Claus, Boot, Millstein, Closure 3.00
Santa Claus, By Square Chimney, Closure 200.00
Santa Claus, Leaving Chimney 95.00
Santa Claus, Paneled Coat, Closure 175.00
Santa Claus, With Double Cuff, Closure 150.00
Santa Claus, With Plastic Head, Closure 75.00
School, House, Milk Glass 75.00
Skookum, By Tree Stump, Replacement Closure 300.00
Soldier, On Monument, Replacement Closure 900.00
Spirit Of Goodwill, Great Paint, Closure 85.00
Spirit Of St. Louis, Glass, Pink, Closure 150.00
Spirit Of St. Louis, Green, Closure 350.00
Spirit Of St. Louis, Pink 75.00
Streamline, Miniature, Closure 3.00
Submarine, Glass 50.00
Submarine, Hull, Closure 400.00
Suitcase, Milk Glass, Closure 150.00
Tank, Man In Turret, Closure 3.00
Tank, Two Guns, Closure 40.00
Tank, War, Miniature, Closure 3.00
Tank, With Man, Closure 40.00
Tank, World War I, Closure 100.00
Telephone, Candlestick, 7 3/4 In. ....*Illus* 350.00
Telephone, Crosetti's, Desk Type 20.00
Telephone, Large, Glass, Closure ....75.00 to 88.00
Telephone, Lynn Type, Sunken Dial, Closure 35.00
Telephone, Lynn Type, Sunken Dial, No Closure 25.00

Back   Side

Candy Container, Locomotive, Lithographed Tin Closure, 3 In.

Telephone, Redlich's, Closure	75.00
Telephone, Ruby Flashed, Closure	50.00
Telephone, Victory Glass, Closure	3.00
Telephone, Victory Glass, Paper Label, Red Flashed, Closure	50.00
Toonerville, Depot Line, Closure	675.00
Trunk, Clear Glass, Round Top, Handle, Closure	125.00
Trunk, Milk Glass, Gold Trim, Closure	150.00
Uncle Sam, By Barrel, Closure	450.00
Volkswagen, No Closure	20.00
Wagon, Western-Type Stage Coach, Closure	150.00
Windmill, Screw On Closure	25.00
World Globe On Stand	500.00

CANNING JAR, see Fruit Jar
CASE, see Gin

COCA-COLA

Coca-Cola was first served in 1886 in Atlanta, Georgia. John S. Pemberton, a pharmacist, originated the syrup and sold it to others. He was trying to make a patent medicine to aid those who suffered from nervousness, headaches, or stomach problems. At first the syrup was mixed with water; but in 1887, Willis E. Venable mixed it with carbonated water, and Coca-Cola was made. Pemberton sold his interest in the company to Venable and a local businessman, George S. Lowndes, in 1888. Later that year, Asa Griggs Candler, an owner of a pharmaceutical company, and some business friends became partners in Coca-Cola. A short time later they purchased the rest of the company. After some other transactions, Asa Candler became the sole owner of Coca-Cola for a grand total of $2,300. The first ad for Coca-Cola appeared in the *Atlanta Journal* on May 29, 1886. Since that time the drink has been sold in all parts of the world and in a variety of bottles. The *waisted* bottle was first used in 1916. Over 1,000 commemorative Coca-Cola bottles have been issued since 1949. The company advertised heavily, and bottles, trays, calendars, signs, toys, and lamps, as well as thousands of other items, can be found. See listings under Go-Withs at the back of the book.

Coca-Cola written in script was trademarked in 1893. *Coke* was registered in 1945. There is a national club with a newsletter, The Coca-Cola Collectors Club, P.O. Box 49166, Atlanta, GA 30359-1166. You can learn from the national about local meetings. Price guides and books about the history of Coca-Cola are listed in the Bibliography. The Schmidt Coca-Cola Museum in Elizabethtown, Kentucky, is associated with Coca-Cola bottlers. The Coca-Cola Company Archives (One Coca-Cola Plaza, Atlanta, GA 30313) can answer questions about Coca-Cola memorabilia. The World of Coca-Cola Museum on Martin Luther King Dr. in Atlanta has exhibits of interest to collectors.

COCA-COLA, 75th Anniversary, Staunton, Consolidated, Wometco, Chattanooga, Atlanta	6.00
100th Anniversary, 9 Bottle Set, Wooden Base & Acrylic Cover, 1986	395.00
Albermarle, N.C., Square Slug Plate	20.00
Arizona State Fair, 10 Oz.	7.00
Arlington Ballpark	4.00
Astrodome, 30th Anniv., 1965-1995, Contents, 8 Oz.	3.00
Auburn Tigers	10.00
Baltimore, Md., Amber, Logo At Top	100.00
Barcelona, 1992	3.00
Basket Village, U.S.A.	2.50
Beckley, W.Va., Hobbleskirt	15.00
Biedenham, 85th Anniversary, Hutchinson	15.00
Big Boy, ABM, Embossed	5.00
Big Chief, Green, Indian Picture, Crown Top	35.00
Binghamton Bottling Co., Inc., Yellow Olive, Crown Top, Contents, 6 1/2 Oz.	70.00
Bluefield, W.Va., Hobbleskirt, 1923	15.00
Boston, Massachusetts, Star Market 70th Anniversary, 1915-1985, 10 Oz.	8.00
Byerly's New Orleans Saints	2.00
Camden Yards, Oriole Park, July 13, 1993, Contents, 8 Oz.	9.00
Canada, Blue, Straight Sided, ABM, 1915	15.00 to 20.00
Carl Perkins, Memphis, Tenn., 10 Oz.	22.00
Casco, India, Aqua	55.00
Chase City, Va., Aqua, Contents, 6 Oz.	10.00

Chattanooga, Tenn., Amber, Straight Sided Embossed Shoulder, ABM, 6 1/2 Oz. 40.00
Chattanooga, Tenn., Light Amber 55.00
Cherokee, Strip.. 3.00
Christmas, Contents, 1988.. 40.00
Christmas, Mexico, Santa-Polar Bear, 1993 .... 75.00
Christmas, Santa Claus, 1991 .... 2.00
Christmas, Springtime In Atlanta, 10 Oz... 40.00
Church Of God 1886, 1986 Centennial Celebration, 10 Oz.. 5.00
Cincinnati Reds World Champs 3.00
Clarksville, 200 Years, 1784-1984, 10 Oz. 10.00
Cleveland, Ohio, Amber, Coca-Cola In Script, 1910 .... 25.00
Clifton Forge, Va., Straight Sided 25.00
Cola Clan Convention, Short, 1981, 10 Oz. 10.00
Cola Clan Convention, Short, 1982, 10 Oz. 15.00
Cola Clan Convention, Short, 1983, 10 Oz. 25.00
Cola Clan Convention, Short, 1984, 10 Oz. 25.00
Cola Clan Convention, Short, 1985, 10 Oz. 30.00
Cola Clan Convention, Short, 1986, 10 Oz. 20.00
Cordele, Ga., 1985 State Junior & Senior Little League Champs, 10 Oz. 7.00
Cornelia, Ga., Centennial Celebration 1887-1987, 10 Oz. 20.00
Dallas Cowboys, 25 Years In The N.F.L., 10 Oz... 10.00
Danville, Va., Aqua, 6 Oz.. 8.00
Denver Broncos 2.00
Dubois, Pa., Tom Mix 6th Annual National Festival, 10 Oz. 20.00
Eagle, ABM, Embossed 5.00
East Tennessee State Univ., 75th Anniv, 1911-1986, 10 Oz. 8.00
Ethiopia, 100 Anniv., 6 1/2 Oz... 20.00
Fayetteville, N.C., Ice Blue, Straight Sides 20.00
Florida Gator South East Conference Champs 12.00
Florida Panthers 3.00
Florida State University 2.00
Freedom Bowl, Iowa Hawkeyes, Big 10 Conference, 10 Oz. 8.00
Ft. Smith 90th, CA Panthers... 3.00
Geneva, N.Y., Clear, 6 1/2 Oz... 35.00
Georgia Southern Eagles, 1985 National Football Champs, 10 Oz............................... 8.00
Git-N-Go 2.00
Golden Eagles, Univ. Of So. Mississippi, N.I.T. Champions, 10 Oz............................. 100.00
Goshen Indiana, Everett A Super-Market, 1935-1985, 10 Oz...................................... 150.00
Green, Coca-Cola In Script, 1920, 23 1/2 Oz.. 75.00
Green, Korean Label, Cap, 13 1/2 In..*Illus* 25.00
Greenville, Ohio, Annie Oakley Day, 10 Oz... 125.00
Greenville, S.C., Aqua, Script 35.00

Coca-Cola, Green,
Korean Label, Cap,
13 1/2 In.

Coca-Cola, Jacksonville
Bottling Co., Jacksonville,
Fla., 7 1/4 In.

Coca-Cola, Marlins, Inaugural
Season, 1993, Coca-Cola
Classic, 7 1/2 In.

Coca-Cola,	*Coca-Cola, Minnesota*	*Coca-Cola, Penn*	*Coca-Cola,*
Memphis, Tenn.,	*Twins, Rod Carew,*	*State, Joe Paterno,*	*Super Bowl*
Amber, 7 1/4 In.	*WLLO Radio*	*1986 NCAA*	*XVIII, 1984,*
		National Champions	*Tampa, Florida*

Harrisburg, Pa., Amber, BIMAL 32.00
Harrisburg, Pa., Soda Water, Aqua 5.00
Hart Co., Georgia A.A.A. State Basketball Champions, Orange, 10 Oz. 20.00
Honolulu, Territory Of Hawaii, Embossed, Hobbleskirt, 6 Oz. 9.50
Hoover Dam, 50th Golden Anniversary, 10 Oz. 80.00
House For Coca-Cola, August 3, 1977, Amber, With Tag .... 120.00 to 140.00
Houston, Texas, Introducing New Coke, May 6, 1985, 10 Oz. 7.00
Houston Convention Invit., 1979 .... 30.00
Houston Rockets Champs, Miniature 20.00
Hucks Convention Store 3.00
Hutchinson Biedenharn Candy Co. 150.00
J.S. Francis, Avon Park, Fla., Emerald Green, 1923 .... 10.00
Jackson, Tenn., Aqua, Circle Arrow, BIMAL 125.00
Jackson, Tenn., Red Amber, Circle Arrow, BIMAL 125.00
Jacksonville Bottling Co., Jacksonville, Fla., 7 1/4 In. ....*Illus*   25.00
Jimmy Carter, 39th President Of The United States, 10 Oz. 200.00
Johnny Lee, Project Entertainment Recreation Assoc. Club, 10 Oz. 45.00
K.B. Co., Hobbleskirt, 1915 .... 15.00
Kansas City Chiefs ....3.00 to 5.00
Knoxville, Tenn. 45.00
Lenox Square Mall Anniversary 35 Years 20.00
LSU Tigers 2.00
Macon, Georgia, Cherry Blossom Festival, 10 Oz. 8.00
Mardi Gras 2.00
Marlins, Inaugural Season, 1993, Coca-Cola Classic, 7 1/2 In. ....*Illus*   2.00
McDonald's 1st Drive In 5.00
Memphis, Tenn., Amber, 7 1/4 In. ....*Illus* 45.00
Mexico 50th Anniversary 50.00
Mexico 50th Anniversary, Cap, Contents 25.00
Minnesota Twins, Rod Carew, WLLO Radio ....*Illus* 12.00
Montgomery, Al., Glass With Class, 10 Oz. 15.00
Mt. Lassen, Susanville, Seltzer 150.00
Nahunta Fire Dept., 35 Years Of Service 65.00
Nashville, Light Amber, 6 1/2 Oz. 50.00
NBA All Stars 3.00
NCAA, Final 4, South Carolina Panthers 2.50
NCAA 1994, Final Four, Charlotte, N.C., Contents, 8 Oz. 7.00
Nehi, ABM, Embossed 5.00
New Bern, N.C., Straight Sides 20.00
New Orleans Jazz 2.00

New York, N.Y., Amber, Crown Top, BIMAL.. 44.00
Norfolk, Va., Aqua, 6 1/2 Oz. ....50.00 to 55.00
NSDA, Anaheim, Sealed, Disney Characters, 1977........................35.00 to 40.00
NSDA, Chicago, Sealed, 1976.. 30.00
NSDA, Chicago, Sealed, 1980.. 30.00
NSDA, Dallas, Sealed, 1975.. 30.00
NSDA, Houston, 1967, No Crown.. 35.00
Ohio State, 25th Anniversary 3.00
Orioles World Series, Commemorative, 1983................................... 20.00
Orlando, Florida, Winning Together, 10 Oz. 40.00
Parkersburg, W.Va., Patent Office, Hobbleskirt................................ 10.00
Parsons, Kansas, 1923.. 10.00
Paul Bear Bryant 10.00
Penn State, Joe Paterno, 1986 NCAA National Champions ....*Illus* 12.00
Penn State, Nittany Lions Champions, 1982 .... 15.00
Phoenix, Ariz., Aqua, BIMAL 45.00
Phoenix Suns, Western Con. Champs, 1993, Contents, 8 Oz. 5.00
Phoenix Suns 25th Anniversary, Contents 25.00
Pittsburgh, Pa., BIMAL, Amber 49.00
Pittsburgh, Pa., Honey Amber 65.00
Polar Bear, Oklahoma Zoo.. 3.00
Pride Of Piedmont, Laurens County, S.C., Yellow, 10 Oz. ....6.00 to 8.00
Proud Past Progressive Future, Holly Hill, S.C., 10 Oz. 300.00
Quincy, Ill, Straight Sides, BIMAL 35.00
Republic Of China, 6 1/2 Oz. 20.00
Republican National Convention 395.00
Richard Petty 2.50
Richmond, Va., Amber, Crown Top 60.00
Richmond, Va., Aqua, Straight Sided... 10.00
Richmond, Va., Hobbleskirt, Dug, 1923.. 5.00
Rochester, N.Y.. 85.00
San Francisco 49ers, Five Time World Champs, Contents, 8 Oz................ 3.00
Savannah, Ga., Straight Sided, Script In Middle 22.00
Scama, 40th Anniversary, 10 Oz. 45.00
Seltzer, Terre Haute, Ind., Etched Palm Tree.................................... 120.00
Shamokin, Pa., Aqua ....10.00 to 55.00
Southwestern, New Mexico, Dug 25.00
Springtime In Tennessee, Gatlinburg, 10 Oz................................... 35.00
Strawberry Festival, 50th West Tenn. Humboldt, 10 Oz. 6.00
Super Bowl XVIII, 1984, Tampa, Florida ....*Illus* 12.00
Super Bowl XXVII 2.00
Talladega, Al., Hutchinson, Block Type.. 1650.00
Tallapoosa, Ga., The Dogwood City, 1860-1985, 10 Oz. 10.00
Tennessee Homecoming, 1986 .... 10.00
Texas A & M, 100 Years Of Football, Gold.. 50.00
Texas Rangers 3.00
Texas Tech Lady 2.00
Township Of Springfield, N.J. 15.00
Ty Cobb, The Georgia Peach, Royston, Ga., 10 Oz........................... 250.00
University Of Tennessee Vols, 1985 S.E.C. Football Champ, 10 Oz............. 10.00
University Of Vermont ....3.00 to 4.00
University Of Virginia, Peach Bowl, 8 Oz. 10.00
Wal-Mart 25th Anniversary, 1987 .... 35.00
Wassau, Wis., Muskie Center, 2 Small Fish Neck............................ 67.00
Westminster, Md., Script, Slug Plate, 24 Oz...................................... 90.00
Wilbur Kurtz, Amber, 1977 .... 35.00
Wilmington, N.C... 45.00
Winthrop College, 100 Years 1886-1986, 10 Oz.............................. 15.00
World Cup Soccer 2.50
World Of Coke, 1st Anniversary.. 16.00
World Of Coke, 2nd Anniversary... 15.00
World Of Coke, 3rd Anniversary ....9.00 to 10.00
World Of Coke, 4th Anniversary 5.00

World's Largest Easter Egg Hunt, Homer, Ga., 10 Oz. 65.00
Wyeths Bros., Philadelphia, Pa., Sailing Ship, PL 4.00
YMCA Scuba Program 25th Anniversary, 10 Oz. 50.00

COLLECTORS ART

Collectors Art bottles are made of hand-painted porcelain. The bird series was made in the 1970s. The first issued was the bluebird, then the meadowlark, canary, hummingbird, parakeet, and cardinal. Only 12 birds were issued each year and each was limited to 1,200 pieces. The later editions included bulls (1975), dogs, other animals, and a 1971 Corvette Stingray.

COLLECTORS ART, Afghan Hound, 1975, Miniature 22.00
Angus Bull, 1975, Miniature 17.00
Basset Hound, 1977, Miniature 22.00
Blue Bird, 1971, Miniature 24.00
Blue Jay, 1972, Miniature 28.00
Brahma Bull, 1975, Miniature 32.00
Bunting, 1973, Miniature 18.00
Canary, 1971, Miniature 26.00
Cardinal, 1971, Miniature 28.00
Charolais Bull, 1975, Miniature 26.00
Chipmunks, 1972, Miniature 18.00
Collie, 1976, Miniature 22.00
Corvette Stingray, Blue, 1971 .... 40.00
Corvette Stingray, Red, 1971 .... 22.00
Daohshund, 1977, Miniature 24.00
Dalmatian, 1976, Miniature 30.00
Doberman, Black, 1976, Miniature 24.00
Doberman, Red, 1976, Miniature 25.00
Goldfinch, 1972, Miniature 22.00
Goodyear Tires, 1971 .... 23.00
Hereford, 1972 .... 36.00
Hummingbird, 1971, Miniature 22.00
Irish Setter, 1976, Miniature 20.00
Koala, 1972, Miniature 35.00
Longhorn Bull 30.00
Meadowlark, 1971, Miniature 25.00
Mexican Fighting Bull, 1975, Miniature 30.00
Oriole, 1972, Miniature 24.00
Parakeet, 1971, Miniature 23.00
Pointer, Brown, White, 1976, Miniature 20.00
Poodle, 1976, Miniature 20.00
Rabbits, 1972, Miniature 46.00
Raccoons, 1973, Miniature 28.00
Robin, 1972, Miniature 18.00
Schnauzer, 1976, Miniature 22.00
Shepherd, Black, 1976, Miniature 30.00
Shepherd, Brown, 1976, Miniature 22.00
Skunks, 1972, Miniature 20.00
St. Bernard, 1977, Miniature 23.00

COLOGNE

Our ancestors did not bathe very often and probably did not smell very good. It is no wonder that the perfume and cologne business thrived in earlier centuries. Perfume is a liquid mixture with alcohol. Cologne is a similar mixture but with more alcohol, so the odor is not as strong or as lasting. Scent was also popular. It was a perfume with some ammonia in the mixture so it could be used to revive someone who felt faint. The mixture dictated the type and size of bottle. Scent bottles usually had screw tops to keep the ammonia smell from escaping. Because its odor did not last as long as that of perfume, cologne was used more often and was sold in larger bottles. Cologne became popular in the United States about 1830; the Boston and Sandwich Glass Company of Sandwich, Massachusetts, was making cologne bottles at that time. Since cologne bottles were usually put on display, they were made with fancy shapes, brightly colored glass, or elaborate labels. Blown figural and scroll bottles were favored. The best-known cologne bottle is the 1880 Charlie Ross bottle. It has the embossed face of Charlie, a famous kidnap victim—a strange shape to choose for a cologne bottle! Today the name *perfume* is sometimes used incorrectly as a generic term meaning both cologne and perfume. Old and new bottles for cologne, perfume, and scents are collected. Related bottles may be found in the Perfume and Scent categories.

COLOGNE, 6-Sided, J.M. Farina, OP, 5 In. 15.00
8-Sided, Amethyst, Smooth Base, 4 In. 66.00
8-Sided, Cobalt Blue, Smooth Base, 6 7/8 In. 154.00
8-Sided, Corset Waist, Amethyst, 6 1/2 In. 852.50
8-Sided, Corset Waist, Amethyst, Rolled Lip, 6 1/2 In. 852.50
8-Sided, Corset Waist, Aqua, OP, c.1850, 4 1/2 In. 385.00
8-Sided, Corset Waist, Cobalt Blue, c.1865-1880, 5 7/8 In. ....*Illus* 578.00
8-Sided, Corset Waist, Cobalt Blue, OP, 1850, 6 In. 825.00
8-Sided, Corset Waist, Cobalt Blue, Purple Tint, 4 5/16 In. 357.50
8-Sided, Corset Waist, Cobalt Blue, Rolled Lip, c.1870, 4 5/8 In. 577.00
8-Sided, Corset Waist, Cobalt Blue, Rolled Lip, OP, c.1850, 6 In. 825.00
8-Sided, Corset Waist, Cobalt Blue, Smooth Base, 5 3/4 In. 550.00
8-Sided, Corset Waist, Opalescent, Light Green, Tooled Mouth, 4 3/4 In. 440.00
8-Sided, Corset Waist, Purple Amethyst, 4 1/2 In. 467.00
8-Sided, Corset Waist, Teal Green, Tooled Mouth, 4 3/4 In. 385.00
8-Sided, Teal Green, Corset Waist, Rolled Lip, 4 5/8 In. 797.00
12-Sided, Amethyst, 4 1/2 In. .... 185.00 to 190.00
12-Sided, Amethyst, Sandwich Glass Works, Stopper, 7 In. 176.00
12-Sided, Amethyst, Smooth Base, 4 3/4 In. 88.00
12-Sided, Amethyst, Smooth Base, 7 1/4 In. 137.50
12-Sided, Amethyst, Tooled & Flared Lip, 1870, 9 1/4 In. 198.00
12-Sided, Amethyst, Tooled Mouth, Sandwich, 7 1/4 In. 154.00
12-Sided, Cobalt Blue, 4 3/4 In. 88.00
12-Sided, Cobalt Blue, 8 3/4 In. 330.00
12-Sided, Cobalt Blue, Flared Lip, Toilet Water, c.1860, 6 3/4 In. 220.00
12-Sided, Cobalt Blue, Paneled, Ring Neck, Stopper, Toilet Water, 1850, 6 3/4 In. 319.00
12-Sided, Cobalt Blue, Rolled Lip, 7 1/8 In. 132.00
12-Sided, Cobalt Blue, Sandwich, 5 3/4 In. 132.00
12-Sided, Cobalt Blue, Sloped Shoulders, Sandwich, 4 5/8 In. 110.00
12-Sided, Cobalt Blue, Smooth Base, 6 1/2 In. 99.00
12-Sided, Cobalt Blue, Tooled Mouth, Sandwich, 4 3/4 In. 93.00
12-Sided, Cobalt, Shouldered Style, Sandwich, 7 1/2 In. 400.00
12-Sided, Deep Teal Green, 4 3/4 In. 88.00
12-Sided, Lavender, Rolled Mouth, Pontil, 7 1/8 In. 550.00
12-Sided, Medium Blue Green, Sandwich, Tooled Mouth, 5 In. 44.00
12-Sided, Milk Glass, Tooled Lip, 5 5/8 In. 253.00
12-Sided, Opalescent, Robin's Egg Blue, Sandwich, Tooled Mouth, 7 1/2 In. 467.00
12-Sided, Pale Blue Green, Rolled Mouth, Pontil, 7 3/8 In. 412.50
12-Sided, Pink Amethyst, 6 1/2 In. 110.00
12-Sided, Pink Amethyst, Sloped Shoulders, Rolled Lip, 7 1/2 In. 357.00
12-Sided, Sapphire Blue, 1860-1870, 7 1/2 In. 143.00
12-Sided, Sapphire Blue, American, 1860-1870, 8 3/4 In. 176.00
12-Sided, Sapphire Blue, Rolled Lip, 1870, 7 1/2 In. 170.00
12-Sided, Sapphire Blue, Sandwich Glass Works, 5 5/8 In. 231.00
12-Sided, Sapphire Blue, Sandwich, Collared Mouth, 8 5/8 In. 302.00
12-Sided, Sapphire Blue, Smooth, Base, 9 In. 357.50
12-Sided, Sapphire Blue, Tooled Lip, 11 3/8 In. 550.00
12-Sided, Sloping Shoulders, Cobalt Blue, 6 In. 148.00
12-Sided, Teal Green, Rolled Lip, 1860-1870, 6 3/8 In. 132.00
12-Sided, Teal Green, Sloped Shoulders, Rolled Lip, 6 1/4 In. 231.00
12-Sided, Teal Green, Smooth Base, 4 3/4 In. 110.00
12-Sided, Teal Green, Tooled Lip, Smooth Base, 11 In. 715.00
6 Draped Panels, Deep Plum-Puce, Flared Lip, Pontil, 1850-1860, 6 In. 1265.00
8 Pillar Mold Design, Canary Yellow, Flared Lip, Pontil, 5 In. 60.50
8 Pillar Mold Design, Green, Flared Lip, Cut Scallops, Cut Star Base, 7 In. 132.00
12 Diamond Pattern, Emil Larson, New Jersey, Pontil, c.1930, 6 In. 143.00
14 Ribs, Swirled To Left, Cobalt Blue, Rolled Lip, Pontil, 19th Century, 6 1/4 In. 3575.00

Cologne, 8-Sided,
Corset Waist, Cobalt
Blue, c.1865-1880,
5 7/8 In.

Cologne, Eau De, Pretty
Girl, Label Under Glass,
Pontil, No Stopper,
1800-1910, 6 In.

Cologne, Lightner's
Rose Geranium
Perfumes, Detroit,
Milk Glass, Stopper,
6 1/4 In.

Cologne, Opalescent
Turquoise Blue, No
Stopper, Sandwich,
5 3/8 In.

Amber, Laid On Ring Top, Smooth Base, 9 In. 25.00
Amethyst, 3-Piece Mold, Toilet Water, Cobalt Stopper, Pontil, 7 In. 330.00
Amethyst, 3-Piece Mold, Toilet Water, Flared Mouth, Stopper, Pontil, 6 1/2 In. 231.00
Amethyst, 3-Piece Mold, Toilet Water, Pontil, 5 5/8 In. 204.00
Amethyst, 3-Piece Mold, Vertical Rib, Toilet Water, Pontil, 5 5/8 In. 303.00
Amethyst, Beads & Flutes, Tooled Lip, Cylinder, c.1870, 10 In. 1650.00
Amethyst, Deep Purple, Indented Panels, Tooled Lip, 1870, 6 In. 275.00
Amethyst, Herringbone Type Corners, Tooled Mouth, 7 1/2 In. 385.00
Amethyst, Label, Tooled Mouth, Smooth Base, 9 3/4 In. 1430.00
Amethyst, Ribbed, Sandwich, OP, 5 7/8 In. 300.00
Amethyst, Rolled Lip, Pontil, 1855-1865, 8 7/8 In. 100.00
Animal, Cobalt Blue, Applied Ears, Mouth & Legs, Blown, Europe, 4 1/2 x 6 1/2 In..... 210.00
Aqua, Basket Weave, Open Pontil.. 22.00
Aqua, Dancing Indians, Sheared Lip, OP 95.00
Aqua, Knight, Standing Between 2 Columns, Rolled Lip, Pontil, 3 7/8 In. 125.00
Barrel, Cobalt Blue, 3-Piece Mold, Toilet Water, Tooled Flared Mouth, Pontil, 7 In. 412.00
Barrel, Lavender Blue, 3-Piece Mold, Toilet Water, Flared Mouth, Stopper, 5 In. 252.00
Blown, 3-Piece Mold, Flared Lip, Pontil 77.00
Blown, Cobalt Blue, 3-Piece Mold, Flared Lip, 6 1/2 In. 253.00
Bottle, Long Neck With Bulb, Label Panels, Yellow Olive, Pontil, 8 In....................... 1072.00
Bulbous, Cobalt Blue, 3-Piece Mold, Toilet Water, Pontil, 5 5/8 In. 121.00
Bust Of Woman, Gold Trim, c.1880-1890, 9 In. 385.00
Charley Ross, Tooled Lip, 1890-1900, 4 1/2 In... 132.00
Charley Ross, Tooled Lip, 1890-1900, 5 5/8 In. 121.00
Charley Ross, Tooled Lip, 1890-1900, 5 In... 83.00
Charley Ross, Tooled Lip, 1890-1900, 6 1/8 In.. 121.00
Clambroth, Opalescent, Beaded Flute Pattern, 5 5/8 In. 72.00
Cobalt Blue, 3-Piece Mold, Flared Lip, OP, Stopper, Toilet Water, 6 1/4 In................. 275.00
Cobalt Blue, 3-Piece Mold, Flared Lip, Pontil, Stopper, Toilet Water, 6 3/4 In. 715.00
Cobalt Blue, 3-Piece Mold, Swirled Rib, Flared Lip, Pontil, Toilet Water, 7 In............. 660.00
Cobalt Blue, 3-Piece Mold, Toilet Water, Pontil, Glass Stopper, 5 In. 330.00

Cobalt Blue, 3-Piece Mold, Toilet Water, Pontil, Flared Lip, 5 3/4 In. 275.00
Cobalt Blue, 3-Piece Mold, Toilet Water, Pontil, 5 1/8 In. 495.00
Cobalt Blue, 3-Piece Mold, Toilet Water, Ribbed Stopper, Pontil, 6 3/4 In. 277.00
Cobalt Blue, 3-Piece Mold, Toilet Water, Stopper, Pontil, 6 3/4 In. 412.50
Cobalt Blue, Beads & Flutes, Tooled Lip, c.1870-1880, 9 1/4 In 1210.00
Cobalt Blue, Beads & Flutes, Tooled Lip, Cylinder, c.1870, 5 3/4 In. 467.50
Cobalt Blue, Blown, Pontil, 10 3/4 In. 66.00
Cobalt Blue, Herringbone Corners, Smooth Base, 5 5/8 In. 77.00
Cobalt Blue, Tooled Mouth, Star Shaped Kick Up Base, 4 1/8 In. 154.00
Corset Waist, Cobalt Blue, 8-Sided, 1880, 5 7/8 In. 578.00
Corset Waist, Cobalt Blue, c.1870, 4 3/4 In. 550.00
Cylindrical, Amethyst, Rolled Lip, OP, 11 1/8 In. 358.00
Cylindrical, Amethyst, Rolled Lip, OP, 1860-1870, 11 1/8 In. 358.00
Cylindrical, Amethyst, Rolled Lip, Pontil, 8 1/8 In. 104.00
Cylindrical, Electric Blue, Smooth Base, 5 1/2 In. 71.50
Cylindrical, Opalescent, Pastel Blue, Turquoise Blue, Rolled Lip, Pontil, 9 1/2 In. 550.00
Cylindrical, Opalescent, Powder Blue, Pontil, 1840-1860, 14 3/8 In. 495.00
Cylindrical, Opaque Blue, Blown, Deep Pontil, 10 1/4 In. 60.00
Cylindrical, Opaque Blue, Sandwich Type, Tapered, Pontil, 1840-1860, 11 7/8 In. 176.00
Eau De, Clear, Label Under Glass, Stopper, 1800-1900, 6 In. 147.00
Eau De, Pretty Girl, Label Under Glass, Pontil, No Stopper, 1800-1910, 6 In. ....*Illus* 148.00
Emerald Green, Tooled Mouth, Sandwich, 10 1/4 In. 605.00
Geometric, Amethyst, 3-Piece Mold, Blown, Flared Lip, 6 In. 357.00
Honey Amber, Tooled Lip, Sandwich, Stopper, 1865, 2 3/4 In. 225.00
Indian, Standing, Aqua, OP .... 95.00 to 115.00
Jockey Club, Red, Green & Gold, Label Under Glass, 7 In. 295.00
Lalique, Helene, Eau De Toilette, Frosted Sepia, Stopper, Panels, 1950, 12 In. 747.00
Lavender, 3-Piece Mold, Vertical Rib, Toilet Water, Type 4, 5 1/2 In. 385.00
Lavender Blue, 3-Piece Mold, Toilet Water, Pontil, 5 1/2 In. 275.00
Lightner's Rose Geranium Perfumes, Detroit, Milk Glass, Stopper, 6 1/4 In. ......*Illus* 275.00
Melon Ribbed, 16 Vertical Ribs, Dark Puce, Flared Lip, OP, 3 1/4 In. 1155.00
Milk Glass, Beaded Ribs, Sandwich, 10 1/2 In. 132.00
Milk Glass, Gold, Black & Pink, Label Under Glass, Tooled Lip, 6 1/8 In 330.00
Milk Glass, Opalescent, Star, Vertical Rib, Rolled Lip, 6 1/2 In 110.00
Milk Glass, Rib With Dot, Tooled Lip, 5 3/4 In. 72.00
Milk Glass, Vertical Ribs, Opalescent, Star Banners, c.1870, 5 3/4 In. 132.00
Milk Glass, Vertical Ribs, Spiral Band Of Stars, 7 1/2 In. 150.00
Milk Glass Over Clear Over Cobalt Blue, Overlay Gilt, Stopper, Pontil, 1850s 400.00
Monument, Amethyst, Boston, 1860, 9 1/8 In. 825.00
Monument, Amethyst, c.1870, 8 In. 1100.00
Monument, Amethyst, Tooled Lip, 1870, 8 In. 1100.00
Monument, Cobalt Blue, Cologne Water For The Toilet Label, Rolled Lip, 6 1/2 In. 798.00
Monument, Cobalt Blue, Flared Lip, c.1870, 12 In. 825.00
Monument, Cobalt Blue, Rolled Lip, c.1870, 6 1/2 In. 798.00
Monument, Cobalt Blue, Tooled Flared Mouth, 6 3/8 In. 55.00
Monument, Cobalt Blue, Tooled Lip, 12 In. 1100.00
Monument, Cobalt Blue, Tooled Lip, 1870, 8 In. 605.00
Monument, Cobalt Blue, Tooled Lip, c.1870, 12 In. 1100.00
Monument, Cobalt, Purple, Boston, 1860, 8 1/8 In. 633.00
Monument, Emerald Green, Tooled Lip, 1870, 6 1/4 In. 1430.00
Monument, Milk Glass, Tooled Lip, 1865-1875, 6 1/2 In. 104.00
Monument, Opalescent Blue Milk Glass, Falcon, Wreaths, Pontil, 5 In. 2585.00
Monument, Peacock Green, Boston, 8 1/8 In. 2970.00
Monument, Peacock, Tooled Lip, c.1850-1860, 11 In. 1375.00
Opalescent Turquoise Blue, No Stopper, Sandwich, 5 3/8 In. ....*Illus* 143.00
Opaque Powder Blue, Rolled Lip, Partly Faded Label, 8 In. 110.00
Pale Aqua, Fancy, Rolled Lip, American, 1840-1860 .... 132.00
Pale Aqua, Rolled Lip, Pontil, 1840-1860 ....*Illus* 132.00
Paneled, 6-Sided, Deep Plum Puce, Pontil, 1850, 6 In. 1265.00
Paneled, 12-Sided, Amethyst, New England, c.1860, 11 1/2 In. 275.00
Paneled, 12-Sided, Amethyst, Rolled Lip, c.1860, 7 In. 297.00
Paneled, 12-Sided, Cobalt Blue, New England, c.1860, 7 1/4 In. 297.00
Paneled, 12-Sided, Cobalt Blue, Toilet Water, 2-Piece Mold, Flared Mouth, 5 3/4 In. ... 121.00

Cologne, Pale Aqua,
Rolled Lip, Pontil,
1840-1860

Cologne, Pocahontas
Indian, Light Green,
Molded Pontil, 5 In.

Cologne, Teal Green,
Label, Rolled Lip,
Sandwich, 1870, 6 1/2 In.

Paneled, 12-Sided, Green, Amethyst, Pontil, 4 1/2 In. 357.50
Paneled, 12-Sided, Light Sapphire Blue, OP, Cylindrical, 8 In. 264.00
Paneled, 12-Sided, Opalescent Pastel Blue, Tooled Lip, c.1860, 7 3/16 In. 385.00
Paneled, 12-Sided, Peacock Blue, Rolled, Flared Lip, c.1860, 7 In.............................. 412.50
Paneled, 12-Sided, Peacock Blue, White Streaks, Tooled Lip, c.1860, 4 In. 242.00
Paneled, 12-Sided, Peacock Blue-Green, c.1860, 11 In... 770.00
Paneled, 12-Sided, Purple Amethyst, Pontil, c.1860, 4 3/4 In. 209.00
Paneled, 12-Sided, Sapphire Blue, Cylindrical, 9 1/2 In.. 687.00
Paneled, 12-Sided, Yellow Green, Tooled Lip, c.1860, 5 In. 357.50
Pendulum Shape, Hanging Basket In Center, 5 1/4 In.. 30.00
Pocahontas Indian, Light Green, Molded Pontil, 5 In.................................*Illus* 300.00
Polygonal, Teal Blue, White Flecks, 4 3/4 In... 468.00
Purple, 16 Ribs, Swirled Left, Flared Lip, Pontil, Toilet Water, 6 In............................ 550.00
Purple, 3-Piece Mold, Toilet Water, Polished Lip, 5 3/8 In. 258.00
Rectangular, Beveled Edged, Pontil, Blown, Late 18th Century, 6 In. 467.00
Refreshing, Green, 8 3/4 In... 26.00
Ricksecker's Sweet Clover Cologne, N.Y., Swirled Multicolor, Handles, 8 1/2 In. 275.00
Robert T. Turlington, Balsam Of Life, London, Guitar Shape, 2 1/2 In....................... 10.00
Sandwich Type, Canary Yellow, Pontil, Square, Single Flutes, Toilet Water, 8 1/4 In. .. 55.00
Sapphire Blue, 16 Ribs, Toilet Water, Rolled Lip, Pontil, 6 1/8 In. 523.00
Sapphire Blue, 19 Ribs, Swirled Left, Toilet Water, Pontil, 5 3/4 In. 385.00
Sapphire Blue, 3-Piece Mold, Ribbed, Toilet Water, Pontil, Type 4, 6 In. 210.00
Sapphire Blue, 3-Piece Mold, Swirled Left, Toilet Water, Pontil, 5 1/2 In. 198.00
Sapphire Blue, 3-Piece Mold, Toilet Water, Pontil, Stopper, 6 In............................... 302.50
Sapphire Blue, 3-Piece Mold, Vertical Rib, Toilet Water, Pontil, 5 5/8 In. 357.00
Scroll, Rococo, Flared Lip, OP, Flint.. 80.00
Teal Green, Label, Rolled Lip, Sandwich, 1870, 6 1/2 In.............................*Illus* 330.00
Triangular, Stylized Leaf Motif, Lavender, Tooled Mouth, 7 5/8 In. 77.00
Turquoise Blue, Slight Opalescent, Sandwich, 4 1/8 In. 275.00
Vaseline, Boston & Sandwich Glass Co., Bell Form, Vertical Ribs, Pontil, Toilet Water, 5 In. 77.00
Woman's Bust, Tree Trunk Shape, Gold Trim, Stopper, 1880, 9 In............................. 385.00

──────────────────────────── **CORDIAL** ────────────────────────────

Cordials are liqueurs that are usually made to be drunk at the end of the meal. They consist of
pure alcohol or cognac, plus flavors from fruits, herbs, flowers, or roots. A cordial may also
be a medicinal drink. Curacao is a cordial containing orange peel, Creme de Menthe contains
mint, Triple Sec has orange and cognac, and Kummel has coriander and caraway seeds.

CORDIAL, Apricot, Paramont Distillers, Inc., Paper Label, 11 In. ....*Illus* 35.00
   California Blackberry, D.B. Perry Pharmacist, Bay City, Mich., Cork, 6 In...........*Illus* 25.00

Cordial, Apricot,
Paramont
Distillers, Inc.,
Paper Label,
11 In.

Cordial, California
Blackberry, D.B.
Perry Pharmacist,
Bay City, Mich.,
Cork, 6 In.

Cordial, Wishart's Pine
Tree Tar, Philadelphia,
Emerald Green,
Pat. 1859, 8 In.

Cordial, Wishart's
Pine Tree Tar,
Philadelphia, Blue
Green,
Pat. 1859, 8 In.

California Fruit Co., Cherry, Victorian Woman, Cherry Blossoms, Contents, Fifth	35.00
Cherry, Victorian Blond Woman Label, Foil Over Top, Contents	35.00
Clarks California Cherry, Amber, Scrolled, Large	45.00
Cone's Cholera & Dysentery Label, Dried Contents, Underhill Druggist	15.00
Dr. Convers Invigorating, Oval, 6 1/8 In.	190.00
Dunbar & Co., Wormwood, Boston, Green Aqua, Applied Mouth, 9 3/8 In.	176.00
Dunbar & Co., Wormwood Cordial, Boston, Teal, 9 5/8 In.	160.00
Emerald Green, Silver Overlay, Handles, Monkey Smoking Cigar Stopper, 11 In.	578.00
Enameled, Woman & Floral Design, Pewter Collar, Pontil, 18th Century, 6 1/2 In.	385.00
Eubanks Topas Cinchona, Amber, Square, Large	45.00
Fosgates Anodyne, Dug	30.00
Gardiner's Rheumatic, London, 8-Sided, 6 1/2 In.	15.00
J.N. Kline & Cos., Aromatic Digestive, Amber, 5 1/2 In.	275.00
J.N. Kline & Cos., Aromatic Digestive, Deep Cobalt Blue, 5 1/2 In.	264.00
J.N. Kline's Aromatic Digestive, Blue, 5 1/4 In.	650.00
L.Q. Wishart's Pine Tree Tar, Philad., Emerald Green, 9 3/4 In.	154.00 to 176.00
McLean's Strengthening, Blue Aqua, Applied Top, Whittled, 9 In.	55.00
McLean's Strengthening Cordial & Blood Purifier, Light Blue, 8 In.	34.00
Mortimore's Bitter Cordial & Blood Purifier, Aqua, OP, 7 7/8 In.	154.00
Mrs. E. Kidder Dysentery Cordial, Boston, Aqua, Pontil, Cylinder, 7 1/2 In.	120.00
Mrs. Metler's Dysentery Cordial, 6 3/4 x 2 1/2 In.	110.00
Mrs. S.A. Allen's Worlds Hair Restorer, New York, Amethyst, 7 1/4 In.	135.00 to 176.00

Mrs. S.A. Allen's Worlds Hair Restorer, New York, Red Puce, 7 1/4 In.	187.00
Wishart's Pine Tree Tar, Philadelphia, Amber, 9 5/8 In.	60.00
Wishart's Pine Tree Tar, Philadelphia, Blue Green, Pat. 1859, 8 In. *Illus*	143.00
Wishart's Pine Tree Tar, Philadelphia, Emerald Green, 9 5/8 In.	252.00
Wishart's Pine Tree Tar, Philadelphia, Emerald Green, Pat. 1859, 8 In. *Illus*	242.00
Wishart's Pine Tree Tar, Philadelphia, Medium Olive Green, Whittled, Pt.	350.00
Wishart's Pine Tree Tar, Philadelphia, Sapphire, 9 5/8 In.	798.00
Wishart's Pine Tree Tar, Philadelphia, Yellow Green, 1859, 7 3/4 In.	121.00
Wishart's Pine Tree Tar, Philadelphia, Yellow Green, Olive Tone, 7 3/4 In.	187.00
Yamara Medicine Co., Chicago, Ill, Tooled Lip, 9 1/4 In.	1045.00
Zollickoffer's Antirheumatic, Philadelphia, Olive Green, Pontil, 6 1/8 In.	1540.00
Zollickoffer's Antirheumatic, Yellow Olive Amber, OP, 1840-1850, 6 1/2 In.	1595.00

COSMETIC

Cosmetics of all kinds have been packaged in bottles. Hair restorer, hair dye, creams, rosewater, and many other product bottles can be found. The early bottles often had paper labels, which add to their value.

COSMETIC, Astol Hair Color Restorer, Cobalt Blue, Light Blue Striations	45.00
Ayer's Ague, Lowell, Mass., Aqua, 7 In.	12.00
Ayer's Hair Vigor, Deep Sapphire Blue, Stopper, 6 1/2 In.	121.00
Ayer's Hair Vigor, Peacock Blue, Rectangular, 6 1/4 In.	44.00
Ayer's Hair Vigor, Peacock Blue, Stopper	72.00 to 79.00
B.G. Noble, Rose Hair Gloss, Aqua, Double Applied Collar, OP, 7 1/4 In.	358.00
Barrow Evans Hair Restorer, Aqua, 6 In.	10.00
Barry's Tricopherous For Skin & Hair, Aqua, Hinged Mold, 6 In.	20.00 to 30.00
Bartine's Lotion, Pale Aqua, Pontil, Burst Bubble Shoulder, Rectangular, 6 5/8 In.	65.00
Bear's Oil, Aqua, OP, Rolled Lip, c.1840, 2 3/4 In.	88.00
Berninghaus's Mexican Shampoo, Cincinnati, Cobalt Blue, 9 1/2 In. *Illus*	45.00
Bishop's Hair Restorer, Cobalt Blue, Sunken Panel, Metal, 6 1/2 In.	80.00
Bogle's Hyperion Fluid For The Hair, Aqua, 5 1/2 In.	75.00
Buckingham Whisker Dye, Amber, 4 7/8 In.	6.00
C.A. Smith's Hair Restorer, Philadelphia, Cobalt Blue, Square Collar, 1880s, 7 In.	210.00
C.S. Emerson's American Hair Restorative, Cleveland, Oh., 6 1/2 In. *Illus*	150.00
Clock's Excelsior Hair Restorer, Aqua, Clouded	15.00
Cranitonic Hair Food, Aqua, 12 Panels, Sample	18.00
D. Mitchell's Tonic For The Hair, Rochester, N.Y., Aqua, 6 1/4 In.	93.50
Dr. B.W. Hair & Son, Asthma Cure, London, Amber, 5 1/4 x 2 In.	120.00
Dr. Campbell's Hair Invigorator, Aurora, N.Y., Aqua, OP, Rectangular, 6 1/8 In.	74.00
Dr. Hay's Hair Health, Amber, Rectangular, 6 1/2 In.	7.00
Dr. Leon's Electric Hair Renewer, Black Amethyst, 7 In.	420.00

Cosmetic, Berninghaus's Mexican Shampoo, Cincinnati, Cobalt Blue, 9 1/2 In.

Cosmetic, C.S. Emerson's American Hair Restorative, Cleveland, Oh., 6 1/2 In.

Cosmetic, Pompeian Cream, Pompeian Mfg. Co., Cleveland, Oh., 3 In.

Dr. Tebbetts' Physiological Hair Regenerator, Amethyst, 7 1/2 In. .... 195.00 to 225.00
Dr. Tebbetts' Physiological Hair Regenerator, Medium Amber, 3 In......................... 62.00
Dr. Tebbetts' Physiological Hair Regenerator, Plum Amethyst, 7 1/2 In. 154.00
Elpsian Mfg. Co., Detroit, Restoring The Skin, Cobalt Blue, Label, 1880, 6 1/2 In. 121.00
Empress Mfg. Co. Instantaneous Hair Color Restorer, N.Y., Amber, 4 1/4 In......... 25.00
Eureka Hair Restorative, P.J. Reilly, San Francisco, Blue Aqua, 7 In. 770.00
Excelsior Hair Tonic, Lombard & Cundall, Olive Amber, OP, 6 1/2 In..................... 2530.00
Fish's Hair Restorative, B.F. Fish, San Francisco, Aqua, 7 1/4 In. 1650.00
Fish's Hair Restorative, San Francisco, Cobalt Blue, 7 1/4 In................................. 6600.00
Florida Water, Larkin Co., Buffalo, Palm Trees & Beach Label.............................. 60.00
Florida Water, Oakley Soap & Perfume, Green Aqua Glass.................................... 20.00
Florida Water, Oakley Soap & Perfumery Co., N.Y., 6 1/2 In. 10.00
Gallagher's Magical Hair Oil, Aqua, Hinged Mold, 6 In.................................... 20.00
Gallagher's Magical Hair Oil, Philad.A, Aqua, c.1860, 6 In. 4.00
Grandjeans Composition For The Hair, Pontil, 3 In.. 176.00
Gray's Hair Restorative, Aqua, Smooth Base, 7 1/2 In..........................25.00 to 35.00
Hair Restorer, Cobalt Blue, Rectangular, 6 3/4 In... 94.00
Hall's Hair Renewer, Teal Blue, Rectangular, 6 5/8 In. 55.00
Hall's Vegetable Hair Renewer, Deep Teal Blue, Tooled Lip, 6 3/8 In. 176.00
Hiawatha Hair Restorative, Mudjekee, Wis., Aqua, Applied Mouth, 6 3/4 In. 72.00
Hill's Hair Dye, No.1, Aqua 7.00
Hurd's Golden Gloss, For Hair, N.Y., Aqua, OP, 6 1/4 In. 140.00
Hurd's Hair Restorer, Aqua, Applied Mouth, Pontil, 8 1/8 In............................... 82.00
Imperial Hair Regenerator, Aqua, 4 3/8 In. 7.00
J. & C. MacGuire Hair Tonic, St. Louis, Mo., Lavender, Rectangular, 6 3/4 In. 440.00
J. Cristadoro's Liquid Hair Dye, No. 2, Aqua, OP, 2 7/8 In. 15.00
Jar, Pomade, 12 Vertical Ribs, Cobalt Blue, Pontil, 3 1/4 In............................... 165.00
Jar, Richard Hudnut Flower Sachet, Floral Tin Cover, Floral Shaped Soap.................. 25.00
Jean Wallace Butler Buena Tonic, Labels, Contents, 6 In................................. 65.00
Kickapoo Sage Hair Tonic, Cobalt Blue, Stopper, 5 1/4 In. 175.00
Kitsap Hair Tonic, Cottel Drug Co., Indian Chief Picture, Rectangular, 7 In............... 16.00
L.S. Bliss, Hatfield, Mass, Unrivaled, Hair Tonic, Aqua, OP, Rectangular, 7 In. 70.00
Lombard & Condall's Hair Restorer, Pink Amethyst.. 140.00
Loxor Cold Cream, Milk Glass, Barrel Shape, 3 1/8 In...................................... 3.00
Madame Yale's Excelsior Hair Tonic, Price 50 Cents, Clear, Amethyst 10.00
Mascara Tonique For The Hair, Rochester, N.Y., Embossed, 6 1/2 In.............. 55.00 to 60.00
Mme. Dejoux Oriental Lotion, Elysign Mfg. Co., Cobalt, Pleated Cloth, 7 In.......... 95.00
Mrs. Garvaise Graham Beauty Doctor, Chicago, Amber, 5 3/4 In........................ 10.00
Mrs. H.E. Wilson's Hair Dressing, Manchester, N.H., Rectangular, 6 3/4 In............. 160.00
Mrs. S.A. Allen's World's Hair Restorer, Deep Cherry Amethyst, 7 1/4 In. 230.00
Mrs. S.A. Allen's World's Hair Restorer, Light Honey, Applied Top, 7 1/4 In............ 110.00
Mrs. S.A. Allen's World's Hair Restorer, Medium Amethyst, 7 1/4 In................... 140.00
Mrs. S.A. Allen's World's Hair Balsam, N.Y., Aqua, Rectangular, 6 3/4 In. 18.00
Mrs. S.A. Allen's World's Hair Restorer, New York, Dark Amethyst, 1860s, 7 1/4 In. 204.00
Mrs. S.A. Allen's World's Hair Restorer, New York, Purple Amethyst, 1870, 7 1/4 In. 242.00
Mrs. S.A. Allen's World's Hair Restorer, New York, Red Puce, 7 1/4 In. 170.00
Mrs. S.A. Allen's World's Hair Restorer, New York, Yellow Amber, 7 1/4 In........... 120.00
Oldridge's Balm Of Columbia, For Restoring Hair, Aqua, Pontil, 5 1/8 In. 253.00
Oldridge's Balm Of Columbia, For Restoring Hair, Phila., Apple Green, 5 1/2 In. 687.00
Oldridge's Balm Of Columbia, For Restoring Hair, Phila., Aqua, Pontil, 5 1/4 In. 253.00
Parker's Hair Balsam, Amber, Label, ABM ....7.00 to 12.00
Parker's Hair Balsam, New York, Amber, Label, Contents, ABM, 7 In. .... 12.00 to 25.00
Perry's Celebrated Hungarian Balm For The Hair, Aqua, Rectangular, 5 3/4 In........ 64.00
Perry's Hungarian Balm For The Hair, Aqua, 5 3/4 In. 85.00
Pompeian Cream, Pompeian Mfg. Co., Cleveland, Oh., 3 In.................................*Illus* .75
Professor Wood Hair Restorative, St. Louis & New York, Aqua 100.00
Professor Wood's Hair Restorative Depot, St Louis & N.Y., Aqua, OP, 8 3/4 In....... 45.00
Professor Wood's Hair Restorative Depot, St. Louis & N.Y., Green Aqua, IP, 9 In... 220.00
Raymond & Co., N.Y., Florida Water, Aqua, Tooled Lip.. 20.00
Renovo For Hair, D. Skidmore & Co., Purple Amethyst, 1865-1875, 7 3/4 In............... 1650.00
Roehl's Reliable Hair Restorer, Amber, Rectangular, 7 7/8 In................................ 22.00
S. Barrow Evans Hair Restorer, Cobalt Blue, Embossed Front Panel......................... 45.00
Shaker Hair Restorer, Medium Amber, Tooled Lip, 7 3/4 In.................................. 210.00

St. Clair's Hair Lotion, Cobalt Blue, Tooled Top, 7 1/4 In. 75.00
Sterling's Ambrosia For The Hair, Aqua, 6 In. 75.00
Swire's Hair Restorer, Deep Cobalt Blue, Rolled Lip, 7 1/4 In. 150.00
Tutts Hair Dye, No.2, Aqua, Square, 3 In. 10.00
Van Deusen's Improved Wahpene, Aqua, OP, Rectangular, 8 In. 195.00
Velvetine Skin Beautifier, 5 1/2 In. 20.00
W.C. Montgomery's Hair Restorer, Philadelphia, Root Beer Amber 135.00
Watkins Dandruff Remover & Scalp Tonic, Winona, Minn., Amber, 6 1/4 In. 20.00
Wm. Roberson's Hair Renewer, Black Amethyst, 6 3/4 In. 300.00

───────────────── **CURE** ─────────────────

Collectors have their own interests and a large group of bottle collectors seek medicine bottles with the word *cure* embossed on the glass or printed on the label. A cure bottle is not a *remedy bottle*. The word *cure* was originally used for a medicine that treated many diseases. A *specific* was made for only one disease. The Pure Food and Drug Act of 1906 made label changes mandatory and the use of the word *cure* was no longer permitted. Related bottles may be found in the Medicine and Bitters categories.

CURE, A.E. Smith's Electric Oil, Philadelphia, Aqua, Cylindrical, OP, 2 1/2 In. 25.00
A.M. Farland, Philadelphia, Blue Green, Pontil 79.00
Adam's Sanatorium, Mexico, Mo., Cobalt Blue, Tooled Lip, 5 1/4 In. 798.00
Alexander's Sure Cure For Asthma, Akron, Oh., Amber, 6 1/4 In. 26.00
Alexander's Sure Cure For Malaria, Akron, Oh., 8 In. 40.00
Arthur's Elixir Of Sulpher, Positively Cures All Throat & Lung Diseases, 8 In. .....*Illus* 12.00
Arthur's Elixir Of Sulphur, Embossed, Oval & Flat Slug Plate 75.00
Ayer's Hair Vigor, Cobalt Blue, Tooled Mouth, Glass Stopper, 6 1/2 In. 121.00
B.B. Roberts & Co., Golden Gate Medical Syrup, Calif., Aqua, 10 In. 50.00
Baker's Vegetable Blood & Liver, Greenville, Tenn., Amber, 9 3/4 In. .... 160.00 to 330.00
Barnett, Magic Cure Liniment, Easton, Pa., Aqua, Label, Contents 35.00
Bear's Oil, Green Aqua, OP, Rolled Lip, 2 5/8 In. 254.00
Bonpland's Fever & Ague Remedy, New York, Aqua, 5 1/4 In. 58.00
Brightbane, The Great Kidney & Stomach, Amber, 8 3/4 In. 82.50
Brown's Blood Cure, Philadelphia, Yellow Green, 6 1/4 In. .... 85.00 to 143.00
Burnett, Boston, Aqua, Rectangular, 8 In. 20.00
Cann's Kidney Cure, Philadelphia, 1876 .... 35.00
Carter's Spanish Mixture, Yellow Olive Green, OP, Cylindrical, 8 In. 535.00
Clay's Sure Cure For Rheumatism, Savannah, Ga., Amber, 8 In. 110.00
Coe's Dyspepsia, C.G. Clark & Co., Aqua, 6 In. 25.00
Craig Kidney Cure Company, Amber, Applied Mouth, 9 1/2 In. .... 137.50 to 143.00
Cramer's Cough Cure, Aqua, 1890, 6 1/4 In. 15.00
Criswell's Bromo Pepsin Cures Headache, Amber .... 4.00 to 12.00
Crystalina The Magic Skin Cure, A.S Hull, 5 In. 25.00
Cuticura System Of Curing Constitutional Humors, Aqua, 2 Labels, 9 13/16 In. 20.00
Damascus, Stoddart Bros., San Francisco, Yellow Amber, 4 1/2 In. 132.00
Davis Drug Co., Rexall Store, Leadville, Col., Medium Amber, 5 In. 44.00
Ditchett's Remedy For Piles, New York, Olive Green, OP, Rectangular, 8 In. 4400.00
Dr. A.M. Loryea & Co., Unkweed Remedy, Oregon, Applied Top, 1860s, 8 In. 660.00
Dr. Ashbaugh's Wonder Of The World, Pittsburgh, Pa., Clear, Amethyst 49.00
Dr. Ball's Hustena Greatest Of All Cough Cures 15.00
Dr. Browder's Compound Syrup Of Indian Turnip, Aqua, OP, 6 7/8 In. 140.00
Dr. C.C. Roc's Liver, Rheumatic & Neuralgic Cure, Knoxville, Tenn., 8 In. 40.00
Dr. C.C. Roc's Liver Rheumatic & Neuralgic, Cullen & Neuman, Aqua, 8 In. .... 35.00 to 45.00
Dr. Culver's Malarial Germ Destroyer, Medium Amber, Tooled Lip, 8 In. 220.00
Dr. D.M. Bye Combination Oil Cure Co., Indianapolis, 7 1/4 In. 62.00
Dr. D.M. Bye Combination Oil Cure Co., Indianapolis, Ind., 6 7/8 In. 64.00
Dr. D.M. Bye Combination Oil Cure Co., Indianapolis, Ind., 7 1/2 In. 65.00
Dr. Daniel's Veterinary Colic Cure, Amber 75.00
Dr. Dewitt's Eclectic Cure, W.J. Parker & Co., Green, 5 5/8 In. 16.00
Dr. Elliot's Speedy Cure, Aqua, Label, 7 1/8 In. 35.00
Dr. Fitler's Rheumatic Remedy, Philadelphia, Smoky Flint Glass 28.00
Dr. Guysott's Yellow Dock & Sarsaparilla, Deep Blue Aqua, IP, 10 1/4 In. 225.00
Dr. H. Kelsey, Lowell, Mass., Aqua, Oval, 6 1/2 In. 26.00
Dr. Henry's Botanic Preparations, Aqua, 6 3/8 In. 71.50

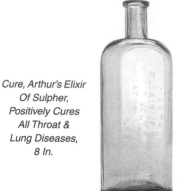

Cure, Arthur's Elixir Of Sulpher, Positively Cures All Throat & Lung Diseases, 8 In.

Cure, L.F. Ganter's Magic Chicken Cholera Cure, Glasgo, Ky., 6 In.

Dr. J. Kauffman's Angeline Internal Rheumatism, Hamilton, Oh., 7 5/8 In. 30.00
Dr. J. Sweet's Celebrated Sprain Liniment, New Bedford, Mass, Aqua, 5 In. 20.00
Dr. J.J. Mc Bridge's, King Of Pain, San Francisco, Aqua, 6 1/4 In............................... 71.50
Dr. Kilmer & Co., Catarrh, Cough Cure Consumption Oil, Aqua, 8 3/4 In. 715.00
Dr. Kilmer's Indian Cough Cure Consumption Oil, Aqua, c.1870, 8 3/4 In. 715.00
Dr. Kilmer's Kidney, Liver & Bladder Cure Specific, Label, Aqua, 8 3/8 In. 18.00
Dr. L.E. Keeley's Double Chloride Of Gold Cure For Drunkenness, 5 1/2 In. 100.00
Dr. Laubach's Eclectic Liniment, Allentown, Aqua, 6 In.. 10.00
Dr. Laubach's Worm, Aqua, 4 5/16 In. 25.00
Dr. Lepper's Oil Of Gladness, Sacramento, Aqua, 5 In. 165.00
Dr. Lesure's, Total Eclipse Spavin Cure, Keene, N.H., Aqua, 5 1/8 In. .... 22.00 to 35.00
Dr. McLane's American Worm Specific, Pontil, 3 7/8 In... 19.00
Dr. Mile's Heart Treatment, Aqua, c.1910, Rectangular, Qt....................................... 412.50
Dr. Mile's New Heart Cure, Aqua, Free Sample, 3 7/8 In. .... 15.00 to 16.00
Dr. Morris's Syrup Of Tar, Dacostas Radical Cure, Indented Panels, 5 1/2 In. 45.00
Dr. Murray's Magic Oil, San Francisco, Blue, 6 In. 38.50
Dr. Peter Fahrney & Sons Co., Chicago, Ill., Cleansing Blood, Amber, 9 In. 410.00
Dr. Pierce's Anuric Tablets For Kidneys & Backaches, Label, Light Green, 3 In. 16.00
Dr. R.C. Flower's Scientific Remedies, Boston, Mass., Amber, 9 1/8 In. 66.00
Dr. Sykes Sure Cure For Catarrh, Aqua, Applied Top, Round, 6 5/8 In. 65.00
Dr. Wistar's Balsam Of Wild Cherry, Philadelphia, Aqua, Pontil, 1860, 6 1/2 In......... 30.00
Dr. Zeublin's Safe & Quick, Sick Headache, Philadelphia, Aqua, Pontil, 3 5/8 In..... 165.00 to 200.00
E. Roussell, Philadelphia, Deep Green, Pontil.. 60.00
Ely's Cream Balm, Catarrh, Amber, 2 1/2 In.. 5.00
Farquar's Medicated California Wine & Brandy, Puce, c.1870, 9 1/2 In. 880.00
Fenning's Fever Cure, Aqua, 6 1/4 In... 19.00
Fitch's Ideal Dandruff Cure Co., 5 5/8 In... 12.00
Foley's Kidney & Bladder Cure, Chicago, Amber, 7 1/2 In. 20.00
Friedenwald's Buchu Gin All Kidney Troubles, Deep Yellow Green, 9 In. 253.00
Fulton's Radical Remedy, Sure Kidney Liver & Dyspepsia Cure, Amber, 8 3/4 In. 330.00
G.W. Merchant, Lockport, N.Y., Deep Blue Green, Applied Mouth, 7 1/4 In. 165.00
German Fir Cough, Dilliard Remedy Co., East Bangor, Pa., Aqua, 6 1/2 In. 110.00
Glover's Imperial Mange, New York, Amber, 6 7/8 In. 12.00
Gray's Balsam Best Cough, Leroy, N.Y., Aqua, Label, Contents, 6 1/4 In. 35.00
Great Blood & Rheumatism, Matt J. Johnson Co., St. Paul, Minn., Aqua, 9 In. ...22.00 to 25.00
Healy & Bigelow's Kickapoo Indian Cough Cure, Aqua, 4 5/8 In. 15.00
Himalaya The Kola Compound, Natures Cure For Asthma, Amber, 7 1/2 In. 20.00
Holman's Natures Grand Restorative, Boston, Mass, Yellow Amber, 7 1/4 In. 1595.00
Holman's Natures Grand Restorative, Boston, Mass., Green, Rectangular, OP, 6 In. . 2530.00
Holmes' Sure Cure Mouthwash, Embossed Set Of Teeth, Macon, Ga. 125.00
Hostetter's Essence Jamaica Ginger, Pittsburgh, Aqua.. 55.00
Howland's Ready Remedy Columbia & Roads, Pa., Aqua, OP, 5 In............................ 100.00

Hynson Westcott & Co., Baltimore, Cobalt Blue 49.00
Kaufman's Angeline Internal Rheumatism, Hamilton, Oh., 7 5/8 In. 40.00
Kendall's Spavin, Enosburg Falls, Vt., Aqua 19.00
L.F. Ganter's Magic Chicken Cholera Cure, Glasgo, Ky., 6 In. ....*Illus* 20.00
L.P. Dodge Rheumatic Liniment, Newburg, Amber, OP, Rectangular, 1850, 5 In. 1650.00
Lactopeptine Best Remedial Agent Digestive Disorders, Cobalt Blue, 7 3/4 In. 55.00
Langenbach's Dysentery, Light Amber, 5 5/8 In. ....28.00 to 37.00
Leonardi's Tasteless Chill, Amber, Stained, 8 1/4 In. 20.00
Long's Vegetable Pain, 25 Cents, Aqua, 5 3/4 In. 20.00
Lorrimer's Medical Institute, Baltimore, Md., Yellow Amber 25.00
Makrauer's Hair Invigorator & Dandruff, Pittsburgh, Rectangular, 6 1/4 In. 15.00
McLean's Strengthening Cordial & Blood Purifier, Light Blue, 8 In. 28.00
Moore's Tree Of Life, Aqua, Rectangular, 8 3/4 In. 715.00
National Kidney & Liver, Amber, Tooled Lip, 9 In. 49.50
Newbro's Herpicide Kills Dandruff Germ, Jug, Aqua, Tooled Top, Gal. 45.00
Newell's Pulmonary Syrup, Redington & Co., Deep Aqua, 7 5/8 In. 66.00
Original Dr. Craig's Kidney Cure, Rochester, N.Y., Amber, 9 1/2 In. 100.00
Piso's Cure For Consumption, Olive, Rectangular, 5 1/16 In. 6.00
Piso's Cure For Consumption, Yellow Green, 5 1/16 In. 10.00
Pratt's Abolition Oil For Abolishing Pain, Deep Aqua, 6 In. 93.50
Price's Patent Candle Co. Limited, Wedge Form, Cobalt Blue, England, 7 3/8 In. 143.00
Prof. Callan's World Renowned Brazillian Gum, Aqua, 4 1/4 In. 15.00
Rhodes Antidote To Malaria, Fever & Ague, Aqua, 1855-1865, 8 1/4 In. 137.00
Rhodes Antidote To Malaria, Fever & Ague, Aqua, Pontil, 8 1/4 In. ....176.00 to 282.00
Rhodes' Fever & Ague Cure, Aqua, Label, Pontil, Wrapper, 1850, 8 1/2 In. 357.00
Rohrer's Expectoral Wild Cherry Tonic, Pyramid, Amber, Pontil, 10 1/2 In. 44.00
Rosewood Dandruff Cure, J.R. Reeves Co., Anderson, Ind., Amethyst, 6 3/8 In. 12.00
S. Grover Graham's Dyspepsia Cure, 6 5/8 In. 11.00
Sallade & Co. Magic Mosquito Bite Cure & Insect Exterminator, N.Y., Aqua, 8 In. 75.00
Sanford's Radical, Cobalt Blue, 7 5/8 In. ....27.00 to 56.00
Saratoga Red Spring, Emerald Green, Qt. 160.00
Scovill's Blood & Liver Syrup, Cincinnati, Oh., Deep Aqua, 9 1/2 In. 35.00
Seaver's Joint & Nerve Liniment, Amber, OP, Cylindrical, 1850, 4 In. 2420.00
Shiloh's Consumption Cure, Leroy, N.Y., Label, 6 3/8 In. 30.00
Sloan's Sure Colic Cure, 3 3/8 In. 12.50
Spark's Kidney & Liver, Camden, N.J., Aqua, 4 1/8 In. 24.00
Stewart D. Howe's Arabian Milk Cure For Consumption, Deep Aqua, 7 5/8 In. 45.00
Thompsonian Appetizer Trade, J.J. Vogt & Co., Cleveland, Yellow Amber, 9 In. 632.00
Vegetable Pulmonary Balsam, Boston, Mass, Aqua, Rectangular, 7 1/4 In. 25.00
W.K. Lewis & Co., Aqua, Rectangular, 5 1/2 In. 22.00
Wait's Wild Cherry Tonic, Great Tonic, Amber, 8 1/2 In. 38.50
Wakelee's Camelline, Cobalt Blue, 4 5/8 In. 99.00
Warner & Co., Tippecanoe, Amber, Pat. Nov. 20, 1883, 1890, 9 In. 94.00
Warner & Co., Tippecanoe, Golden Yellow, 1880-1890, 9 In. 550.00
Warner's Safe Cure, Embossed Safe, Emerald Green, c.1870, 7 In. 88.00
Warner's Safe Cure, Frankfurt, Deep Olive Green, 9 1/2 In. 440.00
Warner's Safe Cure, London, Embossed Safe, Olive Green, Whittled, Pt. ....58.00 to 85.00
Warner's Safe Cure, London, Light Moss Green, Whittled, 7 1/4 In. 90.00
Warner's Safe Cure, London, Safe Picture, Emerald Green, 1/2 Pt., 7 1/4 In. 88.00
Warner's Safe Cure, Medium Pink Puce, Embossed Safe, 9 1/4 In. 330.00
Warner's Safe Cure, Melbourne, Safe Picture, Amber, 9 1/2 In. 60.00
Warner's Safe Cure, Pressburg, Olive Green, 1880s, 9 1/2 In. 1925.00
Warner's Safe Cure, Rochester, Embossed Safe, Amber, 9 3/4 In. ....94.00 to 110.00
Warner's Safe Cure, Rochester, Embossed Safe, Chocolate Amber, 9 3/4 In. 71.50
Warner's Safe Cure, Rochester, Embossed Safe, Medium Red Amber, 11 In. 330.00
Warner's Safe Cure, Rochester, Embossed Safe, Yellow Amber Tone, 7 1/2 In. 88.00
Warner's Safe Cure, Rochester, Safe Picture, Free Sample, 4 1/4 In. 30.00
Warner's Safe Cure, Rochester, Yellow Olive, 9 3/4 In. 242.00
Warner's Safe Diabetes Cure, London, Embossed Safe, Yellow Amber Tone, 9 In. ... 132.00
Warner's Safe Diabetes Cure, London, Embossed Safe, Yellow Amber, 4 5/8 In. 385.00
Warner's Safe Diabetes Cure, Rochester, N.Y., Amber, Applied Mouth, 9 1/2 In. 66.00
Warner's Safe Diabetes Cure, Root Beer Amber, Double Collar, Embossed 75.00
Warner's Safe Diabetes Cure, Embossed Safe, Amber, 9 3/4 In. 60.00

Front   Back

Cure, Wm. Radam's Microbe Killer, Germ Bacteria, Amber, Dec. 12, 1887, 10 In.

Warner's Safe Kidney & Liver Cure, Left Handed, Olive... 118.00
Warner's Safe Kidney & Liver Cure, Red Amber... 30.00
Warner's Safe Kidney & Liver Cure, Rochester, Amber, 9 1/2 In. ....45.00 to 55.00
Warner's Safe Kidney & Liver Cure, Rochester, Amber, Dug, 9 1/2 In. ....9.00 to 22.00
Warner's Safe Nervine, Rochester, Embossed Safe, Green, Applied Mouth, 7 1/2 In... 176.00
Warner's Safe Rheumatic, Label, Amber, 9 1/4 In... 55.00
Warner's Safe Rheumatic, London, Safe Picture, Straw, 9 1/4 In. 120.00
Warner's Safe Rheumatic, London, Yellow Amber, 9 1/2 In. ....125.00 to 550.00
Warner's Safe Rheumatic Cure, Rochester, Embossed Safe, Amber, 9 1/2 In.....45.00 to 56.00
White's Prairie Flower, Toledo, Oh., Deep Aqua, 7 In... 165.00
Wm. Radam's Microbe Killer, Germ Bacteria, Amber, Dec. 12, 1887, 10 In..........*Illus* 440.00
Wooldridge Wonderful Cure, Columbus, Ga., Honey Amber 240.00
World's Greatest Remedy For Cure, c.1890, 5 1/2 In. 715.00

—————————————— CYRUS NOBLE ——————————————

This complicated story requires a cast of characters, Cyrus Noble, a master distiller; Ernest R. Lilienthal, owner of Bernheim Distillery; Crown Distillers, trade name of Lilienthal & Company; Haas Brothers, successor to Lilienthal & Co.; and another Ernest R. Lilienthal, president of Haas Brothers Distributing and grandson of the original Ernest Lilienthal. Cyrus Noble was in charge of the quality of the whiskey made at the Bernheim Distillery in Kentucky. He was said to be a large man, over 300 pounds, and liked to taste his own product. According to the stories, he tasted to excess one day, fell into a whiskey vat, and drowned. The company, as a tribute, named the brand for him in 1871 and so Cyrus Noble Bourbon came into being.

Ernest R. Lilienthal, the original owner of Bernheim Distillery, moved to San Francisco and opened Lilienthal & Company with the trade name of Crown Distillers. Their best-selling brand was Cyrus Noble. It was made in three grades and sold by the barrel. The company later became Haas Brothers Distributing Company.

In 1901 John Coleman, a miner in Searchlight, Nevada, was so discouraged with the results of his digging that he offered to trade his mine to Tobe Weaver, a bartender, for a quart of Cyrus Noble whiskey. The mine was named Cyrus Noble and eventually produced over $250,000 worth of gold.

One of the early bottles used for Cyrus Noble whiskey was amber with an inside screw top; it was made from the 1860s to 1921. Haas Brothers of San Francisco marketed special Cyrus Noble bottles from 1971 to 1980. The first, made to commemorate the company's 100th anniversary, pictured the miner, the unfortunate John Coleman. Six thousand bottles were made and sold, filled, for $16.95 each. Tobe Weaver, the fortunate bartender, was pictured in the next bottle. A mine series was made from 1971 to 1978, the full size about 14 inches high and the miniatures about 6 inches; a wild animal series from 1977 to 1978; and a carousel series in 1979 and 1980. Other series are birds of the forest, olympic bottles, horned animals, and sea animals. W.A. Lacey, a brand of 86 proof blended whiskey distributed by Haas Brothers, was also packed in a variety of figural bottles. They are listed separately under Lacey. Production of both brands of decanters ended in 1981.

CYRUS NOBLE, Assayer, 1972	128.00
Bartender, 1971	145.00
Bear & Cubs, 1978, 1st Edition	114.00
Bear & Cubs, 1978, 2nd Edition	77.00
Beaver & Kit, 1978, 1st Edition	65.00
Blacksmith, 1976	44.00
Buffalo Cow & Calf, 1977, 1st Edition	108.00
Buffalo Cow & Calf, 1977, 2nd Edition	74.00
Burro, 1973	60.00
Carousel, Horse, Black Flyer, 1979	40.00
Carousel, Horse, White Charger, 1979	38.00
Carousel, Lion, 1979	52.00
Carousel, Pipe Organ, 1980	22.00
Carousel, Tiger, 1979	40.00
Deer, White Tall Buck, 1979	72.00
Deer & Mule, 1980	52.00
Delta Saloon, 1971, Miniature	270.00
Dolphin, 1979	46.00
Elk, Bull, 1980	45.00
Gambler, 1974	50.00
Gambler's Lady, 1977, Miniature	44.00
Gold Miner, 1970	172.00
Harp Seal, 1979	53.00
Landlady, 1977	24.00
Middle Of Piano, Trumpeter, 1979	36.00
Mine Shaft, 1978	40.00
Miner's Daughter, 1975	47.00
Moose, 1976, 1st Edition	96.00
Mountain Lion & Cubs, 1977, 1st Edition ....*Illus*	92.00
Mountain Sheep, 1978, 1st Edition	106.00
Music Man, 1978, Miniature	28.00
Oklahoma Dancers, 1978	32.00
Olympic Skater, 1980 ....26.00 to	29.00
Owl In Tree, 1980	37.00
Penguins, 1978	52.00
Sea Turtle, 1979	42.00
Seal Family, 1978	45.00
Snowshoe Thompson, 1972	154.00
South Of The Border, Dancers, 1978 ....*Illus*	37.00
Tonopah, 8-Sided, White, 1972	124.00
USC Trojan, 1980	40.00
Violinist, 1978, Miniature	32.00

Cyrus Noble, Mountain Lion & Cubs,
1977, 1st Edition

Cyrus Noble, South Of The Border,
Dancers, 1978

Walrus Family, 1978 .... 50.00
Walrus Family, 1980, Miniature 48.00
Whiskey Drummer, 1975 .... 40.00
Whiskey Drummer, 1977, Miniature 41.00
Wood Duck 36.00

———————————————— **DANT** ————————————————

Dant figural bottles were first released in 1968 to hold J.W. Dant alcoholic products. The figurals were discontinued after a few years. The company made an Americana series, field birds, special bottlings, and ceramic bottles. Several bottles were made with *errors.* Collectors seem to have discounted this in determining value.

DANT, Alamo, 1969.. 6.00
  American Legion, 1969 .... 10.00
  Atlantic City, 1969... 6.00
  Boeing 747, 1970... 8.00
  Boston Tea Party, Eagle Right, 1968.. 11.00
  Boston Tea Party, Reverse Eagle...*Illus* 11.00
  Burr-Hamilton Duel, 1969... 10.00
  Constitution & Guerriere, 1969... 8.00
  Field Bird Series, No. 1, Ring-Necked Pheasant, 1969..................................... 9.00
  Field Bird Series, No. 2, Chukar Partridge, 1969.. 9.00
  Field Bird Series, No. 3, Prairie Chicken, 1969 .... 9.00
  Field Bird Series, No. 4, Mountain Quail, 1969..*Illus* 9.00
  Field Bird Series, No. 5, Ruffled Grouse, 1969 .... 9.00
  Field Bird Series, No. 6, California Quail, 1969 .... 9.00
  Field Bird Series, No. 7, Bob White, 1969.. 9.00
  Field Bird Series, No. 8, Woodcock, 1969.. 9.00
  Ft. Sill, 1969.. 10.00

Dant, Boston Tea Party,
Reverse Eagle

Dant, Field Bird Series, No. 4,
Mountain Quail, 1969

Dant, Mt. Rushmore, 1969

Indy 500, 1969.. 11.00
Mt. Rushmore, 1969..*Illus* 10.00
Patrick Henry, 1969 .... 8.00
Paul Bunyan, 1969 .... 8.00
San Diego Harbor, 1969.. 7.00
Washington At Delaware, 1969 .... 8.00

———————————— DAVIESS COUNTY ————————————

Daviess County ceramic bottles were made from 1978 to 1981. The best-known were the American Legion Convention bottles. About 14 figural bottles were made, including a series of large tractor trailers and Greensboro Golf Tournament souvenirs.

DAVIESS COUNTY, American Legion, Boston, 1980................................ 21.00
American Legion, Hawaii, 1981... 23.00
American Legion, Houston, 1979.. 22.00
American Legion, New Orleans, 1978... 22.00
Greensboro Open, Ball On Tee, 1981 .... 27.00
Greensboro Open, Golf Cart, 1980 .... 28.00
Greensboro Open, Raining, 1979... 49.00
Iowa Hog, 1978... 25.00
Jeep CJ-7, 1979.. 32.00
Kentucky Long Rifle, 1978... 59.00
Mallard, Decoy, 1980... 37.00
Oil Tanker, Gulf, 1979 .... 36.00
Pontiac Trans Am, 1980 .... 27.00
Porsche 935, Red, 1979.. 52.00

———————————— DECANTER ————————————

Decanters were first used to hold the alcoholic beverages that had been stored in kegs. The undesirable sediment that formed at the bottom of old wine kegs was removed by carefully pouring off the top liquid, or decanting it. At first a necessity, the decanter later became merely an attractive serving vessel. A decanter usually has a bulbous bottom, a long neck, and a small mouth for easy pouring. Most have a cork or glass stopper. They were popular in England from the beginning of the eighteenth century. By about 1775 the decanter was elaborate, with cut, applied, or enameled decorations. Various early American glassworks made decanters. Mold-blown decanters were the most popular style and many were made in the East and the Midwest from 1820 to the 1860s. Pressed glass was a less expensive process introduced in about 1850, and many decanters were made by this method. Colored Bohemian glass consisting of two or three cased layers became popular in the late-nineteenth century. Many decanters are now made for home or restaurant use or with special logos to promote products. Bar bottles, decanter-like bottles with brand names in the glass, were used from about 1890 to 1920 in saloons. The law no longer permits the use of bar bottles because no bottle may be refilled from another container. Other decanters may be found in the Beam, Bischoff, and other modern bottle categories.

DECANTER, 4-Piece Mold, Milk Glass, Embossed Flowers, Bulbous Neck 65.00
8-Pillar Mold, Bell Form, Flared Mouth, Stopper, Pontil, 10 3/4 In. 77.00
Belle Of Lincoln, Jack Daniels, ABM, Reproduction, 1970s, 1/2 Gal........................... 25.00
Blown, 2 Applied Rings, Lacy Flower Stopper, 8 1/2 In. 27.00
Blown, 3 Applied Rings, 10 Rib Stopper, 8 3/4 In... 495.00
Blown, 3 Applied Rings, Wheel Stopper, 7 3/8 In.. 93.00
Blown, 3-Piece Mold, 3 Neck Rings, Stopper, Pontil, Qt. 99.00
Blown, 3-Piece Mold, Amethyst, Flared, Stopper, Pontil, Pt... 159.50
Blown, 3-Piece Mold, Applied Neck Rings, Stopper, Pontil, 8 In. 121.00
Blown, 3-Piece Mold, Baroque Form, Shell, Rib, Flared Mouth, Stopper, Pontil, Qt. 55.00
Blown, 3-Piece Mold, Barrel Form, Period Stopper, Pontil, Pt..................................... 143.00
Blown, 3-Piece Mold, Barrel Form, Wheel Stopper, Pontil, Pt...................................... 132.00
Blown, 3-Piece Mold, Barrel, Clear, Flared Mouth, Pontil, Stopper, Pt.......................... 209.00
Blown, 3-Piece Mold, Clear Blue Green, OP, 1820, Pontil, Stopper 3575.00
Blown, 3-Piece Mold, Clear, 3 Neck Rings, Stopper, Pontil, Pt. 110.00
Blown, 3-Piece Mold, Clear, Acorn Stopper, Pontil, Qt., Pair...................................... 3575.00
Blown, 3-Piece Mold, Clear, Flared Mouth, Stopper, Pontil, Pt. 198.00

Decanter, Blown, 3-Piece Mold,   Decanter, Melrose
Olive Amber, Pt.

Blown, 3-Piece Mold, Clear, Flared Mouth, Stopper, Pontil, Qt............................88.00 to 110.00
Blown, 3-Piece Mold, Clear, Flared Mouth, Stopper, Pontil, Pt. 121.00
Blown, 3-Piece Mold, Clear, Stopper, Pontil, Qt. 132.00
Blown, 3-Piece Mold, Cobalt Blue, Stopper, Pontil, 1/2 Pt. 1540.00
Blown, 3-Piece Mold, Flared Mouth, Stopper, Pontil, Hexagonal, 8 3/4 In................... 77.00
Blown, 3-Piece Mold, Flared Mouth, Stopper, Pontil, Pt.. 77.00
Blown, 3-Piece Mold, Horn Of Plenty Design, Stopper, Pontil, Qt. 1045.00
Blown, 3-Piece Mold, Medium Gray Blue, Stopper, Pontil, 1/2 Pt................................ 935.00
Blown, 3-Piece Mold, Olive Amber, Pt...*Illus* 440.00
Blown, Applied Drapery Type Design, Rigaree, Continental, 7 3/4 In. 154.00
Blown, Flattened Chestnut, Teal, Handle, Metal Stopper 120.00
Blue, Deep Cobalt, Applied Ring Neck, Pontil, 8 1/4 In. 357.00
Burgermeister, Famous Cities, Los Angeles, Ceramarte, Brown, 7 In., Pair 21.00
Chestnut, Globular, Aquamarine, OP, Cylindrical, 9 1/4 In. 2090.00
Cobalt Blue, White Swirl Design, 1830-1850, OP, Pt. 240.00
Cut Glass, Bulbous, 3 Applied Neck Rings, Pontil, Qt. 247.50
Cut Glass, Bulbous, Fern Designs, Flared Mouth, Stopper, Pontil, Qt........................... 363.00
Emerald Green, Handle, Metal Top & Closure, OP, 1830-1840 .... 230.00
Famous Burgermeister Cities, Los Angeles, Brown, Ceramarte, 7 In., Pair................ 21.00
Grim Reaper, 4 Shot Glasses, Brown Black, Bisque, 7 In. 82.50
Hamm's, Bear Shape, Ceramarte, 1973, 11 In... 37.00
Hamm's Bear, Figural, Ceramarte, 1972, 10 1/4 In.. 47.00
Lalique, Wine, Stopper, Stylized Grapes, 1920, 9 3/4 In. 1552.00
Melrose ....*Illus* 10.00
Old J.H. Cutter, Stopper, Embossed, Back Bar... 88.00
Old Style Bourbon, Tom Moore Eitel Bros., Chicago, Handle.................................... 70.00
Olive Amber, Gold Gilt, Flared Lip, 9 3/4 In. 220.00
Paul Jones, Mushroom Stopper, Pinch 40.00
Paul Jones, Pinch, Blown Stopper.. 60.00
Pinch, Half Post, Sea Green, Pewter Cap, Germany, 18th Century, 11 In...................... 500.00
Pinch, Silver Overlay 1900 Man Golfing Picture, Qt.. 69.00
Rye, Deep Ruby, Silver Overlay Around Neck, Tooled Lip, Stopper, 8 1/8 In............... 72.00
Very Old Corn From Casper, Winston, N.C., Etched, Handle 320.00
Whiskey, Black Amethyst Glass, 8 1/2 In. 110.00
Whiskey, Bulbous Base, Cover, Fluted, White, Orange Enamel, 3 1/4 In. 275.00
Whiskey, Cheleme, Clear & Yellow Green, 12 Ribs, Enameled, Backbar, 7 3/4 In. 83.00
Wine, Clear, Etched Bear, Flowers & 1826, OP, 11 7/8 In.. 237.00

DEMIJOHN

A demijohn is a very large bottle that is usually blown. Many held alcoholic beverages, molasses, or other liquids. It was usually bulbous with a long neck and a high kick-up. Early examples have open pontils. Many were covered with wicker to avoid breakage when the bottles were shipped. A demijohn could hold from one to ten gallons. Most early demijohns were made of dark green amber or black glass. By the 1850s the glass colors were often aqua, light green, or clear.

DEMIJOHN, Apple Shape, Yellow Green, 20 Embossed In Slug Plate, OP, 5 Gal. 145.00
Apple Shape, Yellow Green, Slug Plate, OP, 5 Gal. 110.00
Aqua, 3-Piece Mold, 14 In. 22.00
Aqua, Rolled Lip, Pontil, 4 In. 121.00
Bread Loaf Shape, Medium Blue Green, Wicker, 1830, 9 x 11 x 6 1/2 In. 385.00
Dark Amber, 3-Piece Mold, 1 Gal. 28.00
Deep Olive Green, Round Collar Lip, Pontil, Semi-Globular, 10 3/4 In. 187.00
Emerald Green, 3-Piece Mold, OP, 3 Gal. 75.00
Emerald Green, Cylinder, OP, Gal. 60.00
Green, 2-Piece Mold, OP, 3 Gal. 85.00
Kidney Shape, 19.87 Embossed In Slug Plate, OP, 5 Gal. 190.00
Kidney Shape, Olive Green, Pontil, 16 1/2 In. 192.50
Kidney Shape, Orange Amber, Whittle Marks, Qt. 29.00
Kidney Shape, Slug Plate, Drip Plate, OP, 5 Gal. 170.00
Lemon Citron, Squatty, 1/2 Gal. 49.00
Light Green, Dip Mold, Pontil, Gal. 80.00
Olive Amber, Dip Mold, IP, 2 Gal. 95.00
Olive Amber, OP, 2 Gal. 45.00
Olive Green, Applied Wide String Lip, Europe, Early 18th Century, 18 In. 605.00
Olive Green, Tapered Lip, c.1780-1800, 17 1/4 In. 1595.00
Orange Amber, Dip Mold, 3 Gal. 65.00
Secire Levaer, Olive Green, Stopper & Cap, Missing Lock & Key, 1800s, 17 In. 182.00
Stoddard, Apple Form, Red Amber, Seed Bubbles, New Hampshire, 1860, 19 In. 495.00
Stoddard, Seed Bubbles, Pontil, Gal. 85.00
Yellow, 13 In. 15.00
Yellow Olive, Dip Mold, OP, 2 Gal. 39.00
DRUG, see Bitters; Cure; Medicine

--------------------------- **EZRA BROOKS** ---------------------------

Ezra Brooks fancy bottles were first made in 1964. The Ezra Brooks brand was purchased by Glenmore Distilleries Company of Louisville, Kentucky, in 1988, three years after Ezra Brooks had discontinued making decanters. About 300 different ceramic figurals were made between 1964 and 1985. The dates on the bottles are within a year of the time they appeared on the market. Bottles were often announced and then not produced for many months. Glenmore sold the Ezra Brooks label to Heaven Hill Distillery in Bardstown, Kentucky, who sold it to David Sherman Corporation of St. Louis, Missouri, in 1994.

EZRA BROOKS, 100th Award, 1972 .... 25.00
African Lion, 1980 .... 20.00
American Legion, Champaign, Urbana, 1983 .... 25.00
American Legion, Chicago, Salute, 1972 .... 51.00
American Legion, Denver, 1977 .... 20.00
American Legion, Hawaii, 1973 .... 12.00
American Legion, Houston, 1971 .... 34.00
American Legion, Miami Beach, 1974 .... 12.00
American Legion, New Orleans, 1978 .... 39.00
American Legion, Salt Lake City, 1984 .... 46.00
American Legion, Seattle, 1983 .... 33.00
American Legion, Water Tower, 1982 .... 21.00
AMVET, 1974 .... 10.00
AMVET, Polish Legion, 1978 .... 12.00
Antique Cannon, Gold, 1969 ....*Illus* 11.00
Arizona, Desert Scene, 1969 .... 11.00
Auburn, Boat Tail, 1932 Model, 1978 .... 25.00
Auburn, U-War Eagle, 1982 .... 22.00
Badger, Boxer No. 1, 1973 .... 15.00
Badger, Football, 1975 .... 17.00
Badger, Hockey, 1975 .... 17.00
Baltimore Oriole, 1979 .... 29.00
Bareknuckle Fighter, 1972 .... 24.00

Ezra Brooks, Clown, No. 4, Keystone Cop, 1980

Ezra Brooks, Antique Cannon, Gold, 1969

Ezra Brooks, Club, No. 3, U.S.A. Map, 1972

Basketball Player, 1974	18.00
Beaver, 1973	12.00
Betsy Ross, 1975	12.00
Big Daddy Lounges, 1969	11.00
Bordertown Nevada, 1970	11.00
Bowler, 1973	12.00
Brahma Bull, 1972	17.00
Bronco Buster, 1974	15.00
Bucket Of Blood, 1970	9.00
Buffalo Hunt, 1971	12.00
C.B. Convoy Radio, 1976	10.00
Canadian Honker, 1975	15.00
Card, Jack Of Diamonds, 1969	12.00
Casey At Bat, 1973	32.00
Charlois, 1973	14.00
Cheyenne Shootout, 1970	12.00
Chicago Fire Team, 1974	27.00
Christmas Tree, 1980	20.00
Cigar Store Indian, 1968	10.00
Clown, No. 1, Smiley, 1979	27.00
Clown, No. 2, Cowboy, 1979	26.00
Clown, No. 3, Pagliacci, 1979	19.00
Clown, No. 4, Keystone Cop, 1980 ....*Illus*	29.00
Clown, No. 5, Cuddles, 1981	27.00
Clown, No. 6, Tramp, 1981	28.00
Clown With Accordion, 1972	27.00
Clown With Balloons, 1974	25.00
Club, No. 1, Distillery, 1970	12.00
Club, No. 2, Birthday Cake, 1971	14.00
Club, No. 3, U.S.A. Map, 1972 ....*Illus*	17.00
Clydesdale, 1974	19.00
Conquistadors, Drum & Bugle, 1972	12.00
Corvette, 1957 Model, Yellow, 1976	123.00
Corvette Mako Shark, 1962 Model, 1979	27.00
Creighton, Blue Jay, 1976	25.00
Dakota Cowboy, 1975	35.00
Dakota Cowgirl, 1976	30.00
Dakota Grain Elevator, 1978	28.00
Dakota Shotgun Express, 1977	20.00
Deadwagon, Nevada, 1970	11.00
Deer, Whitetail, 1974 ....*Illus*	22.00
Delta Belle, Riverboat, 1969	12.00
Dirt Bike, 1973	16.00
Dollar, Silver 1804, 1970	10.00
Dummy Gallon, 1969	123.00

Dummy Gallon, 1970 .... 57.00
Dusenberg, Model SJ, 1971 .... 34.00
Eagle, Gold, 1971 .... 20.00
Elephant, Asian, 1973 ....*Illus* 19.00
Elephant, Big Bertha, 1970 .... 15.00
Elk, 1972 .... 30.00
English Setter Bird Dog, 1971 .... 15.00
Equestrian, 1974 .... 12.00
F.O.E. Eagle, 1978 .... 18.00
F.O.E. Eagle, 1979 .... 24.00
F.O.E. Eagle, 1980 .... 38.00
F.O.E. Eagle, 1981 .... 37.00
Fire Engine, 1971 .... 22.00
Fireman, 1975 .... 22.00
Flintlock Dueling Pistol, 1968 .... 14.00
Football Player, 1974 .... 14.00
Ford Mustang Indy Pace Car, 1979 ....25.00 to 32.00
Ford Thunderbird, 1956 Model, Blue, 1977 .... 80.00
Ford Thunderbird, 1956 Model, Yellow, 1977 .... 67.00
Foremost Astronaut, 1970 .... 11.00
Fox, Redtail, 1979 .... 36.00
Fresno Grape, 1970 .... 12.00
Fresno Grape, With No Gold, 1970 .... 60.00
Gamecock, 1970 .... 16.00
Gator, Florida, No. 1, Passing, 1972 .... 15.00
Gator, Florida, No. 2, Running, 1973 .... 15.00
Gator, Florida, No. 3, Blocker, 1975 .... 23.00
Gavel, President, 1982 .... 55.00
Gavel & Block, V.I.P., 1982 .... 16.00
Georgia Bulldog, 1972 .... 22.00
Glass, Decanter, 1964 .... 14.00
Glass, Decanter, 1965 .... 15.00
Go Big Red, No. 1, Football, 1970 .... 28.00
Go Big Red, No. 2, With Hat, 1971 .... 21.00
Go Big Red, No. 3, Football, 1972 .... 23.00
Golden Grizzly Bear, 1968 .... 8.00
Goldpanner, 1970 .... 8.00
Gopher, Minnesota Hockey Player, 1975 .... 19.00
Grandfather Clock, 1970 .... 10.00
Greater Greensboro Open, 1972 ....25.00 to 40.00
Greensboro, Cup, 1975 .... 28.00
Greensboro Open, Club & Ball, 1977 .... 23.00
Greensboro Open, Golfer, No. 2, 1973 .... 27.00
Greensboro Open, Map, 1974 .... 37.00

Ezra Brooks, Deer,
Whitetail, 1974

Ezra Brooks, Kachina,
No. 9, Watermelon, 1980

Ezra Brooks, Elephant,
Asian, 1973

Hambletonian, Race Track, 1971 .... 15.00 to 27.00
Happy Goose, 1975 .... 15.00
Hardy, Oliver, 1976 .... 22.00
Harold's Club Dice, 1968 .... 12.00
Hereford, 1972 .... 17.00
Historical Flask, 1970 .... 6.00
Hog No. 3 .... 42.00
Horseshoe Club, 1970 .... 14.00
Hunter & Dog, 1973 .... 20.00
Idaho, Skier, 1972 .... 12.00
Indian, Ceremonial, 1970 .... 20.00 to 25.00
Indy Pace Car, Corvette, 1978 .... 47.00
Indy Pace Car, Ford Mustang, 1970 .... 25.00
Indy Race Car, No. 3, Norton Spirit, 1982 .... 74.00
Indy Race Car, No. 21, 1970 .... 44.00
Indy Race Car, Penske Pacemaker, No. 1, 1982 .... 75.00 to 128.00
Indy STP No. 40, 1983 .... 90.00
Iowa Farmer, 1977 .... 42.00
Iowa Farmer's Elevator, 1978 .... 32.00
Jayhawk, Kansas, 1969 .... 12.00
Jester, 1972 .... 12.00
Kachina, No. 1, Morning Singer, 1971 .... 90.00
Kachina, No. 2, Hummingbird, 1973 .... 85.00
Kachina, No. 3, Antelope, 1975 .... 84.00
Kachina, No. 4, Maiden, 1975 .... 35.00
Kachina, No. 5, Longhair, 1976 .... 48.00
Kachina, No. 6, Buffalo Dancer, 1977 .... 47.00
Kachina, No. 7, Mudhead, 1978 .... 55.00
Kachina, No. 8, Drummer, 1979 .... 72.00
Kachina, No. 9, Watermelon, 1980 ....*Illus* 31.00
Katz Cats, Gray, Tan, 1969 .... 11.00
Katz Cats, Philharmonic, 1970 .... 12.00
Keystone Cops In Car, 1972 .... 49.00
Kitten On Pillow, 1975 .... 13.00
Liberty Bell, 1970 .... 9.00
Lincoln Continental, 1979 .... 27.00
Lion On Rock, 1971 .... 12.00
Liquor Square, 1972 .... 10.00
Loon, 1979 .... 25.00
M & M, Brown Jug, 1974 .... 18.00
Macaw, 1980 .... 48.00
Maine Lighthouse, 1971 .... 27.00
Maine Lobster, 1970 .... 24.00
Maine Potato, 1973 .... 10.00
Man O'War, Horse, 1969 ....*Illus* 18.00
Masonic, Fez, 1976 .... 10.00
Max The Hat Zimmerman, 1976 .... 28.00
Missouri Mule, 1972 .... 13.00
New Hampshire, Old Man Of The Mountain, 1970 .... 12.00
New Hampshire, Statehouse, 1969 .... 11.00
North Carolina Bicentennial, 1975 .... 12.00
Nugget Classic, 1970 .... 12.00 to 30.00
Nugget Gold Rooster, No. 1, 1969 .... 24.00 to 40.00
Oil Gusher, 1969 .... 10.00
Old Ez Owl, No. 1, Barn Owl, 1977 .... 25.00
Old Ez Owl, No. 2, Eagle, 1978 .... 55.00
Old Ez Owl, No. 3, Snowy, 1979 .... 31.00
Old Ez Owl, No. 4, Scops, 1980 .... 22.00
Old Ez Owl, No. 5, Great Gray, 1982 .... 30.00
Panda, 1972 .... 17.00
Penguin, 1973 .... 12.00
Penny-Farthington Bike, 1973 .... 12.00
Phoenix Bird, 1971 .... 24.00

Phonograph, 1970 ....22.00 to 25.00
Pirate, 1971... 10.00
Pistol, Made In Japan, 1968 .... 40.00
Political, Democratic & Republican Conventions, 1976, Pair.................... 28.00
Potbelly Stove, 1968... 10.00
Quail, California, 1970 .... 12.00
Raccoon, 1978 .... 42.00
Ram, 1973 .... 18.00
Razorback Hog, Arizona, 1979 ....20.00 to 35.00
Reno Arch, 1969... 11.00
Saddle, Silver, 1973... 25.00
Sailfish, 1971 .... 12.00
Salmon, Washington, 1971 .... 27.00
San Francisco, Cable Car, Gray, Green, Brown, 1968 .... 9.00
Sea Captain, 1971 .... 14.00
Seal, Gold, 1972.. 10.00
Senator, 1972.. 10.00
Setter, 1974 .... 16.00
Shark, White, 1977 .... 13.00
Shriner, Clown, 1978... 15.00
Shriner, Golden Pharaoh, 1981... 26.00
Shriner, King Tut Tomb Guard, 1979 .... 22.00
Shriner, Sphinx, 1980 .... 12.00
Silver Spur, 1971.. 16.00
Ski Boot, 1972 .... 12.00
Slot Machine, Liberty Bell, 1971 .... 20.00
Snow Egret, 1981.. 20.00
Snow Leopard, 1980.. 32.00
Snowmobile, 1972 ....*Illus* 16.00
South Dakota Air National Guard, 1976... 22.00
Spirit Of '76, Drummer, 1974... 10.00
Spirit Of St. Louis, 1977 .... 12.00
Stagecoach, 1969... 13.00
Stan Laurel, 1976...*Illus* 22.00
Statehouse, 1971... 41.00
Stonewall Jackson, 1974... 26.00
Strongman, 1974 .... 25.00
Tank, Military, 1972... 36.00
Tecumseh, 1969... 10.00
Telephone, 1971 .... 16.00
Tennis Player, 1973... 14.00
Terrapin, Maryland, 1974 .... 16.00
Ticker Tape, 1970.. 8.00

Ezra Brooks, Stan Laurel, 1976

Ezra Brooks, Man O'War, Horse, 1969

Ezra Brooks, Snowmobile, 1972

Ezra Brooks, Tiger, Bengal, 1979

Tiger, Bengal, 1979 ....*Illus*   27.00
Tiger, On Stadium, 1973 ....   16.00
Tonapah, 1972 ....   15.00
Totem Pole, No. 1, 1972 ....   12.00
Totem Pole, No. 2, 1973 ....   15.00
Tractor, Fordson, 1971 ....20.00 to 24.00
Train, Casey Jones Locomotive, 1980 ....   20.00
Train, Iron Horse Engine, 1970 ....   9.00
Trojan, Horse, 1974 ....   18.00
Trojan, USC, 1973 ....   24.00
Trout & Fly, 1970 ....   12.00
Truckin' An' Vannin', 1977 ....   11.00
Turkey, White, 1971 ....   26.00
Vermont Skier, 1973 ....   14.00
VFW, Blue, 75th Anniversary, 1973 ....   10.00
VFW, Cobalt Blue, Red, White & Gold, No. 185, 1973 ....   75.00
Virginia, Cardinal, 1973 ....   17.00
Virginia Mountain Lady, 1972 ....   20.00
Walgreen Drugs, 1974 ....   34.00
Water Tower, Chicago, 1969 ....   12.00
Weirton Steel, 1974 ....   18.00
West Virginia Mountain Man, 1971 ....   62.00
Whale, 1973 ....   21.00
Wheat Shocker, Kansas, 1971 ....   8.00
Whooping Crane, 1982 ....   19.00
Wichita Centennial, 1970 ....   10.00
William Penn, 1981 ....   66.00
Winston Churchill, 1969 ....   9.00
Zimmerman Top Hat, 1968 ....   10.00

――――――――――――――――――――――――― FAMOUS FIRSTS ―――――――――――――――――――――――――

Famous Firsts Ltd. of Port Chester, New York, was owned by Richard E. Magid. The first figural bottles, issued in 1968, were a series of race cars. The last figurals were made in 1985.

FAMOUS FIRSTS, Animals, Mother & Baby, 1981, Miniature 220.00
    Balloon, 1971 ....   34.00
    Bell, Alpine, 1970 ....   18.00
    Bell, St. Pol, 1970 ....   22.00
    Bennie Bowwow, 1973 ....   16.00
    Bersaglieri, 1969 ....   34.00
    Bucky Badger Mascot 12.00
    Bugatti Royale, 1930-1973 ....   340.00
    Butterfly, 1971 ....   22.00
    Cable Car, 1973 ....   50.00
    Centurian, 1969 ....   40.00
    China Clipper, 1979 ....   130.00
    Circus Lion, 1979 ....   25.00

Circus Tiger, 1979 .... 25.00
Corvette Stingray, 1953 Model, 1975 ....*Illus* 109.00
Corvette Stingray, 1963 Model, 1977 .... 106.00
Dino Ferarri, Red, 1983 .... 51.00
Dino Ferarri, White, 1975 .... 31.00
Don Sympatico, 1973 .... 18.00
Duesenberg, 1980 .... 102.00
Duesenberg, 50th Anniversary, Red, 1982 .... 280.00
Egg House, 1975 .... 16.00
Fireman, 1980 .... 73.00
Fireman, 1981 .... 73.00
Garibaldi, 1969 .... 37.00
Golfer, He, 1973 .... 34.00
Golfer, She, 1973 .... 34.00
Hen, Filamena, 1973 .... 22.00
Hippo, Baby, 1980 .... 60.00
Honda Motorcycle, 1975 .... 71.00
Hurdy Gurdy, 1971 .... 18.00
Indy Racer, No. 11, 1971 .... 18.00
Liberty Bell, 1976, Miniature ....*Illus* 9.00
Lockheed Transport, Jungle, 1982 .... 63.00
Lockheed Transport, Marine Gray, 1982 .... 81.00
Lockheed Transport, USAF Rescue, 1982 .... 82.00
Locomotive, Clinton, 1969 .... 26.00
Lotus, Racer, No. 2, 1971 .... 112.00
Marmon Wasp, No. 32, 1968 .... 76.00
Marmon Wasp, No. 32, Gold, 1/2 Pt., 1971 .... 30.00
Minnie Meow, 1973 .... 18.00
Mustang, P-51-D, Fighter Plane, 1974 ....*Illus* 122.00
Napoleon, 1969 .... 24.00
Natchez Riverboat, 1975 .... 47.00
National Racer, No. 8, 1972 ....*Illus* 76.00
Panda, Baby, 1981 .... 86.00
Pepper Mill, 1978 .... 20.00
Phonograph, 1969 .... 48.00
Porsche Targa, 1979 .... 65.00

*Famous Firsts, Corvette
Stingray, 1953 Model, 1975*

*Famous Firsts, Mustang,
P-51-D, Fighter Plane, 1974*

*Famous Firsts, National
Racer, No. 8, 1972*

*Famous Firsts, Liberty
Bell, 1976, Miniature*

*Famous Firsts, Telephone,
French, 1973*

Renault Racer, No. 3, 1969	77.00
Riverboat, Robert E. Lee, 1971	77.00
Rooster, Ricardo, 1973	18.00
Roulette Wheel, 1972	22.00
Scale, Lombardy, 1970	22.00
Sewing Machine, 1979, 200 Ml.	32.00
Ship, Sea Witch, 1976	79.00
Ship, Sea Witch, 1980, 200 Ml.	32.00
Skier, He, 1973	20.00
Skier, She, 1973	21.00
Spirit Of St. Louis, 1969	132.00
Spirit Of St. Louis, 1972, Miniature	84.00
Spirit Of St. Louis, Golden, 1977	99.00
Stamps, 1847, 1980	26.00
Swiss Chalet, 1974	32.00
Telephone, Floral, 1973	25.00
Telephone, French, 1969	63.00
Telephone, French, 1973 ....*Illus*	63.00
Telephone, Johnny Reb, 1973	24.00
Telephone, Yankee Doodle, 1973	28.00
Tennis, He, 1973	27.00
Tennis, She, 1973	27.00
Warriors, 1979, Miniature	26.00
Winnie Mae, Airplane, 1972	112.00
Winnie Mae, Airplane, 1972, Miniature	66.00
Yacht America, 1970, 24 In.	33.00
Yacht America, 1978	31.00

--------------------------------- **FIGURAL** ---------------------------------

Figural bottles are specially named by the collectors of bottles. Any bottle that is of a recognizable shape, such as a human head, a pretzel, or a clock, is considered to be a figural. There are no restrictions as to date or material. A *Soaky* is a special plastic bottle that holds shampoo, bubble bath, or another type of bath product. Figurals are also listed by brand name or type in other sections of this book. More figural bottles may be listed in the Bitters, Cologne, Perfume, and Pottery categories.

FIGURAL, 3 Children, Holding Globe, France	100.00
Alligator, Standing, Tooled Lip, Clear, 10 In.	660.00
Ballon Captif, 1878, Hot Air Balloon, Suspended, Dense Cobalt Blue, 8 3/4 In.	7150.00
Banjo, Amethyst, 9 In.	40.00
Banjo, Yellow Olive Green, Monogram MFJ, 8 In.	30.00
Barrel, Rooster, A Merry Christmas, Happy New Year, Amber, 1/2 Pt.	303.00
Barrel, Yellow Topaz, Straight Sided, 10 Rings, Top & Base, 10 1/2 In.	135.00
Basket Decanter, Tooled Lip, Clear, 1885-1900, 6 1/4 In.	144.00
Bather, On The Rocks, Tooled Mouth, Clear, 11 5/8 In.	60.00
Bear, Kummel, Black Amethyst, Tooled Lip, c.1900, 11 In.	55.00
Bear, Kummel, Milk Glass, Applied Face	650.00
Bell, Advertising, Gayner Glass Works, Salem, N.J., Clear, 6 1/4 In.	143.00
Bell, Melvale Pure Rye, Clear, Cut Glass, Bar, Qt.	59.00
Big Ben Tower, Clear, Ground Lip, 9 3/8 x 2 In.	27.00
Binoculars, Clear, Original Cap, Whiskey, ABM	12.00
Book, Coming Thro' The Rye, Pottery, Blue Glaze, 1880, 5 x 3 1/2 x 1 3/4 In.	220.00
Boot, Woman's, Clear, BIM, 12 In.	30.00
Buddha, Cobalt Blue, Milk Glass Head, Ground Stopper	350.00
Building, Home Of Schenley, Original Cap, ABM, 12 1/4 In.	10.00
Bust, Military Figure, Embossed, Alleroe Calliano 1897, 12 In.	24.00
Bust Of George Washington, Aqua, 1930-1950, 10 1/2 In.	27.50
Bust Of Louis Adolphe Thier, Tooled Lip, Pontil, 11 In.	165.00
Cabin, Smokin', Alfred Andersen & Co., Amber, Square Collar Lip, 7 In.	231.00
Cannon, JT Gayen Whiskey, Amber, 14 In.	880.00
Cat, Sitting, 11 1/2 In. ....*Illus*	45.00
Cherub, Holding Medallion, Emerald Green, Stopper, 1910, 11 In.	193.00
Cherub, Holding Medallion, Emerald Green, Stopper, 1890, 11 In. ....*Illus*	193.00

*Figural, Cat, Sitting,
11 1/2 In.*

*Figural, Cherub, Holding
Medallion, Emerald Green,
Stopper, 1890, 11 In.*

*Figural, Coachman, Pottery,
Tan, Brown Glaze,
1840-1860, 10 3/4 In*

Cherub, Holding Medallion, Purple Amethyst, Stopper, 1910, 11 In............................. 198.00
Cherub, Holding Medallion, Milk Glass, Stopper, 11 In.. 104.00
Children, Climbing Tree, Clear, ABM, 14 1/2 In. 18.00
Chinaman, Boot Blacking Bottle, Amber, Ground Lip, 4 3/8 In. 198.00
Chinese Man, Sitting Cross Legged, On Barrel, Cobalt Blue, Metal Stopper, 5 5/8 In... 3575.00
Christmas Tree, Embossed Branches, Multicolored Painting, Signed S.I.V., 11 In. 180.00
Claw On Globe, Creme De Menthe, Deep Emerald Green, 5 In................................... 35.00
Claw On Globe, Creme De Menthe, Topaz, Enameled Letters, 11 In............................ 25.00
Clock, Pumpkin Seed, 1/2 Pt. 45.00
Clown, Removable Head, Yellow, 16 In.. 55.00
Coachman, Brown & Yellow Rockingham Glaze, Bennington, 1849, 10 1/2 In. 797.00
Coachman, Pottery, Tan, Brown Glaze, 1840-1860, 10 3/4 In. ....*Illus* 220.00
Coachman, Van Dunck, 8 1/2 In...*Illus* 85.00
Continental Soldier, Old Continental Whiskey, Deep Yellow, 1860s, Rectangular....... 1430.00
Crab, Yellow Green, Pontil, Tooled Lip, Embossed Deponirt, c.1920, 8 1/8 In. 275.00
Crying Baby, T.P.S. & Co., New York, Pat. June 2nd, 1874, 6 1/8 In. ....40.00 to 85.00
Cucumber, Medium Sapphire Blue, 10 Ribs, American, 1900s, 7 3/4 In........................ 77.00
Dachshund, Whiskey, Opalescent Glass, Italy, 18 In.. 90.00
Decanter, Ear Of Corn, Lime Green, Gold Paint, Tooled Lip, Ear Of Corn Stopper, 9 In. 137.00
Duck, Atterbury, Milk Glass, Ground Mouth, 11 5/8 In... 357.00
Dutchman's Pipe, Amber Stem, 6 In. 57.00
Eiffel Tower, Clear, c.1890, 13 3/4 In. 45.00
Elephant ....*Illus* 10.00
Elephant, Seated On Drum, Ground, Polished Lip, Clear, 9 3/4 In............................... 578.00
Fat Dutchman, Milk Glass, Ground Mouth, 10 In.. 930.00
Fat Man, Van Dunck's Genever Whiskey, Amber, 1885, 8 1/2 In................................. 77.00
Fish, White & Blue Paint, Clear Glass, Metal Screw Cap, 8 3/4 In. 88.00
Geo. Washington, Cobalt Blue, Label, Cork Closure, 10 In.. 95.00
George Washington, Amethyst, Wheaton, Reproduction.. 10.00
Globe, America, Africa, Europe, Asia, Aqua, Burst Top Lip, Europe, 1880, 3 In. 176.00
Globe, J. Raynald The World, Aqua, Round Collar, 1870, 2 3/8 In.............................. 330.00
Grandfather Clock, Milk Glass, Original Paint.. 125.00
Grandfather Clock, Tooled Lip, Candleholder Stopper, 12 1/4 In. 165.00
Grant's Tomb, Milk Glass, Pewter Cap, 10 In... 350.00
Grape Clusters & Leaves, Imperial Levee, Golden Amber, Applied Ring Lip, IP, 9 1/2 In. 2750.00
Greek God Face, Rectangular, Pontil, 9 7/8 In. 55.00
Guitar, Screw Cap, 5 x 2 3/4 In. 30.00
Gun, Colonial Bar, Pewter Screw Cap, 1900, 10 1/4 In. 1760.00
Hamm's, Bartender Bear, 1973 .... 135.00
Hand Holding Bottle, Cobalt Blue, Pontil, Europe, 1860, 9 1/2 In................................ 1100.00
Hand Holding Bottle, Medium Yellow Amber, 7 1/8 In. 176.00
Hot Air Balloon, Pumpkin Seed, Embossed, The A. Colburn Co., Screw Cap............... 38.00

Figural, Coachman,   Figural, Elephant   Figural, Negro Waiter, Black
Van Dunck, 8 1/2 In.   Head, Clear, 12 In.

Indian Queen, see Bitters, Brown's Celebrated
Jester & Clown, Lamp Pole Between Them, Clear & Frosted, OP 250.00
Joan Of Arc, Broken Sword, Amber, OP 425.00
Joan Of Arc, Clear, Broken Sword, OP 165.00
Joan Of Arc, Full Sword & Armor, Green 425.00
John Bull, Big Bill, Amber, Tooled Lip, 11 1/2 In. 220.00
Klondike, Nugget Form, Milk Glass, Metal Screw Cap, 1880-1900, 6 In. 44.00
Lady's Leg Cocktail Shaker, Chrome High Heel Shoe, Screw On Cap, 15 1/4 In. 72.00
Lantern, Amber, Metal Case, Late 19th Century, 6 In. 143.00
Liberty Bell, Proclaim Liberty Throughout All The Land, Aqua, Tooled Lip, 8 3/4 In. . 220.00
Life Preserver, Flask, Embossed Stars & Roping, 1/2 Pt. 100.00
Life Preserver, Flask, Merry Christmas & Happy New Year, No Cap, 1/2 Pt. 245.00
Man, Smoking Pipe, Amber, Germany, 1890, 11 1/2 In. 825.00
Man, Standing, Smoking Pipe, Amber Variant, 11 1/2 In. 700.00
Megaphone, Deep Citron, Teardrop Stopper, Refired Pontil, Bubbles, 11 In. 40.00
Mennon Hard Hat, Smiling Man, Orange Hard Hat, Clear, c.1950, 3 x 3 x 9 In. 15.00
Mermaid, Brown, Tan Rockingham Glaze, Flask, England, 1850-1880, 8 1/4 In. 187.00
Monkey, Chestnuts, Embossed Monkey, Woman's Buttocks On Reverse, 5 In. 60.00
Monument, Clear, Amethystine Tint, Sheared Collar, 9 3/4 In. 880.00
Monument, Milk Glass, c.1870-1880, 10 In. 632.50
Moses, Poland Water, Blue Aqua, Applied Tapered Collar, Qt. 115.00
Negro Waiter, Black Head, Clear, 12 In. ....*Illus* 150.00
Negro Waiter, Pink Milk Glass Head, 14 1/4 In. 72.00
Nugget Pocket, Milk Glass, Ground Lip, Metal Screw Cap, 5 7/8 In. 78.00
Octopus, Flask, Pocket, Gold, Original Red Paint, 1901, 4 3/8 In. 495.00
Oil Derrick, Bowen's Genuine Crude Oil Hair Grower, Label, Contents 50.00
Old Crow Kentucky Straight Bourbon, Ceramic, Royal Doulton, 12 1/2 In. 155.00
Pig, Anna Pottery, Latest & Only Reliable Railroad & River Guide, 1884, 6 1/2 In. 1650.00
Pig, Dark Brown Glaze, Gray, 7 5/8 In. 633.00
Pig, Drink While It Lasts From This Hog's ..., Bubbles, Clear, 6 3/4 In. 120.00
Pig, Good Old Bourbon In A Hog's, Yellow Amber, 6 5/8 In. 225.00
Pig, Good Old Bourbon In A Hog's ..., Amber, Tooled Lip, 6 1/2 In. 264.00
Pig, Pink Tone, Something Good In A Hog's, Hand Points To Mouth, 4 1/2 In. 100.00
Pig, Pottery, Orange Brown Mottled Glaze, Dicky Clay Co., 6 1/2 In. 358.00
Pig, Pottery, Railroad, Brown Albany Slip Glaze, 8 In. 1980.00
Pig, Pottery, Yellow Brown Glaze, Camark, 1900s, 9 In. 200.00
Pig, Standing On Hind Legs, 9 In. 50.00
Pig, White, Black Spots, Stoneware, Limaville, Oh., 1880 .... 1400.00
Pineapple, Amber, 9 1/8 In. 93.50
Pineapple, Yellow Amber, 9 1/8 In. 176.00
Pipe, Flask, Clear, Amber Mouthpiece, 6 In. 45.00
Pistol, C.P.P. Co., Amber, Fancy Handle 80.00
Pistol, Purple Amethyst, 7 3/4 In. 275.00
Pistol, Sapphire, Turquoise Blue, 10 In. 550.00

Polar Bear, Milk Glass, 4 In. 220.00
Policemen, Cobalt Blue, Billy Club Stopper.. 300.00
Portly Woman, Long Dress, Umbrella, 8 1/2 In. 522.50
Pretzel, Pottery, Flask... 65.00
Rebecca At The Well, Clear & Frosted, OP, 7 3/4 In. 95.00
Revolver, Ground Threaded Mouth, 4 3/4 In. 15.00
Santa, Ruby Red, Frosted 75.00
Santa Claus, German Perfume 50.00
Santa With Tree, Tooled Mouth, 1890-1910, 7 3/8 In. 633.00
Shoe, Tripple Extract, Upper Ten, 3 In. ....*Illus* 25.00
Skeleton, Porcelain, Tan & White, Glazed, Stopper, 1920 .... 60.00
Skeleton In Cape, Word Spirits, Brown & White Bisque, Glazed, Stopper, 8 In. 170.00
Smelling Salts, Bullet Shape, Cobalt Blue, 3 7/8 In. 110.00
Soaky, Alvin Chipmunk 15.00
Soaky, Bambi, 1960s 23.00
Soaky, Bozo 15.00
Soaky, Bullwinkle, No Clothes... 40.00
Soaky, Casper The Friendly Ghost... 25.00
Soaky, Chipmunks, Alvin, Simon, Theodore, 3 Piece 65.00
Soaky, Creature From The Black Lagoon.. 85.00
Soaky, Deputy Dawg.. 20.00
Soaky, Dick Tracy, 1960s ....45.00 to 80.00
Soaky, Donald Duck... 18.00
Soaky, Felix The Cat.. 35.00
Soaky, Frankenstein, 1960s...70.00 to 75.00
Soaky, Lippy The Lion... 45.00
Soaky, Mighty Mouse 33.00
Soaky, Mr. Magoo, 1960s 54.00
Soaky, Porky Pig.. 15.00
Soaky, Pumpkin Puss, Purex, 1960s.. 45.00
Soaky, Rocky The Squirrel.. 30.00
Soaky, Rocky, 1960s 40.00
Soaky, Snow White, Movable Arms 20.00
Soaky, Spouty Whale, Unused 8.00
Soaky, Tweety, 1960s 30.00
Soaky, Wolfman, Blue Pants, 1963 ....85.00 to 90.00
Soaky, Woody Woodpecker 18.00
Soaky, Yoda, Star Wars 10.00
Statue Of Liberty, Milk Glass, 9 1/4 In. 100.00
Theodore Roosevelt, Clear.. 45.00
Victorian Lady, Winter Clothes, 6 1/2 In. 40.00
Violin, Amber, 7 1/2 In. 10.00
Violin, Cocoa Nut Oil, C. Toppan, Aqua, Fluted Sides, IP, 7 1/2 In. 125.00
Violin, Dark Purple, Whittled, Hanger, Pontil, 9 3/4 In. 85.00

Figural, Shoe, Tripple Extract,
Upper Ten, 3 In.

Figural, Woman's
Face, Jug, Old
Plantation
Distilling Co.,
Souvenir, Sunny
California

Violin, Green, 7 1/2 In.	7.50
Violin, Green, Music Notes, 10 In.	35.00
Violin, Light Blue, Music Notes, 10 In.	35.00
Violin, Light Green, 7 1/4 In.	33.00
Violin, Medium Amber, 7 7/8 In.	33.00
Warship, Green Aqua, Tooled Lip, c.1925, 13 5/8 In.	357.00
Whisk Broom, Flask, Pt.	16.50
Whiskey Barrel, Horizontal, Long Neck, Embossed, Grace & Ducan, N.Y., Aqua	55.00
Windmill, Threaded Cap, National Wholesale Liquor Co., Baltimore, Md., ABM	18.00
Woman, Nude, Milk Glass Case, 16 In.	325.00
Woman, On Head, On Ball, 16 1/2 In.	35.00
Woman, Seated, On Wicker Basket, Tolled, Flared Lip, Pontil, 8 1/2 In.	88.00
Woman, Standing, Alsace D.D. Depose, Blue Milk Glass, Crown Stopper, 1890s, 13 In.	385.00
Woman's Face, Jug, Old Plantation Distilling Co., Souvenir, Sunny California.....*Illus*	357.00

FIRE GRENADE

Fire grenades were popular from about 1870 to 1910. They were glass containers filled with a fire extinguisher such as carbon tetrachloride. The bottle of liquid was thrown at the base of a fire to shatter and extinguish the flames. A particularly ingenious *automatic* type was hung in a wire rack; theoretically, the heat of the fire would melt the solder of the rack and the glass grenade would drop into the fire. Because they were designed to be destroyed, not too many have survived for the collector. Some are found today that still have the original contents sealed by cork and wax closures. Handle these with care. Fumes from the contents are dangerous to your health.

FIRE GRENADE, American Fire Extinguisher, Railroad, Deep Yellow Green, 4 1/2 In.	425.00
American Fire Extinguisher Co., Hand, Clear, Tooled Lip, c.1890, 6 In., Pt.	1210.00
Bardinet, Bordeaux, Amber, 4 In. ....*Illus*	25.00
Barnum's Hand Fire Ext. Diamond, Yellow Amber, 6 In.	330.00
Diamond Fire Extinguisher, Pat'd June 29th 1869, Aqua, 6 In., Pt.	1210.00
Extincteur Protector, Cobalt Blue, Ground Lip, 5 3/4 In.	1073.00
Firex, Cobalt Blue, 4 In.	65.00
Firex, Cobalt Blue, Ground Lip, 3 3/4 In.	45.00
Firex, Turquoise Blue, Tooled Lip, 5 1/2 In.	550.00
Harden, Star In Star, Turquoise Blue, Contents, Qt.	165.00
Harden Hand, Star, Yellow Green, c.1885, 6 1/2 In., Pt.	742.50
Harden's, Star, Tubular, Clear, Embossed Star, 16 7/8 In.	253.00
Harden's Hand, Clear, Aqua, 6 1/2 In.	110.00
Harden's Hand, Cobalt Blue, Ground Lip, 6 5/8 In.	176.00
Harden's Hand, Fire Extinguisher, Bulbous, Turquoise Blue, Footed, 6 In.	66.00

Fire Grenade, Bardinet,
Bordeaux, Amber, 4 In.

Fire Grenade, Harden's Hand, Star,
Deep Turquoise, Contents, 1885-1895, 8 In.

*Fire Grenade, Hayward's
Hand, Cobalt Blue, 1890, 6 In.*

*Fire Grenade, Hayward's Hand,
Yellow Amber, Pat. Aug. 8, 1871, 6 1/8 In.*

Harden's Hand, Medium Amber, 6 5/8 In.	1155.00
Harden's Hand, Medium Cobalt Blue, Footed Base, 1871-1875, 4 3/4 In.	88.00 to 99.00
Harden's Hand, Pat. No. 1, Aug. 8, 1871, Turquoise Blue, Contents, Pt.	198.00
Harden's Hand, Quilted, Footed, Sapphire Blue, 1880-1900, 4 1/2 In.	209.00
Harden's Hand, Star In Circle, Turquoise, 1885-1895, 6 5/8 In.	210.00
Harden's Hand, Star, Clear, Vertical Rib Pattern, Ground Lip, 6 7/8 In.	1018.00
Harden's Hand, Star, Deep Cobalt Blue, 1885-1895, Pt., 6 5/8 In.	198.00
Harden's Hand, Star, Deep Cobalt Blue, 6 1/2 In.	90.00
Harden's Hand, Star, Deep Turquoise, Contents, 1885-1895, 8 In. .....*Illus*	165.00
Harden's Hand, Star, Embossed, Cobalt Blue, c.1900, 6 3/4 In.	231.00
Harden's Hand, Star, Medium Cobalt Blue, Ground Lip, 6 1/2 In.	188.00
Harden's Hand, Star, Medium Turquoise Blue, Qt.	93.50
Harden's Hand, Star, Yellow Green, May 27, 84, 7 7/8 In.	203.00
Harden's Star, Amber, Contents, Qt.	239.00
Harden's Star, Cobalt Blue	150.00
Hayward, Clear, Design H Pat., 1880-1890, Pt., 5 7/8 In.	77.00
Hayward's Hand, Aqua, Qt.	110.00
Hayward's Hand, Aqua, Vertical Pleats, 6 In.	130.00
Hayward's Hand, Clear, Aug. 8, 1871, Pt., 6 1/8 In.	110.00
Hayward's Hand, Clear, Pat. Aug. 8, 1871, 6 In.	253.00
Hayward's Hand, Cobalt Blue, 1890, 6 In. .....*Illus*	231.00
Hayward's Hand, Cobalt Blue, Pat. Aug. 8, 1871, Pt.	275.00
Hayward's Hand, Light Yellow, Lime Green, Pt., 6 1/8 In.	203.50
Hayward's Hand, Turquoise, Pat. Aug. 8, 1871, Pt.	330.00
Hayward's Hand, Yellow Amber, Pat. Aug. 8, 1871, 6 1/8 In. .....*Illus*	132.00
Hayward's Hand, Yellow Olive, Pat. Aug. 8, 1871, 6 In.	121.00
Healy's Hand, Yellow Olive Tone, Bubbles, 1880-1890, Qt., 10 3/4 In.	963.00
Heathmans, Swift, Pink Gasoline Puce, England, c.1885, Pt.	798.00
Horizontal Rib, Deep Sapphire Blue, Bubbles, 1875-1890, 6 In.	110.00
Imperial, Medium Green, Ground Lip, England, c.1890, 6 5/8 In.	182.00
Imperial, Pale Green, Crown Within Buckled Belt	200.00
Kalamazoo, Medium Cobalt Blue, Qt.	275.00
Kalamazoo Automatic & Hand, Medium Cobalt Blue, Tooled Lip, 11 In.	232.00
Kalamazoo Rockford, Cobalt	400.00
L'Urbaine, Yellow, Amber Tone, France, c.1880-1900, 6 1/2 In.	825.00
Light Green, 7 In. .....*Illus*	285.00
London Fire Appliance Co., Yellow Olive, England, c.1885, Qt.	468.00
Magic Fire Extinguisher Co., Yellow Amber Tone, Ground Lip, 6 1/8 In.	495.00
Magic Fire Extinguisher Co., Yellow, c.1875-1885, Pt.	495.00
Merryweather, London, Root Beer Amber, Ground Lip, 6 1/2 In.	990.00
NHS, Monogram, Yellow Amber, Some Label & Contents, 7 In.	154.00
Rockford Automatic, Hand, Kalamazoo, Cobalt Blue, 11 In.	350.00 to 412.50
S.F. Hayward, Fire Bomb, Amber, 6 In. .....*Illus*	240.00

Fire Grenade,
Light Green, 7 In.

Fire Grenade, S.F. Hayward,
Fire Bomb, Amber, 6 In.

S.F. Hayward, Yellow Green, Diamond Panels, Globular, 1870, 6 1/4 In. 298.00
Systeme Labbe Paris, Medium Orange Amber, Pt., 5 5/8 In. 303.00
Vertical Rib, Turquoise Blue, Foil Neck Seal, Contents, England, c.1880, Pt. 605.00
FITZGERALD, see Old Fitzgerald

────────────────────────── **FLASK** ──────────────────────────

Flasks have been made in America since the eighteenth century. Hundreds of styles and variations were made. Free-blown, mold-blown, and decorated flasks are all popular with collectors. Prices are determined by rarity, condition, and color. In general, bright colors bring higher prices. The numbers used in the entries in the form McK G I-000 refer to the book *American Bottles and Flasks* by Helen McKearin and Kenneth M. Wilson. Each flask listed in that book is sketched and described and it is important to compare your flask with the book picture to determine value, since many similar flasks were made.

Many reproductions of flasks have been made, most in the last 20 years, but some as early as the nineteenth century. The reproduction flasks that seem to cause the most confusion for the beginner are the Lestoil flasks made in the 1960s. These bottles, sold in grocery stores, were filled with Lestoil, a liquid cleaner, and sold for about 65 cents. Three designs were made, a Washington Eagle, a Columbia Eagle, and a ship Franklin Eagle. Four colors were used—purple, dark blue, dark green, and amber—and mixes were also produced. Over one million of the flasks were made and they now are seen at the collectible shows. The only mark on the bottles was the name Lestoil on the stopper. Other reproductions will be found marked *Nuline* or *Taiwan.*

FLASK, 10 Diamond Pattern, Golden Amber, Sheared Mouth, Pontil, 5 In. 660.00
10 Diamond Pattern, Yellow, Olive Tone, 1825-1835, 1/2 Pt., 5 1/4 In. 357.00
12 Ribs, Swirled To Right, Aqua, Rolled Mouth, Pontil, 8 1/4 In. 132.00
14 Ribs, Swirled To Left, Bright Yellow Green, Midwest, OP, 4 In. 1265.00
16 Diamond, Teardrop Shape, Aqua, Pontil, 6 1/4 In. 100.00
16 Ribs, Ribbed & Swirled To Right, Blue Aqua, Applied Mouth, Pontil, 7 In. 121.00
16 Ribs, Swirled To Left, Aqua, Tooled Mouth, Pontil, 8 3/4 In. 110.00
16 Ribs, Swirled To Left, Pale Blue Green, Applied Mouth, Pontil, 9 In. 121.00
16 Ribs, Swirled To Right, Pale Green, Round Collared Mouth, Pontil, 7 1/2 In. 121.00
16 Ribs, Swirled To Right, Sapphire Blue, Pontil, 3 In. 231.00
16 Ribs, Vertical, Amethyst, Sheared Lip, Pontil, 6 3/8 In. 688.00
16 Ribs, Vertical , Pale Blue Green, Rolled Mouth, Pontil, 8 In. 198.00
16 Ribs, Vertical, Sapphire Blue, Flared Lip, Pontil, 4 7/8 In. 1265.00
18 Ribs, Ribbed & Swirled To Right, Green Aqua, Rolled Mouth, Pontil, 6 7/8 In. 550.00
18 Ribs, Swirled To Right, Teardrop Form, Cobalt Blue, Midwest, Pontil, 6 1/2 In. 264.00
18 Ribs, Vertical, Light Amethyst, Sheared Mouth, Midwest, Pontil, 7 In. 1100.00

20 Ribs, Vertical, Keene, N.H., Olive Amber, Applied Mouth, Pontil, Pt. 2310.00
24 Ribs, Swirled To Left, Aqua, Midwest, Pontil, 8 In. 99.00
24 Ribs, Swirled To Left, Aqua, Pontil, 7 3/4 In. 121.00
24 Ribs, Swirled To Left, Aqua, Pontil, Midwest, 6 7/8 In. 121.00
24 Ribs, Swirled To Left, Deep Brown Amber, Midwest, OP, 5 1/2 In. 523.00
24 Ribs, Swirled To Left, Globular, Golden Amber, Pontil, 7 5/8 In. 440.00
24 Ribs, Swirled To Left, Golden Amber, Midwest, Pontil, 5 1/4 In. 220.00
24 Ribs, Swirled To Left, Golden Amber, Pontil, 4 7/8 In. 253.00
24 Ribs, Swirled To Left, Golden Amber, Red Tone, Rolled Mouth, Pontil, 8 In. 275.00
24 Ribs, Swirled To Left, Golden Amber, Rolled Mouth, Pontil, 7 7/8 In. 715.00
24 Ribs, Swirled To Left, Pale Blue Green, Rolled Mouth, Pontil, 7 1/8 In. 242.00
24 Ribs, Swirled To Left, Puce, Midwest, Pontil, 7 3/4 In. 363.00
24 Ribs, Swirled To Left, Yellow Amber, Olive Tone, Pontil, 8 3/4 In. 440.00
24 Ribs, Swirled To Left, Yellow Olive, Rolled Mouth, Pontil, 7 7/8 In. 935.00
24 Ribs, Swirled To Right, Golden Amber, Midwest, Pontil, 8 1/4 In. 385.00
24 Ribs, Vertical, Golden Amber, Midwest, Pontil, 4 7/8 In. .... 132.00 to 176.00
24 Ribs, Vertical, Olive Yellow Green, Midwest, Pontil, Early 19th Century 275.00
26 Ribs, Swirled To Right, Aqua, Applied Mouth, Pontil, 7 1/2 In. 132.00
Admiral Dewey, Eagles & Flags, Canteen Form, Label Under Glass, Pocket, 1/2 Pt. 275.00
B.P. & B, Scroll, Pontil, 5 7/8 In. 346.00
Berges & Garrissere Wholesale Wines & Liquor, Salinas City, Pt. 35.00
Bird On A Branch, Label Under Glass, Metal Screw Cap, Pocket, 4 In. 220.00
Bishop Holding A Staff, Cobalt Blue, Continental, 3-Piece Mold, OP, 4 3/4 In. 467.50
Brandes Bros., New York, Amber, Strap, 1/2 Pt. 17.00
C.P. Moorman, S.F. Coffin, Yellow Amber, c.1872-1880 .... 400.00
Calabash, Aqua, Applied Mouth, Pontil, 7 3/4 In. 187.00
Chestnut, 10 Diamond, Amber, 4 3/4 In. 3410.00
Chestnut, 10 Diamond, Amber, 4 5/8 In. 1210.00
Chestnut, 15 Diamond, Pontil, 5 In. 165.00
Chestnut, 16 Ribs, Medium Purple Amethyst, 6 1/2 In. 187.00
Chestnut, 18 Ribs, Pale Green, Midwest, Pontil, 7 In, Pt. 126.00
Chestnut, 18 Ribs, Pale Green, Swirl, Midwest, Pontil, 6 3/8 In. 165.00
Chestnut, 24 Ribs, Swirled To Right, Golden Amber, Handle, 1845-1860, 8 1/4 In. 660.00
Chestnut, Deep Cobalt Blue, 6 5/8 In. 82.50
Chestnut, Deep Forest Green, Pontil, New England, c.1830, 8 1/4 In. 121.00
Chestnut, Flat, Medium Yellow Olive Amber, 9 3/4 In. 159.50
Chestnut, Green Aqua, Rolled Lip, OP, 1780-1810, 5 1/2 In. 73.00
Chestnut, Medium Amber, Flattened, Handle, 7 1/2 In. 62.00
Chestnut, Medium Yellow Green, Pontil, Applied String Mouth, 9 3/4 In. 132.00
Chestnut, Medium Yellow Olive, Pontil, 1780-1810, 5 1/8 In. 104.00
Chestnut, Olive Green, New England, OP, 10 1/2 In. 45.00
Chestnut, Painted Floral Design, Yellow Olive Green, 5 In. 120.00
Chestnut, Yellow Olive, Pontil, 8 1/4 In. 142.00
Chestnut, Yellow Olive, Pontil, New England, c.1830, 9 5/8 In. 187.00
Chestnut, Yellow, Amber Tone, OP, 1780-1810, 6 1/2 In. 149.00
Cluster Of Acorns, Leaves, Coat Of Arms, Cobalt Blue, OP, 1/2 Pt. 121.00
Cluster Of Grapes, Standing Lion, Ca., Deep Cobalt Blue, Pontil, Continental, 1/2 Pt.. 132.00
Cobalt Blue, 12 Vertical Ribs, Blown, Pontil, 1/4 Pt. 220.00
Cobalt Blue, 26 Horizontal Ribs, Blown, Sheared Lip, Pontil, 1/2 Pt. 413.00
D.H. Barry, Martinsburg, W.Va., Coffin, Round Slug Plate, 1/2 Pt. 30.00
D.H. Seem, Bangor, Pa., Aqua, Strap, Pt. 35.00
Dr. H.C. Porter & Son Druggists, Towanda, Pa., Amber, Pt. 25.00
Drunk Against Lamppost, Dog, Wire Loop Cork, Pumpkinseed 425.00
E. Son & H., Coffin, Amber, Round Shoulder, 1/2 Pt. 60.00
Eagle Picture, Screw Cap Outer Shot Glass That Threads Onto Neck, Pumpkinseed 100.00
Early Morning, Clock & Star 30.00
Edward Oullahan, Pioneer Liquor House, Stockton, Cala., E In Diamond, 1/2 Pt. 160.00
End Of Day, White, Red & Green Flecks, Yellow & Green Overlay, Pontil, 1/2 Pt. 253.00
Expanded Diamond Design, Blown, Sheared Lip, Pontil, 5 In. 165.00
Fair View Works, Wheat Price & Co., Wheeling, Va., Aqua, Pontil, Pt., 6 In. 110.00
Farmville Dispensary, Farmville, Va., Strap Side, Pt. 30.00
Flowers Manufacturing Co., Greenville, Tenn., Shoofly, 1/2 Pt. 15.00
Forest Lawn, J.V.H., Olive Green, IP, 7 1/2 In. 330.00

Frey & Co., Aurora, Ill, Coffin, 1/2 Pt.. 30.00
G.A.R., 1861-1866 Veteran, Cloth Strap, Emblem 450.00
G.A.R., 29th National Encampment, 1895, Eagle Flag, Cannons, Metal Cap, 1/2 Pt....... 595.00
Gasoline Puce, OP, Pocket, c.1830, 5 1/8 In.. 1320.00
General Fitzhugh Lee, Hanley Bros. Wines & Liquors, Label Under Glass, 5 1/8 In.... 440.00
Geo. Eyssell Union Depot Drug Store, Kansas City, Mo., Shoofly, 1/2 Pt. 75.00
Geo. W. Robinson, W.Va., Aqua, Strap Side, Applied Top, Burst Bubble, Pt. 70.00
Globular, Folded Lip, Dark Amber, 11 1/2 In.. 385.00
Globular, Olive Green, Bulbous, Pontil, Cylindrical, New England, 2 1/2 In. 743.00
Goldberg, Bowen & Co., San Francisco, Coffin, Pt. 80.00
Golden Star, Sun Colored Amethyst.. 39.00
Goodale, Rochester, N.Y., Aqua, Pt. 28.00
GW Chesley, Sacramento, Cal., Pumpkinseed, Pt. ....90.00 to 100.00
H. Brickwedel, Golden Amber, Union Oval, Pt.. 400.00
H. Brickwedel, San Francisco, Yellow Amber, Pt. 425.00
Hand Made Sour Mash, 7 Yrs. Old, Pumpkin Seed, Clear.. 35.00
Henry Chapman & Co., Amber, Tear Drop, Label, Stopper... 190.00
Henry Chapman & Co., Montreal, Amber, Screw Threads Cap, Pocket 179.00
Henry Chapman & Co., Teardrop, Amber, Glass Stopper, Label, 5 3/4 In. 265.00
Henry McGee Family Liquor Store, Amber, Slug Plate, Qt. 65.00
Hildebrandt Posner & Co., Dark Amethyst, Monogram, 1/2 Pt. 300.00
Hoyt Brothers, Lynn, Mass., Pumpkinseed, Pt... 20.00
It's A Long Time Between Drinks, Playing Cards Face, Label Under Glass, 5 In......... 660.00
J.H. Cutter Portland, Amber, Resin Fill, Coffin, Pt... 500.00
J.J. Flanighan & Co., Scranton, Pa., Yellow-Amber, Strap, Pt....................................... 39.00
Kentucky Dew, J.W. Fletcher, Brunswick Bar, Cumberland, Md., 1/2 Pt. 19.00
Klondike Nugget, Milk Glass, Outside Threads, Ground Lip, Cap, Crude 49.00
Lilienthal & Co., San Francisco, Golden Amber, Union Oval Applied Top 250.00
Mallard Distilling Co., Baltimore & N.Y., Baby Bottle Shape, 6 1/4 In....................... 12.00
McCarty & Torreyson, Sunburst, Aqua, Pontil, 7 1/2 In. 907.00
McK G I-001, Washington & Eagle, Blue Green, Pontil, Pt. 1320.00
McK G I-001, Washington & Eagle, Pale Blue Green, Pontil, Pt............................*Illus* 935.00
McK G I-002, Washington & Eagle, Aqua, Pontil, Pt.. 231.00
McK G I-002, Washington & Eagle, Green Aqua, Pt... 357.50
McK G I-002, Washington & Eagle, Green Aqua, Pontil, Pt. ....204.00 to 357.00
McK G I-002, Washington & Eagle, Light Green, Pontil, Pt. 264.00
McK G I-002, Washington & Eagle, Pale Green, Pontil, Pt... 302.50
McK G I-002, Washington & Eagle, Pale Green, OP, Pt. 209.00
McK G I-003, Washington & Eagle, Aqua, Pontil, Pt.. 522.50
McK G I-005, Washington & Eagle, Green Aqua, Pontil, Pt. 4125.00
McK G I-006, Washington & Eagle, Amethystine Tint, Pontil, Pt.................................. 960.00
McK G I-006a, Washington & Eagle, Pale Lavender Tint, Pontil, Pt. 1760.00
McK G I-007, Washington & Eagle, Green Aqua, Pontil, Pt. ....330.00 to 1100.00

*Flask, McK G I-001, Washington &
Eagle, Pale Blue Green, Pontil, Pt.*

*Flask, McK G II-024, Double
Eagle, Medium Yellow, Pt.*

McK G I-008, Washington & Eagle, Green Aqua, Pontil, Pt. 19800.00
McK G I-009, Washington & Eagle, Green Aqua, Pontil, Pt. 935.00
McK G I-009, Washington & Eagle, Light Green, Pontil.. 990.00
McK G I-010, Washington & Eagle, Deep Aqua, Pontil, Pt.. 412.50
McK G I-010, Washington & Eagle, Light Emerald Green, Open Pontil...................... 357.00
McK G I-011, Washington & Eagle, Aqua, OP, Pt. 770.00
McK G I-011, Washington & Eagle, Aqua, Pontil, Pt.. 330.00
McK G I-011, Washington & Eagle, Blue Aqua, Pontil, Pt.. 247.00
McK G I-011, Washington & Eagle, Deep Aqua, Pontil, Pt... 660.00
McK G I-012, Washington & Eagle, Deep Aqua, Pontil, Pt... 880.00
McK G I-013, Washington & Eagle, Pale Green, Yellow, Pontil, Pt. 1100.00
McK G I-014, Washington & Eagle, Aqua, Pontil, Pt... 192.00
McK G I-014, Washington & Eagle, Emerald Green, Pontil, Pt. 4675.00
McK G I-014, Washington & Eagle, Gray, Amethyst Tint, Pontil, Pt........................... 1320.00
McK G I-014, Washington & Eagle, Green Aqua, OP, Pt... 285.00
McK G I-014, Washington & Eagle, Pale Green Aqua, Open Pontil, Pt. 242.00
McK G I-016, Washington & Eagle, Aqua, Pontil, Qt. 77.00
McK G I-017, Washington & Taylor, Medium Apricot Puce, Pontil, Pt........................ 412.00
McK G I-017, Washington & Taylor, Yellow, Pontil, Pt. 2640.00
McK G I-018, Washington & Monument, Green, Yellow Tint, Pontil, Pt. 4675.00
McK G I-020, Washington & Monument, Green Aqua, Pontil, Pt. 143.00
McK G I-020, Washington & Monument, Lavender, Open Pontil, Pt............................ 5500.00
McK G I-020, Washington & Monument, Medium Cobalt Blue, Pontil, Pt. 27500.00
McK G I-021, Washington & Monument, Amethystine Tint, Open Pontil, Qt. 357.00
McK G I-021, Washington & Monument, Gray Aqua, Pontil, Qt. 209.00
McK G I-022, Washington & Taylor, Light Green, Pontil, Qt. 357.00
McK G I-024, Washington & Taylor, Blue Green, Pontil, Pt.. 550.00
McK G I-024, Washington & Taylor, Deep Golden Amber, Olive, Pontil, Pt. 357.50
McK G I-024, Washington & Taylor, Light Amethyst, Pontil, Qt. 2530.00
McK G I-024, Washington & Taylor, Light To Medium Blue Green, Pontil, Pt............ 440.00
McK G I-025, Washington, Classical Bust, Aqua, Pontil, Qt. 121.00
McK G I-025, Washington, Classical Bust, Blue Green, Pontil, Qt.............................. 880.00
McK G I-026, Washington & Eagle, Aqua, Sheared Mouth, Pontil, Qt. 198.00
McK G I-026, Washington & Eagle, Deep Blue Green, Pontil, Qt............................... 1540.00
McK G I-026, Washington & Eagle, Sheared Mouth, Pontil, Qt.................................. 2750.00
McK G I-026, Washington & Eagle, Vaseline, Pontil, Qt.. 2750.00
McK G I-028, Albany Glass Works, Ship, Honey Amber, Repro, 1/2 Pt...................... 20.00
McK G I-028, Washington & Sailing Ship, Aqua, Pontil, Pt. 198.00
McK G I-028, Washington & Sailing Ship, Cornflower Blue, Pontil, Pt...................... 220.00
McK G I-028, Washington & Sailing Ship, Dense Amber, Pontil, Pt. 1100.00
McK G I-028, Washington & Sailing Ship, Golden Amber, IP, Pt. 935.00
McK G I-028, Washington & Sailing Ship, Light Green, Yellow Striations, IP, Pt. 2200.00
McK G I-031, Washington & Jackson, Deep Olive Green, Open Pontil, Pt. 286.00
McK G I-032, Washington & Jackson, Aqua, Pontil, Pt., 6 5/8 In. 110.00
McK G I-032, Washington & Jackson, Medium Yellow Olive, OP, Pt.......................... 154.00
McK G I-032, Washington & Jackson, Olive Amber, Pontil, Pt. 264.00
McK G I-033, Washington & Jackson, Yellow Amber, Pontil, Pt. 137.50
McK G I-034, Washington & Jackson, Dark Olive Yellow Green, Open Pontil, 1/2 Pt.. 275.00
McK G I-034, Washington & Jackson, Dark Olive Yellow Green, 1/2 Pt...................... 250.00
McK G I-034, Washington & Jackson, Deep Yellow Olive, Pontil, 1/2 Pt. 242.00
McK G I-034, Washington & Jackson, Medium Amber, Pontil, 1/2 Pt......................... 231.00
McK G I-035, Washington & Tree, Calabash, Aqua, Pontil................................99.00 to 121.00
McK G I-036, Washington & Tree, Calabash, Aqua, Pontil, Qt..................................... 143.00
McK G I-037, Washington & Taylor Never Surrenders, Dyottville, Aqua, Qt.............. 82.00
McK G I-037, Washington & Taylor Never Surrenders, Burgundy, Pontil, Qt. 2420.00
McK G I-037, Washington & Taylor Never Surrenders, Citron, Qt............................... 242.00
McK G I-037, Washington & Taylor Never Surrenders, Clear, Qt................................. 935.00
McK G I-037, Washington & Taylor Never Surrenders, Copper Puce, Qt.................... 1650.00
McK G I-037, Washington & Taylor Never Surrenders, Copper Topaz, Qt. 990.00
McK G I-037, Washington & Taylor Never Surrenders, Golden Yellow, Qt. 550.00
McK G I-037, Washington & Taylor Never Surrenders, Light Green, Qt...................... 242.00
McK G I-037, Washington & Taylor Never Surrenders, Medium Puce, Pontil, Qt........ 2310.00
McK G I-037, Washington & Taylor Never Surrenders, Medium Brown Amber, Qt. 907.00

McK G I-037, Washington & Taylor Never Surrenders, Medium Pink Amethyst, Qt. ... 2970.00
McK G I-037, Washington & Taylor Never Surrenders, Medium Puce, Pontil, Qt........ 2420.00
McK G I-037, Washington & Taylor Never Surrenders, Sapphire Blue, Pontil, Qt. 1320.00
McK G I-037, Washington & Taylor Never Surrenders, Medium Yellow Green, Qt...... 357.00
McK G I-037, Washington & Taylor Never Surrenders, Pale Green, Yellow Ton, Qt.... 110.00
McK G I-037, Washington & Taylor Never Surrenders, Plum Amethyst, Pontil, Qt. 2750.00
McK G I-037, Washington & Taylor Never Surrenders, Sapphire Blue, Pontil 850.00
McK G I-038, Washington & Taylor Never Surrenders, Amethyst, Pt. 2420.00
McK G I-038, Washington & Taylor Never Surrenders, Blue Green, Pontil, Pt. 275.00
McK G I-038, Washington & Taylor Never Surrenders, Copper, Pt. 275.00
McK G I-038, Washington & Taylor Never Surrenders, Deep Amethyst, Pt. 1210.00
McK G I-038, Washington & Taylor Never Surrenders, Olive Green, Pontil, 1850, Pt. . 550.00
McK G I-038, Washington & Taylor Never Surrenders, Deep Plum Amethyst, Pt........ 467.00
McK G I-038, Washington & Taylor Never Surrenders, Deep Yellow Olive, Pontil, Pt. 715.00
McK G I-038, Washington & Taylor Never Surrenders, Emerald Green, Pontil, Pt. 330.00
McK G I-038, Washington & Taylor Never Surrenders, Light Sapphire Blue, Pt.......... 303.00
McK G I-038, Washington & Taylor Never Surrenders, Olive Yellow, Pt. 880.00
McK G I-038, Washington & Taylor Never Surrenders, Root Beer Amber, Pt............. 550.00
McK G I-039, Washington & Taylor, Blue Green, Pontil, Qt. ....215.00 to 633.00
McK G I-039, Washington & Taylor, Deep Lavender Blue, Open Pontil, Qt. 1925.00
McK G I-039, Washington & Taylor, Green, Amber Striations, Pontil, Qt................. 385.00
McK G I-039, Washington & Taylor, Medium Blue Green, Open Pontil, Qt. 632.00
McK G I-039b, Washington & Taylor, Medium Yellow Green, Pontil, Qt.................... 660.00
McK G I-040, Washington & Taylor, Citron Yellow, Open Pontil, Pt...................... 632.00
McK G I-040, Washington & Taylor, Green, OP, Pt.. 660.00
McK G I-040, Washington & Taylor, Medium Sapphire Blue, OP, Pt...................... 660.00
McK G I-040, Washington & Taylor, Medium Sapphire Blue, Open Pontil, Pt............. 330.00
McK G I-040a, Washington & Taylor, Deep Yellow Olive, Pontil, Pt. 385.00
McK G I-040a, Washington & Taylor, Yellow Olive Green, Pontil, Pt....................... 412.00
McK G I-040b, Washington & Taylor, Medium Cobalt Blue, Pontil, Pt........................ 2090.00
McK G I-040c, Washington & Taylor, Blue Green, OP, Pt. 143.00
McK G I-040c, Washington & Taylor, Medium Blue Green, OP, Pt. 209.00
McK G I-040c, Washington & Taylor, Medium Emerald Green, Pt. ....302.00 to 385.00
McK G I-040c, Washington & Taylor, Medium Green, Open Pontil, Pt. 440.00
McK G I-041, Washington & Taylor, Yellow Olive, Pontil, 1/2 Pt. 770.00
McK G I-042, Washington & Taylor, Cobalt Blue, Pontil, Qt. ....1210.00 to 3410.00
McK G I-042, Washington & Taylor, Light Shading To Medium Teal Blue, Pontil, Qt.   495.00
McK G I-042, Washington & Taylor, Medium Blue Green, Pontil, Qt. 825.00
McK G I-042, Washington & Taylor, Medium Blue, Open Pontil, Qt. 3575.00
McK G I-043, Washington & Taylor, Dark Green, Qt. 1100.00
McK G I-043, Washington & Taylor, Medium Smokey Gray Amethyst, Pontil, Qt. 4400.00
McK G I-044, Washington & Taylor, Cobalt Blue, Pontil, Pt. 1210.00
McK G I-044, Washington & Taylor, Light Yellow Green, Pontil, Pt. 231.00
McK G I-045, Washington & Taylor, Light Yellow Green, Qt..................................... 209.00
McK G I-046, Washington & Taylor, Black, Qt. 1815.00
McK G I-048, Washington & Taylor, Medium Blue Green, Pontil, Pt...................... 264.00
McK G I-048, Washington, Father Of His Country, Blue Teal, Pontil, Pt................ 253.00
McK G I-048, Washington, Father Of His Country, Black Glass, Qt............................ 1815.00
McK G I-048, Washington, Father Of His Country, Medium Blue Teal, Pt.................. 253.00
McK G I-048, Washington, Father Of His Country, Medium Blue Green, Pontil, Pt..... 341.00
McK G I-051, Washington & Taylor, Deep Yellow Green, Blob Lip, OP, Qt. 467.50
McK G I-051, Washington & Taylor, Deep Yellow Green, OP, Qt. 440.00
McK G I-051, Washington & Taylor, Sapphire Blue, Pontil, Qt................................. 2640.00
McK G I-052, Washington & Taylor, Dense Amber, IP, Pt. 522.50
McK G I-052, Washington & Taylor, Golden Amber, Pt... 440.00
McK G I-052, Washington & Taylor, Golden Yellow Amber, Pontil, Pt...................... 440.00
McK G I-054, Washington & Taylor, Blue Green, Pontil, Qt. ....22.00 to 286.00
McK G I-054, Washington & Taylor, Cobalt Blue, Qt.. 990.00
McK G I-054, Washington & Taylor, Copper, Tapered Ring Lip, Qt. 825.00
McK G I-054, Washington & Taylor, Dark Red Puce, Qt... 1760.00
McK G I-054, Washington & Taylor, Emerald Green, Qt.. 550.00
McK G I-054, Washington & Taylor, Light Copper, Qt. 825.00
McK G I-054, Washington & Taylor, Light Yellow Green, Pontil, Qt. 143.00

McK G I-054, Washington & Taylor, Medium Green, Qt. 209.00
McK G I-054, Washington & Taylor, Olive Yellow, Qt. 495.00
McK G I-054, Washington & Taylor, Wine Amethyst, OP, Qt. 2310.00
McK G I-054, Washington & Taylor, Yellow, Qt. 495.00
McK G I-055c, Washington & Taylor, Light Green, Applied Mouth, Pontil, Pt. 187.00
McK G I-056, Washington & Taylor, Yellow, Olive Tone, Pontil, 1/2 Pt. 9350.00
McK G I-057, Washington & Sheaf, Aqua, Pontil, Qt. 55.00
McK G I-060, Washington & Washington, Ice Blue, IP, Qt. 880.00
McK G I-062, John Q. Adams & Bust, Green Aqua, Pontil, Pt. 10450.00
McK G I-063, Wm. H. Harrison & Cabin, Blue Aqua, Pontil, Pt. 26400.00
McK G I-064, Jackson & Eagle, Green Aqua, Pontil, Pt. 935.00
McK G I-065, Jackson & Eagle, Green Aqua, Pontil, Pt. 1430.00
McK G I-065, Jackson & Eagle, Pale Blue Green, Pontil, Pt. 385.00
McK G I-067, Jackson & Eagle, Aqua, Pontil, Pt. 2805.00
McK G I-067, Jackson & Eagle, B & M, Pontil, Pt. 11000.00
McK G I-068, Jackson & Flowers, Aqua, Pontil, Pt. 1210.00
McK G I-068, Jackson & Flowers, Deep Aqua, Pontil, Pt. 1155.00
McK G I-071, Taylor & Ringgold, Rough & Ready, Aqua, Sheared Lip, OP, Pt. 121.00
McK G I-071, Taylor & Ringgold, Rough & Ready, Aqua, OP, Pt. 132.00
McK G I-071, Taylor & Ringgold, Rough & Ready, Clear, Gray Tint, OP, Pt. 330.00
McK G I-071, Taylor & Ringgold, Rough & Ready, Aqua, Pt. 93.50
McK G I-071, Taylor & Ringgold, Rough & Ready, Aqua, Pontil, Pt. 154.00
McK G I-071, Taylor & Ringgold, Rough & Ready, Gray Clear Glass, Pt. 121.00
McK G I-071, Taylor & Ringgold, Rough & Ready, Pale Lavender, Pontil, Pt. 1430.00
McK G I-072, Taylor & Ringgold, Rough & Ready, Amethystine, OP, Pt. 385.00
McK G I-073, Taylor & Monument, Amethyst, Pontil, Pt. 9350.00
McK G I-073, Taylor & Monument, Aqua, Pontil, Pt. 132.00
McK G I-073, Taylor & Monument, Gray Green, Pontil, Pt. 715.00
McK G I-075, Taylor & Corn, Aqua, OP, Pt. 467.00
McK G I-075, Taylor & Corn, Olive, OP, Pt. .... 5115.00 to 7975.00
McK G I-076, Taylor & Eagle, Blue Aqua, OP, Pt. 3575.00
McK G I-076, Taylor & Eagle, Blue Aqua, Pontil, Pt. 4400.00
McK G I-077, Taylor & Eagle, Aqua, OP, Qt. 1155.00
McK G I-077, Taylor & Masterson, Rough & Ready, Milky Swirls, 8 1/4 In., Qt. 990.00
McK G I-078, Taylor & Ramsay, Aqua, Pontil, Pt. 935.00
McK G I-079, Grant & Eagle, Aqua, Pt. 160.00
McK G I-079a, Grant & Eagle, Aqua, Pt. 220.00
McK G I-080, Lafayette & Clinton, Coventry, Yellow Olive, Pontil, Pt. 522.50
McK G I-080, Lafayette & Clinton, Light Yellow Olive, Pontil, Pt. 1760.00
McK G I-081, Lafayette & Clinton, Medium Yellow Olive, Pontil, 1/2 Pt. 880.00
McK G I-081, Lafayette & Clinton, Olive Amber, Pontil, 1/2 Pt. 1430.00
McK G I-081, Lafayette & Clinton, Olive, OP, 1/2 Pt. 1100.00
McK G I-081a, Lafayette & Clinton, Yellow Olive, Pontil, 1/2 Pt. 2310.00
McK G I-082, Lafayette & Clinton, Olive Yellow, Pontil, 1/2 Pt. 2420.00
McK G I-083, Lafayette & Masonic, Olive, 1/2 Pt. .... 2970.00 to 4125.00
McK G I-084, Lafayette & Masonic, Olive, 1/2 Pt. 1815.00
McK G I-084, Lafayette & Masonic, T.S., Olive Green, Pontil, 1/2 Pt. 1870.00
McK G I-084, Lafayette & Masonic, Yellow Olive, Pontil, 1/2 Pt. 825.00
McK G I-085, Lafayette & Liberty, Deep Yellow Amber, Pontil, Pt. 330.00
McK G I-085, Lafayette & Liberty, Deep Yellow Olive, Pontil, Pt. 770.00
McK G I-085, Lafayette & Liberty, Yellow Amber, Olive, Pontil, Pt. 550.00
McK G I-085, Lafayette & Liberty, Yellow Olive, Pontil, Pt. 522.00
McK G I-086, Lafayette & Liberty, Deep Yellow Olive, Pontil, 1/2 Pt. 467.50
McK G I-086, Lafayette & Liberty, Golden Yellow Amber, Pontil, 1/2 Pt. 660.00
McK G I-086, Lafayette & Liberty, Medium Yellow Olive, Pontil, 1/2 Pt. 357.00
McK G I-086, Lafayette & Liberty, Olive Amber, Pontil, 1/2 Pt. 550.00
McK G I-086, Lafayette & Liberty, Yellow Amber, Pontil, 1/2 Pt. 467.00
McK G I-086, Lafayette & Liberty, Yellow Olive, Pontil, 1/2 Pt. .... 522.50 to 660.00
McK G I-087, Lafayette & Liberty, Light Yellow Olive, Pontil, 1/2 Pt. 4400.00
McK G I-087, Lafayette & Liberty, Yellow Green, Olive, Pontil, 1/2 Pt. 3575.50
McK G I-088, Lafayette & Masonic, Dark Olive Green, Variant, Pontil, Pt. 16500.00
McK G I-088, Lafayette & Masonic, Olive Green, OP, Pt. 1045.00
McK G I-088, Lafayette & Masonic, Olive Yellow, Pontil, 1/2 Pt. 1045.00

McK G I-089, Lafayette & Liberty, Deep Yellow Olive, Pontil, 1/2 Pt. 1485.00
McK G I-089, Lafayette & Masonic, Olive, OP, 1/2 Pt. 1595.00
McK G I-090, Lafayette & Eagle, Aqua, Pontil, Pt. ....187.00 to 308.00
McK G I-091, Lafayette & Eagle, Aqua, Pontil, Pt. ....302.50 to 385.00
McK G I-092, Lafayette & Eagle, Pale Green, Pontil, Pt. 2090.00
McK G I-093, Lafayette & Eagle, Deep Green Aqua, Pontil, Pt. 1320.00
McK G I-093, Lafayette & Eagle, Light Blue Green, Pontil, Pt. 1540.00
McK G I-093, Lafayette & Eagle, Light Green, Pontil, Pt. 1045.00
McK G I-094, Franklin & Dyott, Aqua, Sheared Mouth, Pontil, 6 3/4 In. 165.00
McK G I-094, Franklin & Dyott, Deep Golden Amber, Pontil, Pt. 1430.00
McK G I-096, Franklin & Dyott, Pale Aqua, Pontil, 8 In. 137.00
McK G I-097, Franklin & Franklin, Aqua, OP, Qt. ....154.00 to 175.00
McK G I-097, Franklin & Franklin, Deep Aqua, Pontil, Qt. 1705.00
McK G I-097, Franklin & Franklin, Emerald Green, Pontil, Qt. 1530.00
McK G I-097, Franklin & Franklin, Green, Pontil, Qt. 320.50
McK G I-098, Franklin & Dyott, Light Green, Pontil, Pt. ....1732.50 to 2530.00
McK G I-098, Franklin & Dyott, Light To Medium Blue Green, Pontil, Pt. 1320.00
McK G I-099, Jenny Lind, Deep Aqua, Calabash, IP. 121.00
McK G I-099, Jenny Lind, Deep Emerald Green, Calabash, Pontil 1210.00
McK G I-099, Jenny Lind, Emerald Green, Calabash, Pontil, Qt. 1210.00
McK G I-099, Jenny Lind, Lime Citron, Calabash, OP. 1595.00
McK G I-099, Jenny Lind, Pale Yellow Green, Calabash, Pontil, Qt. 220.00
McK G I-099a, Jenny Lind, Aqua, Pontil, Qt. 3300.00
McK G I-101, Jenny Lind, Deep Aqua, Pontil, Qt. 77.00
McK G I-102, Jenny Lind & Glasshouse, Aqua, Pt. 121.00
McK G I-102, Jenny Lind & Glasshouse, Deep Aqua, Pontil, Qt. 231.00
McK G I-104, Jenny Lind & Glasshouse, Root Beer Amber, Calabash, Pontil, Qt. 12100.00
McK G I-104, Jenny Lind & Glasshouse, Root Beer Amber, Pontil, Qt. 1210.00
McK G I-104, Jenny Lind, Calabash, Sapphire Blue, IP, Qt. 1540.00
McK G I-105, Jenny Lind & Glasshouse, Pale Blue Green, IP, Qt. 231.00
McK G I-107, Jenny Lind, Calabash, Aqua, Applied Mouth, Pontil, Qt. 33.00
McK G I-108, Jenny Lind & Lyre, Deep Aqua, Pontil, Pt. 467.00
McK G I-109, Jenny Lind & Lyre, Deep Aqua, Pontil, Qt. 935.00
McK G I-110, Jenny Lind & Lyre, Aqua, OP, Qt. 1375.00
McK G I-110, Jenny Lind & Lyre, Aqua, Pontil, Qt. 880.00
McK G I-111, Kossuth & Frigate, Light Green, Pontil, Pt. 605.00
McK G I-112, Kossuth & Frigate, Aqua, Calabash, OP, Pt. ....198.00 to 231.00
McK G I-112, Kossuth & Frigate, Deep Olive Yellow, Calabash, IP, Qt. 1320.00
McK G I-112a, Kossuth & Frigate, Deep Aqua, Pontil, Qt. 220.00
McK G I-113, Kossuth & Tree, Blue Green, Pontil, Qt. 209.00
McK G I-113, Kossuth & Tree, Olive Yellow, Calabash, Pontil, Qt. 253.00
McK G I-113, Kossuth & Tree, Yellow Apricot, Calabash, OP, Qt. 330.00
McK G I-114, Byron & Scott, Light Olive Yellow, Pontil, 1/2 Pt. 143.00
McK G I-115, Wheat Price, Short Haired Bust, Pale Blue Green, Pontil, Pt. 1320.00
McK G I-117, Columbia & Eagle, Aqua, Pontil, Pt. 660.00
McK G I-117, Columbia & Eagle, Light Gray Blue, Pontil, Pt. 19800.00
McK G I-118, Columbia & Eagle, Pale Vaseline, Pontil, 1/2 Pt. 4675.00
McK G I-121, Columbia & Eagle, Aqua, Pontil, Pt. ....220.00 to 302.50
McK G I-122, Columbia & Eagle, Pontil, Pt. 8250.00
McK G I-123a, Cleveland & Stevenson, Amber, 1/2 Pt. 412.50
McK G I-123a, Cleveland & Stevenson, Barrel, Aqua, Pt. 203.50
McK G I-126, William Jennings Bryan & Eagle, Yellow Amber, 1/2 Pt. 1430.00
McK G II-001, Double Eagle, Pale Green Vaseline, Pontil, Pt. 264.00
McK G II-002, Double Eagle, Brilliant Blue Aqua, Pontil, Pt. 242.00
McK G II-002, Double Eagle, Green Aqua, Pontil, Pt. 165.00
McK G II-003, Double Eagle, Aqua, Pontil, Pt. 187.00
McK G II-004a, Double Eagle, Pale Green, Pontil, Pt. 320.50
McK G II-005, Double Eagle, Light Yellow Green, Pontil, Pt. 4125.00
McK G II-006, Eagle & Cornucopia, Pale Green, Pontil, Pt. 330.00
McK G II-007, Eagle & Sunburst, Emerald Green, OP, Pt. 17600.00
McK G II-007, Eagle & Sunburst, Grass Green, Pontil, 8 1/4 In. 2750.00
McK G II-007, Eagle & Sunburst, Light Blue Green, Pontil, Pt. 660.00
McK G II-007, Eagle & Sunburst, Pale Green, Pontil, 7 3/4 In. 3740.00

McK G II-007, Eagle & Sunburst, Pontil, 9 3/4 In. 1045.00
McK G II-008, Eagle & Scrolled Medallion, Pontil, Pt. 6050.00
McK G II-009, Eagle & Snake, Pale Vaseline, Pontil, Pt. 7150.00
McK G II-010, Eagle & Sheaf Of Wheat, Pale, Light Green, Pontil, Pt. 935.00
McK G II-011, Eagle & Cornucopia, Aqua, OP, 1/2 Pt. 137.50
McK G II-011a, Eagle & Cornucopia, Deep Blue Aqua, Pontil, 1/2 Pt. 187.00
McK G II-012, Eagle & Cornucopia, Deep Green Aqua, Pontil, 1/2 Pt. 550.00
McK G II-013, Eagle & Cornucopia, Blue Aqua, Pontil, 1/2 Pt. 412.50
McK G II-014, Eagle & Cornucopia, Deep Blue Aqua, Pontil, 1/2 Pt. 330.00
McK G II-015, Eagle & Cornucopia, Deep Blue Aqua, Pontil, 1/2 Pt. 660.00
McK G II-015a, Eagle & Cornucopia, Green Aqua, Pontil, 1/2 Pt. 440.00
McK G II-018, Eagle & Cornucopia, Deep Red Amber, Pontil, 1/2 Pt. 2090.00
McK G II-019, Eagle & Morning Glory, Aqua, Pontil, Pt. 181.50
McK G II-019, Eagle & Morning Glory, Aqua, Pt. ....330.00 to 550.00
McK G II-019, Eagle & Morning Glory, Deep Aqua, Pontil, Pt. 550.00
McK G II-020, Double Eagle, Blue Aqua, Pontil, Pt. 2200.00
McK G II-021, Eagle & Prospector, Blue Aqua, Pt. ....95.00 to 132.00
McK G II-022, Eagle & Lyre, Light Green, Pontil, Pt. 770.00
McK G II-022, Eagle & Lyre, Pale Blue Green, Pontil, Pt. .... 187.00 to 302.50
McK G II-023, Eagle & Floral, Green Aqua, Pontil, Pt. 880.00
McK G II-024, 10 Diamond, Expanded, Golden Amber, Pontil, Midwestern, 5 1/4 In... 935.00
McK G II-024, 10 Diamond, Expanded, Yellow Amber, Pontil, Midwestern, 5 1/2 In... 2640.00
McK G II-024, Chestnut, 10 Diamond, Golden Amber, Pontil, Midwestern, 6 1/2 In..... 7150.00
McK G II-024, Chestnut, 24 Rib, Broken Swirl Left, Amber, Pontil, Midwestern.......... 1100.00
McK G II-024, Double Eagle, Aqua, Pontil, Pt. ....110.00 to 121.00
McK G II-024, Double Eagle, Deep Aqua, Pontil, Pt.......................100.00 to 132.00
McK G II-024, Double Eagle, Medium Yellow Green, Pontil, Pt. 357.00
McK G II-024, Double Eagle, Medium Yellow, Pt. ....*Illus* 28800.00
McK G II-024, Double Eagle, Sapphire Blue, Pontil, Pt. 2200.00
McK G II-025, Double Eagle, Aqua, Qt. 110.00
McK G II-026, Double Eagle, Blue Aqua, OP, Qt.. 154.00
McK G II-026, Double Eagle, Golden Amber, Red Tint, Pontil, Qt........................... 1760.00
McK G II-026, Double Eagle, Golden Amber, Red Tone, Pontil, Qt. 1760.00
McK G II-026, Double Eagle, Green Aqua, OP, Qt. 154.00
McK G II-026, Double Eagle, Light Blue Aqua, Qt. 225.00
McK G II-026, Double Eagle, Medium Yellow Olive, IP, Qt. 2090.00
McK G II-027, Eagle & Farley & Taylor, Aqua, IP, 2 1/2 Qt. 3850.00
McK G II-029, Double Eagle, Vertically Ribbed, Aqua, Pontil, Pt. 467.50
McK G II-031, Double Eagle, Aqua, OP, Qt. 143.00
McK G II-031, Double Eagle, Vertically Ribbed, Yellow Green, Pontil, Qt.................. 3575.00
McK G II-033, Eagle & Louisville, Aqua, 1/2 Pt. 132.00
McK G II-033, Eagle & Louisville, Golden Amber, 1/2 Pt. 1320.00
McK G II-033, Eagle & Louisville, Pale Blue Green, 1/2 Pt. 132.00
McK G II-034, Eagle & Louisville, Vertically Ribbed, Aqua, IP, Pt. 330.00
McK G II-035, Eagle, Louisville, Ky., Aqua, Plain Reverse, Qt. 110.00
McK G II-036, Eagle & Louisville, Aqua, Pt. 77.00
McK G II-037, Eagle & Ravenna, Olive Yellow, IP, Pt. 990.00
McK G II-038, Eagle & Dyottville, Aqua, Pt. 121.00
McK G II-040, Double Eagle, Deep Yellow Green, Pontil, Pt. 467.50
McK G II-040, Double Eagle, Light Yellow Green, Citron, Pontil, Pt. 203.50
McK G II-042, Eagle & Frigate, TWD, Aqua, Pontil, Pt.. 220.00
McK G II-047, Eagle & Tree, Aqua, Pontil, Qt. 357.50
McK G II-048, Eagle & Coffin & Hay, Citron, Pontil, Qt. 242.00
McK G II-048, Eagle & Coffin, Deep Blue Green, Pontil, Qt. 2310.00
McK G II-048, Eagle & Coffin, Emerald Green, Pontil, Qt. 1375.00
McK G II-048, Eagle & Coffin, Light Citron, Pontil, Qt. 242.00
McK G II-048, Eagle & Coffin, Light To Medium Green, OP, Qt. 825.00
McK G II-048, Eagle & Flag, Light To Medium Green, OP, Qt. ....*Illus* 825.00
McK G II-049, Eagle & Coffin, Striated Clambroth, Pontil, Pt. 1760.00
McK G II-050, Eagle & Coffin, Aqua, Pontil, 1/2 Pt. 275.00
McK G II-052, Eagle & Flag, Golden Amber, Pontil, Pt.............................2530.00 to 4400.00
McK G II-052, Eagle & Flag, Golden Amber, Pt. 2530.00
McK G II-053, Eagle & Flag, Aqua, Pontil, Pt.. 154.00

McK G II-054, Eagle & Flag, For Our Country, Aqua, Pontil, Pt. 110.00
McK G II-055, Eagle & Grapes, Aqua 85.00
McK G II-055, Eagle & Grapes, Deep Golden Amber, Pontil, Qt. 1210.00
McK G II-055, Eagle & Grapes, Green Aqua, Pontil, Qt. 82.00
McK G II-055, Eagle & Grapes, Olive Yellow, Pontil, Qt. 2200.00
McK G II-056, Eagle & Grapes, Yellow Olive, Pontil, 1/2 Pt. 3850.00
McK G II-057, Eagle & Cornucopia, Yellow Forest Green, Pontil, Pt. 49500.00
McK G II-058, Eagle & Cornucopia, Light Yellow Olive, Pontil, 1/2 Pt. 6380.00
McK G II-058, Eagle & Cornucopia, Olive Yellow, Pontil, 1/2 Pt. 6050.00
McK G II-060, Eagle & Oak Tree, Deep Amber, Pontil, 1/2 Pt. 1320.00
McK G II-060, Eagle & Oak Tree, Deep Golden Amber, Pontil, 1/2 Pt. 770.00
McK G II-060, Eagle & Oak Tree, Golden Amber, Sheared Lip, OP, 1/2 Pt. 1100.00
McK G II-060, Eagle & Oak Tree, Olive Amber, Pontil, 1/2 Pt. 1375.00
McK G II-061, Eagle & Willington, Deep Forest Green, Qt. 209.00
McK G II-061, Eagle & Willington, Deep Golden Amber, Olive, Qt. 176.00
McK G II-061, Eagle & Willington, Deep Olive Green, Pontil, Qt. 264.00
McK G II-061, Eagle & Willington, Deep Yellow Olive, Qt. 154.00
McK G II-061, Eagle & Willington, Olive Amber, Qt. .... 121.00 to 187.00
McK G II-061, Eagle & Willington, Olive Green, Sloping Collared Mouth, Qt. 121.00
McK G II-061, Eagle & Willington, Yellow Amber, Qt. 220.00
McK G II-061, Eagle, Willington, Yellow Amber, Olive Tone, Qt. 77.00
McK G II-062, Eagle & Willington, Bright Green, Pt. 165.00
McK G II-062, Eagle & Willington, Deep Yellow Green, Olive Tone, Pt. 77.00
McK G II-062, Eagle & Willington, Deep Yellow Olive, Pt. .... 100.00 to 165.00
McK G II-062, Eagle & Willington, Forest Green, Pt. 302.00
McK G II-062, Eagle & Willington, Yellow Olive, Pt. .... 99.00 to 154.00
McK G II-063, Eagle & Willington, Deep Forest Green, 1/2 Pt. 187.00
McK G II-063, Eagle & Willington, Deep Olive Green, 1/2 Pt. 176.00
McK G II-063, Eagle & Willington, Deep Yellow Amber, 1/2 Pt. .... 104.00 to 105.00
McK G II-063, Eagle & Willington, Medium Olive Green, 1/2 Pt. 176.00
McK G II-063, Eagle & Willington, Olive Amber, 1/2 Pt. 132.00
McK G II-063, Eagle & Willington, Olive Green, 1/2 Pt. 187.00
McK G II-063, Eagle & Willington, Olive, 1/2 Pt. 176.00
McK G II-063, Eagle & Willington, Yellow Olive, 1/2 Pt. 137.50
McK G II-063a, Eagle & Willington, Deep Forest Green, 1/2 Pt. 176.00

Flask, McK G II-048,
Eagle & Flag, Light To
Medium Green, OP, Qt.

Flask, McK G IV-015,
Masonic & Eagle, Aqua,
Pontil, Pt.

McK G II-064, Eagle & Willington, Deep Golden Amber, Olive, Pt. 137.50
McK G II-064, Eagle & Willington, Medium Green, Pt. 330.00
McK G II-064, Eagle & Willington, Olive Amber, Pt. 137.00
McK G II-064, Eagle & Willington, Yellow Olive, Pt. ....165.00 to 396.00
McK G II-064, Eagle & Wilmington, Olive Green, Pt. 110.00
McK G II-065, Eagle & Westford, Deep Olive Amber, 1/2 Pt. 165.00
McK G II-065, Eagle & Westford, Olive Amber, 1/2 Pt. ....121.00 to 154.00
McK G II-065, Eagle & Westford, Yellow Olive, 1/2 Pt. 132.00
McK G II-066, Eagle & Anchor, Yellow, Qt. 825.00
McK G II-068, Eagle & Anchor, Olive Amber, IP, Pt. 95.00
McK G II-069, Eagle & Cornucopia, Deep Aqua, Pontil, 1/2 Pt. 385.00
McK G II-069, Eagle & Cornucopia, Pale Blue Green, Pontil, 1/2 Pt. 357.50
McK G II-071, Double Eagle, Deep Yellow Olive, Pontil, 1/2 Pt. 220.00
McK G II-071, Double Eagle, Medium Olive Amber, Sheared Lip, OP, 1/2 Pt. 154.00
McK G II-071, Double Eagle, Olive Amber, OP, 1/2 Pt. 253.00
McK G II-071, Double Eagle, Yellow Olive Amber, Pontil, 1/2 Pt. 132.00
McK G II-071, Double Eagle, Yellow Olive, Pontil, 1/2 Pt. 148.50
McK G II-072, Eagle & Cornucopia, Olive Amber, Pontil, Pt. 165.00
McK G II-072a, Eagle & Cornucopia, Olive Amber, Pt. 88.00
MoK G II-073, Eagle & Cornucopia, Deep Blue Aqua, Pontil, Pt. 143.00
McK G II-073, Eagle & Cornucopia, Golden Amber, Whittled, Pontil, Pt. 110.00
McK G II-073, Eagle & Cornucopia, Light Yellow Olive, Pontil, Pt. 143.00
McK G II-073, Eagle & Cornucopia, Medium Yellow Olive, OP, Pt. ....132.00 to 198.00
McK G II-073, Eagle & Cornucopia, Yellow Olive, Pontil, Pt. ....99.00 to 154.00
McK G II-075, Eagle & Cornucopia, Olive Amber, Pontil, Pt. 1980.00
McK G II-076, Eagle & Concentric Ring, Light Green, Pontil, Qt. 3850.00
McK G II-076, Eagle & Concentric Ring, Light Yellow Green, Qt. 2640.00
McK G II-076a, Eagle & Concentric Ring, Yellow Green, Pontil, Pt. 9350.00
McK G II-078, Double Eagle, Yellow Olive, Pontil, Qt. 132.00
McK G II-079, Double Eagle, Yellow Olive, Pontil, Qt. 143.00
McK G II-080, Double Eagle, Light Yellow Olive, Pontil, Qt. 467.50
McK G II-081, Double Eagle, Yellow Amber, OP, Pt. 209.00
McK G II-086, Double Eagle, Forest Green, Pontil, 1/2 Pt. 440.00
McK G II-086, Double Eagle, Yellow Amber, Olive Tone, Pontil, 1/2 Pt. 100.00
McK G II-087, Double Eagle, Forest Green, Pontil, 1/2 Pt. 440.00
McK G II-095, Double Eagle, Green Aqua, 1/2 Pt. 88.00
McK G II-096, Double Eagle, Golden Amber, 1/2 Pt. 220.00
McK G II-101, Double Eagle, Aqua, Oval, Qt. 55.00
McK G II-103, Double Eagle, Dark Green, Qt. 220.00
McK G II-103, Double Eagle, Deep Olive Amber, Qt. 143.00
McK G II-105, Double Eagle, Emerald Green, Pt. 121.00
McK G II-106, Double Eagle, Dark Olive Green, Pt. 187.00
McK G II-106, Double Eagle, Deep Olive Green, Pt. 105.00
McK G II-106, Double Eagle, Medium Yellow Olive Green, Applied Mouth, Pt. 132.00
McK G II-107, Double Eagle, Dark Olive Green, Pt. 187.00
McK G II-109, Double Eagle, Light Sapphire Blue, 1/2 Pt. 1870.00
McK G II-126, Double Eagle, Aqua, 1/2 Pt. 55.00
McK G II-128, Double Eagle, Yellow, Olive Tone, 1/2 Pt. 660.00
McK G II-138, Eagle, Orange Amber, 1/2 Pt. 149.00
McK G II-139, Eagle, Olive Yellow, Pontil, 6 In., Pt. 82.00
McK G II-142, Eagle & Indian Shooting Bird, Blue Aqua, Qt. 100.00
McK G III-001, Cornucopia & Medallion, Pale Blue Green, Pontil, 1/2 Pt. 3300.00
McK G III-002, Cornucopia & Medallion, Grass Green, Pontil, 8 In. 5720.00
McK G III-003, Double Cornucopia, Pale Yellow Green, Pontil, Pt. 4950.00
McK G III-004, Cornucopia & Urn, Deep Yellow Olive, Pontil, Pt. 88.00
McK G III-004, Cornucopia & Urn, Light Yellow Olive, Pontil, Pt. ....88.00 to 100.00
McK G III-004, Cornucopia & Urn, Medium Green, Pontil, Pt. 330.00
McK G III-004, Cornucopia & Urn, Yellow Olive, Pt. ....72.00 to 85.00
McK G III-006, Cornucopia & Urn, Medium Emerald Green, OP, Pt. 237.00
McK G III-007, Cornucopia & Urn, Deep Olive Green, Pontil, 1/2 Pt. 66.00
McK G III-007, Cornucopia & Urn, Deep Yellow Olive Amber, 1/2 Pt. 99.00
McK G III-013, Cornucopia & Urn, Light To Medium Yellow Green, Pontil, 1/2 Pt. 577.00
McK G III-014, Cornucopia & Urn, Emerald Green, Pontil, 1/2 Pt. 357.50

McK G III-016, Cornucopia & Urn, Aqua, IP, Pt. 208.00
McK G III-016, Cornucopia & Urn, Blue Aqua, IP, Pontil 187.00
McK G III-016, Cornucopia & Urn, Blue Green, IP, Pt. 715.00
McK G III-016, Cornucopia & Urn, Dark Olive, Pontil, 7 1/8 In. 385.00
McK G III-016, Cornucopia & Urn, Olive Brown, Pontil, 7 1/4 In. 495.00
McK G III-018, Cornucopia & Urn, Light Blue Green, Pontil, Pt. .... 357.50 to 522.50
McK G IV-001, Masonic & Eagle, Deep Aqua, Pt. 165.00
McK G IV-001, Masonic & Eagle, Pontil, Pt. 715.00
McK G IV-001a, Masonic & Eagle, Medium, Deep Blue Green, Pontil, Pt. 412.50
McK G IV-002, Masonic & Eagle, Olive Green, Qt. 2750.00
McK G IV-002, Masonic & Eagle, Yellow Olive, Pontil, Pt. 3575.00
McK G IV-003, Masonic & Eagle, Deep Yellow Olive, Pontil, Pt. 4125.00
McK G IV-003, Masonic & Eagle, J.KB., Yellow Green, Pontil, Pt. 110.00
McK G IV-003, Masonic & Eagle, Olive Amber Shaded To Olive Green, Gray Slag Lip, Pt. 2640.00
McK G IV-003, Masonic & Eagle, Yellow Green, Pontil, Pt. 1100.00
McK G IV-003, Masonic, J.K.B., Deep Yellow Green, Pontil, Pt. 880.00
McK G IV-004, Masonic, J.K.B., Deep Gray, Pontil, Pt. 880.00
McK G IV-005, Masonic & Eagle, Yellow Green, Pontil, Pt. 412.50
McK G IV-007, Masonic & Eagle, Amethyst Striations, Pontil, Pt. 4125.00
McK G IV-007, Masonic & Eagle, Green, OP, Pt. 357.50
McK G IV-007, Masonic & Eagle, Light Blue Green, Pontil, Pt. 330.00
McK G IV-007, Masonic & Eagle, Medium Yellow Green, Pontil, Pt. 330.00
McK G IV-007, Masonic & Eagle, Yellow Green, Pontil, Pt. 715.00
McK G IV-007a, Masonic & Eagle, Tooled, Pontil, Pt. 220.00
McK G IV-008a, Masonic & Eagle, Green Aqua, Pontil, Pt. 495.00
McK G IV-008a, Masonic & Eagle, Light Yellow Green, Pontil, Pt. 198.00
McK G IV-012, Masonic & Eagle, Blue Green, Pontil, Pt. 3850.00
McK G IV-014, Masonic & Eagle, Light Yellow Green, Pontil, 1/2 Pt. 632.00
McK G IV-014, Masonic & Eagle, Yellow Green, Pontil, 1/2 Pt. 495.00
McK G IV-015, Masonic & Eagle, Aqua, Pontil, Pt. ....*Illus* 3850.00
McK G IV-016, Masonic & Eagle, Aqua, Pontil, Pt. 2640.00
McK G IV-016, Masonic & Eagle, Deep Yellow Olive, Pontil, Pt. 2530.00
McK G IV-016, Masonic & Eagle, Medium Olive Green, Pontil, Pt. 3300.00
McK G IV-017, Masonic & Eagle, Deep Yellow Olive, Pontil, Pt. 215.00
McK G IV-017, Masonic & Eagle, Olive Amber, Pontil, Pt. 143.00
McK G IV-017, Masonic & Eagle, Olive Green, 7 5/8 In, Pt. 137.00
McK G IV-017, Masonic & Eagle, Yellow Amber, Olive Tone, Pontil, Pt. .... 137.00 to 176.00
McK G IV-017, Masonic & Eagle, Yellow Amber, Olive, Pontil, Pt. .... 187.00 to 209.00
McK G IV-017, Masonic & Eagle, Yellow Olive Tone, Pontil, Pt. 187.00
McK G IV-018, Masonic & Eagle, Olive Amber, Pontil, Pt. 132.00
McK G IV-018, Masonic & Eagle, Yellow Amber, Olive, Pontil, Pt. 176.00
McK G IV-019, Masonic & Eagle, Olive Amber, Pontil, Pt. 137.50
McK G IV-021, Masonic & Eagle, Medium Yellow Olive Amber, Pontil, Pt. 154.00
McK G IV-021, Masonic & Eagle, Yellow Olive, Pontil, Pt. 137.50
McK G IV-022, Masonic & Eagle, Colorless, Pontil, Pt. 5500.00
McK G IV-024, Masonic & Eagle, Deep Yellow Olive, Pontil, 1/2 Pt. 242.00
McK G IV-024, Masonic & Eagle, Yellow Olive, Pontil, 1/2 Pt. .... 88.00 to 154.00
McK G IV-026, Masonic & Eagle, Aqua, Pontil, 1/2 Pt. 1100.00
McK G IV-026, Masonic & Eagle, Deep Yellow Olive, Pontil, 1/2 Pt. 440.00
McK G IV-026, Masonic & Eagle, Green Aqua, Pontil, Pt. 148.50
McK G IV-027, Masonic & Eagle, Green Aqua, Pontil, Pt. .... 302.00 to 302.50
McK G IV-027, Masonic & Eagle, Variant, Pale Blue, Pontil, Pt. 357.50
McK G IV-028, Double Masonic, Blue Green, Pontil, 1/2 Pt. 210.00
McK G IV-028, Double Masonic, Deep Aqua, Pontil, 1/2 Pt. 137.00
McK G IV-028, Double Masonic, Deep Grass Green, Pontil, 1/2 Pt. 1045.00
McK G IV-028, Double Masonic, Light Blue Green, Rolled Lip, Pontil, 1/2 Pt. 277.00
McK G IV-028, Double Masonic, Yellow Amber, OP, Pt. 137.50
McK G IV-028a, Double Masonic, Aqua, Pontil, 1/2 Pt. 1100.00
McK G IV-028a, Double Masonic, Emerald Green, Pontil/1/2 Pt. 605.00
McK G IV-028a, Double Masonic, Light Blue Green, Pontil, 1/2 Pt. 231.00
McK G IV-028a, Double Masonic, Light Shaded To Blue Green, Pontil, Pt. 308.00
McK G IV-028a, Double Masonic, Medium Blue Green, Pontil, Pt. 308.00
McK G IV-028a, Double Masonic, Olive Green, Amber, OP, Pt. 308.00

Flask, McK G IX-002, Scroll, Sapphire Blue, Sheared Lip, IP, Qt.

Flask, McK G X-006, Cannon, A Little More Grape, Strawberry Puce, Pontil, 1/2 Pt.

McK G IV-029, Double Masonic, Light Olive Yellow, Pontil, 1/2 Pt. 7150.00
McK G IV-030, Crossed Keys Masonic, Olive Yellow, Sheared Mouth, Pontil, 1/2 Pt...33000.00
McK G IV-031, Masonic & Eagle, Green Aqua, Pontil, Pt. 3025.00
McK G IV-032, Masonic & Eagle, Brilliant Golden Amber, Pontil, Pt. 187.00
McK G IV-032, Masonic & Eagle, Deep Red Amber, Pontil, Pt. 467.50
McK G IV-032, Masonic & Eagle, Golden Amber, Pontil, Pt. 520.00
McK G IV-032, Masonic & Eagle, Golden Amber, Red Tint, Pontil, Pt. 1100.00
McK G IV-032, Masonic & Eagle, Light Blue Green, Pontil, Pt. 302.50
McK G IV-032, Masonic & Eagle, Red Amber, Pontil, Pt. 385.00
McK G IV-032, Masonic & Eagle, Yellow Amber, Pontil, Pt. 467.00
McK G IV-033, Masonic & Eagle, Light Green, Pontil, Pt. 935.00
McK G IV-034, Masonic Arch & Frigate, Aqua, Rolled Lip, OP, Pt............................. 330.00
McK G IV-034, Masonic Arch & Frigate, Green Aqua, Pontil, Pt. 198.00
McK G IV-036, Masonic Arch & Frigate, Pale Yellow Green, Pontil, Pt........... 190.00 to 605.00
McK G IV-037, Masonic Arch & Eagle, Aqua, OP, Pt... 330.00
McK G IV-037, Masonic Arch & Eagle, Aqua, Pontil, Pt. 121.00
McK G IV-038, Union & Clasped Hands, Yellow Olive, Pontil, Qt............................ 1017.00
McK G IV-039, Union & Clasped Hands, Yellow Olive, Pontil, Qt. 1045.00
McK G IV-042, Masonic Clasped Hands & Eagle, Calabash, Citron, Pontil, Qt. 209.00
McK G IV-043, Masonic & Seeing Eye, Olive Amber, Pt.. 154.00
McK G IV-043, Masonic & Seeing Eye, Yellow Olive, Pontil, Pt. 176.00
McK G IX-002, Scroll, Bright Yellow Green, IP, Qt.. 715.00
McK G IX-002, Scroll, Clambroth, Pontil, Qt. 577.50
McK G IX-002, Scroll, Deep Yellow Green, IP, Qt. 270.00
McK G IX-002, Scroll, Moonstone, Lavender Tint, Pontil, Qt..................................... 495.00
McK G IX-002, Scroll, Sapphire Blue, IP, Qt... 412.00
McK G IX-002, Scroll, Sapphire Blue, Sheared Lip, IP, Qt. ....*Illus* 2310.00
McK G IX-003, Scroll, Blue Green, IP, Qt... 203.00
McK G IX-003, Scroll, Brilliant Citron, Pontil, Qt... 935.00
McK G IX-003, Scroll, Deep Aqua, Red Iron Pontil, Qt. 95.00
McK G IX-003, Scroll, Deep Root Beer Amber, Pontil, Qt... 330.00
McK G IX-003, Scroll, Medium Yellow Green, IP, Qt. 412.00
McK G IX-004, Scroll, Deep Root Beer Amber, Pontil, Qt... 550.00
McK G IX-006, Scroll & Louisville, Light Yellow Green, IP, Qt. 270.00
McK G IX-008, Scroll, Light To Medium Yellow Olive, Pt., 7 In. 231.00
McK G IX-010, Scroll, Cobalt Blue, Pontil, Pt.. 2530.00
McK G IX-010, Scroll, Deep Root Beer Amber, OP, Pt. 385.00
McK G IX-010, Scroll, Golden Amber, Pontil, Pt. ....357.50 to 522.00
McK G IX-010, Scroll, Medium Golden Amber, OP, Pt. 247.50
McK G IX-010, Scroll, Milky Lavender, Pontil, Pt. 660.00

McK G IX-010, Scroll, Sapphire Blue, Pontil, Pt. 1980.00
McK G IX-010c, Scroll, Blue Green, Pontil, Pt. 352.00
McK G IX-011, Scroll, Cobalt Blue, IP, Pt. 2420.00
McK G IX-011, Scroll, Light Yellow Olive, Pontil, Pt. 880.00
McK G IX-011, Scroll, Light Yellow Olive, Sheared Mouth, Pontil, Pt. 880.00
McK G IX-011, Scroll, Medium Sapphire Blue, Pontil, Pt. 687.50
McK G IX-015, Scroll, Green Yellow, Pontil, Pt. 385.00
McK G IX-019, Scroll, Sapphire Blue, Pontil, Pt. 1760.00
McK G IX-020, Scroll, Bright Olive Yellow, Pontil, Pt. 825.00
McK G IX-020, Scroll, Citron, Pontil, Pt. 825.00
McK G IX-020, Scroll, Sheared Mouth, Pontil, Pt. 825.00
McK G IX-026, Scroll, S, McKee, Green Aqua, Pontil, Pt. 715.00
McK G IX-028, Scroll, Rough & Ready, Blue Aqua, Pontil, Pt. 935.99
McK G IX-029, Scroll, Aqua, OP, 2 Qt. .... 253.00 to 605.00
McK G IX-030, Scroll, Aqua, Pontil, Gal. 2200.00
McK G IX-031, Scroll, Dark Golden Amber, Pontil, 1/2 Pt. 522.50
McK G IX-034, Scroll, Citron, Pontil, 1/2 Pt. 880.00
McK G IX-034, Scroll, Golden Amber, Pontil, 1/2 Pt. 467.00
McK G IX-035, Scroll, Medium Golden Amber, Pontil, 1/2 Pt. 385.00
McK G IX-037, Scroll, Golden Yellow, Pontil, 1/2 Pt. 198.00
McK G IX-039, Scroll, B.P. & B, Light Moonstone, Pontil, 1/2 Pt. 412.50
McK G IX-041, Scroll, Bright Light Golden Yellow, Pontil, 1/2 Pt. 5225.00
McK G IX-043, Scroll, J.R. & Son, Deep Green Aqua, Pontil, Pt. 412.50
McK G IX-044, Scroll, Light Sea Green, Pontil, Pt. 605.00
McK G IX-045, Scroll, Medium Blue Green, Pontil, Pt. 1870.00
McK G IX-046, Scroll, Aqua, OP, Qt. 880.00
McK G IX-046, Scroll, Corset Waist, Deep Green Aqua, Pontil, Qt. 852.50
McK G IX-046, Scroll, Corset Waist, Pale Blue Green, Pontil, Qt. 660.00
McK G IX-047, Scroll, R. Knowles & Co., Aqua, Pontil, Pt. 852.50
McK G IX-047, Scroll, R. Knowles & Co., Pale Yellow Green, Pontil, Pt. 154.00
McK G IX-048, Scroll, McCarty & Torreyson, Deep Aqua, Pontil, Pt. .... 275.00 to 990.00
McK G IX-048, Scroll, McCarty & Torreyson, Pale Green, IP, Pt. 962.00
McK G IX-049, Scroll, McCarty & Torreyson, Deep Aqua, Pontil, Qt. 990.00
McK G IX-050, Scroll, McCarty & Torreyson, Deep Aqua, Sheared Lip, IP, Qt. 1018.00
McK G IX-050, Scroll, McCarty & Torreyson, Pale Blue Green, Pontil, Qt. 522.50
McK G IX-051, Scroll, Hearts & Flowers, Green Aqua, Pontil, Qt. 522.50
McK G V-001, Success To The Railroad, Locomotive, Aqua, Pt. 187.00
McK G V-001, Success To The Railroad, Medium Sapphire Blue, Base, Pontil, Pt. 2310.00
McK G V-001a, Success To The Railroad, Sapphire Blue, Pt. 3025.00
McK G V-001b, Success To The Railroad, Apricot, Pontil, Pt. 5225.00
McK G V-003, Success To The Railroad, Light Yellow Amber, Pontil, Pt. 605.00
McK G V-003, Success To The Railroad, Light Yellow Olive, Pontil, Pt. 187.00
McK G V-003, Success To The Railroad, Light Yellow Amber, Pontil, Pt. 605.00
McK G V-003, Success To The Railroad, Light Yellow Olive, Pontil, Pt. 187.00
McK G V-003, Success To The Railroad, Yellow Amber, OP, Pt. 303.00
McK G V-003, Success To The Railroad, Yellow Olive Amber, Pontil, Pt. 132.00
McK G V-003, Success To The Railroad, Yellow Olive Green, Pontil, Pt. 143.00
McK G V-003, Success To The Railroad, Yellow Amber, Pontil, Pt. 210.00
McK G V-003, Success To The Railroad, Yellow Amber, OP, Pt. 300.00
McK G V-004, Success To The Railroad, Golden Yellow, Olive Tint, Pontil, Pt. 605.00
McK G V-005, Success To The Railroad, Deep Olive Amber, Pontil, Pt. 165.00
McK G V-005, Success To The Railroad, Deep Olive Green, Pontil, Pt. 143.00
McK G V-005, Success To The Railroad, Deep Yellow Olive, Pontil, Pt. 165.00
McK G V-005, Success To The Railroad, Deep Yellow Olive, Pt. 522.00
McK G V-005, Success To The Railroad, Forest Green, Pontil, Pt. 495.00
McK G V-005, Success To The Railroad, Light Yellow Olive, Pontil, Pt. 77.00
McK G V-005, Success To The Railroad, Olive Green, Pontil, Pt. 55.00
McK G V-005, Success To The Railroad, Yellow Olive, Pontil, Pt. .... 165.00 to 522.50
McK G V-006, Success To The Railroad, Medium Yellow Olive, Pontil, Pt. 165.00
McK G V-006, Success To The Railroad, Olive Green, Sheared Lip, Pontil, Pt. 330.00
McK G V-007, Horse Pulling Cart, Olive-Green. 120.00
McK G V-008, Success To The Railroad, Olive Amber, Sheared Lip, OP, Pt. 231.00
McK G V-008, Success To The Railroad, Yellow Amber, Pontil, Pt. 154.00

McK G V-009, Horse Pulling Cart & Eagle, Yellow Olive, Pontil, Pt............................ 220.00
McK G V-010, Lowell Railroad & Eagle, Olive Amber, Pontil, 1/2 Pt. 302.00
McK G VI-001, Monument, A Little More Grape, Apricot Copper, Pontil, 1/2 Pt. 4400.00
McK G VI-001, Monument, A Little More Grape, Strawberry Puce, OP, 1/2 Pt............ 6820.00
McK G VI-002, Balto & Fells Point, Smokey Citron, Pontil, 1/2 Pt............................. 2420.00
McK G VI-004, Corn For The World, Amber, Qt.. 395.00
McK G VI-004, Corn For The World, Aqua, Qt..115.50 to 143.00
McK G VI-004, Corn For The World, Golden Amber, Qt. 605.00
McK G VI-004, Corn For The World, Golden Yellow, IP, Qt................................ 1981.00
McK G VI-004, Corn For The World, Ice Blue Aqua, Qt................................... 330.00
McK G VI-004, Corn For The World, Medium Blue Green, Qt. 1980.00
McK G VI-004, Corn For The World, Olive Yellow, IP, Qt................................ 495.00
McK G VI-004, Corn For The World, Yellow Amber, Red Tone, Qt........................... 357.50
McK G VI-004, Corn For The World, Yellow Apricot, Qt................................ 825.00
McK G VI-004, Corn For The World, Yellow Olive, Pontil, Qt............................ 143.00
McK G VI-004a, Corn For The World, Aqua, Qt. 275.00
McK G VI-006, Corn For The World, Aqua, Pt.. 165.00
McK G VI-007, Corn For The World, Bright Green, Pontil, 1/2 Pt. 467.50
McK G VII-001, Cabin Tippecanoe & North Bend, Forest Green, Pontil, Pt............16500.00
McK G VII-003, E.G. Booz Old Cabin Whiskey, Medium Amber........................ 1485.00
McK G VII-004, E.G. Booz Old Cabin Whiskey, Medium Honey Amber, Qt................ 2550.00
McK G VIII-001, Sunburst, Pale Blue Green, Pontil, Pt................................ 357.50
McK G VIII-002, Sunburst, Grass Green, OP, Pt.. 522.00
McK G VIII-002, Sunburst, Light Green, Pontil, Pt..................................... 412.50
McK G VIII-002, Sunburst, Medium Blue Green, Pontil, Pt............................. 330.00
McK G VIII-002, Sunburst, Medium Green, Pontil, Pt................................. 737.00
McK G VIII-003, Sunburst, Medium Yellow Olive, OP, Pt............................. 385.00
McK G VIII-003, Sunburst, Olive Amber, Pt... 605.00
McK G VIII-003, Sunburst, Olive Green, OP, Pt....................................... 467.00
McK G VIII-003, Sunburst, Yellow Olive, Pontil, Pt. 522.50
McK G VIII-005a, Sunburst, Light Yellow Olive, Pontil, Pt............................ 1540.00
McK G VIII-005a, Sunburst, Olive Amber Shaded To Olive Green, OP, Pt. 825.00
McK G VIII-005a, Sunburst, Yellow Amber, Pontil, Pt. 880.00
McK G VIII-007, Sunburst, Olive Amber, Pontil, Pt...........................550.00 to 1100.00
McK G VIII-008, Sunburst, Medium Yellow Olive Amber, Pontil, Pt. 522.00
McK G VIII-008, Sunburst, Olive Green, OP, Pt... 231.00
McK G VIII-008, Sunburst, Yellow, Pontil, Pt. 2640.00
McK G VIII-009, Sunburst, Olive Amber, Pontil, 1/2 Pt. 198.00
McK G VIII-009, Sunburst, Olive Green, OP, 1/2 Pt...........................220.00 to 330.00
McK G VIII-009, Sunburst, Yellow Amber, Pontil, 1/2 Pt. 302.00
McK G VIII-010, Sunburst, Yellow Olive Amber, OP, 1/2 Pt. 522.00
McK G VIII-011, Sunburst, Sea Green, Pontil, 1/2 Pt. 3300.00
McK G VIII-012, Sunburst, Deep Olive Green, Pontil, Pt. 6050.00
McK G VIII-014, Sunburst, Light Emerald Green, Pontil, 1/2 Pt. 742.00
McK G VIII-014, Sunburst, Medium Blue Green, Pontil, 1/2 Pt........................ 660.00
McK G VIII-014a, Sunburst, Bright Green, Pontil, 1/2 Pt. 1210.00
McK G VIII-015a, Sunburst, Pale Green, Pontil, 1/2 Pt. 990.00
McK G VIII-016, Sunburst, Clear Olive Green, Sheared Lip, OP, 1/2 Pt. 292.00
McK G VIII-016, Sunburst, Forest Green, Pontil, 1/2 Pt. 495.00
McK G VIII-016, Sunburst, Medium Olive Green, 1/2 Pt.....................231.00 to 412.50
McK G VIII-016, Sunburst, Medium Olive Green, Pontil, 1/2 Pt. 412.00
McK G VIII-016, Sunburst, Olive Amber, Pontil, 1/2 Pt. 400.00
McK G VIII-016, Sunburst, Olive Amber, Pontil, Pt. 401.50
McK G VIII-016, Sunburst, Olive Green, OP, 1/2 Pt. 297.00
McK G VIII-016, Sunburst, Yellow Olive, Pontil, 1/2 Pt. 220.00
McK G VIII-018, Sunburst, Light Yellow Olive, Pontil, 1/2 Pt........................ 253.00
McK G VIII-018, Sunburst, Olive Amber, Pontil, 1/2 Pt. 357.50
McK G VIII-018, Sunburst, Yellow Amber, Pontil, 1/2 Pt. ....302.00 to 357.00
McK G VIII-018, Sunburst, Yellow Olive, Pontil, 1/2 Pt. 550.00
McK G VIII-022, Sunburst, Pale Green, Pt., 7 In. 159.00
McK G VIII-025, Sunburst, Aqua, Pontil, 1/2 Pt. 176.00
McK G VIII-025, Sunburst, Deep Wine, Pontil, 1/2 Pt................................. 3025.00
McK G VIII-025, Sunburst, Medium Pink Puce, Pontil, 1/2 Pt......................... 2640.00

McK G VIII-026, Sunburst, Aqua, Pontil, Pt. 303.00
McK G VIII-026, Sunburst, Deep Yellow Olive, Pontil, Pt. 3575.00
McK G VIII-026, Sunburst, Green, OP, Pt. 181.00
McK G VIII-026, Sunburst, Light Blue Green, Pontil, Pt. 357.50
McK G VIII-026, Sunburst, Pale Aqua, Pontil, Pt. 302.00
McK G VIII-026, Sunburst, Yellow With Amber Tone, Sheared Mouth, Pontil, Pt. 2640.00
McK G VIII-029, Sunburst, Blue Green, OP, Pt. 302.00
McK G VIII-029, Sunburst, Blue Green, Pontil, 1/2 Pt. 198.00
McK G VIII-029, Sunburst, Deep Aqua, Pontil, 3/4 Pt. 77.00
McK G VIII-029, Sunburst, Deep Green Aqua, Pontil, 1/2 Pt. 176.00
McK G VIII-029, Sunburst, Green Aqua, Pontil, Pt. 137.50
McK G X-001, Stag & Willow Tree, Aqua, Pontil, Pt. 165.00
McK G X-001, Stag & Willow Tree, Good Game, Aqua, Pt. 231.00
McK G X-003, Sheaf Of Rye & Grapes, Aqua, Pontil, 1/2 Pt. 143.00
McK G X-004, Cannon, A Little More Grape, Copper, Pontil, Pt. 6050.00
McK G X-004, Cannon, A Little More Grape, Olive Green, Pontil, 7 1/8 In. 2805.00
McK G X-005, Cannon, A Little More Grape, Aqua, Pontil, Pt. 467.00
McK G X-005, Cannon, A Little More Grape, Olive, Pontil, Pt. 2750.00
McK G X-006, Cannon, A Little More Grape, Strawberry Puce, Pontil, 1/2 Pt. ...... *Illus* 3025.00
McK G X-009, Sailboat & Star, Clear Green 60.00
McK G X-010, Sheaf Of Rye & Star, Aqua, Pontil, Pt. .... 385.00 to 605.00
McK G X-011, Sheaf Of Rye & Star, Aqua, Pontil, 1/2 Pt. 385.00
McK G X-012, 2 Men Arguing, Cobalt Blue, Pontil, 1/2 Pt. 605.00
McK G X-014, Murdock & Cassel, Light Blue Green, Pontil, Pt. .... 797.00 to 1650.00
McK G X-015, Summer & Winter, Citron, Moss Green Tone, Pontil, Pt. 605.00
McK G X-015, Summer & Winter, Pale Green, Pontil, Pt. 187.00
McK G X-016, Summer & Winter, Aqua, OP, 1/2 Pt. 165.00
McK G X-017, Summer & Winter, Blue Green, Pontil, Pt. 330.00
McK G X-017, Summer & Winter, Medium Green, Pontil, Pt. 907.00
McK G X-019, Summer & Winter, Aqua, Qt. 132.00
McK G X-019, Summer & Winter, Burnt Orange Amber, Qt. 880.00
McK G X-019, Summer & Winter, Golden Olive Amber, Pontil, Qt. 770.00
McK G X-019, Summer & Winter, Medium Green, Pontil, Qt. 1045.00
McK G X-021, American Steamboat & Sheaf Of Rye, Deep Blue Aqua, Pontil, Pt. 14300.00
McK G X-021, American Steamboat & Sheaf Of Rye, Pale Yellow Green, Pontil, Pt. 4180.00
McK G X-022, Log Cabin & Hard Cider, Deep Blue Aqua, Pontil, Pt. 5500.00
McK G X-024, Jared Spencer & Medallions, Light Olive Yellow, Pontil, Pt. 66000.00
McK G X-025, Medallions & Diamond Diapering Decorative, Olive, Pontil, Pt. 52800.00
McK G X-026, Beads & Pearls, Diamond Diapering Decorative, Olive, Pontil, Pt. 29700.00
McK G X-027, Flag & Stoddard, Olive Amber, Sheared Mouth, Pontil, Pt. 5500.00
McK G X-027, Flag, Stoddard, Olive Amber, OP, Pt. 8525.00
McK G X-028, Flag & Stoddard, Deep Olive Green, 1/2 Pt. 6600.00
McK G XI-002, For Pike's Peak, Prospector, Light Blue Green, Pt. 385.00
McK G XI-002, For Pike's Peak, Prospector, Light Yellow Green, Applied Lip, Pt. 550.00
McK G XI-005, For Pike's Peak, Prospector, Aqua, 1/2 Pt. 121.00
McK G XI-005, For Pike's Peak, Prospector, Aqua, Pt. 121.00
McK G XI-005, For Pike's Peak, Prospector, Aqua, 1/2 Pt. 143.00
McK G XI-007, For Pike's Peak, Prospector, Deep Olive Amber, Qt. 880.00
McK G XI-008, For Pike's Peak, Prospector, Aqua, Qt. 165.00
McK G XI-008, For Pike's Peak, Prospector, Eagle, Deep Aqua, Qt. 85.00
McK G XI-009, For Pike's Peak, Prospector, Aqua, Pt. 50.00
McK G XI-010, For Pike's Peak, Prospector, Aqua, 1/2 Pt. 275.00
McK G XI-011, Prospector & Eagle, Aqua, Pt. 209.00
McK G XI-013, Prospector & Eagle, Yellow Olive, Qt. 632.00
McK G XI-016, Prospector & Eagle, Aqua, Pt. 264.00
McK G XI-017, Prospector & Eagle, Green, Pt. 198.00
McK G XI-018, Prospector & Eagle, Aqua, 1/2 Pt. 105.00
McK G XI-020, For Pike's Peak, Prospector, Aqua, 1/2 Pt. 132.00
McK G XI-021, For Pike's Peak, Prospector, Aqua, OP, Pt. 121.00
McK G XI-021, For Pike's Peak, Prospector, Aqua, Pt. .... 72.00 to 132.00
McK G XI-022, For Pike's Peak, Prospector, Medium Amber, Pt. 825.00
McK G XI-024, For Pike's Peak, Prospector, Light Cornflower Blue, Qt. 440.00
McK G XI-026, For Pike's Peak, Prospector, Aqua, 1/2 Pt. 121.00

McK G XI-030, For Pike's Peak, Prospector, Aqua, Qt... 50.00
McK G XI-032, For Pike's Peak, Prospector, Eagle, Aqua, Sheared Lip, IP, Pt............. 220.00
McK G XI-034, For Pike's Peak, Prospector, Aqua, IP, Qt...................................... 220.00
McK G XI-034, For Pike's Peak, Prospector, Medium Lime Green, Qt....................... 303.00
McK G XI-035, For Pike's Peak, Prospector, Light Cornflower Blue, Pt.................... 990.00
McK G XI-036, For Pike's Peak, Prospector, Aqua, 1/2 Pt....................................... 143.00
McK G XI-040, Prospector & Eagle, Aqua, Qt.. 275.00
McK G XI-040, Prospector & Eagle, Hunter, Olive Green, 1870, Pt........................ 935.00
McK G XI-041, For Pike's Peak, Prospector, Aqua, Pt.. 137.00
McK G XI-044, Prospector & Eagle, Aqua, IP, Qt... 1650.00
McK G XI-045, Prospector & Eagle, Deep Aqua, IP, Pt.. 715.00
McK G XI-045, Prospector & Eagle, Deep Aqua, Pt... 440.00
McK G XI-046, For Pike's Peak, Prospector, Deep Aqua, Qt.................................... 198.00
McK G XI-046, For Pike's Peak, Prospector, Deep Blue Aqua, Qt............................ 176.00
McK G XI-046, For Pike's Peak, Prospector, Yellow Olive Green, Pt........................ 605.00
McK G XI-046, For Pike's Peak, Prospector, Yellow Amber, Pt............................... 550.00
McK G XI-047, For Pike's Peak, Prospector, Amber, Qt... 412.00
McK G XI-047a, For Pike's Peak, Prospector, Aqua, 27 Oz..................................... 880.00
McK G XI-050, For Pike's Peak, Prospector , Yellow Olive, Pt............................... 550.00
McK G XI-050, For Pike's Peak, Prospector, Aqua, Pt.. 137.50
McK G XI-050, For Pike's Peak, Prospector, Deep Aqua, IP, Pt.............................. 275.00
McK G XI-050, For Pike's Peak, Prospector, Deep Yellow Olive, Pt.............. 660.00 to 715.00
McK G XI-050, For Pike's Peak, Prospector, Olive Green, Pt.................................. 396.00
McK G XI-050, For Pikes Peak, Olive Green, Prospector, Pt.................................. 550.00
McK G XI-052, For Pike's Peak, Prospector, Aqua, OP, 1/2 Pt............................... 319.00
McK G XI-052, For Pike's Peak, Prospector, Aqua, Pt.. 143.00
McK G XII-002, Clasped Hands & Eagle, Waterford, Light Yellow, IP, Qt............... 852.00
McK G XII-002, Clasped Hands & Eagle, Waterford, Aqua, IP, Qt.......................... 154.00
McK G XII-006, Clasped Hands & Eagle, Deep Golden Yellow, Qt.......................... 357.00
McK G XII-006, Clasped Hands & Eagle, Yellow Green, 8 3/4 In............................ 137.00
McK G XII-013, Union, Clasped Hands & Eagle, Aqua, Qt....................................... 77.00
McK G XII-013, Union, Clasped Hands & Eagle, Yellow Green, Qt.......................... 495.00
McK G XII-015, Union, Clasped Hands & Eagle, Light Blue Green, Qt...................... 605.00
McK G XII-021, Union, Clasped Hands & Eagle, Amber, Pt.................... 110.00 to 250.00
McK G XII-021, Union, Clasped Hands & Eagle, Medium Amber, Pt........................ 121.00
McK G XII-024, Union, Clasped Hands & Eagle, Amber, Pt..................................... 143.00
McK G XII-025, Union, Clasped Hands & Eagle, A & D H C, Aqua, Pt...................... 85.00
McK G XII-025, Union, Clasped Hands & Eagle, Yellow Olive, Pt........................... 440.00
McK G XII-028, Union, Clasped Hands & Eagle, Amber, Pt..................................... 121.00
McK G XII-029, Union, Clasped Hands & Eagle, Aqua, 1/2 Pt................................. 50.00
McK G XII-030, Union, Clasped Hands & Eagle, Amber, 1/2 Pt.............................. 330.00
McK G XII-031, Clasped Hands & Eagle, Citron, 1/2 Pt... 450.00
McK G XII-031, Clasped Hands & Eagle, Golden Amber, 1/2 Pt............................. 110.00
McK G XII-031, Union, Clasped Hands & Eagle, Amber, 1/2 Pt.............................. 132.00
McK G XII-031, Union, Clasped Hands & Eagle, Bright Citron, 1/2 Pt..................... 451.00
McK G XII-033, Union, Clasped Hands & Eagle, Golden Amber, 1/2 Pt................... 143.00
McK G XII-038, Union, Clasped Hands & Cannon, FA & Co., Yellow Amber, Qt....... 935.00
McK G XII-039, Union, Clasped Hands & Cannon, FA & Co., Deep Amber, Pt.......... 660.00
McK G XII-042, Union, Clasped Hands & Cannon, FA & Co., Aqua, 1/2 Pt.............. 121.00
McK G XII-043, Union, Clasped Hands & Eagle, Aqua, Qt....................................... 66.00
McK G XII-043, Union, Clasped Hands & Eagle, Deep Golden Amber, IP, Qt........... 192.50
McK G XIII-001, Not For Joe, Girl On A Bicycle, Golden Amber, Applied Mouth, Pt. . 1100.00
McK G XIII-003, Girl Riding Bicycle, Eagle, A. & D.H. Chamber, Pa., Aqua, Pt......... 264.00
McK G XIII-004, Hunter & Fisherman, Blue Green, Pontil, Qt.................................. 385.00
McK G XIII-004, Hunter & Fisherman, Deep Puce Apricot, IP, Qt............................ 374.00
McK G XIII-004, Hunter & Fisherman, Light Blue Green, Qt................................... 253.00
McK G XIII-004, Hunter & Fisherman, Medium Blue Green...................................... 357.00
McK G XIII-004, Hunter & Fisherman, Medium Strawberry Puce 302.50
McK G XIII-004, Hunter & Fisherman, Orange Amber 242.00
McK G XIII-004, Hunter & Fisherman, Red Amber, OP.. 346.00
McK G XIII-004, Hunter & Fisherman, Strawberry Puce To Dark Puce, IP 302.00
McK G XIII-004, Hunter & Fisherman, Yellow Amber, IP... 231.00
McK G XIII-005, Hunter & Fisherman, Pale Green, OP 110.00

McK G XIII-008, Sailor & Banjo Player, Yellow Olive Green, OP, 1/2 Pt. 632.00
McK G XIII-011, Soldier & Dancer, Pale Blue Green, Pt. 121.00
McK G XIII-012, Soldier & Dancer, Aqua, OP, Pt... 121.00
McK G XIII-013, Soldier & Dancer, Olive Green, Pt... 522.00
McK G XIII-016, Soldier & Hound, Medium Sea Green... 225.00
McK G XIII-016, Soldier & Hound, Yellow, Olive Tone, IP, Qt. 440.00
McK G XIII-017, Horseman & Hound, Amber, Smooth Base, 7 3/4 In....................... 27.00
McK G XIII-017, Horseman & Hound, Pale Yellow Green, Pt. 187.00
McK G XIII-018, Horseman & Hound, Aqua, 1/2 Pt. 275.00
McK G XIII-019, Flora Temple, Copper, Applied Mouth, Ring Lip, Qt. 467.00
McK G XIII-019, Flora Temple, Golden Yellow, Qt.. 341.00
McK G XIII-021, Flora Temple, Amber, Pt.. 176.00
McK G XIII-021, Flora Temple, Copper Amber, Pt. 176.00
McK G XIII-022, Flora Temple, Standing Horse, Topaz, Puce Tones, Pt. 412.00
McK G XIII-023, Flora Temple, Smokey Yellow Olive.. 187.00
McK G XIII-023, Flora Temple, Yellow Olive, Harness Trot 2.19 3/4, Pt. 187.00
McK G XIII-024, Flora Temple & Horse, Light Copper, Pt. 231.00
McK G XIII-027, Will You Take A Drink Duck, Aqua, Qt... 165.00
McK G XIII-029a, Will You Take A Drink, Duck, Aqua, 1/2 Pt. .... 522.00 to 715.00
McK G XIII-034, Sheaf Of Grain, Aqua, OP, Qt.. 330.00
McK G XIII-034, Sheaf Of Grain, Light Green, OP, Qt... 1375.00
McK G XIII-035, Sheaf Of Grain, Westford Glass Co., Olive Amber, Pt. 66.00
McK G XIII-035, Sheaf Of Grain, Westford Glass Co., Red Amber, Pt....................... 132.00
McK G XIII-035, Sheaf Of Grain, Westford Glass Co., Yellow Olive, Pt........... 110.00 to 165.00
McK G XIII-036, Sheaf Of Grain, Westford Glass Co., Red Amber, Pt....................... 110.00
McK G XIII-036, Sheaf Of Grain, Westford Glass Co., Dark Yellow Olive, Pt. .... 99.00 to 154.00
McK G XIII-037, Sheaf Of Grain, Westford Glass Co., Dark Olive Amber, 1/2 Pt........ 99.00
McK G XIII-037, Sheaf Of Grain, Westford Glass Co., Dark Olive, 1/2 Pt. 165.00
McK G XIII-037, Sheaf Of Grain, Westford Glass Co., Olive Amber, 1/2 Pt. 121.00
McK G XIII-037, Sheaf Of Grain, Westford Glass Co., Red Amber, 1/2 Pt.................. 88.00
McK G XIII-038, Sheaf Of Grain & Star, Medium Blue Green, Pontil, Qt. 275.00
McK G XIII-040, Sheaf Of Grain & Star, Blue Green, Pontil, 1/2 Pt. 412.50
McK G XIII-042, Sheaf Of Grain & Star, Blue Aqua, Pontil, Qt.................................. 66.00
McK G XIII-045, Sheaf Of Grain & Star, Golden Amber, IP, Qt................................. 412.50
McK G XIII-046, Sheaf Of Grain & Tree, Black Cherry Red, OP................................ 1100.00
McK G XIII-046, Sheaf Of Grain & Tree, Deep Amethyst, Black, Pontil, 9 In.............. 495.00
McK G XIII-047, Sheaf Of Grain & Tree, Medium Green, Pontil, Qt.......................... 275.00
McK G XIII-048, Anchor & Sheaf Of Grain, Baltimore Glass, Golden Amber, Qt........ 330.00
McK G XIII-048, Anchor & Sheaf Of Grain, Golden Amber, Qt................................. 330.00
McK G XIII-049, Anchor & Sheaf Of Grain, Medium Apricot, 1/2 Pt.......................... 457.00
McK G XIII-053, Baltimore Glassworks & Resurgam, Variant, Aqua 85.00
McK G XIII-053, Eagle & Anchor, Resurgam, Aqua, Pt.. 55.00
McK G XIII-053, Eagle & Anchor, Resurgam, Olive Green, Pt.................................. 825.00
McK G XIII-054, Anchor & Eagle, Resurgam, Yellow Amber, Pt............................... 357.50
McK G XIII-055, Isabella & Anchor, Aqua, Pontil, Qt. 165.00
McK G XIII-056, Sheaf Of Grain, Glass Works, Aqua, Pt. .... 154.00 to 242.00
McK G XIII-057, Isabella & Anchor, Aqua, Pontil, 1/2 Pt. 440.00
McK G XIII-058, Spring Garden & Anchor, Apricot Yellow, Pt................................. 286.00
McK G XIII-058, Spring Garden & Anchor, Yellow, Pale Olive, Pt. 880.00
McK G XIII-060, Spring Garden & Anchor, Log Cabin, Medium Apricot, OP, Pt. 2200.00
McK G XIII-060, Spring Garden & Anchor, Log Cabin, Aqua, 1/2 Pt. 132.00
McK G XIII-064, Anchor, Amber, Qt.. 55.00
McK G XIII-083, Star & Ravenna, Deep Aqua, OP, Pt. 242.00
McK G XIII-089, Rough & Ready, Deep Aqua, Qt... 605.00
McK G XIV-001, Traveler's Companion & Star, Deep Olive Amber, Qt........... 143.00 to 159.50
McK G XIV-001, Traveler's Companion & Star, Deep Yellow Olive, Qt. 121.00
McK G XIV-001, Traveler's Companion & Star, Deep Olive, Qt................................ 104.00
McK G XIV-001, Traveler's Companion & Star, Deep Yellow Olive Amber, Qt. 148.00
McK G XIV-001, Traveler's Companion & Star, Honey Amber, IP, Pt........................ 550.00
McK G XIV-001, Traveler's Companion & Star, Honey Amber, IP, Qt........................ 550.00
McK G XIV-001, Traveler's Companion & Star, Red Amber, Qt................................ 38.50
McK G XIV-002, Traveler's Companion, Ravenna, Aqua, IP, Qt. 95.00
McK G XIV-002, Traveler's Companion, Ravenna, Blue Aqua, Pt. 852.00

McK G XIV-003, Traveler's Companion, Ravenna, Amber 210.00
McK G XIV-003, Traveler's Companion, Ravenna, Yellow Olive Tone, Pt................... 880.00
McK G XIV-003, Traveler's Companion, Ravenna, Yellow Amber, IP, Pt. 550.00
McK G XIV-005, Traveler's Companion, Lancaster, Aqua, Pt................................ 412.00
McK G XIV-005, Traveler's Companion, Lancaster, Blue Green, Pt........................... 385.00
McK G XIV-006, Traveler's Companion, Lockport, Deep Blue Green, Pontil, Pt......... 1870.00
McK G XIV-006, Traveler's Companion, Lockport, Yellow Green, Pt. 1650.00
McK G XIV-007, Traveler's Companion, Deep Aqua, Pontil, 1/2 Pt............................ 198.00
McK G XIV-007, Traveler's Companion, Golden Amber, IP, 1/2 Pt............................ 412.00
McK G XIV-008, Traveler's Companion, Aqua, 1/2 Pt. 165.00
McK G XIV-009, Traveler's Companion, Pale Blue Green, Pontil, 1/2 Pt..................... 302.50
McK G XV-001, Clyde Glass Works, N.Y., Golden Amber, Pt............................ 110.00
McK G XV-006, Granite Glass Co., Stoddard, N.H., Olive Amber, Pontil, Qt.............. 605.00
McK G XV-017, Ravenna Glass Works, Deep Golden Amber, IP, Pt. 825.00
McK G XV-018, Geo. W. Robinson Co., W.Va., Strapside, Aqua, Qt...................... 165.00
McK G XV-023, Union Glass Works, Medium Olive, Yellow Tint, Pt. 385.00
McK G XV-023, Union Glass Works, Olive Green, Pt................................... 742.00
McK G XV-025, Old Rye, Wheeling, Va., Deep Yellow Olive, Pt............................ 770.00
McK G XV-028, Zanesville Cut Glass Works, Aqua, Pt................................. 100.00
McKinley Label Under Glass Whiskey, Clear, Pewter Screw Cap, 1/2 Pt................... 412.50
Meahring, Harrisburg, Strap, Qt. 29.00
Medium Cobalt Blue, Teardrop, Tooled Lip, Pontil, 8 In. 143.00
Merry Christmas, Happy New Year, Wreath, Pumpkinseed, 1/2 Pt.......................... 30.00
Merry Christmas, Pumpkinseed 18.00
Merry Christmas & Happy New Year, Lima, Oh., Yellow, Gold, Red, Blue, 5 7/8 In.. 77.00
Merry Christmas Happy New Year, Label Under Glass, Pt. 175.00
Miller's Extra, Dark Amber, Pt.. 195.00
Moffett & Bros., Forrest St., Balto, Md., Embossed, Qt............................ 40.00
Mountain, Trees, Deer, Cobalt Blue, Continental, 2-Piece Mold, 4 3/4 In................. 467.50
Neller & Shirmer, San Francisco, Flat, Slug Plate, Screw Top, Pt. ....35.00 to 45.00
New Louvre, San Jose, W.T. Ferguson, Tooled Top, 1/2 Pt........................... 55.00
Picnic, Ladies, Amber, Purse, 1/2 Pt.. 20.00
Pitkin Type, 16 Ribs, Amber, Pontil, 5 1/2 In.................................... 275.00
Pitkin Type, 20 Broken Ribs, Swirled To Right, Sea-Green, OP, 4 1/4 In..................... 660.00
Pitkin Type, 24 Ribs, Swirled To Left, Yellow Green, Pontil, 6 5/8 In............................ 242.00
Pitkin Type, 30 Broken Ribs, Swirled To Left, Pontil............................... 550.00
Pitkin Type, 30 Ribs, Swirled To Right, Brilliant Blue Green, Pontil, 6 1/2 In.............. 192.50
Pitkin Type, 31 Broken Ribs, Swirled To Left, Emerald Green, OP, 6 1/4 In............... 522.50
Pitkin Type, 31 Ribs, Swirled To Right, Yellow Olive, Pontil, 5 7/8 In. 1760.00
Pitkin Type, 32 Ribs, Swirled To Left, Brilliant Blue Green, Pontil, 6 3/4 In............... 357.50
Pitkin Type, 32 Ribs, Swirled To Left, Golden Amber, Pontil, 6 1/2 In................. 385.00
Pitkin Type, 32 Ribs, Swirled To Right, Brilliant Blue Green, Pontil, 6 7/8 In.............. 522.50
Pitkin Type, 36 Broken Ribs, Amber, Tubular Pontil, 6 In. 770.00
Pitkin Type, 36 Broken Ribs, Golden Olive, Pontil, 5 3/4 In. 880.00
Pitkin Type, 36 Broken Ribs, Swirled To Left, Emerald Green, Pontil, 6 7/8 In. 440.00
Pitkin Type, 36 Broken Ribs, Swirled To Left, Medium Olive Yellow, OP, Pt. 220.00
Pitkin Type, 36 Broken Ribs, Swirled To Left, Olive Green, OP, 7 3/8 In. 137.50
Pitkin Type, 36 Broken Ribs, Swirled To Right, Olive Green, OP, 1/2 Pt. 192.50
Pitkin Type, 36 Broken Ribs, Swirled To Right, Light Olive Amber, 5 In 605.00
Pitkin Type, 36 Ribs, Swirled To Left, Golden Amber, Pontil, 5 3/4 In. 440.00
Pitkin Type, 36 Ribs, Swirled To Left, Olive Green, Sheared Mouth, Pontil, 5 In. 935.00
Pitkin Type, 36 Ribs, Swirled To Left, Yellow Amber, Pontil, 7 In. 275.00
Pitkin Type, 36 Ribs, Swirled To Left, Yellow Olive, Pontil, 4 7/8 In. 264.00
Pitkin Type, 36 Ribs, Swirled To Left, Yellow Olive, Pontil, 5 1/4 In................. 286.00
Pitkin Type, 36 Ribs, Swirled To Left, Yellow Olive, Pontil, 6 11/2 In. 264.00
Pitkin Type, 36 Ribs, Swirled To Right, Deep Forest Green, Pontil, 5 3/8 In.............. 434.50
Pitkin Type, 36 Ribs, Swirled To Right, Forest Green, Pontil, 6 1/4 In. 412.50
Pitkin Type, 36 Ribs, Swirled To Right, Forest Green, Pontil, 5 5/8 In. 418.00
Pitkin Type, 36 Ribs, Swirled To Right, Olive Green, New England, Pontil, 5 In......... 198.00
Pitkin Type, 36 Ribs, Swirled To Right, Olive Green, Pontil, 4 1/4 In. 1320.00
Pitkin Type, 36 Ribs, Swirled To Right, Yellow Olive, Pontil, 5 1/2 In. 412.50
Pitkin Type, 36 Ribs, Swirled To Right, Yellow Olive, Pontil, 7 1/8 In. 412.50
Pitkin Type, 36 Ribs, Swirled To Right, Yellow Olive, Tubular Pontil, 6 1/2 In........... 385.00

Pitkin Type, 36 Ribs, Swirled To Right, Yellow Olive, Pontil, 5 1/4 In. 275.00
Pitkin Type, 36 Ribs, Swirled To Right, Yellow Olive, Pontil, 5 3/4 In. 198.00
Pitkin Type, 36 Ribs, Swirled To Right, Yellow Olive, Pontil, 4 7/8 In. 308.00
Pitkin Type, 38 Broken Ribs, Swirled To Right, Medium Olive Green, OP, Pt. 192.50
Pumpkinseed, Screw Top Cover, Amber, 4 1/2 In. 20.00
Pumpkinseed, Sloping Collar With Ring 10.00
Pumpkinseed, Spider Web, 1/4 Pt. 12.00
Pumpkinseed, Teardrop, Honey Amber 25.00
R & G A Wright, Philadelphia, Barrel, Aqua, OP, Applied Lip, 4 In. 285.00
Red, White Looping, Blown, Sheared Lip, Pontil, Europe, 1/2 Pt. 193.00
Redware, Eagle & Pluribus Unum, 1850-1870, 7 1/4 In. 440.00
Redware, Olive Multicolored Glaze, Concentric Ring, Continental, 1760-1800, 7 In. ... 198.00
Redware, Orange Lead Glaze, Green, Brown, 18th Century, 7 1/2 In. 825.00
Ribbed, Diamond Pattern, Ca., Pontil, Continental, 1/4 Pt. 77.00
Richmond P. Hobson, Hanlen Bros. Wines & Liquors, Label Under Glass, 1/2 Pt. 363.00
Robert J. Crispin, Wellington Hotel, Salt Lake City, Aqua, Coffin, 9 1/4 In. 70.00
Rockingham, Brown, Embossed Eagle Both Sides, 1850-1880, 7 1/2 In. 357.00
S.W. Robinson, Dealer In Wines & Liquors, Richmond, Va., Strap Side, Pt. .... 105.00 to 160.00
San Francisco, Pumpkinseed, 1890, 6 5/8 In. 121.00
Scroll, 4 Petal Flowers, Aqua, Pontil, 5 3/4 In. 275.00
Scroll, Amber, Pontil, 7 In. 220.00
Scroll, Amethyst, Pt. 55.00
Scroll, Aqua, Louisville Glass Works, Pontil, 7 In. 126.00
Scroll, Aqua, Pontil, 5 5/8 In. 55.00
Scroll, Aqua, Pontil, 5 7/8 In. 104.00
Scroll, Deep Grass Green, 8 1/2 In. 935.00
Scroll, Grass Green, Sheared Lip, Pt. 550.00
Spider Web, Pumkinseed, Pt. 12.00
Star In Circle, Amber, Pt. 10.00
Try It, Amber, Pumpkinseed, 1/2 Pt. 45.00
Union Pacific Tea Co., Elephant, Pumpkinseed, 1/2 Pt. 75.00
W.W. Ward Grotto, Marysville, Pt. 65.00
Warner & Co. Tablet, Philadelphia, Ground Lip, Screw Threads, 2 1/2 In. 8.00
Whiskey, Iridized, Metal Cap, 4 3/4 In. 48.00
Woman, Label Under Glass, Metal Screw Cap, Pocket, 5 5/8 In. 275.00
Woman, Victorian Dress, Label Under Glass, Metal Screw Cap, Pocket, 6 In. 357.50
Yellow Green, 3-Piece Mold, Rolled Mouth, Pontil, Pt. 6050.00

FOOD

Food bottles include all of the many grocery store containers, such as those for catsup, horseradish, jelly, and other foodstuffs. Vinegar bottles and a few other special bottles are listed under their own headings.

FOOD, A. Schlueter & Co., Fine Flavoring Extracts, Milwaukee, Amber, BIMAL, 13 In. 18.00
Abner Royce Orange Extract 12.00
Acker's Select Tea, Yellow Green, Crown Lid, Embossed, Square, 1910s, 8 1/2 In. 330.00
Apothecary, Horlicks Malted Milk, Label Under Glass, Glass Lid, 6 3/4 In. 187.00
As You Like It Horse-Radish, Stoneware, Brown, Tan, Stenciled, 1/2 Pt. 19.00
Baker's Flavoring Extracts, Baker Extract Co., Rectangular, BIMAL, Qt. 1.00
Beech-Nut Brand Tomato Catsup, 10 In. .... *Illus* 35.00
Berry, Aqua, Petal Design Shoulder, Graphite Pontil, 11 3/4 In. 45.00
Berry, Deep Root Beer Amber, Fluted Neck, 11 1/4 In. 303.00
Big Ben, Pure Apple Butter, Roson-Reichardt Brok. Co., 8 In. .... *Illus* 12.00
British Admiralty Lime Juice, Deep Olive Amber, V & Anchor, Seal, 10 3/8 In. 165.00
Brooke's Lemons, Sweetened Lemon Juice, Fancy Shape, Amethyst, 11 1/2 In. 38.00
Brown's Jamaica Ginger, OP 22.00
California Perfume Co., see Avon, California Perfume Co.
Capers, Dark Emerald Green, 9 In. 22.00
Capers, Deep Emerald, Fluted, 8 In. 12.00
Capital Queen Olives 8.00
Challenge Queen Olives, Milwaukee, Wis., Label 30.00
Chicago Horseradish, Blue Aqua, Man & 2 Jackasses, Embossed 135.00
Chinese Condiment Sauce, Embossed Fishing Boat, 6-Sided, Whittled, Bubbles 35.00

Food, Beech-Nut Brand Tomato
Catsup, 10 In.

Food, Big Ben, Pure Apple Butter,
Roson-Reichardt Brok. Co., 8 In.

Cohen Cook & Co., Ketchup, Aqua, Teardrop Shape, IP, 8 1/2 In.	140.00
Colburn's Fountain, Aqua, Jar, Applied Mouth, Stopple, Qt.	220.00
Cutting & Co. Worcestershire Sauce, Aqua, Whittled, Round, 7 1/2 In.	65.00
D. Ghiradelli & Co., San Francisco, Spice, Light Aqua, 7 1/4 In.	80.00
D. Miller & Co. Shaker, OP, Whittled, 8 Panel, Aqua, 7 In.	650.00
D. Mitchell's Flavoring Extract, Rochester, N.Y., OP, Oval, 5 1/2 In.	55.00
Dr. Pierce's Delicious Flavoring Extracts, Rectangular, Panels, 10 1/4 In.	15.00
Durkee Challenge Sauce, Sample	10.00
E.B. Millar, Raspberry Extract	10.00
Emperor Olive Oil, Spurlock-Neal, Nashville, Tenn., Olive Picture, Label	25.00
Eno's Fruit Salt, Top	10.00
Extract, Hire's.	10.00
Fletcher's Tiger Sauce, Deep Aqua, Crude	8.00
Folger's Golden Gate Flavoring, Sun Colored Amethyst	2.50
Foote & Jenks Red Fruit Coloring	10.00
Forget-Me-Not Horseradish, Aqua, Applied Crown, 6 Oz.	7.00
French's Extract, Cork	18.00
Giessen's Union Mustard, N.Y., Embossed Eagle, S-Base, 4 5/8 In. 65.00 to	88.00
Ginger, Zipper Pattern	40.00
Golden Star Honey, Embossed Star, Light Sun Colored Amethyst	10.00
Gordon & Dilworth, Queen Olives, Yellow Green, Label, 1880s, 10 1/2 In.	66.00
Green & Clark, Missouri Cider, Amber, Aug. 27, 1878, Qt.	65.00
Heinz & Noble, Aqua, Rectangular, Celery Sauce Shape, 9 1/4 In.	130.00
Heinz Catsup, Roped Corners, Globular, No Top	15.00
Heinz Chili Sauce, Labels	18.00
Heinz Tomato Ketchup, Pittsburgh, U.S.A., Clear, Barrel Juice Dispenser	165.00
Heinz's Chili Sauce, Pittsburgh, Pa., 8 In. *Illus*	115.00
Horlick's Malted Milk, Jar, Embossed, Glass Top	135.00
Horse Radish, Saginaw Beef Co., Saginaw, Mich., 6 1/2 In. *Illus*	28.00
Horse Radish Warranted Pure By Remington & Co., N.Y., Aqua, 6 In.	93.00
Hunt, Mustard Pot, Blue Glaze, Stenciled Dogs, Horses, Men & Wild Boar	20.00
I. Rokeach & Sons, Inc., Oil Refiners, Brooklyn, N.Y., Embossed, Clear, 10 1/2 In.	16.00
J. Fan Prunes Dente Bordeaux, Aqua, Pontil, France, c.1860, 10 In.	82.50
J. McCollick & Co., N.Y., Medium Blue Green, IP, c.1860, Cylindrical, 11 1/4 In.	1210.00
Jar, A. Doufour & C. Bordeaux, Light Yellow, Apple Green, 4 3/4 In.	71.50
Jar, Elephant Peanuts, Round	290.00
Jar, Olive Green, Wide Mouth, Cylinder, OP, 5 1/2 In.	180.00
Jelly, Jar, Banner Shield, Tin Cover, Opalescent Rim, 3 4/8 In.	38.00
JFG Peanut Butter, Globe, 1 Lb.	15.00
Jumbo Brand Pepper Sauce, 3 Oz.	30.00
Jumbo Peanut Butter, Fishbowl Bail, Lid	95.00
Jumbo Peanut Butter, Garrett & Co., Weldon, N.C., 4 3/4 In. *Illus*	9.00
Jumbo Peanut Butter, Lid, 7 Oz.	27.00
Junins Catsup, Balto, Md., Embossed, Corker	30.00

Food, Heinz's Chili Sauce,
Pittsburgh, Pa., 8 In.

Food, Horse Radish, Saginaw
Beef Co., Saginaw, Mich., 6 1/2 In.

Food, Jumbo Peanut Butter, Garrett
& Co., Weldon, N.C., 4 3/4 In.

Food, My Wife's Salad Dressing,
Chicago, 8 In.

L.F. Mustard, Barrel, OP, 2 x 4 1/4 In. 21.00
Label Only Food Bottle, Bright Yellow Green, Applied Mouth, 11 18 In. 132.00
Label Only Food Bottle, Clear, Tooled Lip, 7 3/8 In. 253.00
Lake's Celebrated Radish, Denver, Colo., Horse Picture 32.00
Larkin Co., Buffalo, Deep Emerald Green, No Stopper, 3 In. 25.00
Lord Ward's Worcestershire Sauce, Aqua, Whittled, Round, 8 3/4 In. 45.00
Mason's Wine Essences, Nottingham, Blue, Oval, Indented Front Panel, 5 In. 12.00
Mayonnaise, Jar, Paper Label, Lithographed Lid 8.00
Mayor Walnut Oil Co., Kansas City, Mo., Amber, Rectangular 15.00
McCormick & Co., Sweitzers Ginger, Embossed, Label 15.00
Moxie Nerve Food, Lowell, Mass., Aqua, Applied Blob, 10 In. 150.00
Mustard, H.J. Neuhauser, Pontil, Rolled Lip, 1850-1860, 5 In. 93.50
Mustard Jar, Battleship Main, Milk Glass .... 121.00 to 302.50
My Wife's Salad Dressing, Chicago, 8 In. .... *Illus* 25.00
Nemo Korn Syrup, Boston, Round, Pt. 12.00
Old English Table Salt, Glasgow, Jar, Aqua, Glob Top, Convex Panels Around 40.00
Old Judge Coffee, Jar, Owl Picture, Qt. 20.00
Old Manse Syrup, Oelerich & Berry Co., Paper Label, 7 In. .... *Illus* 25.00
Pacific Oysters, Jar, Snap Missing, Pt. 15.00
Pepper Sauce, see Pepper Sauce category
Perrine's Apple Ginger, Philadelphia, Applied Tapered Lip, 10 In. 308.00
Pickle, see Pickle category
Platts Oysters, Jar, Health Seal, Bubble Front, OP, Pt. 85.00

Food, Old Manse Syrup,	*Food, Tic Tic Relish,*	*Food, Tiger Catsup,*
Oelerich & Berry Co.,	*Embossed Clock, Pat. No.*	*Burlington Canning Co.,*
Paper Label, 7 In.	*95888, Paper Label, 4 In.*	*10 1/2 In.*

Pride Of Long Island Tomato Catsup, Label.. 32.00
Pure Honey, Beehive, Dug, 1/2 Lb. 12.00
Pure Olive Oil S.S.T., Bulbous, Light Green, BIM, Embossed, 12 In. 28.00
Pure Olive Oil SSP, Citron, Bulbous, Long Neck, 11 1/4 In. 35.00
Queen Jelly, Patented 1873, Lid.. 12.00
Reddington & Co., Ess Of Jamaica Ginger, San Francisco, Aqua, Drippy Top.............. 24.00
Refrigerator, Sparkletts, Telephone Private Exchange, Albany, Aqua, ABM 20.00
Reliance Coffee, Jar, Paper Label, Lithographed Cover..................................... 25.00
Roses Lime Juice, Brown, Lime Foliage, Embossed, 13 1/2 In................................. 110.00
Royal Mint Sauce, H.C. Mfg. Co., Detroit, Green, c.1880-1900, 6 7/8 In..................... 121.00
San Jose Fruit Packing Co., Jar, Cover, Milk Glass Insert, Eagle & 2 Bears, 1/2 Pt. ... 120.00
Sauer's Peppermint Extract, Label 10.00
Seely's Lemon Extract, 1875.. 24.00
Shriver's Oyster Ketchup, Baltimore, Deep Olive Amber, IP, c.1860, 7 1/4 In. 1430.00
Souder's Elegant Flavoring Extracts, Royal Remedy Co. Dayton, Ohio, Oval............... 15.00
Souvenir Of Sand Mountain's Best Sorghum, Vt. Cobb, Jug, Stoneware, Tan, Pt...... 29.00
Special Brand Extract Jamaica Ginger, Aqua 7.50
St. Louis Cider, Green & Clark, Pottery, Blue Neck Band 65.00
Stoddard, Clover Leaf, Amber, Olive Tint, Rolled Lip, c.1870, 8 In. 577.50
Stork Pure Foods, Jelly Jar, Label... 15.00
Sylmar Brand, Los Angeles Olive Growers, Label, 1900, Pt.................................... 50.00
Syrup, Pillar Mold, Pewter Spout & Lid, Blown Handle, Pontil, c.1850, 9 1/2 In.......... 440.00
Tic Tic Relish, Embossed Clock, Pat. No. 95888, Paper Label, 4 In....................*Illus* 20.00
Tiger Catsup, Burlington Canning Co., 10 1/2 In..*Illus* 20.00
Towels Log Cabin, Maple Syrup, Jug, Handle, Tan & White, Ovoid, 8 In. 30.00
Warranted Pure Honey, 1 Lb. 12.50
Wells Miller Provost, Sauce, Emerald Green, 8 Fluted Sides, OP, 8 In. 357.00
Wendell & Espy Mince Meat, Philadelphia, Aqua, Square, 8 1/8 In. 357.50

———————————————— **FRUIT JAR** ————————————————

Fruit jars made of glass have been used in the United States since the 1850s. More than 1,000 different jars have been found with varieties of closures, embossing, and colors. The date 1858 on many jars refers to a patent and not the age of the bottle. Be sure to look in this listing under any name or initial that appears on your jar. If not otherwise indicated, the jar listed is of clear glass and quart size. The numbers used in the entries in the form RB-0 refer to the book *Red Book of Fruit Jars Number 7* by Douglas M. Leybourne Jr. A publication for collectors is *Fruit Jar Newsletter,* 364 Gregory Avenue, West Orange, NJ 07052-3743.

FRUIT JAR, A. Stone & Co., Philada, Aqua, IP, Wax Seal Ring, Qt., RB-2743 .... 100.00
   A. Stone & Co., Philada, Aqua, Threaded Glass Stopper, Cylindrical, Qt., RB-2747..... 352.00

Fruit Jar, Ball Perfect Mason,
Green, 7 In., RB-339

Fruit Jar, Beaver, Clear, Facing Left,
Metal Cover, 5 1/2 In., RB-426

A. Stone & Co., Philada, Aqua, Wax Sealer, Qt.Plus, RB-2743-1 .... 204.00
A.B.C., Pat. April 15th, 1884, Aqua, Ground Lip, Glass Lid, Qt., RB-4-2 .... 231.00 to 250.00
A.B.C. Pat. April 15th, 1884, Aqua, Metal Clamp, Glass Lid, Qt., RB-4-1 .... 275.00
Air Tight, Deep Aqua, Barrel, IP, Wax Seal Ring, Qt., RB-51 .... 650.00
All Right, Aqua, Metal Cap & Wire Clamp, Qt., RB-61 .... 207.00
All Right, Patd Jan 28th 1868, Deep Aqua, Repro Cap & Wire, Qt., RB-51 .... 110.00
All Right, Patd. Jan 26th 1868, Cornflower, Repro Lid, Wire Closure, Qt., RB-59 .... 187.00
Allen, Pat. June 1871, Aqua, Repro Metal Clamp, Square, Qt., RB-57 .... 100.00
Allen's Pat. June 1871, Aqua, Square, Glass Lid, Repro Metal Clamp, Qt., RB-57 ..... 100.00 to 160.00
Almy, Aqua, Glass Screw On Lid, Pt.Plus, 6 In., RB-63 .... 66.00
American, Eagle, Light Green, Glass Lid & Wire, Australia, 1/2 Gal., RB-73 ... 135.00 to 148.00
Apple Green, Pat. Oct. 19, 1858, Glass Lid, Cylindrical, Qt., RB-1212 .... 182.00
ARS, Script, Aqua, Applied Collared Mouth, Glass A. Kline Stopper, Qt., RB-94.......... 66.00
Aseptic Products Co., Amber, Square, Pt., RB-98-2 .... 16.00
Atherholt Fisher & Co., Philada, Aqua, Oct.27, '63, Stopper, Qt., RB-103 .... 633.00
Atlas, Good Luck, Clear, Qt., RB-130-1 .... 4.00
Atlas, Good Luck, Clear, T-Dimples, 1/2 Pt., RB-131 .... 11.00
Atlas, H.A. Mason, Clear, Ground Pontil, Band, 1/2 Pt., RB-133 .... 7.00
Atlas, H.A. Mason, Mini-Bank, Clear, Slotted Lid, 1/2 Pt., RB-133 .... 10.00
Atlas E-Z Seal, Aqua, 1/2 Pt., RB-121 .... 12.00
Atlas E-Z Seal, Aqua, Amber Swirls, Lid, Qt., RB-109 .... 25.00
Atlas E-Z Seal, Golden Amber, Glass Lid, Wire Bail, Qt., RB-114 .... 55.00
Atlas E-Z Seal, Lightning Closure, Clear, 1/2 Pt., RB-110 .... 5.00
Atlas Junior Mason, Clear, 1/2 Pt., RB-139 .... 15.00
Atlas Mason, Erased Whitney, Aqua, Qt., RB-144 .... 30.00
Atlas Strong Shoulder Mason, Clear, Unslotted Lid, Sample, 1/2 Pt., RB-162 .... 20.00
Atlas Strong Shoulder Mason, Light Cobalt Blue, Qt., RB-161 .... 15.00
Automatic Sealer, Aqua, Glass Lid, Wire Bale, Qt., RB-177 .... 160.00
B. G. Co., Golden Amber, Embossed, Wax Sealer Mouth, Qt., RB-465 .... 55.00
B.B. Wilcox 18, Aqua, Glass Lid, Wire Bail, Qt., RB-3008 .... 82.00
Ball, Aqua Moonstone, ABM Lip, 1915-1925, 1/2 Gal. 198.00
Ball, Light Green, Amber Striations, Swirled Coloring, Zinc Cap, Qt., RB-191 .... 88.00
Ball, Mason, Green Aqua, Yellow Striations, Zinc Lid, 1920s, Qt. 44.00
Ball Ideal, Blue, 1/2 Pt., RB-217 .... 50.00
Ball Ideal, Blue, Glass Top, Pat. July 14, 1908, Qt., RB-220....................................... 5.00
Ball Ideal, Clear, Lightning, Banded Neck, 1/2 Pt., RB-216 .... 6.00
Ball Ideal, Clear, T-Boss, Pt., RB-240 .... 20.00
Ball Ideal, Clear, T-Boss, Qt., RB-240.. 12.00 to 15.00
Ball Mason, Glass-Handled Mug, Pt. 15.00
Ball Mason, Groman, Harvey, Clear, Unthreaded Stopper, 1946, Pt. 15.00

Ball Mason, John Ketchem, 40 Years & Counting, Clear, Gold Green Label, Pt. 20.00
Ball Mason, Scholes, Addison B., Happy Sailing, 1963-1984, Pt.................................. 20.00
Ball Mason, Wade, Bill, 47 Years Service, Man's Bust, Glass-Handled Mug, Pt. 20.00
Ball Mason, Yellow Green, Qt., RB-294 .... 20.00
Ball Perfect Mason, Blue, Square, Qt., RB-344.. 8.00
Ball Perfect Mason, Forest Green, Qt., RB-343 .... 80.00
Ball Perfect Mason, Green, 7 In., RB-339...*Illus* 45.00
Ball Perfect Mason, Olive Amber, Pt., RB-339.. 110.00
Ball Perfect Mason, Yellow Amber, Zinc Lid, Qt., RB-339.................................38.00 to 66.00
Ball Square Mason, Pt., RB-383... 15.00
Ball Standard, Medium Olive Green, Amber Swirls, Wax Sealer, Qt., RB-386............ 250.00
Ball Sure Seal, Blue, Bulged Neck, Pt., RB-389-1 .... 10.00
Ball Sure Seal, Blue, Erased Sanitary, Pt., RB-390... 30.00
Baltimore Glass Works, Aqua, J.D. Willoughby Pat. Jan. 4, 1859, Stopper, RB-399.... 240.00
Banner, Clear, Glass Screw On Lid, RB-403 .... 115.00
Banner, Reisd, Jan 22, 1867, Aqua, Glass Lid, Qt., RB-403.. 121.00
BBGMCo., Monogram, Aqua, Glass Lid, Metal Screw Band, 1/2 Gal., RB-195............. 88.00
BBGMCo., Monogram, Aqua, Ground Mouth, Cylindrical, 1/2 Pt., RB-195 .... 523.00
BBGMCo., Monogram, Aqua, Lined, Porcelain, Aqua, Zinc Lid, Qt., RB-2373............... 165.00
BBGMCo., Monogram, Golden Amber, Ground Mouth, Cylindrical, Qt., RB-195-2 ...... 4675.00
Beaver, Clear, Facing Left, Metal Cover, 5 1/2 In., RB-426....................................*Illus* 395.00
Beaver, Pale Yellow Tint, Glass Lid, Zinc Screw Band, Canada, 1/2 Gal., RB-424-1.... 44.00
Beechnut, T.M., Leaves, Pat. Oct. 23, 1900, Pontil, No Vacuum Cap, 1/2 Pt., RB-432. 6.00
Bennett's, No. 1, Aqua, Cylindrical, Qt., RB-444.. 396.00
Bennett's, No.1, Over Ghosted Embossing, Aqua, Pat.Feb.6th, 1866, Qt., RB-445....... 247.00
Bennett's, No.2, Reversed, Aqua, No Stopper, Qt., RB-446 .... 330.00
Best, Root Beer Amber, Insert, Zinc Screw Band, Canada, Qt., RB-453 ....*Illus* 220.00
Bloeser, Pat Sept. 27 1887, Aqua, Glass Lid, Wire Bail, Qt., RB-468 .... 605.00
Boldt Mason, Aqua, Qt., RB-480 .... 25.00
Bosco Double Seal, Pt., RB-485 .... 45.00
Bosco Double Seal, Qt., RB-485...30.00 to 35.00
Brackett's Perfection, Aqua, Tooled Lip, Tin Push On Lid, Qt., RB-504..................... 467.00
Brighton, Clamp Pat. March 30th, 1886, Wire Bail, Glass Lid, Embossed, RB-512....... 150.00
Buckeye No. 1, J. Adams Pat'd May 20, 1862, Glass Lid, Qt., RB-528.............185.00 to 210.00
Buckeye No. 2, Deep Aqua, Glass Lid, Repro Metal Yoke Clamp, 1/2 Gal., RB-527.... 100.00
Burns Mf'g. Co., Patent Nov. 27, 1883, Aqua, Ground Mouth, Cylindrical, Qt., RB-545 495.00
C F J Co., see Fruit Jar, Mason's CFJ Co.
C.F. Spencer's Patent, Rochester, N.Y., Aqua, 1/2 Gal., RB-2682............................... 44.00
C.F. Spencer's Patent, Rochester, N.Y., Aqua, Tin Lid, Qt., RB-2682.............132.00 to 165.00

Fruit Jar, Best, Root Beer Amber, Insert,
Zinc Screw Band, Canada, Qt., RB-453

Fruit Jar, Chef, The Berdan Co.,
7 In., RB-590

C.F. Spencer's Patent, Rochester, N.Y., Deep Aqua, 1/2 Gal., RB-2682 .... 77.00
C.K. Halle & Co., Cleveland, Oh., Aqua, 1863-1880, Cylindrical, Qt., RB-1176 .... 215.00
Calidad Coronado, Qt. 15.00
Canton, Domestic, Amethyst Tint, Ground Lip, Patd. Dec. 31, 1889, Pt., RB-566........ 170.00
Canton, Pat. Appd For, Glass Lid, Wire Bail, Slug Plate, Qt., RB-563-1 .... 110.00
Canton Domestic, Amethyst Tin, Patd. Dec. 31, 1889, Glass Lid, Pt., RB-566............ 187.00
Canton Domestic, Clear, Glass Lid, Wire Bail, Qt., RB-565 .... 66.00
Canton Fruit Jar, Qt., RB-561.. 150.00
Cassidy, Pat. Sept. 22, 1885, Ground Mouth, Wire Bail, Cylindrical, 1/2 Gal., RB-573. 715.00
Champion, Aqua, Ground Mouth, Iron Clamp, Qt., RB-583.. 73.00
Chef, The Berdan Co., 7 In., RB-590..*Illus* 4.00
Clarke Fruit Jar Co., Aqua, Metal Cam Lever On Wire Bail, No Lid, Qt.RB-603 .... 50.00
Clarke Fruit Jar Co., Cleveland, Oh., Aqua, 1 1/2 Pt., RB-603.................................... 115.00
Cohansey, Aqua, Glass Lid, Wire Clamp, Pt., RB-629 .... 44.00
Cohansey, Pat. Mch 20, '77, Barrel, Aqua, Wax Sealer, Qt., RB-433-1 .... 84.00
Cohansey Glass Mfg., Barrel, Qt., RB-631 .... 65.00
Cohansey Glass Mfg. Co., Pat. Mar. 20, '77, Aqua, Barrel, Wax Sealer, Qt., RB-633-1 143.00
Cohansey Mfg. Co., Patent Feb. 12, 1867, Aqua, Metal, Cover, Pt., RB-630 .... 55.00
Commodore, Aqua, Bell Shape, Repro Closure, 1865, Qt., RB-646.............................. 853.00
Commonwealth Fruit Jar, Aqua, Australia, Qt. Plus 325.00
Commonwealth Jar, Yellow Green Tint, Glass Lid, Wire Bail, Australia, Qt., RB-650. 71.00
Crystal, Aqua, Zinc Lid, 1873-1890, 1/2 Gal., RB-705... 22.00
Crystal Jar, Sun Colored Amethyst, Glass Lid, 1/2 Gal., RB-709 .... 16.50
Crystal Jar C G, Aqua, Ground Lip, Screw Cap, Qt., RB-708 .... 83.00
Crystal Jar C G, Clear, Glass Lid, Qt., RB-708... 33.00
Cunningham & Co., Pittsburgh, Pa., Deep Aqua, 1870-1875, 1/2 Gal., RB-722........... 121.00
Cunningham & Co., Pittsburgh, Yellow Amber, Qt., RB-723 .... 55.00
Dandy, Trademark, Light Yellow Amber, Wire Bail, No Lid, Cylindrical, Qt., RB-751. 116.00
Deep Aqua, Unembossed, Applied Collared Mouth, Pontil, 1/2 Gal. 83.00
Delicious Crushed Fruits, Pale Aqua, 1886-1900, 1/2 Gal., RB-769 .... 88.00
Dexter, Aqua, Cloudy, Qt., RB-772 .... 20.00
Dexter, Aqua, Glass Lid, Metal Screw Band, 1/2 Gal., RB-772.................................... 22.00
Dexter, Surrounded By Fruit, Aqua, Ground Mouth, Cylindrical, Qt., RB-773 .... 33.00
DG Co., Monogram, Aqua, Zinc Lid, Cylindrical, 1/2 Gal., RB-776............................. 44.00
Dictator D, Patent, D.I. Holcomb, Dec. 14th, 1869, Aqua, c.1869, Qt., RB-783-1 .... 33.00
Dillon G. Co., Fairmount, Ind., Emerald Green, Applied Groove Ring, 1/2 Gal.RB-790 253.00
Dillon G. Co., Fairmount, Ind., Light Green, Embossed, Wax Sealer, 1/2 Gal., RB-790 16.50
Dillon G. Co., Fairmount, Ind., Light Green, Wax Sealer, Cylindrical, 1/2 Gal., RB-790 33.00
Drey Perfect Mason, Clear, 1/2 Pt., RB-843-1 .... 25.00
E.C. Flaccus Co., Milk Glass, Glass Insert, Metal Screw Band, Pt., RB-1014 .... 358.00
E.C. Flaccus Co., Clear, 1898-1910, Pt., RB-1016.. 44.00
Eagle, Aqua, Applied Mouth, No Closure, Qt., RB-871... 55.00
Eagle, Reisd June 16th 1868, Aqua, Glass Lid, Repro Metal Yoke, Qt., RB-873 .... 121.00
Eclipse, Patd.Sept.12, 1882, Green, Glass Lid, 1/2 Gal., RB-885 .... 357.00
Economy Sealer Patd Sept. 15th 1885, Aqua, No Closure, Qt., RB-908 .... 66.00
Electric, Globe, Aqua, Pat. Appl. For, Glass Lid, Wire Bail, Qt., RB-922.............. 86.00 to 95.00
Electric, World Globe, Aqua, Glass Lid, Wire Clamp, Qt., RB-921 .... 143.00
Empire, Aqua, Applied Mouth, Reproduction Willoughby Stopple, Qt., RB-927 .... 275.00
Empire, F.A. Bunnell's, Aqua, Glass Lid, Reproduction Metal Clamp, Qt., RB-929 ..... 303.00
Empire, F.A. Bunnell's, Feb. 13th, 1866, Aqua, Glass Lid, Metal Yoke, Qt., RB-929 ... 242.00
Espy Phil, Aqua, Embossed, Qt., RB-936 .... 175.00
Eureka, Pat. Dec. 27th, 1864, Aqua, Ground Lip, Qt., RB-948...................................... 110.00
Excelsior, Aqua, Ground Mouth, No Closure, 1/2 Gal., RB-958 .... 38.00
Excelsior, Aqua, Qt., RB-957 .... 575.00
Excelsior, Patd Aug. 8th, 1862, Aqua, Glass Lid, Metal Screw Band, Qt., RB-956........ 231.00
Excelsior Improved, Aqua, Glass Lid, Zinc Band, Qt., RB-961.................................... 33.00
F. & J. Bodine, Philadelphia, Aqua, No Closure, Qt., RB-474...................................... 72.00
F.C.G. Co., Yellow Amber, Groove Ring Wax Sealer, Qt., RB-989 .... 148.00
Fahnestock Albree & Co., Aqua, Pontil, Qt.Plus, RB-971 .... 121.00
Farm Family, Ground Mouth, Glass, Cover, Cylindrical, Pt. 550.00
Federal, Green Tint, 7 In., RB-996 ....*Illus* 138.00
Flaccus Bros., Steer Head, Touch Haze, No Glass Cap, 1/2 Pt., RB-1008.................... 25.00
Flaccus Bros., Steers Head, Clear, Glass Lid, Pt.RB-1014 .... 55.00

KOVELS'
25-YEAR BOTTLE
MARKET REPORT

Bottle collecting has been a major hobby in the United States since the 1950s, but the type of bottle that is most popular has changed over the years. At first collectors wanted 18th- and early 19th-century blown bottles and historical flasks, 19th-century fruit jars, and inks. Blob-top sodas were saved by a few, usually collectors who did not live on the East Coast, where other bottles are plentiful. In those days of excavations in major cities, the heavy glass soda and pottery bottles were being unearthed daily.

Another group of collectors started around the same time in the 1950s. They were buying the brand new figural bottles created by Avon Cosmetics, Jim Beam, Ezra Brooks, and other liquor companies. These bottles were regularly discontinued, so they were called "limited editions." The craze for modern bottles became so frenzied in the early 1980s there were arrests for selling fake bottles with forged papers of authenticity.

Today the high prices of bottles made before 1904, when the automatic bottle machine came into general use, have caused beginning collectors to concentrate on other types. Milk bottles with applied color labels, food jars with paper labels still in place, and the commemorative soda bottles for brands like Coca-Cola and Pepsi-Cola, attract the new young collectors. Bottle collecting is again a growing hobby, with more shows, more collectors, and more clubs.

About 1850, glass barber bottles were being made in the major American glasshouses. Glass collectors have searched for these elaborate bottles since the 1920s, and they are still paying good prices. This 11-inch aqua hobnail bottle brought $57 in 1992. The blue-and-white-stripe bottle is a rare form of blown glass, and it sold for $350.

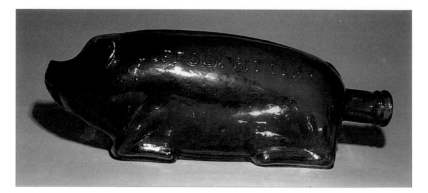

Pig-shape bottles made of glass or pottery have always brought high prices. In 1975 this 10-inch Suffolk Bitters bottle sold for $750. Today it is worth thousands of dollars.

Bitters bottles have been the queens of bottles since the early bottle-collecting days. More than 1,000 different varieties are known. This National Bitters ear of corn bottle was shown in our 1977 book, with no price listed, but a similar one sold for $1,600 that year.

This is the tenth time we have written a book devoted exclusively to bottles and bottle prices. The first edition, published in 1971, was called *The Official Bottle Price List.* We realized that bottle collecting had become one of the major hobbies in America by the late 1960s, and we were sure there would be collectors who wanted a special book just about bottles. The next edition of the book was done in 1973, and we have continued to write a new book every two or three years.

As bottle collecting changed through the years, the books about bottles have continued to help collectors to understand the hobby. The first book to classify bottles was a book about bitters written in 1947 by James Thompson. Our 1971 book listed 135 books in the bibliography. So many of these were privately printed books with small distribution that we decided to include six companies that sold the books about bottles.

Information about bottles could be found in other places. The Antique Bottle Collectors Association of California first met in 1959. *Western Collector* magazine started the "Bottle World" section in 1965. By 1967 our book *Know Your Antiques* included a section on how to date a bottle. The Federation of Historical Bottle Clubs, now known as the Federation of Historical Bottle Collectors, started in 1972, and clubs formed in hundreds of cities. Bottles were dug from dumps, privies, and swamps, or found in basements or old stone walls. Modern bottles—Avon, Ezra Brooks, Jim Beam, and thirty-three other brands—were also listed in our first bottle book. The interest, and the prices, for modern bottles peaked in 1982.

There have been several events and landmark auctions that have affected bottle collecting. The most important was the Gardner auction. Bottle scholar Charlie Gardner started collecting in the 1930s and amassed a collection of more than 3,000 bottles of all types. When he sold his collection

These bottles were sold in 1987 at these prices. Left to Right: Bitters, Seaworth, figural, lighthouse, amber, 6½ in. $2,400; flask, McK G 1-042, Washington & Taylor, cobalt blue, qt. $400; ink, Harrison's Columbian, cylindrical, sapphire blue, 2¼ in. $250; cologne, monument, tooled mouth, cobalt blue, 11⅞ in. $225; bitters, Herkules, flat panels, emerald green, 7½ in. $800; fruit jar, my choice, applied mouth, yellow amber, ½ gal. $850; blown, hat, 3 mold, rolled rim, cobalt blue, 2½ in. $250; flask, black girl, crawling on flask, brown glaze, pottery, 6 in. $850.

at auction in 1975, he grossed over $1.2 million. Many records were set at the Gardner sale. A cobalt blue Columbia pint flask (McKearin GI-119) brought a world record price for a flask at $21,000. The Jared Spencer olive amber flask (McKearin GX-24) was $26,000; a similar flask with medallions and diamonds (McKearin GX-25) sold for $16,000; a sapphire blue Old Homestead Wild Cherry Bitters Patent, ¾ quart was $16,500; and the Genl Scotts New York Artillery bitters (Ring number S78) was $11,000.

Each of the bottles sold at the sale had a round paper sticker that said "Gardner collection." The sticker was numbered to match the sale catalog. Several inexpensive bottles from that auction sold again in 1995. The golden amber East India Root Bitters bottle that sold for $95 in 1975 sold for $385, and the Sharp's Mountain Herb Bitters bottle that cost $40 was sold in 1995 for $121.

In 1983, the historical flasks owned by Edmund and Jayne Blaske were auctioned. At that sale twenty bottles were sold that had come from the Gardner collection. Probably the most famous bottle, the Jared Spencer

The Pineapple Bitters is another popular bottle. This 9-inch amber bottle sold for $250 in 1975. This year amber pineapple bottles sold for about $75 to $300. Examples in rare colors sold for more; an olive green for $1,430 and a blue green for $4,510.

Rare bitters bottles were bringing thousands of dollars by 1992. The root beer–color Dr. S. Mansfield Highland Bitters was $2,500 at a bottle show that year.

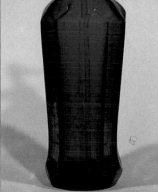

Only the old Coca-Cola bottles like this Winona, Minnesota, seltzer bottle were seen at the shows in the 1970s. This bottle sold for $35. This year, collectors are also buying the new commemorative Coke bottles.

The only candy containers seen at the bottle shows in the 1970s were made of glass, like this 4-inch-high Billiken screwtop figural bottle. It sold for $45 in 1975. Today at the shows, all sorts of candy containers made of plastic, papier-mache, or glass are sold.

(McKearin GX-24), was the world record holder at $26,000. It was resold later for less at $16,000. The similar diamond and medallion flask (GX-25) brought $21,000, an increase of $5,000. The Andrew Jackson, eagle portrait flask (McKearin GI-69) that was $25,000 resold for $22,000. The cabin-shape Jacob's Cabin Tonic Bitters (McKearin GVII-6) that was $4,000 brought $11,000.

Prices for bottles have fluctuated through the years. Inflation has caused some prices to rise, although changing tastes and changing demand have been major factors also. But some things have remained the same. Flasks still command the very highest prices. Blown or mold-blown bottles made before the automatic bottling machine of 1904 are top sellers. Cobalt blue and bright yellow or green examples are still top sellers, too. Condition is of prime importance—no chips or cracks, no scratches or cloudy appearance, no bubbles or other flaws from the manufacturing. Although repairs and repolishing are possible, today the best bottles are those known to be in untouched pristine condition. A known repair will lower value. Yet there are still great finds. A collector-dealer stopped at a church rummage sale in 1995 and bought a Constitution Bitters bottle for less than $10. It was probably a donation from an elderly parishioner who kept the colorful bottle on a shelf. The collector made a substantial profit when the bottle auctioned for $3,080 a few months later.

If the bitters bottle is the queen of the bottles, the historic flask is the king, with a record price of $66,000 set in 1993 for an olive yellow Jared Spencer flask. Other flasks are less expensive. This example of a 5 1/2-inch-high flask with label under glass pictures a woman. It was only $40 in 1975. Today it would bring $200 to $600.

Nineteenth-century blown food bottles of all types are now selling for hundreds of dollars. A label adds extra value. The Lutz Brothers Tomato Catsup is fluted and has an open pontil. It is worth more than $200.

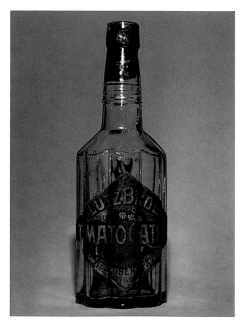

The machine-made Beechnut brand catsup bottle was worth $12 in 1987. It would be about $50 today because of the labels.

The most expensive fruit jars have always been those in unusual colors. Best is cobalt blue or milk glass. This amber jar embossed "Globe, Patent May 25, 1866" sold for $63 in 1992. Clear glass fruit jars can be found for as little as fifty cents. Rare fruit jars sell for $100 to $500, although a few have brought more than $1,000.

We pictured this Shrewsbury Brand, E. C. Hazard & Company beets bottle on the cover of our 1982 book. The company put its paper label on a plain canning jar. Most of the value is the early label, not the bottle. An advertising collector or a collector of labeled bottles would pay $75 for it.

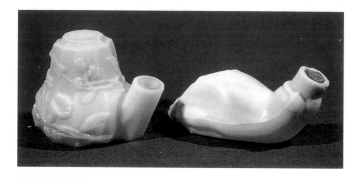

There are many inkwell, inkstand, and ink bottle collectors who now compete with pen collectors to find the best of the old glass inks. These milk glass teakettle inks were pictured in our 1975 book. Today each would be worth about $350 to $400.

Inks came in varied sizes, with different labels. Many were made of cobalt blue glass, which is always popular with collectors. This labeled quart of Signet ink was in our 1979 book.

An early collector removed the label from this Carter's ink bottle, but it still sold for $85 in 1987. Today it is worth up to $250.

Mr. and Mrs. Carter's ink bottles have been listed in almost every edition of the bottle price list because they are so easy to identify and so popular with collectors. There are several versions, one type made in Germany, another in Japan. This German set was in the 1982 book. Today it is worth $200.

Figural bottles have "crossover" appeal. Bottle enthusiasts buy them, decorators like them for window displays, and many collectors can't ignore a figural of special interest, like a baseball player or the Statue of Liberty. The 12-inch-high brandy bottle shaped like a Spanish dancer sold for $45 in 1992. The milk glass Statue of Liberty bottle has always been expensive and hard to find.

In 1973, bottle collectors were little concerned with labels and boxes, so this Log Cabin Extract bottle with original label, instructions, and box was worth only $75. Many medicine bottles are still found with original packaging and contents.

Even rare color milk bottles, like this green Weckerle quart bottle, were ignored by collectors in the sixties, but by 1975, milk bottles were offered at the shows and there was even a newsletter for collectors. The price today for the green milk bottle, $100.

The applied color label (ACL) or pryro-glaze (pyro) label first gained attention among milk bottle collectors. Unusual names or color graphics added to the value. A green glass bottle with a yellow pyro "Sun Valley" has two value plusses. This half-gallon bottle was only $70 in 1982. It's at least $100 today.

Most mineral water bottles have thick walls, sloping shoulders, and tapered collars. Most were made in a mold and had the embossed name of the company and city. A few were made in figural shapes. The best known are the Poland Water bottles from Poland Springs, Maine. The company, run by Hiram Ricker, designed the bottle in 1876 to look like Moses. The design is based on the biblical passage that tells how Moses struck the rock and water flowed forth. More than forty versions of the Moses bottle have been made.

Small comic ceramic bottles were popular giveaways in the days just before and after Prohibition. The Wee Scotch and the 19th Hole miniatures are typical of this kind of bottle. Most were made in Germany or Japan. Today comic miniatures sell for $75 and up.

Miniature jugs were also give-aways. Collectors of both pottery and bottles search for these jugs. Each one has a message, often like "Compliments, James B. Weaver." In 1975 we listed the 4½-inch-tall motto jug for $18, Old Continental for $17.50, and James Weaver for $7.50. Today each would cost more than $50.

Nailsea-type bottles are easy to identify. Look for the mulitcolor loopings. This flask sold for $480 in 1992.

The cathedral-shape pickle bottle did hold pickles in the 19th century. This 12-inch-deep aqua bottle was shown in our 1977 book. The large pickle bottles sell today for about $150 to $600.

It makes sense to clearly identify a bottle that holds poison. Some were shaped like skulls, some had raised bumps, some had cross-hatching or a raised skull and crossbones. Many had the raised word "poison." Cobalt blue was a popular color. As the 19th-century embossed, colored bottles became more expensive, collectors turned to paper-labeled clear bottles from the 20th century. This Bugine bottle was only $5 in 1987. The skull shape bottle was $300 in 1975. Both are worth much more today.

Soda is water that has been carbonated. The process was known in England in 1807. A heavy bottle was needed, so the blob-top soda bottle was made. It had a sloping shoulder and a large, fat blob-top. Collectors sometimes paint the raised printing white so it will show in a photograph like this one. The bottles say "Seitz and Bros., Easton, Pa." and "Union Glassworks, J & A Dearborn."

Some bottles were made of heavy pottery or stoneware. They were inexpensive to manufacture and were popular for beer and household chemicals. The bottles were often made with two-tone brown glaze and a printed label. This bottle says "Old Jug Lager."

In the day of the local neighborhood bar, it was not uncommon for the owner to give regular customers a special Christmas-gift bottle. John Schuldt of Meriden, Connecticut, included the words "A Merry Christmas and a Happy New Year" on his bottle. The bottle sold for $35 in 1975.

Vinegar and other food products have long been packed in clear glass jars with paper labels. This "Home Guard" bottle is a commercial fruit jar with a special paper label. It sold for $5 in 1987. It's not much more today.

Bottle collectors seem to divide into two groups—those who want old bottles and those who want modern ceramic bottles. The special bottles made by Jim Beam, Ski Country, Ezra Brooks, and others were at the height of their popularity in the 1980s; then interest dwindled. Today a few of these bottles are going up in price, especially those with sports-related themes. This Ski Country redwing blackbird bottle, the Old Commonwealth "Lunch Time," and the Old Mr. Boston Bart Starr bottles are all from the past twenty years. They were sold filled at the liquor store.

Flaccus Bros., Steers Head, Clear, Pt., RB-1007-1 .... 75.00
Flaccus Bros., Steers Head, Milk Glass, Lid, Pt., RB-1013 .... 250.00
Flaccus Bros., Steers Head, Yellow, Amber Tone, Ground Lip, Pt., RB-1014 .... 415.00
Flaccus Bros., Trade Mark, Clear, Simplex Glass Lid, 1898-1910, Pt., RB-1014.......... 66.00
Foster, see Fruit Jar, Sealfast
Franklin, Aqua, c.1865, 1/2 Gal., RB-1033..11.00 to 33.00
Franklin Dexter, Aqua, Glass, Metal Screw Band, Qt., RB-1034.................................. 16.50
Franklin Dexter, Aqua, Ground Mouth, Glass Lid, Metal Band, Qt., RB-1033-2.......... 27.50
Free-Blown, Blue, Amber Striation In Neck, Pontil, Cylindrical, 2 Qt. 5500.00
Free-Blown, Light Sapphire Blue, Rolled Mouth, Pontil, 1 Qt................................... 4675.00
Fridley & Cornman's, Patent Oct. 25th, 1859, Ladies Choice, Aqua, Qt., RB-1038 ...... 880.00
Fruit Keeper, Aqua, Glass Lid, Wire Clamp, Cylindrical, Qt., RB-1042....................... 38.00
G J Co., Aqua, Zinc Lid, Qt., RB-1109... 33.00
Garden Walk, Pt. 40.00
Gem, Aqua, CFJ Co., Nov.30, 1858, RB-1078 .... 80.00
Gem, Aqua, Glass Lid, Zinc Band, 1867-1890, Pt., RB-1053...................................... 33.00
Gilberds Improved Jar, Aqua, Ground Mouth, Cylindrical, Qt., RB-1108......... 143.00 to 231.00
Gilberds Improved Star, Aqua, Glass Lid, Wire Clamp, Cylindrical, 1/2 Gal., RB-1108 242.00
Gilberds Star, Aqua, Wire Bail Around Jar, Qt., RB-1107.. 200.00
Gilchrist, see Fruit Jar, GJ Co.
Glassboro Trademark Improved, Yellow Green, Glass Lid, Screw Band, Qt., RB-1114 22.00
Globe, Aqua, Wire & Iron Clamp, c.1900, Qt., RB-1124 .... 88.00
Globe, Blue, Glass Lid, Qt., RB-1123 .... 25.00
Globe, Brands, 1/2 Gal., RB-1124 .... 104.00
Globe, Wide Mouth, Lid, Qt., RB-1124... 150.00
Globe, Yellow Amber, Glass Lid, Wire Bail, 1/2 Gal., RB-1123 .... 104.00
Globe, Yellow Amber, Glass Lid, Wire Bail, Cylindrical, 1886-1900, Qt., RB-1123 ..... 116.00
Good House Keepers, 1/2 Pt., RB-1141-3 .... 30.00
Griffin's Pat. Oct. 7 1862, Aqua, Glass Lid, Iron Clamp, Qt. Plus, RB-1154 .... 94.00
Haine's 3 Patent March Lst 1870, Aqua, Glass Lid, Qt., RB-1170 .... 50.00
Haine's N.E. Plus Ultra, Aqua, Glass Lid, 2 Qt., RB-1173.. 395.00
Hamilton No. 3 Glass Works, Canada, Aqua, Glass Lid, 1/2 Gal., RB-1196 .... 110.00 to 165.00
Hannum & Hauk, Cleveland, O. 42.00
Hansee's PH, Palace Home, Pat. Dec. 19, 1899, Glass Lid, Wire, Qt., RB-1206 ...70.00 to 94.00
Hartell's, Deep Amethyst, Ground Lip, Glass Screw Lid, Qt., RB-1212 .... 1375.00
Hartell's, Grass Green, Lid, 2 Qt., RB-1212 .... 500.00
Hero, Patd Feby 12th, 1856, Apple Green, Screw Band, Qt., RB-1241-1....................... 413.00
Hero Cross, see Fruit Jar, Mason's Cross
Hilton's, Pat. 1868, Aqua, 1868-1880, Cylindrical, Qt., RB-1256 .... 203.50
Howe, Scranton, Pa., Green Aqua, Glass Lid, Wire Bail, Qt., RB-1274 .... 66.00
Howe Jar, Scranton, Pa., Aqua, Glass Lid, Wire Bail, Qt., RB-1274 .... 88.00

Fruit Jar, Federal,
Green Tint, 7 In.,
RB-996

Fruit Jar, J.C. Baker's, Blue,
Patent Aug. 14, 1860, Wire
Bail, Lid, 8 In., RB-188

Fruit Jar, Long Neck,
11 1/2 In.

Fruit Jar, Mason, Black, Qt.

Fruit Jar, Mason, Cornflower Blue, 1858, Qt.

Imperial, Pat. April 20th 1886, Glass Lid, Wire Clamp, Small Mouth, Pt., RB-1293 ..... 100.00
Imperial Trademark, Thomas Pat. July 12, 1892, Aqua, Glass Lid, Qt., RB-1291 .... 578.00
Improved Standard, Pat. April 17th, 1888, Aqua, Original Lid, Qt., RB-1307............. 633.00
Independent Jar, Clear, Glass Lid, 1880-1900, Qt., RB-1308 .... 16.00
J.C. Baker's, Blue, Patent Aug. 14, 1860, Wire Bail, Lid, 8 In., RB-188 ....*Illus* 400.00
J.C. Baker's, Pat. Aug.14, 1860, Aqua, Glass Lid, Ground Lid, Qt., RB-188 .... 159.00
J.J. Squire, March & Sept. 1865, Aqua, Glass Lid, Qt., RB-2696 .... 143.00
J.T. Kinney, Trenton, N.J., Aqua, A.Kline Stopper, Qt., RB-1420................................. 187.00
Johnson & Johnson, Amber, Contents, Label, 1/2 Pt., RB-1342.................................... 25.00
Johnson & Johnson, Cobalt Blue, Lid & Ring, Pt., RB-1344... 325.00
Kerr Self Sealing, Mason, Clear, Round, 1/2 Pt., RB-1374.. 4.00
Kerr Self Sealing, Mason, Sky Blue, 1925-1935, 1/2 Gal., RB-1371 .... 40.00
Kerr's 75th Anniversary, 1903-1978, Clear, Pt., RB-1388.. 40.00
King, Pat. Nov. 2, 1869, Deep Aqua, Glass Lid, Iron Yoke, Qt., RB-1418 .... 264.00
Kline's Pat. Oct. 27. 63, Aqua, Blown Glass Stopple, Qt., RB-1422 .... 72.00
Knott's Swindler, Palatine, W.V., Wax Sealer, Stenciled, 48 Oz... 300.00
Knowlton Vacuum, Pale Blue, Glass Lid, Perforated Zinc Cover, Pt., RB-1432 .... 33.00
Knox Mason, Clear, Marked Metal Lid, Band, 1/2 Pt., RB-1434.................................... 15.00
L & W's, Aqua, Wax Sealer Mouth, 1/2 Gal., RB-1528 .... 44.00
L'Ideale, Green, Lid, France, Liter, RB-1488 .... 50.00
Lafayette, Aqua, 3 Piece Glass & Metal Stopper, 1885-1900, 1/2 Gal., RB-1452......... 154.00
Lafayette, Aqua, Tooled Mouth, 3 Piece Metal & Glass Topper, Pt., RB-1452............. 242.00
Lafayette, Extra Spiced OK Pickles Label, Pat. June 28, 1892, Aqua, Qt., RB-1466..... 198.00
Lafayette, Pat. Sept. 2, 1884, Aqua, Glass & Metal Winged Stopper, Qt., RB-1452...... 99.00
Lafayette, Patent Pending, Aqua, Glass Stopper, Metal Glass Closure, Qt., RB-1450 ... 578.00
Lafayette Profile, Aqua, 1/2 Gal., RB-1450... 900.00
Leader, 2 Line, Amber, Swirly Light Amber, Bail, Qt., RB-1466 .... 85.00
Leader, Amber, 1/2 Gal., RB-1465 .... 225.00
Leader, Pat. June 28, 1892, Amber, Glass Lid, Metal Closure, Qt., RB-1465 .... 143.00
Leader, Yellowish Amber, Lid, Wire, Qt., RB-1466 .... 253.00
Long Neck, 11 1/2 In..*Illus* 110.00
Ludlow's Patent, June 28 1859 & Aug. 6 1861, Aqua, Glass Lid, Qt., RB-1547.......... 104.00
Ludlow's Patent August 6 1861, Aqua, Glass Lid, Iron Clamp, 1/2 Gal., RB-1547.... 66.00
Ludlow's Patent June 28 1859, Light Green, Glass Lid, 1/2 Gal., RB-1546............... 176.00
Lynchburg Standard Mason 5, Aqua, Qt., RB-1594 .... 18.00
Lyon & Bossard's, East Stroudsburg, Pat. Apr. 15, 1884, Aqua, Qt., RB-1595 .... 467.00
Magic Star, Medium Amber, Lid & Clamp, RB-1609.. 1000.00
Magic Star, Pat. March 30th, 1886, Aqua, Glass Lid, Qt., RB-1606 .... 143.00
Marion, Aqua, Block Letters, Ground Top, Qt., RB-1624 .... 12.00
Mascot Trademark, Pat. Improved, Milk Glass Lid, Metal Screw Band, Qt., RB-1631 .. 264.00
Mason, Amber, Pat. 1858, Qt., RB-1939 .... 115.00
Mason, Black, Qt. ....*Illus* 4000.00
Mason, Christmas, Embossed, Pt., RB-1780.. 45.00

Mason, Citron, 1910-1930, 1/2 Gal., RB-1644... 99.00
Mason, Cornflower Blue, 1858, Qt. ....*Illus* 110.00
Mason, I.G. Co., Fancy Monogram... 37.00
Mason, Ohio Quality, Clear, Pt. 4.00
Mason, Porcelain Lined, Aqua, 1/2 Gal., RB-2132 .... 125.00
Mason, U.G. Co., Aqua, Reverse Heel, Qt. 12.00
Mason, Union Stoneware Co., Red Wing, Minn., 1/2 Gal., RB-2133 .... 185.00
Mason, Union, Shield, Aqua, Zinc Lid, Qt., RB-2133 .... 132.00
Mason, Zinc Lid, 1858, Midget, RB-1941 .... 23.00
Mason CC GC, Amethyst, Qt., RB-1937 .... 30.00
Mason SGW Monogram, Sun Colored Amethyst, 1/2 Gal., RB-1658 .... 100.00
Mason's, Cross, Hero, Aqua, Glass Lid, Wire Bail, 1/2 Gal., RB-1243 .... 38.00
Mason's, Moon, Pat. Nov. 30th, 1858, Ball, Aqua, Zinc Screw Lid, 1/2 Gal., RB-1919 187.00
Mason's 1, Patent Nov. 30th, 1858, Aqua, Unlined Zinc Lid, 1/2 Gal., RB-1776 .... 357.00
Mason's 2 Patent Nov. 30th, 1858, Med. Yellow Olive, Ground Lip, Pt., RB-2032 ... 495.00
Mason's 3 Patent Nov. 30th, 1858, Aqua, Ground Lip, Screw Cap, Midget, RB-2038 182.00
Mason's CFJ Co., Cross, Patent Nov. 30th 1858, Amethyst, Lid, Qt., RB-1920............ 198.00
Mason's CFJ Co., Medium Amber, Burst Bubble, Qt., RB-1711.................................... 140.00
Mason's CFJ Co., Patent Nov. 30, 1858, Yellow, Amber, Zinc Lid, Qt., RB-1920 .... 467.00
Mason's CFJ Co., Patent Nov. 30th 1858, Lime Green, Ground Top, Qt., RB-1920..... 240.00
Mason's CFJ Co., Patent Nov. 30th 1858, Yellow, Ground Mouth, Lid, Qt., RB-1920.. 187.00
Mason's CFJ Co. Improved, Amber, Ground Lip, 1/2 Gal., RB-1711 .... 126.00
Mason's CFJ Co. Improved, Midget, RB-1711 .... 13.00
Mason's Cross Patent Hero, Olive Green, Amber Swirls, 2 Qt., RB-1942.................. 1000.00
Mason's Cross Patent Nov. 30th, 1858, Amber, Qt., RB-1694 .... 148.00
Mason's Cross Patent Nov. 30th, 1858, Amber, Qt., RB-1940 .... 148.00 to 210.00
Mason's Crowleytown, Nov. 30th, 1858, Aqua, Pat., Qt., RB-1771........................... 450.00
Mason's Improved, Yellow Amber, Glass Insert, Screw, 1/2 Gal., RB-1695..... 170.00 to 187.00
Mason's Improved, Yellow Amber, Insert, Zinc Band, c.1880, 1/2 Gal., RB-1694 .... 99.00
Mason's Keystone, Metal Insert, Qt., RB-1737 .... 200.00
Mason's Keystone, Patd. Jan. 19, 1869, Aqua, Qt., RB-1737 .... 105.00
Mason's Keystone, Yellow Green, 1880-1910, Qt., RB-1737 .... 522.00
Mason's Patent Nov. 30th, 1858, Amber, Ground Lip, Screw Lid, 1/2 Gal., RB-1784 330.00
Mason's Patent Nov. 30th, 1858, Aqua, 1/2 Gal., RB-1848....................................... 250.00
Mason's Patent Nov. 30th, 1858, Aqua, Glass Lid, Screw Band, 1/2 Gal., RB-1773... 198.00
Mason's Patent Nov. 30th, 1858, Aqua, Ground Lip, 1/2 Gal., RB-1787 .... 253.00
Mason's Patent Nov. 30th, 1858, Black Amethyst, Midget Pt., RB-1787 .... 73.00
Mason's Patent Nov. 30th, 1858, Cobalt Blue, Midget Pt., RB-1787........................... 55.00
Mason's Patent Nov. 30th, 1858, Cornflower Blue, Qt.......................................*Illus* 2000.00
Mason's Patent Nov. 30th, 1858, Emerald Green, Zinc Lid, Qt., RB-1787...........*Illus* 193.00

*Fruit Jar, Mason's Patent Nov.
30th, 1858, Emerald Green,
Zinc Lid, Qt., RB-1787*

Fruit Jar, Moore's Patent Dec. 3d, 1861,
Aqua, Glass Lid, Qt., RB-2204

Fruit Jar, Potter & Bodine's Air-Tight,
Pat. April 18, 1859, Philadelphia, 6 In.

Mason's Patent Nov. 30th, 1858, Medium Emerald Green, Zinc Lid, Qt., RB-1784 ... 193.00
Mason's Patent Nov. 30th, 1858, Opalescent Milk Glass, Reproduction, 1/2 Gal. 94.00
Mason's Patent Nov. 30th, 1858, Tudor Rose, Reverse, Immerser Lid, RB-1875 .... 175.00
Mason's Patent Nov. 30th, 1858, Yellow Amber, 1/2 Gal., RB-1782...................... 110.00
Mason's Patent Nov. 30th, 1858, Yellow Amber, Ground Lip, 1/2 Gal., RB-1784 ..... 302.50
Mason's Patent Nov. 30th, 1858, Yellow, Olive Tone, Ground Lip, Qt., RB-1787 ..... 303.00
Mason's Patent Nov. 30th, 1858, Zinc Lid, Midget, RB-1787................................ 187.00
Mason's Union, Shield, Aqua, 1865-1890, 1/2 Gal., RB-2133 .... 77.00
Mason's Union, Shield, Aqua, No Lid, Qt., RB-2133 .... 82.00
Mason's Unlettered Cross, Patent Nov. 30th, 1858, Amber, Qt., RB-1940-1............. 90.00
Mastodon, T.A. Evans & Co., Aqua, Applied Wax Sealer Ring, Qt., RB-2135 .... 180.00
Millville, Qt., RB-2181 .... 28.00
Millville, Whitall's Patent, Aqua, Glass Lid, Iron Clamp, 1/2 Pt., RB-2185............... 165.00
Millville, Whitall's Patent, June 18, 1861, Aqua, Embossed, 1/2 Pt., RB-2185............ 242.00
Millville Atmospheric, Aqua, Glass Lid, Iron Clamp, 1/2 Gal., RB-2181 .... 77.00
Millville Atmospheric, Aqua, Glass Lid, Iron Clamp, Qt., RB-2181 .... 33.00
Millville Atmospheric, Whitall's Pat. June 18th, 1861, Aqua, Qt., RB-2181-1 .... 77.00
Millville Atmospheric, Whitall's Pat. June 18th, 1864, Aqua, 1/2 Qt., RB-2180 .... 187.00
Millville Wit. Co. Improved, Aqua, Ground Lip, Qt., RB-2187 .... 50.00
Model Jar, Patent August 27, 1867, Rochester, N.Y., Aqua, Qt., RB-2195 .... 110.00
Moore's, Pat. Dec. 3, 1861, Aqua, Original Clamp, 1/2 Gal., RB-2204........................ 85.00
Moore's, Patent, Dec. 3, 1861, Aqua, Glass Insert, Iron Yoke, Qt., RB-2204............... 77.00
Moore's Patent Dec. 3d, 1861, Aqua, Glass Lid, Qt., RB-2204 ....*Illus* 99.00
Moore's Patent Dec. 3d, 1861, Glass Lid, Metal Yoke, Qt., RB-2204 .... 88.00
Mrs. G.E. Haller, Brandied Pears, Martha Washington, 1876 Centennial, RB-1178 ...... 35.00
Mrs. G.E. Haller, Pat. Feb. 25 '73, Aqua, Clear Blown Stopple, Qt., RB-1178 .... 66.00
My Choice, Aqua, Applied Collared Mouth, Qt., RB-2217...................................... 137.00
Myers Test, Aqua, Glass Lid, Repro Brass Clamp, Qt., RB-2219-1 .... 94.00
Myers Test, Deep Aqua, Ground Mouth, Tin Cover, Qt., RB-2219-1 .... 110.00
Myers Test Jar, Aqua, Cylindrical, 1/2 Gal., RB-2218.. 110.00
Myers Test Jar, Aqua, Metal Cap & Clamp, c.1869, 1/2 Gal., RB-2218 .... 88.00
NE Plus Ulta Air Tight, Aqua, Embossed, 2 Qt... 1500.00
NE Plus Ultra Air Tight, N.J., Deep Aqua, Green, IP, Applied Mouth, Pt. 770.00
New Paragon, Aqua, Glass Lid, Metal Band, 1870-1880, Qt., RB-2289 .... 99.00
New Paragon 3, Aqua, Glass Lid, Metal Band, Cylindrical, 1/2 Gal. 88.00
Newman's, Pat. 1859, Deep Aqua, 1859-1870, Cylindrical, Pt., RB-2240 .... 847.00
Newman's, Patent Dec. 20th, 1859, Aqua, Qt., RB-2242....................................... 605.00
Newman's, Patent Dec. 20th, 1859, Cornflower Blue, Tin Lid, Qt., RB-2240............... 705.00
Nonpareil, Patented July 17, 1866, Aqua, No Lid, Qt., RB-2250 .... 330.00

Pacific San Francisco Glass Work, Pat. Feb. 9th, 1864, Sapphire Blue, Qt. 400.00
Patented June 27, 1865, Aqua, Clear Lid, Iron Clamp, 1/2 Gal. Plus, RB-2301 .... 237.00
Patented Oct. 19, 1858, Apple Green, Ground Mouth, Glass Lid, 1/2 Gal., RB-1212 .. 66.00
Pearl, Aqua, Qt., RB-2318 .... 35.00
Peerless, Aqua, Glass Lid, Iron Yoke Clamp, Qt., RB-2322 .... 110.00
Penn, Aqua, Applied Wax Sealer, Qt., RB-2326 .... 60.00
Perfect Seal, Pat. Pend., Script, Medium Amber, Clear Lid, Qt., RB-2334 .... 187.00
Perfection, Aqua, Glass Lid, Wire Bail, 1/2 Gal., RB-2330 .... 38.00 to 44.00
Petal, Deep Blue Aqua, IP, 1855-1865, 1/2 Gal. 468.00
Petal, Emerald Green, Red, Applied Mouth, IP, 8 1/2 In. 1595.00
Porcelain, Lined, Glass Screw Cap, Aqua, Midget, RB-2373 .... 852.00
Porcelain Lined, Pat. Nov. 1867, Aqua, Ground Lip, Zinc Screw Cap, Midget 121.00
Port Q, Wax Sealer, Qt., RB-2379 .... 25.00
Potter & Bodine, Philadelphia, Aqua, Ground Lip, Qt., RB-2381 .... 132.00
Potter & Bodine, Philadelphia, Aqua, Qt., RB-2381 .... 132.00
Potter & Bodine's Air-Tight, Pat. April 18, 1859, Philadelphia, 6 In. .... *Illus* 450.00
Presto Supreme Mason, Glass Lid, Band, 1/2 Pt., RB-2408 .... 10.00
Puritan, L.S. Co., Aqua, Glass Lid, Metal Closure, 1/2 Gal., RB-2425 .... 137.00
Rau's Improved Pat. Applied For Grove Ring, Amethyst, 1/2 Gal., RB-2469 .... 83.00
Robert Arthur's Pat. 2nd January, 1855, Yellow Pottery, Wax Groove, Qt., RB-98 ... 275.00
Royal, Aqua, Glass Lid, Zinc Collar, Preserve Contents, Qt. RB-2514 .... 121.00 to 165.00
Royal, Aqua, Ground Mouth, Glass Lid, Repro. Metal Screw, 1/2 Gal., RB-2514 .... 100.00
Royal Of 1876, Green Aqua, Ground Mouth, No Closure, 1/2 Gal., RB-2515 .... 66.00
Safety, Golden Yellow, Glass Lid, Wire Bail, Qt., RB-2534 .... 132.00
Safety, Patent Applied For, Amber, Glass Lid, Wire Clamp, Qt., RB-2534 .... 143.00
Safety, Yellow Amber, 1870-1890, Qt., RB-2534 .... 143.00
Safety, Yellow Amber, Glass Lid, Wire Bail, Qt., RB-2534 .... 143.00
Safety, Yellow Amber, Glass Lid, Wire Bail, Cylindrical, 1890, 1/2 Gal., RB-2534 ...... 187.00
Safety Valve, Greek Key Design, Aqua, 2 Qt., RB-2539 .... 25.00
Safety Valve, Green, Clear Lid, Unembossed, 1/4 Pt., RB-2538 .... 15.00
Safety Valve, Pat. May 21 1895, Aqua, Greek Key, Lid, Bail, 1/2 Gal., RB-2538 .... 55.00
Safety Valve, Sun Colored Amethyst, Clear Lid, 1/4 Pt., RB 2538 .... 20.00
Schaffer, Rochester, N.Y., JCS Monogram, Aqua, Glass Lid, Wire Bail, Qt., RB-2562 247.00
Scranton, Aqua, Original Metal, Wood Closure, Qt., RB-2576 .... 743.00
Sealfast, C.S. & B. Cummings, ABM Lip, Glass Lid, Wire Bail, Qt., RB-2586 .... 100.00
Sealtite, Clear, Pt., RB-2603 .... 17.00
SKO Queen, Trademark, Clear, Lightning Closure, 1/2 Pt., RB-2445 .... 8.00
Smalley Full Measure, Monogram, Golden Amber, Incorrect Lid, Qt., RB-2648 .... 55.00
Standard, W. McC & Co., Aqua, Applied Wax Sealer Mouth, Qt. 330.00
Star, Clear, Lid, Qt., RB-2718 .... 95.00
Star, Clear, Metal Cover, 5 1/2 In. .... *Illus* 395.00
Star Glass Co., New Albany, Ind., Green Aqua, Applied Wax Sealer, 1/2 Gal., RB-2729 50.00
Stark, Glass Lid, Metal Clamp, Cylindrical, 1900-1920, Qt., RB-2732 .... 165.00
Steer's Head, see Fruit Jar, Flaccus Bros.

Fruit Jar, Star, Clear, Metal Cover, 5 1/2 In.   *Fruit Jar, Tight Seal, Aqua, 5 In.*

Stevens Tin Top, Aqua, c.1875, Qt., RB-2738 .... 77.00
Stone Mason, Union Stoneware, Red Wing, Gray Glaze, Qt., RB-2754 .... 165.00
Sun Trademark, Aqua, Glass Lid, Metal Yoke Clamp, Cylindrical, Pt., RB-2761 .... 148.00
Sun Trademark, Green Aqua, Glass Lid, Metal Yoke Clamp, 1/2 Gal., RB-2761 .... 176.00
Sure Seal, Bamberger, L. Co., Blue, 7 In., Pt., RB-2773-1 .... 10.00
Swayzee's Improved Mason, Deep Green, Qt., RB-2780 .... 30.00
T.M. Sinclair & Co. Ltd., Cedar Rapids, Iowa, Pork & Beef Packers, Qt., RB-1308 ..... 60.00
The Chief, Deep Aqua, Ground Mouth, Tin, Cover, Cylindrical, 1/2 Gal., RB-594........ 303.00
The Empire, Pat. Feb. 13, 1866, Aqua, Glass Lid, Metal Yoke, Qt., RB-927 .... 105.00
The Nifty, Clear, 1900-1920, Qt., RB-2248 .... 137.00
The Pearl, Aqua, Glass Lid, Metal Screw Band, 1/2 Gal., RB-2318 .... 77.00
The Queen, Aqua, Glass Lid, Metal Screw Band, Qt., RB-2433 .... 33.00
The Reservoir, Aqua, Collared Mouth, Cylindrical, Stopper, 1/2 Gal., RB-2494 .... 352.00
The Valve Jar Co., Philadelphia, Pat. Mar. 10, 1868, Aqua, Wire Closure, Qt., RB-2874 176.00
Tight Seal, Aqua, 5 In...*Illus*   2.00
Tillyer, Aqua, Glass Lid, Wire Clamp, 1870-1890, Qt., RB-2810 .... 66.00
Trademark Lightning, Amber, Glass Amber Lid, Wire Bail, Pt., RB-1499 ....55.00 to 82.00
Trademark Lightning, Citron, RB-1499... 155.00
Trademark Lightning, Dark Amber, Qt., RB-1499 .... 100.00
Trademark Lightning, Deep Purple Amethyst, Qt., RB-1499 .... 214.00
Trademark Lightning, Golden Amber, Glass Lid, Wire Bail, 1/2 Gal., RB-1498 .... 38.00
Trademark Lightning, Yellow Amber, Ground Lip, 1/2 Gal., RB-1499 .... 77.00
Trademark Lightning Putnam, Aqua, 1/2 Pt., RB-1491-1 .... 80.00
Trademark Lightning Putnam, Aqua, Ground Lip, 1/2 Pt. 104.50
Trademark Lightning Putnam, Yellow Amber, Qt., RB-1499........................ 88.00
Trademark The Dandy, Gilberds, Pat. Oct. 13th, 1885, Amber, Qt., RB-751 .... 253.00 to 385.00
Trademark The Dandy, Golden Amber, Glass Lid, Wire Bail, Qt., RB-751 .... 71.00
Trademark The Dandy, Yellow, Amber, Gilberds, Pat. Oct. 13, 1885, Qt., RB-751 ..... 230.00
Triumph No. 2, Aqua, Pressed Down Wax Seal Ring, 3-Piece Mold, Qt., RB-2815...... 550.00
Turn Mold, Golden Amber, Applied Wax Sealer, 1/2 Gal. 73.00
Unembossed, Aqua, Groove Ring Wax Sealer, Red, IP, 1/2 Gal., RB-3061 .... 94.00
Unembossed, Aqua, OP, Hand Formed Groove Ring Wax Sealer, 1/2 Gal., RB-3061 .. 204.00
Union 1, Deep Aqua, Applied Wax Sealer, Qt., RB-2845................................ 60.00
Union 1, L & C., Sun Colored Amethyst, Wax Seal Ring, 1/2 Gal., RB-2836.............. 467.00
Union 5, Aqua, Applied Wax Sealer, Qt., RB-2852 .... 38.00
Vacuum Seal, Sun Colored Amethyst, 1904, Cylindrical, Qt., RB-2870 .... 66.00
Valve Jar Co., Philadelphia, Aqua, Glass Lid, Wire Coil Clamp, 1/2 Gal., RB-2873...... 165.00
Valve Jar Co., Philadelphia, Patd Mar.10th, 1868, Aqua, Glass Lid, Qt., RB-2873 .... 176.00
Van Vliet, Aqua, Glass Lid, Metal Yoke Clamp & Wire, Pt., RB-2878 .... 303.00
Van Vliet, Aqua, Metal Yoke Clamp, Wire Bail, Qt., RB-2878.......................... 358.00
Van Vliet Jar Of 1881, Aqua, Glass Lid, Wire & Metal Yoke, Qt., RB-1879.... 467.00 to 523.00
Victor, M In Diamond, Aqua, Patent Feb. 20, 1900, 1/2 Gal., RB-2887 .... 22.00
Victor, M In Diamond, Pat. 1899, Glass Lid, Metal Yoke Clamp, 1899, Pt., RB-2886... 66.00
Victory, Aqua, Glass Lid, Zinc Band, 1867, Qt., RB-2889............................. 33.00
Victory 1, Aqua, Glass Lid, Metal Screw Band, Qt., RB-2893 .... 60.00
W.H. Glenny Son & Co., Aqua, Applied Mouth, Kline Stopper, Qt., RB-1120.............. 121.00
W.W. Lyman, Pat. Feb. 9th, 1864, Aqua, Ground Lip, Qt., RB-1571 .... 55.00
Wax Seal Groove, 3-Piece Mold, Cornflower Blue, Whittled, Qt., RB-3063 .... 633.00
Weideman Boy Brand, Cleveland, 7 1/2 In., RB-2931 ....*Illus*   6.00
Western Pride, Star, Patented June 22, 1875, Aqua, Glass Lid, Qt., RB-2945............. 55.00
Whitmore's Patent, Rochester, N.Y., Aqua, Glass Lid, Repro Clamp, Qt., RB-2964 ... 187.00
Whitmore's Patent, Rochester, N.Y., Aqua, Wire Bail, Cylindrical, Qt., RB-2965....... 385.00
Whitmore's Patent, Rochester, N.Y., Wire Bail, Qt., RB-2964.......................... 385.00
Winslow, Aqua, Metal Clamp, Incorrect Closure, 1 1/2 Pt., RB-3023................... 137.00
Winslow, Patented Nov. 29th, 1870, Aqua, Glass Lid, Wire Clamp, Qt., RB-3023 .... 231.00
Winslow Improved Valve Jar, Aqua, Ground Mouth, Qt., RB-3021 .... 88.00
Winslow Improved Valve Jar, Green Aqua, No Closure, Pt., RB-3021 .... 385.00
Wm. L. Haller, Carlisle, Pa., Aqua, Applied Mouth, 1/2 Gal., RB-1179...................... 319.00
Wm. L. Haller, Carlisle, Pa., Aqua, Applied Mouth, Qt., RB-1179 .... 143.00 to 578.00
Wm. L. Haller, Carlisle, Pa., J.D. Willoughby Pat. Jan. 4, 1859, Aqua, Qt., RB-1179 ... 578.00
Woodbury, Aqua, Glass Lid, Vent Hole, Metal Band Clamp, Pt., RB-3027 .... 55.00
Woodbury, WGW, Aqua, 1885-1900, Qt., RB-3028.............................22.00 to 44.00
Woodbury Improved, 7 1/2 In., RB-3029.......................................*Illus* 25.00

Fruit Jar, Weideman Boy Brand, Cleveland,
7 1/2 In., RB-2931

Fruit Jar, Woodbury Improved,
7 1/2 In., RB-3029

Woodbury Trademark Sterilizer, Aqua, Vented Glass Lid, Cap, 5 1/2 In., RB-3031.... 143.00
Woods, Aqua, Rolled Mouth, Cylindrical, 1860-1880, 7 1/2 In., RB-3032 .... 330.00
Yeoman's Fruit Bottle, Aqua, 1/2 Gal., RB-3040 .... 50.00
Yeoman's Fruit Bottle, Aqua, 1860-1880, 1 1/2 Pt., RB-3040-1 .... 55.00

GARNIER

The house of Garnier Liqueurs was founded in 1859 in Enghien, France. Figurals have been made through the nineteenth and twentieth centuries, except for the years of Prohibition and World War II. Julius Wile and Brothers, a New York City firm established in 1877, became the exclusive U.S. agents for Garnier in 1885. Many of the bottles were not sold in the United States but were purchased in France or the Caribbean and brought back home. Only miniature bottles were sold in the United States from 1970 to 1973. From 1974 to 1978, Garnier was distributed in the United States by Fleischmann Distilling Company. In 1978 the Garnier trademark was acquired by Standard Brands, Inc., the parent company of Julius Wile Sons and Company and Fleischmann Distilling Co., and few of the full-sized bottles were again sold in the United States. Standard Brands later merged with Nabisco Brands, Inc. In 1988 Nabisco sold the Garnier Liqueurs trademark to McGuiness Distillers, Ltd. of Alberta, Canada. No new decanters are being made.

GARNIER, Acorn, 1910	43.00
Aladdin's Lamp, 1963	61.00
Alfa Romeo, 1913 Model, 1969	27.00
Alfa Romeo, 1924 Model, 1969	30.00
Apollo, 1969	22.00
Aztec, 1965..	18.00
Baby Foot, 1963..	16.00
Bacchus, 1967	25.00
Baseball Player, 1970	20.00
Bellows, 1969..	19.00
Blue Bird, 1970...	60.00
Bouquet, 1966...	22.00
Bulldog, ...	20.00
Bullfighter, 1963...	22.00
Burmese Man, 1965	20.00
Butterfly, 1970, Miniature	10.00
Candlestick, Bedroom, 1967	24.00
Candlestick, Glass, 1965	20.00
Cannon, 1964..	55.00
Cardinal, 1969	16.00
Cards, Miniature, 1970	14.00
Carrossee Coach, 1970..	28.00
Cat, 1930	76.00

Cat, Black, Gray, 1962	23.00
Chalet, 1955	46.00
Chimney, 1956	60.00
Chinese Man, 1970	22.00
Chinese Woman, 1970	21.00
Christmas Tree, 1956	64.00
Citroen, 1922 Model, 1970	27.00
Clock, 1958	24.00
Clown, No. 20, 1910	43.00
Clown, With Tuba, 1955	20.00
Clown's Head, 1931	76.00
Coffee Mill, 1966	26.00
Coffeepot, 1962	34.00
Collie, 1970	20.00
Country Jug, 1937	32.00
Diamond Bottle, 1969	14.00
Drunkard, Millord, 1956	24.00
Duck, No. 21, 1910	12.00
Duckling, 1956	40.00
Egg House, 1956	74.00
Eiffel Tower, 1950	22.00
Elephant, No. 66, 1932	9.00
Empire Vase, 1962	14.00
Fiat, 1913 Model, Nuevo, 1969	28.00
Fiat, 1924 Model, 1969	27.00
Football Player, 1970	18.00
Ford, 1913 Model, 1969	28.00
German Shepherd, 1970	20.00
Goldfinch, No. 11, 1970	15.00
Goose, 1955	18.00
Greyhound, 1930	75.00
Guitar & Mandolin,	19.00
Harlequin, No. 166, 1958	37.00
Hockey Player, 1970	20.00
Hula Hoop, 1959	30.00
Humoristiques, 1934, Miniature	30.00
Hunting Vase, 1964	29.00
Inca, 1969	17.00
Indian, 1958	18.00
Indian Princess	14.00
Indy 500, No. 1, 1970	33.00
Jockey, 1961	28.00
LaDona, 1963	36.00
Lafayette, 1949	20.00
Laurel Crown, 1963	22.00
Locomotive, 1969	22.00
Log, Quarter, 1958	30.00
Log, Round, 1958	25.00
Loon, 1970	14.00
Maharajah, 1958	74.00
Marquis, 1931	74.00
Marseilles, 1970	20.00
Meadowlark, 1969	15.00
MG, 1913 Model, 1970	27.00
Mocking Bird, 1970	40.00
Montmartre, 1960	17.00
Napoleon, 1969	27.00
Oasis, 1959	20.00
Oriole, 1970	14.00
Packard, 1930 Model, 1970	28.00
Painting, 1961	28.00
Parrot, 1910	34.00
Pelican, 1935	52.00

Penguin, 1930 .... 77.00
Pheasant, 1969 .... 26.00
Pistol, Horse, 1964 .... 20.00
Poodle, Black, 1954 .... 15.00
Poodle, White, 1954 .... 15.00
Rainbow, No. 142, 1955 .... 28.00
Renault, 1911 Model, 1969 .... 29.00
Roadrunner, 1969 .... 16.00
Robin, 1970 .... 14.00
Rooster, Black, 1952 .... 16.00
Rooster, Maroon, 1952 .... 22.00
Soccer Shoe, 1962 .... 37.00
Soldier, Faceless, 1949 .... 61.00
SS France, 1962 .... 102.00
SS Queen Mary, 1970 .... 28.00
Stanley, 1907 Model, 1970 .... 27.00
Tam Tam, 1961 .... 52.00
Taxi, Paris, 1960 .... 54.00
Trout, 1967 .... 20.00
Vase, Miniature, 1935 .... 10.00
Violin, 1966 .... 37.00
Watch, Blue, 1966 .... 26.00
Watch, Tan, 1966 .... 25.00
Watering Can, 1958 .... 17.00
Woman, With Jug, 1930 .... 51.00
Young Deer, 1964 .... 30.00

---------------------------------- **GEMEL** ----------------------------------

Gemel bottles are made in pairs. Two bottles are blown separately then joined together, usually with the two necks pointing in different directions. Gemels are popular for serving oil and vinegar or two different types of liqueurs.

GEMEL, Emerald Green, Blown, Pontil, Rolled Lips, c.1860, 4 3/4 In. 176.00
Opalized Green Aqua, White Nailsea Type Loopings, Pontil, 9 In. 88.00

---------------------------------- **GIN** ----------------------------------

The word *gin* comes from the French word *genieve*, meaning juniper. It is said that Count de Morret, a brother of King Henry IV, made a drink of distilled spirits, juniper berries, and other substances. One of the earliest types of gin was what today is called *Geneva* or *Holland's* gin. It is made from a barley malt grain mash and juniper berries. The alcohol content is low and it is usually not used for cocktails. In some countries it is considered medicine. In England and America, the preferred drink is dry gin, which is made with juniper berries, coriander seeds, angelica root, and other flavors. The best dry gin is distilled, not mixed by the process used during Prohibition to make *bathtub* gin. Another drink is Tom gin, much like dry gin but with sugar added. Gin bottles have been made since the 1600s. Most of them have straight sides. Gin has always been an inexpensive drink, which is why so many of these bottles were made. Many were of a type called *case bottles* today. The case bottle was made with straight sides so that 4 to 12 bottles would fit tightly into a wooden packing case.

GIN, A.M., No. 19 Broad Street, N.Y., Pottery, Amber, Handle 375.00
Avan Hoboken & Co., Rotterdam, Olive Green, Case, Applied Lip & Seal, 11 In. 40.00
Berzogthum Nassas, Lion Crest, With Selters, Pottery, Handle 20.00
Bininger, see Bininger category
Blankenheym & Nolet, Yellow Olive 25.00
Blankenheym & Nolet Schiedam, Pottery, Handle, 12 In. 10.00
Blown, Olive Amber, String Lip, Tapered Square, OP, Late 18th Century, 13 1/4 In. 210.00
Boll & Dunlop Rotterdam Holland, Medium Olive, Tapered, 11 In. 90.00
Booth & Sedgwick's, London, Cordial, Emerald Green, Whittled, 9 3/4 In. 121.00
Booth & Sedgwick's, London, Cordial, Emerald Green, IP, Square, 9 3/4 In. ... 145.00 to 153.00
Booth & Sedgwick's, London, Cordial, Olive Green, Pontil, c.1865, 7 1/2 In. 154.00
Carbon's Medicate Gin, Square 8.00
Case, Amber, Dip Mold, Pontil, England, 8 In. 357.00

Case, Cosmopoliet, Olive Amber, 10 1/2 In.. 121.00
Case, Emerald Green, 10 1/4 In. 137.50
Case, Green Amber, 9 1/2 In.. 25.00
Case, Houtman, Double Palm Tree, Label, BIM 50.00
Case, Light Olive Amber, Tapered Form, Pontil, 10 In. 77.00
Case, Light Olive Green, OP, 9 1/2 In. 108.00
Case, Light Olive, Smooth Base, Tapered Lip, 9 1/4 In. 17.00
Case, Medium Olive Amber, 9 3/4 In. 66.00
Case, Olive Amber, Backward F On Base, Shingled Sides, 9 1/2 In. 25.00
Case, Olive Amber, Tapered, Pontil, 1750-1800, 9 In. 88.00
Case, Olive Green, Dip Mold, Pontil, Continental, 17 3/4 In........................ 578.00
Case, Straight Lip, Dutch, 1850-1870 .... 15.00
Case, Tapered Body, Dutch, Olive Green, OP, c.1810, 13 1/3 In..............*Illus* 90.00
Case, Tapered Gin Form, Yellow Olive, Applied Mouth, Pontil, 9 1/2 In. 77.00
Case, Tapered, Palm Boom, C. Myer & Co., Schiedam, Olive Green, Seal, 11 1/2 In.... 125.00
Case, Yellow Amber, Double Collar, Medicine Top.. 30.00
Case, Yellow Olive Amber, Flared & Rolled Lip, OP, Dutch, 1760-1780, 9 In............. 88.00
Case, Yellow Olive Amber, OP, Flared & Rolled Lip, Dutch, 9 1/2 In. 99.00
Case, Yellow Olive Green, OP, Rolled Lip, Swirl Of Bubbles, 10 1/8 In. 143.00
Case, Yellow Olive, Dip Mold, Pontil, Holland, 10 3/8 In. 110.00
Charles London Cordial, Emerald Green, Square, 1870s, 9 1/2 In. 93.50
Chocolate Amber, String Lip, Straight Sided, Square, Pontil, Europe, 13 3/4 In. 990.00
Cononet, Aqua, BIMAL, Square, 8 1/2 In. 22.00
Dip Mold, Medium Olive Amber, Continental, 1780-1820, 9 5/8 In. 40.00
Dip Mold, Medium Olive Green, Continental, 1760-1780, 9 7/8 In. 55.00
Dip Mold, Yellow Green, England, 1780-1820, 10 1/8 In. 75.00
Dr. Bouver's Buche, Amethyst, Fancy Neck & Shoulders, Square, 11 1/2 In............... 22.00
E.H. Co. Dry Gin, Aqua, 4-Odd Sided, Tooled Top 45.00
E.N. Cook & Co., Distillers, Buffalo, N.Y., Root Beer Amber, Bubbles, Applied Top... 160.00
Fairchild's Excelsior, Aqua, Square, Crude Applied Top 165.00
Gin Cocktail, S.M. & Co., New York, Yellow Amber, Ribbed, Pontil, 10 In. 577.00
Golden Amber, Dip Mold, Laid-On Lip, OP, 1790-1830, 11 In. 120.00
Golden Gate Distilling Co., Olive Green, Tapered Sides, 1893-1904, 10 3/4 In........... 185.00
Gordon's Distilled London Dry Gin, Display 27.50
Gordon's Dry Gin, ... 10.00
Green, Dip Mold, OP 65.00
Hartwig Kantorowicz, Paris, Milk Glass, Case ....45.00 to 65.00
Hulsikamp & Zoon & Molyn Rotterdam, Applied Handle, Stamped, 5 1/2 In............. 45.00
Ilers Eagle, With Order Form, Qt. 50.00
J.H. Friedenwald & Co., Kidney & Liver Troubles, Yellow Green, 10 In. 660.00
J.J. Melchers, Schiedam, Olive Green, Tapered Case, Waves Of Bubbles, 10 5/8 In..... 175.00
J.J.W. Peters, Embossed Dog, Bird, Yellow Olive, Whittled, Case, 8 1/2 In. 120.00
J.J.W. Peters, Hamburg, Amber, Embossed Dog, Holding Bird In Mouth, Pt. 40.00

Gin, Case, Tapered Body, Dutch,
Olive Green, OP, c.1810, 13 1/3 In.

Gin, Pelican, Holland

London Jockey Club House, Olive Amber, Embossed Horse & Rider, 14 1/2 In. 1320.00
London Royal Imperial Gin, Cobalt Blue, Applied Mouth, 9 3/4 In. 440.00
London Royal Tiger, Aqua, Applied Top, Square 110.00
Medium Olive Amber, 15 1/5 In. 522.50
Olive Amber, Applied Collar, Square, OP, Europe, 16 In. 523.00
Olive Amber, Dip Mold, OP, 10 In. 100.00
Olive Amber, Rolled Lip, OP, 10 1/2 In. 75.00
Olive Black, St. Angeline Side, 10-Sided, Cylindrical, Long Neck, Scalloped Base 95.00
Olive Green, Pontil, 1780-1830, 10 1/8 In. 88.00
Paul Jones & Co., Red Star Gin, Aqua, Tooled Top, Case 55.00
Pelican, Holland ....*Illus* 20.00
Pond's Gin-Ger-Gin, Aqua, Tooled Top, Stopper, Case 70.00
Ruhl & Co., Case, Juniper Leaf Gin, Philadelphia, Amber, Embossed 18.00
S.B. Rothenberg, Milk Glass, Applied Seal On Reverse 95.00
Square, Tapered, Yellow Olive, Pontil, 16 1/4 In. 770.00
Tan King Hoeij, Samarang, Olive Green, Case, Seal, 11 In. 45.00
Tapered Form, Yellow Olive, Flared Mouth, Pontil, 15 3/4 In. 770.00
Yellow Olive, Blown, Pontil, 1780-1890, 9 5/8 In. 770.00
Yellow Olive Amber, Dip Mold, Case, Holland, 12 3/8 In. 176.00
Yellow Olive Amber, Dip Mold, Case, Holland, 15 1/8 In. 440.00
Yellow Olive Green, Applied String Lip, Europe, 1770-1790, 12 1/2 In. 1210.00
Yellow Olive Green, String Lip, OP, Rectangular, Europe, 1770-1790, 10 3/4 In. 303.00

———————————————— **GINGER BEER** ————————————————

Ginger beer was originally made from fermented ginger root, cream of tartar, sugar, yeast, and water. It was a popular drink from the 1850s to the 1920s. Beer made from grains became more popular and very little alcoholic ginger beer was made. Today it is an alcohol-free carbonated drink like soda. Pottery bottles have been made since the 1650s. A few products are still bottled in stoneware containers today. Ginger beer, vinegar, and cider were usually put in stoneware holders until the 1930s. The ginger beer bottle usually held 10 ounces. Blob tops, tapered collars, and crown tops were used. Some used a cork, others a Lightning stopper or inside screw stopper. The bottles were of shades of brown and white. Some were salt glazed for a slightly rough, glassy finish. Bottles were stamped or printed with names and usually the words *ginger beer.*

GINGER BEER, Adams' Brewed, Glastonbury, Pottery, Black Print, 6 3/4 In. 65.00
Blackwood's, Royal Edinburgh, Winnipeg, Canada, Qt. 110.00
Bull Dog, Wolverine Ginger Ale Co., Detroit, Green, 7 In. ....*Illus* 6.00
Chelmsford Spring, Old English, Knight On Horse, Stopper, Stoneware 70.00
Chelmsford Spring Co., Old English, Knight On Horse, Stoneware, Porcelain Top 49.00
Crown Ginger Beer Co., Cleveland, O., Brown, Black, 7 In. 35.00
E.G. Lyons & Co., San Francisco, Aqua, Oval, 7 7/8 In. 10.00
F. Brown's, Philadelphia, Aqua, Oval, Square Collar, 5 1/2 In. 10.00
Genuine Sanford's, Ginger French Brandy & Choice Aromatics, Aqua, 1876, 6 In. 10.00
H. Goulds, English Home Brewed 20.00
Hart & Co., Pottery, Blue Top, Eagle Transfer, 6 3/4 In. 465.00
Henry-Brown Co., Sierra Club, Glendale, Calif., Tan, Black, 6 3/4 In. 85.00
Hostetter's Essence, Pittsburg, Aqua, 5 5/8 In. 38.50
J.A. Folger & Co., San Francisco, Aqua Oval, 5 7/8 In. 5.00
J.S. Briggs, Watertown, N.Y., Pottery 42.00
Jamaica, E. Frese, San Francisco, Aqua, Applied Top 40.00
Jamaica, Wenzel, San Francisco, Aqua, Oval, Applied Top 50.00
John Noble, Dublin Stout, Pottery, Black Print, 9 In. 16.00
McMillan & Kester's, San Francisco, Aqua, Oval, 5 1/2 In. 10.00
Middletons, N.Y., Tan & Brown, Stenciled 39.00
Original Sparkling Drink, Pottery, Pale Blue Top, Windmill Picture, 7 In. 124.00
P. Pfannebecker, Stoneware, Cobalt Neck, Qt. 79.00
Pink's, Chichester 22.00
R.M. Bird & Co., Picture Of Flying Bird, Tan 35.00
Redington & Co., San Francisco, Aqua, 9 In. 12.00
Redington & Co., San Francisco, Aqua, Oval, 5 3/8 In. 15.00
Sanford's, Aqua, Rectangle, 1876, 6 1/2 In. 5.00
Seber's Old English, T.J. Bottling Co., Lorain, Oh., 7 In. ....*Illus* 10.00

Ginger Beer, Bull Dog, Wolverine Ginger Ale Co., Detroit, Green, 7 In.

Ginger Beer, Seber's Old English, T.J. Bottling Co., Lorain, Oh., 7 In.

Sir Arthur's Original English Brewed, Rex Water Co., N.Y., U.S.A.	44.00
Stockport Hop Bitters Co., Stoneware, Marked	55.00
Sullivan's Brewed, Pottery, Man With Flowers Picture, Swing Stopper, 8 In.	62.00
Terris Maple Leaf, St. John, N.B., Tan Top, Stoneware	48.00
Thos. Permberton & Co., Pottery, Green Top, Black Transfer, 8 1/2 In.	403.00
Victor Brewery Co., Ltd., Pottery, Viking Picture, 6 3/4 In.	65.00
W. Atkinson & Sons, Pottery, Castle Picture, 8 In.	58.00
W. Robson, Sunderland, Pottery, Screw Stopper, 8 1/4 In.	39.00
W. Underwood, Carlisle, Pottery, Black Transfer, Swing Stopper, 9 In.	58.00
Washington Bottling Co., Washington, D.C., Stoneware, Tan, Stenciled	79.00

GLUE

Glue and paste have been packaged in bottles since the nineteenth century. Most of these bottles have identifying paper labels. A few have the name embossed in the glass.

GLUE, Siliceous Cement, Aqua, Embossed, 3-Sided, OP, 3 1/2 x 2 In.	36.00
Te-Nex-Ine, Pyramid, Aqua, Cone, 2 7/8 In.	20.00
Upton's Refined Liquid, Aqua, 12-Sided, OP, 3 1/8 x 2 1/2 In.	38.00

GRENADIER

The Grenadier Spirits Company of San Francisco, California, started making figural porcelain bottles in 1970. Twelve soldier-shaped fifths were in Series No. 1. These were followed by Series 2 late in 1970. Only 400 cases were made of each soldier. The company continued to make bottles in series, including the 1976 American Revolutionary Army regiments in fifths and tenths, and many groups of minibottles. They also had series of club bottles, missions, foreign generals, horses, and more. The brothel series was started in 1978 for a special customer, Mr. Dug Picking of Carson City, Nevada. These are usually sold as *Dug's Nevada Brothels* and are listed in this book under Miniature. The Grenadier Spirits Company sold out to Fleishmann Distilling Company and stopped making the bottles about 1980. Jon-Sol purchased the remaining inventory of bottles.

GRENADIER, Pontiac Trans Am, 1979	31.00
San Fernando Mfg. Co., 1976	66.00
Santa Claus, Blue Sack, 1978	33.00
Santa Claus, Green Sack, 1978 ....*Illus*	28.00
Soldier, 1st Pennsylvania, 1970	30.00
Soldier, 3d Guard	27.00
Soldier, Billy Mitchell, 1975	38.00
Soldier, Comte DeRochambeau, 1978	30.00
Soldier, Count Pulaski, 1978	54.00
Soldier, General MacArthur, 1975	26.00
Soldier, Jeb Stuart, 1970	28.00

Grenadier, Santa Claus, Green Sack, 1978   *Grenadier, Soldier, Texas Ranger, 1977*

Soldier, Napoleon, 1969 .... 34.00
Soldier, Ney, 1969 .... 21.00
Soldier, Officer, 1st Guard Regiment, 1971 .... 25.00
Soldier, Robert E. Lee, 1976 .... 36.00
Soldier, Scots Fusilier, 1971 .... 21.00
Soldier, Scots Fusilier, 1975 .... 22.00
Soldier, Teddy Roosevelt, 1976 .... 30.00
Soldier, Teddy Roosevelt, 1977 .... 30.00
Soldier, Texas Ranger, 1977 ....*Illus* 35.00
Soldier, Texas Ranger, 1979 .... 33.00
Soldier, Wisconsin, 6th, 1975 .... 13.00
Washington Blue Rifles, Miniature 13.00
Washington On Horse, 1974 .... 24.00
HAIR PRODUCTS, see Cosmetic; Cure
HAND LOTION, see Cosmetic; Cure

─────────────────────────── **HOFFMAN** ───────────────────────────

J. Wertheimer had a distillery in Kentucky before the Civil War. Edward Wertheimer and
his brother Lee joined the business as young men. When Edward Sr. died at age 92, his son
Ed Wertheimer Jr., became president. Edward Jr.'s sons, Ed Wertheimer III and Thomas
Wertheimer, also worked in the family company. L. & E. Werthcimer Inc. made the prod-
ucts of the Hoffman Distilling Company and the Old Spring Distilling Company, including
Old Spring Bourbon, until 1983 when the company was sold to Commonwealth Distillery.
Hoffman Originals, later called the Hoffman Club, was foundcd by the Wertheimers in
1971 to make a series of figural bottles. The first was the Mr. Lucky series, started in 1973.
These were leprechaun-shaped decanters. Five series of leprechauns were made. Other
series include wildlife, decoy ducks (1977–1978), Aesop's fables, C.M. Russcll (1978),
rodeo (1978), pool-playing dogs (1978), belt buckles (1979), horses (1979), Jack Richardson animals, Bill Ohrmann animals (1980–1981), cheerleaders (1980), framed pistols
(1978), political (1980), and college football (1981–1982). The miniature Hoffman bottles
include series such as leprechauns (1981), birds (1978), dogs and cats (1978–1981),
decoys (1978–1979), pistols on stands (1975), Street Swingers (musicians, 1978–1979),
pistols (1975), wildlife (1978), and horses (1978).

HOFFMAN, Aesop's Fables, Hare & The Tortoise, 1978 .... 17.00
  Alaska Pipeline, 1975 .... 24.00
  Animal, Bear & Cub Fishing, 1978 .... 38.00
  Animal, Bobcat & Pheasant, 1978 .... 47.00
  Animal, Doe & Fawn, 1975 .... 32.00
  Animal, Falcon & Rabbit, 1978 .... 37.00
  Animal, Fox & Eagle, 1978 .... 47.00
  Animal, Fox & Rabbit, 1981 .... 44.00
  Animal, Jaguar & Possum, 1978 .... 28.00

Animal, Lion & Crane, 1979 .... 24.00
Animal, Lion & Dall Sheep, 1977, 3 Piece 176.00
Betsy Ross, 1974 .... 48.00
Big Red Machine, 1973 .... 44.00
Bird, Blue Jay, 1979 .... 36.00
Bird, Canada Geese, 1980 .... 20.00
Bird, Dove, Open Wing, 1979 .... 15.00
Bird, Egret, Baby, 1979 .... 17.00
Bird, Love, 1979 .... 16.00
Bird, Swan, Closed Wing, 1980 .... 18.00
Bird, Titmice, 1979 .... 29.00
College, Auburn Tigers, Helmet, 1981 .... 24.00
College, Clemson Tigers, 1981 .... 30.00
College, Georgia Bulldogs, Helmet, 1981 ....*Illus* 37.00
College, Kansas State Wildcats, Helmet, 1981 .... 22.00
College, Kentucky Wildcats, Helmet, 1981 .... 24.00
College, LSU Tiger, No. 2, 1981 .... 28.00
College, Missouri Tiger, Helmet, 1981 .... 22.00
College, Nebraska Cornhusker, Helmet, 1981 .... 39.00
College, Oklahoma Sooners, Helmet, 1981 .... 40.00
College, Tennessee Volunteers, Helmet, 1981 .... 31.00
Convention, Leprechaun On Barrel, 1982 .... 42.00
Cowboy & Puma, 1978 ....*Illus* 360.00
Duck, Decoy, Blue Bill, 1978, Miniature, Pair 14.00
Duck, Decoy, Blue Wing Teal, 1978, Pair 17.00
Duck, Decoy, Canada Goose, 1977 .... 18.00
Duck, Decoy, Canvasback, 1978, Miniature, Pair 14.00
Duck, Decoy, Golden Eye, 1978, Miniature, Pair 14.00
Duck, Decoy, Loon, 1978 .... 32.00
Duck, Decoy, Mallard, 1977, Miniature, Pair 14.00
Duck, Decoy, Merganser, 1978 .... 20.00
Duck, Decoy, Merganser, Hooded, 1978, Miniature, Pair 13.00
Duck, Decoy, Merganser, Red Breast, 1978, Miniature, Pair 12.00
Duck, Decoy, Pintail, 1977, Miniature, Pair 13.00
Duck, Decoy, Redhead, 1977, Miniature, Pair 13.00
Duck, Decoy, Ruddy Duck, 1978, Miniature, Pair 13.00
Duck, Decoy, Swan, White, 1978 .... 22.00
Duck, Decoy, Widgeon, 1978 .... 28.00
Duck, Decoy, Wood Duck, 1977 .... 37.00
Duck, Mallard, Open Wing, 1980 .... 20.00
Lady Godiva, 1974 .... 32.00
Mr. Baker, 1978 .... 36.00
Mr. Barber, 1980 .... 31.00
Mr. Bartender, 1975 .... 32.00
Mr. Blacksmith, 1976 .... 26.00

Hoffman, College, Georgia Bulldogs,
Helmet, 1981

Hoffman, Cowboy & Puma,
1978

Hoffman, Mr. Carpenter,
1979

Hoffman, Mr. Guitarist,
1975

Hoffman, Mr. Cobbler,
1973

Mr. Butcher, 1979 .... 28.00
Mr. Carpenter, 1979...*Illus* 31.00
Mr. Charmer, 1974 .... 21.00
Mr. Cobbler, 1973...*Illus* 20.00
Mr. Dancer, 1974.. 21.00
Mr. Dentist, 1980.. 25.00
Mr. Doctor, 1974 .... 32.00
Mr. Electrician, 1978 .... 37.00
Mr. Farmer, 1980 .... 26.00
Mr. Fiddler, 1974.. 23.00
Mr. Fireman, 1976... 71.00
Mr. Guitarist, 1975 ....*Illus* 25.00
Mr. Harpist, 1974.. 19.00
Mr. Lucky, 1973.. 27.00
Mr. Lucky & Rockwell, 1980, Miniature 50.00
Mr. Mailman, 1976.. 34.00
Mr. Mechanic, 1979 .... 32.00
Mr. Organ Player, 1979.. 29.00
Mr. Photographer, 1980 .... 28.00
Mr. Pilot, Miniature 26.00
Mr. Plumber, 1978 .... 28.00
Mr. Policeman, 1975... 38.00
Mr. Policeman, Retired, 1986, Miniature... 23.00
Mr. Railroad Engineer, 1980 .... 29.00
Mr. Salesman, 1982, Miniature... 17.00
Mr. Sandman, 1974... 20.00
Mr. Saxophonist, 1975... 30.00
Mr. Stockbroker, 1976.. 40.00
Mr. Tailor, 1979 .... 29.00
Mr. Teacher, 1976 .... 22.00
Mr. Tourist, 1980..27.00 to 40.00
Mrs. Lucky, 1974... 19.00
Mrs. Lucky, Retired, 1981, Miniature.. 18.00
Pistol, Civil War Colt, Framed, 1978 .... 28.00
Pistol, Civil War Colt, With Stand, 1975, Miniature................................ 16.00
Pistol, Colt 45 Automatic, Framed, 1978 .... 28.00
Pistol, Colt 45 Automatic, With Stand, 1975, Miniature.......................... 17.00
Pistol, Derringer, Silver, Framed, 1979.. 25.00
Pistol, Dodge City Frontier, Framed, 1978 .... 29.00
Pistol, Dodge City Frontier, With Stand, 1976, Miniature 17.00
Pistol, German Luger, Framed, 1978 .... 18.00

Pistol, German Luger, With Stand, 1975, Miniature 14.00
Pistol, Kentucky Flintlock, With Stand, 1975 .... 27.00
Pistol, Lawman, With Stand, 1978, Miniature .... 29.00 to 32.00
Pistol, Tower Flintlock, With Stand, 1975 .... 27.00
Political Donkey, 1980 .... 16.00
Political Elephant, 1980 .... 16.00
Rodeo, All Around Clown, 1978 .... 42.00
Rodeo, Bareback Rider, 1978 .... 40.00
Rodeo, Belt Buckle, Saddle Bronc, 1979 .... 43.00
Rodeo, Bull Rider, 1978 .... 46.00
Rodeo, Calf Roping, 1978 .... 42.00
Rodeo, Saddle, 1978 .... 33.00
Rodeo, Steer Wrestler, 1978 .... 35.00
Russel, Buffalo Man, 1976 .... 34.00
Russel, Bust, 1978 .... 31.00
Russel, Cowboy, 1978 .... 34.00
Russel, Flathead Squaw, 1976 .... 24.00
Russel, Half Breed Trader, 1978 .... 40.00
Russel, I Rode Him, 1978 .... 40.00
Russel, Indian Buffalo Hunter, 1978 .... 31.00
Russel, Last Of 5000, 1975 .... 20.00
Russel, Northern Cree, 1978 .... 33.00
Russel, Prospector, 1976 .... 27.00
Russel, Red River Breed, 1976 .... 35.00
Russel, Scout, 1978 .... 37.00
Russel, Stage Coach Driver, 1976 .... 30.00
Russel, Stage Robber, 1978 .... 40.00
Russel, Trapper, 1976 .... 30.00
Soldier, Concord, 1973 .... 25.00
Soldier, Queen's Ranger, 1978, Miniature, 4 Piece 53.00
Street Swingers, Train, I Think I Can, 1981 .... 70.00
Truck Distillery, 1981 .... 60.00

—————————————————— HOUSEHOLD ——————————————————

Many household cleaning products have been packaged in glass bottles since the nineteenth century. Shoe polish, ammonia, stove blacking, bluing, and other nonfood products are listed in this section. Most of these bottles have attractive paper labels that interest the collector.

HOUSEHOLD, Acme Blacking, Philadelphia 3.00
Ammonia For Washing, San Francisco, Dark Aqua, Applied Collar, Pt. 30.00
Bait Trap, McSwain Glass Co., Medium Yellow, Ground Lip, 12 In. 220.00
Black Cat Stove Enamel, 6 In. 5.00
Carter's Photo Library Paste, Embossed Cap With Applicator, Label 35.00
Clear, Metal Cover, 4 1/2 In. 49.00
Crystal Cleaner, Embossed Winchester, Paper Label, Box, 5 In. 110.00
Eclipse French Satin Gloss, Olive Green, 4 1/2 In. 30.00

Household, Standard
Ammonia, Puhl-Webb Co.,
Chicago, Ill., Green, 9 1/2 In.

Household,
Golden Key Ammonia,
Paper Label, 8 In.

Favorite Sewing Machine Oil, 4 1/2 In. 7.50
Furniture Reviver, Merten Moffitt & Co.'s, San Francisco, Amber, Rectangular, 6 In. . 45.00
Golden Key Ammonia, Paper Label, 8 In. ....*Illus* 10.00
Howe & Stevens Dye, Aqua, Crude 8.50
Lysol, Label, BIMAL, 1906, Sample 12.00
Mason's Shoe Dressing, Bright Drying, Olive Green, 4 In. 30.00
Shulite For Shoes, R.M. Hollingshead Co., Camden, N.J., Olive Green, 3 3/4 In. 30.00
Standard Ammonia, Puhl-Webb Co., Chicago, Ill., Green, 9 1/2 In. ....*Illus* 25.00
Stoddard Blacking, Golden Amber, OP 45.00
Tin Inhaler, Warner's Azmola, Wm. R. Warner & Co., Canada, Yellow, 4 In. 94.00

---------------------------------- **INK** ----------------------------------

Ink was first used about 2500 B.C. in ancient Egypt and China. It was made of carbon mixed with oils. By the fifteenth century, ink was usually made at home by the housewife who bottled it for later use. In the late eighteenth century, ink was sold by apothecary shops and bookstores. The first patented ink was made in England in 1792. Ink bottles were first used in the United States about 1819. Early ink bottles were of ceramic and were often imported. Small ink bottles were made to be opened and used with a dip pen. Large ink bottles, like the cathedral shaped Carter's inks, held a quart of ink to be poured into small bottles with dips. Inks can be identified by their shapes. Collectors have nicknamed many and the auctions often refer to *teakettles, cones, igloos,* or *umbrellas.*

Ink bottles were made to be hard to tip over. Some inks, especially English examples, were made with *bust-off* tops. The glass was cracked to open the bottle and the rough edge remained. In general the shape tells the age. Cones and umbrellas were used from the early 1800s to the introduction of the automatic bottle machine in the early 1900s. Hexagonal and octagonal bottles were preferred from about 1835 to 1865. Igloos, or turtles, were introduced in 1865 and were very popular for schools until about 1895. Barrels were made from 1840 to 1900. Square bottles became popular after 1860. Rectangular was the shape chosen in the 1900s. Figural bottles, especially ceramic types, were also made.

For further research, consult the book *Ink Bottles and Inkwells* by William E. Covill Jr. There is a national club, The Society of Inkwell Collectors, 5136 Thomas Avenue South, Minneapolis, MN 55410.

INK, 3-Piece Mold, Medium Olive Green, Seed Bubbles, Spout, Master........................ 60.00
8-Sided, Burst-Top, Slanted Base, England, 2 1/2 In. 15.00
10-Sided, Blue Green, Pontil, 3 1/8 In. 357.00
12 Vertical Ribs, Cylindrical, Cobalt Blue, Sheared Mouth, 2 1/4 In. 165.00
12-Sided, Bright Yellow Green, Applied Sloping Mouth, Master, 4 3/8 In. 110.00
12-Sided, Emerald Green, Pontil, Rolled Lip, c.1860, 1 3/4 In. 242.00
16-Lobed Daisy Flower, Sapphire Blue, Ground Pontil 120.00
18 Vertical Ribs, Aqua, Pontil, Bubbles, 1860, 1 7/8 In. 264.00
A & F, Cone, Aqua, Pontil 20.00
American Ink Co., Denver, USA, Round, Amber, Master, 8 1/2 In. 45.00
American Standard Ink, Frederick, Md., Yellow Green, Spout, Master, 10 In. 264.00
American Standard Ink, Frederick, Md., Square, Aqua, 1880, 2 1/2 In. 25.00
American Standard Ink, Frederick, Md., Square, Aqua, 2 3/4 In. 20.00
Aqua, Funneled Top, Pontil, 1 In. 231.00
Arnolds Ink, Bakelite, Round, 2 1/4 In. 35.00
Barrel, Pat. Oct. 17, 1865, Aqua, 4 In. 302.50
Bauman's Ink, Pittsburgh, Cone, Aqua, 12 5/8 In. 100.00
Bertinguiot, Black Glass, Sheared & Tooled Lip, Pontil, 1840-1855, 2 1/8 In. 303.00
Bertinguiot, Cylindrical, Domed Form, Olive Amber, Pontil, c.1860, 2 x 2 1/4 In. 154.00
Bertinguiot, Cylindrical, Olive Amber, Pontil, 2 In. 210.00
Bertinguiot, Deep Olive Amber, OP, Sheared Top, Bubbles, 1850s, 2 1/4 In. 176.00
Bertinguiot, Light Olive Green, OP 325.00
Bertinguiot, Medium Olive Amber, OP, 1850, 2 In. 110.00
Bertinguiot, Medium Olive Yellow, Tooled Lip, Pontil, 2 In. 231.00
Birdcage, Aqua, Embossed Door & Feeders Each End...................................... 120.00
Birdcage, Clear, Smooth Base, 1880, 3 3/4 In. 154.00
Bixby's Mucilage, Cone, Aqua, Label, Contents 14.00
Blackstone's, BIMAL, 3 Oz. 10.00
Blake, N.Y., Umbrella, 6-Sided, Aqua, Hexagonal, 2 7/8 In. 413.00

Blankenhey & Nolet, Dark Olive Amber, 3-Piece Mold, Globby Top, Case, Qt........... 10.00
Boss Bros. & Co., Crock, Flat Lip, Master.. 20.00
Building, Aqua, Smooth, 4 7/8 In.. 286.00
Building, Pat. Apr. 11, 1876, Clear, America, 3 1/4 In. 1017.00
Butlers, Cincinnati, 12-Sided, Aqua, Rolled Lip, OP, 1850, 2 1/4 In. 165.00
C.R. Cie, Umbrella, 6-Sided, Black Olive Amber, Pontil, 2 3/8 In................................. 550.00
Cabin, Aqua, Applied Square Collar, Patd March 1871, 2 1/2 In...................... 187.00
Cabin, Aqua, Ne Plus Ultra Fluid On Roof, 2 1/2 In... 165.00
Cabin, Aqua, Square Collar, 1870, 2 3/4 In.. 275.00
Cabin, Aqua, Tiny Bubbles, Smooth Base, England, 1870, 2 1/4 In. 1970.00
Cabin, Clear, Smooth Base, Ground Lip, c.1885, 3 1/4 In. 605.00
Cabin, Log, Ground Lip, Clear, 3 1/8 In.. 880.00
Cabin, S.I. Comp. On Roof, Aqua, Square Collar, 2 3/4 In....................................... 253.00
Cabin, Square Collar, Smooth Base, 1870-1880, 2 1/4 In. 100.00
Cabin, Square, Aqua, America, c.1890, 2 3/8 In.. 275.00
Cabin, Tooled Flared Lip, OP, c.1840, 3 7/8 In. 143.00
Cabin, Tooled Lip, 1880-1890, 1 1/2 In.. 440.00
Carter Ink, 6-Sided, Cobalt Blue, 6 In..*Illus* 240.00
Carter's, 6-Sided, Clover Leaf Design, Cobalt Blue, 2 7/8 In...................................... 132.00
Carter's, 6-Sided, Clover Leaf Motif, Cobalt Blue, 2 7/8 In....................................... 148.00
Carter's, 6-Sided, Clover Leaf Motif, Cobalt Blue 129.00
Carter's, 6-Sided, Clover Leaf Motif, Cobalt Blue, 2 3/4 In., C-555 .... 154.00
Carter's, 6-Sided, Clover Leaf Motif, Medium Sapphire Blue, c.1900-1910, 3 In. 412.00
Carter's, 6-Sided, Cobalt Blue, ABM 160.00
Carter's, 6-Sided, Sapphire Blue, Cloverleaf Design, Labels, 1900, 3 In. 413.00
Carter's, Amber, Embossed, Master, 5 In... 35.00
Carter's, Aqua, Master, Pt., 7 1/2 In.. 20.00
Carter's, Cathedral, 9 1/2 In. 125.00
Carter's, Cathedral, Cobalt Blue, ABM, Pour Spout, 1910-1930, 7 7/8 In. 165.00
Carter's, Cathedral, Cobalt Blue, Master, 1/2 Pt.. 231.00
Carter's, Cathedral, Cobalt Blue, Master, 7 7/8 In.. 187.00
Carter's, Cathedral, Cobalt Blue, Master, 8 In.. 165.00
Carter's, Cathedral, Cobalt Blue, Master, 9 3/4 In....................................66.00 to 100.00
Carter's, Cathedral, Master, Ca-Rt-Er, Cobalt Blue, Carter's On Base, c.1925, 6 1/4 In. 220.00
Carter's, Cone, Yellow Amber, Embossed, Tool Top 30.00
Carter's, Cylinder, Blue Green, Leadville Co., 5 1/2 In... 35.00
Carter's, Fluid Oz Embossed Side, Cylindrical, Milk Glass, ABM, 5 1/2 In. 10.00
Carter's, Fountain, Smooth Base, 1880, 2 1/2 In. 132.00
Carter's, Label, Master, Cobalt Blue, 9 3/4 In.. 176.00
Carter's, Light Green, Front & Back Labels, Spout, Cap, Qt. 75.00
Carter's, Light Green, Spout, Cap, Labels, Qt... 75.00
Carter's, Ma & Pa Carter, White Porcelain, Painted, Germany, 1900-1915, Pair.......... 187.00
Carter's, Ma Carter, Bisque, Germany, 3 5/8 In. 75.00
Carter's, Pa Carter, Bisque, Germany, 3 5/8 In.. 145.00
Carter's, Turtle, Aqua, Sheared Lip, Cylindrical, 1870, 1 3/4 In.................................. 363.00
Carter's 1897, Cone, Amber 10.00
Carter's Indelible Ink, 8-Sided, 1 3/4 In... 13.00
Carter's Ink, Emerald Green, Spout 82.50
Carters, Igloo, Round Collar Lip, 1880, 4 In.. 231.00
Cathedral, Cobalt Blue, Tooled Lip, 7 7/8 In.. 154.00
Caw's, Aqua, Tooled Top, Embossed... 33.00
Chest, Aqua, Ground Lip, 1880-1900, 3 In... 210.00
Clark Ink Co., Spout, Embossed, 7 1/4 In.. 38.50
Cobalt Blue, Pontil, 1 3/4 In. 120.00
Cobalt Blue, Pontil, Tooled Rim, Applied Knob, 2 In.. 104.00
Collins Ink Co., Louisville, Ky., Cone, Aqua, Green Streaks, Burst Top, 4 In. 280.00
Cone, Aqua, Flared Lip, Pontil, 2 1/8 In... 165.00
Cone, Bright Green.. 30.00
Cone, Cobalt Blue, Tooled Lip, 2 1/2 In... 60.00
Cone, LB Monogram, Aqua 75.00
Cone, Light Emerald Green, OP, 1845-1860, 2 1/4 In. 66.00
Cone, Mucilage, Aqua, 18 Vertical Ribs, Rolled Lip, OP, 2 1/8 In................................ 73.00
Cone, Root Beer Amber, Pontil, Sheared Lip, 2 3/8 In.. 176.00

Ink, Carter Ink,
6-Sided, Cobalt Blue,
6 In.

Ink, Crescent Fre-Flo,
Fountain Pen Ink,
3 In.

Ink, Paul's Safety Bottle &
Ink Co., Wrap Around
Label, 1880-1900, 8 In.

Cone, Sapphire Blue, Rolled Lip, OP, Dug, 1850, 2 1/4 In. 440.00
Cone, Yellow Amber, Rolled Lip, OP, 2 3/8 In.................. 605.00
Cone, Yellow Olive Amber, Pontil, 1830-1845, 1 5/8 In. 413.00
Cornflower Blue, Milk Glass Neck, Round, Sheared Top 44.00
Cottage, Aqua, America, c.1890, 2 5/8 In......................... 440.00
Cottage, Aqua, Pat.Mar 14, 1871, Applied Mouth, 2 1/2 In. 468.00
Cottage, Aqua, Sheared Lip, 2 5/8 In................................. 495.00
Cottage, Aqua, Tooled Lip, 2 1/2 In. 176.00
Cottage, Aqua, Tooled Lip, 2 5/8 In. 440.00
Cottage, Bank Of England Ink, Aqua, Tooled Lip, 3 5/8 In.......................... 1925.00
Cottage, Clear, Tooled Lip, 4 7/8 In. 385.00
Cottage, Ne Plus Ultra Fluid, Blue Aqua, Sheared Lip, 2 5/8 In.................................. 467.00
Crescent Fre-Flo, Fountain Pen Ink, 3 In. ....*Illus* 165.00
Cut Glass, Diamond Pattern, Fluted Neck, Twisted Pontil 16.00
Cylindrical, Blue Green, Flared Lip, Pontil.................. 25.00
Cylindrical, Cobalt Blue, Vertical Ribs, 3-Piece Mold, Blown, 1 5/8 In. 192.00
Cylindrical, Dark Olive Amber, 3-Piece Mold, Pontil, 1 7/8 In. 110.00
Cylindrical, Deep Olive Green, Applied Disk Lip, 3-Piece Mold, OP, 1 3/4 In. 330.00
Cylindrical, Dense Olive Green, 3-Piece Mold, Pontil, 1 9/16 In............................... 77.00
Cylindrical, Green, 2 3/8 In.. 35.00
Cylindrical, Milk Glass, 5 1/2 Oz. 10.00
Dark Olive Amber, 3-Piece Mold, OP, 1 3/4 In. 148.00
Dark Olive Amber, 3-Piece Mold, Pontil, 1 3/4 In.. 357.50
Davids, Medium Blue Green, Tooled Lip, 1875-1890, 1 5/8 In.................................... 440.00
Davids', Turtle, Aqua, Sheared Rolled Lip... 100.00
Davids' & Black, N.Y., Light Bright Green, Applied Mouth, Pontil, 4 5/8 In. 121.00
Davids' Black Marking Ink, Thaddeus Davids Co., N.Y., Cobalt Blue, Spout, Label ... 66.00
Deep Amber, 3-Piece Mold, Pontil, 1 5/8 In... 286.00
Deep Cobalt Blue, Pontil, 2 In. 198.00
Deep Olive Amber, 3-Piece Mold, Pontil, 1 1/2 In... 77.00
Deep Olive Amber, Tooled Disc Lip, 3-Piece Mold, Pontil, 1 7/8 In...................... 88.00
Deep Yellow Amber, Tooled Disc Lip, 3-Piece Mold, Blown, 1800-1820, 2 In. 88.00
Deep Yellow Olive, 3-Piece Mold, 1820, 1 1/2 In. 100.00
Deep Yellow Olive Green, 3-Piece Mold, Pontil, GIII-29, 1 1/2 In. 88.00
Dense Olive Amber, 3-Piece Mold, Pontil, 1 5/8 In.. 143.00
Dense Olive Amber, 3-Piece Mold, Pontil, 2 In... 176.00
Domed, Bisque, Cream Color, 3 Purple Diamonds, 2 In. 148.00
Domed, Medium Amber, Sheared & Ground Lip, 1880, 1 7/8 In................................. 132.00
Dr. Blocksom's Chemical Warehouse, Zanesville, 12-Sided, Aqua, OP, 4 1/4 In. 231.00
Drape Pattern, Aqua, OP, Applied Mouth, 2 1/4 In....................................... 275.00
Drum Form, Medium Green, 3-Piece Mold, Pontil, 1 1/4 In............................... 132.00
E. Waters, Aqua, Rolled Lip, OP, 1840-1855, 3 1/8 In. 440.00
E. Waters, Troy, N.Y., 6-Sided, Aqua, Conical Paneled, Partial Label, 1 7/8 In. 1705.00

E. Waters, Troy, N.Y., 6-Sided, Aqua, OP, 3 In. 1430.00
E. Waters, Troy, N.Y., Aqua, Applied Mouth, Pontil, 4 1/4 In. 385.00
E. Waters, Troy, N.Y., Aqua, Fluted Shoulders, Square Collar, 1860, 5 1/8 In. 633.00
E. Waters, Troy, N.Y., Aqua, Pontil, Applied Mouth, 6 3/4 In. 468.00
E. Waters, Troy, N.Y., Cylindrical, Aqua, Applied Tapered Lip, OP, 2 1/2 In. 413.00
E. Waters, Troy, N.Y., Cylindrical, Aqua, Fluted Shoulder, 7 3/4 x 5 1/2 In. 1540.00
E. Waters, Troy, N.Y., Yellow Green, Applied Lip, IP, Master, 6 1/2 In. 2145.00
E.S. Curtis Chemical Powder Half Gross, Cylindrical, Flared Lip, Pontil, 1860, 4 1/2 In. 308.00
Estes, N.Y., 8-Sided, Aqua, OP, 1850, 1 1/4 In. 297.00
F M & Co., Aqua, Dagger Picture, Bell, Whittled, 3 In. 30.00
F. Klett & Co., Superior, Aqua, Pontil, 4 1/4 In. 104.00
Farley's, 8-Sided, Amber, OP, 1850, 1 3/4 In. 578.00
Farley's, 8-Sided, Deep Olive Amber, Pontil, c.1860, 1 3/4 x 1 7/8 In. 522.00
Farley's, 8-Sided, Root Beer Amber, Pontil, c.1840-1850, 2 In. 440.00
First Premium Steel Pen Ink, 6-Sided, Amber, 2 1/2 In., C-180 .... 94.00
Forest Green, Large IP, 8 1/2 x 3 In. 50.00
Fort Pitt Blockhouse, ... 100.00
Fountain, 8-Sided, Clear, 3 3/4 In. 132.00
Fountain, Cylindrical, Green Aqua, Acorn Type Finial, Blown, 2 1/4 In. 110.00
Fountain, Short Stem, 2 Lobed Bowl, Prunts, Pontil, 4 1/8 In. 715.00
Geometric, 3-Piece Mold, Blown, Tooled Lip, Clear, 1 7/8 In. 715.00
Gibb, Umbrella, 6-Sided, Deep Aqua, 2 5/8 In. 110.00
Gleich's Black Writing Ink, Label, Spout, Embossed 50.00
Globe, America, Africa, Europe, Aqua, Smooth Base, 3 In. 247.00
Green, Blown, Folded Lip, 2 1/2 In. 55.00
H.G. Hotchkiss, Lyons, N.Y., Smoky Sapphire, Blue, Applied Mouth, Master, 9 In. 78.00
Haley Ink Co., USA, Embossed, Qt. 19.25
Harrison, Clear, Rough ABM Lip, 1905-1910, 1 3/8 In. 50.00
Harrison's Columbian, 8-Sided, Aqua, OP, 1840, 3 1/8 In. 66.00
Harrison's Columbian, 8-Sided, Aqua, Pontil, 3 1/2 In. 40.00
Harrison's Columbian, 8-Sided, Aqua, Rolled Lip, OP, 1 5/8 In. 100.00
Harrison's Columbian, 8-Sided, Backwards N In Ink, Aqua, OP, 3 7/8 In. 154.00
Harrison's Columbian, 12-Sided, Aqua, 2 Pontils, 5 3/4 In. 450.00
Harrison's Columbian, 12-Sided, Aqua, Applied Mouth, Pontil, 7 In. 110.00
Harrison's Columbian, 12-Sided, Aqua, Applied Mouth, Pontil, 9 In. 522.00
Harrison's Columbian, 12-Sided, Aqua, Applied Mouth, Pontil, 11 1/2 In. 770.00
Harrison's Columbian, 12-Sided, Aqua, Applied Tapered Collar, OP, 7 1/2 In. 253.00
Harrison's Columbian, 12-Sided, Aqua, IP, 7 1/2 In. 121.00
Harrison's Columbian, 12-Sided, Aqua, Pontil, 4 1/2 x 2 1/2 In. 176.00
Harrison's Columbian, 12-Sided, Aqua, Pontil, 5 7/8 In. 44.00
Harrison's Columbian, Aqua, 1 7/8 In. 220.00
Harrison's Columbian, Cobalt Blue, OP, c.1855, 4 In. 742.00
Harrison's Columbian, Cobalt Blue, OP, Whittled, c.1845-1860, 2 1/8 In. 825.00
Harrison's Columbian, Cobalt Blue, Pontil, 4 In. 357.00
Harrison's Columbian, Cobalt Blue, Pontil, Master, 5 3/4 In. 1018.00
Harrison's Columbian, Cobalt Blue, Pontil, Rolled Lip, 2 In. 660.00
Harrison's Columbian, Cylindrical, Cobalt Blue, Applied Mouth, Pontil, 4 In. 440.00
Harrison's Columbian, Cylindrical, Cobalt Blue, Applied Mouth, Pontil, 5 3/4 In. 302.00
Harrison's Columbian, Cylindrical, Cobalt Blue, Rolled Mouth, Pontil, 2 In. 605.00
Harrison's Columbian, Cylindrical, Deep Cobalt Blue, Applied Mouth, Pontil, 7 In. .. 935.00
Harrison's Columbian, Cylindrical, Sapphire Blue, IP, 7 In. 1980.00
Harrison's Columbian, Igloo, Aqua, Sheared & Tooled Lip, 1875, 1 1/2 In. 172.00
Harrison's Columbian, Light Sapphire Blue, Rolled Mouth, Pontil, 2 In. 467.00
Harrison's Columbian, Medium Sapphire Blue, OP, 4 1/2 In. 1100.00
Harrison's Columbian, Medium Sapphire Blue, Rolled Lip, OP, 2 In. 210.00
Harrison's Columbian, Sapphire Blue, Partial Label, Flared Mouth, Pontil, 7 In. 5775.00
Harrison's Columbian, Sapphire Blue, Pontil, c.1840-1850, 4 1/8 In. 798.00
Higgs, Umbrella, 12-Sided, Deep Green Aqua, 2 1/4 In. 132.00
Hoffman's Carmine, Embossed, Yellow Label, Half Contents 20.00
House, Aqua, Smooth Base, 2 7/8 In. 330.00
Hover, Philadelphia, Cylindrical, Aqua, Pour Spout, Applied Mouth, 9 In. 143.00
Hover, Philadelphia, Green, Flared Lip, OP, 4 1/2 In. 125.00
Hover, Philadelphia, Light To Medium Blue Green, Flared Lip, Pontil, 1855, 6 In. 176.00

Hover, Philadelphia, Medium Emerald Green, Pontil, Master, 9 In. 440.00
Hover, Philadelphia, Umbrella, 12-Sided, Emerald Green, Rolled Lip, OP, 1 7/8 In. 385.00
Hyde 61 Fleet St., London, Cobalt Blue, Pour Lip, 12 Panel, Master, 8 1/4 In. 180.00
Igloo, Dark Aqua, Scalloped Sides, Embossed Bird On Branch 125.00
Igloo, Deep Cobalt Blue, Ground Lip, 2 In. 1540.00
Igloo, Domed Type, Deep Golden Amber, Tooled Mouth, 1 3/4 In. 187.00
J. & I.E.M., Amber Turtle, Ground Lip, 1 5/8 In. 275.00
J. & I.E.M., BIMAL, Deep Root Beer, Olive Amber, Tooled Lip, 1 3/4 In. 187.00
J. & I.E.M., BIMAL, Golden Yellow Amber, Tooled Lip, 1 3/4 In. 440.00
J. & I.E.M., BIMAL, Medium Yellow Amber, Ground Lip, 1 3/4 In. 253.00
J. & I.E.M., Igloo, Bright Blue, Domed Form, Ground Mouth, 1865-1880 .... 1210.00
J. & I.E.M., Igloo, Citron, Domed Form, Sheared Mouth, 1 5/8 In. 550.00
J. & I.E.M., Igloo, Light Golden Amber, Domed Form, Sheared Mouth, 1 1/2 In. 132.00
J. & I.E.M., Igloo, Medium Blue Green, Ground Mouth, 1 1/2 In. 121.00
J. & I.E.M., Igloo, Yellow, Green, Domed Form, Sheared Mouth, 1 1/2 In. 550.00
J. & I.E.M., Turtle, Amber, BIMAL, Embossed 143.00
J. & I.E.M., Turtle, Aqua, BIMAL, Embossed 55.00
J. & I.E.M., Turtle, Light Yellow Apple Green, Tooled Lip, 1 5/8 In. 248.00
J. & I.E.M., Turtle, Medium Emerald, Teal Green, 1 5/8 In. 550.00
J. & I.E.M., Aqua, OP, Rolled Lip, 2 7/8 In. 110.00
J.A. Williamson Chemist, Medium Blue Green, Applied Spout, 7 1/2 In. 132.00
J.J. Butler, Cincinnati, Oh., 12-Sided, Pale Apple Green, OP, Rolled Lip, 2 1/4 In. 302.50
J.J. Butler, Cincinnati, Oh., Cone, Aqua, Pontil, 2 1/2 In. 440.00
J.J. Butler, Cincinnati, Oh., Square, Aqua, OP, 1850, 2 3/4 In. 132.00
J.K. Palmer, Chemist, Boston, Olive Amber, Pontil, c.1855, 9 In. 412.00
J.S. Dunham, St. Louis, 12-Sided, Aqua, Rolled Lip, OP, 1850, 2 7/8 In. 297.00
J.S. Dunham, Umbrella, 8-Sided, Aqua, OP, 2 3/4 In. 143.00
J.S. Dunham, Umbrella, 8-Sided, Deep Aqua, Pontil, 2 5/8 In. 275.00
J.S. Dunham, Umbrella, Aqua, OP 375.00
J.S. Mason, Philadelphia, Medium Emerald Green, 4 3/8 In. 275.00
J.W. Ely, Cincinnati, Oh., Rolled Lip, Aqua, 2 5/8 In. 302.50
James Kidder, Jr., East Boston, Cylindrical, Aqua, Tapered Collar, OP, 1850, 8 In. 187.00
James S. Mason & Co., Umbrella, 8-Sided, Aqua, OP, 2 3/8 In. 110.00
Keene, Medium Olive, Disk Lip, 2 5/8 x 1 7/8 In. 200.00
Keene, New Hampshire, Red Amber, 3-Piece Mold, OP, 1 3/4 In. 688.00
Kirkland's Writing Fluid, Cone, Aqua, Applied Square Cover, 2 5/8 In. 40.00
Kirkland's Writing Fluid, Poland, Oh., Cylindrical, Aqua, OP, 2 3/8 In. 320.00
Kiryland's Ink W & H, Igloo, Aqua, Smooth Based, 1870-1880, 2 1/4 In. 137.00
Kwikstick, Cone, Applicator Cap, 2 1/2 In. 30.00
L.R. Goodhue, Umbrella, 6-Sided, Aqua, 2 1/4 In. 210.00
Lady's Slipper Form, Fiery Opalescent, Ground Mouth, 3 1/4 In. 467.00
Light Green Aqua, Tooled Lip, Pontil, 1840-1870, 4 In. 198.00
Light Yellow Green, Pontil, 2 1/4 In. 110.00
Linn Smith & Co., Philadelphia, Yellow Amber, OP, Flared Lip, 4 5/8 In. 253.00
Llewellyn, 1410 Chestnut St., Tan, Spout, Pt. 59.00
Locomotive, American, c.1874-1880, Aqua, 2 In. 330.00
Locomotive, Aqua, Smooth Base, 2 1/8 In. 853.00
Locomotive, Figural, Aqua, 2 3/8 x 2 7/8 In. 1870.00
Maxwell's Record & Copying, Olive Amber, Applied Mouth, Pontil, 9 1/2 In. 132.00
Medium Olive Green, Tooled Disc Mouth, 3-Piece Mold, OP, 1 3/4 In. 121.00
Medium Yellow Amber, Tooled Disc Lip, 3-Piece Mold, Pontil, 1 5/8 In. 88.00
Medium Yellow Olive, 3-Piece Mold, Pontil, 1 1/2 In. 165.00
Milky Opalescent, Sheared & Ground Lip, 3-Piece Mold, 1 5/8 In. 220.00
Morrell, London, Teakettle, Stoneware, Brown 150.00
Mt. Vernon Glass Co., Deep Olive Green, 3-Piece Mold, Cylindrical, OP, 1 3/4 In. 495.00
Olive Green, 8-Sided, Burst Top, 3 In. 22.00
Olive Green, Whittled, Spout, Cork, Open Pontil, Master 187.00
Opdyke Bros., Barrel, Aqua, 1870, Square, 2 1/2 In. 310.00
Opdyke Bros., Barrel, Aqua, Tooled Lip, 2 1/2 In. .... 165.00 to 198.00
P. & J. Arnold, England, Cylinder, 4 1/2 In. 40.00
P. & J. Arnold, London, Stoneware, Master, Qt. 15.00
Palmer Chemist, Olive Green, Spout, Cylindrical, Master, 9 1/2 In. 275.00
Paperweight, Aqua, Pontil, 2 7/8 In. 198.00

Paperweight, Green Aqua, Tooled Flared Mouth, Cylindrical, 4 1/2 In.	330.00
Paris Depose, Deep Cobalt Blue, Sheared & Ground Lip, France, 1880s, 2 7/8 In.	165.00
Patterson's Excelsior, 8-Sided, Aqua, Pontil, 2 5/8 In.	412.00
Paul's Safety, Clear, Tooled Lip, Wrap Around Label, Master, 1900, 8 1/4 In.	110.00
Paul's Safety Bottle & Ink Co., Wrap Around Label, 1880-1900, 8 In. *Illus*	110.00
Penn Mfg. Works, P. Garrett, 8-Sided, Milk Glass, Stopper, 2 3/4 In.	66.00
Petal Foot, Pontil, Flaring Lip, 3-Piece Mold, c.1840	1430.00
Pitkin Type, 28 Ribs, Swirled To Left, Deep Yellow Olive, Pontil, 1 1/2 In.	632.00
Pitkin Type, 36 Ribs, Medium Olive Green, Swirled To Right, 1 5/8 In.	715.00
Pitkin Type, 36 Ribs, Swirled To Left, Medium Yellow Olive, Pontil, 1 5/8 In.	275.00
Pitkin Type, 36 Ribs, Swirled To Left, Yellow Olive Green, Pontil, 1 5/8 In.	742.00
Pitkin Type, 36 Ribs, Swirled To Right, Conical Form, Yellow Olive, Pontil, 1 1/2 In..	705.00
Pitkin Type, Cylindrical, Yellow Olive, Tooled Mouth, Pontil, 2 In.	715.00
Pitkin Type, Yellow Olive Green, Pontil, Tooled Disc Lip, c.1800, 1 5/8 x 2 1/8 In.	605.00
Pomeroy's Fountain Pen Ink, Round Shoulder, 2 3/4 In.	40.00
Potain, Paris, Hand Form, Pink Milk Glass, Ground Lip, 1870, 4 x 2 In.	275.00
Pressed Glass, 8-Sided, Hinged Cover, Deep Ice Blue, 2 7/8 In.	210.00
R.B. Snow, St. Louis, 12-Sided, Umbrella, Light Green, Pontil, 1 3/4 In.	231.00
R.F., Deep Amethyst Black, Tooled Flared Lip, Pontil, 2 In.	104.00
Round, Cobalt Blue, Spout, 1 1/2 In.	22.00
Round, Green, OP, 3 In.	75.00
S. Fine Blk. Ink, Medium Emerald Green, Rolled Lip, OP, 1840-1860, 3 In.	357.00
S. Fine Blk. Ink, Medium Green, Rolled Lip, OP, 3 In.	495.00
S.I. Comp., Cottage, Aqua, Tooled Lip, 2 3/4 In.	357.00
S.I. Comp., Cottage, Milk Glass, Rolled Lip, 2 3/4 In.	440.00
S.I. Company, Barrel, 2 1/4 In.	77.00
S.O. Dunbar, Taunton, Mass., Aqua, Pour Spout, Applied Mouth, Pontil, 8 1/2 In.	38.00
S.O. Dunbar, Taunton, Umbrella, Aqua, 8-Sided, OP, 2 3/8 In.	143.00
S.O. Dunbar's Black, Aqua, 6 3/4 In.	55.00
S.S. Stafford's, Cobalt, Pour Spout, Qt.	50.00
S.S. Stafford's Inks, Cobalt, Pour Spout, Qt.	60.00
S.S. Stafford's Inks, Inc., Cobalt, Label, Qt.	40.00
San Francisco, California Ink Co., Cottage, Amber, 2 1/4 In.	1100.00
Sanborn & Carter's Superior Black Record Ink, 6-Sided, Blue Green, 2 3/8 In.	154.00
Sandwich Glass, Blue, White Mottled Flecks, Circular, 2 5/8 In. Diam.	20350.00
Sanford Co., Boat, Aqua, BIMAL, Embossed	22.00
Sanford's & Library Paste, Amber, ABM Label, Master, 9 3/8 In.	83.00
Sanford's Ink & Library Paste, Yellow, Cylinder, 9 1/4 In.	19.00
Sanford's Inks & Library Pastes, Label, Cap & Contents, 1/2 Pt.	25.00
Schmidts, Igloo, Aqua, Smooth Base, 1870-1880, 1 3/4 In.	198.00
Scott, 417 Strand, 1820s	405.00
Ship Captains, White, Green Swirled Ribbons, 1870, 5 1/2 In.	385.00
Signet Ink & Mucilage, Cobalt, ABM	18.00
Square, Aqua, Brown Body Swirls, 3-Sided Vertical Ribs	45.00
Stafford's, Cobalt Blue, Pt.	45.00
Stafford's, Emerald Green, Master, Pt.	100.00
Stafford's Ink, Amber, BIMAL, Pt.	27.50
Stafford's Ink, Teal Green, Pouring Lip, Master	85.00
Stafford's Jet Black Writing Ink, Cobalt Blue, Label	50.00
Stafford's Writing Ink, Unchangeable Black, Cork, Partial Label	12.50
Stoddard, 8-Sided, Stoddard Dot, OP, Red Amber, 2 1/2 In.	650.00
Stoddard, 12-Sided, Olive Amber, Rolled Lip, OP, 1840, 2 1/2 In.	467.00
Stoddard, Cone, Olive Amber, Sheared Lip, OP, Cylindrical, 2 1/4 In.	210.00
Stoddard, Cone, X On Base, Olive Green	210.00
Stoddard, Cone, Yellow Olive, Pontil, 2 In.	302.00
Stoddard, Globe, Red Amber, Handle	225.00
Stoddard, Umbrella, 8-Sided, Pontil	150.00
Stoddard Type, Cylindrical, Amber, Master, Pt.	29.00
Stoneware, Gray, Cobalt Blue Slip, 3 Quill Holes, Center Hole, 1 7/8 In.	221.00
Stoneware, Ross Brothers & Co., Binghamton, N.Y., Saltglaze, Gray, 7 In.	60.50
Stoneware, Ross Brothers & Co., Binghamton, N.Y., Bottle, Dark Brown Albany	93.50
T & M, Bright Green, Umbrella Form, Pontil, Rectangular, 2 1/4 In.	110.00
T. David & Co., Aqua, Pat. Nov. 7, '76	15.00

Teakettle, 6-Sided, Aqua, Ground Lip, 2 1/8 In. 154.00
Teakettle, 6-Sided, Canary Yellow, Ground, Polished Lip, 2 1/8 In. 253.00
Teakettle, 6-Sided, Deep Cobalt Blue, Gilt Design, 1 7/8 In. 495.00
Teakettle, 6-Sided, Medium Green Aqua, Ground Lip, 2 1/4 In. 687.50
Teakettle, 6-Sided, Medium Honey Amber, Ground Lip, 2 1/2 In. 231.00
Teakettle, 6-Sided, Yellow Green, Sheared Lip, 1 7/8 In. 495.00
Teakettle, 8-Sided Facets, Deep Puce-Amethyst 550.00
Teakettle, 8-Sided, Aqua, Concave Upper Panels, Ground Lip, Iridescent, 2 1/8 In. 132.00
Teakettle, 8-Sided, Cobalt Blue, Ground Lip, 2 1/8 In. 522.00
Teakettle, 8-Sided, Deep Cobalt Blue, Gilt Design, Sheared Lip, 2 3/8 In. 440.00
Teakettle, 8-Sided, Deep Emerald Green, Oval, 1 3/4 In. 1210.00
Teakettle, 8-Sided, Deep Opaque Powder Blue, Polished Lip, 2 5/8 In. 577.50
Teakettle, 8-Sided, Fiery Opalescent Green, Floral Design, Sheared Lip, 2 5/8 In. 358.00
Teakettle, 8-Sided, Fiery Opalescent Robin Egg Blue, Sheared Lip, 2 5/8 In. 440.00
Teakettle, 8-Sided, Ghosted Ellipse On Each Panel, Deep Amethyst, 2 In. 121.00
Teakettle, 8-Sided, Ground Mouth, Amethyst, 2 3/4 In. 302.00
Teakettle, 8-Sided, Light Blue Green, Ground Mouth, 2 In. 388.00
Teakettle, 8-Sided, Pillow, Carved Tassels, Emerald Green, 1 1/4 In. 705.00
Teakettle, 10-Sided, Aqua, Ground Mouth, 2 3/8 In. 66.00
Teakettle, 10-Sided, Floral, Leaf Design, Opalescent, Green, Blue, Amethyst, 2 In. 385.00
Teakettle, 3 Cobalt Blue Enamel Bands, Clear, c.1890, 2 In. 330.00
Teakettle, 5-Lobed Body Form, Raised Floral, Leaf Design, Fiery Opalescent, 2 In. 302.00
Teakettle, Amethyst, Ground Mouth, Brass Collar, 2 In. 440.00
Teakettle, Aqua, A.M. Embossed On Base & Top, Ground Lip, 2 In. 110.00
Teakettle, Aqua, Sheared Lip, 2 1/8 In. 302.50
Teakettle, Aqua, Vertical Ribbed, 2 In. 55.00
Teakettle, B-D On Clear Panels, Ground Lip, 1 1/2 In. 330.00
Teakettle, Barrel Form, Deep Sapphire Blue, Ground Lip, 2 1/8 In. 1008.00
Teakettle, Barrel, Cobalt Blue, Metal Lid, c.1890, 2 1/4 In. 1155.00
Teakettle, Barrel, Medium Blue, Rectangular, 1870, 2 1/8 In. 1100.00
Teakettle, Barrel, Medium Purple Amethyst, Sheared Lip, 2 1/4 In. 1650.00
Teakettle, Barrel, Sapphire Blue, 2 3/8 In. 1100.00
Teakettle, Barrel, Sapphire Blue, Ground Lip, 2 1/8 In. 660.00
Teakettle, Brilliant Turquoise, Diamond Pattern On Panels, 1890, 2 3/8 In. 665.00
Teakettle, Bust Of Ben Franklin, Pale Aqua, Ground Lip, 4 In. 302.00
Teakettle, Clambroth, 7 Lobes At Base, 7 Leaf Flutes On Dome, Gray Blue, 2 3/4 In. ... 935.00
Teakettle, Clear, Cobalt Blue Overlay, Allover Cut Thumbprint, 1875, 2 1/2 In. 770.00
Teakettle, Cobalt Blue, Curved Spout 300.00
Teakettle, Cobalt Blue, Gilt, Polished Pontil, Brass Lid, 1 1/2 In. 550.00
Teakettle, Cobalt Blue, Ground Mouth, England, 2 In. 550.00
Teakettle, Cobalt Blue, Jelly Mold, Long Spout 390.00
Teakettle, Cobalt Blue, Victorian Designs, Soapstone Base, Polished Lip, 3 1/2 In. 632.00
Teakettle, Conical, Polished Diamond Design, Amethyst, 2 In. 605.00
Teakettle, Deep Amethyst, Ground Lip, 1870, 2 In. 413.00
Teakettle, Deep Cobalt Blue, Sheared Lip, 2 1/8 In. 252.00
Teakettle, Elks Pride Whiskey, Elk's Head, Brown & Cream, Stenciled 289.00
Teakettle, Emerald, Teal Green, Ground Lip, 2 In. 338.00
Teakettle, Fiery Opalescent, Milk Glass, Pear Shape, Sheared Lip, 2 3/4 In. 330.00
Teakettle, Medium Cobalt Blue, Ground Lip, 2 1/8 In. ....198.00 to 358.00
Teakettle, Medium Yellow Green, Original Neck Ring, 1870-1890, 2 3/4 In. ....*Illus* 935.00
Teakettle, Melon Form, Canary Yellow, Brass Lid, 2 3/4 In. 797.00
Teakettle, Milk Glass, Opalescent, Powder Blue Milk Glass, Ground Lip, 2 3/8 In. 220.00
Teakettle, Opalescent Milk Glass, Ribbed, 1875-1895, 3 In. 495.00
Teakettle, Opalescent, Allover Gold Flowers, Blue Ridges 690.00
Teakettle, Opalescent, Powder Blue, Ground Lip, 2 3/8 In. ....358.00 to 440.00
Teakettle, Opaque Lavender, Polished Lip, 2 3/8 In. 385.00
Teakettle, Opaque Lime Green, 1870-1890, 2 In. ....550.00 to 665.00
Teakettle, Opaque Mint Green, Pear Shape, Sheared Lip, 2 1/2 In. 385.00
Teakettle, Pale Green, Brass Neck Ring, 2 1/8 In. 523.00
Teakettle, Porcelain, White, Allover Floral Design, 1 1/2 In. 468.00
Teakettle, Purple Amethyst, Ground Lip, c.1870, 2 In. 715.00
Teakettle, Sandwich Glass Works, Milk Glass, Opalescent, Ground Lip, 2 In. 303.00
Teakettle, Snail Shape, Ground Lip 250.00

Teakettle, Tan, Mottled White, Brown Glaze, 2 1/8 In. 132.00
Thaddeus Davids & Co., N.Y., 3-Piece Mold, Green, IP, Spout, Partial Label 77.00
Thaddeus Davids' Steelpen Ink, Emerald Green, Pontil, Label, Master, 5 3/8 In. 230.00
Tinta, American, Pontil, 1855, 1 3/4 In. 253.00
Tippecanoe, Cabin, c.1840 .... 2100.00
Turtle, Amber, Ground Lip, 1 3/4 In. 188.00
Turtle, Aqua, Ground Mouth, 2 In. 550.00
Turtle, Medium Purple Amethyst, Ground Lip, 1 7/8 In. 1485.00
Turtle, Pewter, 20-Sided, 1880, 2 1/4 In. 231.00
Umbrella, 6-Sided, Aqua, Pontil, 3 1/8 In. 176.00
Umbrella, 6-Sided, Medium Cobalt Blue, Pontil, 2 1/2 In. 935.00
Umbrella, 6-Sided, Medium Sapphire Blue, 2 5/8 In. 264.00
Umbrella, 8 Concave Panels, Light Sapphire Blue, OP, 2 3/16 In. 1650.00
Umbrella, 8-Sided, 2 1/2 In. 660.00
Umbrella, 8-Sided, Amber, OP, Sheared Lip, 1850, 2 1/2 In. 165.00
Umbrella, 8-Sided, Amber, Pontil, Rolled Lip, c.1855, 2 1/2 In. 154.00
Umbrella, 8-Sided, Amethyst, 2 1/2 In. 522.00
Umbrella, 8-Sided, Aqua, OP, 3 1/8 In. 204.00
Umbrella, 8-Sided, Aqua, Rolled Lip, OP, 2 3/4 In. 523.00
Umbrella, 8-Sided, Black Amethyst, Applied Mouth, 2 1/4 In. 495.00
Umbrella, 8-Sided, Blue Aqua, OP, Rolled Lip, 2 1/2 In. 231.00
Umbrella, 8-Sided, Blue Emerald Green, 2 5/8 In. 110.00
Umbrella, 8-Sided, Bright Green, Olive Tone, Sheared Mouth, Pontil, 2 1/4 In. 495.00
Umbrella, 8-Sided, Bright Light Blue, Pontil, 2 1/2 In. 165.00
Umbrella, 8-Sided, Cobalt Blue, 2 5/8 In. 220.00
Umbrella, 8-Sided, Deep Amber, OP, 2 5/8 In. 413.00
Umbrella, 8-Sided, Deep Brilliant Blue, Rolled Lip, OP, 1850, 2 1/2 In. 220.00
Umbrella, 8-Sided, Deep Chocolate Amber, OP, 2 1/2 In. 198.00
Umbrella, 8-Sided, Deep Cobalt Blue, Rolled Lip, 2 3/8 In. 358.00
Umbrella, 8-Sided, Deep Cobalt Blue, Tooled Lip, 2 1/2 In. 550.00
Umbrella, 8-Sided, Deep Emerald, OP, 2 3/8 In. 198.00
Umbrella, 8-Sided, Deep Olive Green, Pontil, 2 3/8 In. 231.00
Umbrella, 8-Sided, Deep Purple Amethyst, Tooled, 2 5/8 In. 605.00
Umbrella, 8-Sided, Deep Red Amber, Pontil, 2 1/2 In. 302.00
Umbrella, 8-Sided, Deep Red Puce, Pontil, Rolled Lip, 2 1/2 In. 633.00
Umbrella, 8-Sided, Deep Sapphire Blue, OP, 2 1/2 In. 853.00
Umbrella, 8-Sided, Deep Yellow Green, Pontil, 2 7/8 In. 187.00
Umbrella, 8-Sided, Deep Yellow Green, Pontil, c.1860, 4 3/8 x 2 In. 187.00
Umbrella, 8-Sided, Deep Yellow Olive, Sheared Mouth, Pontil, 2 1/4 In. 302.00
Umbrella, 8-Sided, Deep Yellow Olive Amber, Reverse S4, OP, 2 1/2 In. 209.00
Umbrella, 8-Sided, Emerald Green, OP, 1840-1860, 2 3/8 In. 467.00
Umbrella, 8-Sided, Golden Yellow Amber, Pontil, 2 1/4 In. 132.00
Umbrella, 8-Sided, Light Apple Green, 2 5/8 In. 523.00
Umbrella, 8-Sided, Light Emerald Green, OP, 2 1/2 In. 231.00
Umbrella, 8-Sided, Light Emerald Green, Rolled Lip, OP, 2 1/4 In. 935.00
Umbrella, 8-Sided, Light To Medium Emerald Green, OP, 2 1/2 In. 121.00
Umbrella, 8-Sided, Light Yellow Amber, Pontil, 2 3/8 In. 770.00
Umbrella, 8-Sided, Light, Medium Yellow Green, IP, 2 3/8 In. 412.00
Umbrella, 8-Sided, Medium Amber, Rolled Lip, OP, 2 3/8 In. 132.00
Umbrella, 8-Sided, Medium Cobalt Blue, 2 1/2 In. 605.00
Umbrella, 8-Sided, Medium Root Beer Amber, OP, 2 3/8 In. 121.00
Umbrella, 8-Sided, Medium Sapphire Blue, 2 3/4 In. 660.00
Umbrella, 8-Sided, Medium To Deep Yellow Green, Outward Folded Lip, 2 3/4 In. 577.00
Umbrella, 8-Sided, Medium Yellow Olive, Rolled Lip, 2 5/8 In. 137.00
Umbrella, 8-Sided, Medium Yellow Root Beer Amber, OP, 2 In. 121.00
Umbrella, 8-Sided, Red Amber, Pontil, 2 1/2 In. 154.00
Umbrella, 8-Sided, Red Amber, Pontil, 2 3/8 In. 132.00
Umbrella, 8-Sided, Rich Emerald Green, Pontil, 2 1/4 In. 357.00
Umbrella, 8-Sided, Root Beer Amber, OP, 2 3/8 In. 176.00
Umbrella, 8-Sided, Yellow Amber, OP, 2 1/4 In. 797.50
Umbrella, 8-Sided, Yellow Amber, OP, Sheared Lip, 2 3/8 In. 99.00
Umbrella, 8-Sided, Yellow Olive, Rolled Lip, OP, 1850, 2 3/8 In. 357.00
Umbrella, 8-Sided, Yellow Olive Green, OP, Sheared Lip, 2 1/2 In. 209.00

Umbrella, 8-Sided, Yellow, 7-Up Green, 2 5/8 In... 242.00
Umbrella, 8-Sided, Yellow, Amber Tone, Rolled Lip, Pontil, 1855, 2 3/8 In. 825.00
Umbrella, 12-Sided, Aqua, OP, 2 In. 55.00
Umbrella, 12-Sided, Aqua, OP, Rolled Lip, 3 1/8 In... 220.00
Umbrella, 12-Sided, Aqua, Pontil, 1 7/8 In. 30.00
Umbrella, 12-Sided, Emerald Green, OP, Rolled Lip, 2 In. 242.00
Umbrella, 12-Sided, Light Green, Rolled Lip, OP, 2 5/8 In. ....*Illus* 264.00
Umbrella, 12-Sided, Light To Medium Green, OP 175.00
Umbrella, 12-Sided, Light Yellow Green, Pontil, 2 1/8 In..................................... 231.00
Umbrella, 12-Sided, Medium Emerald Green, Pontil, 1 7/8 In. 267.00
Umbrella, 12-Sided, Medium Emerald Green, OP, 2 In.. 242.00
Umbrella, 12-Sided, Medium Green, Yellow Tone, OP, 2 1/8 In............................ 303.00
Umbrella, 12-Sided, Root Beer Amber, Rolled Lip, Pontil 358.00
Umbrella, 16-Sided, Deep Olive Amber, Pontil, 2 In... 468.00
Umbrella, 16-Sided, Medium Root Beer Amber, OP, Sheared Lip, 1830-1860, 2 In. 495.00
Umbrella, 16-Sided, Yellow Amber, Sheared Lip, OP, 1850, 2 1/4 In........................... 495.00
Umbrella, Aqua, Pontil, Jumbo, 3 1/8 In.. 245.00
Umbrella, Aqua, Vertical Ribs, Pontil, Rolled Lip, 2 3/8 In. 413.00
Umbrella, Black Olive Amber, OP, Rolled Lip, 2 1/2 In... 467.00
Umbrella, Deep Yellow Olive Green, Pontil, 2 5/8 In.. 121.00
Umbrella, E. Water's, Troy, N.Y., 6-Sided, Aqua, Pontil, 2 1/2 In. 1100.00
Umbrella, Medium Orange Amber, Sheared Top, OP, Whittled, 2 1/2 In...................... 303.00
Umbrella, Medium Pink Puce, Hexagonal, Pontil, 2 1/2 In.................................... 3245.00
Umbrella, S.O. Dunbar, 8-Sided, Aqua, Pontil, 2 3/8 In. 121.00
Umbrella, S.O. Dunbar, 8-Sided, Tontine, Aqua, Rolled Lip, OP, 1850, 2 3/16 In......... 132.00
Umbrella, Yellow Olive Green, 3 Piece Mold, Pontil, 1 1/2 In...............................*Illus* 100.00
Umbrella, Yellow Olive Green, OP, Rolled Lip, c.1855, 2 1/2 In............................. 302.50
Umbrella, Yellow Olive Green, OP, Sheared Lip, 2 5/8 In. 154.00
Underwood's, Aqua, 2 3/4 In... 42.00
Underwood's, Master, Cobalt Blue, Tooled Mouth, Cylindrical, Pontil, 9 1/4 In. 137.00
Underwood's Ink, 8-Sided, Cover, Aqua, 2 1/4 In.. 30.00
Underwood's Inks, Embossed, 16 Oz.. 22.00
Underwood's Inks, Spout, Cobalt, Qt.. 145.00
Vertu Bordeaux, Medium Gasoline Pink Puce, Pontil, France, 2 1/8 In...................... 231.00
W.E. Bonney, Aqua, Barrel Master, Pour Spout, 6 1/8 In. 275.00
W.E. Bonney, Barrel, Rolled Lip, OP, 1850, 2 5/8 In. 231.00
Ward's Ink, Boston, Green, Spout, Qt. 71.00
Wedding Cake Shape, Aqua, 3 Tiers 60.00
Williams, Aqua, BIMAL, 1/2 Pt.. 21.00
Williams & Carlton, Hartford, Ct., Cylindrical... 50.00
Wood's Black Co., Portland, Aqua, Rolled Lip, 2 1/2 In....................................... 303.00
Wood's Black Ink, Portland, Aqua, OP, Rolled Lip, c.1850, 2 1/2 In. 253.00
Worden's, Threaded Metal Cap, Aqua, Round Shoulder, 2 5/8 In. 30.00
Yellow Amber, 3-Piece Mold, 1830, 1 3/8 In. 110.00
Yellow Amber, Pontil, Pour Spout, 9 1/2 In. 105.00

*Ink, Teakettle, Medium
Yellow Green, Original Neck
Ring, 1870-1890, 2 3/4 In.*

*Ink, Umbrella,
12-Sided, Light Green,
Rolled Lip, OP, 2 5/8 In.*

*Ink, Umbrella, Yellow
Olive Green, 3-Piece
Mold, Pontil, 1 1/2 In.*

Yellow Emerald Green, Spout, IP, 9 1/2 In. 115.00
Yellow Green, Bubbles, Pour Spout, Master 45.00
Zierlein, St. Louis, Aqua, OP, 1850, Square, 2 5/8 In. 286.00

———————————————————— **JAR** ————————————————————

Jar is the name for a container of a special shape. It has a wide mouth and almost no neck.
Today we see jars of cold cream, but in earlier days jars made of glass or ceramic were
used for storage of home-canned produce and for many commercial products.

JAR, Berry, Blue Green, Applied Top, 1870s, 11 1/2 In. 83.00
Black Amethyst, Blown, Pontil, Sheared & Tooled Rim, 5 3/8 In. 210.00
Blueberry, Amber, Cylindrical, 11 1/4 In. 308.00
Brytstele Bath, Razor, Green & Tan Pottery, Lid, England, 3 1/4 In. 253.00
Bust Of Queen Mary, Medium Green, 1870-1900, England, 4 1/8 In. 675.00
Cheese, Northampton Sanitary Dairy, 1/2 Pt. 15.00
Cigar, William Tegge & Co., 50 Cigars, Slug Plate, No Cover, Round, 5 In. 45.00
D & Co., Green Tint, Whittled, Wide Mouth, OP, 4 3/4 In. 15.00
Edgefield, S.C., Stoneware, Green & Brown, Slip Floral Sides, Handle, 1850, 14 In. 660.00
Edgefield, S.C., Stoneware, Green, 2 Lug Handles, Ovoid, 1850, 11 1/2 In. 550.00
McMechens Always The Best Old Virginia, Wheeling, Square, Glass Cover, 5 In. 75.00
Mercantile Air Tight Havana Cigars, St. Louis, Mo., Amber, Embossed Lid............... 65.00
O.L. & A.K. Ballard, Burlington, Vt., Blue, Salt Glaze, 2 Gal. 90.00
Phoenix Surgical Dressing Co., Milwaukee, Wis., Amber, Qt. 350.00
Quong Hop & Co., San Francisco, Embossed Chinese Characters, Wire & Bail, Pt. 39.00
Salt Glazed, Blue Floral, J.S. Taft & Co., Keene, N.H., 3 Gal. 350.00
Stoneware, Butter, Brown, Tan Glaze, 6 3/4 In. 44.00
Stoneware, Butter, Cream Glaze, Black Transfer, Original Lid, Wire Handle, 7 In. 88.00
Stoneware, Light Green, Kaolin Floral Around, Handle, 7 In. 1760.00
Storage, Blown, Dark Olive Green, Sheared Mouth, Pontil, 9 1/2 In. 132.00
Storage, Blown, Emerald Green, 4-Sided, Cylindrical Neck, Folded Rim, 1860, 9 In. .. 154.00
Storage, Blown, Olive Green, Sheared Lip, OP, 1780-1830, 11 In. 220.00
Storage, Blown, Tapered Gin Form, Flared Mouth, Yellow Olive, Pontil, 10 In........... 550.00
Storage, Blown, Yellow Green, Olive Tone, Flared Mouth, Pontil, 12 In. 357.00
Storage, Deep Aqua, Sheared Lip, Pontil, 1800s, 11 1/8 In... 110.00
Storage, Deep Olive Amber, Wide Mouth, Pontil, 8 1/8 In. 385.00
Storage, Deep Yellow Olive Amber, Tooled Lip, 11 3/4 In. 132.00
Storage, Deep Yellow Olive Amber, Wide Mouth, Pontil, Continental, 9 In. 198.00
Storage, Deep Yellow Olive Amber, Wide Mouth, Pontil, 13 3/8 In. 550.00
Storage, Green, Wide Mouth, New England, Gal.. 90.00
Storage, Honey Amber, Folded Out Lip, Cylindrical, Pontil, 9 1/2 In........................... 413.00
Storage, Incised Bird, New York, Tan Salt Glaze, 1825... 413.00
Storage, Medium Emerald Green, OP, 14 1/4 In. 88.00
Storage, Medium Olive Amber, Pontil, 10 1/8 In... 143.00
Storage, Medium Yellow Green, Tooled & Flared Lip, Pontil, 1800-1820, 6 In............ 357.00

Jar, Tobacco,
Lid, 7 In.

Jug, Wm. Radam's Microbe
Killer, #2 Pottery, Cork,
Gal., 11 In.

Jug, Old Governor Sour
Mash, A. Graf & Co.,
St. Louis, 1879, 7 1/2 In.

Storage, Medium Yellow Olive Amber, Wide Mouth, Pontil, Holland, 9 In. 165.00
Storage, Olive Amber, Pontil, 1870s, 11 In. 187.00
Storage, Petal Form Flutes On Shoulder, Yellow Olive, IP, 1/2 Gal. 2750.00
Storage, Stoddard Preserve, Octofoil Body, Red, Orange, Amber, 8 In. 300.00
Storage, T.F. Reppard, Greensboro, Pa., Cobalt Blue Worm Lines, Stenciled 145.00
Storage, Yellow Olive Green, Pontil, 1810-1840, 15 1/2 In. 193.00
Storage, Yellow Olive Green, Tooled Lip, 9 1/2 In. 110.00
Storage, Yellow Olive, Wide Mouth, Pontil, 8 3/4 In. 176.00
Tobacco, Globe Tobacco Co., Detroit, Mich., Yellow Topaz, Paneled, Cover & Handle   90.00
Tobacco, Lid, 7 In. ....*Illus*   35.00
Tobacco, Los Equalitos, Factory No. 63, 9th District Of Pa., Yellow, Screw Lid, 5 1/2 In.   165.00
Tobacco, U.S.T. Co., Sapphire Blue, Melon Ribbed, Metal Lid Handle, 5 3/4 In. 176.00
Tobacco, Wm. S. Kimball & Co., Rochester, NY, Yellow, Metal Screw Lid, 5 3/4 In. ... 143.00
Tobacco, Wm. S. Kimball & Co., Yellow Amber, 8-Sided, Ground Top, 6 In. 50.00
Weir, Brown Over Cream, Clamps, Qt. 15.00
Wide Mouth, Blown, Floral Design, Deep Yellow Olive, Pontil, 8 5/8 In. 1100.00
Yellow Olive, Blown, Cylindrical, Squat, 6 1/2 In. 984.00
Yellow Olive, Blown, Pontil, 1730-1750, Cylindrical, 6 1/2 In. 880.00
Yellow Olive, Blown, Pontil, 1775-1825, Cylindrical, 5 In. 275.00
JIM BEAM, see Beam

---------------------------------- JUG ----------------------------------

A jug is a deep container with a narrow mouth and a handle. It is usually made of pottery. Jugs were often used as containers for liquor. Messages, mottoes, and the name of the distillery or bar are often printed on the jug.

JUG, AB & D Sands Druggist, N.Y., Blue Design, Debossed, 2 Gal. 250.00
B.F. Baldwin, Marion, Ind., Miniature 75.00
Bellarmine, Tan, Brown Glazes, Germany, 8 3/4 In. 302.00
C. Rhodes Maker, Edgefield, S.C., Stoneware, Brown, Floral, 1850, 8 In. 6050.00
Cannitzer & Luca Liquor Dealer, Evan, Col., Gal. 500.00
Chas. D. Kaier Co., Mahanoy City, Pa., Stoneware, Cone Top, Gal. 32.00
Chinn's Cave House, Brooklyn Bridge, Ky., Brown, 1/2 Pt. 195.00
Cobalt Floral Design, Tan Salt Glaze, J. Campbell, Utica, N.Y., 1825-1829, 12 1/2 In. 330.00
Dark Green Glaze, JHL, Handle, 1880, 11 1/2 In. 550.00
Deodorizer, Pullman Company, Blue, Brown Top, Handle, 1/2 Gal. 120.00
E.B. Taylor, Richmond, Va., Stoneware, Blue Stenciled, Gal. 143.00
F.W. Baker, Nash., Tn., Crock, Gal. 115.00
Face, Pottery, Dark Brown Alkaline Glaze, China Teeth, N. Carolina, 1930s, 7 In. 1210.00
Face, T.A. Mullin's, Phoenix, Ala., 4 1/4 In. 7150.00
Golden Hills, Toledo, Ohio, Blue Stenciled, 1905-1914, 1/2 Pt. 80.00
Grotesque Devil, Green Glaze, Clay Ball Teeth, Lanier Meaders, 1988, 10 1/2 In. 687.00
Grotesque Devil, Green Matte Glaze, Rock Teeth, Lanier Meaders, 1970, 9 1/2 In. 1155.00
Grotesque Devil, Light & Dark Matte Green Glaze, Lanier Meaders, 1970, 9 1/2 In. 1870.00
H.F. Phillips & Stein, Richmond, Va., Stoneware, Blue Stenciled, 1 Gal. 611.00
I.C. Shore & Co., Rocky Mount, N.C., Stoneware, Cream, Wire Wooden Handle, Gal. .. 176.00
Kaolin Floral Design, Dark Green Brown Alkaline Glaze, c.1850, 8 In. 6050.00
Kaolin Floral Design, Light Dark Green Alkaline Glaze, c.1850, 8 In. 3575.00
Kaolin Slip Floral Design, Light Green Alkaline Glaze, c.1850, 7 In. 4950.00
Mi. Hessberg & Son, Bristol Tenn-Va., 2-Tone, Gal. 225.00
Old Governor Sour Mash, A. Graf & Co., St. Louis, 1879, 7 1/2 In. ....*Illus* 125.00
Poe & Co., N.C., Redware, Handle, 3/4 Gal. 160.00
Powers, Weightman, Rosengarten Co., Phila., Mercury Stencil, Tan White, 1/2 Pt. 35.00
Raxtum Ft. Edward, N.Y., Blue Floral, Salt Glaze, Gal. 200.00
Salt Glaze, Applied Hunting, Port Dundas Glasgow Pottery Co., 4 1/2 In. 85.00
Salt Glaze, Applied Relief Stags & Dogs Around, England, 8 In. 62.00
Salt Glaze, Hunting, George Slaying Dragon, England, 4 3/4 In. 50.00
Salt Glaze, Hunting, Mr. John, 1891 Inscription, England, 7 1/2 In. 62.00
Salt Glaze, Man & Woman Among Bullrushes, England, 6 In. 163.00
Salt Glaze, Orange Peel, Man Holding Pipe, Conical, England, 7 1/2 In. 70.00
Salt Glaze, Tan, Grapes & Vines, England, 7 3/4 In. 78.00
Souvenir, Pensacola, Fla., Brown & White Handle, Red Paint, Gold Trim, 1/2 Pt. 50.00
Strohacker & Ellis Dealers In Fine Liquors, 2-Color Beehive, McComb Pottery, 5 In. .. 135.00

Victoria, King Design, Flask Type, Brown, Cream, Handle, 9 In. 60.00
Wm. Radam's Microbe Killer, #2 Pottery, Cork, Gal., 11 In..................................*Illus* 65.00

--- LACEY ---

Haas Brothers of San Francisco, California, was established in 1851. They made W.A.
Lacey and Cyrus Noble bottles in the 1970s. The firm discontinued its ceramic business
about 1981 and destroyed all of the molds. Lacey bottles include the log animal series
(1978–1980) and the tavern series (1975). Other Lacey bottles may be listed in the Cyrus
Noble category.

LACEY, Bank Exchange, Exterior, 1976 .... 22.00
  Bank Exchange, Interior, 1976.. 22.00
  Continental Navy, 1976... 11.00
  Faro Bank, 1975 .... 20.00
  Harold's Club, 1970, Miniature 21.00
  Rabbit, Log, 1978 .... 29.00
  Rabbit, Log, 1980 .... 29.00
  Raccoon, Log, 1978... 45.00
  Raccoon, Log, 1980... 45.00
  Squirrel, Log, 1979... 29.00
  Tennis Player, 1976, Pair 33.00
  Tun Tavern, No. 1, 1975.. 11.00
  Tun Tavern, No. 2, U.S. Marines, 1975 .... 17.00
  Willits Frontier, 1976 .... 116.00

--- LAST CHANCE ---

Last Chance Whiskey was presented in ceramic figural bottles in 1971 and 1972. One
series of 8-ounce bottles called Professionals pictured a doctor, dentist, banker, entertainer,
politician, and salesman. Another series was a group of six bottles that joined together to
form a long bar scene. Two versions of this bar scene were made, one with and one without a frame.

LAST CHANCE, Banker, 1972 .... 12.00
  Bar Scene, 1971, Miniature.. 76.00
  Bar Scene, With Frame 150.00
  Professionals, 1971, Miniature 12.00
  Wyoming Stockgrowers 48.00

--- LEWIS & CLARK ---

Lewis & Clark bottles were created by Alpha Industries of Helena, Montana. The first bottles, full-length representations of historical figures, were made from 1971 to 1976. The
pioneer series of 1977–1978 was released in two-bottle sets. Each bottle was 13 inches
high and two placed together created a scene. For example, one was an Indian (bottle)
offering to sell some furs to a white man (bottle). A set of six troll bottles was made in
1978–1979.

LEWIS & CLARK, Barnyard Clown, 1981 .... 38.00
  Bighorn, 5 Piece.. 97.00
  Blinking Owl, 1981 .... 40.00
  Charbonneau, 1973.. 52.00
  Cook, 1977 .... 48.00
  Cousin, 1979 .... 20.00
  Cowboy, 1977... 42.00
  Curlee Indian Scout, 1974.. 42.00
  Daughter Troll, 1978 .... 24.00
  Family, 1978, Pair 115.00
  General Custer, 1974 .... 30.00
  Grandfather, 1978 .... 19.00
  Grandmother, 1979 .... 18.00
  Hobo, 1981 .... 38.00
  Indian, 1978.. 68.00
  John Lennon 46.00
  Lewis & Clark, Miniature, 5 Piece 100.00

Major Reno, 1976	27.00
Meriwether Lewis, 1971	48.00
Montana, 1976	50.00
Mr. & Mrs., 1978	18.00
Mr. & Mrs., 1979	18.00
Plaque Peace Pipe, 1978	44.00
Prowling Panther, 1982	44.00
Sacajawea, 1972	76.00
Sheepherder	44.00
Sitting Bull, 1976	86.00
States, 1981, Miniature	8.00
States, 1984, Miniature	8.00
Trader, 1978	64.00
Trooper, 1976	33.00
William Clark, 1971	49.00
York, 1972	44.00

————————————————— **LIONSTONE** —————————————————

Lionstone Distilleries Inc. of Lawrenceburg, Kentucky, started making porcelain figural bottles to hold their whiskey for national sale in 1969. The first bottles were Western figures, each with a black label that told the historical facts about the figure. About 15, 000 bottles were made for each of the first six subjects, the cowboy, proud Indian, casual Indian, sheriff, gentleman gambler, and cavalry scout. About half of the bottles were never filled with liquor because they leaked. These *leakers* were used by bars as display items on shelves and were clearly labeled with decals stating that they were for display only. More bottles were made for the series, about 4,000 of each. The set had 16 bottles. Lionstone then made a series of race cars (1970–1984), more Western figures (1970–1976), a Western bar scene (1971), birds (1970–1977), circus figures (1973), dogs (1975–1977), European workers (1974), oriental workers (1974), Bicentennial series (1976), clowns (1978–1979), sports series (1974–1983), and others. They also made many miniature bottles. The whiskey was distilled in Bardstown, Kentucky, but the bottles were made in Chicago. Over 800 styles were made. No decanters were made in 1995. Lionstone was sold to Barton Brands in December 1979. It was sold back to Mark Slepak, the original owner, in December 1983. Collectors can contact the company at 1955 Raymond Drive, Suite 102, Northbrook, IL 60062.

LIONSTONE, AMVET Riverboat, 1983	12.00
Annie Christmas, 1969	20.00
Annie Oakley, 1969 ....*Illus*	18.00
Backpacker, 1980	28.00
Bar Scene, 1970, 4 Piece	460.00
Bar Scene & Nude, With Frame, 1970	500.00
Barber, 1976	40.00

Lionstone, Annie Oakley, 1969

Lionstone, Belly Robber, 1969

Bartender, 1969	27.00
Baseball Players, 1974	80.00
Basketball Players, 1974	48.00
Bass, No.1, 1983	50.00
Belly Robber, 1969 ....*Illus*	22.00
Betsy Ross, 1975	18.00
Bird, Blue Jay, 1971	20.00
Bird, Canada Goose, 1980	50.00
Bird, Cardinal, 1973	27.00
Bird, Eastern Bluebird, 1972	29.00
Bird, Western Bluebird, 1972	27.00
Blacksmith, 1973	23.00
Brooks Robinson, 1983	82.00
Buccaneer, 1973	24.00
Buffalo Hunter, 1973	30.00
Calamity Jane, 1973	22.00
Cherry Valley, Gold, 1971	23.00
Dog, Boxers, 1974	63.00
Duck, Canvasback, 1981	32.00

-------------------------------- **LUXARDO** --------------------------------

In 1821 Girolamo Luxardo began making a liqueur from the marasca cherry. The company literature calls this famous drink *the original maraschino*. The business has remained in the family through five generations. Decorative Luxardo bottles were first used in the 1930s at Torreglia near Padua, Italy. Most of the Luxardo bottles found today date after 1943. The date listed here is the first year each bottle was made. The bottles are still being made and some are sold at stores in the United States and Canada. Bottles are of glass or ceramic and come in many sizes, including miniatures. Many of the bottles were pictured in the now-out-of-print book *Luxardo Bottles* by Constance Avery and Al Cembura (1968).

LUXARDO, African Head	22.00
Apothecary Jar, 1960	22.00
Autumn Wine Pitcher, 1958	36.00
Bacchus, 1969	27.00
Baroque Gold, Ruby, 1957	24.00
Bizantina, 1959	34.00
Bulldog, Miniature	24.00
Candlestick, Alabaster, 1961	34.00
Ceramic Barrel, 1968	28.00
Clock, 1960	24.00
Clown, Miniature	19.00
Coffeepot, 1962	14.00
Duck, Green, 1960	48.00
English Bull, Miniature	7.00
Faenza, 1972	9.00
Fakir, 1960	32.00
Frog, Miniature	8.00
Fruit, 1968	35.00
Gambia, 1961	12.00
Gondola, 1959	26.00
Gondola, 1970	26.00
Maraboo, 1957	37.00
Mayan, 1960	22.00
Modern, 1960	50.00
Penguin, 1968	29.00
Pheasant, Black, 1968	177.00
Pierrot, 1959	12.00
Tower Of Flowers, 1968	24.00
Venus, 1959	25.00
Venus, 1969	20.00
Wobble Bottle, 1957	12.00
Zodiac, 1970	32.00

—————————————— MCCORMICK ——————————————

It is claimed that the first white men to find the limestone spring near Weston, Missouri, were Lewis and Clark on their famous expedition. Over 20,000 gallons of fresh water gush from the spring each day. An Indian trading post was started near the spring by a man named McPhearson about 1830. His friend Joseph Moore decided to establish a town and paid a barrel of whiskey for the land. Bela Hughes and his cousin Ben Holladay came to the new town in 1837. They soon had a dry goods store, a drugstore, a tavern, and a hotel. They even built a Pony Express station. In 1856, Ben Holladay and his brother David started a distillery to make bourbon using the spring water. David's daughter later married a man named Barton and the distillery was renamed Barton and Holladay. It was sold in 1895 to George Shawhan but closed from 1920 to 1936. The property became a cattle and tobacco farm.

In 1936, after the repeal of Prohibition, Isadore Singer and his two brothers purchased the plant and began making Old Weston and Old Holladay bourbon. About 1939 they bought the name *McCormick* from a nearby distillery founded years before by E.R. McCormick. Legend says that Mrs. McCormick would not allow her husband to reopen the distillery because she had "gotten religion." The Singer brothers' new distillery used part of the grain for the mash, and their cattle feed lot used the leftover parts.

During World War II, alcohol was needed by the government and Cloud L. Cray bought the distillery to make industrial alcohol at a company he called Midwest Solvents. After the war, Bud and Dick Cray, sons of Cloud Cray, started making bourbon at the old plant by old-fashioned methods, producing about 25 barrels a day. The bourbon was sold in Missouri, Kansas, Iowa, and Oklahoma. The old plant, listed in the National Register of Historic Sites, is open for tours. In about 1980 the company, under the direction of the new president, Marty Adams, started marketing on a national instead of a local scale, and it is now selling in all of the states. They have a full line, including wine, beer, and many alcoholic beverages such as rum, tequila, vodka, dry gin, blended whiskey, and brandy that are now sold under the McCormick name.

McCormick Distilling Company, now a subsidiary of Midwest Grain Products, has created many types of figural bottles for their bourbon, ranging from a bust of Elvis Presley (made in 1979) to a musical apple (1982). The company discontinued making decanters in 1987.

MCCORMICK, 50th Anniversary, 1986	397.00
Alabama	30.00
Arizona Wildcat	40.00
Baylor Bear, 1972	29.00
Belle Jug	34.00
Betsy Ross, 1975	25.00
Betsy Ross, 1976, Miniature	30.00
Bing Crosby, Golf	54.00
Blue Bird, 1971	22.00
California Bears	24.00
Capt. John Smith, 1977	17.00
Chair, Queen Anne, 1979	48.00
Christmas House, 1984	46.00
Christmas Tree	145.00
Cowboy Hall Of Fame, 1983	90.00
Deer Trophy Plaque, 1983	92.00
Eleanor Roosevelt, 1977	23.00
Elvis With Teddy Bear	500.00
Fire Extinguisher, 1983	40.00
FOE, 1984	76.00
FOE, 1985 *Illus*	76.00
FOE, 1986	27.00
Frontiersman Davey Crockett, 1975	26.00
Georgia Tech	32.00
Graceland Gate	127.00
Hank Williams Jr., Bocephus, 1980 *Illus*	80.00
Hank Williams Sr., 1980	85.00
Henry Ford, 1977 *Illus*	30.00
Hound Dog	495.00

McCormick, FOE,
1985

McCormick, Hank Williams Jr.,
Bocephus, 1980

McCormick, Henry Ford,
1977

Ice Box, 1983	32.00
Iowa Hawkeye, 1974	76.00
Iowa Northern Panther, 1974	44.00
Jimmy Durante	39.00
Johnny Rogers, No. 1, 1972	188.00
Joplin Miner, 1972	23.00
Jug, Bourbon, 1967	14.00
Jug, Gin, 1967	10.00
Jug, Vodka, 1967	10.00
Julia Bullette, 1974	97.00
Kansas City Chiefs, 1969	30.00
Kansas City Club, 1982	27.00
Kansas City Royals, 1971	14.00
King Arthur, 1979	40.00
Kit Carson, 1975	25.00
Meriwether Lewis, 1978	22.00
Merlin, 1979	34.00
Michigan Wolverine, 1974	24.00
Minnesota Gopher, 1974	35.00
Mississippi Rebel, 1974	30.00
Missouri, China, 1970	12.00
Missouri, Glass, 1971	7.00
Muhammad Ali, 1980	74.00
Nebraska Football Player, 1972	37.00
New Mexico Lobo, 1973	40.00
Old Holiday, 1956	16.00
On Rising Sun, 1984	500.00
Oregon Duck, 1974	43.00
Oregon St. Beaver, 1974	38.00
Packard, Hood Ornament, 1985	30.00
Packard, Model 1937, Black, 1980	46.00
Packard, Model 1937, Cream, 1980	46.00
Packard, Model 1937, Gold	79.00
Packard, Model 1937, Silver	79.00
Paul Bunyan, 1979	32.00
Pendleton Roundup	54.00
Pony Express, 1978	67.00
Pony Express, 1980	67.00
Quail Gamal, 1982	50.00
Quail Gamal, 1984	48.00
Queen Guinevere, 1979	27.00

Robert E. Lee, 1976	42.00
Robert Peary, 1977	26.00
Rose Garden, 1980, Miniature	22.00
Samuel Houston, 1977	27.00
Sargeant, 1983	107.00
Seal With Ball	54.00
Sir Lancelot, 1979	25.00
Skibob, 1971	13.00
Skier Club Of Kansas City	77.00
Spirit Of 76, 1976	52.00
TCU Horned Frogs, 1972	28.00
Telephone Operator, 1982	60.00
Texas 150th Anniversary	22.00
Texas Long Horns, 1972	30.00
Texas Tech Raider, 1972	24.00
Thelma Lu	30.00
Tom Sawyer, 1980	27.00
Tom T. Hall, 1980	66.00
Train, Locomotive, 1969	19.00
Train, Mail Car, 1969	38.00
U.S. Marshall, 1979	36.00
Victorian, 1984	20.00
Washing Clothes, 1980	37.00
Washington, 1975	24.00
Washington, 1976	24.00
Weston, 1856, Miniature	150.00
Willie Weary, 1981	92.00
Woman Feeding Chickens, 8 Piece	28.00
Wood Duck, 1980	30.00
Wood Duck, 1984	300.00
World's Greatest Fan	18.00

MEDICINE

If you have friends with scrofula or cattarh, they probably can find a medicine from the nineteenth century. The extravagant claims for cures and the strange names for diseases add to the fun of collecting early medicine bottles. Bottles held all of the many types of medications used in past centuries. Most of those collected today date from the 1850–1930 period. Some of the names, like Kickapoo Indian Oil, Lydia Pinkham's Female Compound, or Wahoo Bitters, have become part of the slang of America. Bitters, cures, sarsaparilla, and tonics are listed under their own headings in this book. Apothecary and other drugstore bottles are listed here. Collectors prefer early bottles with raised lettering. Labeled bottles in original boxes are also sought. For more information, look for *The Bottle Book, A Comprehensive Guide to Historic, Embossed Medicine Bottles* by Richard E. Fike.

MEDICINE, A. McEckron's R.B. Liniment, N.Y., Aqua, Pontil, 6 In.	83.00
A.A. Cooley, Hartford, Con., Olive, 4 1/2 In.	187.00
A.E. Roedel Druggist, Cheyenne, Wyo., 5 5/8 In.	35.00
A.H. Lewis Medicine Co., St. Louis, Mo., 5 7/8 In.	5.00
A.M. Cole, Virginia City, Aqua, 8 1/2 In.	1430.00
Al. S. Lamb Druggist, Aspen, Colo., Clear, Square Collared Lip	385.00
Allerho For Rheumatism & Neuritis, Rochester, ABM, Cork, 7 3/4 x 3 In.	12.00
American Compound, Philadelphia, Aqua, OP, 5 7/8 In.	93.50
American Drug Co., Los Angeles, Calif., 3 1/2 In.	6.00
American Panacea, Richardson & Co., Aqua, OP, 6 3/8 In.	1210.00
American Rob, Dr.'s J & M, New York, Aqua, Pontil, 7 5/8 In.	253.00
Anderson's Dermador, Ice Blue, Cylinder, 4 1/4 In.	120.00
Anti Scorbutic Drops, Prepared By Dr. Roberts, Bridgeport, Flint, OP, Early 1800s	130.00
Apothecary, A.M. Cole, Virginia City, Nevada, Amethyst Tint, 6 1/2 In.	27.50
Apothecary, A.M. Cole, Virginia City, Nevada, Medium Amber, 5 3/4 In.	357.50
Apothecary, Bell Shape, Hot Drops Label Under Glass.	20.00
Apothecary, Blown, Cobalt Blue, Syr Scillae, Knobbed Stopper, 7 In.	187.00
Apothecary, Chloroform, Poison, Cobalt Blue, Pontil, England, 6 In.	77.00

Medicine, Apothecary,
Classical Bust,
Milk Glass, Pontil,
4 5/8 In.

Medicine, Apothecary, Ex.
Cannab, Pottery, Enam-
eled, Lavender Wrap,
1870, 3 3/4 In.

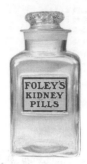

Medicine, Apothecary,
Foley's Kidney Pills, Label
Under Glass, Glass Stopper,
11 In.

Medicine, Apothecary, Horlick's
Malted Milk, Glass Lid,
1880-1910, 6 3/4 In.

Medicine, Apothecary, Tabellae
Ipecacuan, Sapphire Blue, Pontil,
1870-1890, 10 1/4 In.

Apothecary, Classical Bust, Milk Glass, Pontil, 4 5/8 In. ....*Illus*	55.00
Apothecary, Clear, Cobalt Blue Applied Bands, Blown, Lid, 1860s, 9 3/4 In.	330.00
Apothecary, Cobalt Blue, Label, 7 3/4 In.	88.00
Apothecary, Cobalt Blue, OP, Stopper, 8 1/2 In.	78.00
Apothecary, Cobalt Blue, Paper Label, Stopper, England, 6 3/4 In.	121.00
Apothecary, Cobalt Blue, Stopper, 4 1/8 In.	176.00
Apothecary, Cobalt, OP, BIM, 7 1/2 In.	45.00
Apothecary, Coles Drug Store, Timmonsville, S.C., 6 1/4 In.	15.00
Apothecary, Cornflower Blue, 6 3/8 In.	49.50
Apothecary, Ex. Cannab, Pottery, Enameled, Lavender Wrap, 1870, 3 3/4 In. ....*Illus*	578.00
Apothecary, Fl. Ex. Colch. S. Label, Blue, Gold, Red, Black, Stopper, Pontil, 8 In.	88.00
Apothecary, Foley's Kidney Pills, Label Under Glass, Glass Stopper, 11 In. ....*Illus*	303.00
Apothecary, Forest Green, Label, Stopper, 4 1/4 In.	71.50
Apothecary, Globe Shape, Golden Amber, Clear Lid & Pedestal, ABM, 12 3/4 In........	275.00
Apothecary, Globe, Golden Amber, Pedestal, Clear Lid, 1890s, 12 1/2 In., 3 Piece	303.00
Apothecary, Green, Stars, Marked I, 40 Oz.	20.00
Apothecary, Hanover Drug Co., Wilmington, N.C., 5 1/2 In.	12.00
Apothecary, Hick's Capudine Liquid For Headaches, Gripp, Amber, Man's Head, Pt. .	299.00
Apothecary, Horlick's Malted Milk, Glass Lid, 1880-1910, 6 3/4 In. ....*Illus*	187.00
Apothecary, Lime Green, Whittled, Bubbles, 4 1/2 In.	35.00

Apothecary, Milk Glass, Applied Pedestal, Stopper, 1870-1880, 12 3/4 In. 550.00
Apothecary, Off & Vaughn Drug Co., Los Angeles, 6 In. 15.00
Apothecary, Olive Amber, AQ Destill., Gold & Black Label, England, 13 In. 330.00
Apothecary, Olive Amber, Part Enameled Label, 1840-1860, 13 In. 357.00
Apothecary, Opalescent Powder Blue, Label, Stopper, 4 1/4 In. 187.00
Apothecary, P. Gentian, Cobalt Blue, Label Under Glass, Stopper, OP, Qt. 159.00
Apothecary, P. Ipecac C, Cobalt Blue, Pontil, Stopper, England, 8 1/2 In. 264.00
Apothecary, Pottery, Blue Wrap, Ex. Cannab Ind., Lid, 1870-1890, 5 1/4 In. 1265.00
Apothecary, Ruby Red, BIMAL, 4 x 8 1/4 In. 245.00
Apothecary, Sapphire Blue, Label Under Glass, 8 1/2 In. 88.00
Apothecary, Sapphire Blue, White, Label, Stopper, 6 3/4 In. 66.00
Apothecary, Sapphire Blue, Wide Mouth, Mushroom Shaped Stopper, Qt. 55.00
Apothecary, Syr Auranl, Purple, Blown Stopper, England, 7 5/8 In. 154.00
Apothecary, Syr Rhoead, Cobalt Blue, Pontil, Blown Stopper, 7 3/4 In. 143.00
Apothecary, Syr Scillae, Cobalt Blue, Pontil, Blown Stopper, 6 7/8 In. 121.00
Apothecary, Tabellae Ipecacuan, Sapphire Blue, Pontil, 1870-1890, 10 1/4 In. ......*Illus* 264.00
Apothecary, Vin Opii, Pontil, Glass Stopper, England, 5 In. 77.00
Apothecary, W.R. Warner & Co., Pat Sept 18 1875, Tinct. Ipecac C, Stopper, 10 In. 100.00
Apothecary, W.R. Warner & Co., Pat.Sept. 18, 1875, Pedestal, Stopper, 11 In. 100.00
Apothecary, W.T. Co., Cobalt Blue, Label Under Glass, TR Mirra, Stopper, 9 1/8 In. .. 110.00
Apothecary, White Porcelain, Label, Stopper, 4 1/2 In. 77.00
Apothecary, White Pottery, Cobalt Blue, Label Under Glass, Stopper, 2 3/8 In. 165.00
Apothecary, White, Brown, Label, Stopper, 2 3/8 In. 170.50
Apothecary, Wm. H. Keith & Co., San Francisco, Aqua, Applied Mouth, 6 1/4 In. 45.00
Apothecary, Wm. R. Perston's Catholicon, Portsmouth, N.H., Aqua, OP 200.00
Apothecary, Yellow Amber, Pontil, Rolled Lip, c.1860, 9 In. 143.00
Apothecary, Yellow Green Gold, Label Under Glass, Stopper, 6 3/4 In. 82.50
Apothecary, Yellow Green, 1880-1910, 12 In. 66.00
Apothecary, Yellow Green, Potass. Bichrom, Label Under Glass, Stopper, 1880, 7 3/4 In. . 110.00
Ayer's Hair Vigor, Cobalt Blue, Stopper, Tooled Lip, 6 3/8 In. 121.00
Ayers Cherry Pectoral, Lowel, Mass., Aqua, 6 1/8 In. ....12.00 to 18.00
Ayers Cherry Pectoral, Lowel, Mass., Aqua, 7 3/16in. 14.00
B & S Homeopathic Cough & Croup Syrup, BIMAL, 3 5/16 In. 6.00
B.O. & G.C. Wilson Botanic Druggists, Boston, Mass., 6 1/2 x 2 1/2 In. 72.00
Bach's American Compound, Auburn, N.Y., Aqua, 7 3/4 In. ....88.00 to 108.00
Baker's Bamboo Brier Compound, Binghampton, Green Aqua 30.00
Baker's Vegetable Blood & Liver Cure, Greenville, Tenn., Amber, 9 1/2 In. 160.00
Banpland's Fever & Ague Remedy, Aqua, Rectangular, 5 1/4 In. ....44.00 to 88.00
Barry's Tricopherous For The Skin & Hair, New York City, Aqua, 6 In. 32.00
Battery Jar, F.G. Otto & Sons, N.Y., Electro-Therapy, 5 In. ....*Illus* 35.00
Berlin Series, Embossed Bull's Eyes, Aqua, 5 1/4 In. 18.00
Bicknell Dysentery Syrup, E. Suttons, Providence, R.I., Aqua, Rectangular, 6 3/8 In... 22.00
Billings Clapp & Co. Chemists, Boston, Aqua, Rectangular, 10 3/16 In. 10.00
Bogle's Hyperion Fluid For The Hair, Aqua, 5 1/2 In. 75.00
Bohamansson Druggist, Arcata, Cal., Green, Tooled Mouth, 4 1/2 In. 198.00
Bohmansson Co., Eureka, Cal., Tooled Lip, 8 1/8 In. 33.00
Bohmansson Druggist, Arcata, Cal., Green, Tooled Top, 4 1/2 In. 198.00
Boland's Bitter Wine Of Iron Pectoral 20.00
Botanic Blood Balm For All Blood Tumors, B.B.B., Amber, Contents, 1915, 8 1/2 In. . 45.00
Braddock's Pulmonary Cough Mixture, Hartford, Ct., Rectangular, 5 3/8 x 2 1/8 In. .. 145.00
Brandt's Purifying Extract, M.T. Wallace, Brooklyn, N.Y., Pontil, 10 In. 250.00
Brant's Indian Balsam, 8-Sided, Aqua, OP, 7 3/8 In. ....272.00 to 297.00
Brant's Purifying Extract, Brooklyn, N.Y., Aqua, Double Collar, 9 3/4 In. 88.00
Brant's Purifying Extract, M.T. Wallace & Co., Brooklyn, N.Y., Aqua, 10 In. ..88.00 to 265.00
Brioschi Effervescent Preparation, Cobalt Blue, Round, Label, 9 In. 45.00
Bromated Pepsin, Humphrey's Medical Co., New York, Cobalt Blue, 4 1/4 In. 35.00
Bromo Caffeine, Cobalt Blue, 3 1/8 In. 20.00
Bromo-Seltzer, Cobalt Blue, Measuring Cap, 5 In. 8.00
Bromo-Seltzer, Emerson Drug Co., Baltimore, Md., Cobalt Blue, Tin Lid, 7 3/4 In. 20.00
Brother Benjamin, Great Tonic Herbalo, Aqua, 8 5/8 In. 38.50
Brown & Ward, Directions, Round, OP, 2 In. 30.00
Browns Blood Treatment, Philadelphia, Emerald Green, 6 1/8 In. 200.00
Brunet's Universal Remedy, Philada., Pa., Aqua, OP, 1845-1860, 8 In. 264.00

Medicine, Battery Jar, F.G. Otto & Sons, N.Y., Electro-Therapy, 5 In.

Medicine, Converse Treatment Institute, Mt. Vernon, Oh., Stopper, 9 1/2 In.

Medicine, Hopkin's Chalbeath, Baltimore, Emerald Green, Pontil, 7 1/4 In.

Brush's Elixir Prophylactic, For Prevention Of Sea Sickness, Amber, 6 3/4 In............... 75.00
Budd's Wound Nerve & Bone Liniment, Aqua, 5 3/8 In. 522.50
Burks Med. Co., Maple Balsam, New York & Chicago, Label, Contents, 6 1/4 In. 17.00
Burnett's Cocaine, 7 In..20.00 to 35.00
Burnett's Cocaine, Boston, Aqua, 6 3/4 In. 45.00
Burr's Liniment, Aqua, Pontil, Applied Mouth, 6 In... 100.00
Burrow's Infants Friend, Albany, N.Y., 8-Sided, Aqua, Pontil, 4 1/8 In...................... 330.00
C. Heimstreet & Co., Troy, N.Y., Cobalt Blue, 8-Sided, Pontil, 7 In................ 176.00 to 264.00
C. Sines Tar Wild Cherry & Hoarhound, Philadelphia, Pa., Aqua, OP, 5 In............... 59.00
C.A.P. Mason-Alpine Hair Balm, Providence, R.I., Olive, OP, 6 7/8 In. 6050.00
California Fig Syrup, Wheeling, West, V.A., 6 7/8 In... 10.00
Canchalacocue, Sargent & Co., N.Y., Aqua, Pontil, 7 3/4 In. 83.00
Carter's Spanish Mixture, Olive Green, IP, 8 In.. 275.00
Carter's Spanish Mixture, Yellow Olive Green, OP, 8 In.. 533.50
Celebrated H.H.H. Horse Medicine, D.D.T., 1868, Aqua, 7 3/4 In. 88.00
Celery Compound, Stalk Of Celery, Yellow Amber, 10 In. ....55.00 to 88.00
Central Pharmacy, Preiss & Pironi, Los Angeles, Amber, 1880s Style, 4 1/4 In........... 65.00
Chamberlain's Cough Remedy, Aqua, Label, Contents, Wrapper, 5 3/4 In. 18.00
Chapman's Genuine, Boston, Olive Yellow, Pontil, 8 1/8 In.. 2035.00
Chas. Clarke, Glacier Pharmacy, Hood River, Ore., 5 In. 14.00
Chesbrough Mfg. Co., Vaseline, Amber, 2 3/4 In... 20.00
Chill Killer, J.D. Burke, Montgomery, Ala., Yellow Amber, 5 3/4 In............................. 95.00
Christies Ague Balsam, New York, Deep Aqua, OP, 7 1/4 In..............................65.00 to 93.00
Circassian Lymph, T & S, Aqua, Violin Shape, Pontil, 6 5/8 In. 176.00
Citrate Of Magnesia, H.P. Wakelee Druggist, Cobalt Blue, 7 1/4 In. 121.00
City Drug Store, Angels Camp, Cal., Clear, Amethyst Tint, 5 5/8 In................................ 77.00
Clark Stanley's Snake Oil Liniment, Best Horse Liniment, BIM, Label, 6 1/2 In. 25.00
CMF, Chas. M. Fassitt, Druggist, Ruby Hill, Nev., Monogram, 4 1/4 In. 853.00
Colgate's Smelling Salts, Emerald Green, Label, Stopper, 3 In..................................... 95.00
Compound, Chlorine Toothwash, Rushton & Aspinwall, Amber, 1840, 5 7/8 In. 7425.00
Comstock & Brother, Turkish, Aqua, Applied Double Collar, OP, 7 In......................... 385.00
Congreves Celebrated Balsomic Elixir For Coughs & Asthma, 4 7/8 In.................... 15.00
Connell's Brahminical Moon Plant East Indian Remedies, Stars, Amber, 8 1/4 In. .. 495.00
Converse Treatment Institute, Mt. Vernon, Oh., Stopper, 9 1/2 In. ....*Illus* 25.00
Corbin's German Drops, Syracuse, N.Y., Aqua, Pontil, 6 1/4 In................................... 187.00
Crane & Brigham, San Francisco, Embossed Bay Leaf, Amber, 10 In. 825.00
Croff's Liniment, Queensbury, N.Y., Aqua 138.00
Cumberland River American Oil, Kentucky, Aqua, Pontil, 6 3/4 In............................ 198.00
Curatine For The Blood, Liver & Kidneys, Baltimore, Md., Aqua, 9 1/4 In................. 137.50
Curo Medicine Co., Helena, Mont., Aqua, Dug 20.00
Curtis & Perkins Cramp & Pain Killer, Bangor, Me., Aqua, Pontil, 4 1/2 In. 65.00

Cutler Bros. & Co. Vegetable Pulmonary Balsam, Boston, Aqua 30.00
Damascus Stoddart Bros., San Francisco, Arabian Knight, Camel, Amber, 4 1/2 In. 104.50
Davis & Lawrence Co., LIM Chemists, Montreal, Honey Amber, Opalescent, 8 In. 40.00
Davis Vegetable Pain Killer, Aqua, Graphite Pontil, 6 In. .... 68.00 to 75.00
Delmonico's Syrup, Pectoral, N.Y., 7 x 2 3/8 In. 150.00
Dickey Pioneer, Mortar & Pestle, Cobalt Bluc, 5 5/8 In. .... 71.00 to 110.00
Dickey Pioneer, Mortar & Pestle, Sapphire Blue, 5 7/8 In. .... 50.00 to 70.00
Ditchett's Remedy For The Piles, N.Y., Olive Green, OP, 8 In. 4400.00
Doct. Harrison's Chalybeate Tonic, Teal, 9 In. 100.00
Doct. Robt. B. Folger's Olosaonian, New York, Aqua, OP, 7 3/4 In. .... 55.00 to 125.00
Doctor Geo. W. Blocksom, Druggist, Zanesville, Aqua, IP, 12-Sided, 6 3/4 In. 385.00
Doherty Apothecary, Atlantic City, N.J., Cobalt Blue, 4 7/8 In. 75.00
Dr. A. Roger's Liverwort Tar & Canchalagua, New York, Aqua, 8 In. 85.00
Dr. A.L. Adam's Liver Balsam, Blue Aqua, IP, 7 1/8 In. 110.00
Dr. Alain, Deep Cobalt Blue, Pontil, Cylindrical, 3 In. 577.50
Dr. Atwood's Rheumatic Liniment, Chas' Town, Mass., Aqua, Pontil, 6 In. 105.00
Dr. B. Sherman, Medium Amber, 9 5/8 In. 77.00
Dr. Baker's Compound, New York, Aqua, Pontil, c.1845, 7 3/4 In. 495.00
Dr. Baker's Pain Panacea, Deep Blue Aqua, OP .... 45.00 to 58.00
Dr. Birmingham's Antibilious Blood Purifier, Yellow Green, 8 1/2 In. 770.00
Dr. Blair's Ru-Mex-Ol For Blood, Freeport, Ill., Trial Mark, Rawleigh's Copycat 18.00
Dr. Blendigo's Celery Tonic Peptonized, Chicago, Ill., Amber, 9 1/2 In. 225.50
Dr. Browder's Compound Syrup Of Indian Turnip, Aqua, Pontil, 7 In. 165.00
Dr. Brunet's Pulmonary Syrup, Tombstone Shape, Whittled, Clear, 1850s, 7 In. 119.00
Dr. Brunet's Worm Syrup, Aqua, OP, 1840-1855, 6 3/4 In. 275.00
Dr. C.F. Basford's Home Guard, Blue Aqua, Pontil, 4 1/2 In. 275.00
Dr. C.J. Weatherby Is Labratory, Kansas City, Mo., Amber, 6 In. 125.00
Dr. C.P. French Druggist, Denver, Col., Aqua, 6 In. 85.00
Dr. Clarke's Compound Syrup Of Wild Cherry & Tar, 8-Sided, Pontil 50.00
Dr. Cooper's Ethereal Oil For Deafness, Aqua, OP, 2 5/8 In. 440.00
Dr. Crook's Wine Of Tar, Light Apple Green, Label, Whittled, 8 3/4 In. 150.00
Dr. D. Fahrney & Son, Cleansing The Blood, Apricot Amber, 9 1/4 In. 412.50
Dr. D. Jayne's Carminative Balsam, Philadelphia, Cylinder, Aqua, 4 3/4 In. ...... 22.00 to 38.00
Dr. D. Jayne's Expectorant, Phila., Aqua, OP 38.50
Dr. D. Jayne's Indian Expectorant, Philadelphia, Aqua, Flared Lip, 6 In. .... 100.00 to 240.00
Dr. D.C. Kellinger's Remedies, New York, Aqua, OP, 8 3/4 In. 220.00
Dr. D.C. Kellinger's Remedies, New York, Cylindrical, 7 In. 48.00
Dr. Daniels Ostercocus, Nerve & Muscle Liniment, 5 3/4 In. 15.00
Dr. Daniels Wonder Worker Liniment, Cure For Men Or Beast, Mass., 6 3/8 In. 42.00
Dr. Davis's Depurative, Phila., Green, c.1850, 9 1/2 In. 2695.00
Dr. Drakes German Coup Remedy, Aqua, 6 3/8 In. 25.00
Dr. Duncan's Expectorant Remedy, Light Green Aqua, OP, 8 1/8 In. 210.00
Dr. G. Gould's Pin Worm Syrup, Aqua, OP, 5 In. 17.00
Dr. G.A. Zimmerman's East Indian Castor Oil, Johnstown, Pa., Blue, 5 1/2 In. 45.00
Dr. H.F. Perry's Dead Shot Vermifuge, Aqua, OP, 4 In. 84.00
Dr. Hayden's Viburnum Compound, Aqua, BIM, Cylinder, 7 1/4 In. 7.00
Dr. Henley's Celery, Beef & Iron, Amber, 11 3/4 In. .... 71.50 to 121.00
Dr. Henley's Dandelion Tonic, Amber, 9 In. 55.00
Dr. Hitzfeld, Denver, Colo., For External Use Only, Cobalt Blue, 3 1/2 In. 180.00
Dr. Hooker's Cough & Croup Syrup, Aqua, Pontil, 5 5/8 In. 125.00
Dr. Hough's Anti Scrofula Syrup, Aqua, OP, 9 5/8 In. 176.00
Dr. Humphrey's Medicated Gin, Philadelphia, Penna., Aqua, Fancy, ABM, Qt. 39.00
Dr. Ira Warren's Inhaling Balm, Aqua, OP, 7 1/2 In. 126.00
Dr. J. Gesteria, Regulator Gesteria Formula, Amber, 5 In. 18.00
Dr. J. Hedges, Fever & Ague, Annihilator, New York, Aqua, OP, 7 1/4 In. 264.00
Dr. J. McLintock's Family Medicines, Amethyst Tint, OP, 7 1/4 In. 85.00
Dr. J.S. Woods, Albany, N.Y., Green, Tombstone Form, IP, 8 1/2 In. .... 1980.00 to 3850.00
Dr. J.W. Bull's Cough Syrup, Baltimore, Aqua, 5 3/4 In. 20.00
Dr. J.W. Bull's Vegetable Pills, 8-Sided, Ground Top, 2 1/2 In. 20.00
Dr. J.W. Poland, Olive Amber, Flattened Collar, c.1870, 7 3/4 In. 302.50
Dr. J.W. Poland, Stoddard, Pontil, Oval, 1855-1865, 8 In. 1300.00
Dr. J.W. Poland's Humor Doctor, Aqua, Applied Top, 8 3/4 In. 69.00
Dr. James Cannabis Indica, Craddock & Co., Aqua, 1875-1885, 7 3/4 In. 303.00

Dr. James Fig Laxative, Pittsburgh, Box 17.00
Dr. Jones Liniment, Embossed Beaver, Aqua, 6 3/8 In. .... 15.00 to 18.00
Dr. Kellinger's Magic Fluid, New York, Aqua, OP, 4 7/8 In. 110.00
Dr. Kennedy's Rheumatic Liniment, Roxbury, Mass, Aqua, 6 1/2 In. .... 20.00 to 25.00
Dr. Kennedy's Salt Rheum Ointment, Aqua, Cylinder, 3 1/2 In. 70.00
Dr. Kilmer's Female Remedy, Binghamton, N.Y., Aqua, 8 5/8 In. 52.00
Dr. Kilmer's Great Nerve Restorer, Green, 9 1/3 In. 10.00
Dr. Kilmer's Ocean Weed Heart Remedy, Aqua, Embossed Heart, 7 1/8 In. ...... 45.00 to 120.00
Dr. Kilmer's Ocean Weed Heart Remedy, Aqua, Embossed Heart, 8 1/2 In. 118.00
Dr. Kilmer's Swamp Root Kidney, Liver Bladder Remedy, Aqua, Sample, 4 1/4 In..... 22.00
Dr. Kilmers Autumn Leaf Ext For Uterine Injection, Aqua, 4 1/2 In. 20.00
Dr. King's Croup & Cough Syrup, Aqua, Pontil, 5 In. 83.00
Dr. Larbor's Extract Of Lungwort, C.J. Roosevelt, New York, Aqua, Pontil, 6 1/8 In. 154.00
Dr. Larookah's Indian Vegetable Pulmonic Syrup, Aqua, Large 55.00
Dr. Larookah's Indian Vegetable Pulmonic Syrup, Deep Aqua, 8 1/4 In. 86.00
Dr. Lesure's Veterinary Fever Drops 15.00
Dr. Liebig's Wonderful German Invigorator No. 1, S.F., Cal., Blue Aqua, 7 3/4 In.... 220.00
Dr. M. Bowman's Genuine Healing Balsam, Smoky Clear, 8-Sided, Pontil, 5 3/4 In.. 125.00
Dr. M.M. Fenner's People Remedies, Fredonia, Ny., Amber, Oval, 8 1/2 In.............. 20.00
Dr. Markley's Family Medicines, Lancaster, Pa., Aqua, Pontil, 7 1/8 In. 77.00
Dr. McLean's Liver & Kidney Balm, St. Louis, Aqua, Oval, 8 3/4 In. 15.00
Dr. McMunn's Elixir Of Opium, Aqua, OP, 4 1/4 In. 40.00
Dr. Miles Heart Treatment, Aqua, Label & Contents 121.00
Dr. Mintie's Nephreticum, San Francisco, Aqua, 6 1/2 In. 160.00
Dr. Mott's Wild Cherry Tonic, Spruance Standley & Co., Yellow Amber, 9 1/8 In. 800.00
Dr. Murray's Magic Oil, San Francisco, Cal., Blue Aqua, Applied Top, 6 1/4 In. 176.00
Dr. Myers Bilious King, Smith Myers & Co., Amber, 1870-1880, 9 In. 84.00
Dr. N. Angell's Rheumatic Gun, Deep Aqua, Pontil, 7 In. 302.50
Dr. Perry's Last Chance Liniment, Aqua, 5 3/4 In. 55.00
Dr. Peter's Uterine, Rectangular 35.00
Dr. Pierce's Anuric Tablets, Citron, Embossed Kidney, Green, 3 1/16 In. 25.00
Dr. Pierce's Favorite Prescription, Citron, Cork, ABM, 8 1/4 In. 25.00
Dr. Pierce's Golden Medical Discovery, Aqua, 8 3/8 In. .... 15.00 to 30.00
Dr. Pierce's Pile Cure, Label, Box 30.00
Dr. Pierce's Tablets For Kidneys & Backache, Cylinder, Yellow, 3 In. 40.00
Dr. Pinkham's Emmenagogue, Aqua, Rectangular, 1850, 6 In................................ 94.00 to 176.00
Dr. Porter, New York, Aqua, Rolled Lip, Pontil, Rectangular, 4 1/8 In. .... 17.00 to 32.00
Dr. Porter's Antiseptic Oil, Contents 8.00
Dr. R.C. Flower's Scientific Remedies, Boston, Mass., Amber, 9 1/8 In. 66.00
Dr. Roback Swedish Remedy, 6-Sided, Aqua, Pontil, 4 1/2 In. 143.00
Dr. Rogers Liverwort, Tar & Canchalague, Cincinnati, Apple Green, Hinged Mold 35.00
Dr. S. Hart, Vegetable Extract, New York, Aqua, Pontil, 7 1/2 In. 110.00
Dr. S.A. Weaver's Canker & Salt Rheum Syrup, Aqua, Pontil, 9 1/4 In.................... 132.00
Dr. S.S. Fitch, Broadway, N.Y., Aqua, Oval, OP 54.00
Dr. Sanford's Liver Invigorator, New York, Aqua, Apple Green7 1/2 In................... 75.00
Dr. Sawen's Magic Balm, Aqua, Label, 5 In. 12.00
Dr. Seth Arnold's Balsam, 8-Sided, Aqua, Pontil, 2 1/2 In. 50.00
Dr. Shoop's Prescription Of Rheumatism, Label, Contents 15.00
Dr. Steph. Jewett's Celebrated Pulmonary Elixir, Rindge, N.H., Aqua, Pontil, 5 In.. 100.00
Dr. Thatcher's Liver & Blood Syrup, Chattanooga, Tenn., Amber, 8 In. 35.00
Dr. Tobias New York Venetian Liniment, Aqua 40.00
Dr. VD Bell's Mouth Elixir, Bell Shape, Clear 20.00
Dr. W. Burton's Syrup, Philada, Pale Green, Pontil, 6 1/4 In. 440.00
Dr. W.B. Farrell's Arabian Liniment, Chicago, Aqua, 3 7/8 In. 125.00
Dr. W.S. Love's Vegetable Elixir, Baltimore, Olive Green, OP, 7 In. 6875.00
Dr. W.S. Lunt's Ague Killer, Findlay, O., Deep Blue Aqua, OP, 6 3/4 In.................... 303.00
Dr. White's Dandelion Alterative, Indianapolis, Aqua, Rectangular, 9 1/4 In. ...98.00 to 100.00
Dr. White's Dandelion Compound, Blood Purifying Tonic, Label, Blue 25.00
Dr. Wistar's Balsam Of Wild Cherry, Philadelphia, Aqua, OP, 6 1/4 In. .... 45.00 to 57.00
Drs. J. & M. Rob, N.Y., Whittled Aqua, Applied Mouth, Pontil, 7 5/8 In. 253.00
Duff Gordon Sherry Medical Department, Deep Olive Green, 9 3/4 In...................... 500.00
Duncan's Cough Balsam, Nashville, Tenn., Label, Contents 37.00
Durand & Tourtelot Pharmaceutists, Philadelphia, Clear, 5 1/2 x 2 In. 65.00

Dyers' Healing Embrocation, Providence, R.I., 12-Sided, Aqua, OP, 4 1/4 In............. 220.00
E. Anthony, New York, Sapphire Blue, OP, 6 1/4 In. 550.00
E.T. Sudness Lion Drug Store, Salt Lake City, Utah, Embossed Lion, 5 1/2 In........... 85.00
Edward H. Hance, Philadelphia, Aqua, Oval, 10 1/2 In. 29.00
Elysian Mfg. Co. Chemists & Perfumers, Detroit, U.S.A., Cobalt Blue, 6 1/2 In. 121.00
F.F. Muller Drug Store, Elko, Nev., 3 1/2 In. 247.00
F.J. Macke Midland Drug Store, Leadville, Col., 4 1/2 In...................... 85.00
Farquar's Medicated-California Wine & Brandy, Puce, 9 1/2 In. 880.00
Fenner's Pleasant Worm Syrup, Label, Contents...................................... 42.00
Flagg's Cough Killer, Chicago, Ill... 30.00
Fleming & Meadville Druggist, Denver, Amber, 5 3/4 In................................ 250.00
Flip, Converse Treatment Institute, Mt.Vernon, Oh., Figural, Hat, Pontil, 3 3/8 In........ 258.00
Folga's Olosonian, New York, Aqua, 6 In. 68.00
Fowler's Itch Killer, Cornflower Blue, Crude, 5 3/4 In. 45.00
Frey's Vermifuge, Baltimore, Aqua, Hinged Mold, 4 1/4 In......................... 20.00
Friedenwald's Buchu-Gin, Yellow Green, 10 In............................... 660.00
Frontier Asthma Co., Buffalo, Amber, Square.. 15.00
G.E. Briggs, Cobalt Blue, OP, Label, 6 In.. 1485.00
G.H. Markley Druggist, Lansing, Iowa, Dose Cup.................................. 35.00
G.W. Davis Inflammatory Extirpator & Cleanser, Aqua, OP, 4 In. 58.00
G.W. Merchant, Chemist, Lockport, N.Y., Emerald Green, Whittled, 5 1/2 In. 132.00
G.W. Merchant, Chemist, Lockport, N.Y., Green, IP, 7 In.............................. 220.00
G.W. Merchant, Chemist, Lockport, N.Y., Teal Blue, IP, 5 1/2 In. 577.00
G.W. Merchant, Chemist, Lockport, N.Y., Teal Blue, Whittled, 7 1/4 In.............. 165.00
G.W. Merchant, Chemist, Lockport, N.Y., Teal Green, Crude, 5 3/4 In...............77.00 to 90.00
G.W. Merchant, Chemist, Lockport, N.Y., Yellow Green, OP, 5 1/2 In................ 400.00
G.W. Merchant, Lockport, N.Y., Emerald Green, 5 3/4 In. 302.50
G.W. Merchant, Lockport, N.Y., Emerald Green, c.1870, 5 1/2 In. 60.50
G.W. Merchant, Lockport, N.Y., Emerald Green, Pontil, Applied Mouth, c.1855, 5 In. 140.00
Gargling Oil, Lockport, N.Y., Blue Green, 7 1/2 In. 65.00
Gargling Oil, Lockport, N.Y., Emerald Green, 7 In.................................... 358.00
Gees Lobelline Cough Syrup, Yellow Green, Sunken Panel, 5 In. 14.00
Genuine J. Russell Spalding, Boston, Mass., Aqua, OP, 5 In........................ 42.00
George Dowden Chemist & Druggist, Richmond, Va., Aqua, Pontil, 4 3/4 In............ 198.00
GFP For Women, Gerstle Medicine Co., Chattanooga, Tenn........................... 45.00
Gibb's Bone Liniment, 6-Sided, Olive Green, OP, 6 1/4 In. 880.00
Gladstone Celery Compound, Mastico, Danville, Il., Amber, 7 3/8 In.............. 50.00
Globe Tobacco Co., Detroit, Mich., Yellow Topaz, Paneled, Handle 80.00
Glover's Imperial Distemper Remedy, New York, Teal Blue, 5 In. 80.00
Gove's Pharmacy, Est.1876, San Francisco, 7 3/4 In................................ 49.50
Green's Lung Restorer, Oroville, Cal., U.S.A., Aqua, 8 In. 104.50
Greenes Vegetable Alternative & Restorative Syrup, Cincinnati, Oh., Aqua, 9 In..... 500.00
Greenlund's Caldwell, Idaho, Purple, 5 In.. 20.00
Guaranty Rheumatic Remedy Company, Amber, Rectangular, 7 1/4 In. 55.00
Gun Wa's Chinese Remedy, Amber, Crude Applied Top, 7 3/4 In..............330.00 to 485.00
H. Lake's Indian Specific, Aqua, OP, 8 1/8 In.................................467.50 to 715.00
H.H. Warner & Co., Tippecanoe, Pat. Nov. 20, '83, Yellow, Applied Mouth, 8 3/4 In.. 154.00
H.H. Warner & Co., Tippecanoe, Pat. Nov. 20, 83, Medium Amber, 9 In.............. 88.00
Hale, Helena, Mont., 5 1/2 In... 50.00
Hall's Balsam For The Lungs, Aqua, OP, Original Label, 6 1/2 In. 110.00
Hall's Pulmonary Balsam, Aqua, 6 3/8 In 137.50
Hammer Druggist, McGregor, Iowa, Embossed, 6 1/2 In. 35.00
Harper Headache Remedy, Washington, D.C., 6 1/4 In.............................. 18.00
Hartford's Balsam Of Myrrh, Label, ABM, Contents................................ 9.00
Haskin's Nervine, Binghampton, Lime Green, 8 1/2 In.............................. 45.00
Hawe's Healing Extract, A.F. Whittemore, Essex, Conn., Aqua, OP, 3 3/8 In............ 231.00
Healy & Bigelow Kickapoo Indian Sagwa, Aqua, Label, 8 1/2 In.............50.00 to 154.00
Henley's Celery Beef & Iron, Amber, Applied Top, Kickup Base, 11 3/4 In............ 121.00
Henley's Royal Balsam, Woodward & Quivey, Aqua, Applied Top, 1866, 7 In........... 660.00
Henry J. Schnaidt Druggist, Parkston, S.D., 8 7/8 In. 150.00
Herters Headache Medicine, Washington, D.C., BIM, 5 In. 5.00
Hilmer's Laboratory, San Francisco, Aqua, 9 1/8 In................................. 27.50
Hobensack's Medicated Worm Syrup, Philad., Aqua, OP, Embossed, 4 3/4 In...35.00 to 85.00

Holman's Natures Grand Restorative, Boston, Mass., Yellow Olive, OP, 6 1/2 In. 3575.00
Hopkin's Chalbeath, Baltimore, Emerald Green, Pontil, 7 1/4 In. ....*Illus* 88.00
Houck's, Patent, Panacea, Baltimore, Aqua, Pontil, 6 1/2 In. 93.50
Hough's Life Preserver, Vegitable, Keene, N.H., Olive Green, c.1840, 6 1/4 In. 7700.00
Howards Vegetable Cancer & Canker Syrup, Amber, Rectangular, 7 1/4 In. . 852.50 to 880.00
Howland's Ready Remedy, Columbia, Aqua, Pontil, 5 In. 100.00
Hub Punch, C.H. Graves & Sons, Boston, Amber, Cylinder, 1875, 9 1/8 In. ....*Illus* 83.00
Hull's Salicine Mixture, Radway & Co., Aqua, Pontil, 7 In. 302.50
Humphrey's Homeopathic Veterinary Specific, Horse, Partial Label, 3 1/2 In. 20.00
Hunt's Liniment, C.E. Staton, Sing Sing, N.Y., Aqua, 5 In. ....35.00 to 40.00
Hunter's Pulmonary Balsam, Bangor, Me., Aqua, Pontil, Flared Lip, 5 7/8 In............. 60.00
Husband's Calcined Magnesia, Label, BIMAL, Stamp Top, 4 In. 12.00
Hyatt's Infallible Life Balsam, Aqua, 9 1/2 In. 35.00
Hyatt's Infallible Life Balsam, Green Aqua, Applied Top, 9 1/2 In. 45.00
Hyatt's Infallible Life Balsam, N.Y., Yellow Green, IP, 9 1/2 In. 1155.00
Hypophosphites & Cod Liver Oil, John Wyeth, Cobalt Blue, Rectangular, 8 3/4 In...... 25.00
I. Covert's Balm Of Life, Olive Amber, Pontil, 6 In. 1375.00
Imperial Blood & Liver Tonic, King Of All Tonics, Dr. R. Drake, Amber, 9 In............ 143.00
Indian, see also Medicine, Healy & Bigelow
Indian Wigwam Remedies Compound Mineral Springs, Denver, Colo, Amber, 8 In. ... 750.00
Indian's Panacea, Olive Green, Pontil, 8 In. 4400.00
J & H, Philadelphia, 12-Sided, OP, 6 1/4 In.. 70.00
J. & C. Maguire C., St. Louis, Purple Lavender, 6 3/4 In. 440.00
J. & C. Maguire Chemists & Druggists, St. Louis, Mo., Cobalt Blue, 7 3/4 In. 1250.00
J.B. Wheatley Compound Syrup, Dallasburgh, Ky., Aqua, Pontil, 5 7/8 In. 72.00
J.C. DuBose Compound Syrup Of Iceland Moss, Aqua, Pontil, 5 3/4 In. 220.00
J.K. Palmer, Olive Amber, Pontil, Doctor Gay's Blood Purifier, c.1855, 9 1/4 In........ 467.00
J.L. Leavitt, Boston, Olive Amber, IP, 8 3/8 In..............................132.00 to 154.00
J.L. Parson Leadville Druggist, Durango, Col., Amethyst, 6 7/8 In. 125.00
J.R. Nichols & Co., Chemists, Boston, Blue, Indented Panels, Rectangular, 9 1/4 In. 143.00
J.S. Spear, Boston, Rectangular, 4 In. 65.00
J.W. Bull's Compound, Pectoral, Baltimore, Aqua, OP, 5 1/2 In. 93.50
Jacob's Cholera & Dysentry Cordial, Aqua, Open Pontil, 7 3/8 In............................ 88.00
Jadwin's Subduing Liniment, Honesdale, Pa., 4 In. 7.00
Jno. Wyeth & Bro., Cobalt Blue, Dose, Cap.. 20.00
John Gilbert & Co., Philadelphia, Aqua, OP, 9 1/2 In. 176.00
John J. Smith, Louisville, Ky., Aqua, Cylinder, 6 In.. 10.00
John Q. Hill, Apothecary, Worcester, Mass., Olive Amber, IP, 9 In. 357.50
John Wyeth & Bro., Cobalt Blue, Pat.May 16th 1899, Square 19.00

*Medicine, Hub Punch, C.H. Graves & Sons,
Boston, Amber, Cylinder, 1875, 9 1/8 In.*

*Medicine, Kaytonik, Coughs,
Cobalt Blue, 7 In.*

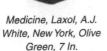

Medicine, Laxol, A.J. White, New York, Olive Green, 7 In.

Medicine, Liquozone, The Liquid Ozone Co., Chicago, U.S.A., Amber, 8 1/2 In.

Medicine, Rheumatic Syrup, R.S. Co., Rochester, N.Y., Amber, 1882, 9 5/8 In.

Jones & Elmes Veterinary Surgeons, St. Albans, Luton, Cobalt Blue, 8 1/2 In. 100.00
Jones Drops For Humors Or Anti Impetigines, Aqua, OP, 4 3/4 In. 154.00
Julius Deetkew Pharmacist, Deadwood, S.D., Aqua, 4 1/4 In. 65.00
Julius Hospital, Wurzburg, Pius Emblem, Claret, Kidney Shape 95.00
Kalmus Chemical Co., Cincinnati & New York, Green, 8 In. 10.00
Kaytonik, Coughs, Cobalt Blue, 7 In. ....*Illus* 15.00
Kelly's Rheumatic Syrup, Aqua, 5 1/4 In. 7.50
Kendall's Blister For Horses, Horse On Box 30.00
Kendall's Spavin Cure For Human Flesh, Enosburg Falls, Vt., Amber, 5 1/4 In. 14.00
Keystone Drug Co., Mont., Deer Lodge, 2 7/8 In. 7.00
Kickapoo Oil, see Medicine, Healy & Bigelow
Kilmer's Autumn Leaf Extract For Uterine Injection, Binghamton, N.Y., Aqua, 4 1/2 In. 35.00
Kobolo Tonic Medicine Co., Chicago, Ill., Milk Glass, 8 3/4 In. 264.00
Kodol Dyspepsia Cure, Aqua, Contents, Label 38.00
Kraums New Red Blood, Emporia, Kan. 20.00
L.P. Dodge Rheumatic Liniment, Newburg, Amber, OP, 5 In. 1650.00
L.W. Leithhead Drug Co. Wholesale Druggist, Duluth, Minn., Cobalt Blue 100.00
Laughlin & Bushfield Wholesale Druggist, Wheeling, W. Va., Blue Aqua, IP, 7 5/8 In. 148.50
Laxol, A.J. White, New York, Olive Green, 7 In. ....*Illus* 75.00
Lee's Pharmacy, Seattle, Wash., 1 Oz., 3 1/2 In. 5.00
Lee's Pharmacy, Seattle, Washington, 3 1/2 In. 5.00
Lewis Drug Co., Ely, Nev., Flags, Fireworks, 4 1/2 In. 176.00
Lighting Hot Drops, No Relief, No Pay, Herb Medicine Co., Springfield, Oh., Aqua, 5 In. 7.50
Lilly Syrup, J. Fish, Rochester, N.Y., Olive Green, OP, 1840, 5 3/4 In. 7150.00
Lindsey's Blood Searcher, Pittsburgh, Aqua, Crude Applied Top, 8 1/2 In. .... 65.00 to 71.50
Liquozone, The Liquid Ozone Co., Chicago, U.S.A., Amber, 8 1/2 In. .... *Illus* 1.00
Little's White Oil, Scottsville, Va., Aqua, Pontil, 6 1/16 In. 302.50
Lockport, N.Y., Blue Green, 5 1/4 In. 24.00
Lord's Opodeldoc, Rolled Lip, Aqua, OP, 5 In. 21.00
Lorree's Ohio Liniment 100.00
Loudon & Co. Indian Expectorant, Philada., Aqua, Oval, 7 1/2 In. 168.00
Lydia E. Pinkham's Vegetable Compound, Aqua, Label, Contents, 1915, 8 1/4 In. 45.00
Lynn's Sore Throat & Bronchitis Remedy, Mo., Label, Contents 40.00
Lyon's Powder, B & P, Emerald Green, OP, Rolled Lip, 4 1/4 In. 220.00
Lyon's Powder, B & P, N.Y., Olive Green, OP, 4 1/16 In. 150.00
Lyon's Powder, B & P, N.Y., Puce Orange, OP, 4 1/16 In. 198.00
Lyon's Powder, B & P, N.Y., Yellow Green, OP, 4 1/16 In. 180.00
Lyon's Powder, B & P, Olive Green Rolled Lip, OP, 4 1/4 In. 200.00
Lyon's Powder, B & P, Puce, Rolled Top, Bubbles, Whittled, OP, 4 1/4 In. .... 85.00 to 198.00

M.A.C. For Dyspepsia & Constipation, Smith Bros., 8 3/4 In. 30.00
Maple Balsam, Burks Medicine Co., New York, Label, Tooled Top, 6 1/4 In. 17.00
Masta's Indian Pulmonic Balsam, Lowell, Mass., Aqua, Pontil, 5 5/8 In. 142.00
McCrum's, Lexington, Va., BIMAL, Embossed, 6 In. 5.50
McGuire Druggist, Petaluma, Cal., 6 1/2 In. 35.00
Medical Department, U.S. Army, 4 3/4 x 3 1/2 In. 15.00
Medical Department, U.S.N., Clear, Embossed, 500 Cc, Square, 7 3/4 In. 65.00
Melvin & Badger Apothecaries, Boston, Mass., Cobalt Blue, White Wash Lotion, 5 In. 60.00
Meritol American Drug & Press Assn., Decorah, Iowa, Rectangular, Amber, 6 3/8 In. . 25.00
Mexican Mustang Liniment, Lyon Mfg. Co., Aqua, 5 1/2 In. 45.00
Mexican Mustang Liniment, Lyon Mfg. Co., N.Y., Aqua, 4 In. ....85.00 to 110.00
Miracol Embrocation For Rheumatism, Amber, Triangular, 5 In. 35.00
Moe Hospital, Sioux Falls, South Dakota, 4 1/2 In. 12.00
Moore & Thurston Western Liniment, Green Aqua, OP, 4 5/8 In. 412.50
Moore's Revealed Remedy, Shield & Monogram, Amber, 9 In. 385.00
Moore's Tree Of Life, Aqua, Label, Contents, 8 3/4 In. 715.00
Morse's Celebrated Syrup, Prov., R.I., Aqua, IP, 9 1/4 In. 154.00
Morse's Compound Syrup Of Yellow Dock Root Syrup, Prov., R.I., Aqua, OP, 9 1/2 In. 165.00
Morse's Indian Root Pills, Amber, 2 1/2 In. 12.00
Mother's Worm Syrup, Edward Wilder & Co., Cabin, Windows, Clear....................... 45.00
Mother's Friend, Aqua, 1890, Pt.... .... 5.00
Mrs. Winslow's Soothing Syrup, Aqua, 5 In.. 5.00
Mrs. Winslow's Soothing Syrup, Curtis & Perkins, Aqua, OP, 5 1/16 In. ....21.00 to 30.00
Muegge Druggist, We Never Sleep, Baker, Ore., Emerald Green, 6 Oz. 125.00
Murine Eye Remedy Co., Embossed, Graphic Label, Trial Size 15.00
Myers' Rock Rose, New Haven, Aqua, Pontil, 9 In. 258.50
Myers' Rock Rose, New Haven, Emerald Green, IP, 1845-1860, 9 In. ....1320.00 to 1650.00
N.Y. Pharmacal Association Lactopeptine, Cobalt Blue, 7 3/8 In............................. 80.00
Nerve & Bone Liniment, OP, Aqua, 4 In. ....10.00 to 15.00
North Beach Drug Store, Citrate Magnesia, SCA, 7 1/2 In. 49.50
Nubian Tea For The Liver, Amber, Embossed Head, Amber, 8 In. 75.00
Nyal's Compound Larkspur Lotion, Amber, BIMAL, Label, 6 9/16 In. 18.00
Ober & McConkey's For Specific Fever & Ague, Baltimore, 6-Sided, Aqua, Pontil, 7 In. 231.00
Owens Montgomery, Butte, Mont., Purple, 6 1/4 In. 35.00
Owl Drug Co., Amethyst, 1 Wing, Tooled Top, 9 7/8 In. 80.00
Owl Drug Co., Cobalt Blue, Label, Square, Qt. 300.00
Owl Drug Co., Cobalt Blue, Rectangular, 6 1/4 In. 150.00
Owl Drug Co., Cobalt Blue, Rectangular, 9 3/8 In. 475.00
Owl Drug Co., Milk Glass, 4 In. ....35.00 to 45.00
Owl Drug Co., Milk Glass, 5 1/2 In. ....40.00 to 65.00
Owl Drug Co., Rectangular, 8 1/4 In. 20.00
Owl Drug Co., Screw Top, 3 5/8 In. 10.00
Owl Drug Company, Milk Glass, 6 In. 275.00
Owl Pharmacy, W.H. Davis, Everett, Wash., Owl Picture, Tooled Top, 1900s, 7 In...... 50.00
P.R. Clarke, Pure Castor Oil, Sharon, Opalescent Aqua, Eagle, Flag, Stoddard, 5 In..... 100.00
P.T. Wright & Co., Pectoral Syrup, Philadelphia, Aqua, OP, 6 1/4 In. ....88.00 to 110.00
Paine Drug Co., Rochester, N.Y., Yellow Green, 6 1/8 In. 1210.00
Paine's Celery Compound, Amber, Square, 9 1/2 In. ....7.00 to 10.00
Panopeton Bread & Beef Peptone, Fairchild, WT & Co., Amber, 5 3/8 In. 80.00
Paregoric, Advertising & Doses For Infants, Violet, Swirls....................................... 200.00
Pawnee Indian Too-Re, Dark Aqua, 7 3/8 In. 35.00
Peerless Special Capsules, Remedy For Gonorrhea, Brooklyn, Contents, Box, 5 In. .. 30.00
Phalon's Chemical Hair Invigorator, Broadway, N.Y., Aqua, 5 1/2 In. 62.00
Phillip's Milk Of Magnesia, Light Blue, 5 In.. 30.00
Phillip's Milk Of Magnesia, Light Blue, 7 In... 35.00
Phillips' Emulsion Cod Liver Oil, New York, Amber To Brown, Crude 20.00
Pioneer, Seattle, Wash., Mortar & Pestle, Light Cobalt Blue, 5 1/4 In. 176.00
Planter's Old Time Remedies, Cuban In Sombrero, Label 35.00
Pratt & Butcher Magic Oil, Brooklyn, Ny, Aqua, Pontil.. 56.00
Prof. H.K. Flagg's Balm Of Excellence, Aqua, 6-Pointed Star, OP, 6 3/4 In............... 176.00
R.F. Kinsell, Yellow Green, Applied Ring Lip, Pontil, Cylindrical, 9 1/2 In. 633.00
R.W. Davis Drug Co., Chicago, U.S.A., Milk Glass, 11 In...............................60.50 to 71.50
Ralph F. Burnham Pharmacist, Auburn, Me., Honey Amber, Embossed, 6 3/4 In. 35.00

Ramon's Santonine Worm Syrup, Tenn. 15.00
Rawleigh's Effervescent Salts, ΛBM, 7 1/2 In. 7.00
Reed & Carnrick Pharmacists, New York, Honey Amber, Maltine Shape, Whittled... 25.00
Reed & Carnrick Pharmacists, New York, Honey Amber, Tombstone, 7 3/4 In. 30.00
Reeve's Ambrosia, Aqua, Rectangular, 7 1/4 In. 42.00
Rev. T. Hill's Vegetable Remedy, Green 8.00
Rexall UD Compound Cathartic Pills, Box, 2 3/4 In. 5.00
Rheumatic Syrup, R.S. Co., Rochester, N.Y., Amber, 1882, 9 5/8 In. ....*Illus* 143.00
Rhodes' Antidote To Malaria Fever & Ague, Aqua, OP, 8 1/4 In. 297.00
Robert's Drug Store, Goldfield, Nev., 1905, 5 In. 100.00
Roberts, Goldfield, Nev., Sun Colored, Amethyst, 3 5/8 In. 66.00
Roberts & Nelden, Salt Lake City, Cobalt Blue, 2 7/8 In. 55.00
Rowland's Tonic Mixture Of Vegetable Febrifuge, Aqua, 6-Sided, 5 3/4 In. 170.00
Rumford Chemical Works, Green, 7 1/2 In. 25.00
Rushton's Cod Liver Oil, New York, Aqua, Open Pontil, 10 In. 165.00
S.A. Palmer Druggist, Santa Cruz, Calif., Amber, 4 1/8 In. 45.00
S.A. Palmer Druggist, Santa Cruz, Calif., Amber, 5 1/2 In. 35.00
Samuel Sime Pharmacien Chemist, Philadelphia, Aqua, Bulbous Neck, OP, 9 In. 124.00
Sanitarium, Yellow Green, Triangular, Replaced Collar 40.00
Sanitol For The Teeth, Milk Glass, Stopper, Rectangular, 6 In. 23.00
Schenck's Pulmonic Syrup, Philad., Aqua, OP, 7 1/4 In. 75.00
Scott's Pharmacy, Fort Collins, Colo., 4 13/16 In. 8.00
Scott's Red Oil Liniment, Philadelphia, Aqua, 4 7/8 In. 90.00
Seaver's Joint & Nerve Liniment, Amber, Ground Lip, 4 In. 25.00
Selden's Magic, Fluid, N.Y., Aqua, 7 3/8 In. 154.00
Seminole Indian Liver & Tonic, Lides Lab., Columbus, BIM, 7 3/4 In. 25.00
Shaker Cherry Pectoral Syrup, Canterbury, N.H. No. 1, Aqua, OP, 5 1/2 In. .. 105.00 to 165.00
Shaker Fluid Extract, Valerian, Aqua, 3 3/4 In. 46.00
Silver Pine Healing Oil, Aqua, 6 In. 9.00
Simmon's Liver Regulator, Zeilin & Co., Aqua, Applied Top, 9 In. 15.00
Sloan's Nerve & Bone Linament, Label, Box, Sample, 4 In. 25.00
Sloan's Ointment, Aqua, OP, 2 5/8 In. 110.00
Smith's Anodyne Cough Drops, Montpelier, Aqua, OP, 5 7/8 In. 110.00
Smith's Green Mountain Renovator, Amber, 7 1/2 In. 1175.00
Smith's Green Mountain Renovator, Amber, IP, c.1850, 6 3/4 In. 1017.00
Smith's Rheumatic Cure, South Londonderry, Vt., Aqua, 8 In. 128.00
South Carolina Dispensary, Aqua, Palm Tree, 6 In. ....75.00 to 121.00
Spirit Camphor, Milford Drug Co., Milford, Ind., Free-Blown, Aqua, Cylinder, 5 In.... 45.00
St. Andrews Life Root, Amber, Double Ring Lip, 9 In. 90.00
St. Joseph Cough Syrup, Amber, Label, Cork Type, 5 1/4 In. 4.00
Strong, Cobb & Company, Wholesale Druggist, Cleve., Jug, Cream, Handle, 1/2 Gal. 65.00
Strong & Cobb, Wholesale Druggist, Cleveland, O., Electric Blue 65.00
Strong & Cobb White, Wholesale Druggists, Cleveland, Oh., Cornflower Blue 65.00
Strong & Cobb White, Wholesale Druggists, Cleveland, Oh., Golden Amber.............. 19.00
Suire Eckstein & Co. Druggists, Cincinnati, Oh., Sapphire Blue, 1845-1855, 6 1/2 In. 523.00
Swaim's Panacea, Aqua, BIMAL, Label, 7 In. 40.00
Swaim's Panacea, Olive Amber, Pontil, 7 1/2 In. 302.00
Swaim's Panacea, Philadelphia, Indented Panels, Yellow Olive, 7 In. 413.00
Swaim's Vermifuge, Dysentery Cholera Morbus Dyspepsia, Aqua, OP, 4 1/4 In. 247.00
T. Morris Perot & Co., Druggists, Philada, Rectangular, 4 3/4 In. 60.00
T.H. VanHorn Druggist, Lockport, N.Y., Aqua, 10 x 4 In. 30.00
Tarrant Druggist, New York, Rolled Lip, 5 In. ....21.50 to 25.00
Taylor's Cherokee Remedy Of Sweet Gum & Mullein, Aqua, Rectangular, 4 7/8 In... 8.00
Thatcher's Liver & Blood Syrup, Sample, Amber, 3 5/16 In. 25.00
Thos. Woodliff Druggist, Virginia City, Nevada, 3 1/2 In. 45.00
Tippers White Oils, Embossed Embro, Birmingham, Cobalt Blue, Square, 7 In. 90.00
Tonopah Co., Tonopah, Nevada, Pale Amethyst Tint, 7 3/8 In. 82.50
Tr. Hyoscyam, Label Under Glass, Gold Trimmed Label, Square, Stopper, 7 3/4 In...... 26.00
Trommer Extract Of Malt Co., Fremont, Ohio, Apricot Yellow, Whittled, 8 1/4 In...... 45.00
Turf Oil, Dove & Co., Richmond, Va., 3-Sided, Aqua, OP, 4 1/2 In. 71.50
U.S.A. Hosp. Dept., Amber, 9 1/4 In. 357.50
U.S.A. Hosp. Dept., Cobalt Blue, Applied Mouth, 9 In. 1320.00
U.S.A. Hosp. Dept., Cobalt Blue, Flared Lip, 1860, 7 1/8 In. 1045.00

U.S.A. Hosp. Dept., Inside Oval, Aqua, 1860-1875, 7 3/4 In. 154.00
U.S.A. Hosp. Dept., Olive Amber, Applied Mouth, 9 1/4 In. 385.00
U.S.A. Hosp. Dept., Olive Green, 9 7/8 In. 578.00
U.S.A. Hosp. Dept., Olive Green, Bubbed, 9 1/4 In. ....412.50 to 495.00
U.S.A. Hosp. Dept., Sapphire Blue, Oval, 1865, 3 1/2 In. ....300.00 to 357.00
U.S.A. Hosp. Dept., Sapphire Blue, Tooled Lip, 2 1/2 In. 358.00
U.S.A. Hosp. Dept., Yellow Amber, Seed Bubbles, 9 3/8 In. ....330.00 to 357.00
U.S.A. Hosp. Dept., Yellow, Amber Tint, c.1875, 8 7/8 In. 357.50
Universal Cough Remedy, J.W. Hunnewell & Co., Boston, Mass., Aqua, Pontil, 4 In. 110.00
Valentine Hassuc's Lung & Cough Syrup, Red Amber, Glob Top, 11 3/4 In. 357.00
Van Buskirk's Fragrant Sozodont For Teeth & Breath, 5 1/2 In. 15.00
Van Deusen's Improved Wahpene, Aqua, OP, c.1855, 8 In. ....154.00 to 200.00
Vaughn's Vegetable Lithontripic Mixture, Buffalo, Aqua, Pontil, 8 In. ....100.00 to 467.00
Vegetable Pulmonary Balsam, Reed Cutler & Co., Boston, Mass., Aqua, Pontil, 7 In. 198.00
Vick's Drops, Embossed, Cobalt, 1 7/8 In. 8.00
Vick's Drops, Cobalt Blue, 2 In. 35.00
Victor Laxative Fig Syrup, Contents, Label 15.00
Vine & Dot, Pine Trees, Sapphire Blue, Pontil, 4 1/8 In. 137.00
W. Goldstein's IXL Florida Water, Aqua, 9 1/4 In. 55.00
W.E. Hagan & Co., Troy, N.Y., 8-Sided, Cobalt Blue, 6 3/4 In. 143.00
W.F. Lawrence's Genuine Preparations, Epping, N.H., Aqua, 5 5/8 In. 175.00
W.H. Bovee & Co., San Francisco, Green Aqua, OP, 6 3/4 In. 302.50
W.H. Brown & Bro. Druggist, Baltimore, Aqua, OP, 11 5/8 In. ....82.50 to 142.00
W.T. & Co., Teal Green, Bitters Type, Square, Pt. 45.00
W.T. Wenzell, San Francisco, Aqua, Crude, 5 5/8 In. 45.00
Walter E. Day Pharmacist, Hopkinton, Mass., Light Amber, 5 In. 35.00
Ward's Liniment, Aqua, IP, 5 In. 40.00
Warner's Bromo Soda, Phila., St. Louis, Cobalt Blue, 7 In. 50.00
Warner's Safe Kidney & Liver Cure, Rochester, N.Y., Yellow, 9 3/4 In. ....30.00 to 82.00
Washington Purifier, M.A. MickleJohn N.O., Olive Green, Square, 1870, 8 In. 4400.00
West Indian Toothwash, R.B. Dacosta, Philada., Aqua, Hinged Mold, 3 3/4 In. 20.00
Western Liniment, Moore & Thurston, Green Aqua, Rectangular, OP, 4 5/8 In. 413.00
Westlake's Vegetable Ointment, Lima, N.Y., Aqua, OP, 3 1/8 In. 110.00
Wheeler's Teaberry Toothwash, Philada., Aqua, OP, 1835-1845, 4 In. 121.00
Whitlock's, U-Gar-Gl, Little Cherokee, Cherokee Remedy Co., Chicago, 7 In. ....*Illus* 20.00
Wing & Sisson Druggists, Coxsackie, N.Y., Aqua, OP, 5 5/8 In. 68.00
Winslow's Improved, Olive Amber, 5 In. 330.00
Wm. E. Zoeller, Pittsburgh, Pa., Hostetter Shape 50.00
Wm. Radam's Microbe Killer, Amber, Pat. Dec. 12, 1887, 10 In. 440.00
Youatt's Gargling Oil, Comstock & Bro., Aqua, OP, Rectangular, 7 5/8 In. 75.00
Youatt's Gargling Oil, Comstock & Bro., Aqua, OP, Whittled, 9 In. 195.00

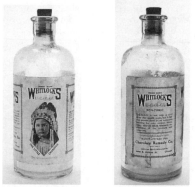

Front   Back

Medicine, Whitlock's, U-Gar-Gl, Little Cherokee,
Cherokee Remedy Co., Chicago, 7 In.

MICHTER'S

Michter's claims to be America's oldest distillery, established in Schaefferstown, Pennsylvania, in 1753, before it was even the state of Pennsylvania. The building was named a national historic landmark in 1980. Special ceramic jugs were first made in 1955 and figural decanters were made beginning in 1977. One of the most famous series was King Tut (1978–1980). About 3,000 were made of the large size. Miniature bottles were also made. Production ended in 1989.

MICHTER'S, 230th Anniversary, 1983	22.00
Amish Buggy	57.00
Auto, York Pulman, 1977	58.00
Barn, Daniel Boone, 1977	27.00
Canal Boat, 1977	26.00
Casinos, 1980	27.00
Christmas, Bell, 1983	53.00
Christmas Ornament, 1984	30.00
Christmas Tree, 1978	50.00
Christmas Wreath, 1980	34.00
Conestoga Wagon, 1976	62.00
Covered Bridge, 1984	47.00
Doughboy, 1979 ....*Illus*	23.00
Easton Peace Candle, 1979	20.00
Goddess Selket, 1980	32.00
Halloween Witch, 1979	55.00
Hershey Trolley, 1980 ....*Illus*	48.00
Ice Wagon, 1979 ....*Illus*	19.00
Indian Kneeling	52.00

Michter's, Doughboy, 1979

Michter's, Hershey Trolley, 1980

Michter's, Ice Wagon, 1979

Michter's, Policeman, New York, 1980

Jug, 1955	62.00
Jug, 1957, 1/2 Gal.	70.00
Jug, 1957, Qt.	20.00
Jug, Sheridan, 1970, Qt.	12.00 to 22.00
Jug, Sheridan, 1976, Qt.	10.00
Jug, Sheridan, 1978, Qt.	10.00
King Tut, 1978	64.00
King Tut, Miniature	17.00
Knights Of C, 4th Degree	112.00
Liberty Bell, Brown, 1976	43.00
Liberty Bell, With Cradle, 1976	14.00
Liberty Brown, Bisque, 1975	77.00
Packard, Fleetwood, 1979	25.00
Penn State Nittany Lion, 1978	48.00
Pennsylvania, Keystone State, 1980	20.00
Pennsylvania Hex, 1977	12.00
Pitt Panther, 1977	53.00
Policeman, New York, 1980 ....*Illus*	32.00
Reading, Pagoda, Pa., 1977	24.00
Stagecoach, 1978	50.00
USC Trojan	35.00

─────────────── **MILK** ───────────────

The first milk bottle we have heard about was an earthenware jar pictured on a Babylonian temple stone panel. Evidently, milk was being dipped from the jar while cream was being churned into butter.

Milk came straight from the cow on early farms; but when cities started to grow in America, a new delivery system was needed. The farmer put the milk into large containers. These were taken to the city in horse-drawn carts and delivered to the consumer. The milkman took a slightly dirty dipper and put it into the milk, ladling a quantity into the customer's pitcher.

Flies, dirt, horse hairs, and heat obviously changed the quality of the milk. By the 1860s iceboxes were developed. One type of milk can claimed to keep milk from becoming sour in a thunderstorm. In 1895, pasteurization was invented and another source of disease from milk was stopped. The first milk bottle patent was issued in the 1880s to the Warren Glass Works Company. The most famous milk bottle was designed in 1884 by Dr. Harvey D. Thatcher, a physician and druggist from Potsdam, New York. His glass bottle had a *Lightning* closure and a picture on the side of a cow being milked. In 1889 The Thatcher Company brought out the bottle with a cap that is still used.

The characteristic shape and printed or embossed wording identify milk bottles for collectors. The round bottle was the most popular until 1936, when the squat round bottle was invented. In 1940 a square squat bottle became the preferred shape. A slug plate was used in the manufacture of a special type of round milk bottle. The manufacturer would change the name embossed on the bottle by changing a metal plate in the glass mold. The letters *ISP* mean *inserted slug plate.* In the following list of bottles, the words *slug plate* are used. Amber-colored glass was used for a short time. Makers claimed it resisted spoiling. A green bottle was patented in 1929. *Pyro* is the shortened form of the word *pyroglaze,* an enameled lettering used on milk bottles after the mid-1930s. Before that, the name had been embossed. Some bottle collectors now refer to these as *ACL,* Applied Color Label. In this listing, color refers to the applied color of the label not to the color of the glass.

Cop the top, babyface, toothache, and *cream top* are some of the terms that refer to the shapes of bottle necks popular in the 1930s. Near the top of the bottle there was an indentation so the cream, which separated from the standing milk, could be poured off with little trouble. Today, with homogenized milk, few children realize that the cream on natural milk will rise to the top. The glass bottle was displaced by cartons by the 1960s. There are two newsletters for collectors, The Milk Route, 4 Ox Bow Road, Westport, CT 06880-2602 and The MOOSletter, 240 Wahl Avenue, Evans City, PA 16033.

MILK, A.G. Smalley, Tin Cap, 1898, Pt.	125.00
A.G. Smalley, Tin Top, 1898, 1/2 Gal.	125.00

Front   Back

*Milk, Bangor Dairy, Bangor, Mich.,
For Mothers Who Care,
Black Label, 9 1/2 In.*

*Milk, Bean's
Dairy, Bendon,
Mich.,
Light Liquid*

*Milk, Belle Isle
Creamery
Co., Detroit,
Mich., 9 1/2 In.*

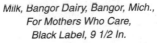

A.G.S. & Co., Clear, Original Metal Handle, Qt. 110.00
AIA Dairy, Embossed, 1/2 Pt. 25.00
Alex Campbell Milk Co., Qt. 25.00
Allentown Dairy Co., Aristocrat Milk Over Circle, Orange, Round, Qt. 18.00
Allwin Dairy, Clintondale, N.Y., Red, Round, Qt. 18.00
Alpenrose, The Very Best, Portland, Ore., Red, Square, Pt. 12.00
Amarillo Milk Co., Amarillo, Texas, Pt. 25.00
American Dairy Co., San Jose, Calif., Slug Plate, Embossed, Round, Qt. 7.00
Anderson Erickson Dairy Co., Des Moines, Iowa, Orange, Square, Qt. .... 18.00 to 50.00
Anderson Gold Star Dairy, Las Vegas, Nev., Red, Square, 48 Ml. 18.00
Andrews Dairy, Canandaigua, N.Y., Cow, Barn, Pasture Scene, Round, Qt. 48.00
Arden, In Oval, Red, Square, 1/2 Pt. 20.00
Arizona Creamery, Phoenix Store, V-Shaped Ribs, Embossed, Pt. 38.00
Arlington Country Dairy, Marcey Bros.Inc., Clarendon, Va., Embossed In Circle, Pt. .. 11.00
Associated Bottle Supply Co., 2 Neck Rings, Embossed, Pt. 12.00
Athens Co-Op Creamery, War Bonds For Victory, Uncle Sam, Green, Qt. 60.00
Athens Co-Operative Creamery, Green, Round, Qt. 18.00
Azdella Dairy, East Liverpool, Oh., Green, Round, Qt. 20.00
Babcock Dairy, Brown, Round, Pt. 18.00
Baer's Dairy, Meeker, Colo., Upright Smiling Bear, Black, Qt. 38.00
Bailey's Dairy, Riverside, Calif., Slug Plate, Embossed, Qt. 25.00
Baker Farm, Exeter, N.H., Square, Cream Top, Qt. 15.00
Baldwin Dairy Farms, Pasteurized Homogenized Milk, White, Square, Qt. 15.00
Bangor Dairy, Bangor, Mich., For Mothers Who Care, Black Label, 9 1/2 In. ....*Illus* 18.00
Barker Dairy, Ogden, Utah, In Slug Plate, Embossed, Round, Qt. 40.00
Bean's Dairy, Bendon, Mich., Light Liquid ....*Illus* 50.00
Beitsinger's Dairy Imperial, Pa., Green Glass, Squatty, Qt. 65.00
Belle Isle Creamery Co., Detroit, Mich., 9 1/2 In. ....*Illus* 13.00
Belle Springs, B In Bell Emblem Over Bell, Slug Plate, Embossed, Round, Qt. 12.00
Bellview Dairy, Himrod, N.Y., Amber Glass, White, Square, Qt. 10.00
Benware Creamery, Malone, N.Y., Orange, Round, Pt. 18.00

Blais Dairy, Lewiston, Maine, Baby Top, Red, Square, Qt. 65.00
Blais Dairy Farm, Lewiston, Maine, Jersey Milk, Cow's Head, Orange, Black, Qt. 38.00
Blue Ribbon Dairies, Sumter, S.C., Guard Your Health, Blue, Qt. 30.00
Borden's, Anchor Hocking Glass Co., Ruby Red Glass, c.1950, Qt. 770.00
Borden's Condensed Milk Co., Clear, Tooled Lip, Metal Lid, Wire Bail, Qt. 27.50
Borden's Condensed Milk Co., Embossed Eagle, Bail & Tin Lid, Qt. 65.00
Borden's Milk, Glass Label, Display 225.00
Boyles' Dairy, Topeka, Kansas, Quality Dairy Products, White, Square, Qt. 18.00
Broguiere's, Celebrate An American Tradition, Black, 1920, Square, Qt. 20.00
Broguiere's, Family Owned & Operated, Black, 1920, 48 Ml. 30.00
Broguiere's, God Bless America, Black, 1920, Square, Qt. 30.00
Broguiere's, Merry Christmas & A Happy New Year Rinse, Red, 1920, Square, Qt. 25.00
Broguiere's, Milk Or Nothin', Red, 1920, Square, Qt. 12.00
Broguiere's, Montebello, Calif., Baby In High Chair, Square, Qt. 12.00
Broguiere's, Salutes U.S. 1992 Summer Olympic Teams, Red, 1920, Square, Qt. 15.00
Brookfield, Babyface, 1/2 Pt. ....30.00 to 58.00
Brookfield Dairy, Double Baby Top, Red, Square, Qt. 65.00
Brookside Farm, Westminster, Mass., Cow's Head, Maroon, Square, Qt. 8.00
Brown's Dairy, Cazenovia, N.Y., Red, Round, Qt. 28.00
Burroughs Brothers, Knightsen, Calif., 2 Kids In Buggy, Red, Round, Qt. 10.00
California Dairies, Alameda, Calif., Cow Picture, Pt. 15.00
Cambridge Dairy, Black & Orange, Qt. 35.00
Cambridge Dairy, Where Quality Products Are Produced, Orange, 1892, Round, Qt.... 35.00
Capital Dairy, Chicago, Cream, 1/2 Pt. 32.00
Carnation, Fresh Milk Over Circle, Red, Square, 1/2 Pt. 30.00
Carnation, Fresh, Red, Square, 48 Ml. ....25.00 to 30.00
Carnation, In Script, Embossed, Round, Qt. ....25.00 to 30.00
Carnation, Script, Between 2 Body Belts, Round, 1/2 Pt. 20.00
Carnation Dairy, Milk Glass, Red Carnation Spray, Qt. 48.00
Carnation Fresh Milk, Amber Glass, Rectangular, White, 1/2 Gal. 15.00
Carnival Golden Guernsey Dairy Products, Algoma, Wis., Orange, 1/3 Pt. 24.00
Castle Rock Barbecue, It Is Smart To Drink Milk, Man & Woman, Green, Round, 1/3 Qt. 25.00
Cedar Grove Dairy, Memphis, Tenn., Slug Plate, Embossed, Qt. 12.00
Chase Bros. Dairy, Yellow, Amber, Rectangular, 1/2 Gal. 15.00
Chestnut Farms Chevy Chase Dairy, Washington, D.C., Safe For Babies, Round, Qt. 17.00
Chicago Sterilized Milk Co., Aqua, Blob Top, No Closure, Qt. 65.00
Citizen's Dairy, Albion, N.Y., Orange, Round, Pt. 18.00
City Dairy, Please, Keep Me Healthy, Mom, Meal, Bed, Or Any Time, 9 In. ....*Illus* 18.00
Clare, King & Queen Picture, Red, Qt. 280.00
Cloverleaf, Blue Ribbon Farms, Stockton, Calif, Red, Round, 1/3 Qt. 15.00
Cloverleaf Dairy Co., Addison, Illinois, Green, Orange, Square, Qt. 8.00
Cloverleaf Farms, Stockton, Calif., Protect Our Children, Orange, Round, Pt. 12.00

Front   *Back*

Milk, City Dairy, Please, Keep Me Healthy, Mom,
Meal, Bed, Or Any Time, 9 In.

Coleman Dairy Co., Belvidere, Ill., Grade A Dairy Products, Red, Rectangular, 1/2 Gal.   20.00
College Dairy For High Quality Dairy Products, Green, Square, Qt. 22.00
Collegian Dairy Products, Laramie, Wyo., Cream Separator, Turquoise 75.00
Columbia Dairies, Columbia, S.C., Drum Majorette, Aqua Green, Round, Qt...............   25.00
Columbia Dairies, Columbia, S.C., Green, Short, Round Qt. 18.00
Colvert's Pasteurized Milk, Amber, White, Qt. 10.00
Consumer's Co-Op Dairy, Astoria, Ore., Slug Plate, Embossed, Round, Qt. 35.00
Coray's Dairy, Fall River, Mass., Milk For Mother's Who Care, Orange, Round, Qt.....   18.00
Cosgrove, Tin Top, Registered, Pt. 45.00
Creamer, All-Star Dairies, Red, 2 In..   11.00
Creamer, Borden's, Red, 1/2 Oz...   15.00
Creamer, Brookside Creamery, Manville, N.J., Red, 2 In..   23.00
Creamer, Colvert's Pasteurized Dairy Products, Red, Round, 1/2 Oz. 20.00
Creamer, Country Club Dairy, Brown, 2 In. 26.00
Creamer, Creamland Albuquerque, Green, Round, 1/2 Oz. 20.00
Creamer, Dairy Products, Brand, Red...   20.00
Creamer, Dolly Madison Dairies, Orange, 2 In. 11.00
Creamer, Forner-Lakeside Dairies, Red, 2 In. 13.00
Creamer, Gerber's Central, Red, Round, 1/2 Oz...   20.00
Creamer, Golden Royal, Red, Round, 1/2 Oz...   20.00
Creamer, Jersey Farms, Red, 1 3/4 In. 18.00
Creamer, Maple Shade, Orange, 2 In..   29.00
Creamer, Mell-O, Red, Round, 1/2 Oz..   20.00
Creamer, Potomac Valley, White China, Cobalt Blue, 1830, 3 3/4 In. 77.00
Creamer, Quality Dairy, None Better, Red, Round, 1/2 Oz. 12.00
Creamer, Rosebud Creamery, Sideways, Maroon...   20.00
Creamer, Sangamon Dairy, Red 15.00
Creamer, Sanitary Farm Dairies, Red, Round, 1/2 Oz...   20.00
Creamer, Sealtest, In Script, Orange, Round, 1/2 Oz..   20.00
Creamer, Shamrock Dairy, Green, Round, 1/2 Oz..   18.00
Creamer, Suncrest Farms & Mowrer's, Inc., Red, 2 In...   27.00
Creamer, Tastemark Cream, Red, 1/2 Oz. 20.00
Creamer, Valley Farm Dairy Products, Orange, 1/2 Oz..   20.00
Creamer, Walnut Dairy Farm, Orange, 2 In..   25.00
Cresent Milk, Reno, Nev., 1/2 Pt...   12.00
Crown Dairy, Picanniny Picture, Red & Black, Qt..   438.00
Curles Neck Dairy, Cop The Cream, Embossed, Square, Qt. 40.00
Dacry Protected W.B. Brown & Sons Inc., 2-Sided Babyface, Yellow, Orange, Qt. ...   75.00
Dairlee Milk, Double Baby Top, Red, Square, Qt. 65.00
Dairy Products Co., Morristown, Tenn., Loving Cup, Red, Square, Qt. 7.00
Dairyland Creamery, Coos Bay, Ore., Embossed, 1/2 Pt..   26.00
Dairyland Pasteurized Milk, Sioux Falls, S.D., Orange, Round, Qt. 35.00
Dairylea, Owl & Figures, 1/2 Pt...   12.00
Damascus Fresh Dairy Products, Amber, Square, Pt...   80.00
Darigold, Quality Homogenized Milk, Portland, Ore., Amber, Square, Qt. 12.00
Diamond Creamery Co., Sioux Falls, Embossed, Qt..   58.00
Diamond Dairy, W. Bridgewater, Mass., Red, Cream Top, Qt..   15.00
Dickert Dairy, Helena, Montana, Child Crawling To Bottle, Red, Qt. 5.00
Dodds Lakeview Farm, North Hero, Vt., Orange, Cow, Round, Qt. 55.00
Douglaston Manor Farm, Pulaski, N.Y., Black, Round, Qt. 10.00
Drew's Dairy Inc., Pasteurized Milk & Cream, Modern Dairy Bldg. Scene, Orange, Qt.   18.00
Dublin Co-Op, Buy War Bonds, 5 Cents Deposit, Red, Qt...   35.00
Dublin Co-Op Dairies, Pasteurized Milk & Cream, 5 Cents, Red, Round, Pt. 45.00
Dupont, Repaund Farms, Gibbstown, N.J., 1/2 Pt...   30.00
E.H. Vela, Tuolumne, Calif., Pt...   65.00
E.R. Warner Dairy, Store Bottle Neck Deposit, Brown, Round, Qt. 18.00
E.X. Mayer, Golden Amber, Machined Mouth, Cylindrical, 1810-1830, Qt. 44.00
Early Dawn Co-Op Dairy, Waynesboro, Va., Red, Square, Qt..   6.00
East Providence Dairy, Cream Top, Red, Square, Qt. 30.00
Ebling's Golden Jersey, Red, Round, Qt. 12.00
Eden Dairy, Pueblo, Colorado, In Slug Plate, Embossed, Round, Qt. 50.00
Edward Schlaepfer, Leadville, Colorado, Qt. 100.00
Elgin Dairy, Butte, Mont., Square, Qt..   18.00

Milk, Empire State Dairy Co., Brooklyn, Strictly Pure Milk, 1900-1920, 9 In.

Milk, Ferndale Dairy, First In Quality, Grand Ledge, Mich., Amber, 8 1/2 In.

Milk, Fleming's Guernsey, Pasteurized Milk, Nature Gives It, Evart, Mich., 10 In.

Elmog Dairy, Coatsville, Pa., It Whips On Cream Top, Qt.	35.00
Embassy Dairy, Washington, D.C., Babyface, Qt.	65.00
Empire Dairy, Oelwein, Iowa, Pasteurized Milk & Cream, Drink More Milk, Qt.	48.00
Empire State Dairy Co., Brooklyn, Strictly Pure Milk, 1900-1920, 9 In. ....*Illus*	66.00
Enid Cooperative Creamery Assn., Enid, Ok., Farm, Milkman, Orange, Dacro Top, Qt.	30.00
Equity Top Of Ohio, Remember They Need The Best, Round, Gal.	70.00
Eureka Dairy, Amethyst, Embossed, Slug Plate, Pt.	20.00
Eureka Dairy, Keystone Weber, Amethyst, Embossed, Churn Shape, Slug Plate, Pt.	20.00
F. Buzzelli & Sons, Niagara Falls, N.Y., Babyface, Pink, ABM, Qt.	60.00
Farmer's Dairy, Howell And Demarest, 14 And 16 Jefferson Market, Tin Lid, 1/2 Pt.	24.00
Farmer's Dairy Association, Fresh Homogenized Milk, Amber, White, Square, Qt.	15.00
Farmer's Delight Dairy, Leechburg, Pa., It's Pasteurized, Orange, Round, Qt.	20.00
Farmers Cooperative Dairy, Greenville, Ohio.	10.00
Farmers Creamery, Livingston, Montana, Embossed, 1/2 Pt.	38.00
Farmers Dairy Co., Inc., Baby's Picture, Black, Pt.	17.00
Federal Dairy, Dish Of Ice Cream, Amber, Square, Qt.	18.00
Federal Dairy, Ice Cream Quality, Amber, White, Square, Qt.	18.00
Ferndale Dairy, First In Quality, Grand Ledge, Mich., Amber, 8 1/2 In. ....*Illus*	15.00
Fleming's Guernsey, Pasteurized Milk, Nature Gives It, Evart, Mich., 10 In. ....*Illus*	25.00
Forest Lake Dairy Co., Palmer, Mass, Orange, Square, Qt.	6.00
Forgey's, Logansport, Ind., Orange, Creamed Cottage Cheese Daily, Round, 12 Oz.	30.00
Forgey's Dairy, Logansport, Ind., Orange, Square, 1/2 Gal.	22.50
Four Mile Dairy, Canon City, Colorado, Pasteurized Products, Round, Qt.	35.00
Fraleigh Farm, Millbrook, N.Y., Maroon, Round, Qt.	18.00
Framer's Dairy, Howell & Demarest, Tin Stopper, 1/2 Pt.	95.00
Frasure & Brown Dairy, Logan, Ohio, Woman At Gate, Red, Square, Qt.	8.00
Frasure-Brown, Logan, Oh., Embossed, 1/2 Pt.	24.00
Fredericks Farm Dairy, Conyngham, Pa., Round, Pt.	15.00
Fredericktown Ice & Dairy Co., Slug Plate, Embossed, Qt.	15.00
Fredericktown Ice & Dairy Co., Wash & Return, In Slug Plate, Embossed, Round, Qt.	15.00
Fredricks Farm Dairy, Conyngham, Pa., Ayshire Cow, Brown, Round, Qt.	32.00
Fresh Milk From Atzingen Gannon Whitehouse, Jersey City, Cream Top, Round, Qt.	25.00
Frye's Dairy, Double Baby Top, Square, Qt.	75.00
G.A. Perret's Dairy, Dinsmore, Fla., Fresh Jersey Milk, Maroon, Round, Qt.	14.00
Gagnon's Huron, S.D., Invest In Victory, Planes, War Bonds, Red, Blue, Qt.	75.00
Garner Dairy Co., Protects Damage From Light, Amber, White, Square, Qt.	12.00
Garst Bros. Dairy Inc, Oval, Cream Separator, Turquoise	65.00
Gascoyne Dairy, Cream Separator, Red, Qt.	80.00

Genessee Valley Dairy, Mt. Morris, N.Y., Blue, Round, Qt.	12.00
Glendale Dairy, Decatur, Alabama, Orange, Round, Pt.	32.00
Gold Medal, Award Ribbon, Crown City Dairy Co., 1/3 Qt.	20.00
Gold Medal, Crown City Dairy Co., Embossed, Round, 1/3 Qt.	20.00
Gold Spot Dairy Products, Stillwater, Okla., Orange, Rectangular, 1/2 Gal.	75.00
Gold Spot Homogenized & Pasteurized Milk, Orange, Pt.	10.00
Golden Arrow, Finest Quality, Amber, Yellow, Square, Qt.	12.00
Golden State Dairy, Blake-Hart, California, Qt.	30.00
Golden State Dalry, California, Red, 1/2 Pt.	30.00
Grandy, Guardian Of Health, Tanks Picture, Red, 1/2 Pt.	180.00
Gray's Harbor Dairy Products, ISP, 1/2 Pt.	7.00
Greenleaf Dairy, Petersburg, Va., Cop The Cream, Green, Square, Qt.	65.00
Gridley Dairy Co., Amethyst, Pt.	17.50
H.B. Day, Aqua, Cylindrical, 1880-1910, 10 1/4 In.	55.00
Hagerstown Dairy Company, In Shield-Like Design, Round, 1/2 Pt.	8.00
Haleakala Dairy, Makawao, 1 Embossed Ring, 1/2 Pt.	12.00
Haleakala Dairy, Orange & Gray, Orange, 1963, 1/2 Pt.	8.00
Haleakala Dairy, Square, 1958, Qt.	20.00
Hancock Dairy, Port Crane, N.Y., Black, Square, Qt.	7.00
Helfand Dairy Products, Dartmouth, Mass., This Milk Is Safe, Pure, Red, Round, Qt.	18.00
Highfield Dairy, Sharon, Conn., Guernsey Milk, Green, Square, Qt.	8.00
Highland Hill Dairy, Calif., In Slug Plate, Embossed, Round, Pt.	20.00
Highland Pacific Dairy, Mt. Vernon, Wash., Green, Round, Qt.	35.00
Hillcrest Dairy, Pennington, N.J., Green, Glazed, Qt.	38.00
Hillside Dairy, Pueblo Health Dept., Trophy, Cow, Milkman, Brown, Nearly Mint, Qt.	28.00
Hilo Dairymen's Center, Round, Pt.	35.00
Hilton Dairy, Madison, Maine, Our Pasteurized Milk Solves The Problem, Maroon, Qt.	18.00
Hirschman's Dairy, Florence, N.J., Red, Round Pt.	15.00
Horne's Dairy, Skowhegan, Maine, Yellow, Round, Pt.	20.00
Hosfler's Dairy, Buffalo, N.Y., Orange, Square, Qt.	7.00
Hover, Pelican, Red, Qt.	100.00
Hunts Dairy, Skowhegan, Me., Drink More Milk For Health, Orange, 1/2 Pt.	26.00
Inderkum's Dairy, Sacramento, Cow's Head, Red, C.T., Qt.	25.00
J.H. Rich Dairy, Banner Over Neck, Embossed, Pt.	13.00
Jersey Farms, Yuma, Ariz., Amber, Square, Qt.	25.00
Jersey Milk, Cream & Butter Co., Oakland, Cal., Ribbed Neck, Embossed, Pt.	28.00
Keating Dairy, Yankton, S.D., Fancy Shield, Boy Drinking Milk, Red, Round, Qt.	75.00
Keystone Dairy Co., 1/2 Pt.	7.00
Klondike Farm, Elkin, N.C., Golden Guernsey, Green, Round, Qt.	25.00
Knowles Jersey Dairy, Gunnison, Colo.	85.00
Korters Pasteurized Milk, Moscow, Idaho, Squat, Square, Yellow, 1/2 Pt.	28.00
L.H. Todd Roswell Dairy, New Mexico, Light Purple, Pt.	45.00
Lackawanna Dairy Co. Inc., Lackawanna, N.Y., Embossed, 1/2 Pt.	24.00
Leafy Lane Dairy, Princeton, Ill., Amber, Qt.	18.00
Linger Light Dairy, New Castle, Pa., A Home Owned Company, Red, 1/2 Pt.	24.00
Live Oak Riviera Farms, Santa Barbara, Eagle, Red, 1/2 Pt.	30.00
Logan's Morning Star Dairy, Red, Yellow, Square, Qt.	8.00
Lost River Milk, Black, Twin Lightning Bolts, 8 1/2 In., Pt.	9.00
Lotus Lawn Dairy, Oshkosh On Ft. Shoulder, Orange, Round, Qt.	12.00
Lowell Creamery, Lowell, Mich., His Gift To Mankind, Louis Pasteur, 9 In. .... *Illus*	50.00
Lucerne, Homogenized Vitamin D Milk, Red Plastic Handle, Square, Gal.	30.00
Ludwig Lane Dairy Co., Toledo, Ohio, Best For You & Baby Too, Brown, Round, Qt.	25.00
Mackenzie Guernsey, Keen, N.H., Acre Wide Farm, Cows Head, Orange, Qt.	26.00
Magnolia, Script, Slug Plate, Round, 1/2 Pt.	7.00
Manor Croft Dairies Ltd.	45.00
Maple Dairies, Tyrone, Pa., Cream Top Says It Whips, Embossed, Qt.	35.00
Maple Grove Dairy, Ludington, Mich., Green, Short, Round Qt.	18.00
Marble Farms Dairy, Yellow & Blue Lettering, Square, Embossed	15.00
Marble Farms Dairy, Yellow Lettering, Square, 1/2 Gal.	15.00
Marigold Dairy Products, Red & Blue, Square, Qt.	22.00
Marland Dairy, Andover, Mass., Orange, Tall Round, Qt.	18.00
Marshall's Dairy, Victoria, Va., Orange, Round, Qt.	25.00
Mayflower, Farm Scene, Red, Squatty, Qt.	60.00

Milk, Lowell Creamery,
Lowell, Mich.,
His Gift To Mankind,
Louis Pasteur, 9 In.

Front   Back

Mayflower, For Purity, Woman's Head, Red, Square, 1/2 Pt.	12.00
Mayflower Milk, Fresh From The Farms, Red, Squatty, 48 Ml.	60.00
McCarty Dairy, Fillmore, N.Y., Buy Locally, Profit Locally, Deposit, Black, Qt.	18.00
McClain Dairy Farm, Gadsden, Al., Embossed, Qt.	20.00
McMurtrie Dairy, Bishop, Cal., Red, 7 1/8 In.	49.50
Meadow Dairies, Leakville, N.C., Qt.	5.00
Meadow Gold, Cream Top, Qt.	25.00
Meadow Gold, Himes Bros.Dairy Co., Dayton, Amber, Square, Qt.	18.00
Meadow Gold, Square, 1/2 Gal.	12.00
Medo-Land, It's A Real Treat, Maroon, Round, 48 Ml.	15.00
Medo-Land, Maroon, 1/2 Pt.	15.00
Metzger's, Baby's Head, Embossed, Pt.	60.00
Michigan State College Creamery, E. Lansing, Mi., Green, Cap, Round, Qt.	60.00
Michigan State Dairy Dept., Beaumont Tower Picture, Green, Square, Qt.	35.00
Mid Valley Farm, Boy & Girl, Milk Green, Square, 1/2 Pt.	6.00
Midland Creamery Co., Colorado Springs, Colorado, Short, Round Qt.	32.00
Midwest, Plymouth, Wisconsin, Brown, Round, Qt.	25.00
Mill Stream Dairy, Black, Round, Qt.	25.00
Miller Dairy, Miller's Pasteurized, This Is Where You Come In, Red, Round, Qt.	55.00
Miller's Dairy, Culver, Ind., Embossed, SP, Round, Pt.	30.00
Mission Creameries, Inc., Red, Qt.	10.00
Mission Milk Creameries Inc., Orange, Round, Qt.	11.00
Mission Milk Creameries Inc., Red, Round, Qt.	10.00
Mission Milk Creameries Inc., Tower & Building, 1/2 Pt.	18.00
Model Dairy, Bowling Green, Oh., Cream Separator, Red, Qt.	80.00
Model Dairy, Galveston, Tx., Keep His America, Soldier, Orange, Dacro, Qt.	25.00
Monterey Bay Milk Distributors Inc., 1/4 Pt.	20.00
Morningside Farm, Stockton, Calif., Dairy Farm Scene, Orange, Qt.	28.00
Morningside Farms, Stockton, Calif, Orange, Round, Qt.	10.00
Mountain Dairies, M. Burgmann Inc., Amethyst, Slug Plate, Embossed, Round, Qt.	24.00
Mountain Meadow Dairy, Bisbee, Arizona, Yellow, Black, Qt.	68.00
Mountain View, Just Honest Milk, Square, Orange, Round, 1/2 Pt.	10.00
Mt. Diablo Dairy, Danville, Calif., Clear, 1 Qt.	55.00
Mt. Union, Pa., Keep 'em Flying, Red Pilot, Slogans, Hobnail Neck, 9 1/2 In.	85.00
Mt. Williams Dairy, Williamstown, Mass., Orange, Square, Qt.	7.00
Mt. Williams Dairy, Williamstown, Mass., Yellow, Square, Qt.	6.00
National Dairy, Property Of Honolulu, Red Block Letters	85.00
Newport Dairy, Newport, Ky., Neck Hobnails, Embossed, Qt.	15.00
Niday's Dairy, Molalla, Ore., Cow's Head, Blue, Square, Plastic Handle, Gal.	30.00
Norris Creamery Inc., Phone 330, Harriman, Tennessee, Embossed, Qt.	58.00
North Yarmouth Dairy Inc., Round, 1/3 Pt.	24.00
Northside Dairy, Aurora, Ind., Qt.	20.00
Northside Dairy, Boy & Girl Faces, Red & Black, Round, Pt.	13.50
Norway Creamery Inc., Norway, Maine, Pasteurized For Better Health, Orange, Qt.	18.00

Oakleigh Farms Quality Products, Red, Tall Round, Pt. 18.00
Oatman's Dairy, Cream, Dark Brown, Cardboard Cover, Pt. 28.00
Page's Dairy, Rome, N.Y., Red, Square, Qt. 7.00
Palmerton Sanitary Dairy, Palmerton, Pa., Red, Cream Top, Qt. 15.00
Paramount Dairy, Ogden, Salt Lake City, Red, Qt. 38.50
Paterson Dairy, Clifton, Arizona, Orange, Qt. 75.00
Penn Acres Dairy, Ainsworth, Nebraska, Baby Drinking Nursing Bottle, Red, Qt. 78.00
Peplau's Dairy, New Britian, Ct., Orange, Tall Round, Pt. 15.00
Phelp's Dairy, Waycross, Ga., We Appreciate Your Patronage, Orange, Qt. 25.00
Pine State Dairy, Bangor, Me., Pine Trees, Babyface, Square, Qt. 80.00
Plain, Early Bottle, Amethyst, Embossed, Round, Qt. 9.00
Poinsettia Dairy Products, Orange, Tall Round, Qt. 18.00
Polks Best, Indianapolis, Cream Top, Round, Qt. 40.00
Poplar Hill Dairy, Hobbs, Pa., Frederick, Md., Child & Adult Drinking Milk, Red, Qt. 48.00
Port Colbourne, Tank, Boy & Go-Cart Picture, Both Need Fuel, Red, Pt. 240.00
Portland Damascus Milk Co., Slug Plate, Embossed, Round, Ribbon Overlay, Pt. 12.00
Price's Farm Dairy, Hazelton, Pa., Qt. 24.00
Producer's Pasteurized Milk, Greenville, Texas, Red, Qt. 75.00
Property Of Lawnfield Farm, Henniker, N.H., Powell & Lockwood, Tin Top, 1890s... 140.00
Pure Milk Dairy, In Slug Plate, Embossed, Round, Qt. 15.00
Quality Dairy Co., Connellsville, Pa., Orange, 1/2 Pt. 6.00
Ray Riderdy, Cohoes, N.Y., Pt. 8.00
Realicious Cooperative Dairies, Soldier & Sailor, Green, Pt. 35.00
Red River Lumber Co., Westwood, Calif., Sided, Qt. 80.00
Red Rock, Slug Plate, Embossed, Round, Qt, ... 25.00
Reehl's Dairy, Multi-Vitamin Mineral, Amber, Square, Qt. 10.00
Renovo Milk Co., Renovo, Pa., 1/2 Pt. 25.00
Return To H.B. Day, Grass Green, Cylindrical, 10 1/4 In. 198.00
Reuger's Premium Milk Dairy, Evergreen Park, Ill., Qt. 18.00
Richmond Dairy, Cream Separator, Qt. ....*Illus* 80.00
Richmond Dairy Co., Embossed Circle, 1/4 Pt. 27.50
Ridgecroft Farms, Spencerport, N.Y., Red, Square, Qt. 8.00
River Edge Dairy, Somerville, N.J., Cow Head, Red, Round, Qt. 30.00
Riverdale Farms, West Lebanon, N.Y., Garrignes Jr., Cow Face, Brown, Round, Qt.... 15.00
Riverview Dairy, Wash & Return, Slug Plate, Embossed, Round, Pt. 15.00
Roanoke Milk & Ice Cream Co., Roanoke, Va., Baby, Black, Round, Qt. 35.00
Roberos Dairy, Serving Savannah Since 1920, Orange, Square, Qt. 8.00
Robinson & Woolworth, Whiteman, New York, Pat. April 3, 1889, 8 1/2 In.........*Illus* 99.00
Roof Garden, Fish Co., Tucson, Ariz., War Slogan, White, Round, 1/4 Pt. 45.00
Royal Crest Inc., Denver, Colorado, Black, Square, 48 Ml. 18.00
Ruff's Dairy, St. Clair, Mich., Building My Future Safety When I Play, 9 In.........*Illus* 15.00
Ruff's Dairy, St. Clair, Michigan, Orange, Square, Qt. 7.00
Saco Dairy, Maine, Babyface Neck, 52 Seal, Qt. 99.00
Sacramento 5 Cents Store Bottle, Ribs, Embossed, Round, Pt. 20.00
San A Pure Co., Findlay, Oh., Cream Separator, Red, Qt. 80.00
San Bernardino Creamery, 1/4 Pt. 30.00
San Bernardino Creamery, Crown Top, Embossed, Slug Plate, Pt. 10.00
San Bernardino Creamery, In Slug Plate, Embossed, Round, Qt. 30.00
Sanitary Dairies Co., Uniontown, Pa., Everyone Cheers, Orange, Round, Qt. 18.00
Sanitary Milk Co., Canton, Oh., Embossed On Shoulders, Square, 1/2 Gal. 20.00
Sardis Creamery, Sardis, Miss., Grade A Pasteurized, Embossed, Qt. 35.00
Scholl's Cafeterias Grill & Farm, Red, Round, 1/2 Pt. 18.00
Scott Powell Dairies, Philadelphia, 1/2 Pt. 7.00
Seeman's Pasteurized Milk, Loyal, Wis., We Are Bringing You Health, Orange, Qt. 18.00
Seneca Guernsey Farms, Geneva, N.Y., Blue, 5 Cent Deposit, Qt. 25.00
Seward Dairy, Seward, Ala., Slug Plate, Cap, Qt. 125.00
Sgr., Weldonian, Wellsville, N.Y., Red, Qt. 12.00
Shanklin Dairies, Blue, Square, Qt. 7.00
Shellback Ranch, Cheyenne, Wy., Barn & Cows, Orange & Black, Round, 1/2 Pt. 12.00
Shrum's Dairy, Jeannette, Pa., Cream Separator, Turquoise Green 55.00
Shy-Der's 100% Pure Undiluted Health Juices, 5 Cents, Green, Round, Qt. 15.00
Simon's Dairy, Vernon Center, N.Y., Tree, Cow Barn Scene, Orange, Qt. 15.00
Smith Bros. Dairy, Amber, Yellow, Square, Qt. 15.00

Smith's Haleakala Dairy, 4-Ring, Embossed, Pt. 200.00
Snider Dairy & Produce Co., In Slug Plate, Embossed, Round, Qt............................. 12.00
Snider Dairy & Produce Co., Slug Plate, 1/2 Pt. 25.00
Somerset Farms Dairy, Middlebush, N.J., Amber, Square, Qt. 12.00
Southwest Dairy Products Co., Embossed, Round, Pt... 60.00
Sparkle Blue Boy Dairy, Rochester, N.Y., Blue Lettering, Square, Qt. 15.00
Spokane Bottle Exchange Inc., Blue, Round, Qt... 15.00
St. Mary's Dairy, George M. Erich, St. Mary's, Pa., Maroon, Qt. 18.00
Stalker's Dairy, Ravenna, N.Y., Maroon, Square Qt... 6.00
State Creamery, Elkhart, Ind., Label, Contents, 1/2 Pt. 45.00
Stokely's Dairy, Newport, Tenn., Red Shield, Qt. 48.00
Stoney Brook Farm, West Newton, Pa., Growing Children With Milk, Red, Qt. 22.00
Sunland Dairy, Yuma, Ariz., Amber, White, Square, Qt. 25.00
Sunnydale Dairy, Union City, Ind., Better Dairy Products, Qt. 38.00
Sunnymede Farm, Bismarck, Mo., Missouri Pacific Lines, Red, Squatty, 1/2 Pt. 28.00
Sunrise Dairy, Red, Squatty, Qt. 30.00
Sunrise Farm Dairy, Baltic, Ct., Orange Sunrise, Square, 1/2 Pt. 7.00
Sunset Creamery, Roswell, N.M., Setting Sun, Glazed, Orange, Qt............................ 42.00
Sunset Dairy, Tucson, Arizona, Amber, White, Square, Qt... 25.00
Sunshine Dairy, Florida, Cream Top, Qt. 32.00
Sunshine Farms, Lafayette, Ind., Try Our Cottage Cheese, Red, Glaze, Qt................. 32.00
Superior Milk, Pueblo, Colo., Green, Qt. 30.00
Superior Quality Dairy Farms, Machined Mouth, Cardboard Cap, 1900-1930, Qt. 66.00
Supreme Dairy, Peru, Ill., Baby In Crib With Baby's Choice, Blue, Qt. 24.00
Supreme Ice Cream, Alliance, Oh., Taste Tells With Ice Cream, Maroon, Qt. 25.00
Sutter's Dairy, Bethlehem, Pa., Slug Plate, Babyface, Qt. 85.00
Sweet Clover Dairy, De Pere, Wis., Clover Ground, Child, Orange, 1/2 Pt.................... 28.00
T & M Dairy, Hanover, N.H., Qt. 55.00

Milk, Richmond Dairy, Cream Separator, Qt.

Milk, Robinson & Whiteman, New York, Pat. April 3, 8 1/2 In.

Milk, Ruff's Dairy, St. Clair, Mich., Building My Future Safety When I Play, 9 In.

Milk, Twin Pines, An Employee Independent Cooperative

Taylor's Dairy, Amber, Square, 1/2 Pt.	35.00
Terrace Farm Dairy Co., Slug Plate, Embossed, Qt.	18.00
Terry Dairy Co., Little Rock, Ark., Pasteurized Milk & Cream, Embossed, Qt.	35.00
Thatcher's Dairy, Embossed Man Milking Cow, 1884, Qt.	250.00
Tidey's Home Dairy, Eau Claire, Mich., Safe Milk Bottled On Our Farm, Red, Qt.	18.00
Tin Top & Handle, Pat. 1898, Pt.	150.00
Titusville Dairy Co., Titusville, Pa., Drakes Oil Derrick, Red, Square, 1/2 Pt.	10.00
Titusville Dairy Products Co., Titusville, Pa., Red & Black, Qt.	50.00
Tomek & Sons Dairy, Trumbull, Conn., Embossed, Round, Pt.	24.00
Tri-State Milk Bottle Supply Co., Ashland, Ky., Embossed, Qt.	30.00
Triangle Dairy, Fulton, N.Y., Maroon, Yellow, Square, Qt.	8.00
Tro Fe Dairy, Gadsen, Al., Trophy Front, Crystal Ball, Round, Qt.	40.00
Twin Lakes Dairy, Monticello, Ind., Brown, Cows Head, Square, Qt.	15.00
Twin Pines, An Employee Independent Cooperative *Illus*	13.00
Twin-Cities Milk Corp., Johnstown, N.Y., Embossed, Round, Qt.	7.00
Union Milk Co., Ltd., Calgary, Round, Qt.	15.00
Universal Store Bottle, 5 Cents, Embossed, Round, Qt.	15.00
Universal Store Bottle, Ribbed, 5 Cents, Embossed, Round, 1/2 Pt.	9.00
Vale Edge Dairy, A Bottle Of Health, Brown, Round, Qt.	35.00
Valley Gold, Albuquerque, N.M., Orange In Blue Shield, Square, Qt.	12.00
Valley Rogue Farm, Grants Pass, Ore., Golden Guernsey Logo, Orange, Qt.	40.00
Victoria Guernsey, Over Calif. Poppy, San Bernardino, Calif, Orange, Squatty, Qt.	45.00
Waihee Dairy, Square, 1956, Pt.	25.00
Waihee Dairy, Square, 1964, Qt.	20.00
Walnut Crest Farm, Westbrook, Maine, Guernsey Milk From Our Herd, Red, Qt.	32.00
Wanzer's Kazol, Amber, ABM, Qt.	77.00
Wanzer's On Milk Is Like Sterling On Silver, Gal.	22.00
Wauregan Dairy Farm, Wauregan, Conn., Red, Square, Cream Top, Qt.	17.00
Wayne County Hospital Diet Kitchen, Black, Round, 1/2 Pt.	50.00
Weeks Creamery Inc., Store Bottle, Black, Orange, Round, Qt.	28.00
West End Dairy, C.C. Rebert, Hanover, Pa., Embossed, Pt.	20.00
Westview Dairy, Salisbury, N.C., Black, Round, Qt.	30.00
Wheeler & Taylor, Pasteurized Milk, Keene, N.H., Orange, Squatty, Qt.	15.00
White Spring's Farm, Geneva, N.Y., Cream Separator, Turquoise	55.00
White's Farm Dairy, Quality Products, Babyface, Red, Yellow, Square, Qt.	80.00
Whiteholm Jersey Farm, Black, Tall Round, Qt.	18.00
Willow Farm Products, LaGrange, Ill., Qt.	28.00
Willow Farms Dairy, Westminister, Md., Warner, Embossed, Qt.	35.00
Willowdale Dairy, Keyser, W.Va., E.A. Warnick, ISP, Embossed, Qt.	58.00
Wilson Dairy Co., Amber, Qt.	325.00
Winnisimet Dairy, Tiverton, R.I., Indian Brave, Brown & Red, Round, Pt.	48.00
Wm. E. Hemming, Whiteboro, N.Y., Tin Top, Pt.	45.00
Wm. Green Jr., Schenectaday, N.Y., 1/2 Gal.	25.00
Wm. Weckerle & Sons, Emblem, Amber, Qt.	60.00
Wm. Weckerle & Sons, W. 806 Jefferson St., Amber, ABM, Qt.	75.00
Wood County Dairymen, Parkersburg, W.Va., Safety Ring, Pt.	24.00
Woodland, Clare, Mi., Green & Red, Cap, Round, Pt.	13.50
Woodson Dairy, Red Hill, Pa., Orange, Square, Pt.	7.00
Yoder Dairy, Amber, Logo, Enameled, Square, ABM, Qt.	5.50
York Dairy Co., Inc., Brooklyn, N.Y.Deposit, Round, Pt.	12.00
Zehner's Dairy, Farmer To Consumer, Red, Round, Qt.	18.00
Zenda Farms, Golden Guernsey, Clayton, N.Y., Orange, Tall Round, Pt.	12.00

———————————————— **MILK GLASS** ————————————————

It makes perfect sense to think that white milk-colored glass is known as *milk glass* to collectors. But not all milk glass is white, nor is all white glass milk glass, so the name may cause a little confusion.

The first true milk glass was produced in England in the 1700s. It is a semi-opaque glass, often with slight blue tones. The glass reached the height of its popularity in the United States about 1870. Many dishes and bottles were made. Both new versions of old styles and new styles have been made continuously since that time, many by the Westmoreland and the Kemple glass companies. These pieces, many very recent, often appear at antiques sales.

Figural bottles of milk glass were used by Westmoreland to hold their food products, especially mustard. Today it is considered correct to talk about blue milk glass or black milk glass. This is glass made by the same formula but with a color added. It is not correct to call a glass that is white only on the surface *milk glass*. Bottles made of milk glass may also be found in this book in the Cologne, Cosmetic, and Figural categories.

MILK GLASS, Alba Lotio, Triangular, 8 1/2 In.	36.00
Apothecary, R.S. Reed's Sons, Atlantic City, N.J., Dragon, Stopper, Oval	89.00
Aqua De Colognia La Carmella, Square, 7 1/2 In.	58.00
Champlin's Liquid Pearl, Rectangular, 5 In.	24.00
Cut Oval Design Each Side, Square Lip, 7 3/4 In.	30.00
De Colonia, Embossed, Square, Aqua, 7 1/2 In.	16.00
Embossed Flowers & Vines, 4-Piece Mold, Oval, Bulbous Neck, 8 In.	65.00
G.W. Laird Perfumer, N.Y.	17.00
Hogan's Magnolia Balm, Part Label, Rectangular, 5 In.	24.00
Libby, McNeil & Libby, Chicago, Maggi Shape, Square, 4 1/2 In.	30.00
Murine Eye Remedy, Rectangular, Tooled Top, 4 In.	8.00
Prof. Hubert's Malvinian Lotion, Toledo, Ohio	25.00
Rolling Pin, Blown, English Flags & A Friends Gift, Pontil, 1870-1890, 14 In.	100.00
Sanitol For The Teeth	15.00
Silkodono For The Hair & Scalp	15.00
Velvetina Skin Beautifier, Goodrich Drug, Omaha, USA	17.00

MINERAL WATER

Although today it is obvious which is soda water and which is mineral water, the difference was not as clear in the nineteenth and early-twentieth centuries. Mineral water bottles held the fresh natural spring waters favored for health or taste. Even though some had a distinct sulfur or iron taste, the therapeutic values made them seem delicious. Some mineral waters had no carbonation, but many were naturally carbonated. Soda water today is made with artificial carbonation and usually has added flavor.

Mineral water was mentioned by the ancient Greeks, and the Romans wrote about visiting the famous springs of Europe. Mineral springs were often the center of resorts in nineteenth-century America, when it was fashionable to "take the waters." Often the water from the famous springs was bottled to be sold to visitors. Most of the mineral water bottles collected today date from the 1850–1900 period. Many of these bottles have embossed lettering and blob tops. The standard shape was cylindrical with thick walls to withstand the pressure of carbonation. Most were made in a snap case mold although a few can be found with open or iron pontils. Common colors are clear, pale aqua, and light green. More unusual are dark green, black, and amber bottles, while cobalt blue ones are rare. The bottles were sealed with a cork. A few places, like Poland Springs and Ballston Spa, made figural bottles. Related bottles may be found in the Seltzer and Soda categories.

MINERAL WATER, A. Monroe & Co., Eureka H.B., Calif., Gravitating Stopper, 7 In.	330.00
A.W. Cudworth & Co., San Francisco, Aqua	25.00
A.W. Rapp, N.Y., Philadelphia, Sapphire Blue, Applied Mouth, IP, Pt.	154.00
Adirondack Spring, Westport, N.Y., Emerald Green	385.00
Adirondack Spring, Westport, N.Y., Emerald Green, Qt.	88.00 to 303.00
Adirondack Spring, Whitehall, N.Y., Emerald Green, Bubbles, Pt.	222.00
Alburgh Springs, Vt., Yellow Amber, Qt.	523.00
Artesian Spring, Ballston, N.Y., Olive Emerald Green, 1870, Pt.	105.00
Artesian Spring, Sweet Springs Co., Amber, Pt.	120.00
Artesian Spring Co., Ballston Spa, Yellow Green, Pt.	118.00
Artesian Spring Co., Ballston, N.Y., Medium Aqua, Pt.	66.00
Artesian Water, Louisville, Ky., Amber, Red Lip, 12-Sided, Whittled, Pt.	320.00
Artesian Water, Louisville, Ky., Black Amber, Pontil Mug Base, 7 3/4 In.	193.00
Artesian Water, Louisville, Ky., Orange Amber, Fluted Panel Base, IP	55.00
Artesian Water, Louisville, Ky., Root Beer Amber, 12-Sided, Red IP, Pt.	180.00 to 280.00
B & G Superior, San Francisco, Cobalt Blue, 6 3/4 In.	220.00
B & G Superior, San Francisco, Medium Emerald Green, 6 7/8 In.	303.00
B & G Superior, San Francisco, Medium Sapphire Blue, 6 7/8 In.	209.00
B.J. McGee Benicia, Deep Aqua, 7 1/2 In.	55.00

Bailey's Island Spring Water, Red Amber, Blob Top, 9 In. 400.00
Baldwin, Tuthill & Co., Medium Emerald Green, IP, 7 In. 72.00
Ballston Spa, Emerald Green, Cylindrical, Pt. ....77.00 to 88.00
Ballston Spa, Lithia, Aqua, Pt. 88.00
Ballston Spa, Lithia, Emerald Green, 1860-1880, Pt. 88.00
Ballston Spa, Yellow Green, Cylindrical, Pt. 77.00
Bedford Springs Co., Aqua, Shark Fin Inside, Qt., M-7 .... 88.00
Blount Spring Natural Sulphur Water, Cobalt Blue, 7 1/2 In. 120.00
Blue Lick Water, Kentucky, Deep Emerald Green, Blob Top, 1850s, 7 7/8 In. 2530.00
Bolen Waack & Co., Emerald Green, 1860-1880, 1/2 Pt. 110.00
Bridgeport Aerated Water Co., Light Green, Torpedo 15.00
Buffalo, Lithia, Natures Materia Medica, Aqua, Woman With Pitcher, 1/2 Gal. 33.00
C & K Eagle Works, Deep Cobalt Blue, 7 1/8 In. 99.00
C & K Eagle Works, Sac City, Calif., Medium Blue, Dug 60.00
C.B. Hale & Co., Camden, N.J., Emerald Green, IP, 6 3/4 In. 220.00
C.B. Owen & Co. Bottlers, Cincinnati, Cobalt Blue, Cylindrical, 1860, 7 1/2 In. 298.00
C.H. Haake, Deep Yellow Olive, Qt. 22.00
C.M. Henderson's Bonanza, Blue Aqua, 7 In. 88.00
C.W. Weston & Co., Saratoga, N.Y., Olive Green, Qt. 154.00
Caladonia Spring, Wheelock Vt., Honey Amber, Cylindrical, c.1870, Qt. 797.50
Caladonia Spring, Wheelock, Vt., Yellow Amber, 1865, Qt., 9 1/2 In. 660.00
Carter's Spanish Mixture, Deep Yellow Olive, OP, 8 1/8 In. 357.00
Champion Spouting Spring, Saratoga, N.Y., Aqua, Pt. 132.00
Champion Spouting Spring Co., Saratoga, N.Y., Aqua, Tooled Collar, Pt. 495.00
Champlain Spring, Medium Green, Cylindrical, Qt. 302.00
Chase & Co., San Francisco, Deep Emerald Green, 7 1/4 In. 110.00
Clarke & Co., N.Y., Deep Olive Amber, Pt. 66.00
Clarke & Co., N.Y., Medium Blue Green, IP, Pt. 210.00
Clarke & Co., N.Y., Yellow Olive, 1860-1880, Qt. 242.00
Clarke & Co., N.Y., Yellow Olive, Pt. ....44.00 to 88.00
Clarke & Co., New York, Olive Green, Smooth Base, Pt. 78.00
Clarke & White, N.Y., Dark Emerald Green, Qt.Variant, Qt. 187.00
Clarke & White, N.Y., Deep Olive Green, Qt. 187.00
Clarke & White, N.Y., Forest Green, Bubbles, 1870s, Qt. 132.00
Clarke & White, N.Y., Olive Amber, Pontil, Bubbles, Qt. 88.00
Clarke & White, N.Y., Olive Amber, Qt. 121.00
Clarke & White, N.Y., Yellow Olive, Pontil, Qt. 66.00
Clarke & White, Yellow Olive Green, Whittle, Sand Pontil, Qt. 115.00
Classen & Co., San Francisco., Calif., Aqua 25.00
Colbert Spring Water Co., Aberdeen, S.D., Aqua, Contents, ABM, Gal. 45.00
Cold Indian Spring Water Co., Aqua, Indian Picture, Tooled Top, 12 1/4 In. 110.00
Congress & Empire Spring, Deep Emerald Green, Cylindrical, Qt. 99.00
Congress & Empire Spring, Hotchkiss Sons, Emerald Green, Qt. 140.00
Congress & Empire Spring Co., Deep Olive Green, Qt. 303.00
Congress & Empire Spring Co., Emerald Green, Sloping Collar, Ring, Pt. 33.00
Congress & Empire Spring Co., Forest Green, Qt. 99.00
Congress & Empire Spring Co., Hotchkiss Sons Congress Water, Green, Pt. 128.00
Congress & Empire Spring Co., Hotchkiss' Sons, Yellow Olive, Pt. 77.00
Congress & Empire Spring Co., Olive Green, Pt. 88.00
Congress & Empire Spring Co., Olive Green, Qt. 99.00
Congress & Empire Spring Co., Olive Yellow, Cylindrical, Qt. 319.00
Congress & Empire Spring Co., Orange Amber, Bubbles, Pt. 330.00
Congress & Empire Spring Co., Saratoga, N.Y., Emerald Green, Pt., 7 5/8 In. 121.00
Congress & Empire Spring Co., Saratoga, N.Y., Emerald Green, Pt. 55.00
Congress & Empire Spring Co., Saratoga, N.Y., Emerald Green, Qt. 303.00
Congress & Empire Spring Co., Saratoga, N.Y., Green, Pt. 38.00
Congress & Empire Spring Co., Saratoga, N.Y., Medium Yellow Olive, 7 In. 93.50
Congress & Empire Spring Co., Saratoga, N.Y., Reverse Congress, Green, Pt. 35.00
Congress & Empire Spring Co., Yellow Olive, 1/2 Pt. ....88.00 to 192.50
Congress Spring Co., Saratoga, N.Y., Emerald Green, Blob Top 27.50
Copper's Well Water, Miss., Honey Amber, Double Collar, Cylindrical, 9 5/8 In. 165.00
Crone & Brigham, San Francisco, Dark Aqua, Applied Top, Large 50.00

Crump & Fox, Bernardston, Mass., Superior Mineral Water, Green, IP .... 675.00 to 750.00
Crump & Fox, Bernardston, Mass., Superior, Emerald Green, Bubbles, Whittled 750.00
Crystal Palace Premium Soda Water, Blue Green, Cylindrical, IP, 7 1/2 In. 357.00
Crystal Water Co., Pittsburgh, Pa., Porcelain Stopper, Blob Top, 14 1/2 In. 20.00
D. Tullman's Mineral Water Works, Hutchinson 35.00
D.A. Knowlton, Saratoga, N.Y., Olive Green, 1860-1880, Pt.............................. 55.00
D.A. Knowlton, Saratoga, N.Y., Olive Green, Cylindrical, Qt. ....50.00 to 132.00
Darien Mineral Springs, Darien Centre, N.Y., Aqua, 7 5/8 In.......... 385.00
Deep Rock Artesian Fresh, Los Angeles, Calif., Red, Green, 1/2 Gal. 65.00
Deep Rock Spring, Oswego, N.Y., Aqua, Qt. 302.50
Deep Rock Spring, Oswego, N.Y., Golden Amber, 1860-1880, Pt. 275.00
Deuell Brothers, Aqua, Squat 29.00
Diehl's, Pat. 1840, Medium Green, 6 1/2 In.............. 165.00
Dr. Struves, Yellow Olive, 1/2 Pt.............. 88.00
E-Piece Mold, Olive Amber, Pontil, Qt. 30.00
Ebberwein, Meineke, Savannah, Cobalt Blue, Blob Top 85.00
Empire Spring Co., Saratoga, N.Y., Emerald Green, 1880s, Qt........................ 55.00
Empire Spring Co., Saratoga, N.Y., Emerald Green, Qt. 72.00
Empire Spring Co., Saratoga, N.Y., Emerald Green, Whittled, Qt.............. 78.00
Empire Spring Co., Saratoga, N.Y., Golden Amber, Qt....... 187.00
Eureka Spring Co., Deep Aqua, Pt......... 363.00
Eureka Springs, A Pleasant Laxative Tonic And Diuretic 75.00
Evergreen, Applied Tapered Top, Graphite Pontil, 1850s, 7 1/4 In. 154.00
Evergreen, Graphite Pontil, Blob Top, 7 1/2 In. 143.00
Excelsior Spring, Saratoga, N.Y., Aqua, 1860-1880, Qt. 66.00
Excelsior Spring, Saratoga, N.Y., Emerald Green, Pt............. 120.00
Excelsior Spring, Saratoga, N.Y., Emerald Green, Qt............. 220.00
Excelsior Spring, Saratoga, N.Y., Emerald Green, Qt., 9 3/8 In. 302.00
Excelsior Spring, Saratoga, N.Y., Teal Blue, Cylindrical, Pt. 143.00
Excelsior Spring, Saratoga, N.Y., Yellow Green, Pt............. 55.00
Excelsior Spring, Saratoga, N.Y., Yellow Green, Qt. 198.00
Excelsior Springs Mo. Mineral Waters, Jug, Brown Top, Stoneware, Qt. 175.00
Fouts Springs Natural, Aqua, Tooled Lip, Blob Top, Qt. 20.00
Frank Bros., Reno, Nevada, Pale Aqua, 8 In................ 154.00
Franklin Spring, Ballston Spa, Saratoga, N.Y., 1860-1880, Yellow Green, Pt............. 550.00
Franklin Spring, Ballston Spa, Saratoga, N.Y., Emerald Green, Pt........... 625.00
Franklin Spring, Ballston Spa, Saratoga, N.Y., Yellow Green, 1860-1880, Pt............. 385.00
Frost's Magnetic Spring, Aqua, 1860-1880, Qt........... 242.00
G K W, Blue Aqua, Whitney Glass Works, Glassboro, N.J., Qt. 44.00
G. Ebberwein, Savannah, Ga., Cornflower Blue, Monogram, Blob Top 27.50
G.W. Weston & Co., Saratoga, N.Y., Dark Green, Pontil, Qt........... 165.00
G.W. Weston & Co., Saratoga, N.Y., Dark Olive Green, Qt. 88.00
G.W. Weston & Co., Saratoga, N.Y., Olive Amber, Pt.....................121.00 to 176.00
G.W. Weston & Co., Saratoga, N.Y., Olive Amber, Qt.............. 303.00
G.W. Weston & Co., Saratoga, N.Y., Olive Green, Pt......................143.00 to 176.00
G.W. Weston & Co., Saratoga, N.Y., Olive Green, Qt., 9 5/8 In. 187.00
G.W. Weston & Co., Saratoga, N.Y., Yellow Olive Green, Pt. 88.00
G.W. Weston & Co., Saratoga, N.Y., Yellow Olive Green, Qt.......... 60.50
Gettysburg Katalysine Water, Yellow Olive Green, Qt........... 143.00
Geyser Spring, Aqua, Pt. 30.00
Geyser Spring, Saratoga Springs, Aqua, Qt., 9 3/8 In. 100.00
Goldstein's IXL, Applied Top........ 125.00
Guilford Mineral Spring Water, Grass Green 65.00
Guilford Mineral Spring Water, Guilford, Vt., Deep Emerald Green, Crude, Qt. 75.00
Guilford Mineral Spring Water, Guilford, Vt., Green, Yellow, Flat 40.00
Haas Bros. Natural, Cobalt Blue, 7 1/4 In.......... 88.00
Haddock & Sons, Torpedo, Yellow Olive, 4-Piece Mold, Pontil, 6 7/8 In. 935.00
Hanbury Smith's, Bright Yellow Green, Pt................ 66.00
Hanbury Smith's, Yellow Olive, Pt........... 77.00
Hassinger & O'Brien, 17 & O'Fallon Sts., St. Louis, Aqua, Blob Top, IP 30.00
Hawthorn Springs, Saratoga, N.Y., Black Glass, Pt........... 28.00
High Rock Congress Springs, Saratoga, N.Y., Yellow Olive, Pt. 190.00
High Rock Congress Springs, Black Amber, Pt.......... 990.00

High Rock Congress Springs, Olive Amber, Pt. 75.00
High Rock Congress Springs, Rock Design, 1767, Root Beer Amber, Pt. 204.00
High Rock Congress Springs, Rock Design, Yellow Olive, Pt. 165.00
High Rock Congress Springs, Saratoga, N.Y., Chocolate Amber, 7 7/8 In. 143.00
High Rock Congress Springs, Saratoga, N.Y., Root Beer Amber, Pt. 88.00
High Rock Congress Springs, Saratoga, N.Y., Teal Blue Green, Cylindrical, Pt. 935.00
High Rock Congress Springs, Saratoga, N.Y., Teal, 7 3/4 In. .... 231.00 to 253.00
High Rock Congress Springs, Saratoga, N.Y., Yellow Amber, 7 7/8 In. 330.00
High Rock Congress Springs, Yellow Green, Qt. 110.00
High Rock Congress Springs, Yellow Olive Amber, Pontil, Pt. 140.00
Highland Spring Water, St. Paul, Minn., Square, 1/2 Gal. 10.00
Hull's Salicine Mixture, Radway & Co., Aqua, Pontil, 7 In. 303.00
Humbolt's Artesian Mineral Water, Eureka, Calif. 70.00
Hutchinson & Co., Chicago, Cobalt Blue, Seed Bubbles, IP, 7 1/4 In. 253.00
Hygeia, Woman Pouring A Cup, Olive Green, 11 1/2 In. 121.00
Isham's California Water Of Life, Aqua, 1/2 Gal. 50.00
J & A Dearborn, N.Y., Sapphire Blue, 6-Sided, IP, 7 In. 187.00
J & A Dearborn, New York, Sapphire Blue, 8-Sided, IP, 7 In. 170.00
J. Boardman, N.Y., Cobalt Blue, 8-Sided, IP, 7 1/2 In. 210.00
J. Boardman, N.Y., Emerald Green, 8-Sided, 7 3/4 In. 495.00
J. Boardman, N.Y., Sapphire Blue, Blob Top, 8-Sided, IP, c.1860, 7 In. 176.00
J. Boardman, N.Y., Star, Sapphire Blue, IP, 7 1/2 In. 357.00
J. Kennedy, Pittsburg, Medium Blue Green, Tapered Top, IP 49.00
J. Smith & Co., Neshannock, Pa., Aqua, 9 3/8 In., Qt. 88.00
J.E. Feldmann, Richfield Springs, Green, 12 In. .... *Illus*   25.00
J.N. Gerdls, San Francisco, Deep Aqua, 8-Sided, 7 1/4 In. 66.00
Jackson's Napa Soda, Aqua, 7 In. 715.00
John Clarke, N.Y., Olive Green, Applied Tapered Ring Lip, Pontil, 1834, Qt. 165.00
John Clarke, N.Y., Yellow Olive Amber, 3 Mold, Sand Pontil, Qt. 125.00
John Ryan Excelsior, Savannah, Ga., Cobalt Blue, 1859, 7 1/8 In. 121.00
John Ryan Excelsior, Savannah, Ga., Cobalt Blue, Blob Top, 7 1/2 In. 180.00
Johnston & Co., Philadelphia, Green 17.00
Kernan & Co., Hutchinson 10.00
Kissingen Water, Hanbury Smith, Deep Yellow Olive, Pt. 90.00
Kissingen Water, Hanbury Smith, Yellow Green, Olive Tone, Pt. 44.00
Kissingen Water, Hanbury Smith, Yellow Olive, Pt. 83.00
Korrylutz Lithia Water, N.Y., Deep Orange Amber, 9 1/4 In. 110.00
L.A. Lomax, Chicago, A & D.H. Co., Amber, Whittled, Qt. 176.00
L.J. Miday & Co., Canton, Oh., Aqua, Qt. 99.00
L.T. Crawford, Hartford, Conn., Cobalt Blue, Blob Top, IP, 7 1/4 In. 324.50
Lithia Mineral Spring Co., Gloversville, Aqua, Pt. 430.00

*Mineral Water, J.E.
Feldmann, Richfield
Springs, Green, 12 In.*

*Mineral Water, Silver Rock,
Silver Rock Mineral Springs,
N.Y., Paper Label, 9 In.*

*Mineral Water, Sparkling
Sal-U-Taris, 100% Natural
Alkaline, Amber, 11 1/2 In.*

Lynch & Clarke, Green Olive Amber, Sand Pontil, Pt. 365.00
Lynch & Clarke, N.Y., Deep Olive Green, Pontil, Cylindrical, 1840, Pt. 1265.00
Lynch & Clarke, N.Y., Medium Yellow Green, Pontil, Pt. 253.00
Lynch & Clarke, N.Y., Olive Amber, Long Neck, Pontil, Pt. 365.00
Lynch & Clarke, N.Y., Olive Amber, Pontil, 9 3/8 In. 578.00
Lynch & Clarke, N.Y., Yellow Olive Amber, Pontil, Applied Mouth, Pt. .... 280.00 to 347.00
Lynch & Clarke, N.Y., Yellow Olive Amber, Pontil, Pt. 250.00
Lynch & Clarke, N.Y., Yellow Olive, Pontil, Pt. 264.00
Lynch & Clarke, New York, Olive Green, Pontil, Qt. 685.00
Lynch & Clarke, New York, Yellow Olive Green, Pontil, Pt. 258.00
Lynde & Putnam, San Francisco, Deep Teal Blue, IP, 7 3/8 In. 121.00
M.T. Crawford, Hartford, Conn, Cobalt Blue, Blob Top, 10-Sided, c.1860, 7 1/4 In. 324.50
Magnetic Spring, Henniker, N.H., Yellow Amber, Qt. 660.00
Martin Petersen, San Rafael, Ca., Aqua, Tooled Lip, Hutchinson, 6 3/4 In. 66.00
Massena Spring, Blue Green, Cylindrical, Qt. 88.00
Massena Spring, Golden Amber, c.1880, Qt. 99.00
Massena Spring, Monogram, Teal Blue, 9 7/8 In. 165.00
Meincke & Ebberwein, Savannah, Geo., Electric Cobalt Blue, 1882, 7 7/8 In. 66.00
Middletown Healing Springs, Middletown, Vt., Golden Amber, Qt. 55.00
Middletown Healing Springs, Middletown, Vt., Grays & Clark, Amber..................... 75.00
Middletown Healing Springs, Middletown, Vt., Yellow Amber, 9 1/2 In. 550.00
Middletown Healing Springs, Red Amber, Whittled, Qt. 74.00
Middletown Mineral Spring Co., Nature's Remedy, Yellow Emerald Green............... 340.00
Milton Aerated Water Works Queens Co., Nova Scotia 90.00
Missisquoi A Springs, Amber, Qt. 22.00
Missisquoi A Springs, Golden Yellow Amber, Qt. .... 94.00 to 121.00
Missisquoi A Springs, Olive Green, Qt. 88.00
Missisquoi A Springs, Squaw, Olive Green, Qt. 231.00
Missisquoi A Springs, Yellow Olive, Qt. 77.00
Napa Soda, Napa, Cal., Natural Mineral Water, Light Aqua, Blob Top, 7 In. 220.00
Napa Soda, Natural Sapphire Blue, Metal Closure, 7 1/4 In. 330.00
Napa Soda, Phil Caduc, Medium Green, Blob Top 95.00
Napa Soda, Phil Caduc, Napa, Cal., Blue Aqua, Whittled, Blob Top, 7 In. 100.00
New Almaden, California, W & W, 1870 ....75.00 to 95.00
New Almaden Vichy Water, California, Apple Green, 12 1/2 In. 467.50
New Century, Aqua, 1910, 7 1/8 In. 253.00
Oak Orchard Acid Springs, G.W. Merchant, Lockport, N.Y., Emerald Green, Qt. 66.00
Oak Orchard Acid Springs, Lockport, N.Y., Aqua, Qt. ....77.00 to 88.00
Owen Casey Eagle Soda Works, Sac City, Calif., Aqua 40.00
P. Conway Bottler, Philadelphia, Cobalt Blue, IP 120.00
Pacific Congress, Aqua, Whittled, Long Neck, Blob Top 65.00
Pacific Congress, Deer, Aqua, 7 1/8 In. 33.00
Parker & Son, N.Y., Sapphire Blue, Smooth Base 65.00
Pavilion & U.S. Spring Co., Medium Aqua, Pt. 275.00
Pavilion & U.S. Spring Co., Saratoga, N.Y., Deep Aqua, Pt. 264.00
Pavilion & U.S. Spring Co., Yellow Green, Pt. 110.00
Peterman Mineral Springs Co., Mt. Pleasant, Tex., Aqua, Blob Top, Slug Plate........ 15.00
Pluto Water, America's Physic, Light Green, Embossed Pluto, 8 1/4 In. 8.00
Reid & Cecil, Philada., Emerald Green, IP, 7 1/2 In. 110.00
Riddle's, Philadelphia, Emerald Green, 8-Sided, IP, 7 1/4 In. 350.00
Rock Bridge Virginia Alum Water, Emerald Green, 1/2 Gal. 330.00
Roussel's, Philadelphia, IP, Emerald Green 200.00
Rushton & Aspinwall, N.Y., Deep Olive Green, Ten Pin Shape, 7 3/8 In. 770.00
Rutherford's Premium, Cincinnati, Sapphire Blue, 10-Sided, IP, 7 1/4 In. 247.00
S. Grossman, Soda, Philada., Mug Base, Medium Yellow Green, 7 1/2 In. 275.00
Saint Leon Spring Water, Boston, Mass., Emerald Green, Cylindrical, Pt. 385.00
Samuel Soda Springs, Amber, Crown Top, 1900s, 7 In. 55.00
San Francisco Glass Works, Deep Green, 7 1/8 In. 44.00
Saratoga A Spring Co., Emerald Green, Cylindrical, Pt. 275.00
Saratoga A Spring N.Y., Black, 1866, Pt. 468.00
Saratoga A Spring N.Y., Emerald Green, Pt. 253.00
Saratoga Red Spring, Emerald Green, Qt. ....77.00 to 88.00
Saratoga Red Spring, Emerald Green, Whittled, Pt. 143.00

Front   *Back*

Mineral Water, Sparkling Sal-U-Taris, Mineral Springs,
St. Clair, Mich., 1878, 11 in.

Saratoga Seltzer Water, Teal Blue, 1/2 Pt. 50.00
Saratoga Star Spring, Amber, Qt. 94.00
Saratoga Star Spring, Amber, Stoddard, Qt. 75.00
Saratoga Star Spring, Emerald Green, Qt. 66.00
Saratoga Star Spring, Golden Amber, Qt. 88.00
Saratoga Star Spring, Red Amber, Qt. ....130.00 to 165.00
Saratoga Star Spring, Yellow Amber, 7 5/8 In. 60.50
Saratoga Vichy Spouting Spring, Saratoga, N.Y., Amber, 9 5/8 In. 176.00
Saratoga Vichy Spouting Spring, Saratoga, N.Y., Aqua, 7 7/8 In. 77.00
Saratoga Vichy Water, Saratoga, N.Y., Amber, Cylindrical, Qt. 352.00
Saratoga Vichy Water, Saratoga, N.Y., Golden Yellow, Tall Cylinder, 1900, Pt. 99.00
Saratoga Vichy Water, Saratoga, N.Y., Yellow Amber, Beer Shape, Blob Top, Pt. 130.00
Sharon Sulphur Water, Light Blue Green, Pt. 22.00
Silver Rock, Silver Rock Mineral Springs, N.Y., Paper Label, 9 In. ....*Illus* 4.00
Sparkling Sal-U-Taris, Mineral Springs, St. Clair, Mich., 1878, 11 in. ....*Illus* 18.00
St. Regis Water Massena Springs, 1880-1900, Pt. 440.00
Stag's Head, Blue Mountain Forest, Cobalt Blue, Cylindrical, 10 In. 990.00
Star Spring Co., Saratoga, N.Y., Amber, Pt. ....70.00 to 99.00
Star Spring Co., Yellow Golden Amber, Cylindrical, Pt. 121.00
Summit, Medium Yellow Green, 7 1/2 In. 187.00
Twitchell Superior, Philadelphia, Cobalt Blue, IP, 7 1/4 In. 303.00
Twitchell Superior, Philadelphia, Green, IP ....30.00 to 35.00
Utica Bottling, A.L. Edic, Light Green, IP, 6 7/8 In. 77.00
Vermont Springs Saxe & Co., Sheldon, Vt., Emerald, Qt. 75.00
Veronica, Amber, 10 5/8 In. 7.50
Vichy Water, Hanbury Smith, Green, Blob Top. 30.25
Vichy Water, Patterson & Brazeau, N.Y., Yellow Olive, 1860-1880, 1/2 Pt. 165.00
W. Ryer, Union Glass Works, Philadelphia, Brilliant Cobalt Blue, IP, 7 1/8 In. 467.00
Washington Spring, Saratoga, N.Y., Medium Olive Amber, Pt. 413.00
Water From The Celebrated American Chalybeate Spring, Me., Aqua, 12 1/4 In. 75.00
Whimea Co., L.T.D., Aqua, Tooled Lip, Hutchinson, 7 7/8 In. 66.00
White Sulphur Springs, Greenbrier, W.V., Emerald Green, Qt. 176.00
Williams & Severance, San Francisco, Blue, Whittled, Blob Top, 1852, 7 1/2 In. 357.00
Wm. Betz & Co., Pittsburgh, Deep Aqua, 10-Sided, 7 7/8 In. 132.00
Wm. Goldstein's IXL, Florida Water, Aqua. 75.00
Yampah Springs, Glenwood Springs, Col., Amber, Embossed, 9 1/2 In. 60.00

──────────────── **MINIATURE** ────────────────

Most of the major modern liquor companies that make full-sized decanters and bottles
quickly learned that miniature versions sell well too. Modern miniatures are listed in this
book by brand name. There are also many older miniature bottles that were made as give-
aways. Most interesting of these are the small motto jugs that name a liquor or bar, and the

comic figural bottles. Collectors sometimes specialize in glass animal miniatures, beer bottles, whiskey bottles, or other types. Interested collectors can join the Lilliputian Bottle Club, 54 Village Circle, Manhattan Beach, CA 90266-7222; or subscribe to Miniature Bottle Collector, P.O. Box 2161, Palos Verdes, CA 90274.

MINIATURE, A Wee Scotch, Baby Drinking From Whiskey Bottle, Bisque, Germany.....	45.00
Beer, Acme Brewing Co., San Francisco, Calif..	1.00
Beer, Acme Brewing, San Francisco, Calif.	30.00
Beer, Adam Scheidt Brewing Co., Valley Forge, Norristown, Pa.	3.00
Beer, Ballantine Export, Crown, 1940s	8.00
Beer, Black Label, Oh.	5.00
Beer, Blatz Brewing Co., Milwaukee, Wis..	1.00
Beer, Blatz Old Heidelburg, Wis.	7.00
Beer, Blatz, Crown, 1940-1950, 4 1/4 In.	9.00
Beer, Budweiser, Mo.	10.00
Beer, Carling Brewing Co., Cleveland, Oh.	6.00
Beer, Cold Spring Brewing, Cold Spring, Lawrence, Mass...	14.00
Beer, Coors Export Lager, Ceramic, 1940..	35.00
Beer, Coors Golden, Ceramic..	25.00
Beer, Drewery's Ale, Green Label, Mountie, 1940-1950, 4 1/4 In.	11.00
Beer, Eastside Pabst, Calif.	10.00
Beer, Eldelweiss, Ill.	5.00
Beer, Falstaff Brewing Corp., Falstaff, St. Louis, Mo...	1.00
Beer, Haberle's Black River Ale, Syracuse, N.Y., 1940s, 3 In.....................................	15.00
Beer, Hamm's, Minn..	5.00
Beer, High Life, 1930s, Stubby, 3 In.	11.00
Beer, Kingsbury Pale, 1930-1940, 4 In.	9.00
Beer, Meister Brau, Ill...	5.00
Beer, Miller Brewing Co., Miller High Life, Milwaukee, Wis.....................................	1.00
Beer, Miller's High Life, Girl In Moon, Crown, Contents, 4 1/4 In.	5.00
Beer, Old Dutch Ale, Penna.	75.00
Beer, Old Export, Md..	20.00
Beer, Old Original High Life, 1930s, 3 In..	11.00
Beer, Pabst Ale, Wisc.	8.00
Beer, Rainier Brewing, Seattle, Wash., Light Amber..	55.00
Beer, Trophy, Birk Bros. Brewing Co., Chicago, Ill., 1940s, 4 In.	1.00
Bond & Cillard Whiskey, Round, Sample	50.00
Casey's Malt Whiskey, Jug, Tan, Ovoid	89.00
Charles H. Gring, Sinking Springs, Pa., Merry Christmas, Jug, Brown, Cream	300.00
Charles Huster, Youngstown, Ohio, Merry Christmas, Jug, Tan & White....................	175.00
Compliments Of I.W. Harper Nelson Co., Ky., Jug...	55.00
Flask, C.I. Lewis, Philadelphia, Medium Amber, IP, Pocket, Nip	242.00
For Your Baby, Flask, 4 In.	85.00
Gin, Gilbey's, Paper Label, 3 In. ....*Illus*	5.00

Miniature, Gin, Gilbey's,
Paper Label, 3 In.

Miniature, Whiskey, Old Continental, Jug,
Stoneware, 3 1/4 In.

Glad Hand Whiskey Nipper, Porcelain	95.00
H.J. Kuhr, 906 South St., Jug, Dark Black Lettering	60.00
I.W. Harper, Nelson Co., Kentucky, Jug	45.00
Jug, Rutherford, V.E. Day, Fighter Plane, 1945-1995, Set Of 3	35.00
Jug, Whiskey, Stoneware, Brown, Salt Glaze, Sailing Ship, Doulton Lambeth, 2 In.	280.00
Kellogg Hitchcock & Co., Menthol Powder, Flask, Cobalt Blue, 2 1/4 In.	20.00
Man & Woman Dancing, Nip, Germany	95.00
Man Holding Dog, Old Scotch & Little Scotch, Nip, Germany	75.00
Man Sitting On Barrel, What We Want, Nip, Germany	95.00
Merry Christmas, Happy New Year, Label Under Glass, Stopper, 1/2 Pt.	143.00
Merry Christmas, Happy New Year, Thos. Little, Lancaster, Ohio, Label	17.00
Nip, Woman's, Boot Shape, Whiskey	18.00
Nipper, A Little Scotch, Woman & Scottie Dog, Multicolored, Japan, 5 1/2 In.	60.00
Nipper, Gold Water, Miner, Pick & Bottle, Hotel Sutter, San Fran., Germany, 5 In.	60.00
Nipper, Never Drink Water, Boy, Peeing In Creek, Multicolored, Japan, 5 In.	50.00
Nipper, Woman, Carrying Basket, Multicolored, Germany, 7 1/4 In.	60.00
O.L. Lusby, Washington, D.C., Brown, Jug	195.00
Old Continental Whiskey, Jug, Stoneware, Cream, Black Stencil	79.00
Pensacola Golden Corn, Jug, Red, Tan & Green Swirls, Debossed	175.00
Plane, St. Louis	30.00
Plane, Winnie Mae	30.00
Quaker Maid Whiskey, Sample	10.00
Rlcksecker, Cologne, N.Y., Jug, Pottery, Painted Flowers, 4 1/4 In.	120.00
Rynbende, Flamingo, Blown	15.00
Rynbende, Hare, Blown	15.00
Rynbende, Kangaroo, Blown	15.00
Rynbende, Owl, Blown	15.00
Rynbende, Pelican, Blown	15.00
Rynbende, Seal, Blown	15.00
Rynbende, Swan, Blown	15.00
St. Galmler, Dog, Brown	25.00
St. Galmler, Dog, White	25.00
St. Galmier, Duck	25.00
St. Galmier, Monkey	25.00
St. Galmier, Parrot	25.00
Tucker Special, Brown Forman & Co. Distillers, Jug, Clear Glass, Bulldog, Handle	249.00
Warners Tried & True Ointment, Barrel, Aqua, Embossed, 2 1/4 In.	80.00
Whiskey, Applegate & Sons, Louisville, Cylinder, 5 In.	20.00
Whiskey, B.T. & P. Oak Run	125.00
Whiskey, I.W. Harper, Barrel	45.00
Whiskey, Kellogg's Extra, Honey Amber	85.00
Whiskey, Old Continental, Jug, Stoneware, 3 1/4 In. ....*Illus*	30.00

MR. BOSTON, see Old Mr. Boston

NAILSEA TYPE

The intricate glass called *Nailsea* was made in the Bristol district of England from 1788 to 1873. The glass included loopings of white or colored glass worked in patterns. The characteristic look of Nailsea was copied and what is called Nailsea today is really Nailsea type made in England or even America. Nailsea gemel bottles are of particular interest to collectors.

NAILSEA TYPE, Bar, Clear Cranberry, White Looping, Teardrop, Pontil, 7 1/2 In.	145.00
Bar, Clear Cranberry, White Netting, Straight Sided, Pontil, 7 3/4 In.	165.00
Bar, Dark Olive Amber, White Flecks, Pontil, 4 3/4 In.	187.00
Bar, Opaque Cranberry, White Looping, Teardrop, Pontil, 7 1/2 In.	145.00
Boot, White Striations, Pontil	400.00
Decanter, Blue Aqua, White Herringbone Pattern, Pontil, 9 3/8 In.	632.00
Fireplace Bellows, Free-Blown, White & Pink Loopings, 12 1/2 In.	165.00
Flask, Canary Yellow, Swirl, Pontil, 6 3/4 In.	132.00
Flask, Clear, White Looping, Horizontal Ruby Bands, Milk Glass Lip, OP, 6 1/4 In.	264.00
Flask, Clear, White Loopings, Pontil, 1860-1890, 9 3/8 In.	72.00
Flask, Controlled White Looping, Strawberry Puce, Sheared Lip, OP, 4 In.	523.00
Flask, Deep Olive Amber, White Flecks, Pontil, 11 5/8 In.	605.00

Flask, Deep Olive Green, White Dot Pattern, Sheared Lip, 13 Ribbed Neck, 4 7/8 In.... 880.00
Flask, Milk Glass, Pink Loopings, Tooled Mouth, Pontil, Oval, 7 1/8 In. 143.00
Flask, Pocket, Clear, White Loopings, c.1890, 7 3/4 In. 60.50
Flask, Pocket, Cranberry Red, Cased In Clear Glass, White Loopings, Pontil, 6 7/8 In.. 93.50
Flask, Red & Blue Looping, White Ground, Sheared Lip, Pontil, Pt. 310.00
Flask, Red, Blue Looping On White, Sheared Lip, Pontil, Pt.. 310.00
Flask, Ruby Red, White Swirls 295.00
Flask, Teardrop, Milk Glass With Pink, Lavender, Blue Loopings, Pontil, 6 1/4 In. 231.00
Onion, Olive Green, White Fleck In Swirl Pattern, Handle, 6 In......................... 220.00 to 413.00
Perfume Bottle, Seahorse, White & Purple, Clear, Rigaree Chips, 3 1/4 In................... 140.00
Whiskey, Cobalt Blue, White String Swirl, Pontil.. 200.00

NURSING

Pottery nursing bottles were used by 1500 B.C. If a bottle was needed, one was improvised, and stone, metal, wood, and pottery, as well as glass bottles were made through the centuries. A glass bottle was patented by Charles Windship of Roxbury, Massachusetts, in 1841. Its novel design suggested that the bottle be placed over the breast to try to fool the baby into thinking the milk came from the mother. By 1864 the most common nursing bottle was a nipple attached to a glass tube in a cork that was put into a glass bottle. Unfortunately, it was impossible to clean and was very unsanitary. The nursing bottle in use today was made possible by the development of an early 1900s rubber nipple.

Nursing bottles are easily identified by the unique shape and the measuring units that are often marked on the sides. Some early examples had engraved designs and silver nipples but most are made of clear glass and rubber. There is a collectors club, The American Collectors of Infant Feeders, 1849 Ebony Drive, York, PA 17402-4706, and a publication called *Keeping Abreast*. A reference book, *A Guide to American Nursing Bottles* by Diane Rouse Ostrander, is also available.

NURSING, American Feeding 20.00
Baby's Delight, Baby Sitting Up Drinking From Bottle, Embossed 75.00
Betsy Brown Safety Nurser 25.00
Clear, Ground Pontil 135.00
Comfey, Pluto, 6 1/2 In. 15.00
Copeland Spode, Submarine, Blue & White, People Fishing, 1830-1860, 7 1/2 In. 550.00
Dolly, With Puppy 5.00
Flask, Blown, 16 Vertical Ribs, Green Aqua, 6 1/2 In. 88.00
Flask, Blown, 19 Diamond Pattern, Light Aqua, 5 3/4 In. 100.00
Flask, Blown, 20 Vertical Ribs, Green Aqua, 6 1/4 In. 84.00
Flask, Blown, Cobalt Blue, 7 1/4 In. 231.00
Flask, Blown, Diamond Pattern, Green Aqua, 6 1/2 In. 88.00
Franklin, Script, Oval 22.00
Infant Feeder, Best Feeding Bottle, Clear, Japan, Box, 1910-1930, 7 1/4 In................ 100.00
M.S. Burr's Proprietor, Boston, Mass., Aqua, Flowers, Pear Shape, 5 3/4 In. 50.00
Oriental Nurser, Embossed, Clear... 55.00
Queen Victoria, Salt Glaze 1200.00
Rand Bros., Feed The Baby, Clear, Figural Baby Bust, 1890, 4 In............................. 220.00
Riker Hegeman Druggist, N.Y., Pale Green, Graduated Back.................................... 25.00
See-Saw Margery Daw, Rhyme & Children On See-Saw, 6 1/2 In. 25.00
Sonny Boy 18.00
Staffordshire, Submarine, Blue & White, Women By Fountain, 7 5/8 In. 385.00
Submarine, Staffordshire, White, 1830-1860, 6 1/2 In... 165.00
Universal Feeder, 8 Oz. 25.00
Welfare, Double-Ended, England 35.00
White, Blue Oriental Design, Europe, 19th Century, Crazed, 7 In. 357.00
Wm. McCully & Co., Pittsburgh, Pa., Standard, Clear, 1890-1900, 6 1/4 In................. 104.00

OIL

Motor oil, battery oil, and sewing machine and lubricating oils were all sold in bottles. Any bottle that has the word *oil* either embossed in the glass or on the paper label falls in this category. A battery jar has straight sides and an open top. It was filled with a chemical solution. The jars were usually made with a zinc plate or a copper plate plus a suspended carbon plate. With the proper connections the chemicals and metals generated an electric current. Many companies made batteries that included glass jars, and the jars are now appearing at bottle shows. In the Edison battery, the solution was covered with a special protective layer of oil which kept it from evaporating. Edison battery oil jars, dating from about 1889, were specially made to hold the protective oil and can still be found.

OIL, Battery, Leclanche Battery Co., N.Y., Aqua, Ground Lip	40.00
Clarke Stanley's Snake Oil Liniment, Best Horse Liniment In World, Square, 6 In. ...	15.00
Essential Oil, H.B. Hotchkills, Phelps, N.Y., Teal, Spout, 10 1/4 In.	125.00
Gargling Oil, Blue Green, 5 1/2 In.	15.00
Gargling Oil, Deep Blue Green, Medium, Applied Top, 5 5/8 In.	35.00
Gargling Oil, Lockport, N.Y., Cobalt Blue, ABM	20.00
Gargling Oil, Lockport, N.Y., Emerald Green, Crude, 5 1/2 In.	40.00
Gargling Oil, Lockport, N.Y., Teal, 5 5/8 In.	55.00
Gargling Oil, Lockport, N.Y., Yellow Olive	39.00
Gun Oil, Hoppe's No. 9	15.00
J.B. Rhodes Co., Kalamazoo, Mich., Screw Cap, Tube, Qt.	47.50
Kickapoo, Embossed, Label, ABM, Contents, Box	35.00
Little's White Oil, Scottsville, Va., Aqua, Pontil, 6 1/2 In.	303.00
Magassar, Aqua, OP	14.00
Mobil, Gargoyle, Flat Sides, Arctic Grade, Qt	95.00
Prof. DeGrath's Electric Oil, Philadelphia, Hinged Mold, Aqua	20.00
Shell, Raised Logo, Ribbed Design, Qt.	85.00

OLD BARDSTOWN

Old Bardstown was made and bottled by the Willit Distilling Company in Bardstown, Kentucky. Figural bottles were made from about 1977 to 1980. One unusual bottle pictured Foster Brooks, the actor who is best known for his portrayal of drunks.

OLD BARDSTOWN, Affirm & Alydar	152.00
Christmas Card, 1977	16.00
Clemson Tiger	70.00
Delta Queen, 1980	38.00
Fiddle, Miniature	15.00
Fighting Gamecock	152.00
Football Player	37.00
Foster Brooks, 1978	20.00
Georgia Bulldog, 1980	145.00
Horse, Citation, 1979	132.00
Iron Worker, 1978	30.00
Keg With Stand, 1977, 1/2 Gal.	16.00
Keg With Stand, 1977, Gal.	27.00
Kentucky Colonel, No. 1, 1978	15.00
Kentucky Colonel, No. 2, 1979	55.00
Kentucky Derby, 1977	13.00
Surface Miner, 1978	20.00
Tiger, 1979	18.00 to 40.00

OLD COMMONWEALTH

Old Commonwealth bottles have been made since 1975 by J.P. Van Winkle and Sons, Louisville, Kentucky. They also put out bottles under the Old Rip Van Winkle label. An apothecary series with university names and other designs has been made from 1978 to the present. As few as 1,600 were made of some of these designs. Other bottles depict firemen, coal miners, fishermen, Indians, dogs, horses, or leprechauns. Some of the decanters were made with music box inserts. A limited edition Irish decanter is made every year for St. Patrick's Day. The distillery will sell empty bottles to collectors interested in completing a set. Write to 2843 Brownsboro Road, Louisville, KY 40206.

OLD COMMONWEALTH, Alabama Apothecary, 1980	27.00
Auburn Tigers, 1979	38.00
Castles Of Ireland, 1990	30.00
Chief Illini, No. 1, 1979	76.00 to 84.00
Chief Illini, No. 2, 1981	52.00 to 62.00
Clemson Tigers, 1979	76.00

Old Commonwealth, Fireman, No. 3, Valiant Volunteer, 1979

Old Commonwealth, Fisherman, Keeper, 1980

Coal Miner, Coal Shooter, 1983	28.00
Coal Miner, Lump Of Coal, 1977	37.00
Coal Miner, Lump Of Coal, 1981	37.00
Coal Miner, Lunch Time, 1980	40.00
Coal Miner, Lunch Time, 1983, Miniature	41.00
Coal Miner, Pick, 1976	39.00
Coal Miner, Pick, 1982	39.00
Coal Miner, Shovel, 1975	85.00
Coal Miner, Shovel, 1980	84.00
Coins Of Ireland, 1979	22.00
Cottontail Rabbit, 1981	35.00
Crimson Tide, 1981	17.00
Dogs Of Ireland, 1980	19.00
Fireman, Modern No. 2, Nozzle Man, 1983	69.00
Fireman, Modern No. 3, On Call, Boots, Yellow Hat, 1983	70.00
Fireman, Modern No. 4, Fallen Comrade, 1982	70.00
Fireman, No. 1, Cumberland Valley, 75th Anniversary, 1976	115.00
Fireman, No. 2, Volunteer, 1978	74.00
Fireman, No. 3, Valiant Volunteer, 1979 ....*Illus*	76.00
Fireman, No. 4, Heroic Volunteer, 1981	70.00
Fireman, No. 5, Lifesaver, 1983	60.00
Fisherman, Keeper, 1980 ....*Illus*	46.00
Flowers Of Ireland, 1983	25.00
Happy Green, 1986	25.00
Horses Of Ireland, 1981	20.00
Irish At The Sea, 1989	27.00
Irish Idyll, 1982	14.00
Irish Lore, 1988	27.00
Kansas State Wildcats, 1982	39.00
Kentucky Peach Bowl, 1977	32.00
Leprechaun, No. 1, Elusive, 1980	34.00
Leprechaun, No. 2, Irish Minstrel, 1982	34.00
Leprechaun, No. 3, Lucky, 1983	25.00
Louisville Champs, 1980	32.00
LSU Tiger, 1979	50.00
Lumberjack, Old Time, 1979	29.00
Maryland Terps, 1977	28.00
Missouri Tigers, 1979	42.00
Modern Hero, 1982	67.00
Princeton Univ., 1976	20.00
Sons Of Erin, No. 2, 1978	27.00
Sports Of Ireland, 1987	26.00
St. Patrick's Day Parade, 1984	25.00

Statue Of Liberty, Miniature	22.00
Symbols Of Ireland, 1985	27.00
Thoroughbreds, Kentucky, 1977	42.00
Waterfowler, No. 1, Hunter, 1978	47.00
Waterfowler, No. 2, Here They Come, 1980	37.00
Waterfowler, No. 3, Good Boy, 1981	40.00
Western Boot, 1982	22.00
Western Logger, 1980	34.00

OLD CROW

Dr. James Crow of Kentucky was a surgeon and chemist from Edinburgh, Scotland. He started practicing medicine but decided to improve the quality of life by distilling corn whiskey instead. In those days, about 1835, whiskey was made by a family recipe with a bit of that and a handful of the other. The results were uneven. Dr. Crow was a scientist and used corn and limestone water to make a whiskey that he put into kegs and jugs. He used charred oak kegs, and the liquid became reddish instead of the clear white of corn liquor. More experiments led to his development of the first bourbon, named after northeastern Kentucky's Bourbon County, which had been named for the French royal family.

Old Crow became a popular product in all parts of the country and was sold to saloons. Salesmen for competing brands would sometimes try to ruin the liquor by putting a snake or nail into the barrel. In 1870, for the first time, bourbon was bottled and sealed at the distillery. The distillery was closed during Prohibition, and when it reopened in 1933, Old Crow was purchased by National Distilleries. That Old Crow would be packaged in a crow-shaped decanter was inevitable, and in 1954 National Distillers Products Corporation of Frankfort, Kentucky, put Old Crow bourbon into a ceramic crow. Again in 1974 a crow decanter was used; this time 16,800 Royal Doulton bottles were made. The bourbon was sold in the 1970s in a series of bottles shaped like light or dark green chess pieces.

OLD CROW, Chess Set, Pawns	22.00
Chess Set, With Rug, 32 Piece	426.00
Crow, Red Vest, 1974	16.00
Crow, Royal Doulton	76.00

OLD FITZGERALD

Stitzel Weller of Louisville, Kentucky, had a letterhead in 1971 that said *established 1849, America's oldest family distillery.* In 1972 the distillery was sold to Somerset Importers, Ltd., a division of Norton Simon Company, Inc. Somerset Importers continued to market the Old Fitzgerald series until 1978, when they sold it to Julian P. Van Winkle. He had started the series while president of the Old Fitzgerald Distillery. He continued making the decanter series under the brand Old Commonwealth. The Van Winkle series of bottles for both brands included only 20 bottles through 1986. In 1968 the Old Fitzgerald decanter carried the words *plase God.* Federal laws ruled this objectionable and the decanters were changed to read *prase be.* Esmark purchased Norton Simon in 1984, then sold the Old Fitzgerald label to Distillers of England in 1985, who sold it to Guinness Stout of Ireland in 1986. Guinness Stout has since become Guinness PLC of London, and its Louisville distillery is called United Distillers Production, Inc.

An out-of-print pamphlet called *Decanter Collector's Guide* pictures Old Fitzgerald decanters offered since 1951. Most are glass in a classic shape. A series of apothecary jars was made from 1969 to 1983. In 1971, when J. P. Van Winkle Jr. was president, the company, of course, made a Rip Van Winkle decanter. The distillery makes Old Fitzgerald bourbon, Cabin Still bourbon, and W.L. Weller bourbon. The Cabin Still decanters are also listed in this book. These include a series of hillbilly bottles made in the 1950s and 1960s, apothecary jars, and classic glass decanters.

OLD FITZGERALD, America's Cup, 1970 ....*Illus*	19.00
American Sons, 1976	15.00
Around We Go, 1983	22.00
Birmingham, 1972	47.00
Blarney, Irish Toast, 1970	12.00
Candlelite, 1955	20.00
Candlelite, 1961	10.00
Classic, 1972	8.00

Old Fitzgerald, America's Cup, 1970   *Rip Van Winkle, 1971*

Colonial, 1969	7.00
Davidson, N.C., 1972	32.00
Eagle, 1973	10.00
Early American, 1970	6.00
Executive, 1960	8.00
Flagship, 1967	8.00
Gallon In Cradle	17.00
Geese, 1970	8.00
Gold Coaster, 1954	15.00
Gold Web, 1953	14.00
Hostess, 1977	7.00
Huntington, W.V., 1971	27.00
Illinois, 1972	14.00
Irish Charm, 1977	20.00
Irish Counties, 1973	20.00
Irish Luck, 1972	30.00
Irish Patriots, 1971	15.00
Irish Wish, 1975	19.00
Jewel, 1951	10.00
Memphis, 1969	14.00
Nebraska, 1972	29.00
Ohio State, 1970	14.00
Old Fitz 101, 1978	7.00
Old Ironsides	7.00
Pheasant Rising, 1972	10.00
Pilgrim Landing, 1970	19.00
Ram, Bighorn, 1971	9.00
Rip Van Winkle, 1971 ....*Illus*	37.00
Songs Of Ireland, 1974	15.00
Sons Of Erin, 1969	12.00
Tree Of Life, 1964	9.00
Triangle, 1976	6.00
Venetian, 1966	8.00
Vermont, 1970	20.00
Virginia, 1972	19.00
W.V. Forest Festival, 1973	23.00

OLD MR. BOSTON

It seems strange that a liquor company began as a candy factory, but that is part of the history of Old Mr. Boston. The Ben Burk Candy Company started in 1927 making nonalcoholic cordials during Prohibition. After Repeal, they became the first Massachusetts company to get a license for distilled spirits. They built a still and started making gin. One of the first brand names used was Old Mr. Boston. There was even a live Mr. Boston, an actor who made appearances for the company. In the early 1940s the company was sold to

American Distilleries, but four years later Samuel Burk and Hyman Burkowitz, brothers, bought the company back. They expanded the Old Mr. Boston brand to include other beverages, such as flavored cordials and homogenized eggnog. They claim to be the first to introduce the quarter-pint size. In the mid-1960s the company began putting the liquor in decanters that are in demand by today's collectors. No decanters were made after the early 1970s. They also made Rocking Chair Whiskey in a bottle that actually rocked. Traditionally, whiskey barrels were rolled back and forth on ships to improve the taste. Ships' captains liked the improved flavor and when they retired they would tie barrels of whiskey to their rocking chairs. A series of liquors in glass cigar-like tubes called *The Thin Man* were made in the mid-1960s. Glenmore Distilleries acquired Old Mr. Boston in 1969. The brand name was changed to Mr. Boston about 1975.

The Mr. Boston trademark was redesigned in the 1950s and again in the 1970s. Each time he became thinner, younger, and more dapper. The slogan *An innkeepers tradition since 1868* was used in the 1980s. It refers to the year the Old Mr. Boston mark was first registered.

OLD MR. BOSTON, AMVETS, Iowa Convention, 1975	12.00
Anthony Wayne, 1970	10.00
Assyrian Convention, 1975	23.00
Bart Starr, No. 15	47.00
Beckley, W.V.	26.00
Bingo In Illinois, 1974	15.00
Black Hills Motor Club, 1976	22.00
Clown Head, 1973	16.00
Clown Head, Signature, 1974	27.00
Cog Railway, 1978	30.00
Concord Coach, 1976	28.00
Dan Patch, 1970	17.00
Dan Patch, 1973	15.00
Deadwood, South Dakota, 1975	16.00
Eagle Convention, 1976	8.00
Eagle Convention, 75th Anniversary, 1973	16.00
Eagle Convention, 78th Anniversary, 1973	15.00
Eagle Convention, Atlanta, 1972	16.00
Eagle Convention, Boston, 1971	12.00
Green Bay, No. 87	30.00
Greensboro Open, Gold Shoe, 1978	39.00
Greensboro Open, Golf Bag, 1976	34.00
Illinois Capitol, 1970	16.00
Lincoln Horseback, 1972	12.00
Lion Sitting, 1974	16.00 to 22.00
Miss Madison Boat, 1973	36.00
Monticello, 1974	12.00
Mooseheart, 1972	12.00
Nathan Hale, 1975	14.00
Nebraska, No. 1, Gold, 1970	46.00
Nebraska Czechs, 1970	10.00
New Hampshire, 1976	18.00
Paul Revere, 1975	12.00
Polish American Legion, 1976	17.00
President Inauguration, 1953	20.00
Prestige Bookend, 1970	11.00
Race Car, Mario Andretti, No. 9, Yellow	35.00
Red Dog Dan, 1974	12.00
Sherry Pitcher	6.00
Ship Lantern, 1974	20.00
Steelhead Trout, 1976	16.00
Tennessee Centennial	10.00
Town Crier, 1976	12.00
Venus	17.00
W.V. National Guard, 1973	37.00
Wisconsin Football	27.00
York, Nebraska, 1970	15.00

—————————————— OLD RIP VAN WINKLE ——————————————

Old Rip Van Winkle apothecary jars and figurals shaped like Rip Van Winkle were made from 1968 to 1977. J.P. Van Winkle and Sons, Louisville, Kentucky, made these bottles and others under the Old Commonwealth label.

OLD RIP VAN WINKLE, Bay Colony, 1975	15.00
Cardinal, 1974	17.00
Colonial Virginia, 1974	14.00
Kentucky Sportsman, 1973	27.00
New Jersey Bicentennial, 1975	18.00
New York Bicentennial, 1975	19.00
No. 1, Green, 1975	30.00
No. 2, Reclining, 1975	37.00
No. 3, Standing, 1977	24.00
Sanford, N.C., Centennial, 1974	14.00
University Of Kentucky, Wildcat, 1974	30.00

—————————————————— PACESETTER ——————————————————

Bottles shaped like cars and trucks were made under the Pacesetter label from 1974 to about 1983.

PACESETTER, Ahrens Fox Pumper, 1983	120.00
Camero Z-28, Gold, 1982	48.00 to 55.00
Camero Z-28, Platinum, 1982	55.00
Corvette, 1975	29.00
Corvette, 1975, Moving Wheels	65.00
Corvette, 1978, Black, 375 Ml.	42.00
Corvette, 1978, Brown, 375 Ml.	41.00
Corvette, 1978, Gold, Miniature	32.00
Corvette, 1978, White, 375 Ml.	41.00
Corvette, 1978, Yellow, 375 Ml.	42.00
Fire Truck, LaFrance, White, 1982	68.00
Fire Truck, Snorkle, Red, 1982	52.00
Mack Pumper	142.00
Olsonite Eagle, No. 8, 1974	72.00
Pirsch Pumper, Red, 1983	63.00
Pirsch Pumper, White, 1983	63.00
Pontiac Firebird, 1980	40.00
Tractor, Massey Ferguson, 1939	77.00
Tractor, No. 1, John Deere, 1982	132.00
Tractor, No. 2, International Harvester, 1983	105.00
Tractor, No. 3, International Harvester, 1983, Miniature	122.00
Tractor, No. 4, 4-Wheel Drive, Big Red, 1983	120.00
Tractor, No. 4, 4-Wheel Drive, Ford, 1983	85.00
Tractor, No. 4, 4-Wheel Drive, Green Machine, 1983	71.00
Tractor, No. 5, Allis Chalmers, 1983	87.00
Tractor, Steiger, 4-Wheel Drive, 1959	147.00
Truck, Coca-Cola	158.00
Truck, Elizabethtown	127.00
Vukovich, 1974	74.00

————————————————— PEPPER SAUCE —————————————————

There was little refrigeration and only poor storage facilities for fresh meat in the nine-teenth century. Slightly spoiled food was often cooked and eaten with the help of strong spices including pepper. Small hot chili peppers were put into a bottle of vinegar. After a few weeks the spicy mixture was called *pepper sauce*. A distinctive bottle, now known as a pepper sauce bottle, was favored for this mixture. It was a small bottle, 6 to 12 inches high, with a long slim neck. The bottle could be square or cylindrical or decorated with arches or rings. Most were made of common bottle glass in shades of aqua or green. A few were made of cobalt or milk glass. Very early examples may have a pontil mark. More information on pepper sauce can be found in *Ketchup, Pickles, Sauces* by Betty Zumwalt.

PEPPER SAUCE, Aqua, 22 Indented Fluted Ribs, Applied Square Collar, OP, 10 1/2 In. . 220.00

Aqua, 3 Rings On Neck, Fluted Sides, OP	38.00
Aqua, 8-Sided, IP	45.00
Aqua, Round, 20 Rings	8.50
Cathedral, Aqua, 10 In.	160.00
Cathedral, Aqua, 6-Sided, OP, 8 3/4 In.	70.00
Cathedral, Aqua, BIMAL	60.00
Cathedral, Cleveland, Aqua, 1865-1875, 8 1/2 In.	303.00
Cathedral, Light Blue Green, Applied Mouth, c.1870, 10 1/4 In.	258.00
Cathedral, Light Teal, Pontil, Whittled, c.1840-1855, 8 3/4 In.	176.00
Cathedral, Medium Blue Green, OP, c.1860, 8 3/4 In.	121.00
Cathedral, Medium Green, Pontil, Square, Panels, c.1860, 8 3/4 In.	220.00
Cathedral, Opalescent, Bencia Type, Applied Top, OP, 8 3/4 In.	303.00
Fluted, 8 Panels, Pontil, 8 1/2 In.	55.00
Great Atlantic & Pacific Tea Co., Amber, 9 5/8 In.	8.00

PEPSI-COLA

Caleb Davis Bradham, a New Bern, North Carolina, druggist, invented and named Pepsi-Cola. Although he registered the trademark, the word *Pepsi-Cola* in calligraphy script, in 1903, he claimed that it had been used since 1898. A simpler version was registered in 1906. The bottle is marked with the name. The name in a hexagonal frame with the words *A Sparkling Beverage* was registered in 1937. This logo was printed on the bottle. The bottle cap colors were changed to red, white, and blue in 1941 as a patriotic gesture. Until 1951, the words Pepsi and Cola were separated by 2 dashes. These bottles are called *double dash*. In 1951 the modern logo with a single hyphen was introduced. The simulated cap logo was used at the same time. The name *Pepsi* was started in 1911, but it was not until 1966 that the block-lettered logo was registered. Both names are still used. A few very early Pepsi bottles were made of amber glass. Many other Pepsi bottles with local bottlers' names were made in the early 1900s. Modern bottles made for special events are also collected. There is a club, Pepsi-Cola Collectors Club, P.O. Box 1275, Covina, CA 91722. The company has archives at One Pepsi Way, Purchase, NY 10589.

PEPSI-COLA, 1975 World Champions, Cinci. Reds, Bicentennial, July 4, 1976	*Illus*	12.00
2 Full Glasses, Applied Color Label, 10 In.	*Illus*	45.00
Applied Color Label, 3 Colors, 10 In.	*Illus*	18.00
Applied Color Label, 8 1/2 In.	*Illus*	10.00
Charlottsville, Va., Aqua, 6 Oz.		16.50
Desert Storm, 1991, Full Contents, 6 Pack		35.00

Pepsi-Cola, 1975 World Champions, Cincinnati Reds, Bicentennial, July 4, 1976

Pepsi-Cola, 2 Full Glasses, Applied Color Label, 10 In.

Pepsi-Cola, Applied Color Label, 3 Colors, 10 In.

Pepsi-Cola, Applied Color Label, 8 1/2 In.

Pepsi-Cola, Devil Shake, Shake 'n Enjoy, Red Applied Color Label, 9 1/2 In.	Pepsi-Cola, Diet Pepsi, Applied Color Label, 10 In.	Pepsi-Cola, Newport News Bottling Company, 8 1/2 In.	Pepsi-Cola, No Deposit, Short, Cap, 6 In.

Devil Shake, Shake 'n Enjoy, Red Applied Color Label, 9 1/2 In. ....*Illus* 60.00
Diet Pepsi, Applied Color Label, 10 In..*Illus* 5.00
Durham, N.C... 33.00
Escambia, Hutchinson 600.00
Exmore, Va., Drum Style, Aqua... 55.00
Greensboro, N.C., Aqua, Crown Top 16.50
Jessup Bottling Works, Charlottesville, Va., Aqua, Crown Top 41.25
Newport News Bottling Company, 8 1/2 In. ....*Illus* 175.00
No Deposit, Short, Cap, 6 In..*Illus* 3.00
Orange, Va., Block Letter, Aqua.. 9.00
Red, White & Blue Label On Neck, 16 Oz.. 3.50
Red & White Label Oval On Neck, 10 Oz. 3.00
Richard Petty, Long Neck, Set Of 8... 23.00
Richmond, Va., Aqua, Crown Top... 55.00
Richmond, Va., Trademark, Some Contents, 6 1/2 Oz. 50.00
Suffolk, Va., Aqua, Crown Top.. 38.50
Wilmington, N.C., Aqua, Crown Top 38.50

────────────────────── **PERFUME** ──────────────────────

Perfume is a liquid mixture of aromatic spirits and alcohol. Cologne is similar but has more alcohol in the mixture so it is not as strong. Perfume bottles are smaller than colognes and usually more decorative. Most perfume bottles today are from the twentieth century. Some were made by famous glass makers such as Lalique or Webb, and some held expensive perfumes such as Schiaparelli, Nina Ricci's Coeur de Joie, or D'Orsay's Le Lys D'Orsay. DeVilbiss is a manufacturer of the spray tops used on perfume bottles and the name sometimes appears in a description. The word *factice*, which often appears in ads, refers to store display bottles. The club International Perfume Bottle Association publishes a newsletter (3519 Wycliffe Drive, Modesto, CA 95355). The Tops & Bottoms Club has a matching service for Rene Lalique bottles. If you have a bottle without a stopper, or a stopper and no bottle, contact them at P.O. Box 15555, Plantation, FL 33318. Related bottles may be found in the Cologne and Scent categories.

PERFUME, Borghese, Swirled, Swirled Stopper, Metal Collar, Factice, 8 In. 88.00
Bourjois, Evening In Paris, Blue, Long Dabber Stopper, Red Metal Egg, 3 In.............. 121.00
C'Est La Vie, Store Display 400.00
Calendal, Molinard, Frosted, Gilt Metal, Atomizer, Nudes, Lalique, 1927, 5 1/2 In. 460.00
Caron, With Pleasure, Keg Shape, Enameled Gold Bands, Green Stopper, 3 1/2 In. 242.00
Chloe, Store Display, Large 450.00
Chloe, Store Display, Small 275.00

Clam Shell, Blue, English, c. 1870, 2 3/8 In. ....*Illus* 240.00
Corday, Femme Du Jour, Frosted, Purse, Stopper, Metal Overcap, 2 1/8 In. 50.00
Cormac's American Perfumes, N.Y., Paper Label, 2 3/4 In. 35.00
Coty, L'Aimant, Plastic Globe, On Metal Stand, Frosted Stopper, 1 1/8 In.................... 165.00
Coty, L'Or, Teardrop Shape, Baccarat Emblem On Base, 6 3/8 In. 60.00
Coty La Rose Jacqueminot, Gold Label, Frosted Fishscale Stopper, 2 In. 66.00
Cross-Hatched Design, Scalloped Edge Stopper, Pink, 5 7/8 In.................................... 825.00
Cut Glass, Tiara-Like Stopper, Mauve, Czechoslovakia, 6 In....................................... 165.00
Cut Glass, Wheel Cut Rose, Stopper, Czechoslovakia, 5 7/8 In.................................... 231.00
D'Orsay, Toujours Fidele, Pillow Shape, Sitting Dog Stopper, Enameled, 3 1/2 In. 286.00
Dancer Holding A Stem Of Flowers, Stopper, Czechoslovakia, 6 In............................. 770.00
Dorothy Gray, Savoir Faire, Enameled Masks, Overlapping Bows Cape, 3 7/8 In.......... 467.00
Duck Shape, Multiple Facets, Duck's Head Stopper, 6 3/4 In....................................... 100.00
Eisenberg, Woman In Gown Shape, Frosted, Stopper, 2 1/2 In..................................... 522.00
Elizabeth Arden, Blue Glass, Inner Stopper, Turquoise Cap, Horseshoe Box, 2 7/8 In.. 385.00
Elizabeth Arden, Frosted, 2 Women, Whispering, Stopper, 3 7/8 In. 550.00
Elizabeth Arden, It's You, Hand Holding Rose Stopper, White Glass, 3 3/8 In. 935.00
Elizabeth Arden, Memoire Cherie, Frosted, Woman Shaped Stopper, 3 In. 231.00
Elizabeth Taylor, Passion, Violet, Molded Facets Stopper, Store Display, 12 1/2 In. 231.00
Faberge, Flambeau, Whistle Shape, Worn On Chain, Red Foil Box, 3 In. 60.00
Florida Water, Stevens & Stevens Co., 9 In... 10.00
Fragonard, Gamine, Urn Shape, Enameled Gold, Stopper, 4 1/2 In. 275.00
Frosted Overlapping Petals, Ball Shape, Atomizer, France, 20th Century, 4 In. 231.00
Grenoville, Oellet Fane, Frosted Rooster Stopper, 3 3/8 In.. 253.00
Guerlain, Bowtie Shape, Dark Blue, Stopper, 3 1/8 In.. 253.00
Guerlain, Ode, Curvilinear Design, Partly Frosted, Rosebud Stopper, 5 7/8 In.............. 357.00
Guerlain, Une Rose, Floriform Stopper, Contents, Box, 3 7/8 In. 412.00
Houbigant, Essence Rare, Stopper, Silver Label, Store Display, 6 1/2 In...................... 176.00
Houbigant, Le Parfum Ideal, Decanter Shape, Faceted Stopper, Gold Label, 5 In. 198.00
Houbigant, Quelques Fleurs, In Straw Basket, Brass Cap, 1 1/2 In............................. 88.00
Jacqueline Cochran, L'Air Du Temps, Vial Encased In Lucite, Gold Metal Pin Top ... 120.00
Jean Desprez, Bal A Versailles, Gold Metal Cap, Brocade Box, 2 1/8 In...................... 33.00
Kathryn, Forever Amber, Mermaid Torso Shape, Clear Stopper, 5 In. 27.50
Kerkoff, Monogram, Stopper, Square, Paris, 5 1/8 In. 5.00
Lady Posed As Butterfly, Clear Stopper, Green, 6 In. 495.00
Lalique, D'Heraud, Frosted, Gilt Metal, Charcoal Gray, 1924, 6 1/4 In......................... 287.00
Lalique, D'Orsay, Le Lys, Sepia Patina, Label, 1922, 5 1/2 In. 575.00
Lalique, D'Orsay, Le Lys, Sepia Patina, Label, 1922, 7 1/4 In. 345.00
Lalique, D'Orsay, Square, Gold Label, Amber, Glass, Stopper, 3 In. 242.00
Lalique, Dans La Nuit, Worth, Display, Blue Enameled, Clear Stars, 1924, 12 3/4 In.... 1265.00
Lalique, Enfants, Frosted, Metal Atomizer, Cherubs, Sepia, 1931, 4 1/4 In.................. 862.00
Lalique, Epines, Clear & Frosted, Blue Patina Stopper, 1920, 4 In. 517.00
Lalique, Epines, Clear & Frosted, Sepia Pattern, Stopper, 1920, 4 5/8 In. 632.00
Lalique, Fe Reviens, Worth, Display, Contents, Label, 12 1/2 In. 460.00
Lalique, Female Nudes, Gilt Metal, Leather Case, 1925 .... 575.00
Lalique, Figurines, Marcus Et Bardel, Clear & Frosted, Gilt Metal, 1922, 6 In. 316.00
Lalique, Forvil, Design Of Beads In Spirals, Stopper, 8 In... 990.00
Lalique, Perles, Clear & Frosted, Sepia Patina, 1926, 6 5/8 In. 230.00
Lalique, Petites Fueilles, Blue Patina, 1910, 4 In.. 1035.00
Lalique, Worth Fragrances, Amber, Dabber Stopper, Flask, 1930 .... 258.00
Lentheric, Tweed, Wooden Overcap, Contents, Box, 2 3/4 In...................................... 44.00
Lightner's Maid Of The Mist Perfumes, Milk Glass, Cylindrical, 1890, 7 1/4 In. 330.00
Lucien Lelong, Flower Caddy, Cylindrical, Gold Cap, Box, 2 1/2 In., 4 Piece............... 55.00
Lucien Lelong, Jabot, Bow Shape, Frosted, Inner Stopper, 1/2 Oz., 1 1/8 In................. 412.00
Lucien Lelong, Jabot, Gilded Wooden Cap, Hatbox, 1 7/8 In..................................... 198.00
Lucien Lelong, Orgueil, Curvaceous Shape, Encased Gold, Stopper, 3 1/4 In. 198.00
Lucien Lelong, Sirocco, Gold Cap, Green & White Box, 1 5/8 In. 71.50
Lucretia Vanderbilt, Flattened Round Shape, Blue, Dabber, Leather Pouch, 2 3/8 In. .. 275.00
Maggie Noir, Store Display 350.00
Matchabelli, Beloved Golden Autumn, Crown Shape, Hat Box, Ribbon, 1 3/8 In., Pair 143.00
Matchabelli, Prophesy, Crown Shape, Enameled White, Gold Patina, 2 1/2 In............. 231.00
Matchabelli, Windsong, Crown Shape, Green Enamel, Gold Metal Cap, Box, 1 3/4 In. 100.00
Max Factor, Wild Musk, Acorn Shape, On Chain, Celluloid Box, Contents, 1 7/8 In. ... 50.00

Perfume,
Tre Lis, Plume
Stopper, Paper
Label, 6 In.

Perfume, Clam
Shell, Blue,
English, c. 1870,
2 3/8 In.

Maxim's Of Paris, Black, Red Plastic Stopper, Gold Cord, Store Display, 12 In. 187.00
Mercury Glass, Green & Orange Swirl 40.00
Molyneux, Charm, Apothecary Shape, Disc Stopper, Baccarat Emblem, 6 In. 115.00
Monument, Boston & Sandwich Glassworks, Green, c.1860, 8 In. 2970.00
Nina Ricci, Coeur Joie, Marc Lalique Design, 1950 .... 230.00
Nina Ricci, Coeur Joie, Heart Shape, Plastic Heart Box, 1 1/8 In. 275.00
Nina Ricci, Fille D'Eve, Flattened Apple, Frosted, Metal Cap, Green Lined Basket 357.00
Oakley Soap & Perfumery Co., New York, Barrel, Pt. 29.00
Obsession, Men's, Store Display 95.00
Opalescent White, Enameled Floral Panels, Octagonal, Stopper, 3 1/8 In. 170.00
Oscar, Red, Store Display 350.00
Oscar, Store Display, Small 250.00
Oscar De La Renta, Ruffles, Boat Shape, Rectangular Stopper, Display, 10 3/8 In. 176.00
Palmer's Patchouli, Embossed Salon Palmer Perfumer, N.Y., Sept. 23, 1962, 9 In. 495.00
Passion, Store Display 500.00
Patou, Normandie, Liner Ship Shape, Blue & Silver Plinth Base, Long Dabber, 3 In. ... 3300.00
Picturing Victorian Girl, Label, Original Box 40.00
Ralph Lauren, Safari, Cut Glass, Faux Silver, Tortoiseshell Cap, Store Display, 10 1/8 In. 187.00
Renaud, Sweet Pea, Blue Stripes, Brass Cap, Red Leather Case, 2 1/2 In. 38.00
Safuran, My Own Jasmine, Held By Japanese Doll, Gold Cap, Wooden Base, 2 7/8 In. 82.50
Sandwich Glass, Green, 6-Sided, Molded Spire Stopper, 6 1/2 In. 357.00
Schiaparelli, Shocking You, Dress Dummy Shape, Gold Chain, Pouch Box, 2 1/8 In. ... 132.00
Schiaparelli, Shocking, Skyscraper Shape, Ball Top, Sealed, Contents, 7 In. 192.00
Schiaparelli, Succes Fou, Fig Leaf Shape, Green & Gold, Inner Stopper, 3 In. 522.00
Schiaparelli, Zut, Molded Woman's Torso, Green Ribbon, Gold Cap, 2 3/8 In. 715.00
Seely Helotrope Perfume, Paper Label, BIMAL, 3 x 1 1/8 In. 35.00
Suzy, Scarlet De Suzy, Molded Woman's Head, Red Hat, Inner Stopper, 4 1/2 In. 467.00
Tre Lis, Plume Stopper, Paper Label, 6 In. ....*Illus* 10.00
Verlayne, Attente, Fan Shape, Stopper, Overcap, 1946, 3 3/8 In. 121.00
Vigny, Le Golliwogg, Molded, Black Stopper, Red Silk Box, 3 In. 264.00
Vigny, Le Golliwogg, Molded, Frosted, Black Golliwog Stopper, 6 In. 412.00
World Globe Shape, Clear & Frosted, Airplane Stopper, 5 In. 495.00

─────────────────────── **PICKLE** ───────────────────────

Pickles were packed in special jars from about 1880 to 1920. The pickle jar was usually large, from one quart to one gallon size. They were made with four to eight sides. The mouth was wide because you had to reach inside to take out the pickle. The top was usually sealed with a cork or tin cover. Many pickle jars were designed with raised gothic arches as panels. These jars are clear examples of the Victorian gothic revival designs, so they are often included in museum exhibitions of the period. Their large size and attractive green to blue coloring make them good accessories in a room, and designers often use them on a kitchen counter. Bottle collectors realize that pickle jars are examples of good bottle design, that they are rare, and that a collection can be formed showing the works of many glasshouses. Pickle bottles are so popular that they are being reproduced. For more information on pickle jars, see *Ketchup, Pickles, Sauces* by Betty Zumwalt.

PICKLE, Aqua, Plain Base, Qt., 14 In. 15.00
Atmore's, Cathedral, Apple Green, c.1870-1880, 11 1/4 In. 275.00

Barrel, Brilliant Emerald Green, Concentric Rings, Qt. 49.00
Barrel, Emerald Green, Large 75.00
Bunker Hill, Skilton Foote & Co., Amber, 6 3/4 In. ....90.00 to 121.00
Bunker Hill, Skilton Foote & Co., Amber, Square, 6 1/2 In. 58.00
Bunker Hill, Skilton Foote & Co., Aqua, Round, 5 In. 25.00
Bunker Hill, Skilton Foote & Co., Aqua, Tooled Lip, 11 1/2 In. 176.00
Bunker Hill, Skilton Foote & Co., Embossed Monument, Yellow, Applied Top 55.00
Bunker Hill, Skilton Foote & Co., Honey Amber, Smooth Base, Qt. 35.00
Bunker Hill, Skilton Foote & Co., Light Citron Amber, Whittled Glass 75.00
Bunker Hill, Skilton Foote & Co., Yellow-Olive, Wide Mouth, 7 5/8 In. 125.00
C.P. Co., Blue-Aqua, Square, 11 1/4 In. 65.00
Cathedral, Amber, c.1880-1890, 13 1/4 In. 1072.00
Cathedral, Aqua, 11 1/2 In. 605.00
Cathedral, Aqua, 12 3/4 In. 258.50
Cathedral, Aqua, 14 In. 143.00
Cathedral, Aqua, 4 Sided, 11 1/2 In. 176.00
Cathedral, Aqua, 6-Sided, 1 Indented Panel, 13 1/4 In. 440.00
Cathedral, Aqua, 6-Sided, c.1870, 13 1/4 In. 82.50
Cathedral, Aqua, 6-Sided, Rolled Lip, Whittled, c.1870, 12 3/4 In. 132.00
Cathedral, Aqua, Applied Mouth, Whittled, 13 1/8 In. 210.00
Cathedral, Aqua, Applied Top, 9 In. 275.00
Cathedral, Aqua, Applied Top, Bubbles, 11 1/2 In. 94.00
Cathedral, Aqua, Collared Mouth, 11 1/2 In. 257.00
Cathedral, Aqua, Embossed, c.1875, 13 3/4 In. 231.00
Cathedral, Aqua, IP, Rolled Mouth, 11 In. 523.00
Cathedral, Aqua, Rolled Lip, 1865-1875, 8 3/4 In. ....*Illus* 143.00
Cathedral, Aqua, Rolled Lip, 1865-1875, 11 In. ....*Illus* 198.00
Cathedral, Aqua, Rolled Lip, 1865-1875, 13 3/4 In. ....*Illus* 203.00
Cathedral, Aqua, Rolled Mouth, Pontil, 8 5/8 In. 418.00
Cathedral, Benicia Type, Opalescent, Applied Top, 11 1/4 In. 385.00
Cathedral, Clear, Tooled Collared Mouth, 13 In. 165.00
Cathedral, Dark Green, Partial Label, 13 In. 250.00
Cathedral, Emerald Green, 13 1/2 In. 440.00
Cathedral, Emerald Green, IP, Rolled Lip, 14 1/2 In. 1400.00
Cathedral, Emerald Green, Rolled Lip, IP, 12 In. 1375.00
Cathedral, Emerald Green, Rolled Lip, Pontil, c.1870, 9 3/8 In. 440.00
Cathedral, Emerald Green, Whittled, Rolled Lip, 13 In. 1595.00
Cathedral, Gothic Arches, Aqua, Square, c.1880, 11 1/4 In. 275.00
Cathedral, Gothic Pattern, 13 In. 250.00
Cathedral, Green, 6-Sided, c.1870, 13 1/4 In. 192.00
Cathedral, Light Green, 6-Sided, Applied Mouth, 13 In. 253.00
Cathedral, Light Green, 8 1/2 In. ....*Illus* 110.00
Cathedral, Light Green, Rolled Lip, IP, 1855-1865, 11 1/2 In. ....*Illus* 297.00
Cathedral, Light Yellow Green, Rolled Mouth, 1860-1870, 11 5/8 In. 358.00
Cathedral, Olive Amber, Rolled Mouth, Pontil, 14 In. 1650.00

*Pickle, Cathedral, Aqua,
Rolled Lip,
1865-1875, 8 3/4 In.*

*Pickle, Cathedral,
Aqua, Rolled Lip,
1865-1875, 11 In.*

*Pickle, Cathedral,
Aqua, Rolled Lip,
1865-1875, 8 3/4 In.*

Pickle, Cathedral,   Pickle, Cathedral, Light   Pickle, H.J. Heinz Co., Pitts-
Light Green,   Green, Rolled Lip, IP,   burgh, Fresh Cucumber Pickle,
8 1/2 In.   1855-1865, 11 1/2 In.   Improve By Chilling, 8 In.

Cathedral, Whittled, Applied Top, 11 1/2 In. 176.00
Cathedral, Yellow Green, 11 1/2 In. 275.00
Cathedral, Yellow Green, Rolled Lip, c.1870, 13 3/8 In. 1320.00
Cloverleaf, Golden Amber, Rolled Mouth, 8 1/8 In. 495.00
Cruirshank Bros. Co., Pat. Feb. 11, 1886, Stoneware, Wire Handle, Label, 5 1/8 In. ... 88.00
Cylindrical, Aqua, Pontil, 1840-1860, 10 1/4 In. 220.00
E. Gager Manufacturer, Norwalk, Ohio, 3-Sided.. 50.00
E.T. Cowdrey & Co., Boston, Red Label, Aqua, Rolled Lip, 11 5/8 In. 55.00
English Spiced Sweet Mixed, Williams Bros. & Charbonneau, Detroit, Aqua, 11 In. .. 44.00
G.P. Sanborn & Son, Boston, Shield & Star, Amber, Ground Lip, c.1890, 8 In. 148.00
Goofus, Flower On Stem, Ground Top, 14 In. 75.00
H.J. Heinz Co., Keystone Pickling & Preserving Works, Pat.1890, Large Screw Cap.... 10.00
H.J. Heinz Co., Pittsburgh, Embossed Glass Lid, c.1910, 9 1/2 In. 121.00
H.J. Heinz Co., Pittsburgh, Fresh Cucumber Pickle, Improve By Chilling, 8 In. ...... *Illus* 45.00
Henry Kellogg, Philadelphia 150.00
M.C. Co., Cathedral, 6-Sided, c.1890, 13 3/8 In. 231.00
Mason, Original Tin Lid & Handle, 24 In. 40.00
Milwaukee Pickle Co., Wauwatosa, Wis., Amber, 9 1/2 In. 225.00
Pacific Vinegar & Pickle Works, San Francisco, Sun-Colored Amethyst................... 10.00
Parker & Co., Union Brand, Amber, Tapered Cone, 8 In. 40.00
Pioneer Pickle Works, Sacramento, Cal., Mixed Pickles, Aqua, Label, 1880s, 10 3/4 In. 77.00
Plain Pickles From Cohen Cook & Co., New York, Cathedral, Aqua, Rolled Lip, 11 In. 99.00
Richmond Pickle Co., Richmond, Va., Aqua, 3-Sided... 13.75
Shaker Brand, E.D. Pettengill & Co., Amber, Rolled Lip, 7 1/4 In. 440.00
SJG, Cathedral, Aqua, Embossed.. 66.00
Skilton Foote & Co.'s Bunker Hill Pickles, Lighthouse, Amber, c.1890, 11 In. 412.00
Superior Pickles, Cathedral, Aqua, Tooled Lip, c.1880, 13 In. 88.00
T.B. Smith & Co., Philadelphia, Emerald Green, Pontil, 1/2 Gal. 1650.00
W.K. Lewis & Bros., Boston, 5 Vertical Panels, Aqua, IP, 10 1/2 In. 303.00
W.K. Lewis & Bros., Boston, Cathedral, Gherkins, Aqua, c.1875, 11 1/4 In. 93.50
Warsaw Pickle Co., Embossed Statue Of Liberty, 8 1/2 In. 25.00
Weller Pickle Co., Cincinnati, Oh., Aqua, Rectangular... 35.00
Wells Miller & Provost, Emerald Green, Pontil, Applied Mouth, 7 7/8 In. 413.00
Whitney Glass Works, Aqua, Rolled Lip, 14 In. 88.00

─────────────────── **POISON** ───────────────────

Everyone knows you must be careful about how you store poisonous substances. Our
ancestors had the same problem. Nineteenth-century poison bottles were usually made
with raised designs so the user could feel the danger. The skull and crossbones symbol was
sometimes shown, but usually the bottle had ridges or raised embossing. The most interesting poison bottles were made from the 1870s to the 1930s. Cobalt blue and bright green
glass were often used. The bottle was designed to look different from any type of food
container. One strange British poison bottle made in 1871 was shaped like a coffin and was
often decorated with a death's head. Another bottle was shaped like a skull. Poison collec-

tors search for any bottle that held poison or that is labeled poison. Included are animal and plant poisons as well as dangerous medicines. A helpful reference book is *Poison Bottle Workbook* by Rudy Kuhn.

POISON, A.L. Ogg, Cobalt Blue, Square Collar Lip, Square, 1890, 4 5/8 In. 198.00
Acid Vulcanizing Solution, Goodyear Tire Rubber Co., Amber, Blob Top, 4 1/2 In. 25.00
Admiralty, Cobalt, 8 Oz. 43.00
Amber, 3-Sided, 2 3/4 In. 25.00
Amber, Embossed Both Sides, Ridged Borders, 1 1/2 In. 4.50
Amber, Euvalerol, Cylinder, 9 In. 48.00
Amber, Label, Contents, 2 3/4 In. 18.00
Ammonia, Embossed Caution Poisonous, Aqua, Bee Hive On Back, Oval, 6 1/4 In. 45.00
Ammonia, Mfg.'d By S.F. Gaslight Co., Aqua, Qt. 40.00
Anrol Ant Killer, Green 14.00
Antiseptic Tablets, Parke Davis & Co., Amber, Labels, 1890, 4 1/2 In. ....*Illus* 77.00
Aqua, Ribbed, Porcelain Stopper, 10 In. 45.00
Bichloride Of Mercury, John Wyeth & Bros. Inc., Cobalt Blue, ABM, 2 1/4 In. 55.00
Black Flag Powder, Contents, Label, Box. 8.00
Bowman's Drug Store, Cobalt Blue, 4 1/4 In. 325.00
C.L.C. & Co., Embossed Poison, Green, 5 1/2 In. 121.00
C.L.G. Co., Cobalt Blue, 3 Smooth Flat Sides, 3 Ridged Sides 18.50
C.L.G. Co., Cobalt Blue, 6-Sided, 4 In. 35.00
C.L.G. Co., Pat. Applied For, Cobalt Blue, 4 1/4 In. 45.00
C.L.G. Co., Poison On 2-Sides, Olive Green, 6-Sided, 5 In. 110.00
Carbolic Acid, Cobalt Blue, 5-Sided Front, 1 Flat Side, Embossed 38.50
Carbolic Acid, Label, Rigo, Cobalt Blue, Tooled Lip, Canada, 6 7/8 In. 85.00
Carbolic Acid, Morris Drug Co., York, Pa., Skull & Crossbones, Label 12.00
Carbolic Oil, Embossed Poisonous On Shoulder, Cobalt Blue, 8-Sided, 5 7/8 In. 45.00
Cobalt Blue, 3-Sided, 6 1/8 In. .... 90.00 to 100.00
Cobalt Blue, 3-Sided, Label, Cork, ABM, Contents, 3 1/8 In. 100.00
Cobalt Blue, 6-Sided, 4 1/4 In. 40.00
Cobalt Blue, Blob Top, No Stopper, 13 1/2 In. 100.00
Cobalt Blue, Quilted, 7 1/8 In. 55.00
Cobalt Blue, Ribbed, Stopper, Square, 16 Oz. 71.50
Cobalt Blue, Tooled Lip, c.1870-1880, 4 1/4 In. 715.00
Cobalt Blue, Vin Antimon, Three Piece Mold, 14 1/2 In. 100.00
Coffin, Amber, Tooled Lip, 3 1/2 In. 242.00
Coffin, Blue, American, c.1910, 3 5/8 In. 99.00
Costar's, Bug Powder, Aqua 3.00
Cyanide Antiseptic Tablets, Sharpe & Dohme, Baltimore, Amber, Box, 4 In. 77.00
Dark Blue, 6-Sided, 5 In. 40.00
Dead Shot For Bed Bugs, St. Albans, Vt., Aqua, OP, c.1850, 5 In. 176.00
Dead Stuck For Bugs, Aqua, 9 1/4 In. 20.00

*Poison, Antiseptic Tablets,
Parke Davis & Co., Amber,
Labels, 1890, 4 1/2 In.*

*Poison, Dil Acid
Nitric, Cap,
7 In.*

*Poison, Figural, Skull,
Cobalt Blue, Pat. Appl'd For,
4 1/8 In.*

Dept. Of Hospitals, Mercurochrome, Quilted, Red Interior, 4 5/8 In. 40.00
Diamond & Lattice Pattern, Cobalt Blue, Whittled, Stopper, 7 1/4 In. 96.00
Diamond Antiseptic, 3-Sided, Label, 4 3/4 In. 20.00
Dick's Ant Destroyer, Dick & Co., New Orleans, La., Metal Screw Lid, 6 In. 83.00
Dil Acid Nitric, Cap, 7 In. ....*Illus* 12.00
DP Poison, Skull & Crossbones, Coffin Shape, Cobalt Blue, Label, 3 In. 990.00
DP Poison, Skull & Crossbones, Coffin Shape, Cobalt Blue, 3 In. 385.00
Dr. Orestes, Cobalt, Stopper.. 225.00
Dun Drug Co., Green, 3 7/16 In. 225.00
Dutchers Dead Shot For Bed Bugs, St. Albans, Vt., Aqua, OP, 5 In. 330.00
Dykema's, C.L.G. Co., Patent Applied For, Yellow Green, c.1910, 6 3/8 In. 385.00
Eclipse, Cobalt Blue, Wasp Waist, Stopper, 8 Oz. 3495.00
Eli Lilly & Co., Embossed Poison, Amber, 10 1/8 In...:.................................. 121.00
Eli Lilly & Co., Indianapolis, Amber, 2 Embossed Sides, Label, 5 In. 15.00
Embossed Arrow Below Poison, Cobalt Blue, 6-Sided 40.00
Embossed Bud, Aqua, Flared Lip, 4 1/4 In. 132.00
Embossed Caution Not To Be Taken, Emerald Green, c.1910 .... 577.00
Embossed Not To Be Taken, Amber, 6-Sided, 3/12 In. 35.00
Embossed Not To Be Taken, Aqua, Round, 5 1/4 In. 10.00
Embossed Not To Be Taken, Cobalt Blue, 6-Sided, 3 In. 20.00
Embossed Not To Be Taken, Cobalt Blue, 6-Sided, 3 Oz. 40.00
Embossed Not To Be Taken, Cobalt Blue, Swirls, Ribbed, Rectangular, 6 1/2 In......... 24.00
Embossed Not To Be Taken, Emerald Green, BIMAL, Rectangular, 4 1/4 In. 13.00
Embossed Not To Be Taken, Yellow Green, 3 1/ 2 In. 154.00
Embossed Not To Be Taken, Yellow Green, 6-Sided, 6 3/8 In. 50.00
Embossed Poison, Amber, 3 1/4 In.. 77.00
Embossed Poison, Amber, 3-Sided, 3 In. 85.00
Embossed Poison, Amber, 6-Sided, Irregular.. 45.00
Embossed Poison, Amber, Cork & Wire Stopper, 3 1/4 In. 60.00
Embossed Poison, Amber, Tooled Lip, 7 7/8 In. 264.00
Embossed Poison, Amber, Triangular, 3 7/8 In. 770.00
Embossed Poison, Aqua, Round, 5 1/2 In. 28.00
Embossed Poison, Clear, Tooled Lip, 7 7/8 In. 853.00
Embossed Poison, Cobalt Blue, 2 7/8 In. 1540.00
Embossed Poison, Cobalt Blue, 3 3/8 In. 1045.00
Embossed Poison, Cobalt Blue, 6-Sided, 4 1/4 In. 40.00
Embossed Poison, Cobalt Blue, 6-Sided, Stopper, 10 In. 220.00
Embossed Poison, Cobalt Blue, ABM, 2 5/8 In. 93.00
Embossed Poison, Cobalt Blue, c.1890, 7 1/2 In. 797.50
Embossed Poison, Cobalt Blue, Cylinder, 5 1/2 In. ....30.00 to 40.00
Embossed Poison, Cobalt Blue, Lattice & Diamond Pattern, 4 1/8 In. 35.00
Embossed Poison, Cobalt Blue, Ribbed, Stopper 100.00
Embossed Poison, Green, Rolled Lip, Pontil, 5 5/8 In. 66.00
Embossed Poison, Green, Round Cylinder, 5 In.. 30.00
Embossed Poison, Hobnail, Clear, Pontil, 5 1/8 In. 100.00
Embossed Poison, J.F. Hartz Co., Toronto, Cobalt Blue, 6 1/8 In. 605.00
Embossed Poison, J.T.M. & Co., Amber, Applied Mouth, 3 In.............................. 83.00
Embossed Poison, Lattice & Diamond, Cobalt Blue, Stopper, 1890, 7 1/4 In........*Illus* 77.00
Embossed Poison, Not To Be Taken, Green, Ribbed, Oblong, 6 5/8 In........................ 18.00
Embossed Poison, Skull & Cross Bones, Stars, Amber, 4 3/4 In......................413.00 to 595.00
Embossed Poison Not To Be Taken, Cobalt Blue, Oval, 8 1/4 In............................. 26.00
Embossed Poisonous Not To Be Taken, Cobalt Blue, 6-Sided, 6 In. 58.00
Embossed Poisonous Not To Be Taken, Cobalt Blue, England, 3 1/2 In. ....*Illus* 75.00
Embossed Poisonous Not To Be Taken, Green, England, 5 1/2 In. ....*Illus* 50.00
Embossed Poisonous Not To Be Taken, Olive, England, 6 In.............................*Illus* 18.00
Embossed Use With Caution, Cobalt Blue.. 72.00
Fahnestocks Vermifuge, Aqua, OP 20.00
Farmers Rat Paste, Embossed Rat, Cobalt Blue, 2 In. 60.00
Farmers Rat Paste, Embossed Rat, Peach Amber, 2 In.................................30.00 to 55.00
Figural, Skeleton In Cloak, Brown & Tan, Ceramic, 1880-1920, 5 3/4 In. 110.00
Figural, Skull, Cobalt Blue, Flared Mouth, 1880-1900, 4 1/8 In. 187.00
Figural, Skull, Cobalt Blue, Pat. Appl'd For, 4 1/8 In...................................*Illus* 660.00
Figural, Skull, Cobalt Blue, Pat. Appl'd For, Tooled Lip, 4 In. 2090.00

Poison, H.K. Mulford Co.,
Chemists, Phila., Skull &
Crossbones, Cobalt Blue,
3 1/4 In.

Poison, Maorix, Olive,
England

Poison, Jno. Wyeth & Bro.,
Philadelphia, Cobalt Blue,
1890-1910, 2 5/8 In.

Poison, Embossed
Poison, Lattice & Diamond,
Cobalt Blue, Stopper,
1890, 7 1/4 In.

Poison, Embossed
Poisonous Not To Be
Taken, Cobalt Blue,
England, 3 1/2 In.

Poison, Embossed
Poisonous Not To Be
Taken, Green, England,
5 1/2 In.

Figural,	Skull, Cobalt Blue, Pat. Appl'd For, 1890, 4 1/8 In.	660.00
Figural,	Skull, Cobalt Blue, Pat. Appl'd. For, c.1972, 3 7/8 In.	60.00
Figural,	Skull, Cobalt Blue, Pat. June 26th, 1894, 4 In.	1375.00
Figural,	Skull, Cobalt Blue, Tooled Lip, 1870-1880, 4 1/4 In.	715.00
Figural,	Skull, Cobalt Blue, Tooled Lip, 4 1/8 In.	990.00
Figural,	Skull, Embossed Poison, Pat. Appl'd For, Cobalt Blue, c.1910, 4 1/8 In.	522.00
Figural,	Skull, Pat. June 26th, 1894, Cobalt Blue, Tooled, 3 1/2 In.	1375.00
Flask,	2-Piece Mold, Raised Square Pattern, Pontil	231.00
Flask,	Flattened Form, Crossbones Motif, 5 1/2 In.	66.00
Foulston,	Crescent, Embossed Not To Be Taken, Cobalt Blue, 3/1/2 In.	55.00
Friedgen,	C.L.G. Co., Patent Applied For, Yellow Green, c.1910, 2 3/4 In.	852.00
Grasselli Arsenate Of Lead,	Jug, Tan, Large Winged Insect, Handle, Qt	80.00
Green,	6-Sided, 4 1/2 In.	30.00
Green,	6-Sided, 6 1/2 In.	30.00
Green,	Embossed Star Poison, 6 In.	280.00
Green,	Ribbed, Stopper, Wide Mouth, 8 1/2 In.	120.00
Green,	Vertical Ribs, Stopper, Cylinder, 4 1/2 In.	89.00
H.B. Co.,	Stopper, 4 5/8 In.	75.00 to 85.00
H.K. Mulford Co.,	Chemists, Phila., Skull & Crossbones, Cobalt Blue, 3 1/4 In. ....*Illus*	121.00
Hastings,	Worcester, Embossed Not To Be Taken, Yellow Green, c.1910, 5 5/8 In.	440.00
Hunters Domestic Cleansing Ammonia,	Stoneware, Stenciled, Stopper	135.00
Huxley Brand,	Sal-Antiseptious, Cobalt Blue, 5 1/2 In.	22.00
Inmans Household Ammonia,	Marvelous Cleanser, Eagle, Stoneware, Stenciled	100.00

Insecticide Vicat Brevete, Aqua, Embossed Bug, 1870, 4 1/4 In. 132.00
Iodine, Skull & Crossbones, Amber, ABM, 3 In. 6.00
J. Cox, Armadale, Cobalt Blue, Square, 1890, 4 3/4 In. 187.00
J. T. M. Co., Embossed Poison, Amber, 5 In. 467.50
J.G. Godding & Co., Apothecaries, Boston, Cobalt Blue, Ribbed, 6 1/4 In. 425.00
J.T.M. & Co., Milliken's Tri-Seps, Yellow Amber, Label, 3 In. 94.00
J.T.M. & Co., Red Amber, Tooled Lip, 5 In. 523.00
Jacobs' Bed Bug Killer, Amber, Skull & Crossbones, 1890, 5 1/2 In. 1485.00
Jacobs' Biochloride Tablets, Amber, Skull & Crossbones, 8-Sided, 1 1/4 In. 935.00
Jar, Hydrarg Oxyd. Rub, Cobalt Blue, Glass Stopper, 1890s, 4 1/4 In. 220.00
Jeye's Fluid, Amber, Oval, 6 In. 35.00
Jno. Wyeth & Bro., Philadelphia, Cobalt Blue, 1890-1910, 2 5/8 In. .... *Illus* 99.00
Kil-Lol Bug Killer .... 35.00 to 45.00
Killgerm Co., Ltd., Cleckheaton In Script, Amber, 3-Sided, Triangular, 6 In. 60.00
Krieger's Pharmacy, Poughkeepsie, Embossed, Label, 1900 .... 28.00
Lattice & Diamond, Cobalt Blue, Round, 1/2 Gal. 605.00
Lattice & Diamond, Cobalt Blue, Round, Tooled Lip, 1890, 11 1/2 In. 660.00
Lattice & Diamond, Cobalt Blue, Stopper, 1910, 7 In. .... 77.00 to 88.00
Lattice & Diamond, Cobalt Blue, Tooled Lip, c.1890, Cylindrical, 11 1/2 In. 660.00
Lattice & Diamond, Green, 4 1/2 In. 522.50
Lattice & Diamond, H.B. & Co., Cobalt Blue, c.1910, 5 5/8 In. 88.00
Lattice & Diamond, Tooled Top, 4 1/2 In. 55.00
Lattice & Diamond, W.T. Co., Cobalt Blue, Poison Stopper, c.1910, 4 1/2 In. 82.50
Lin Bellad Meth, 3-Piece Mold, Brown, Stopper, 7 1/2 In. 48.00
Liq. Hyd. Perchl, Emerald Green, Stopper, Round, Label Under Glass, 7 In. 125.00
Maorix, Olive, England .... *Illus* 150.00
Marshall's, Amber 40.00
Martin's, S.A.A. Manchester, Embossed Poison, Aqua, 2 Oz. 399.00
Martin's Poison, U-Bend Neck, Lies Horizontally, 4 Oz. 390.00
McCormack & Co., Baltimore, Cobalt Blue, 3-Sided, 3 In. 80.00
McSwain Jr., Roaches, Minnows, Aqua, 12 1/4 In. 100.00
Melvin & Badger Apothecaries, Boston, Mass, Cobalt Blue, 5 In. 55.00
Mercury Bichloride, Amber, Tooled Lip, 3 In. 143.00
Mercury Bichloride, Clear, Tooled Lip, 3 3/8 In. 121.00
Mercury Bichloride, Eli Lilly & Co., Amber, 3-Sided, 8 In. 60.00
Mercury Bichloride, Parke, Davis & Co., Amber, 7 3/4 In. 264.00
Mercury Bichloride, Poison Antiseptics, Label, Amber, 3-Sided, 8 In. 60.00
Mercury Bichloride, Yellow Amber, Tooled Lip, 3 3/8 In. 121.00
Morgan X, 31, Amber, Honey, No Stopper, 6 1/2 In. 100.00
Morris L. Holman Liquid Lye Co., New York, Pat. June 30 1874, Aqua, 6 1/2 In. 80.00
Mulford Co., Chemists, Philadelphia, P.A., Embossed Poison, Cobalt Blue, 3 1/8 In. 137.50
N.B. Co., Embossed Poison, Amber, Pat. Appd. For, c.1910, 2 1/2 In. 110.00
National Casket Co., Capitol Dome & Eagle, 1/2 Gal. 29.00
Norwich Coffin, Cobalt Blue, Tooled Lip, 7 1/2 In. 1320.00
Owl Drug Co., 8 In. 275.00
Owl Drug Co., Cobalt Blue, 2 7/8 In. 104.50
Owl Drug Co., Cobalt Blue, 4 1/2 In. 170.50
Owl Drug Co., Cobalt Blue, 9 1/2 In. 550.00
Owl Drug Co., Cobalt Blue, c.1890, 9 3/4 In. 522.50
Owl Drug Co., Cobalt Blue, Owl On Mortar & Pestle, 7 7/8 In. 121.00
Owl Drug Co., Cobalt Blue, Tooled Lip, Stopper, 9 In. 550.00
Owl Drug Co., Cobalt Blue, Tooled Top, Bubbles, 8 In. 357.00
Owl Drug Co., Dark Cobalt Blue, 1 7/8 In. 65.00
Owl Drug Co., Embossed Owl, Cobalt Blue, 3-Sided, Qt. 795.00
Owl Drug Co., Embossed Owl, Cobalt Blue, 8 In. 325.00
Owl Drug Co., Owl On Mortar & Pestle, Cobalt Blue, 7 3/4 In. 275.00
Owl Drug Co., Skull & Crossbone, Tooled Lip, Stopper, 10 In. 357.50
P.D. & Co., Amber, Tooled Lip, 1910, 5 3/4 In. 77.00
Permal Solution, Cobalt Blue, Oval, 6 1/2 In. 120.00
Plynine, Stenciled, 8 1/4 In. 80.00
Poison Embossed On 2 Panels, Amber, c.1910, 7 7/8 In. 264.00
Poison Embossed On 2 Panels, Amber, Contents, c.1910, 3 3/8 In. 82.50
Poison Embossed On 2 Panels, Cobalt Blue, C.L.G. Co., Pat. Applied For, 1910, 7 1/2 In. 121.00

Poison, Embossed
Poisonous Not To Be Taken,
Olive, England, 6 In.

Poison, S. & D., Poison,
Amber, Tooled Lip,
1890-1910, 4 3/4 In.

Poison, U.D. Co., W.G.W.,
Amber, Tooled Lip,
1890-1910, 3 1/4 In.

Poison Embossed On 2 Panels, Olive Green, Rolled Lip, c.1910, 7 3/4 In. 2145.00
Poison Tincture Iodine, Skull & Crossbones, Amber, Rubber Stopper 30.00
Potassium Permanganate, Embossed Poison, Cobalt Blue, ABM, Labels, Panels, 3 In. ... 35.00
Quilted Design, Cobalt Blue 85.00
Ribbed Center Panel, Emerald Green, 6 1/4 In. 125.00
Row & Co. Dispensing Chemists, Rochampton, Cobalt Blue, Square, England, 3 1/2 In. 242.00
S. & D., Poison, Amber, Tooled Lip, 1890-1910, 4 3/4 In. ....*Illus* 330.00
Seibert Poison Fly Paper 5.00
Sergsoll Elliott, Amber, 6 1/4 In... 110.00
Sheffield Corp., Embossed Poison, Emerald Green, 6 3/4 In. 145.00
Skull & Crossbones, Amber, Tooled Lip, 2 5/8 In.. 88.00
Skull & Crossbones, Bichloride Tablets, Honey Amber, 8-Sided, c.1890, 2 1/4 In. 935.00
Skull & Crossbones, Cobalt Blue, ABM, 2 In. 242.00
Skull & Crossbones, Embossed W.T. Co., Amber, Tooled Lip, Cylindrical, 5 In. 1485.00
Skull & Crossbones, Iodine, Amber, Square.. 3.50
Skull & Crossbones, Pat. June 26th 1894, Blue, Tooled Lip, Smooth Base, 1895 .... 1595.00
Skull & Crossbones, Red, White Transfer On Tin, Screw Cap, Square, 5 1/2 In. 232.00
Stekette's Pin Worm Destroyer, Geo. Stekette, Aqua 10.00
Strychnine, Clear, America, c.1910, 2 3/8 In.. 121.00
Strychnine, Webb & Roger, San Rafael, Calif., Cobalt Blue, Quilted, 3 7/8 In............. 55.00
Submarine, Cobalt Blue, 4 In. 600.00
Submarine, Cobalt Blue, Small 375.00
Sun Drug, Yellow Green, 2 7/8 In... 220.00
Sun Drug, Yellow Green, 3 3/8 In... 303.00
Sun Drug Co., Yellow Green, C.L.G. Co., Pat. Appl'd For, c.1910, 2 3/4 In. 182.00
Sure Death Poison, Fly Paper 5.00
Swift's Arsenate Of Lead, Merrimac Chemical Co., Stenciled Crock, 5 Lbs................ 69.00
Swift's Arsenic Of Lead, Merrimac Chemical Co., Boston, Jar, Handle, 6 1/4 In......... 75.00
Tinct Canthar, Label Under Glass, Clear, Glass Stopper, c.1910, 9 In........................... 143.00
Tincture Iodine, Skull & Crossbones, Glass Rod & Rubber Stopper 55.00
Trilets, Cobalt Blue, 3-Sided.. 10.00
Trilets, Cobalt Blue, 3-Sided, Label, 3 1/4 In.. 38.00
U.D. Co., W.G.W., Amber, Tooled Lip, 1890-1910, 3 1/4 In.................................*Illus* 715.00
U.S.P.H.S., Cobalt Blue, Quilt Pattern, 5 3/8 In. 950.00
Undertakers Supply Co., Chicago, Embalming Fluid, 7 1/2 In. ....60.00 to 75.00
Vapo Cresolene, Blue, 5 1/2 In.. 85.00
Vapo Cresolene Co., U.S. Pat. June 18, 1895, Cobalt Blue, Olive Striations, 5 1/4 In... 132.00
W.H. McCarthy, Sydney, Cobalt Blue, Square Collar Lip, 1890, 3 3/8 In. 187.00
Wm. Radams Microbe Killer, Jug, No.3, Tan, Stenciled, Gal. ....295.00 to 395.00
Wm. Radams Microbe Killer, Jug, White Glazed, Gal. ....110.00 to 130.00
Wm. Radams Microbe Killer, Man Beating Skeleton, Amber, 10 1/4 In...................... 55.00

Wrights Lysol, Amber, 4 In.	50.00
X M In Circle, Cobalt Blue, Triangular	9.00
Yellow, Fluting On Back And Shoulders, 5 1/2 In.	100.00

----------------------------- POTTERY -----------------------------

Many bottles were made of pottery. In this section we have included those that have no brand name and do not fit into another category. Many figural flasks, such as those made at the Bennington, Vermont, potteries or the Anna pottery, are listed. Another section lists stoneware bottles

POTTERY, Anderson Club 1880 Pure Bourbon, P.F. Harris, St. Louis, Mo., Gilt On Handle..	38.00
Coachman, Figural, Rockingham Glaze, Mark On Base, 1849, 10 3/8 In.	220.00
J. Russell & Son Brewery, Malton, Triangle Trade Mark, Debossed, Blob Seal	140.00
J.C. Schnell's Sour Mash, Kiln Dried, Grain Whisky, Debossed.............................	40.00
Jar, Apothecary, Pulv. Kaolin Label, Forest Green Wrap, 9 3/4 In.	83.00
Jar, Tobacco, Dunhill My Mixture, Cream, Red Black Bands, Egg Shape, Store Type...	80.00
Jug, C.G. Ritter & Co., Gold Lettering, Painted Flowers, 2 Tone, 8 3/4 In.	150.00
Jug, Handle, White & Cobalt Blue, 8 In.	154.00
Jug, Peoria, Stamped Side & Bottom, 1 Gal.	65.00
Jug, Rickseckers, Cologne, N.Y., Flattened Sides, Flowers, Handle, 1/4 Pt.................	90.00
Knadler & Lucas Pure Maple Syrup, Louisville, Ky., Qt...............................	80.00
Mermaid, Figural, Brown Albany Glaze, 7 1/2 In.	104.50
Sink & Frisbie, Debossed, Kiln Mark...	22.00
Sulzberger Pure Horse Radish, As You Like, No Lid.....................................	42.00

------------------------- PURPLE POWER -------------------------

Purple power is the Kansas State University slogan. A series of bottles was made from 1970 to 1972 picturing the wildcat at a sporting event. They were distributed by Jon-Sol.

PURPLE POWER, Football Player, 1972	15.00
On Basketball, 1971	17.00
Wildcat Walking, 1970..	19.00
SANDWICH GLASS, see Cologne; Scent	

--------------------------- SARSAPARILLA ---------------------------

The most widely distributed syphilis *cure* used in the nineteenth century was sarsaparilla. The roots of the smilax vine were harvested, cleaned, dried, and sold to apothecaries and drug manufacturers. They added alcohol and other flavorings, such as the roots of yellow dock, dandelion, or burdock or the bark from prickly ash, sassafras, or birch trees. A few makers also added fruit or vegetable juice and clover blossoms. All of this was mixed to make the medicine called *sarsaparilla*. It was claimed to cure many diseases, including skin diseases, boils, pimples, piles, tumors, scrofulous conditions including king's evil (a swelling of the neck), and rheumatism. It could cleanse and purify the blood, a process doctors thought should take place regularly for good health. The first labeled sarsaparilla was made in the early 1800s. Some bottled products called sarsaparilla are still made today. The bottles were usually rectangular with embossed letters, or soda-bottle shaped. Most were light green or aqua but some amber and cobalt bottles were made. Later bottles had paper labels.

SARSAPARILLA, A.H. Bull Extract Of Sarsaparilla, Hartford, Conn., Aqua, OP, 7 In. ..	90.00
Ayers, Lowell, Mass., Aqua, 8 1/2 In.	15.00
Bristol's Genuine, New York, Aqua, 10 1/2 In.	56.00
Brown's Sarsaparilla For The Kidneys Liver & Blood, Aqua....................................	20.00
Buffum Sarsaparilla & Lemon, Pittsburgh, Cobalt Blue, 10-Sided, IP, 7 1/2 In.	330.00
Buffum Sarsaparilla & Lemon, Pittsburgh, Deep Cobalt Blue, 7 5/8 In.........................	2365.00
Buffum Sarsaparilla & Lemon Mineral Water, Pgh, Sapphire, IP, 10-Sided, Squatty.	525.00
Dalton's Sarsaparilla & Nerve Tonic, Belfast, Maine, U.S.A., Label, Aqua, 9 3/16 In.	30.00
Dr. Belding's Sarsaparilla Of Wild Cherry, 9 1/2 x 2 3/4 In.	37.00
Dr. Belding's Wild Cherry, Diagonal Fancy Script Emblem, 8 3/4 x 3 In.	50.00
Dr. Buchan's, Felton Grimwade, Melbourne, Blue 9 1/4 In.	145.00
Dr. Denison's Emerald Green, Pontil, 7 3/8 In.	1540.00
Dr. Guysott's, Aqua, Oval, Applied Top	50.00
Dr. Guysott's, Yellow Dock & Sarsaparilla, Cincinnati, O., Aqua, IP, 9 1/4 In. ..77.00 to 121.00

Sarsaparilla, Dr. Kings,   Sarsaparilla, Dr. Townsend's,   Sarsaparilla, Old Dr. J.
Label, Box, 9 In.   Albany, N.Y., Blue Green,   Townsend's, Aqua, Metallic
                          Whittled, 1855, 9 3/4 In.   Pontil, 1855-1860, 9 3/4 In.

Dr. Guysott's, Yellow Dock & Sarsaparilla, New York, Olive Amber, Pontil, 9 1/4 In. 1980.00
Dr. Guysott's, Yellow Dock & Sarsaparilla, New York, Blue Green, 9 1/4 In. 605.00
Dr. Guysott's, Yellow Dock & Sarsaparilla, Oval, Aqua, 9 1/2 In............. .... 70.00
Dr. J. Townsend's, Albany, N.Y., Aqua, IP, Whittled, 9 1/4 In................................. 318.00
Dr. J. Townsend's, Emerald Green, IP, 9 1/4 In. 235.00
Dr. Kings, Label, Box, 9 In. ....*Illus* 125.00
Dr. Myer's Vegetable Extract, Wild Cherry Dandelion, Buffalo, IP, 9 7/8 In...253.00 to 350.00
Dr. Myer's Vegetable Extract Sarsaparilla, Wild Cherry Dandelion, Aqua, 9 1/4 In.. 303.00
Dr. Russell's Balsam Of Horehound, Aqua, Pontil, 9 1/4 In. 440.00
Dr. Schwartze's Compound, Washington, D.C., Aqua, Pontil, 7 3/4 In. 357.00
Dr. Townsend's, Albany, N.Y., Amber, Pontil, 9 1/8 In................................. 605.00
Dr. Townsend's, Albany, N.Y., Amber, Pontil, Square, 1860, 9 1/2 In. 495.00
Dr. Townsend's, Albany, N.Y., Aqua, 9 1/4 In................................. 121.00
Dr. Townsend's, Albany, N.Y., Aqua, Embossed 3 Sides, BIMAL, 4 1/2 In................ 75.00
Dr. Townsend's, Albany, N.Y., Aqua, IP, 9 1/2 In. 220.00
Dr. Townsend's, Albany, N.Y., Aqua, Whittled, Graphite Pontil 450.00
Dr. Townsend's, Albany, N.Y., Blue Green, Whittled, 1855, 9 3/4 In...................*Illus* 231.00
Dr. Townsend's, Albany, N.Y., Cornflower Blue, Blob Top, IP, 1860, 9 1/2 In............ 1430.00
Dr. Townsend's, Albany, N.Y., Deep Green, IP, 1840-1855, 9 3/8 In. 237.00
Dr. Townsend's, Albany, N.Y., Emerald Green, 1855-1860, 9 1/2 In. 154.00
Dr. Townsend's, Albany, N.Y., Emerald Green, IP, c.1845, 9 3/4 In. .... 187.00 to 220.00
Dr. Townsend's, Albany, N.Y., Emerald Green, IP, Whittled, 9 1/2 In. 385.00
Dr. Townsend's, Albany, N.Y., No. 1, Olive Amber, Pontil................................. 185.00
Dr. Townsend's, Albany, N.Y., Olive Amber, 1840-1855, 9 1/2 In. 187.00
Dr. Townsend's, Albany, N.Y., Olive Amber, Pontil, 9 5/8 In. 110.00
Dr. Townsend's, Albany, N.Y., Olive Green Graphite Pontil, Embossed...................... 245.00
Dr. Townsend's, Albany, N.Y., Olive Green, Nail Heads All Sides, Pontil, 9 3/8 In. 265.00
Dr. Townsend's, Albany, N.Y., Olive Green, Pontil, 9 1/4 In. 247.50
Dr. Townsend's, Albany, N.Y., Olive, Applied Mouth, 9 In. 176.00
Dr. Townsend's, Albany, N.Y., Olive, Pontil, Square, 9 1/2 In. 198.00
Dr. Townsend's, Albany, N.Y., Root Beer Amber, c.1845, 9 3/8 In................................. 495.00
Dr. Townsend's, Albany, N.Y., Teal Blue, Applied Mouth, 1860-1870, 9 1/2 In.......... 330.00
Dr. Townsend's, Aqua, Miniature 80.00
Dr. Townsend's, Emerald Green, Pontil, c.1850, 9 1/4 In. 319.00
Dr. Townsend's, New York, Bright Aqua, 9 5/8 In. 110.00
Dr. Wilcox Compound Extract, Blue Green 350.00
Dr. Wynkoop's Katharismichonduras, N.Y., Blue, Rectangular, 1850, 10 In............ 8525.00
Enameled White & Gold, Pewter Top, 11 1/2 In.. 139.00
Gleason's Sarsaparilla & Lemon, Rochester, N.Y., Blue, 10-Sided, 1850, 7 3/4 In. 357.00
Gooch's Extract Of Sarsaparilla, Cincinnati, O., Gray Cast, 9 1/8 In......................... 66.00
Hood's, Lowell, Mass., Aqua, 8 1/2 In.. 15.00

I.D. Bull's, Hartford, Con., Aqua, OP, 1835-1845, 7 In. 110.00
I.D. Bull's, Hartford, Con., Aqua, Pontil, 6 7/8 In. 143.00
John Bull Extract Of Sarsaparilla, Aqua, IP, 8 7/8 In. 150.00
John Bulls Extract, Blue Green, IP 255.00
Log Cabin, Olive Amber 95.00
Log Cabin, Rochester, N.Y., 6-Sided, Amber, 9 In. 93.00
Log Cabin, Rochester, N.Y., Amber, 9 In. 154.00
Log Cabin, Rochester, N.Y., Brown, Embossed.. 140.00
Masury's Compound, Rochester, N.Y., Aqua, Pontil, 11 1/4 In. .... 220.00 to 242.00
Morsio's Compound Syrup, Amber, 4-Sided, 9 5/8 In. 82.00
Old Dr. J. Townsend, N.Y., Yellow Green, 9 1/2 In. 130.00
Old Dr. J. Townsend's, Aqua, Metallic Pontil, 1855-1860, 9 3/4 In. ....*Illus* 303.00
Old Dr. J. Townsend's Sarsaparilla, New York, Blue, IP, 9 7/8 In. 440.00
Old Dr. Townsend's, Aqua, Square, IP, 1845-1860, 9 1/2 In. 209.00
Premium Sarsaparilla & Lemon Soda, Chas. Cable & Son, Blue Green, IP, 7 1/8 In.. 412.00
Radway's Sarsaparillian Resolvent, Aqua, 7 1/2 In. 26.00
Sand's, Aqua, OP, Applied Top, Whittled 45.00
Sirson & Streets, Stoneware, Gray Glaze, Cobalt Blue Wash, 9 1/4 In. 495.00
Taylor's Sarsaparilla Root Beer, Trenton, N.J., Aqua, Miniature 15.00
Turner's, Buffalo, N.Y., Aqua, Whittled, IP, 1850, Gal. 1950.00
Turner's, Oval, Aqua, 12 1/2 In. 302.00
Warner's Log Cabin, Olive Amber, 9 In. 85.00
Wm. Foster, Stoneware, Gray Glaze, Black Brown Glaze Lettering, 10 1/4 In. 413.00
Woodman's, Amber, Tapered Ring Lip, Pontil, 1840, 8 In. 7150.00
Wynkoop's Katharismic, New York, Sapphire Blue, 1845-1860, 10 In. 7150.00
Yager's, Amber 78.00

———————————————— SCENT ————————————————

Perfume and cologne are not the same as scent. Scent is smelling salts, a perfume with
ammonia salts added for a sharp vapor that could revive a person who was feeling faint.
Because our female ancestors wore tightly laced corsets and high starched collars, the
problem of feeling faint was common. Scent bottles were sometimes small mold-blown
bottles in the full spectrum of glass colors. Sometimes the bottles were free blown and
made in elaborate shapes to resemble, perhaps, a seahorse. By the mid-nineteenth century
molded scents were made, usually of dark green, cobalt, or yellow glass. These were rather
squat bottles, often with unusual stoppers. There is much confusion about the difference
between cologne and scent bottles because manufacturers usually made both kinds.
Related bottles may be found in the Cologne and Perfume categories.

SCENT, Applied Milk Glass Rigaree, Footed, Pontil, 2 7/8 In. 60.00
Cobalt Blue, 24 Ribs, Swirled To Left, Globular, Pontil, 2 1/8 In. 110.00
Cobalt Blue, 24 Ribs, Swirled To Right, Pontil, 2 1/2 In. 209.00
Concentric, Coin, Blue, Pontil, 2 1/4 In. 467.50
Concentric, Coin, Emerald Green, Pontil, 2 In. 522.50
Cut Glass, Emerald Green, Barrel Form, Ground Mouth, 2 In. 100.00
Pink Stripes, Braided Gold & White Threads, Pontil, 4 1/4 In. 130.00
Ribbed, Swirled To Right, Pontil, Tooled Lip, 6 1/4 In. 165.00
Ribbed, Vertically, 26 Ribs, Amethyst, Pontil, 3 In. 264.00
Sandwich Glass, Sapphire Blue, 6-Sided, Cap, 2 1/4 In. 70.00
Sunburst, 12 Rays, Blue, Pontil, 2 3/4 In. 330.00
Sunburst, 12 Rays, Emerald Green, Pontil, 2 7/8 In. 495.00
Sunburst, Cobalt Blue, Pontil, 2 7/8 In. 357.00
Sunburst, Cobalt Blue, Pontil, 3 In. 303.00
Sunburst, Cobalt Blue, Tooled Mouth, 1870, 3 In. 440.00
Sunburst, Coin, Green, Pontil, 1 3/4 In. 302.50
Sunburst, Deep Amethyst, Pontil, 2 5/8 In. 660.00

———————————————— SEAL ————————————————

Seal or sealed bottles are named for the glass seal that was applied to the body of the bottle. While still hot, this small pad of glass was impressed with an identification mark. Seal
bottles are known from the second century but the earliest examples collectors can find
today date from the eighteenth century. Because the seal bottle was the most popular con-

tainer for wine and other liquids shipped to North America, broken bottles, seals alone, or whole bottles are often found in old dumps and excavations. Dutch gin, French wine, and English liquors were all shipped in large seal bottles. Seal bottles also held rum, olive oil, mineral water, and even vinegar. It is possible to date the bottle from the insignia on the seal and from the shape of the bottle.

SEAL, A. Kelly Applied Spirits Bottle, Yellow Olive, Applied Mouth, Pontil, 10 1/2 In..... 110.00
A.S.C.R., 3-Piece Mold, Deep Olive Amber, Pontil, England, 11 3/8 In. 94.00
A.S.C.R., Deep Olive Amber, Pontil, England, 10 1/2 In. 165.00
Ambrosial, B.M. & FAW & Co., Chestnut, Yellow Amber, Pontil, 8 7/8 In................... 165.00
Apothecary, Ryks Eigendon, Aqua, Flared Lip, Pontil, Holland, 5 3/8 In. 88.00
Auchen Lech, Black Glass, Pewter Top & Ring, England, 1717, 5 5/8 In...............*Illus* 8250.00
Black Glass, T.G. In Shoulder Seal, Applied String Lip, Cylindrical, OP, 8 1/4 In........ 770.00
Brynker, Deep Yellow Olive, Cylindrical, 11 3/4 In. 110.00
Burger Spital, Wurzburg, Bird Design, Red Amber, Pontil, 1880, 6 3/4 In................... 578.00
Chateau Laffite, Large Oval Seal, 1903, 11 In.. 48.00
Chestnut Grove, C.W., Chestnut, Amber Shaded To Yellow Amber, Pontil, 8 7/8 In.... 104.00
Comet, Deep Yellow Olive, Applied Mouth, 12 1/2 In. 231.00
D Sears 4, Yellow Green, Pontil, Cylindrical, 10 7/8 In... 110.00
D Sears 6, Yellow Green, Pontil, 10 3/4 In. 77.00
E.G. 1762, Mallet, Applied String Lip, Olive Green, OP, 8 1/2 In. 1430.00
Emanuel College, Deep Yellow Olive, Pontil, 11 In. 121.00
Embossed Star, Deep Olive, Pontil, 1820, 9 1/4 In. 385.00
F.G. 1760, Onion, Deep Olive Green, String Lip, Pontil, Europe, 6 In. 1595.00
H. Ricketts & Co., Deep Olive Amber, Pontil, Applied Mouth, 8 3/4 In 231.00
HHC, Deep Olive Amber, Pontil, Applied Mouth, England, 10 3/4 In............................ 204.00
Ino Walley Budleigh 1763 Applied Spirits Bottle, Deep Olive Amber, Pontil, 9 In... 1100.00
J.F.T. & Co., Philadelphia, Golden Yellow Amber, Vertical Rib, Handle, Pontil, 7 In. .. 605.00
M.W. Applied Spirits Bottle, Olive Amber, Sheared Mouth, Cylindrical, Pontil, 10 1/4 In. 198.00
Manufacture De Tabac De Natchitoches, Olive Amber, Blown In Turn Mold, 9 1/2 In. 770.00
Napa Valley, San Francisco, Calif., Green, Turn Mold, Embossed Seal 25.00
Nathan's Bros., Philadelphia, Amber, 1863, 9 1/2 In.. 121.00
Old Mill Whitlock & Co., Medium Red Amber, Handle, Neck Band & Medal, 8 In. 880.00
P.F. Heering, Amber, Bubbles, Whittled, Long Ribbon Seal... 215.00
P.F. Heering, Blown, Olive Amber, Pontil, 1800-1830, 9 1/2 In. 154.00
PHO, England, c.1765, 10 1/2 In. 295.00
Railway Bell, A. Dabell, Gray Green Slip Glaze, Bell Shape, 9 1/4 In............................ 403.00
Robt. Cochran Junr., Armagh Grocery Tea Wine, Olive Amber, England, 9 3/8 In. 605.00
Royal Crown Over A Bore, Olive Amber, Pontil, England, 8 In.................................... 550.00
Seltzer & Miller, Philadelphia, Yellow Amber, 1880, 9 1/4 In. 121.00
Tabac De A. Delpit, Nouville, Orleans, Deep Olive Amber, 1860-1870, 10 1/2 In. 605.00
TC & CR, Deep Yellow Olive, Cylindrical, Pontil, 10 5/8 In.. 110.00
Trelaske, Deep Olive Green, Pontil, 10 7/8 In. 88.00
W. Stannus, Dark Yellow Olive, Pontil, c.1722, 7 1/2 In.. 1760.00

Seal, Auchen Lech, Black Glass, Pewter Top & Ring, England, 1717, 5 5/8 In.

Seltzer, G.N. & Co.,
Detroit, Mich., Cobalt
Blue, 10 1/2 In.

Seltzer, New York
Seltzer Water Co.,
Detroit, Michigan, 11 In.

Seltzer, Sparkling Seltzer
Water, Bohemian Bottling
Works Co., Detroit, 11 In.

─── SELTZER ───

The word *seltzer* was first used for mineral water with medicinal properties at Selters, Germany. Seltzer was thought to be good for intestinal disorders. The word soon was used for any of the artificially carbonated waters that became popular in the nineteenth century. Seltzer bottles were advertised in Philadelphia by 1816. *Soda* and *seltzer* mean the same thing. Collectors want the bottles that say *seltzer* and the special pump bottles that dispensed it. These pump bottles were usually covered with a metal mesh to keep glass from flying in case of an explosion. The top of the bottle was a spigot and carbonation was added to the water when the spigot was pressed. Related bottles may be found in the Coca-Cola, Mineral Water, Pepsi-Cola, and Soda categories.

SELTZER, 7-Up, New Orleans, Pink Rose, 3/4 In. Lip	30.00
Beaufont Lithia Water Co., Richmond, Va., Stenciled Elk Head	132.00
Big Chief, Coca-Cola Bottling Co., Sacramento, Calif.	80.00
C. Frieds, Brooklyn, N.Y., Dark Green	12.00
California Natural, Green Aqua, Whittled, Bubbles, Bear On Log	300.00
Carson Brewing Co., Carson City, Nevada, ACL	150.00
Carson Brewing Company, Carson City, Nev., Blue	80.00
Clarksons, Leeds, Amber	12.00
Coca-Cola Bottling Corp, Rochester, Clear, Metal Spout, 7 In.	198.00
Cripple Creek Bottling Works, Original Metal Top	350.00
Fountain Mineral Water, Bronx, N.Y., Czechoslovakia	15.00
G.N. & Co., Detroit, Mich., Cobalt Blue, 10 1/2 In. *Illus*	85.00
Green, Pewter Fittings, 1930	160.00
Green Saratoga, Wyo.	30.00
H & C, Bear On Back, Green Aqua, Whittled, Blob Top, 7 1/2 In.	187.00
Jas. Doughan, Parlor City Bottling Works, N.Y., Pewter Fittings, Qt.	35.00
Jay-Eff, Sparkling Beverage, Brooklyn, N.Y., Bright Blue	22.00
Mt. Lassen Siphon Water, Susanville Coca-Cola Bottling Co., Susanville, Calif.	100.00
New York Seltzer Water Co., Detroit, Michigan, 11 In. *Illus*	10.00
Pablo & Co., Elysian Fields, Mineral & Seltzer Water, Aqua, Blob Top, 7 1/4 In.	100.00
Puroxia, 1930	50.00
Ray Bottling Works, Brooklyn, N.Y., Aqua, Czechoslovakia	15.00
Saratoga Seltzer Water, Blue Green, Blob Top, Pt.	128.00
Sparkling Seltzer Water, Bohemian Bottling Works Co., Detroit, 11 In. *Illus*	40.00
Star Bottling Works, Medford, Ore., Acid Etched, Base Footed	50.00

─── SKI COUNTRY ───

Ski Country bottles are issued by The Foss Company of Golden, Colorado. The first bottles were made in 1973. By 1975 the company wrote us that they were making about 24 different decanter designs in each size each year, plus one decanter in the gallon size. The firm has marketed many series of decanters. The National Ski Country Bottle Club, at 1224 Washington Avenue, Golden, CO 80401, will send lists and information.

SKI COUNTRY, Animal, Antelope, Pronghorn, 1979	47.00
Animal, Badger Family, 1981	38.00
Animal, Basset Hound, 1978	40.00
Animal, Bear, Brown, 1974 ....*Illus*	34.00
Animal, Bobcat, 1981	72.00
Animal, Buffalo, Stampede, 1982	65.00
Animal, Buffalo, Stampede, 1982, Miniature	16.00
Animal, Bull Rider, 1980	87.00
Animal, Bull, Charolais, 1974	44.00 to 55.00
Animal, Circus, Tiger, On Ball, 1975	28.00 to 45.00
Animal, Cow, Holstein, 1973	95.00
Animal, Coyote, Family, 1978	42.00
Animal, Deer, White-Tailed, 1982	134.00
Animal, Elk, American, 1980	178.00
Animal, Ferret, Blackfooted, 1976, Miniature	42.00
Animal, Giraffe, Circus Wagon, 1977	36.00
Animal, Goat, Mountain, 1975 ....*Illus*	62.00
Animal, Kangaroo, 1974	27.00
Animal, Moose, Bull, 1982	104.00
Animal, Otter, River, 1979	70.00
Animal, Raccoon, 1975	42.00
Animal, Sheep, Dall, Grand Slam, 1980	165.00
Animal, Sheep, Desert, Grand Slam, 1990	100.00
Animal, Sheep, Rocky Mountain, 1981	70.00
Animal, Skunk, Family, 1978, Miniature	35.00 to 38.00
Animal, Squirrel, Plaque, 1983	130.00
Animal, Walrus, Alaskan, 1985	50.00 to 60.00
Bird, Blackbird, Red Wing, 1977	44.00 to 54.00
Bird, Blue Jay, 1978	85.00
Bird, Cardinal, 1977	90.00
Bird, Cardinal, 1979, Miniature	56.00
Bird, Chickadee, 1981	62.00
Bird, Condor, California, 1973	38.00 to 74.00
Bird, Dove, Peace, 1973	45.00
Bird, Duck, Blue Wing Teal, 1976	199.00 to 300.00
Bird, Duck, Canvasback, 1981	40.00
Bird, Duck, Green Wing Teal, 1985	58.00
Bird, Duck, Mallard Drake, 1973	46.00
Bird, Duck, Mallard Family, 1977	44.00
Bird, Duck, Mallard, Banded, 1980	57.00

*Ski Country, Animal,
Bear, Brown, 1974*

*Ski Country, Animal,
Goat, Mountain, 1975*

*Ski Country, Bird, Owl,
Great Gray, 1985*

Bird, Duck, Merganzer, Female Hooded, 1981 .... 50.00
Bird, Duck, Merganzer, Male Hooded, 1983 .... 76.00 to 82.00
Bird, Duck, Pintail, 1/2 Gal., 1979 .... 129.00
Bird, Duck, Pintail, 1978 .... 55.00
Bird, Duck, Red Head, 1974 .... 70.00
Bird, Duck, Widgeon, 1979 .... 51.00
Bird, Duck, Wood Duck, Banded, 1982 .... 62.00
Bird, Duck, Wood, 1974 .... 158.00
Bird, Duck, Wood, Plaque, 1980 .... 297.00
Bird, Eagle, Bald, On Water, 1981 .... 118.00
Bird, Eagle, Birth Of Freedom, 1976 .... 117.00
Bird, Eagle, Birth Of Freedom, 1976, Miniature 72.00
Bird, Eagle, Birth Of Freedom, 1977, Gal. 1670.00
Bird, Eagle, Harpy, 1973 .... 82.00
Bird, Eagle, Majestic, 1971 .... 319.00
Bird, Eagle, Majestic, 1973, Gal. 1796.00
Bird, Eagle, Mountain, 1973 .... 104.00
Bird, Eagle, On A Drum, 1976 .... 86.00
Bird, Flycatcher, 1979 .... 112.00
Bird, Goose, Canada, 1973 .... 86.00 to 100.00
Bird, Grouse, Ruffled, 1981 .... 55.00 to 65.00
Bird, Grouse, Ruffled, 1981, Miniature 33.00
Bird, Grouse, Sage, 1974 .... 70.00
Bird, Kestrel, Plaque, 1986 .... 63.00
Bird, Meadowlark, 1980 .... 62.00 to 70.00
Bird, Oriole, Baltimore, 1977 .... 52.00
Bird, Owl, Barn, 1979 .... 75.00 to 85.00
Bird, Owl, Great Gray, 1985 .... *Illus* 55.00
Bird, Owl, Great Horned, 1974 .... 44.00
Bird, Owl, Great Horned, 1974, Gal. 1308.00
Bird, Owl, Saw Whet, 1977, Miniature 44.00
Bird, Owl, Screech, Family, 1977 .... 97.00
Bird, Peacock, 1973 .... 88.00
Bird, Pelican, Brown, 1976 .... 57.00 to 67.00
Bird, Pelican, Brown, 1976, Miniature 35.00
Bird, Pheasant, Golden 54.00
Bird, Pheasant, In Corn, 1982 .... 90.00
Bird, Prairie Chicken, 1976 .... 50.00
Bird, Seagull, Plaque, 1985 .... 40.00
Bird, Swallows, Barn, 1977 .... 46.00
Bird, Swan, Black, 1974 .... 37.00
Bird, Turkey, 1976 .... 82.00 to 135.00
Bird, Whooping Crane, 1983 .... 53.00
Bird, Woodpecker, Gila, 1972 .... 54.00
Bird, Woodpecker, Ivory Billed, 1976 .... 52.00
Bonnie, Customer Specialty, 1974 .... 35.00
C.S.M. Burro, Customer Specialty, 1973, Miniature 70.00
Caveman, Customer Specialty, 1974 .... 26.00
Christmas, Cardinal, 1990 .... 67.00
Christmas, Cedar Waxwing, 1985 .... 56.00
Christmas, Woodland Trio, 1980 .... 58.00
Circus, Elephant, 1974 .... 37.00 to 44.00
Circus, Horse, Lipizzaner, 1976 .... 54.00
Circus, Horse, Palomino, 1976 .... 40.00
Circus, Jenny Lind, Blue, 1976 .... 62.00
Circus, Jenny Lind, Yellow, 1976 .... 104.00 to 195.00
Circus, Jenny Lind, Yellow, 1976, Miniature 185.00
Circus, P.T. Barnum, 1976 .... 46.00
Circus, Tom Thumb, 1974 .... 32.00
Clown, 1974 .... 67.00
Clyde, Customer Specialty, 1974 .... 37.00
Fire Engine, 1923 Ahrens-Fox, 1981 .... 185.00
Fish, Salmon, 1977 .... 42.00

Ski Country, Indian, Ceremonial, No. 2, Buffalo, 1980

Ski Country, Indian, Ceremonial, No. 1, Eagle, 1979

Ski Country, Indian, Ceremonial, No. 3, Deer, 1980

Fish, Trout, Rainbow, 1976		65.00
Indian, Ceremonial, No. 1, Eagle, 1979	*Illus*	130.00
Indian, Ceremonial, No. 2, Buffalo, 1980	*Illus*	118.00
Indian, Ceremonial, No. 3, Deer, 1980	*Illus*	93.00
Indian, Ceremonial, No. 4, Wolf, 1981		50.00
Indian, Ceremonial, No. 5, Antelope, 1982		62.00
Indian, Ceremonial, No. 6, Falcon, 1983		105.00
Indian, Ceremonial, Rainbow Dancer, 1984		50.00
Indian, Cigar Store, 1974		48.00
Indian, End Of Trial, 1976		217.00 to 270.00
Indian, Great Spirit, 1976		90.00
Indian, Lookout, 1977		44.00
Indian, North American, Tribes, 1977, 6 Piece, Miniature		120.00
Indian, North American, Tribes, 1977, 6 Piece		148.00
Indian, South West Dancers, 1975		194.00
Indian, Warrior, Hatchet, Chief, No. 1, 1975		83.00
Indian, Warrior, Lance, Chief, No. 2, 1975		81.00
Phoenix Bird, Customer Specialty, 1981		42.00
Political Donkey, Customer Specialty, 1976		31.00
Rodeo Barrel Racer, 1982		60.00
Skier, Blue, Customer Specialty, 1972		27.00 to 42.00
Skier, Gold, Customer Specialty, 1972		70.00
Skier, Red, Customer Specialty, 1972		25.00
Submarine, Customer Specialty, 1976, Miniature		27.00
U.S. Ski Team, Olympic, 1980		37.00

SNUFF

Snuff has been used in European countries since the fifteenth century, when the first tobacco was brought back from America by Christopher Columbus. The powdered tobacco was inhaled through long tubes. The French ambassador to Portugal, Jean Nicot, unknowingly made his name a household word when he sent some of the powdered tobacco to his queen, Catherine de Medici. The stuff became known as *nicotine*. Tobacco was at first considered a remedy and was used in many types of medicines. In the sixteenth and seventeenth centuries, royalty enjoyed snuff and kept it in elaborate gold and silver snuffboxes. Snuff was enjoyed by both royalty and laboring classes by the eighteenth century. The nineteenth-century gentleman no longer used snuff by the 1850s, although poor Southern women used snuff by dipping, not sniffing, and putting it in the mouth, not the nose.

Snuff bottles have been made since the eighteenth century. Glass, metal, ceramic, ivory, and precious stones were all used to make plain or fancy snuff holders. Commercial bottles for snuff are made of dark glass, usually shaped more like a box than a bottle. Snuff was also packaged in stoneware crocks. Most oriental snuff bottles have a small stick with a spoon end as part of the closure. The International Chinese Snuff Bottle Society, 2601 North Charles Street, Baltimore, MD 21218, has a colorful, informative publication.

SNUFF, A. Delpit, New Orleans, Honey Amber, Flared Lip, Rectangular, 1870, 4 In. 440.00
A. Delpit, No. 16, New Orleans, Yellow, IP, c.1855, 4 1/2 In. 1072.00
American Gentleman, Race Dunlap, Boston, Yellow Olive, Pontil, 4 3/8 In. 275.00
Appleby & Helm's Railroad Mills, New York, Amber, Square, 3 1/2 In. 154.00
Apricot, Bubbles, Sheared Top 25.00
Black Glass, Gray Striations, Pontil, Rectangular, 4 In. 385.00
Black Glass, Yellow Olive Green, 4 1/4 In. 99.00
Blown, Light Green, Cylindrical, Pontil, 4 3/4 In. 187.00
Blown, Olive Amber, Beveled Corners, Rectangular, 4 1/8 In. 60.00
Blown, Yellow Olive, New England Type, 8 3/8 In. 350.00
Blown, Yellow Olive, Square, Pontil, 4 7/8 In. 88.00
Cephalick, Yellow Green 750.00
Deep Amber, Flared Lip, Rectangular, OP, 4 1/2 In. 77.00
Dr. Marshall's, OP 29.00
E. Roome, Troy, N.Y., Light Clear Green, Sheared Lip, Rectangular, OP, 4 1/4 In. 825.00
E. Roome, Troy, N.Y., Olive Amber, Rectangular, 4 3/8 In. 357.00
E. Roome, Troy, N.Y., Yellow Olive, Pontil, 4 1/2 In. 132.00
Emerald Green, Rectangular, Flared Lip, 1855-1865, 4 1/8 In. 143.00
First Quality Tobacco Scotch & Ruppert, Olive Amber, Pontil, 4 1/4 In. 110.00
J.J. Mapes, N.Y., Deep Olive Amber, Sheared Lip, Rectangular, OP, 4 1/4 In. 798.00
J.J. Mapes, N.Y., Yellow Olive Amber, Flared Lip, Rectangular, OP, 1840, 4 1/2 In.... 1100.00
J.M. Venabbe & Co., Petersburg, Va., Amber, 1860-1870, 4 1/4 In. 77.00
J.M. Venabbe & Co., Petersburg, Va., Medium Amber, Rectangular, 4 1/4 In. 154.00
Jar, Blown, Deep Yellow Olive, Pontil, 5 7/8 In. 143.00
Jar, Blown, Medium Yellow Olive, Flared Mouth, Pontil, 7 7/8 In. 253.00
Jar, Blown, New England, Yellow Olive, Rectangular, Pontil, 6 3/4 In. 280.50
Jar, Blown, Olive Amber, Rectangular, Pontil, 4 5/8 In. 121.00
Jar, Blown, Yellow Olive, Pontil, 7 1/4 In. 264.00
Jar, Blown, Yellow Olive, Pontil, 8 3/8 In. 242.00
Jar, Blown, Yellow Olive, Rectangular, Pontil, 5 5/8 In. 264.00
Jar, Deep Cobalt Blue, Rolled Lip, 3 1/8 In. 148.50
Jar, Deep Olive Amber, Tooled Lip, OP, 4 3/8 In. 165.00
Jar, Helme's Railroad Mills, Amber, Rectangular, 4 3/8 In. 77.00
Jar, Light Green, Square, Sheared Lip, Pontil, 4 3/8 In. 176.00
Jar, Light Yellow Olive Green, Rectangular, OP, 4 1/2 In. 165.00
Jar, Lorillard Label, New England, Blown, Pontil, Olive Amber, 4 1/2 In. 198.00
Jar, Medium Golden Yellow Amber, Rectangular, OP, 5 1/8 In. 110.00
Jar, Medium Root Beer Amber, Square, OP, 4 1/4 In. 121.00
Jar, Medium Yellow Amber, 4 3/8 In. 303.00
Jar, Olive Amber, Flared Lip, 8 1/2 In. 192.50
Jar, Olive Amber, Flared Lip, Rectangular, Pontil, 4 1/8 In. 77.00
Jar, Olive Amber, OP, 4 3/8 In. 825.00
Jar, Olive Green, Rectangular, Impressed F, Flared Lip, 4 1/8 In. 82.50
Jar, Olive Green, Rectangular, Pontil, 5 7/8 In. 181.50
Jar, Olive Green, Tooled, Flared Lip, Pontil, 5 3/8 In. 302.00
Jar, P. Lorillard Co., Amber, Cover, Bail Handle 11.00
Jar, Weyman's, Pottery, Cover, Flared Lip 15.00
Jar, Yellow Olive Amber, Rectangular, Pontil, 6 1/4 In. 154.00
Jar, Yellow Olive Amber, Sheared Lip, Pontil, 4 1/4 In. 77.00
Jar, Yellow Olive, Pontil, 6 In. 55.00
Jar, Yellow Root Beer Amber, Square, OP, 5 In. 165.00
Jar, Yellow, Amber Tone, Tooled, Flared Lip, OP, 4 1/4 In. 121.00
Jar, Yellow, Amber Tones, Rectangular, Sheared Lip, OP, 7 3/8 In. 192.50
Leonard Appleby Railroad Mills, Apricot Amber, Rectangular, Flared Lip, OP, 4 In. 1760.00
Levi Garrett & Sons, Philadelphia, Yellow Apricot, Square, Sheared Lip, OP, 4 In...... 357.00
Light Olive Green, F On Base, OP 40.00
Olive Amber, 8-Sided, Wide Flared Lip, OP, 4 1/2 In. 605.00
Olive Amber, OP, 4 1/4 In. 45.00
Olive Amber, Rectangular, Pontil, 1810-1830, 4 1/8 In. 77.00
Olive Amber, Wide Flared Lip, 8-Sided, OP, 4 1/2 In. 605.00
Olive Green, Bubbles, Whittled, Pontil, 4 1/4 In. 75.00
Olive Green, Impressed F, Smooth Base, Rectangular, 4 1/8 In. 70.00
Olive Green, Pontil, Tooled & Flared Lip, c.1800, 5 In. 467.00

Olive Green, Rectangular, OP, 4 1/4 In. 88.00
Pale Olive Green, Wide Flared Lip, Rectangular, Pontil, Early 19th Century, 7 In. 330.00
Pale Yellow Green, Rectangular, OP, 4 1/4 In. 128.00
Pale Yellow Green, Wide Flared Lip, Rectangular, Pontil, 7 In. 330.00
Pink Amethyst, Wide Mouth, Pontil, Continental, 8 In. 908.00
Pink Puce, Pontil, Square, Flared & Tooled Lip, c.1820, 4 In. 522.00
True Cephalic, By The King's Patent, Aqua, OP, 3 7/8 In. 60.00
Weyman's Copenhagen, Golden Amber, Fruit Jar Form, Qt. 88.00
Wm. S. Kniball & Co., Stoneware, Cream Tan Glaze, Male Female Figures, 6 7/8 In. 110.00
Yellow Green, Bubbles, Whittled, Pontil, 4 1/4 In. 75.00
Yellow Olive Amber, Large F Impressed Base, Pontil, 4 1/4 In. 45.00

SODA

All forms of carbonated drink—naturally carbonated mineral water, artificially carbonated and flavored pops, and seltzer—are forms of soda. The words are often interchanged. Soda bottles held some form of soda pop or carbonated drink. The soda bottle had a characteristic thick blob top and heavy glass sides to avoid breakage from the pressure of the carbonation. Tops were cleverly secured; the Hutchinson stopper and Coddball stopper were used on many early bottles. The crown cap was not developed and used until 1891. The cork liner inside the crown cap was outlawed in 1969.

The first soda was artificially carbonated in the 1830s by John Matthews. He used marble chips and acid for carbonation. It is said he took all the scrap marble from St. Patrick's Cathedral in New York City to use at his plant, which made, so they say, 25 million gallons of soda water. In 1839 a Philadelphia perfume dealer, Eugene Roussel, had the clever idea of adding flavor to the soda. Soon colors were added and the soft drink industry had begun. The late 1800s saw the beginning of Coca-Cola (1886), Pepsi-Cola (1898), Moxie (1876), Dr Pepper (1885), and others. The English brand Schweppes was already established, but they added artificially carbonated sodas as well.

Collectors search for the heavy blob top bottles and the newer crown top sodas with embossed lettering or silk-screened labels. Recent commemorative bottles are also in demand. In this book, the soda bottle listing includes modern carbonated beverage bottles as well as the older blob tops, Hutchinsons, and other collectible soda bottles. Coca-Cola, Pepsi-Cola, mineral water, sarsaparilla, and seltzer bottles are listed in their own sections. Collector clubs with newsletters include Painted Soda Bottle Collectors Association, 9418 Hilmer Drive, LaMesa, CA 91942; Dr Pepper Collectors Club, P.O. Box 153221, Irving, TX 75015; and the clubs listed in this book in the Coca-Cola and Pepsi-Cola sections.

Collectors refer to *painted label bottles* as *ACL* or *Applied Color Label*. Related bottles may be found in the Coca-Cola, Mineral Water, Pepsi-Cola, Sarsaparilla, and Seltzer categories.

SODA, A & W Root Beer, Amber, Long Neck, Orange & White Label, 12 Oz. 3.00
  A. Hain & Son Lebanon Co., Cobalt, IP, Squatty 300.00
  A. Monroe & Co., Eureka, Calif., Aqua, Hutchinson, 7 1/4 In. 330.00
  A. Shoemaker, Philadelphia, Emerald Green, Bubbles, Whittled, Blob Top, Squatty 75.00
  A.J. Nevers Ginger Ale, Norway, Me., Hutchinson 20.00
  A.R. Cox, Norristown, Pa., Cobalt Blue, IP, c.1860, 7 1/4 In. 140.00
  Aba, Grand Forks, N.D., Aqua, Hutchinson, Mug Base 55.00
  Adam Weiser, Spokane, Wash., Hutchinson, Mug Base 45.00
  Adirondack Spring, Whitehall, N.Y., Emerald Green, Pt. 275.00
  Aerated Soda Water, E.D.K.B., Sapphire Blue, Applied Mouth, IP, 7 1/4 In. 550.00
  Aircraft Beverages, Painted Label, Clear, Red & White Airplane, 24 Oz. 48.00
  Alameda Soda Water, Embossed Shaking Hands, Apple Green, Hutchinson, Bubble 60.00
  Alameda Soda Water Co., Medium Lime Green, 6 1/2 In. 176.00
  Albert King, Claridge, Pa., Hutchinson, Oval Slug Plate 110.00
  Albert Von Harten, Savannah, Ga., Blue Green, Blob Top, 7 1/4 In. 45.00
  Alden Bros., Battle Creek, Mich., Hutchinson, Qt. 35.00
  American Desiccating Co., N.Y., Golden Amber, 7 1/4 In. 82.50
  American Soda Fountain Co., Amber, Blob Top, 9 In. 25.00
  American Works, Aqua, Hutchinson, 6 3/4 In. .... 38.00 to 44.00
  Angel's Brewery & Soda Works, Angels Camp, Purple, 4-Piece Mold, Crown Top 125.00
  Arctic, 2 Bears & Ice, Red & White Label, 1948, 10 Oz. 12.50
  Arctic Soda Works, Honolulu, Hi., Hutchinson 50.00

Soda, Argentina, A
Delightful Beverage,
Argentina Beverage
Co., Detroit, 9 In.

Soda, Big Chief Bev-
erages, Coca-Cola
Bottling Co., Long
Pine, Neb., 9 In.

Soda, Bireley's,
10 In.

Soda, Blackhawk
Ginger Ale, Carse &
Ohlweiler Co., 7 In.

Argentina, A Delightful Beverage, Argentina Beverage Co., Detroit, 9 In. ....*Illus*   38.00
Arizona Bottling Works, Phoenix, Aqua, Hutchinson, 7 In. 145.00
Arthus R. Ashton White Hart Hotel Clane, Tear Drop, 7 1/4 In. 32.00
Artic Beverages, Conroe, Tex., Red & White Polar Bears, ACL 20.00
B & G, San Francisco, Cobalt Blue, Blob Top, Pontil, 1852-1856, 6 5/8in.....................   440.00
B & H, Stockton, Calif., Aqua, Crown Top 25.00
B.W. & Co., New York, Cobalt Blue, IP, 7 3/8 In. 165.00
Bacon's Soda Works, Sonora, Calif., Aqua, Hutchinson, 6 3/4 In..............................   192.00
Barq's, Diamonds, Blue & White Label, 12 Oz. 5.00
Barq's, Textured, White Label, 1940s, 8 Oz. 5.50
Basin Bottling Works, Basin, Wyoming, Crown Top 135.00
Battleship Maine, Remember The Maine, Hutchinson 150.00
Bay City Soda Water Co., San Francisco, Cobalt Blue, Star...................75.00 to 120.00
Bay City Soda Works Co., San Francisco, Sapphire Blue, Blob Top, 7 3/4 In... 150.00 to 220.00
Belmont Soda Works, Horseshoe Trademark, Aqua, Hutchinson 125.00
Big Chief Beverages, Coca-Cola Bottling Co., Long Pine, Neb., 9 In. ....*Illus*   75.00
Big Red, Shield, Red & White Label, 1970s, 10 Oz...2.50 to 5.00
Bireley's, 10 In..*Illus*   5.00
Birmingham Bottling House, Aqua, Blob Top 15.00
Blackhawk Ginger Ale, Carse & Ohlweiler Co., 7 In..*Illus*   12.00
Blob Top Cottle Post & Co., Portland, Ore, Teal Green..   265.00
Boardman, Cobalt Blue, Red IP, Cylindrical, 1/2 Pt..   93.00
Boley & Co., Sac City, Calif., Cobalt Blue, Graphite Pontil, Blob Top, 7 1/4 In............   154.00
Boley & Co., Union Glass Works, Philadelphia, Cobalt Blue, 7 1/4 In. 253.00
Bortner Bottling Works, Hanover, Pa., Aqua, Slug Plate...   8.00
Boylans Birch Cream, 12 Oz. 2.00
Brandon & Kirrymeyer, Leavenworth, Kansas, Aqua, Blob Top, Squatty, 7 1/4 In.......   80.00
Bremenkampf & Regli, Eureka, Nevada, Aqua, 7 In. 187.00
Brighton & South Coast, Aqua, Hamilton Hybrid, Codd, 9 3/4 In. 49.00
Brough, Cleveland, O., Eagle Pictured...   20.00
Brown Stout-Charles Grove, Cola, Pa., Emerald Green, IP, 1840-1855, 7 In...............   104.00
Brownell & Wheaton, New Bedford, Cobalt Blue..   100.00
Brownie, Elf With Bottle, Brown & White Label, 8 Oz. 8.00
Burgin & Sons Glass Works, IP, Green, 7 1/4 In. 70.00
Burke Mt., Mountain & Trees, 7 Oz. 70.00
C. B. Owen & Co. Bottlers, Cincinnati, Cobalt Blue, IP, Squatty 200.00
C. & P.M., Ashland, Pa., Emerald Green, 1855-1870, 7 In. 121.00
C. Brandt, Carlisle, Dyottville Glass Works, Emerald Green, IP..   170.00
C. Leary Root Beer, Stoneware 35.00
C. Whittemore, New York, Emerald Green, IP, 8 1/8 In...   209.00
C.D. Egert & Co., Albany N.Y., Plum Puce, Cylindrical, 1860-1875, 7 In...................   770.00

Cairns Timmermann Block & Co., Sapphire Blue, IP, 1845-1855, 7 3/8 In. 132.00
California Natural Seltzer Water, H & G, Aqua, Blob Top, 7 1/2 In. 187.00
California Soda Works, Aqua, Hutchinson, Eagle 30.00
Camel Bottling Co., Birmingham, Ala., Camel, Hutchinson 30.00
Canada Dry, Grapefruit Soda, Green, 11 In. 1.50
Canada Dry, Green, Red, White & Yellow Label, 1960s, 10 Oz. 4.00
Capitol City, Little Rock, Ark., Hutchinson, Mug Base, 7 In. 18.00
Carl H. Schultz Seltzers, Aqua, 8 1/2 In. 66.00
Carousel Pop Shoppe, Warren, Oh., Red & White Applied Color Label, 10 In. 6.00
Carpenter & Cobb Knickerbocker Soda Water, Blue Green, 10-Sided, IP, 1/2 Pt. 198.00
Carse & Ohlweller, Rock Island, Ill., Aqua 12.00
Caswell Hazard & Co., New York, Ginger Ale, Aqua, 9 In. 10.00
Celro-Kola Co. Inc., Portland, Ore., Amber, 8 1/2 In. 30.00
Champagne Mead, Blue Green, 8-Sided, 7 3/8 In. 38.50
Champion, P & C Scotch Ale, Amber, 6 7/8 In. 357.50
Chapman's, Puce Ten Pin, Flared Applied Mouth, 4 In. 6050.00
Chesterman & Barrow, Sioux City, Ia., Aqua, Hutchinson, SP 15.00
Chico Club, Indian's Head, 7 Oz. 6.00
Christian Schlepegrell Soda Water, Charleston, S.C., Blue, 8-Sided, Pontil, 8 In. 110.00
Christo Mfg. Co., Richmond, Va., Amber, Crown Top, Embossed 44.00
Chuk-Ker, Polo Players On Horses, Black & White Label, 1950s, 10 Oz. 7.50
City Soda Works, Eureka, Aqua, Hutchinson 25.00
Clarkesburg Bottling Works, W. Va., Hutchinson 20.00
Classen & Co., San Francisco, Emerald Green, 7 In. 38.50
Cleminshaw, Troy, N.Y., Aqua, Vertical Ribs, IP, 1/2 Pt. 38.00
Clicquot Club, Eskimo Boy, Red & White Label, 12 Oz. 6.00
CMS Co., Alliance, Oh., Crown, Hutchinston 10.00
Coan, Mahahanoy City, Aqua, Bubbles, Blob Top, Squatty. 40.00
Cock 'n Bull 15.00
College Club, Cap & Diploma, Green, White Label, 6 Oz. 8.50
Columbia Works, San Francisco, Seated Liberty, Aqua, 7 1/4 In. 72.00
Comstock Cove & Co., Boston, Aqua, Blob Top, 7 In. ....50.00 to 55.00
Condarman, Philada, Green, IP, 1/2 Pt. 44.00
Connell & Tallon, Bordentown, N.J., Green, Pick Chips 10.00
Cottle Post & Co., Eagle, Teal Blue, 7 In. 175.00
CoWo Schlieper Soda Water, St. Louis, Mo., Aqua, Blob Top, Graphite Pontil 22.00
Craven, Union Glass Works, Philadelphia, Pa., Sapphire Blue, 7 1/4 In. 110.00
Cream Soda, Chas. F. Youngred Amber, Providence, R.I., Whittled 75.00
Cream Soda, F.M. Hall & Co., Boston, Aqua, Tapered Top 45.00
Crystal Bottling Works, Tucson, Ariz., Pale Aqua, 7 7/8 In. 99.00
Crystal Palace, Premium Soda Water, N.Y., Blue Green, IP, 7 1/2 In. 357.00
Cumberland Valley, Corbin, Ky., Coal Train & Waterfall, ACL. 15.00
D. O'Kane, Dyottville Glass Works, Philadalphia, Green, IP, c.1860, 7 In. 60.00
D.S. & Co., San Francisco, Cobalt Blue, Blob Top, 7 In. 210.00
D.S. & Co., San Francisco, Green, Blob Top, 7 In. 150.00
D.S. Rahn, Pirkiomenville, Pa., Blue Green, 6 7/8 In. 440.00
Dad's Mama, Amber, 32 Oz. 35.00
Dad's Old Fashion Root Beer, Mini 20.00
Dads Root Beer, Boy Picture, Yellow & Red Label, 1960s, 10 Oz. 8.00
Dads Root Beer, Yellow & Red Label, 10 Oz. 5.00
David Engel, Cincinnati, Oh., Horseshoe, Hutchinson 20.00
Dearborn & Co., N.Y., Sapphire Blue, Applied Mouth, IP, 7 3/4 In. 154.00
Delaware Punch, Shield, Ribbon Punchbowl, Cups, Red White Label, 1960s, 10 Oz. .. 5.00
Denhalter Bottling Co., Salt Lake, Utah, Aqua, Hutchinson 17.00
Dennis & Co. Bottlers, Mt. Morris, Ny., Hutchinson, Paneled Base 10.00
Diel & Lord, Nashville, Tenn., Aqua, Blob Top 75.00
Dillon Beverages, Dillon, Mt., Cowboy On Bronco, Red & White, ACL ....12.00 to 20.00
Distilled Soda Water Co., Alaska, Green Swirls Top, Aqua, Hutchinson, 7 1/2 In. 80.00
Dixie Grape, Charlotte, N.C., Yellow, White, Southern Belle, Horse & Carriage, ACL . 20.00
Dixon & Carson, N.Y., Green, 6 7/8 In. 40.00
Donald Duck Cola, ACL, Cap, Contents 24.00
Donati's Bottling WKS, Richmond, Va., BIMAL, Contents, 8 1/2 Oz. 100.00
Dossin's Set-Up, Green, 8 In. ....*Illus* 6.00

Left to Right: *Soda, E.M. Gatchell & Co., Charlestown, S.C., Emerald Green, IP, 7 1/2 In.; Soda, Felix J. Quinn Soda Water, Halifax, N.S., Amber, 8 In.; Soda, Dossin's Set-Up, Green, 8 In.; Soda, H. Schlotterbeck, Ann Arbor, Mich., Green Tint, 8 In.; Soda, Heep Good Beverages, Wenatchee Bottling Co., Wa., 9 1/2 In.*

Double Cola, Oval Shield On Neck, Red & White Label, 1970s, 10 Oz. 5.00
Double Cola, Oval Shield, Red & White Label, 2 Indian Heads, 1950, 12 Oz. 7.50
Double Cola Jr., Painted Label, Bottom Dated 4/7, 7 1/2 Oz. 2.00
Dr Pepper, 10-2-4 On Shield, Red & White Label, 1960s, 10 Oz. 5.50
Dr Pepper, 10-2-4, Salisbury, Md., Clear 5.00
Dr Pepper, 10-2-4, Winchester, Va., Green 8.00
Dr Pepper, Desert Storm, Red, White & Blue Label, July 4, 1991, 12 Oz. 5.00
Dr Pepper, Diet, Green, 10 Oz. 10.00
Dr Pepper, Good For Life, 6 1/2 Oz. 35.00
Dr Pepper, Orange, Va., Aqua, Debossed 9.00
Dr Pepper, Red & White Label, 32 Oz. 4.00
Dr Pepper, Sugar Free, Blue & White Label, 1970s, 10 Oz. 4.00
Dr Pepper, Waco, Texas, 1885-1985 .... 20.00
Dr Pepper Bott. Co., Memphis, Tenn., Pewter Top, Clear, Siphon, Qt. 79.00
Dr. Nut, Punxsutawney, Complimentary, Clear, 1949, 7 Oz. 25.00
Dr. Wells, Sun Rays, Red & White Label, 1940s, 10 Oz. 8.00
Duffy, Dyottville Glass Works, Emerald Green, IP, Crude, Squatty 225.00
Durham's Hi-Tide Beverages, When Your Ship Comes In, 12 In. 10.00
Dyottville Glass Works, Philadelphia, Yellow Green, IP, 1845-1855, 7 1/4 In. 468.00
E. Bigelow & Co., Springfield, Mass., Sapphire Blue, IP, 7 3/8 In. 194.00
E. De Freest Root Beer, Stoneware, Tan Glaze, 9 In. 88.00
E. Duffy & Son, 44 Filbert St., Philadelphia, Blue, Squatty 30.00
E. Duffy & Son, No. 44 Filbert St., Dyottville Glass Works, Emerald Green, IP 225.00
E. Ottenville, Nashville, Tenn., Amber, Block Letters, Blob Top .... 50.00 to 95.00
E. Ottenville, Nashville, Tenn., Cobalt Blue, Blob Top 135.00
E. Ottenville, Nashville, Tenn., Cobalt Blue, Blob Top, Embossed 115.00
E. Ottenville, Nashville, Tenn., Cobalt Blue, Hutchinson, Lacquered, Repaired 95.00
E. Roussel, Philadelphia, Emerald Green, IP, 7 1/2 In. 88.00
E. Smith, Elmira, N.Y., Cobalt Blue, 7 In. 143.00
E.K.B. Aerated Soda Water, Cobalt Blue, IP, Blob Top, 6 3/4 In. 110.00
E.L. Billing's Geysers Soda, Lime Green, 7 1/4 In. 143.00
E.L. Billing's Geysers Soda, Sac City, Aqua, Blob Top, 7 1/4 In. 50.00
E.M. Gatchell & Co., Charleston, S.C., Emerald Green, IP, 1845, 7 1/2 In. .... *Illus* 330.00
Eagle Bottling Works, Tacoma, Washington, Eagle, Embossed, Hutchinson, ... 25.00 '
Eagle Soda Water & Bottling Co., Santa Cruz, Calif., Eagle, Aqua, Hutchinson 85.00 to 125.00
Eastern Cider Co., Golden Amber, 7 1/4 In. 82.00
Einwechter & Fulton Philada, Blue Green, Squatty 29.00
El Dorado, Ice Blue, Blob Top, 7 1/4 In. 95.00
Empire Soda Works, Aqua, Applied Top, 1863, 7 1/4 In. 523.00

Empire Soda Works, San Francisco, Blue Green, 7 1/2 In................................110.00 to 198.00
Empire Soda Works, San Francisco, Green Aqua, Applied Blob Top, 7 1/4 In. ...44.00 to 140.00
Empire Soda Works, San Francisco, Medium Green, Whittled, Blob Top, 7 1/4 In. 220.00
Excelsior Soda Works, Los Angeles, Calif., Aqua, Hutchinson, 6 3/4 In..................... 44.00
F. & L. Schaum, Baltimore Glass Works, Dark Yellow Olive, Cylindrical, 7 In........... 302.00
F. Bauman Soda Works, Santa Maria, Calif., Aqua, 7 1/4 In............................... 88.00
F. Dusch & Son, Richmond, Va., Aqua, Blob Top, Ten Pin Shape 93.00
Faygo Root Beer, Paper Label, Contents, 16 Oz... 3.50
Felix J. Quinn Soda Water, Halifax, N.S., Amber, 8 In................................*Illus* 45.00
Ferber Bros., Phoebus, Va., Aqua, Hutchinson, Embossed In Circle, 7 1/4 In.............. 33.00
Fitzgerald & Co., Amsterdam, N.Y., Aqua, Matthews Gravitating Stopper, Blob Top .. 22.00
Fontinalis Beverages, Carl W. Peterson, Grayline, Mich., Red ACL, 8 1/2 In............. 40.00
Frostie, You'll Love It, Elf, Cream & Red, 10 Oz. 5.00
G. Ebberwein Ginger Ale, Olive Yellow, 7 1/2 In.. 121.00
G. Morris & Co., City Bottling Works, Detroit, Sapphire Blue, Hutchinson, 6 3/4 In. ... 154.00
G. Schnerr & Co., Sacramento, Calif., Apple Green, Hutchinson, 6 7/8 In................... 110.00
G.A.K., Winnemucca, Nev., Aqua, Hutchinson, 1/4 In. Lip................................... 40.00
G.S., Green, 8-Sided, Applied Blob Lip, 7 1/4 In... 715.00
Gardner & Co., Hackettstown, N.J., Sapphire Blue, 10-Sided, c.1865, 6 3/4 In............. 400.00
Genuine Belfast Ginger Ale, John Ryan, Savannah August, Ga., Green Aqua, 9 3/8 In. .. 121.00
Geo. F. Ensminger & Co., Martinsburg, W.Va., Aqua, Gravitating Stopper................. 30.00
Geo. Gemenden, Savannah, Eagle, Emerald Green, IP, 7 1/2 In. ....242.00 to 300.00
Geo. Norris & Son, Detroit, Mich., Aqua, Qt... 10.00
Geo. Schmuck's Ginger Ale, Cleve., O., Amber, Hutchinson, 12-Sided, 7 3/4 In....... 82.00 to 125.00
Geo. Schoch, Philadelphia, Light Blue Green, IP, Squatty, Pt............................ 44.00
Geo. Spreitzer, 1892, Paterson, N.J., Eagle, Hutchinson 25.00
Golden Gate, San Francisco, Green, Blob Top, 1870s, 7 1/8 In............................ 75.00
Golden West Soda Works, San Francisco, Calif., Aqua, Fluted Base, 6 3/4 In. 77.00
Grand Pop Hits The Spot, 6 1/2 Oz... 7.00
H. Aman, Cheyenne, Wyo., Hutchinson, 6 1/2 In.. 100.00
H. Brader & Co., San Francisco, Aqua, 8-Sided, Blob Top, 7 1/4 In..................330.00 to 360.00
H. Brand's & Co., Toledo, Ohio, Coblat Blue, Blob Top, 7 In............................ 100.00
H. Nash & Co. Root Beer, Cincinnati, Sapphire Blue, 12-Sided Panels, IP, 9 7/8 In..... 660.00
H. Schlotterbeck, Ann Arbor, Mich., Green Tint, 8 In..............................*Illus* 250.00
H. Schmidtmann, New York, Aqua, Blob Top.. 45.00
H.L. & J.W., Hartford, Ct., Olive Amber, IP, Squatty, 6 1/2 In. 235.00
H.W. Stoll, Los Angeles, Calif., Aqua, 6 3/4 In.. 121.00
Haddock & Sons, Yellow Olive, Torpedo Shape, Ring Pontil, c.1830, 6 1/4 In............ 850.00
Hamakua Soda Works, Tooled Lip, Hutchinson, 7 5/8 In................................. 275.00
Harmony Club, Orchestra & Notes, Red & White Label, 1945, 7 Oz. 9.50
Harrold & Johnson, Cream Soda, Aqua, Cylindrical, 1/4 Pt. 55.00
Heart Club, Heart & Club, Red & White Label, 12 Oz..................................... 5.00
Heep Good Beverages, Wenatchee Bottling Co., Wa., 9 1/2 In..................... *Illus* 25.00
Henry Lubs, Savannah, Teal, 1885, 7 1/2 In.. 55.00
Henry Schramm, Aqua, Pictured Anvil, Fullersburg, Ill., Hutchinson 35.00
Henry Weinhard, Portland, Or., 6 Pack, Capped & Filled 12.00
Hering & Carpenter, Cumberland, Md., Aqua, Slug Plate 8.00
Hewlett Bros., Salt Lake City, Aqua, Hutchinson, Dug, 6 1/2 In. 25.00
Hickory Bottling, Hickory, N.C., Hutchinson... 25.00
Hill Billy Brew, Hillbilly & Still, Green, Red & White Label, 10 Oz. 8.50
Hippo Size, San Antonio, Tx., Embossed Hippo, Pat.1926................................. 20.00
Hires, Amber, Embossed... 44.00
Hires, The Hires Co., Philadelphia, Pa., 9 3/4 In..............................*Illus* 4.00
Hires Root Beer, Amber, Long Neck, Orange & White Label, 10 Oz......................... 4.00
Hires Root Beer, Contents.. 18.00
Hires Root Beer Extract, Aqua.. 10.00
Holland Rink Bottling Works, Butte, Mont., Hutchinson 25.00
Hollister Works, Aqua, 7 1/4 In... 242.00
Home Bottling Works, Newport News, Va., Embossed In Circle, Hutchinson 55.00
Home Brewing, Richmond, Va., Embossed In Circle, Aqua, Hutchinson, 6 3/4 In. 154.00
Howel's Root Beer, Elf & Tray, Red & White Label, 1940s, 12 Oz. 9.50
Howell & Smith, Buffalo, Sapphire Blue, Cone, Applied Blob Lip, IP, 5 1/2 In............ 330.00
Hoxie, Albany, Aqua, Square Shoulders, Blob Top, 6 1/2 In.............................. 35.00

Humboldt Soda Works, Winnemucca, Nev., Aqua, Slug Plate, 7 3/4 In. .... 140.00 to 155.00
Hygia Soda Works, Kahului, Hawaii, Aqua, Hutchinson, 7 1/4 In...................... 95.00 to 175.00
I.A. Lindestram, Madison, Wi., Aqua, 7 1/4 In. 121.00
I.G. Vreeland, Supr Soda Water, Newark, N.J., Light Green, 7 1/2 In. .... 35.00 to 90.00
Imperial Bottling Works, Portland, Oregon, Hutchinson.. 30.00
Imperial Ginger Ale & Soda Water Co., Oakland, Calif., Aqua, Crown Top 20.00
Ira Harvey, Providence, R.I., Cobalt Blue, IP, Cylindrical, c.1860, 6 3/4 In. 440.00
Italian Soda Water Manufacter, San Francisco, Sapphire Blue, IP, 7 1/4 In. .. 400.00 to 605.00
J. Cosgrove, Charleston, 1866, Sapphire Blue, 1/2 Pt. 100.00
J. Esposito, Koka Nola, Light To Medium Yellow, Hutchinson, 1900-1910, 7 3/4 In. .. 1100.00
J. Esposito, Koka Nola, Philadelphia, Yellow, Hutchinson, Stopper, 7 5/8 In................. 4620.00
J. Harvey & Co., Providence, R.I., Olive Amber, Blob Top, c.1870, Cylindrical, 7 In.. 88.00 to 162.00
J. Lake, Schenectady, N.Y., Sapphire Blue, Graphite Tontil, c.1860, 7 1/2 In............... 525.00
J. Pabst & Sons, Hamilton, Ontario, Hutchinson... 15.00
J. Stouffer, Tannersville, Penn., Green, IP 200.00
J. Tweddle Celebrated Soda Or Mineral Waters, Blue Green, IP, 7 1/2 In. 132.00
J. Wise, Allentown, Pa., Cornflower Blue, Blob Top, 6 3/4 In.. 66.00
J.A. Dearborn, N.Y., Cobalt Blue, IP, 7 1/2 In. 148.00
J.A. Lomax, Chicago, Cobalt Blue, Hutchinson 66.00
J.A. Schiff, Plattsburg, N.Y., Aqua, Hutchinson 12.00
J.F. Batterman, Brooklyn, Blob Top 15.00
J.F. Groghan, Lexington, Ky., Green Aqua, Hutchinson, Mug Base 30.00
J.I. Blivens & Co., Oakland, Calif., Aqua, Hutchinson, Gravitating Stopper................. 40.00
J.J. Harington, Butte, Mont., Aqua, Hutchinson, Dug 50.00
J.M. Wilson, Newport News, Va., Hutchinson, Embossed In Circle............................ 66.00
J.T. Brown, Chemist, Boston, Double Soda Water, Cobalt Blue, c.1870, 9 In. .... 850.00 to 935.00
J.W. Garrison, Louisville, Ky., IP 45.00
J.W. Harris Soda Water, New Haven, Ct., Sapphire Blue, 8-Sided, IP, 7 3/8 In. .. 413.00 to 770.00
J.W. Vetter, Chattanooga, Tenn., Amber, Blob Top 200.00
Jackson's Napa Soda Spring's Natural, Cobalt, Applied Mouth, 7 1/2 In. ..... 770.00 to 825.00
James Ray Ginger Ale, Savannah, Ga., Cobalt Blue, Cylindrical, 7 1/2 In......... 100.00 to 200.00
Jet, Airplane Picture, Faded, Red & White Label, 8 Oz. 12.50
John Graf, Milwaukee, Wis., 8-Sided, Aqua.. 50.00
John M. Krug, Philadelphia, Blue Green, Squatty 59.00
John Moon, Philadelphia, Teal Blue, Blob Top, Cylindrical, IP, 1850, 7 In. 385.00
John Ogden, Pittsburgh, Aqua, IP, Applied Mouth, 7 3/8 In. 88.00
John Ryan, 1866 Excelsior Soda Works, Savannah, Ga., Cobalt Blue, Blob Top ... 50.00 to 55.00
John Ryan, Columbus, Ga., Cobalt Blue, Cylindrical, 7 3/4 In. 44.00
John Ryan, Savannah, Ga., Excelsior, Ginger Ale, 1852, Yellow Olive, 7 1/4 In........... 121.00
John Ryan, Savannah, Ga., Ginger Ale, Olive Yellow, Dug, 1/2 Pt........................... 121.00
John S. Baker Soda Water, Emerald Green, 8-Sided, IP, 7 1/4 In. 154.00
John Seedorf Soda Water, Charleston, S.C., Cobalt Blue, IP, c.1855, 7 1/2 In............. 275.00
K Orange, K On Shield, Black Label, 1950s, 7 Oz. 5.00
K.C. Heart, Kit Carson, Love, Orange & Yellow, 10 Oz. 6.50
Keys, Burlington, N.J., Blue Green, IP, c.1860, 7 In.. 375.00
King-Cola, Royal Drink, Richmond, Va., Washington, D.C., Aqua, 6 1/2 Oz. .... 10.00 to 22.00
Kinsella & Hennessy, Albany, N.Y., Green, IP, 1/2 Pt. 27.00
Knauss & Lichtenwal, Allentown, Pa., Cobalt Blue, Blob Top.................................. 200.00

Soda, Hires,
The Hires Co.,
Philadelphia,
Pa., 9 3/4 In.

Soda, Lincoln,
Lincoln Bottling
Co., Chicago, Ill.,
Blue Applied
Color Label

Soda, M.
Shouler
Bottling, Akron,
Oh., 6 1/2 In.

Top Row, Left to Right: *Soda, Mason's Root Beer, Amber, 11 1/2 In.; Soda, Nezinscot Beverages, Nezinscot Bottling Co., Turner, Maine, 11 In.; Soda, Norton Big Chief Beverages, Norton Coca-Cola, Norton, Ks., 9 1/2 In.; Soda, Old Faithful Beverage Co., Idaho Falls, Red Applied Color Label, 9 1/2 In.*

Knicker-Bocker, Soda Water, Cobalt Blue, 10-Sided, IP, 7 3/8 In. 115.00
Knicker-Bocker, Soda Water, Sapphire Blue, 10-Sided, IP, c.1860, 7 5/8 In. 190.00
Knicker-Bocker, Soda Water, Sapphire Blue, 10-Sided, IP, 1/2 Pt. 330.00
Knicker-Bocker, Soda Water, Saratoga Springs, Sapphire Blue, 10-Sided, IP, 7 In. 385.00
Kroger Bros., Butte, Mt., Aqua, Hutchinson, 6 3/4 In. 100.00
L. Bordonsky & Son, Chicago, Ill, Buffalo, Hutchinson ....⸱....... 20.00
L.C. Smith, Cobalt Blue, IP, 7 1/4 In. .... 170.00 to 210.00
L.J. & A. Dearborn, Albany Glassworks, Indigo Blue, IP 400.00
Lahaina Ice Ltd., Maui, Aqua, Hutchinson, Crude Top 50.00
Lakeview, Lake & Cottage, Green, White & Red Label, 7 Oz. 6.50
Lancaster Glass Works, N.Y., Sapphire Blue, Blob Top, 7 In. 110.00
Leary's Root Beer. 15.00
Leland Ice & Cold Storage Co., Leland, Miss., Hutchinson 30.00
Lincoln, Lincoln Bottling Co., Chicago, Ill., Blue Applied Color Label. ....*Illus* 40.00
Lion Soda Works, Walnut Grove, Ca., Crown Top, Lion's Head Picture. 50.00
Little Tom, Man With Bottle, Red & White Label, 1965, 6 Oz. 5.00
Livermore Soda Works, Livermore, Calif., Aqua, Hutchinson, 6 5/8 In. 240.00
Lone Pine Nebraska Bottling Co., Aqua 10.00
Los Angeles Soda Works, Embossed Star, Applied Top, 6 1/2 In. 45.00
Louis Weber, Louisville, Ky., Amber, Embossed, Whittled, Qt. 75.00
Love, Heart, Kit Carson On Rearing Horse, White Label, 10 Oz. 7.50
Lucky Strike, Nashua, New Hampshire 3.00
Luke Beard, Emerald Green, 10-Pin, Pontil, c.1860, 7 In. .... 160.00 to 200.00
M. Cronan, Sacramento, Calif., Aqua, Hutchinson 6.00
M. Eisen Bottling Works, Leavenworth, Kans., Hutchinson 90.00
M. Keeley, Chicago, Ill., Aqua 12.00
M. McCormack, Cobalt Blue, Blob Top, IP, Embossed. .... 165.00 to 200.00
M. Shouler Bottling, Akron, Oh., 6 1/2 In. ....*Illus* 10.00
Manhattan, City & Skyline Picture, White & Red Label, 7 Oz. 7.00
Martinell's Soda Works, M.S., Blue Aqua, Applied Mouth, 7 1/4 In. 50.00
Mason's Root Beer, Amber, 11 1/2 In. ....*Illus* 5.00
McCarthy & Moore, Waterbury, Ct., Hutchinson, Mug Base 10.00
Meincke & Ebberwein, 1882 Ga. Ginger Ale, Amber, Blob Top, Dug, 8 In. 50.00
Meyer & Rottman, N.Y., Pale Green, IP 65.00
Minneapolis Bottling Works, Minneapolis, Minn., Amber 180.00
Mishler's, Yellow 55.00
Mission, Mission Picture, Black & White Label, 1950s, 10 Oz. 5.50

Monroe Cider & Vinegar Co., Ferndale, Calif., Aqua, Hutchinson, 6 7/8 In. .... 65.00 to 71.00
Monroe's Distilled Soda Water, Eureka, Calif., Aqua, Hutchinson 45.00
Monteith, Philadelphia, Aqua, Blob Top, Whittled 15.00
Moriarty & Carroll, Waterbury, Conn., Hutchinson 15.00
Mountain Dew, Hillbilly With Gun, Green, Red & White Label 7.50
Mountain Dew, Southern 500 .... 12.00
Moxie, Albany, Ice Blue, Square Shoulders, Squatty 35.00
Moxie, Aqua, Tooled Lip, 6 3/8 In. 93.00
Moxie, Blob Top, 6 1/2 In. 10.00
Moxie Nerve Food, Denver, Colo., Amber, Whittled, 10 In. 253.00
Mrs. Geo. Franz, White Plains, N.Y., Tombstone, Hutchinson, Mug Base 10.00
Napa, Natural, Mineral Water, Sapphire Blue, Metal Closure, c.1865, 7 1/4 In. 300.00
Napa, Natural, Philadelphia, Cobalt Blue, 7 In. 253.00
Napa, Natural, Philadelphia, Yellow Green, 7 1/2 In. 440.00
Napa Soda, Phil Caduc, Blue Aqua, Blob Top, 7 In. 230.00
Nash Root Beer, Cobalt Blue 1600.00
National Root Beer, Albany, Label, 12 Oz. 4.00
National Soda Works, Stockton, Calif., Crown Top, Contents 18.00
Negaunee Bottling Works, Negaunee, Mich., Hutchinson, Qt. 35.00
Nehi, White Label, 16 Oz. 4.00
Nehi, Yellow & Red Label, 1950s, 10 Oz. 5.00
Nemo, Sea Captain, Green, White Label, 1954, 7 Oz. 12.50
Neptune Glass Works, Green Aqua, IP, 1845-1855, 7 1/4 In. 253.00
New Almaden Mineral Water, W & W, 1870. .... 95.00
Nezinscot, Indian Girl's Head, Green, Red & White Label, 6 Oz. 12.50
Nezinscot, Indian Girl's Head, Red & White Label, 1950s, 8 Oz. 9.50
Nezinscot Beverages, Nezinscot Bottling Co., Turner, Maine, 11 In. .... *Illus* 3.00
Norris & Co., Detroit, Mich., Cobalt Blue, Hutchinson, Smooth Lip 40.00
Norton Big Chief Beverages, Norton Coca-Cola, Norton, Ka., 9 1/2 In. .... *Illus* 75.00
Norwich Bottling Works, Norwich, N.Y., Orange Amber, Hutchinson, 6 3/8 In. 154.00
Nugrape, Yellow Label, 1970s, 8 Oz. 5.00
O-So Grape, Flat River, Mo., White Label, 1946, 7 Oz. 5.00
O. Tullman's Mineral Water Works, Aqua, Hutchinson, 7 In. 35.00
Oahu Soda Works, Hutchinson, Pale Green, 7 5/8 In. 121.00
Oak Orchard Acid Springs, Deep Root Beer Amber, Qt. 55.00
Oak Orchard Acid Springs, Emerald Green, Applied Mouth, Qt. .... 71.00 to 77.00
Old Faithful Beverage Co., Idaho Falls, Red Applied Color Label, 9 1/2 In. .... *Illus* 72.00
Omaha Bottling Co., Omaha, Neb., Hutchinson 30.00
Orange County Soda Works, Anaheim, Aqua, Crown Top 25.00
Owen Casey Eagle Soda Works, Sac City, Sapphire Blue, c.1870, 7 1/2 In. .... 65.00 to 121.00
Owen Casey Eagle Soda Works, Yellow Olive Green, 7 1/8 In. 577.50
P. Divine Bottler, Philadelphia, Emerald Green, IP, 1845-1855, 6 3/4 In. 38.00
P. Pons & Co., 334 Royal St., New Orleans, Aqua, Pontil, Blob Top 55.00
P.J. Crays Old Fashioned Root Beer, Holyoke Mass, Stoneware, 8 Oz. 65.00
Pacific & Puget Sound Works, Aqua, Hutchinson, 7 In. 176.00
Pacific Glass Works, Blue Green, Blob Top 35.00
Pacific Soda Works, Glassen & Co., San Francisco, Aqua 65.00
Pappy Of Them All, Pat. 1928, Adam's Beverage Co., Double Waisted, 8 3/4 In. 9.00
Pearson Bros., Aqua, Gravitating Stopper, Whittled, Blob Top, 1/4 In. 1540.00
Pearson Bros., Placerville, Calif., Codd 65.00
Pep-Up, Big Boy Beverages Inc., Cleveland, Ohio, 8 In. 8.00
Phil Daniels, Anaconda, Mont., Aqua, Hutchinson, Dug 45.00
Phoenix Bottling Works, Mobile, Ala., Aqua, Hutchinson, Embossed 19.25
Phoenix Glass Works, Brooklyn, N.Y., Aqua, 7 1/4 In. 154.00
Phoenix Glass Works, Brooklyn, Pale Green, IP, c.1855, 7 1/8 In. 400.00
Phosphorize, Cobalt Blue, Embossed Across Shoulder 190.00
Pioneer Brown & Co., Blue Aqua, Applied Blob Top, 7 1/4 In. 1540.00
Pioneer Soda Works, Aqua, Blob Top 20.00
Pioneer Soda Works, Portland, Ore, Anchor, Hutchinson 25.00
Pioneer Soda Works, Reno, Nev., Green Aqua, Hutchinson, 7 In. 357.00
Pioneer Soda Works, San Francisco, Blue Aqua, Blob Top, 7 3/8 In. 132.00
Pioneer Soda Works, San Francisco, Blue Aqua, Hutchinson, 6 7/8 In. 77.00
Polly's Soda Pop, Refresh With Polly's, Independent Bottling Co., 9 1/2 In. 25.00

Pop Kola, Textured, Emblem, White Label, 1940s, 12 Oz. 5.00
Pratt Bros., Pipestone, Minn., Aqua, Hutchinson, 7 In. .... 12.00 to 16.00
Premium Mineral Waters, Peacock Blue, Applied Top, 8-Sided, 7 1/2 In. 85.00
Pride Bottling Co., Chicago, Ill., Deer Embossed, Hutchinson 45.00
Priest's Natural Soda, Aqua, Hutchinson 8.00
Puritan Mfg. Co., Portland, Ore., Crown Top 5.00
Queen City Soda Works, Seattle, Blue Aqua, Hutchinson, 6 7/8 In. 253.00
R.C. & T., New York, Light To Medium Blue Green, 7 1/16 In. 55.00
R.R. Randall & Co., Aqua, Hamilton Hybrid, Codd, 9 3/4 In. 38.00
R.W. Snyder, Battle Creek, Mich., Hutchinson, Qt. 35.00
Red Seal Soda Water Co., Salt Lake City, Sun-Colored Amethyst, Hutchinson 30.00
Richmond Soda Works, F.S.W., San Rafael, Calif., Aqua, Hutchinson, 6 3/4 In. 45.00
Rob't Massenburg, Hampton, Va., Aqua, Hutchinson, Embossed 121.00
Robinson, Wilson & Legallee, Boston, Green, IP, 6 7/8 In. 165.00
Root Beer, Stoneware, 9 3/4 In. 88.00
Rushton & Aspinwald, New York, Olive Green, Tenpin Shape, 7 3/8 In. 770.00
S. Smith, Auburn, N.Y., Von Harten & Grogan, Blue, Tenpin Shape, IP, 1/2 Pt. 264.00
S.D. Harper, Frankford, Dyottville Glass Works, Emerald Green, IP, Squatty 235.00
Sacramento, Eagle On Branch, Green, Blob Top, Pontil 155.00
Saegertown, Man With Sword, Green, Red & White Label, 7 Oz. 6.50
Sammons Bros., Jamestown, Blue Aqua, Hutchinson, 6 3/4 In. 121.00
San Francisco Glass Works, Blue Aqua, 7 1/4 In. .... 40.00 to 50.00
San Francisco Glass Works, Grass Green, Whittled, 7 In. 357.00
Saratoga Seltzer Water, Blue Green, Pt. 302.00
Seitz & Bro. Premium Soda Water, Easton Pa., Cobalt Blue, 8 Sided, IP, 7 1/8 In. 170.00
Sequoia Soda Works, Angels, Calif., Aqua, Crown Top 45.00
Seven-Up, Bubble Girl, Green, Orange & White Label, 7 Oz. 8.00
Seven-Up, Charleston, S.C., Amber, Embossed Twice On Neck 44.00
Seven-Up, Orange & White Label, 1970s, 16 Oz. 3.00
Seven-Up, The Uncola, Green, Orange & White Label, 8 Oz. 3.00
Shero-Cola, Princeton, W.Va. 8.00
Shoshone Bottling Works, Shoshone, Ida., Hutchinson 100.00
Simba Cola, Lion Picture, Green, 1950s, 10 Oz. 8.00
Skipper, Boy & Flag, Red & White Label, 7 Oz. 8.00
Sky High Root Beer, Amber, 64 Oz. 45.00
SLO Soda Works, Hutchinson 45.00
Sloper & Frost, Cobalt Blue, IP, Applied Blob Top, 7 5/8 In. 192.00
Smith & Fotheringham, St. Louis, Sapphire Blue, 10-Sided, IP, 1/2 Pt. 220.00
South Yorkshire Aerated Water Co., Aqua, Hamilton Hybrid, Codd, 10 In. 108.00
Southern, Eagle On Shield With Flags, Sapphire Blue, IP, Cylindrical, 1860, 7 In. 550.00
Southern Bottling Works, Atlanta, Aqua, Hutchinson, 7 1/4 In. 10.00
Southwick & Tupper, N.Y., Cobalt Blue, 10-Sided, 7 3/8 In. 742.50
Sprite, Green, White Label, 1970s, 10 Oz. 3.00
Squeeze, Boy & Girl On Bench, ACL, 10 Oz. 7.00
Squeeze, Boy & Girl On Bench, Blue & White Label, 12 Oz. 8.00
Standard Bottling Works, Minneapolis, Minn., Black Amber 190.00
Star Bottling Works, South Sharon, Pa., Star, Hutchinson 15.00
Stephens & Jose, Virginia City, Nevada, Aqua, Gravitating Stopper 580.00
Stewarts & Stewarts Diet, 12 Oz. 2.00
Suburban Club, Petersburg, W.V., Golfer, Swinging Club, Applied Color Label 10.00
Sun Crest, Blue Applied Color Label, 8 1/2 In. 1.00
Sun Tang, Diamonds, Emblem, Blue & White Label, 1960s, 10 Oz. 5.00
Sun-Drop Lemonade, Roma Bottling Works Co., Pittsburgh, 9 1/2 In. 20.00
Sun-Rise, Snow, Mountain & Sun Rays, Red & White Label, 10 Oz. 6.00
Sunburst, White Label, 1960s, 12 Oz. 5.00
Superior Soda Water, Aqua, IP 50.00
Sweetie Beverage Co., Philadephia, Pa., 8 In. .... *Illus* 55.00
T.W. Gillett, New Haven, Co., Cobalt Blue, 8-Sided, IP, 7 5/8 In. .... 385.00 to 400.00
Tahoe Soda Springs, Natural Mineral Water, Green Aqua, 7 1/8 In. ...... 209.00 to 302.00
Take-Kola, Harrisburg, Va., Aqua, 8-Sided 10.00
Taylor & Co., Valparaiso, Blue Green, 7 1/4 In. 330.00
Taylor & Co. Soda Water, San Francisco, Eureka, Cobalt Blue, 6 3/4 In. 330.00
Taylor & Co. Soda Water, Valparaiso, Chili, Emerald Green, IP, Blob Top, 7 3/8 In. .. 330.00

Soda, Sweetie
Beverage Co.,
Philadephia, Pa.,
8 In.

Soda, Tom
Moore Fine
Beverages,
8 In.

Soda, Virginia
Dare, First Lady
Of The Land,
New Kensington,
Pa., Green,
12 In.

Tennis & Crockett, Hampton, Va., Aqua, Hutchinson, Embossed In Circle	16.50
Thomas Leonard Sonora Soda Works, Medium Green Aqua, 7 In.	55.00
Thos. Burger, South Bend, Ind., Hutchinson	17.00
Thos. Mayer, Dark Green, IP, Slug Plate	66.00
Tifton, Ga., Aqua, Hutchinson	12.00
Tom Moore Fine Beverages, 8 In. ....*Illus*	4.00
Tom Sawyer Root Beer, Mark Twain Picture	100.00
Topp Cola, White Label, 16 Oz.	4.00
Tower Root Beer, Amber, 28 Oz.	125.00
Towne Club, Red & White Label, 12 Oz.	5.00
Triple Extract Syrup Of Moxie, Lowell, Aqua, Cylindrical, Label, 1880, 9 1/2 In.	286.00
Triple L, It's Swell, Green, Red & White Applied Color Label, 12 In.	5.00
Tripple AAA Root Beer, Red & White Label, 1940s, 6 Oz.	8.00
Tripple XXX Root Beer, Red & Yellow Label, 1950s, 8 Oz.	6.50
Twin Lights, Lighthouses, Green, Red & White Label, 7 Oz.	12.50
Union Bottle Works Co., Dupont City, Va., Crown Top, Contents, 7 Oz.	22.00
Union Glass Works Phila., Cobalt Blue, IP	140.00
Union Glass Works Phila., Pink Amethyst, IP, 7 3/4 In.	852.50
Valentine & Vreeland, Newark, N.J., Cobalt Blue, IP, Blob Top, 7 3/8 In.	165.00
Vernor's Ginger Ale, Detroit's Drink, Green, 12 In.	5.00
Vess, Light Green, Cream & Red Label, 10 Oz.	5.00
Vicksburg Steam Bottling Works, Miss., Hutchinson	12.00
Victor Barothy, Chicago, Teepee, Amber, Blob Top	200.00
Vincent's, Patent July 18th, 1876, 6-Sided, 5 3/8 In.	145.00
Virginia Dare, First Lady Of The Land, New Kensington, Pa., Green, 12 In. ....*Illus*	5.00
Voelker & Bro., Cleveland, Ohio, Sapphire Blue, Blob Top	60.00
Vonharten & Grogan, Savannah, Ga., Teal Green, Cylindrical, 1/2 Pt.	66.00
W. Eagle, Vestry Varick, Canal Sts., Union Glass Works, Cobalt Blue, 7 3/8 In.... 110.00 to	132.00
W. Eagle Superior Soda, W.E., Aqua	30.00
W. Eagles Superior, Yellow Green, IP	175.00
W. Morton, Trenton, N.J., Forest Green, Qt., 7 1/2 In.	35.00
W. Riddle, Philadelphia, Turquoise Green, Graphite Pontil, Blob Top, 7 1/4 In.	132.00
W. Ryer, Philadelphia, Cobalt Blue, IP, 7 1/8 In.	467.00
W. Ryer, Union Glass Works, R/Philada., Cobalt Blue, IP, c.1860, 7 1/8 In.	425.00
W. Voight, Detroit, Olive Yellow, 9 In.	715.00
W.C. O'Malley, Clinton, Mass., Blob Top	15.00
W.E. Deamer, Aqua, 7 1/8 In.	60.50
W.H.H., Chicago, Queen Victoria, Ice Blue, Mug Base, Nursing, Salt Glaze, 1840	2000.00
W.M. & D.T. Cox, Port Jervis, N.Y., Yellow Green, IP, Cylindrical, 1/2 Pt.	231.00
Walter & Lauter Reading Pa., W&l, Blue Green	159.00
Walters Napa County Soda, Blue Aqua, Green Striations, Hutchinson, 7 1/4 In.	50.00
Wapa-Koneta, Wapakoneta, Oh., Yellow, Indian Chief & Maiden, ACL	15.00
Warwick Bottling Co., Newport News, Va., Embossed In Circle, Hutchinson	71.00
Welch's, Blue & White Label, 16 Oz.	5.00
Wesley Cunningham, Hampton, Va., Embossed Circle, Hutchinson, Paneled Base	44.00
Wesley Cunningham, Hampton, Va., Hutchinson, Tombstone Slug Plate	88.00
Wheaton, New Bedford, Mass., Whale Design	30.00
White Eagle, Eagle Picture, Red & White Label, 7 Oz.	9.50
Williams & Severance Soda & Mineral Waters, San Francisco, Blue, IP, 1/2 Pt.	357.00
Williams Bros., San Jose, Calif., Aqua, Hutchinson, Gravitating Stopper	30.00

Willibald Kuebler Bottler, Easton, Pa., Aqua, Squatty 12.00
Wishing Well, National Dry Ltd., London, Canada, Green, 9 In..................................... 6.00
Wm. A. Kearney, Shamokin, Pa., Amber, Qt.. 250.00
Wm. Eagle, New York, Cobalt Blue, 8-Sided, IP, 7 1/4 In..................................105.00 to 132.00
Wm. Eagle Premium Soda Water, Teal, Graphite Pontil, 7 1/2 In.............................. 330.00
Wm. Lawrence, Boston, Green, Yellow Tone, IP, 1845-1855, 6 3/4 In......................... 88.00
Wm. Pond, XX Philadelphia Ale & Porter, N.Y., Emerald Green, Small 100.00
Wm. Russel, Baltimore, Yellow Green, 9 In.. 341.00
Wm. Russell, Baltimore, Blue Green, IP.. 150.00
Wm. Russell, Emerald Green, Pontil, 1845-1855, 8 1/8 In. 275.00
Wm. W. Lappeus Premium Soda Or Mineral Waters, Sapphire Blue, 10-Sided, IP, 7 In. 187.00
Wonsitler & Co., Doylestown, Penna., Blue Green, Squatty 89.00
Yuncker Bottling Co., Tacoma, Wash., Hutchinson, 10-Sided Base............................. 30.00
Zetz Seven-Up Bottling Co. Inc., Seltzer, New Orleans, Pink Rose, No Cap............... 30.00
SPIRIT, see Flask; Gin; Seal

———————————————— **STIEGEL TYPE** ————————————————

Henry William Stiegel, an immigrant to the colonies, started his first factory in Pennsylvania in 1763. He remained in business until 1774. Glassware was made in a style popular in Europe at that time and was similar to the glass of many other makers. It was made of clear or colored glass that was decorated with enamel colors, mold blown designs, or etchings. He produced window glass, bottles, and useful wares. It is almost impossible to be sure a piece is a genuine Stiegel, so the knowing collector now refers to this glass as Stiegel type. Almost all of the enamel-decorated bottles of this type that are found today were made in Europe.

STIEGEL TYPE, Amethyst, 12 Diamond, Pontil, Pocket, 4 1/4 In. 3025.00
Amethyst, 12 Diamond, Pontil, Pocket, 4 3/4 In. 2420.00
Amethyst, 16 Ribs Above Expanded Diamond, Sheared Lip, Pontil, 5 In. 413.00
Amethyst, 28 Diamond, Pontil, Pocket, 5 3/8 In. 3850.00
Amethyst, 3 Rows Daisy, Over 30 Flutes, Sheared Lip, Pontil, 5 1/2 In......................... 3130.00
Amethyst, Daisy In Diamond, 1770-1774, 1/2 Pt..14550.00
Amethyst, Deep Purple, Daisy In Diamond, OP, 1770-1774, 4 1/4 In. 1595.00
Amethyst, Diamond Pattern, Teardrop Form, Pontil, 6 In.. 1100.00
Amethyst, Diamonds & Circles Pattern, 7 In., 2 Piece.. 413.00
Amethyst, Expanded Diamond Daisy, Sheared Lip, Pontil, 4 3/4 In............................. 2310.00
Amethyst, Expanded Diamond Pattern, Sheared Lip, OP, 18th Century, 5 1/2 In.......... 6600.00
Amethyst, Flask, Daisy In Hexagon, Pocket, 4 3/8 In.. 4400.00
Amethyst, Flask, Diamond Over Flute, Pontil, Pocket, 5 3/8 In....................................... 6050.00
Amethyst, Flask, Diamond Over Flute, Pontil, Pocket, 4 3/4 In..................................... 4675.00
Brilliant Amethyst, Pattern Molded, Diamond Over Flute, Pontil, 4 1/2 In. 3575.00
Brilliant Amethyst, Perfume, Diamond, 1770, 5 1/2 In..*Illus* 3575.00
Deep Amethyst, Expanded 12 Diamond, Sheared Lip, Pontil, 5 1/2 In. 4675.00
Deep Amethyst, Expanded Diamond Pattern, Sheared Lip, Pontil, 3 1/2 In. 308.00
Deep Amethyst, No Pattern, Sheared Lip, Pontil, 6 1/8 In. 743.00
Deep Amethyst, Pattern Molded, Diamond Over Flute, Pontil, 4 5/8 In........................ 3025.00
Light Amethyst, Pattern Molded, Diamond Over Flute, Pontil, 4 3/4 In........................ 2750.00

Stiegel Type, Brilliant
Amethyst, Perfume,
Diamond, 1770, 5 1/2 In.

Light To Medium Amethyst, Expanded Diamond Daisy, 5 In. 4400.00
Medium Amethyst, OP, 6 In.. 2200.00
Medium Amethyst, Sheared Lip, OP, 6 In.. 2200.00

─────────────────────── **STONEWARE** ───────────────────────

Stoneware is a type of pottery, not as soft as earthenware and not translucent like porcelain. It is fired at such a high temperature it is impervious to liquid and so makes an excel-
lent bottle. Although glazes are not needed, they were often added to stoneware to enhance
its appearance. Most stoneware bottles also have the name of a store or brand name as part
of their decoration.

STONEWARE, Barrel, Doulton & Watts, Salt Glaze, Brown, Applied Sprigging, 16 In. 155.00
Bottle, Gould, Hibberd & Randall Ltd., Isle Of Wight, 7 In. ....*Illus* 35.00
Bottle, J. Hindles Pop, Star, Salt Glazed, Incised.. 180.00
Crock, Blue Floral, 1865, 3 Gal. 225.00
Crock, Blue Floral, 1870, 2 Gal. 275.00
Crock, Carpenter & Co., Boston, Gray, Cobalt Slip Floral Design, Salt Glaze, 12 In. 440.00
Crock, Gray, Cobalt Slip Floral Decoration, Salt Glaze, 13 1/2 In................................... 138.00
Crock, Gray, Salt Glaze, WHH, Cobalt Blue X, Multisided, 9 1/2 In. 121.00
Crock, I.M. Mead & Co., Gray, Cobalt Slip Decoration, Salt Glaze, 9 1/2 In. 100.00
Crock, Incised Man's Head Decoration, Dark Brown, Cylindrical, 7 7/8 In. 220.00
Crock, J.H. Brough & Co., Liverpool, Black Transfer, Table Salt, 1880s, 5 7/8 In......... 231.00
Crock, Liverpool, Black Transfer, Table Salt, 1880s, 5 7/8 In. 231.00
Jar, Dark Gray, Cobalt Slip Stencil, Salt Glaze, 10 In.. 220.00
Jar, Dark Gray, Cobalt Stencil, 7 1/2 In... 220.00
Jar, Dark Gray, Cobalt Stencil, Salt Glaze, 8 1/2 In... 264.00
Jar, Gray, Cobalt Stencil, Salt Glaze, 6 1/8 In.. 275.00
Jar, Gray, Salt Glaze, Cobalt Blue Design, Handle, Egg Shape, 3 Gal. 165.00
Jar, Gray, Salt Glaze, Cobalt Floral, Handle, Egg Shape, Gal. 132.00
Jar, Gray, Salt Glaze, Lyons, Cobalt Blue Floral, Handle, 2 Gal....................................... 310.00
Jar, Gray, Tan, Salt Glaze, 8 1/8 In.. 138.00
Jar, Green, Morgan & VanWinkle Pottery, N.J., Impressed Bird, Gray, 8 7/8 In. 242.00
Jar, Handle, Ovoid, Gray Salt Glaze, Cobalt Blue, New York, 1815-1820, 12 In............. 413.00
Jar, Handle, Ovoid, Tan Salt Glaze, Cobalt Blue, Floral, New York, 1835, 10 3/4 In....... 198.00
Jar, Handle, Ovoid, Tan Salt Glaze, Cobalt Blue, Floral, New York, 1825, 11 1/2 In..... 275.00
Jar, McCarthy & Bayless, Louisville, 3 Qt.. 225.00
Jar, Tan, Brown, Cobalt Stencil, Salt Glaze, 5 1/2 In. 308.00
Jar, Tan, Salt Glaze, Cobalt Blue Floral, Gal. 220.00
Jar, Tan, Salt Glaze, Cobalt Blue Floral Both Sides, 1/2 Gal. 282.00
Jug, A. Moll Grocer, St. Louis, 1/2 Gal... 55.00
Jug, Bellarmine, Brown Speckled Glaze, 1650-1750, 16 x 11 1/8 In............................ 525.00

Stoneware, Gould, Hibberd & Randall Ltd., Isle Of Wight, 7 In.

Stoneware, Jug, C. Rhodes, Edgefield, S.C., Green & Brown Glaze, Strap Handle, 15 In.

Stoneware, Jug, C. Rhodes, Brown & Green Glaze, 1850, 13 In.

Jug, Bellarmine, Brown, Salt Glaze, Applied Face On Neck, Germany, 9 In. 880.00
Jug, Bellarmine, Dark Brown, Light Tan Speckled, 1700-1780, 17 x 10 5/8 In. 450.00
Jug, Bellarmine, Handle, Gray Brown, 8 3/4 In. 577.50
Jug, Bellarmine, Handle, Orange Brown, 16 3/4 In. 715.00
Jug, Blankenheym & Nolet, Brown Speckled Glaze, Dutch, 1860-1890, 9 3/4 In. 30.00
Jug, C. Crolius Manufacturer, N.Y., Gray, Cobalt Slip Cloud Design, Salt Glaze, 12 In. 1100.00
Jug, C. Rhodes, Brown & Green Glaze, 1850, 13 In...*Illus* 15400.00
Jug, C. Rhodes, Edgefield, S.C., Green & Brown Glaze, Strap Handle, 15 In........*Illus* 13750.00
Jug, Catlettsburg Pottery Co., Kentucky, 5 Gal. 650.00
Jug, Cream Color Glaze, Cobalt Stencil, 2 In. 302.00
Jug, G. Benton, L. Stewart, Hartford, Cobalt Stamped 75.00
Jug, Gelfands Quality Products, Brown & White, Lid, 1 Gal. 75.00
Jug, Glens Falls Wine Co., Handle, Creamy Gray Glaze, Blue Lettering, 1/2 Gal. 275.00
Jug, Gray Glaze & Unglazed, J2G In Circle, Germany, 1830-1860, 11 3/4 In. 25.00
Jug, Gray Glaze, Cross In Circle, Blue, Germany, 1780-1830, 11 1/4 In. 45.00
Jug, Handle, Gray Salt Glaze, Cobalt Blue, 1828-1830, 10 3/4 In............................... 242.00
Jug, Handle, Ovoid, Gray Salt Glaze, Floral, N.Y., 1810-1815, 2 Gal. 715.00
Jug, Handle, Ovoid, Gray Salt Glaze, Floral, N.Y., 1810-1820, 13 1/2 In...................... 2090.00
Jug, Handle, Ovoid, Gray Salt Glaze, New York, 1824-1825, 11 1/2 In. 357.00
Jug, Handle, Ovoid, Tan Salt Glaze, Circle, Scallops On Sides, 1810, 3 Gal. 187.00
Jug, Harvest Canteen, Handle, Olive, 10 1/2 In.. 93.50
Jug, Little Falls N.Y., 1 Gal. 40.00
Jug, Miller, Wheeling, Va., Light Brown, Stamped... 125.00
Jug, S.R. Engerman, Dark Gray, Cobalt Slip Stencil, Salt Glaze, 12 In. 192.00
Jug, Schlueter Bros., Yonkers, N.Y. In Script, Blue Flower, Eared, Gal. 250.00
Jug, Tan, Salt Glaze, Impressed Oil, Handle, Egg Shape, 14 In. 413.00
Jug, Tan, Salt Glaze, Whites, Utica, Cobalt Blue Floral, 2 Handles, 5 Gal..................... 550.00
Jug, Wm. Hare, Wilmington, De., 1 Qt. 75.00
Jug, Williams & Reppert, Greensboro, Pa., Cobalt Blue Design, 2 Gal......................... 275.00
Pitcher, Dark Gray, Cobalt Slip Decoration, Salt Glaze, 10 3/4 In. 660.00
Pitcher, Gray, Cobalt Slip Decoration, Salt Glaze, 11 5/8 In.. 660.00

--------------------- **TARGET BALL** ---------------------

Target balls were first used in England in the early 1830s. Trapshooting was a popular sport. Live birds were released from a trap and then shot as they tried to fly away. The target balls, thrown into the air, replaced the live birds. The first American use was by Charles Portlock of Boston, Massachusetts, about 1850. A mechanical thrower was invented by Captain Adam Bogardus and with this improvement, trap shooting spread to all parts of the country. Early balls were round globes but by the 1860s they were made with ornamental patterns in the glass. Light green, aqua, dark green, cobalt blue, amber, amethyst, and other colors were used. Target balls went out of fashion by 1880 when the *clay pigeon* was invented.

TARGET BALL, Amber, Flat On Base, 2 5/8 In. 550.00
Amber, Plain.. 50.00
Bogardus, Apr. 10, 1877, Medium Olive Amber, 2 3/4 In.................................... 330.00
Bogardus, Apr. 10, 1877, Medium Olive Green, 2 3/4 In.................................... 522.50
Bogardus, Diamond Pattern, Olive Green, 2 5/8 In... 660.00
Bogardus, Pat. April 10, 1877, Yellow Olive, Sheared Lip, 2 3/4 In................... 467.00
Cobalt Blue, c.1890, 2 1/4 In.. 143.00
Cobalt Blue, Diamond, 2 1/2 In.. 154.00
Cobalt Blue, Light, Diamond, 2 1/2 In... 176.00
Cobalt Blue, Rows Of Squares, c.1890, 2 1/4 In... 143.00
Deep Emerald Green, Diamond, 2 3/4 In.. 715.00
Diamond, Vertical Line Pattern Center Band, 2 3/4 In... 798.00
Glashuttenewotte Um Charlottenburg, Diamond Pattern, 2 5/8 In. 1980.00
Glass, Range, Medium Sapphire Blue, 1 1/2 In.. 121.00
Ira Paine's, Filled Ball, Amber.. 250.00
Ira Paine's, Yellow Amber, 2 3/4 In... 253.00
L. Jones Gunmaker, Blackburn, Light Gray Sapphire Blue, Diamond, 2 3/4 In........... 154.00
Light Sapphire Blue, Sheared Mouth, Misshapen, 2 1/8 In.. 143.00
Man, Gun, In Circle, Pink Amethyst, 2 3/4 In. 303.00
Man, Gun, In Circle, Sapphire Blue, 2 3/4 In. 605.00

Target Ball, N.B. Glassworks, Perth, Blue, Diamond, England, 1880-1890, 2 3/4 In.

Target Ball, Quentin, Cobalt Blue, France, 3 In.

Tonic, Reed's, Gilt Edge 1878, Amber, 8 1/2 In.

Man, Shooting, 2 Opposite Circles, Pink Amethyst, Swirls Of Color, 2 3/4 In. 412.50
Medium Amber, 2 1/2 In. 467.50
Medium Orange Amber, Diamond, 2 3/4 In. 154.00
Medium Root Beer Amber, 2 3/4 In. 385.00
N.B. Glassworks, Perth, Aqua, Sheared Lip, 2 5/8 In. 110.00
N.B. Glassworks, Perth, Blue, Diamond, England, 1880-1890, 2 3/4 In. ....*Illus* 165.00
N.B. Glassworks, Perth, Cobalt Blue, Sheared Lip, 2 5/8 In. 188.00
N.B. Glassworks, Perth, Diamond, Sheared Mouth, 2 1/2 In. 330.00
N.B. Glassworks, Perth, Medium Cobalt Blue, Sheared Lip, 2 5/8 In. 176.00
N.B. Glassworks, Perth, Medium Sapphire Blue, 1 1/2 In. 121.00
N.B. Glassworks, Perth, Sapphire Blue, Spherical, 2 1/2 In. 198.00
Paine's, Amber 100.00
Purple, Embossed Shooter, England 250.00
Quentin, Cobalt Blue, France, 3 In. ....*Illus* 125.00
Van Gutsem, A St. Quentin, Cobalt Blue, Spherical, 2 1/2 In. Diam. 385.00
Van Gutsem, A St. Quentin, Diamond, Cobalt Blue, 2 1/2 In. 187.00
Van Gutsem, A St. Quentin, Diamond, Deep Cobalt Blue, 2 1/2 In. 198.00
W.W. Greener, London, Pink Amethyst, c.1885, 2 3/4 In. 264.00
W.W. Greener, St. Mary's Works, Cobalt Blue 150.00
W.W. Greener, St. Mary's Works, London, Diamond, Cobalt Blue, 2 3/4 In. 121.00
TOILET WATER, see Cologne

———————————————— **TONIC** ————————————————

Tonic is a word with several meanings. Listed here are medicine bottles that have the word *tonic* either on a paper label or embossed on the glass. In this book *hair tonic* is listed with cosmetics or cure. There may be related bottles listed.

TONIC, Arabian Tonic Blood Purifier Stewards Howe's, New York, Green, Large 38.00
Baldwin's Celery Pepsin & Dandelion, Amber, Spider Web, Long Neck, 8 In. 85.00
Blood Tabs. Blood & System Tonic, Reese Chem.Co., Green, Embossed Heart, 4 In.. 120.00
Brownlow & Raymond Federal Tonic, Cobalt Blue, 10 1/2 In. .... 357.50 to 550.00
C.C. Pendleton's, Amber, Applied, 9 1/2 In. 88.00
Clothworths Oriental, Honey 495.00
Dalton's Sarsaparilla & Nerve Tonic, Full Label, Rectangular, 9 In. 32.00
Dr. Blendigo's Celery, John Scheyer & Co., Amber, 1880-1900, 9 1/2 In. 227.00
Dr. Boyce's Tonic Bitters, Aqua, 12-Sided, 7 1/2 In. 35.00
Dr. H.C. Stewart's, Variant, Embossed 195.00
Dr. Jones Red Clover, Deep Brown, Square, 8 1/4 In. 68.00
Dr. Kurnitzki's Aromatic Wire Grass, Amber, Applied Mouth, 9 3/8 In. 110.00
Dr. Miles Restorative Tonic, Fancy Letters 25.00
Dr. Warren's Tonic Cordial, Cincinnati, O., Aqua, Applied Top, 8 1/2 In. 70.00
Federal, Brownlow & Raymond, Deep Cobalt Blue, 10 1/2 In. .... 357.00 to 550.00

Gogings Iron, Sacramento, Monogram, Aqua, 8 3/8 In. 110.00
Gogings Wild Cherry, Yellow Amber, 8 3/4 In. 105.00
Gold Lion Iron Tonic, Dr. Thenard, Amber, Applied Top, Sunken Sides, 8 3/4 In. 72.00
Hall's Wine, Stephen Smith & Co. Ltd., Olive Green, Bubbles, 12 1/4 In. 55.00
Hop Tonic, Grand Rapids, Mich., Amber, Paneled, Semi-Cabin, 9 1/2 In. 633.00
Indian, Clemen's Tonic, Standing Indian, Aqua, Pontil, 5 3/8 In. 688.00
Indian Clemens, Geo. W. House, Indian Picture, Aqua, Pontil, 5 1/2 In. 688.00
Japanese Remedy, The Mikado Tonic, Golden Amber, Applied Top, Crude, 9 In. 110.00
Japanese Remedy, The Mikado, Yellow Amber, 9 1/2 In. 132.00
Kobolo Tonic Medicine Co., Chicago, Ill., Milk Glass, 8 3/4 In. 264.00
Liebigs Cos Coca Beef Tonic, San Francisco, Aqua, Tooled Lip, 7 1/4 In. 15.00
Lung, Hull, Owbridge's, Deep Lime Green, 5 In. 16.00
Paine's Celery Compound, Crude Applied Top 8.00
Parker's Ginger, N.Y. 10.00
Primley's Iron & Wahoo, Light Yellow Amber, Embossed, Square, 8 1/2 In. 88.00
Reed's, Gilt Edge 1878, Amber, 8 1/2 In. ....*Illus* 20.00
Reed's 1878 Gilt Edge, Golden Amber, Embossing, 9 1/2 In. 50.00
Reno's New Health Uterine, S.B. Leonardi, Aqua, Rectangular 45.00
Risley & Co., Orange, Lady's Leg, Yellow, Cylinder 166.00
Rohrer's Expectoral, Wild Cherry Tonic, Amber, IP 315.00
Rohrer's Expectoral Wild Cherry, Lancaster, Pa., Amber, Rectangular, 10 1/2 In. 187.00
Rohrer's Wild Cherry Tonic, Medium Amber, IP 300.00
Rowand's Improved Tonic, Mixture, Vegetable, Febriafuge, Aqua, 6-Sided, OP, 6 In. 198.00
Schenek's Seaweed, Deep Aqua, 3-Sided, Embossed, 9 1/4 In. 55.00
Seminole Indian Liver & Kidney, Columbus, Miss., Indian Chief Picture, BIM, 11 In. 25.00
Spooners Hygeian, New York, Olive Amber, Ring Lip, 8-Sided, Pontil, 1840, 6 In. 5225.00
Thorn's Hop & Burdock Tonic, Brattleboro, Vt., Honey Amber, 8 In. 74.00
Townsend's Phosphated Cereal, Orange Amber, Applied Mouth, 10 1/8 In. 72.00
Warner's Safe Tonic, Rochester, N.Y., Medium Amber, Applied Mouth, 9 1/2 In. 220.00
Warner's Safe Tonic, Rochester, N.Y., Medium Amber, Whittled, 1870s, 7 1/2 In. 357.00
Web's A No. 1 Cathartic Tonic, Best Liver, Kidney & Blood Purifier, Amber, 9 In. ... 44.00
Web's Cathartic 28.00

———————————————— **VINEGAR** ————————————————

Vinegar was and is sold in glass bottles. Most vinegar packers prefer a large glass jug-shaped bottle with a small handle, the shape used today even for modern plastic vinegar bottles. The collector wants any bottle with the name *vinegar* on a paper label or embossed on the glass. The most famous vinegar bottles were made by National Fruit Product Company for their White House Brand vinegar. Bottles with the embossed brand name and a picture of a house, the trademark, were made in the early 1900s. Jugs in three or four sizes, apple-shaped jars, canning jars, fancy decanters, cruets, a New York World's Fair bottle, rolling pins, vases, a refrigerator water jar, and other fanciful reusable shapes were used until the 1940s. The company is still in business.

VINEGAR, Heinz Pure Malt, Brown, Label, 10 In. ....*Illus* 75.00

*Vinegar, Heinz Pure
Malt, Brown,
Label, 10 In.*

*Vinegar, Paw Paw Brand,
Apple Cider, M. Steffen & Co.,
Chicago, 7 In.*

*Vinegar,
White House
Brand, 7 In.*

Paw Paw Brand, Apple Cider, M. Steffen & Co., Chicago, 7 In. ....*Illus*   12.00
Pride Spirit Vinegar, Richmond Vinegar Co., Richmond, Va., ABM, Label 22.00
W.D. McCullough Pure Vinegar, Beaver, Pa., Dark Brown, Handle, 6 In. 170.00
White House, 2 Handles, Spout, Embossed Leaves, Gal. 33.00
White House, Dark Green..   16.00
White House, Glass Cover, Metal Screw Band...   11.00
White House, Jug, Apple Shape, Spout, 2 Handles, Qt. 46.75
White House, Jug, Apple Shape, Spout, 2 Handles, Pt. ....98.00 to 242.00
White House, Jug, Apple Shape, Spout, 2 Handles, Gal..   35.75
White House, Jug, Apple Shape, Spout, 2 Handles, 1/2 Gal....................22.00 to 41.25
White House, Jug, Script, Wooden Handle, 1/2 Gal...   100.00
White House, Pt..   12.00
White House, Qt...   18.00
White House Brand, 7 In. ....*Illus*   35.000
W.A. LACEY, see Lacey
WATER, MINERAL, see Mineral Water

WHISKEY

Whiskey bottles came in assorted sizes and shapes through the years. Any container for whiskey is included in this category. Although purists spell the word *whisky* for Scotch and Canadian and *whiskey* for bourbon and other types, we have found it simpler in this book to use only the spelling *whiskey*. There is also blended whiskey, which includes blended bourbon, Scotch, Irish, or Canadian. Although blends were made in Scotland and Ireland for many years, it was not a process popular in the United States until 1933. One way to spot very new whiskey bottles is by the size. The 1 3/4-liter bottle is slightly less than a half gallon, the 1-liter bottle slightly more than a quart, and the 3/4-liter bottle almost the same size as a fifth. These bottles were introduced in 1976.

Several years ago there was a contest to find the oldest bourbon bottle made in America. It was thought to be one dated 1882. The contest turned up an even older bottle, a Bininger made in 1848. Bourbon was first made in 1789 in Kentucky. Rum was made in America by the mid-seventeenth century; whiskey made of corn, rye, or barley by the early 1700s. It was the tax on this whiskey that caused the so-called Whiskey Rebellion of 1794.

A museum of interest to collectors is the Seagram Museum, 57 Erb St., Waterloo, Ontario, Canada. See also modern manufacturers categories by brand name.

WHISKEY, 26 Swirled Ribs, Inverted Conical Form, Golden Amber, Pontil, 9 In...........   258.50
3-Piece Mold, Whitney Glassworks, Aqua, Fifth 34.00
4 Aces American Rye, Ace Design, 8 In...   94.00
4 Aces American Rye, British Columbia Dis., Fancy, 1920s, Pt....................................   15.00
A. & R. Postel, Medium Orange Amber, 11 3/4 In...   1705.00
A. Fenkhausen, San Francisco, Pale Yellow, Applied Mouth, 12 In.............................   231.00
A. Fenkhausen, San Francisco, Sample, 5 In. 65.00
A.G. Thomson & Co., Stoneware, Black Transfer, Glasgow, Jeroboam, 7 1/4 In. 108.00
A.P. Simms, Fine Whiskies, Natchez, Miss., Jug, Stoneware, Gal. 65.00
A.V. Mallette, Jug House, Greenville, Miss., Jug, Pictures Mallette, Stoneware, 3 Gal.   275.00
Adolph Harris, San Francisco, Calif., Tooled Top..   35.00
Altschul Distilling Co., Dayton, Oh., Amber...   35.00
Amber, 1-Winged Owl, 1900s, 11 1/2 In..   330.00
B.F. & Co., N.Y., Golden Amber, 26 Vertical Ribs, Ear Handle, Spout, 1850, Large 1760.00
B.F. & Co., New York, Amber, Handle, Pontil, 9 In..   495.00
B.M. & E.A. Whitlock & Co., New York, Barrel, Aqua, Bevel Pontil, c.1860 ....   55.00
B.M. & E.A.W & Co., Ambrosial, Embossed, Free-Blown, Chestnut, Amber, 8 7/8 In...   143.00
Bailey Fulham, Rum, Jug, Stoneware, Tan, Brown, Cork, Square, Handle, Qt. 29.00
Bailey's, Huey & Christ, Philadelphia, Pa..   10.00
Bamford, Locust Blossom Pure Rye, Pittsburg Pa., Jug, Bail Handle, Stoneware, Gal...   80.00
Barkhouse Bros. & Co., Gold Dust Kentucky Bourbon, Golden Amber, 11 3/4 In.......   1760.00
Beer's Green Fredericksburg Bottling Co., San Francisco, Qt...................................   20.00
Bell's Scotch Whiskey, Perth Scotland, Bell, Figural, Brown, Royal Doulton 125.00
Belle Of Anderson, Milk Glass...   120.00
Bennett & Carrol, Pittsburgh, Barrel, Medium Yellow Amber, 9 1/2 In......................   605.00
Bennett & Carrol, Pittsburgh, Barrel, Yellow Amber Chestnut, Flattened, 8 3/8 In.......   907.50
Berry's Diamond Wedding Whiskey, Amethyst, 3 Barrels Design, 12 1/4 In..............   75.00

Whiskey, Cruiskeen Lawn, Mitchell's, Old Irish Whisky, Belfast, 8 In.

Whiskey, Dougherty's Old Rye, Woman Smoking Pipe Label, Backbar, 1875, 8 3/4 In.

Whiskey, For Your Baby, Sayings, 4 In.

Beukers Aromatic Schnapps, Green... 75.00
Bininger, see the Bininger category
Blackberry, Tooled Lip, 1890-1910, 11 1/4 In. 137.00
Bonnie Castle, Stoneware, Castle, Jug, Sepia Transfer, Rear Handle, Pear, 8 1/2 In. 93.00
Booze, Sapphire Blue, Tooled Top, Reproduction 45.00
Buchanan, Cannon Shape, Golden Amber.. 315.00
Budweiser Cafe, San Pablo, Okla., Sun-Colored Amethyst, 6 1/4 In. 55.00
Bulkley & Fiske & Co. Brandy, Medium Amber, Handle, OP, 8 1/2 In........................ 4400.00
C.A. Richardson & Co., Boston, Yellow Amber, c.1880, 7 1/2 In., Pt. 209.00
C.D. Postel, San Francisco, Golden Amber, Applied Mouth, 11 3/4 In. 413.00
C.P. Moorman, San Francisco, Yellow Amber, 7 5/8 In. 385.00
Cabin Whiskey, Cabin, No Embossing, 10 1/2 In. 75.00
Cabinet Whiskey, Cut, Design, Backbar, Qt. 40.00
Campus Gossler Bros. Prop's, N.Y., Amber, 9 3/4 In. 71.50
Cartan, McCarthy & Co, San Francisco, Amber, 12 In.. 176.00
Cartan, McCarthy & Co., San Francisco, Amber, Monogram, Cylinder, 12 In.............. 35.00
Cascade, Jug, Dickel, Gal.. 100.00
Casey & Kavanaugh, Sacramento, Cal., Amber, Fifth 35.00
Casper Co., Inc., 4-Cities, Cobalt Blue, Tooled Lip, 1880, 11 3/4 In. 550.00
Casper Co., Inc., Cobalt Blue, Double Collar Lip, Cylindrical, 1870, 12 In. 523.00
Casper's, Made By Honest North Carolina People, Cobalt Blue, Cylindrical, 12 In....... 275.00
Casper's Whiskey, Made By Honest North Carolina People, Blue, 12 In. ....360.00 to 525.00
Castle, Amber, Inside Threads.. 25.00
Castle Whiskey, San Francisco, Calif., Castle Picture, Tooled Top 40.00
Champion Monogram Kessler & Co., N.Y., Honey Amber, Applied Top, Qt. 25.00
Chapin & Gore, Chicago, Sour Mash, Lettered, Amber, Flask, 1867, Pt. 49.00
Chapin & Gore Sour Mash, Barrel, Amber... 129.00
Chapin & Gore Sour Mash 1867, Barrel, Amber, 8 3/4 In. 110.00
Chapman & Gore, Sour Mash 1867, Amber, Barrel, Embossed 95.00
Chesley's Jockey Club, Sun-Colored Amethyst, 12 In... 209.00
Chestnut Grove, C.W. On Seal, Amber, Pontil, Handle, 9 In. ....77.00 to 165.00
Chestnut Grove, C.W. On Seal, Golden Amber, Handle, OP 155.00
Chestnut Grove, C.W. On Seal, Red Orange Amber, Handle, Whittled, OP, Qt. 100.00
Chestnut Grove, Flattened Chestnut Form, Amber, Embossed, 8 7/8 In. 44.00
Chevaliers Old Castle, San Francisco, Amber, Cylinder, Fifth, 11 1/8 In................. 40.00
Chicken Cock Bourbon, Pinch, Enameled Rooster, Stopper, Backbar, 6 7/8 In. 1018.00
Club House Bourbon, St. Louis, Fifth... 22.00
Coffin-Reddington Co., San Francisco, Jug, Bold Lettering, Oval, Stoneware, Gal....... 110.00
Cordial, see the Cordial category
Coronation King Edward VII, 1902, Jug, Stoneware, 8 In. 155.00
Crown Distilleries, Crown Above CDCO, Medium Amber, 5 3/4 In............................ 220.00
Crown Distilleries, Squatty, Crude Top, IP 14.00
Cruiskeen Lawn, Mitchell's, Old Irish Whisky, Belfast, 8 In................................*Illus* 45.00
Cruiskeen Lawn Old Irish Whiskey, Mitchell's Belfast, Jug, Stoneware, Tan 49.00

Cylinder, Bartletts Glass Ware, Yellow Olive, 11 3/4 In.. 176.00
Cyrus Eaton & Co., Denver, Medium Amber, 1 Qt.. 495.00
D.J. O'Connell, Washington, D.C., Embossed 1 Qt. On 2 Sides, Qt. 11.00
D.P. Roberts, Belle Fourche, S.D., Red Wing, Jug, Stoneware, 1/2 Gal. 175.00
Daly Rye, Light Amber, Crude 16.00
Daniel Schaeffer's Log Cabin Whiskey, Amber, Inside Screw Threads, 11 1/2 In. 715.00
Dark Green, Dutch, Squatty, 1720, 8 In.. 145.00
Davy Crockett, Hey, Grauerholz & Co., Amber, Cylinder, 11 7/8 In. 30.00
Davy Crockett, San Francisco, Cal., Light Orange Amber, Bubbles............................. 49.00
Davy Crockett Pure Old Bourbon, Medium Amber, 12 In.. 110.00
Detrick Distilling Co., Dayton, Jug, Stoneware, May Fortune Ever Smile On You 59.00
Dewar's, Jug, Stoneware, Green Top, Purple Base, Thistle Shape, 1905, 7 1/4 In......... 388.00
Dewar's Perth Whisky, Scotsman, Jug, Green, Salt Glaze, Doulton Lambeth, 12 In..... 360.00
Dewar's Whisky, Jug, Stoneware, Green Top, Salt Glaze, Hunting, 4 In. 140.00
Dewars, Jug, White Label, Stoneware, Uncle Sam, Scotsman & John Bull, 9 1/4 In...... 698.00
Donnelly's Rye, Amber, Inside Thread, Stopper, Rectangular, Contents, Qt. 20.00
Dougherty's Old Rye, Woman Smoking Pipe Label, Backbar, 1875, 8 3/4 In.........*Illus* 220.00
Dougherty's Old Rye Whiskey, Backbar, Clear, Pontil, 1890, 8 3/4 In.......................... 220.00
Duff's Crescent Saloon, Louisville, Pig, Aqua... 140.00
Duff's Malt Whiskey, ... 25.00
Duffy's Malt, Light Amber 25.00
Dyottville Glassworks, Light Olive Green, Seed Bubbles, Iron Pontil, 11 1/2 In. 40.00
Dyottville Glassworks, Philadelphia, Olive Amber, Cylinder, Iron Pontil 40.00
Dyottville Glassworks, Philadelphia, Yellow Citron, Cylinder, Iron Pontil 45.00
E.G. Booz's Old Cabin, Cabin, Yellow Amber, Whittled, 7 3/4 In................................. 1155.00
E.G. Booz's Old Cabin, Golden Amber, Tapered Lip, McK GVII-004, Qt. 1925.00
E.L. Mills Straight Whiskey, J.J. Roben, South Richmond, Va., Jug, Label, Handle 143.00
E.P. Middleton Bro., Philadelphia, Amber, Seal, 1825, 12 In...................................... 209.00
Ebner Bros., Sacramento, Clear, 5 7/8 In... 99.00
Ellison Harvey Co., Richmond, Va., Rectangular, 8 In... 18.00
Evans & Ragland Old Ingledew, La Grange, Ga., Amber, Round Collar, 10 In. 357.00
F. Chevalier & Co., San Francisco, Yellow Olive Green, 12 In. 210.00
F. Chevalier Whiskey Merchants, Flask, Amber, Oval, 1/2 Pt. 20.00
F. Zimmerman, Portland, Or., Golden Amber, Tooled Top, Fifth 15.00
Flask, see the Flask category
For Your Baby, Sayings, 4 In...*Illus* 85.00
Forest Lawn, J.V.H., Medium Olive Green, Iron Pontil, Whittled, 7 1/8 In. 550.00
Forest Lawn, J.V.H., Olive Green, 7 1/2 In.. 412.50
Frank Abadie Wholesale Liquors, Eureka, Nev., Light Amethyst, 1884-1886, 6 In..... 2530.00
G.H. Clark's, Medium Golden Amber, 11 7/8 In. 1018.00
G.H. Moore Old Bourbon & Rye, San Francisco, Honey Amber, Whittle Swirls, Fifth. 35.00
G.O. Blake's Bourbon Co., 2 Barrels, Red Amber, Qt... 385.00
G.O. Blake's Rye & Sour Whisky, A.T. & Co., Amethyst, 12 1/2 In............................. 45.00
G.S.C. Sealed Spirits, Olive Green, Cylindrical, Pontil, 8 3/4 In................................. 99.00
Gavin & L'abbe, Leadville & Cripple Creek, Col., Flask, Pt. 450.00
Genuine Sanfords Ginger French Brandy, Aromatics, Aqua, 1876, 6 1/2 In................. 10.00
Geo. Braun, San Francisco, Medium Amber, Tooled Lip, 11 1/2 In. 50.00
Geo. Cohn & Co., Louisville, Ky., Amber, Flat, Bulbous Neck.................................... 32.00
Geo. Fairbanks, Worcester, Mass, Light Amber, Applied Top, Qt. 400.00
Geo. S. Ladd & Co. Wholesale Liquors, Amber, Bubbles, Fifth, 11 In. 30.00
Gilmore Thomson's Royal Stag, Jug, Pottery, Tan, White, Stag, With Vines 90.00
Gin, see the Gin category
Glen Garry Blended Scotch Whiskey, Brown & Tan 20.00
Glen Garry Blended Scotch Whiskey, Greybeard On Back, Jug, Stoneware, Qt. 59.00
Glen Garry Scotch, Jug, 1 Handle, Pottery, Transfer 20.00
Glen Lossie, Jug, Stoneware, Blue Transfer, Rear Handle, London & Glasgow, 7 In. ... 372.00
Gold Cup, Labbe Tresorcoir, France, Jug, Delft Type Green White, Windmills, 1900s.. 59.00
Golden Dome, Boston, Embossed Capital Dome, Honey Yellow 65.00
Golden Eagle Distilleries Co., San Francisco, Cal., Amber, Cylinder, 11 1/8 In. 130.00
Golden Gate, San Francisco, Amber, Tooled Lip, 12 In... 275.00
Golden Gate, San Francisco, Medium Amber, Tooled Lip, 9 In.................................... 160.00
Golden Wedding, Carnival Glass, Label, Pt. 50.00
Golden Wine Co., Boston, Jug, Stoneware 25.00

Good Samaritan Brandy, N.Y., Olive Amber, 7 In.. 990.00
Grace Bros. Brewing Co., Santa Rosa, Ca., Amber, Porcelain Top, Qt. 20.00
Greeley's Bourbon, Smoky Peach Amber, Peach Swirls... 950.00
Green, Barrel Shape Dispenser, Stopper, Metal Spout 115.00
Grey Beard Heather Dew Whiskey, Jug, 2 Scotsmen Toasting, Transfer..................... 65.00
Greybeard Heather Dew Scotch, Tan & Brown Glaze, Double Handle, 7 In. ...... 16.00 to 18.00
Griffith Hyatt & Co., Baltimore, Root Beer Amber, Pontil, c.1875, 7 1/4 In. 467.00
H. Hiller, Wholesale Retail Liquors, Canton, Miss., Jug, Stoneware, Gal. 130.00
H. Metzler, San Francisco, Amber, Applied Mouth, 11 5/8 In.................................... 2200.00
H. Pharazyn, Right Secured, Philadelphia, P.A., Yellow Amber, 12 1/4 In.................... 1155.00
H.A. Graef's Son, N.Y., Canteen Form, Yellow Olive, 6 1/2 In. 143.00
H.A. Graef's Son, N.Y., Deep Yellow Green, 2 Handles, 6 1/2 In. 440.00
H.C. Brinkman, Wines, Liquors, Savannah Ga., Jug, Stoneware, Gal. 135.00
H.W. Hespendeide & Son Wholesale Liquor Dealers, Bitters Type, Square, Qt........ 25.00
Hanover Rye, Standard Distilling Co., Flask, Amber, Horse Picture, 1/2 Pt. 45.00
Happy Days, Famous Old Rye Whiskey, 8 In. ....*Illus* 120.00
Happy Days Famous Old Rye Whiskey, Jug, Stoneware, Men Drinking, Brown Stencil 99.00
Happy Days Famous Old Rye Whiskey, Jug, Stoneware, Brown, 3 College Men 79.00
Harvard Rye, Klein Bros., Cincinnati, Label, 7 1/2 In. ....*Illus* 35.00
Harvard Rye, Rectangular, 6 1/8 In... 15.00
Hayner Lock Box 290, Dayton, Oh., Stoneware, Gal. 38.50
Heather Dew, Greybeard, Jug, Stoneware, Black Transfer, Glasgow, 7 In.................... 34.00
Henry Campe & Co. Wholesale, San Francisco, Sun-Colored Amethyst, 11 In. 82.50
Henry Chapman & Co., Sole Agents, Montreal, Amber, Teardrop, Pat. 1861, 6 In. 231.00
Henry George Whiskey, White Enameled Letters, Backbar 100.00
Hettermann, Amber, In Wicker Basket, 9 1/4 In. 20.00
Hill & Hill, Sour Mash, Owensboro, Ky., ABM, Box, Pt. 45.00
Hollander Bros., Patterson N.J., Jug, Cobalt Script, Stoneware, Gal........................... 170.00
Hollenback Dietrich & Co., Wholesale Liquor Dealers, Reading, Pa., Strap, Qt. 19.00
I. Goldbery, New York City, Golden Amber, 9 Vertical Panels, Qt............................... 40.00
I. Tracer Co., Cincinnati, Oh., Amber, BIMAL, Cylinder, Qt. 3.50
I.P. Claudius & Co., San Francisco, Calif., Tooled Top.. 35.00
I.W. Harper, Stoneware, Blue Stencil, Qt. 85.00
I.W. Harper Gold Medal, Pottery, Maroon, Square, Qt. 89.00
I.W. Harper Nelson Co. Kentucky Whiskey, Jug, Tan, Brown, Qt. 59.00
Imperial Levee J. Noyes, Amber, Embossed Grapes & Leaves, IP, 1885, 9 3/8 In......... 1430.00
Imperial Levee J. Noyes, Grape & Leaf, Amber, Hollywood, Miss., IP, 9 1/2 In. 1540.00
Imperial Levee J. Noyes, Hollywood, Miss., Yellow Root Beer Amber, 9 3/8 In.......... 2090.00
J'Donnel's, Old Irish, Belfast, Jug, Stoneware, Green Transfer, Harp & Crown, 8 In..... 124.00
J. & E. Mahoney Distillers, Portsmouth & Alexandria, Flask, BIMAL, 1/2 Pt. 4.50
J. Cooney & Co., Wholesale Liquors, Nashville, Tenn., 2 Gal. 150.00
J.B. Cutter Old Bourbon, Amber, Applied Top, Cylinder, Fifth, 11 3/4 In.................... 35.00
J.B. Cutter Old Bourbon, Dark Amber, Applied Top, Cylinder, Fifth 230.00
J.C. Shore & Co., Petersburg, Va., 3-Piece Mold, Qt. 82.50

Whiskey, Happy Days, Famous
Old Rye Whiskey, 8 In.

Whiskey, Harvard Rye, Klein Bros.,
Cincinnati, Label, 7 1/2 In.

J.F. Cutter, Extra, Star & Shield, Amber, Glob Top, Fifth 80.00
J.F. Cutter, Medium Amber, Applied Mouth, 11 3/4 In. 495.00
J.F. Cutter Extra Trade, Medium Golden Amber, 12 In. 60.00
J.F. Cutter Old Bourbon, Portland, Oh., Coffin, Amber, Pt. 430.00
J.H. Cutter, Bird, Medium Amber, 12 In. 110.00
J.H. Cutter, Crown Over Barrel, Amber, 11 7/8 In. 71.50
J.H. Cutter, Medium Amber, 11 5/8 In. ....44.00 to 104.50
J.H. Cutter, Yellow Root Beer Amber, 11 7/8 In. 412.50
J.H. Cutter Old Bourbon, A.P. Hotaling & Co., Glob Top 30.00
J.H. Cutter Old Bourbon, C.P. Moorman, Louisville, Amber, Applied Top, 12 In. 154.00
J.S. Carraway, Fine Whiskies, Harriston, Miss., Jug, Stoneware, Gal. 135.00
J.T. Doores & Co., Distillers & Wholesale Liquor Dealers, Bowling Green, Ky., 1/2 Gal. 175.00
J.T.S. Brown Distillers, Round, 1/2 Pt. 25.00
J.W.M. Field & Sons Wholesale Liquors, Owensboro, N.Y., Gal. 150.00
James Kerr, Gibson Old Rye, Amber, 1880, 8 In., Pt. 165.00
James Woodburn Co., Sacramento, Calif., Deep Amethyst, Tooled Top 20.00
Jesse Moore, Louisville, Ky., Golden Amber, Applied Mouth, 12 In. 88.00
Jesse Moore, San Francisco, Amber, Tooled Lip, Fifth 20.00
Jesse Moore & Co., Louisville, Ky., Golden Amber, Blob Top, 11 3/4 In. 71.50
Jesse Moore-Hunt, Amber 20.00
Jno. H. Graves Old Kentucky, San Jose, Calif., Amber, Fifth, 11 In. 30.00
Jnordhauser Kornschnapps Albert Schultz & Co., Jug, Tan & Brown, Qt. 39.00
John Dewar & Sons, Perth N.B., Jug, Stoneware, Salt Glaze, Doulton Lambeth, 6 In. ... 240.00
John H. Schroeder, St. Louis, Mo., Cylinder, Qt. 20.00
John Lyster Wine & Spirit Merchant Mountrath, Flat Sided, Debossed 90.00
Jos. Leopold, Jug, Gal. 90.00
Jos. Waterman, Philadelphia, Chestnut, Golden Amber, OP, 1850, 8 5/8 In. 605.00
Joseph Fetz, Importer, Amethyst, Cylinder, Fifth 125.00
Jug, Bulbous, Deep Wine, IP, 6 1/4 In. 170.50
Jug, Chestnut Grove, Chestnut Form, Handle, Golden Amber, Pontil, 8 7/8 In. 143.00
Jug, Chestnut Grove, Flattened Form, Golden Amber, Pontil, 9 In. 121.00
Jug, Chestnut Grove, Yellow Olive, Pontil, 8 1/2 In. 550.00
Jug, Chestnut, Ambrosial, Golden Amber, Pontil, 9 In. 132.00
Jug, Crescent Club Whiskey, Stoneware, Tan, Blue Stencil, Ovoid, 3 In. 109.00
Jug, Elliott & Burke, Fine Whiskey, Memphis, Tenn., Stoneware, Brown, 1 Gal. 125.00
Jug, Ewer Form, Handle, Yellow Amber, 9 7/8 In. 165.00
Jug, Free-Blown, Golden Amber, Pontil, 9 In. 203.50
Jug, Free-Blown, Netherlands, Yellow Green, Pontil, 6 In. 77.00
Jug, Golden Amber, Red, Pour Spout, 10 In. 132.00
Jug, Handle, Yellow Olive, 5 1/8 In. 880.00
Jug, Pear Form, Gasoline Apricot, Pontil, 9 1/2 In. 341.00
Jug, Scotch, Tan & Brown Square Handle, 1880 .... 25.00
Kellerstrass Distilling Co., St.Louis, Mo., Patent Applied For, Qt. 5.50
Kellogg's Extra, Medium Amber, 5 In. 55.00
Kellogg's Nelson, Red Amber, Applied Mouth, 11 3/4 In. 357.00
Kellogg's Nelson County, W.L. Co., Amber 40.00
Kellogg's Nelson County Extra Kentucky Bourbon, Tooled Top 35.00
Key & Co.'s Pure Hand Made Corn Whiskey, Jug, Brown Over Cream, 1 Gal. 200.00
Keystone Malt Whiskey, Philadelphia, 1854 .... 15.00
King Blend Whiskey, Backbar, Qt. 35.00
L. Eppinger, Portland, Clear, 1/2 Pt. 104.50
L. Lyons Pure Ohio Catawba Brandy, Cincinnati, Oh., Deep Amber, 13 3/8 In. 231.00
L.K. Lewith Wholesale Liquors, Wilkes-Barre, Pa., Flask, Aqua, Strap, Qt. 35.00
Lady's Leg, Amber, 12 In. 55.00
Lilienthal & Co., San Francisco, Amber, 8 3/8 In. 357.50
Liscapernong, Garrett & Co., Weldon, N.C., Iridized, 11 1/2 In. ....*Illus*   40.00
Livingston & Co., San Francisco, Amber, 7 1/2 In. 1705.00
Loheide & Vorrath, Eureka, Ca., Orange Amber, 11 In. 44.00
Lotus Club Hand Made Sour Mash, Kaufmann Bros., Amethyst, 12 In. 70.00
Louis Taussig & Co., San Francisco, Golden Amber, Pt. 880.00
M. Salzman Co., Amber, Rectangular, Qt. 16.00
Mammoth Cave, Oval, Cover, White Enamel Dots, Backbar 3800.00
Meehan's, Superior Irish Whisky, Jug, Stoneware, Black Transfer, 7 1/2 In. 119.00

Whiskey, Liscapernong,
Garrett & Co., Weldon,
N.C., Iridized, 11 1/2 In.

Whiskey, Nordhausen
Kornschnapps, 8 In.

Whiskey, Old Barbee,
Pharmacy Label Back,
Dated 4-24-28, 8 1/4 In.

Melrose Highland, Streaky Brown Glaze, Jug, Doulton Lambreth, 9 1/2 In.	442.00
Meredith's Diamond Club Pure Rye Whisky, For Medicinal Use, Jug, Green Letters,	65.00
Meredith's Diamond Club Pure Rye Whiskey, Jug, Stoneware, Green Stencil, Qt.	89.00
Meyer Klein Wholesale Liquor Dealer, Omaha, Neb., Qt.	35.00
Meyerfeld Mitchell & Co., Days Of 49 Trademark, Amethyst, 10 7/8 In.	35.00
Miller & Co. Wholesale Liquor Dealers, Sioux City, Ia., Jug, Red Wing, 2 Gal.	350.00
Miller's Extra Trade, Deep Gold Amber, Pt.	467.50
Miller's Extra Trade, Golden Yellow, Olive, 7 3/8 In.	632.50
Miniature, see the Miniature category	
Mist Of The Morning, Barrel Form, Golden Amber, 9 7/8 In.	286.00
Mist Of The Morning, Barrel, Amber, Sloping Collar, c.1880, 10 1/4 In.	192.50
Mohawk Pure Rye Whiskey, Pat. 1868, Indian, Yellow Amber, 12 3/8 In.	1540.00
Monk's Old Bourbon, Medicinal Purposes, Olive Amber, Square, IP, 8 In.	385.00
Mount Vernon Brand Straight Rye Whiskey, Label, Embossed	38.50
Naber, Alfs & Brune Wholesale Liquor, San Francisco, Light Yellow, 11 3/4 In.	770.00
Naber, Alfs & Brune, San Francisco, Medium Orange Amber, Tooled Lip, 11 7/8 In.	302.00
Naber, Alfs & Brune, San Francisco, Medium Amber, Tooled Lip, 11 7/8 In.	154.00
New Louvre, San Jose, Pumpkinseed, 5 1/4 In.	99.00
Nordhausen Kornschnapps, 8 In. *Illus*	18.00
Nuyens Bordeau, Emerald Green, Ornate Shape, 12 In.	29.00
O'Keefe's Malt Whiskey, Oswego, N.Y., Jug, Tan, Brown Top, Design	65.00
Old Barbee, Pharmacy Label Back, Dated 4-24-28, 8 1/4 In., Pt. *Illus*	35.00
Old Bourbon Castle, Chevalier Whiskey Co., Light To Medium Amber, 11 3/4 In.	523.00
Old Cold Spring Sour Mash Whiskey, Jug, Stoneware, Brown, Tan, Qt.	129.00
Old Danton, John P. Dant, Louisville, Ky., Brown & White, Gal.	125.00
Old Henry, Straus Gunst & Co., Richmond, Va., BIMAL, Qt.	22.00
Old Henry, Straus Gunst & Co., Richmond, Va., Cylinder, Fluted Shoulder, Qt.	38.50 to 80.00
Old Homestead Fine Bourbon, Floral Design, Ground Tip	235.00
Old Joe Gideon Bros., St. Louis 1904, Portland, Ore., 1906, Amber, Tooled Mouth	40.00
Old Nector Bourbon Fritzthies Prop., Denver Col., Cylinder, Embossed	325.00
Old Rose Distilleries, Chicago, Jug, 1/2 Gal.	10.00
Old Scotch Whiskey Bonnie Castle, Jug, Pottery, Castle Pictures, Qt.	50.00
Old Valley, Medium Golden Amber, Pt.	577.50
Old Valley Whiskey, Light Yellow Amber, Crude, 1870-1880, 8 In.	1320.00
Orange Amber, Backbar, Petal Shoulders.	19.00
Our Choice, Hencken & Schroder, San Francisco, Medium Golden Amber, 12 In.	577.50
Our Choice, Hencken & Schroder, San Francisco, Medium Amber, 12 1/8 In.	275.00
P. Claudius & Co., Monogram, San Francisco, Red Amber, Tooled Top, Fifth	25.00
Pacific Club, Seattle, Wash., Wicker Cover, Embossed, Fifth.	35.00
Paris Distilling Co., Bourbon Co., Qt.	45.00

Pennsylvania Club Pure Whiskey, Stoneware, Stencil, Swan & Wheat, Qt................. 119.00
Perfection, G.A.F.C. Old Valley, Jug, Stoneware, Blue Transfer, Glasgow, 7 1/4 In. ... 93.00
Phil G. Kelly Straight Whiskey, Richmond, Va., Embossed, Flask, Pt......................... 82.50
Phoenix Old, San Francisco, Bird, Medium Amber, 11 3/4 In.................................... 616.00
Phoenix Old, San Francisco, Circle, Medium Golden Amber, 11 7/8 In......................... 176.00
Phoenix Old Trade, San Francisco, Medium Yellow Amber, 1/2 Pt............................. 44.00
Poteen Trademark Pt'd., Innishowen Ireland, Jug, Stoneware, Tan, Cream, Qt........... 79.00
Pottery, Embossed Eagle, Multicolored, 3 1/2 In.. 35.00
Pure Malt, Bourbon Co., Ky., Amber, 8 5/8 In.. 577.50
Pure Old Rye, Saltzman & Siegelman, Brooklyn, N.Y., Jug, 2-Tone, Qt..................... 45.00
Purola Trade Mark, In Script, Coffin, Cobalt Blue, Zinc Lid, Bubbles, 6 1/2 In. 25.00
Quaker Club Old Rye, S.B. Rothenberg, 4-Piece Mold, Amber, 1890s, 10 In................ 220.00
Queen Victoria, 1837 & 1897, Jug, Barrel, Doulton Lambeth, 7 1/2 In...................... 93.00
R.B. Cutter, Louisville, Ky., Medium Amber, Applied Mouth & Handle, Pontil, 8 1/2 In. 413.00
R.B. Cutter, Louisville, Ky., Pear Form, Golden Amber, c.1880, 8 1/2 In. 264.00
R.B. Cutter Pure Bourbon, Louisville, Ky., Medium Amber, 8 1/2 In........................ 330.00
R.B. Cutter Pure Bourbon, Louisville, Ky., Medium Smoky Pink Puce, 8 3/8 In.......... 660.00
R. Klingholtz Co., Manitowoc, Wis., Jug, Tan, Brown, Handles, Gold Lettering, Qt........ 79.00
R.R. Dinnigan & Co., San Francisco, Calif., Dark Amber, Cylinder, 11 In. 25.00
Rathjen Mercantile Co., San Francisco, Medium Amber, Tooled Lip, 11 In. 55.00
Red Top Rye, Ferd Westheimer & Sons, Olive Green, Whittled, 12 In. 165.00
Red Wing Liquor Co., Red Wing, Minn., Jug, Stoneware, 1/2 Gal. 175.00
Reeds Old Lexington Club, Amber.. 150.00
Relda Pure Rye, 2 Headed American Eagle, Backbar, 11 1/4 In............................... 963.00
Roehling & Shultz, Chicago, Semi-Cabin, Red Amber, 9 1/2 In.............................. 75.00
Rooney's Malt Whiskey, Straus Gunst & Co., Richmond, Va., Pocket, Flask, 1/2 Pt. ... 27.50
Rooney's Malt Whiskey, Straus, Gunst & Co., Richmond, Va., 1/2 Pt. 16.50
Roth & Co., San Francisco, Monogram, Amber, Oval Slug Plate, Fifth 100.00
Roth-Lawton Rye, Rectangular.. 9.00
Rothenberg Co., San Francisco, Cal., Amber, 1/2 Pt. 25.00
Rum, 8-Sided, Gray-Green, Opalescent, Double Ring Lip, OP, England, 1780, 9 In...... 3300.00
Rum, 8-Sided, Greens To Reds, Double Ring Lip, Pontil, England, 1780, 9 1/8 In. 3080.00
S.B. Rothenberg & Co, Old Judge, San Francisco, Golden Amber, 11 3/8 In. 55.00
S.B. Rothenberg & Co, Old Judge, San Francisco, Red Amber, 11 3/4 In.................... 121.00
S.M. & Co., N.Y., Jug, Embossed Seal, Amber, Pontil, 7 1/2 In............................. 715.00
S. Rosenthal & Co., New York & Brooklyn, Medium Golden Amber, 13 1/2 In. 50.00
Sam's Johnson Bar, Reno, Nevada, 1909, 7 1/2 In... 2310.00
Samuel Bros., Louisville, Ky., Medium Amber, Applied Mouth, 11 3/8 In................... 440.00
Shamrock, P. O'Brien & Co., Jug, Stoneware, Green Transfer, Rear Handle, 9 In. 388.00
Sheehan's, Utica, N.Y.. 17.00
Sherman Rye, Orange Amber, Crude, Bubbles 17.00
Silver Leaf Pure Rye, Richmond, Va., Embossed USA & Leaf, 1/2 Pt......................... 44.00
Simmond's Nabob, In Circle, Amber, Cylinder, Fifth, 10 3/8 In 50.00
Simmond's Nabob Trademark, Amber, Man, Servant, Amber, Cylinder, 11 5/8 In. 250.00
Slater's Premium, San Francisco, Amber, 12 In.. 71.50
Sol S. Goldstrom Wholesale Liquor Dealer, South Omaha, Neb., Qt. 20.00
Sol Stern, St. Louis, Embossed Star, Flask, 1860s, Dug...................................... 160.00
Spero's Saloon, San Francisco, Jug, Porcelain, Oil Can Shape, Gilt Handle, 4 In. 245.00
Spruance & Stanley, Amber, Tooled Top, Backbar.. 65.00
Spruance Stanley & Co., San Francisco, Horseshoe, Medium Amber, 11 5/8 In. 110.00
Squatty, Cylindrical, c.1750, 7 3/4 In.. 235.00
St. George Vineyard, San Francisco, Amber, Man On Horse, Cylinder, 11 1/8 In. 90.00
Star, Handle, Conical Vertical Ribbing, Golden Amber, Pontil, 8 1/4 In..................... 110.00
Star, N.Y., Amber, OP, Handle, 8 1/4 In... 357.50
Star, New York, W.B. Crowell Jr., Amber, Pontil, Cone Shape, Handle, 8 1/2 In. 460.00
Star Whiskey, N.Y., W.B. Crowell, Jr., Golden Yellow Amber, 8 1/8 In..................... 467.50
Stoddard, 3-Piece Mold, Deep Olive, Crude, Pontil.. 40.00
Stoddard Type, Olive Amber, Pontil, Fifth 45.00
Stoneware, Flask, Handled, N.Y., Tan & Olive Mottled, 7 1/8 In............................. 264.00
Straus Gunst & Co., Richmond, Va., Amber, Cylindrical, Qt. .... 187.00 to 275.00
Sunny Brook Whiskey, Inspector Back Of Every Bottle, Backbar, 11 In.................... 1100.00
Sunny Side Saloon, Lebanon, Ky., Jug, Stoneware 215.00
Swan Brewery Co., Yellow Green, Applied Mouth, 6 1/4 In. 705.00

T.D. Tweedie Red Hand, San Francisco, Olive Green, Applied Mouth, 7 5/7 In. 110.00
Taussig, Light Amethyst 15.00
Teal, OP, Cylinder, 1/6th 125.00
Trademark Gold Dust Kentucky Bourbon, Cylindrical, Horse, 12 In. 150.00
Tullamore Dew Irish, Whiskeygreen & White, Dogs & Harp 20.00
Turner Brothers, Barrel, Olive Yellow, 9 1/2 In. 297.00
Turner Brothers, N.Y., Barrel, Yellow Olive, 1860-1870, 9 7/8 In. 467.50
U.S. Eagle Mail, 1880-1900, Tooled Lip, 6 1/4 In. 192.50
Udolpho Wolfe's Aromatic Schnapps, Amber, Part Label, 9 3/4 In. 27.00
Udolpho Wolfe's Aromatic Schnapps, Blue Olive, 3 1/2 In. 48.00
Udolpho Wolfe's Aromatic Schnapps, Olive Green, IP 75.00
Udolpho Wolfe's Schiedam Aromatic Schnapps, Light Green, OP 135.00
Udolpho Wolfe's Schiedam Aromatic Schnapps, Pink Amethyst, 1865, 8 1/4 In. 385.00
Udolpho Wolfe's Schiedam Aromatic Schnapps, Root Beer Amber, IP, 7 3/4 In. 165.00
Udolpho Wolfe's Schiedam Aromatic Schnapps, Yellow Olive, 10 In. 45.00
United We Stand Whiskey, Medium Amber, Seed Bubbles, 1884-1888, 11 7/8 In. 1540.00
Universal Beverage, Tonic Schnapps, Clock Face, Deep Amber, Whittled 358.00
Van Schuyver, Amber 19.00
Vic Trolio, Canton, Miss., Whiskey Stoneware, 2 Gal. 39.00
Vidvard & Sheehan, Jug, Yellow Olive, 9 3/4 In. 1705.00
W & Co., N.Y., Pineapple Form, Yellow Olive, IP, 8 3/8 In. 1017.00
W. & Co. Cognac, Medium Amber, Handle, 5 3/4 In. 302.50
W.B. Co., San Francisco, Deep Blue Aqua, Applied Mouth, 6 1/8 In. 633.00
W.J. Van Schuyver, Portland, Crown Over Shield, Medium Amber, 11 3/4 In. 77.00
W.J. Van Schuyver & Co., Portland, Ore, Tooled Top 25.00
Wachenheim & Gilbert, Fine Whiskies, Vicksburg, Miss., Jug, Stoneware, Gal. 85.00
Walter Moise, Wedding Bouquet Rye, Omaha, Neb., Amber, 1890, Pt. 25.00
Wharton's, Chestnut Grove, Amber, Flattened Ewer Shape, Embossed, Handle 425.00
Wharton's, Chestnut Grove, Golden Amber, 10 In. 412.50
Wharton's, Chestnut Grove, Medium Amber, 5 1/8 In. 253.00
Wharton's, Chestnut Grove, Medium Cobalt Blue, 5 1/8 In. 357.50
White Horse Blended Scotch Whiskey, 2 Labels, Gal. 11.00
White Rock Distillery, Kansas City, Mo., Bail Handle, 2 Gal. 130.00
Whitney Glass Works, Aqua, Fifth 65.00
Wicklow Distillery, Old Irish, Owl On Branch, Jug, Stoneware, Black Transfer, 8 In. 147.00
Winedale Co., Oakland, Calif., Golden Amber, Bulbous Neck, 11 1/2 In. 25.00
Wm. D. Barry Reliable Family Liquor Store, Washington, D.C., 8-Sided 16.50
Wm. Edwards & Co. Pure Rye, Justice Scale, Screw Cap, Pottery, Honest Quart 275.00
Wm. H. Daly Sole Importer, N.Y., Olive Green Bell, 9 1/4 In. 935.00
Wm. H. Spears & Co., San Francisco, Clear, 12 In. 231.00
Wm. H. Spears & Co., San Francisco, Golden Yellow Amber, 11 7/8 In. 2805.00
Wm. H. Spears & Co. Old Pioneer, Bear, Amethyst, Cylinder, Fifth, 11 5/8 In. 500.00
Woodfall Manor Whiskey, 3-Piece Mold, Deep Olive Amber, Embossed 36.00
Wright & Greig Ltd., Brown & Tan, Kilted Warrior Both Sides, Jug, Stoneware 89.00
Ziegler & Behnerd, Big Mail Order Liquor House, Huntington, Wire Bail, Gal. 125.00

———————————————— **WILD TURKEY** ————————————————

Wild Turkey is a brand of bourbon made by Austin Nichols Distillery. The company says
the bourbon was originally made as a gift for some hunting companions and so was named
for their favorite gamebird. A crystal bottle with an etched flying turkey design was made
in 1951. The company made turkey-shaped ceramic bottles from 1971 to 1989. The first
bottle, filled with bourbon, sold for $20. In 1981 the company added miniature bottles. For
a short time during the 1980s, the company marketed a line of *go-withs* such as plates and
plaques. After 1989, Wild Turkey sold two limited-edition bottles: a Rare Breed Whiskey
bottle in a teardrop shape, which is still made, and a Kentucky Legend decanter shaped
like a violin, which is no longer in production. Since mid-1994, under the Rare Breed
label, Austin Nichols & Co. Distillery has issued a Kentucky Spirit, single barrel bourbon
in a distinctive bottle with a pewter-style top, available all year around in a gift box. Wild
Turkey figural decanters are no longer being made.

WILD TURKEY, Decanter, Baccarat, Crystal, 1979 .... 226.00
Decanter, Wedgwood, L Ltr. 215.00
Fliers Club, Plaque 77.00

Series 1, No. 1, Standing, Male, 1971..*Illus* 191.00
Series 1, No. 1, Standing, Male, 1981, Miniature.. 192.00
Series 1, No. 2, On Log, Female, 1972 ....*Illus* 146.00
Series 1, No. 2, On Log, Female, 1981, Miniature......................................125.00 to 144.00
Series 1, No. 3, On Wing, 1973..*Illus* 85.00
Series 1, No. 3, On Wing, 1982, Miniature..66.00 to 85.00
Series 1, No. 4, With Poult, 1974 .... 44.00
Series 1, No. 4, With Poult, 1982, Miniature 43.00
Series 1, No. 5, With Flags, 1975.. 27.00
Series 1, No. 5, With Flags, 1983, Miniature 26.00
Series 1, No. 6, Striding, 1976.. 24.00
Series 1, No. 6, Striding, 1983, Miniature.. 26.00
Series 1, No. 7, Taking Off, 1977 .... 25.00
Series 1, No. 7, Taking Off, 1983, Miniature.. 25.00
Series 1, No. 8, Strutting, 1978.. 40.00
Series 1, No. 8, Strutting, 1983, Miniature.. 40.00
Series 2, No. 1, Lore, 1979.. 30.00
Series 2, No. 2, Lore, 1980.. 32.00
Series 2, No. 3, Lore, 1981.. 36.00
Series 2, No. 4, Lore, 1982.. 41.00
Series 3, No. 1, In Flight, 1983 .... 96.00
Series 3, No. 1, In Flight, 1984, Miniature.. 25.00
Series 3, No. 2, With Bobcat, 1983.. 112.00
Series 3, No. 2, With Bobcat, 1985, Miniature.. 25.00
Series 3, No. 3, Turkeys Fighting, 1983.. 110.00
Series 3, No. 3, Turkeys Fighting, 1983, Miniature 25.00
Series 3, No. 4, With Eagle, 1984 .... 90.00
Series 3, No. 4, With Eagle, 1984, Miniature 40.00
Series 3, No. 5, With Raccoon, 1984 .... 76.00
Series 3, No. 5, With Raccoon, 1984, Miniature 25.00
Series 3, No. 6, With Poults, 1984 .... 66.00
Series 3, No. 6, With Poults, 1984, Miniature.. 20.00
Series 3, No. 7, With Fox, 1984, Miniature.. 25.00
Series 3, No. 7, With Fox, 1985.. 78.00
Series 3, No. 8, With Owl, 1985 ....*Illus* 80.00
Series 3, No. 8, With Owl, 1985, Miniature.. 25.00
Series 3, No. 9, With Bear Cubs, 1985.. 83.00
Series 3, No. 9, With Bear Cubs, 1985, Miniature 30.00
Series 3, No. 10, With Coyote, 1986.. 76.00
Series 3, No. 10, With Coyote, 1986, Miniature 25.00
Series 3, No. 11, With Falcon, 1986.. 92.00
Series 3, No. 11, With Falcon, 1986, Miniature 35.00

Wild Turkey, Series 1, No. 1, Standing, Male, 1971;
Wild Turkey, Series 1, No. 3, On Wing, 1973;
Wild Turkey, Series 1, No. 2, On Log, Female, 1972

Wild Turkey, Series 3, No. 8,
With Owl, 1985

Series 3, No. 12, With Skunk, 1986	95.00
Series 3, No. 12, With Skunk, 1986, Miniature	35.00
Series 4, No. 1, Habitat, Female, 1988	90.00
Series 4, No. 1, Habitat, Female, 1988, Miniature	50.00
Series 4, No. 2, Habitat, 1989	100.00
Series 4, No. 2, Habitat, 1989, Miniature	50.00

─────────────── **WINE** ───────────────

Wine has been bottled since the days of the ancient Greeks. Wine bottles have been made in a variety of sizes and shapes. Seal bottles were used from the second century and are listed in their own section in this book. Most wines found today are in the standard shapes that have been used for the past 125 years. The Bordeaux shape has square shoulders and straight sides while the Burgundy shape is broader with sloping shoulders. The Geman or Rhine wine flute bottle is tall and thin. Other wines, such as Champagne, are bottled in slightly different bottles.

WINE, 8-Sided, Olive Amber, Pontil, c.1780, 11 In.	330.00
Bodega Wines & Liquor, Spokane, Wash., Flask Strap Side, 32 Oz.	50.00
Cobalt Blue, BIMAL, 12 In.	125.00
Deep Olive Amber, OP, 6 3/8 In.	77.00
Deep Olive Green, OP, 9 1/4 In., 3 7/8 In. Diam.	55.00
Fisher & Co. Wholesale Wines & Liquors, Jug, Tan, Wire Bail, 1/2 Gal.	89.00
Garrett & Co., American Wines, Golden Amber, Tooled Collar, Cylindrical, 1890, 12 In.	137.50
Golden Wine Co., Boston, Jug, 2-Tone, Gal.	40.00
Gundlach Bundschu, Rhine Farm Sonoma, Light Amber, Tooled Top, 11 3/8 In.	50.00
J. Kellenberger, Durango, Colorado, Clear, Black Swirl Through Lip, 11 3/8 In.	302.00
James Durkin Wines & Liquors, Spokane, Wash., Amber, Embossed Front, Qt.	25.00
Joseph King, England, Olive Green, Applied Lip, Pontil, 1733, 8 In.	1925.00
Langery Wine Co., Spokane, Wash., Tooled Top	35.00
Light Olive Green, Globular, Pontil, 9 1/4 In.	303.00
Medium Olive Amber, Europe, Long Neck, OP, 1780-1800, 10 3/4 In.	176.00
Medium To Deep Green, Long Tapered Neck, OP, Europe, 1780-1800, 10 In.	413.00
Miniature, see the Miniature category	
Olive Amber, Winged Dragon, RHC Monogram Belly Seal, Cylindrical, Pontil, 11 In.	176.00
Oliver Porter & Co. Wine Merchants, Toronto, Jug, Stoneware, Blue Writing, Gal.	75.00
Pernod Fils, Sealed, 1880, 9 1/2 In.	36.00
Rhine Farm, San Francisco, Medium Amber, Tooled Lip, 11 In.	38.00
S.W. Zollinger Wines & Liquors, Harrisburg, Pa., Flask, Qt.	39.00
Saltzman & Siegelman, Brooklyn, N.Y., Brown, Tan, Stenciled, Qt.	29.00
Southern California Wine Co., Los Angeles, Calif., Jug, Brown & Cream, Handle	300.00
Speer's, Elder, N.Y., Light Emerald Green, Tapered Lip With Ring, 11 1/4 In.	413.00
W.C. Peacock & Co., Honolulu, Hi., Golden Amber, Tooled Lip, 11 In.	121.00
W.H. Jones & Co., Importers, Boston, Mass., Shield, Green, Rectangular Base, 10 In.	20.00

─────────────── **ZANESVILLE** ───────────────

The Zanesville Manufacturing Company started making glass in Zanesville, Ohio, in 1815. This glassworks closed in 1838 but reopened from 1842 to 1851. The company made many types of blown and mold blown pieces. At least one other glassworks operated in Zanesville from 1816 to the 1840s. The products of all the Zanesville factories are sometimes identified as *Midwestern* glass and are grouped with pieces made in Mantua, Kent, Ravenna, and other Ohio towns. The blown glass pieces include diamond patterned and ribbed pieces in clear, blue, amethyst, aquamarine, and amber colored glass. Collectors prize the Zanesville swirl pieces and sometimes identify them as *right* or *left* swirl.

ZANESVILLE, 24 Swirled Ribs, Golden Amber, Globe, Pontil, 8 1/4 In.	159.00
24 Swirled Ribs, Amber	230.00
24 Swirled Ribs, Amber, Globular, 7 1/4 In.	660.00
24 Swirled Ribs, Amber, Globular, 7 3/4 In.	770.00
24 Swirled Ribs, Cornflower Blue, Pontil, 8 1/4 In.	5170.00
24 Swirled Ribs, Dark Amber, 4 3/4 In.	192.00
24 Swirled Ribs, Golden Amber, Globe, Pontil, 9 1/2 In.	1540.00
24 Swirled Ribs, Olive Apricot, Globe, Rolled Lip, Pontil, 7 1/2 In.	1375.00

24 Vertical Ribs, Dark Amber, 6 1/2 In. 275.00
Flask, 24 Ribs, Light Blue, Pontil, 8 1/4 In. 605.00
Flask, 24 Swirled Ribs, Aqua 175.00
Flask, 24 Swirled Ribs, Aqua, 7 1/2 In. 192.00
Flask, 24 Swirled Ribs, Aqua, Pontil, 7 1/2 In. 302.00
Flask, 24 Swirled Ribs, Citron, Pontil, 8 1/4 In. 2200.00
Flask, 24 Swirled Ribs, Golden Amber, Globular, 1830-1840, 7 5/8 In. 550.00
Flask, 24 Swirled Ribs, Golden Amber, OP, 8 1/4 In. 660.00
Flask, 24 Swirled Ribs, Golden Amber, Pontil, c.1840, 7 1/2 In. 385.00
Flask, 24 Swirled Ribs, Olive Amber, Pontil, 9 1/2 In. 1045.00
Flask, Chestnut, 10 Diamonds, Amber, Sheared Pontil, 5 In. 1210.00
Flask, Chestnut, 10 Diamonds, Aqua, 1/2 Pt., 5 In. 1237.00
Flask, Chestnut, 10 Diamonds, Aqua, 8 In. 220.00
Flask, Chestnut, 10 Diamonds, Aqua, Pontil, 1/2 Pt., 5 1/4 In. 605.00
Flask, Chestnut, 10 Diamonds, Dark Amber, Pontil, 4 5/8 In. 495.00
Flask, Chestnut, 10 Diamonds, Olive Yellow, 1/2 Pt., 5 3/8 In. 2420.00
Flask, Chestnut, 20 Ribs, Broken Swirl, Golden Amber, 6 /34 In. 935.00
Flask, Chestnut, 24 Ribs, Aqua, Pontil, 5 In. 137.00
Flask, Chestnut, 24 Ribs, Broken Swirl, Dark Amber, Pontil, 6 5/8 In. 2090.00
Flask, Chestnut, 24 Ribs, Dark Amber, OP, 4 7/8 In. 247.00
Flask, Chestnut, 24 Ribs, Golden Amber, OP, 4 3/4 In. 275.00
Flask, Chestnut, 24 Ribs, Olive Amber, OP, 4 7/8 In. 220.00
Flask, Chestnut, 24 Swirled Ribs, Aqua, 7 1/2 In. 522.00
Flask, Chestnut, 24 Swirled Ribs, Dark Amber, Pontil, 4 3/4 In. 412.00
Flask, Chestnut, 24 Swirled Ribs, Golden Amber, 1/2 Pt., 5 In. 275.00

——————————— GO-WITHS ———————————

There are many items that interest the bottle collector even though they are not bottles, all
types of advertising that picture bottles or endorse bottled products like whiskey or beer,
many small items like bottle openers or bottle caps, and related products by well-known
companies like trays and plaques. Collectors call all of these *go-withs*. A variety of the
items are listed here. Many others can be found under company names in other price lists
such as *Kovels' Antiques & Collectibles Price List*. Clubs and publications that will help
collectors are listed in the bibliography and club list.

GO-WITHS, Ashtray, Billing Brewing Co., Metal, Glass Inside, 4 1/2 In. 325.00
Ashtray, Budweiser, A-Eagle Logo, Tin, Burgundy, 1940s, 6 x 3 3/4 In. 44.00
Ashtray, Coca-Cola, Partners, Baseball, Square 75.00
Ashtray, Dr Pepper, Glass 113.00
Bank, Coca-Cola, Truck, Red 22.00
Bank, Coca-Cola, Vending, Plastic, Box, 1950s 500.00
Bank, Truck, Ford Model A, Pickup, Liberty Classics, Hamm's 25.00
Baseball Glove, Child's, Drink Coca-Cola In Bottles, 1920s 965.00
Bicycle, Huffy, Man's, Coca-Cola, Box 400.00
Blotter, Coca-Cola Chewing Gum, 2 Packs Of Gum Picture 2475.00
Blotter, Coca-Cola, 1937 .... 32.00
Blotter, Off To A Fresh Start, Coca-Cola, 1930 .... 40.00
Bookmark, Coca-Cola, Heart Shape, 1900 .... 565.00
Bookmark, Coca-Cola, Owl, Celluloid, 1906 .... 1100.00
Bottle Cap, 7-Up, Plastic Lined, Silver & Red, Unused .... .50
Bottle Cap, Brownie Root Beer, Cork Lined, Brown, Tan, Unused 2.00
Bottle Cap, Canada Dry Ginger Ale, Cork Lined, Green, White & Red, Unused .... .50
Bottle Cap, Clicquot Club Root Beer, Cork Lined, Brown & Silver, Unused 1.50
Bottle Cap, Coca-Cola, Silver 1.00
Bottle Cap, Double Cola, Plastic Lined, Red & Silver, Unused .... .50
Bottle Cap, Fanta Root Beer, Plastic Lined, Silver, Brown & Blue, Unused .... .50
Bottle Cap, Fire Water, Cork Lined, Red & White, Unused 1.50
Bottle Cap, Hires Root Beer, Draft, Cork Lined, Orange, Brown & White, Unused 1.00
Bottle Cap, Kist Orange Soda, Cork Lined, Orange, Black & Silver, Unused 1.50
Bottle Cap, Old Red Eye, Cork Lined, Red & White, Unused 1.50
Bottle Cap, Pepsi-Cola, Cork Lined, Yellow & Red 1.00
Bottle Cap, Pepsi-Cola, Green, 1910 .... 35.00
Bottle Cap, R.C. Free, 1960s 5.00

Bottle Opener, Alligator, Cast Iron, Nickel Plate, 1 1/4 x 6 1/8 In. ....25.00 to 35.00
Bottle Opener, Alligator, Mardi-Gras.. 40.00
Bottle Opener, Anchor, Metal 2.00
Bottle Opener, Auto Jack 30.00
Bottle Opener, Baseball Cap, Cast Iron.. 20.00
Bottle Opener, Blue Gill, Brass 40.00
Bottle Opener, Budweiser Starr, Wall Mount.. 5.00
Bottle Opener, Buffalo, Cast Iron.. 125.00
Bottle Opener, Cactus Drunk 125.00
Bottle Opener, Canada Goose 50.00
Bottle Opener, Cat, Brass 30.00
Bottle Opener, Chinaman... 20.00
Bottle Opener, Coca-Cola, Wall Mount 20.00
Bottle Opener, Colorado Three Star 20.00
Bottle Opener, Cowboy, With Guitar, Cactus, Cast Pot Metal, 4 7/8 In. 395.00
Bottle Opener, Dog, Cast Iron.. 40.00
Bottle Opener, Donkey, Brass...30.00 to 37.00
Bottle Opener, Donkey, Large, Brass.. 60.00
Bottle Opener, Donkey, Small, Cast Iron 125.00
Bottle Opener, Drink Moxie, 100% The Home Of Moxie... 6.00
Bottle Opener, Eagle, Brass 35.00
Bottle Opener, Elephant, Art Deco, Chrome 30.00
Bottle Opener, Elephant, Black 60.00
Bottle Opener, Elephant, Brass 40.00
Bottle Opener, Elephant, Silver... 50.00
Bottle Opener, Elephant, Small, Cast Iron 125.00
Bottle Opener, Fish, Aluminum 20.00
Bottle Opener, Fisherman, Brass 40.00
Bottle Opener, Foundryman, Brass 40.00
Bottle Opener, French Maid 35.00
Bottle Opener, Goat ....55.00 to 60.00
Bottle Opener, Helmet, Fireman's, Base Plate 45.00
Bottle Opener, High Hat Sign Post... 35.00
Bottle Opener, High Life, Girl In Moon, Wooden, Miniature Crown, 4 1/4 In. 5.00
Bottle Opener, Indian, Iroquois Beer.. 25.00
Bottle Opener, Irish Setter, Cast Iron 38.00
Bottle Opener, Isaac Leisy Brewing Co., Figure Of Baseball Pitcher, Pat. 1914........... 32.00
Bottle Opener, Jacob Ruppert Knickerbocker Beer, Figural... 15.00
Bottle Opener, Jimmy Carter, 1976... 40.00
Bottle Opener, Lamp Post Drunk On Ash Tray...25.00 to 30.00
Bottle Opener, Lamp Post Drunk, Intercourse, Pa.. 25.00
Bottle Opener, Lobster 25.00
Bottle Opener, Lovable Bar Bum, Box.. 150.00
Bottle Opener, Mademoiselle, Lamp Post & Sign, Cast Iron, 4 1/2 In. 20.00
Bottle Opener, Monkey, Brass 35.00
Bottle Opener, Monkey, Cast Iron... 265.00
Bottle Opener, Mouse 75.00
Bottle Opener, Old St. Nick, Brass.. 40.00
Bottle Opener, Palm Tree Drunk, Florida 75.00
Bottle Opener, Palm Tree Drunk, Iron 50.00
Bottle Opener, Parrot, With Can Punch... 65.00
Bottle Opener, Peacock, Brass 35.00
Bottle Opener, Pelican, Cast Iron, 3 3/8 x 3 3/4 In. 50.00
Bottle Opener, Praying Jayhawk, Brass... 45.00
Bottle Opener, Pretzel, Brass 25.00
Bottle Opener, Pretzel, Iron, 1951... 40.00
Bottle Opener, Rooster, Chrome Plated 35.00
Bottle Opener, Schlitz Bottle, Wooden, 1939 New York World's Fair, 3 1/2 In. 22.00
Bottle Opener, Schmidt's Of Philadelphia 3.00
Bottle Opener, Toad, Brass 40.00
Bottle Opener, Top Hatter, Brass 40.00
Bottle Opener, Toucan, Cast Iron.. 145.00
Bottle Topper, Ma's Root Beer, 1941.. 12.00

Bottle Topper, NuGrape, Colorful, 1940s 22.00
Bottle Topper, Swallow's Keg Root Beer, 1941, Unused 5.00
Box, Dr. J. Hostetter's Celebrated Stomach Bitters, Wooden, 1 Doz., 11 1/2 x 16 In. 94.00
Box, Hagen's American India Ink, Waterproof Drawing Ink, 1881, 8 x 6 x 4 In. 25.00
Box, Kerr Economy Lids 25.00
Box, Mason Fruit Jars, Lockport, Wooden, 1 Dozen Pints, Black Lettering, 1900-1910. 74.00
Box, Mason Fruit Jars, Lockport, 1 Dozen Quarts, Black Lettering, 1900s 154.00
Broadside, Dr. Brown's Magic Liniment, Woman Waving Wand, 1901, 8 x 10 In........ 20.00
Button, Canada Dry Spur 8.00
Button, Dad's Root Beer 8.00
Button, Muehlebach Beer, Chain Hanger, White Letters, Red Ground, 9 In................. 45.00
Button, Vess Cola 8.00
Calendar, Chas. D. Kaier Co., Mahanony City, Pa., 1912 .... 40.00
Calendar, Chero Cola, 1926, Frame... 449.00
Calendar, Coca-Cola, 1915, 1 Sheet, Matted... 1000.00
Calendar, Coca-Cola, 1921, Top, Frame.. 120.00
Calendar, Coca-Cola, 1947.. 280.00
Calendar, Coca-Cola, 1972.. 25.00
Calendar, Coca-Cola, 1985.. 15.00
Calendar, Coca-Cola, 1986.. 15.00
Calendar, Coca-Cola, July 1922 Sheet, Matted, Frame 1599.00
Can, Coca-Cola, Diamond, Canada, 1960s... 110.00
Can, Pepsi-Cola, Double Dot, Cone Type 283.00
Canteen, Bardwell's Root Beer, Stoneware, Gray, Blue, Metal Wooden Handle, 11 In. 412.00
Card, Coca-Cola, Polar Bear, Gold 800.00
Card, Playing, Coca-Cola, Ballerina, 1943... 220.00
Card, Playing, Coca-Cola, Sealed, 1963... 55.00
Card, Playing, Red Cap Ale, Beer Can Shape, 1960s... 14.00
Card, Playing, Royal Crown, Box 60.00
Card, Playing, Santa, Double Deck, Coca-Cola Tin.. 14.00
Card, Trade, Coca-Cola, Bathtub 1 Side, Girl Serving 2 Men Coke, 1907............... 504.00
Card, Trade, Coca-Cola, Girl At Soda Fountain, 1890s 3800.00
Carrier, Baumeister Root Beer, 6 Pack For 12 Oz. Bottles, Unused 3.50
Carrier, Clicquot Club, 6 Pack For 7 Oz. Bottles, Unused..................................... 3.50
Carrier, Dr. Swett's, From Childhood To Old Age, Cardboard, 3 Sides, 6 Bottles 12.00
Carrier, Nehi Soda, 4 Bottles, 1925 .... 22.50
Carrier, Stadium, Coca-Cola, Metal, Painted, 1950s... 125.00
Carton, Clicquot Club, 6 Pack For 7 Oz. Bottles, Unused...................................... 3.00
Carton, Double Cola, 6 Pack For 10 Oz. Bottles, Unused...................................... 4.00
Carton, Maple Farms Inc., Elmira, N.Y., Batman & Riddler, 1966, Unfolded 3.50
Carton, NuGrape, 6 Pack For 10 Oz. Bottles, Unused 3.50
Chalkboard, Pepsi-Cola, Have A Pepsi, 1950s, 19 x 30 In.................................... 25.00
Chart, Mileage, 7-Up, 1970s.. 50.00
Christmas Ornament, Ball, Coca-Cola, Corning 7.00
Clamp, Kerr Economy, Clear 8.00
Clock, Budweiser, Clydsdales, Wagon, Light-Up, 4 Ft. 400.00
Clock, Busch Bavarian Beer, Metal, Plastic, Mountain Scene, Light-Up, 1950s, 13 In... 18.00
Clock, Coca-Cola, Enjoy Diet Coke, Battery Operated, Round Face, Box 17.50
Clock, Coca-Cola, Light-Up, 1963 .... 125.00
Clock, Coca-Cola, Please Pay Cashier, Counter... 700.00
Clock, Coca-Cola, Regulator, Battery Operated, 1970s... 250.00
Clock, Double Cola, Light-Up, Telechron, Double Glass, Round 375.00
Clock, Dr Pepper, Logo, Telechron, Glass Front, 1940s, Round 235.00
Clock, John Bull Medicine & Co., Seth Thomas, 1880-1900, 22 In. 357.00
Clock, Miller Genuine Draft, Motion, Neon... 65.00
Clock, Molson Beer, Plastic Face, Metal Back, Square, 15 1/4 In........................... 175.00
Clock, Olympia, Plastic, Metal, Bottle Cap Shape, Electric, Light-Up, 1971, 16 In. Diam. 17.00
Clock, Pepsi-Cola, Cash Register/Counter Clock, Light, Menu Slats, 1967, 14 x 7 In.... 190.00
Clock, Phoenix Beer, Square, Tin Face, Wood Case, Paint, 15 1/2 In......................... 235.00
Clock, Teem, Metal, Plastic Face, Square, 15 1/2 In.. 225.00
Clock-Thermometer, Seagram's Whiskey, Banjo Type, Electric............................. 125.00
Coaster, Fox Deluxe, Peter Fox Brewing Co., Chicago, Red & Black, 1940s, 4 In. 8.00
Coaster, Gunther's Beer, Baltimore, Md., Blue & Brown, 4 In. 4.00

Go-Withs, Cup, Coca-Cola, Diet Coke; Go-Withs, Cup, Coca-Cola,
Drink Coke; Go-Withs, Cup, Coca-Cola, Frozen Coke

Coaster, Hampden, Handsome Waiter, 1940s, 4 In.	8.00
Coaster, Old Reading Brewery, Inc., Reading, Pa., 1950s, 4 & 5 In., Pair	15.00
Coaster, Tam-O-Shanter Ale, Rochester, N.Y., 1940-1950, 4 1/4 In.	16.00
Coaster Set, Hamm's Bear, Metal, Different Bear Sport Scenes, 1981, 6 Piece	6.00
Cookbook, Borden's Eagle Brand Magic Recipes, 1946, 28 Pages	9.00
Cookie Jar, Black Label, White Glaze, Logo, West Bend Pottery, 8 x 8 x 7 In.	40.00
Cookie Jar, Budweiser, Champion Clydesdales, Siesta Ware, Wooden Lid, 9 In.	120.00
Cooler, Picnic, Red Vinyl, Late 1940s	175.00
Cooler, Schmidt City Club, Metal, Insulated, Green Paint, 1940-1950, 12 x 8 In.	6.00
Corkscrew, Anheuser-Busch, A-Eagle Logo, Brass, Pat.June 1, 1897, 2 7/8 In.	45.00
Corkscrew, St. Louis ABC Beer, Wooden Handle, 1900s, 5 1/2 In.	12.00
Cribbage Board, Kellogg Whiskey, Wilmerding & Loew, San Francisco	85.00
Cup, Coca-Cola, Diet Coke ....*Illus*	3.00
Cup, Coca-Cola, Drink Coke ....*Illus*	3.00
Cup, Coca-Cola, Frozen Coke ....*Illus*	3.00
Cup, Measuring, Eclectic Medical Company, Richmond, Va., 8 Tsp., 2 Tbsp.	11.00
Cup, Pepsi-Cola, Bottle Caps..*Illus*	10.00
Cup, Pepsi-Cola, Diet Pepsi	10.00
Cup, Pepsi-Cola, Elvis Used In Photo, 3 1/2 In. ....*Illus*	10.00
Cup, Pepsi-Cola, Have A Pepsi	6.00
Cup, Pepsi-Cola, Pepsi Blue	8.00
Cup, Pepsi-Cola, Pepsi Cone ....*Illus*	5.00
Cup, Pepsi-Cola, Pepsi's Best..*Illus*	6.00
Cup & Saucer, Pabst Brewing Co., Milwaukee, Wis.	62.00
Decanter-Stein, Budweiser, Jim Beam, Red Tag, 1983, 7 1/8 In.	160.00
Dice, Coca-Cola, Pair	5.00
Dice, Pepsi-Cola, Pair	5.00
Dispenser, Buckeye Root Beer, Tree Stump, Pump	425.00
Dispenser, Fountain, Coca-Cola, Thin Style, With 5 Flavors, 1970s	250.00
Dispenser, Syrup, Coca-Cola, Logo, Gold Trim, Ornate, 1890s	2200.00
Dispenser, Ward's Lemon Crush, Ball Pump	1522.00
Dispenser, Ward's Lemon Crush, Ceramic Lemon, Brass Pump, 13 x 10 x 8 In.	1430.00
Display, Dr Pepper, 3-D Girl, Cardboard, 18 x 16 In.	600.00
Display, Dr Pepper, Good For Life, Cutout Bottle, Cardboard	152.00
Display Case, Sanford's Ink, Oak, Refinished	395.00
Display Figure, Jim Beam, Cowboy	65.00
Door Push, Pepsi-Cola, Canada, 32 x 3 1/4 In.	65.00
Dose Cup, Padres Wine Bitters Tonic	15.00
Dose Glass, Alter Bismarck Magen Bitters, Etched Bust Of Man	85.00
Dose Glass, H.E. Yardley, Pharmacist, Sacramento, Calif.	50.00
Dose Glass, McLaughlin Of Auburn, Calif.	65.00
Dose Glass, Minneapolis, Minn.	15.00
Dose Glass, Oskaloosa, Iowa	22.00
Dose Glass, Owl Drug, Single Wing	35.00
Dose Glass, Wolfe's Aromatic Schnapps, Multicolored, Footed	45.00
Dose Goblet, Devil Stomach Bitters, Fred Kalina, Pittsburg, Pa., Gray Tint	40.00

Go-Withs, Cup,
Pepsi-Cola, Bottle
Caps

Go-Withs, Cup, Pepsi-Cola,
Pepsi's Best; Go-Withs, Cup,
Pepsi-Cola, Pepsi Cone

Go-Withs, Cup, Pepsi-
Cola, Elvis Used In
Photo, 3 1/2 In.

Dose Goblet, Dr. Harter's, Lavender Tint	40.00
Dose Goblet, Petzold's German Bitters, Lavender Tint	40.00
Eyecup, John Bull, Pat. Aug. 14, 1917, Emerald Green, 2 3/4 In.	60.00
Eyecup, Oftalmol, Amber, 1910-1920, 1 3/8 In.	137.00
Fan, Bourjois Soir De Paris, Silver, Blue, Parisian Symbols, Bottle, 7 3/8 In.	286.00
Fan, Drink Coca-Cola, 1940s	65.00
Figure, Avon, Christmas, 1981	60.00
Figure, Avon, Mother's Love, 1981, Box	5.00
Figure, Avon, Mrs. Albee, Box, 1984	35.00
Figure, Owl, Owl Drug Co., Plaster Of Paris, 1900, 5 1/4 In.	121.00
Figure, Santa Claus, Coca-Cola, 3 In.	60.00
Figure, Snowman, Coca-Cola, 28 In.	60.00
Flyswatter, Bottled Coca-Cola, Clean, Sanitary, Metal, 1930s	330.00
Foam Scraper, Anheuser-Busch, 10 In.	24.00
Foam Scraper, Pabst Blue Ribbon, Blue Letters, White Ground, 8 3/4 In.	12.00
Game, Dominoes, Warner's Products, 28 Wooden Dominoes, 1880s, Box	257.00
Glass, A.B.C., Bohemian Brewing Co., St. Louis, Eagle, Etched Barrel, 3 1/4 In.	50.00
Glass, Arrow 77 Beer, It Hits The Spot, Cumberland, Md., 5 3/4 In.	46.00
Glass, Barrel, Coors, Logo, Gold Lettering & Design, 3 1/8 In.	10.00
Glass, Bartholomay, Rochester Beer & Ale, Frosted, Tire, Wings, Straight-Sided, 4 In.	30.00
Glass, Blatz, Unequal Pioneer Milwaukee Beer, B With Pine Cone, 3 3/8 In.	45.00
Glass, Budweiser Beer, Christmas, Red & Green Enameled, 1940s, 5 3/4 In.	17.00
Glass, Chief Oshkosh Beer, Oshkosh, Wis., 4 1/4 In.	7.00
Glass, Coca-Cola, Churchill Downs, Louisville, Ky., 1990, 3 3/4 In.	7.00
Glass, Coca-Cola, Collegiate Crest, Cal State, Long Beach, Brown, 6 1/8 In.	5.00
Glass, Dakota Beer, Red & White Enameled, 1950s, 4 1/4 In.	17.00
Glass, Dusseldorfer Dieterich Export, Multicolored, Germany, 5 1/2 In.	2.00
Glass, GP, Grand Prize, Beer Within Scroll Border, Barrel, Enameled, 3 1/8 In.	20.00
Glass, Hamm's, From The Land Of Sky Blue Waters, Red & Blue Shell, 3 1/2 In.	14.00
Glass, Hires Root Beer, Hourglass Shape	60.00
Glass, Measuring, Alonzo O. Bliss Co., Washington, D.C., 8 Tsp., 2 Tbsp.	9.00
Glass, Michelob Beer, Red Enamel, Stemmed, 1950s, 7 3/8 In.	2.00
Glass, Moxie, Handle, Orange Band, Logo Around	118.00
Glass, Nehi, Frosted Band Center, Applied Black Lettering	150.00
Glass, Pabst Blue Ribbon, Blue, 3-14-78, 5 5/8 In.	11.00
Glass, Pepsi-Cola, Bullwinkle, White, 6 1/4 In.	11.00
Glass, Pepsi-Cola, Cobalt Blue, Locomotive Logo, 16 Oz.	15.00
Glass, Pepsi-Cola, Locomotive Logo, 12 Oz.	7.50
Glass, Pepsi-Cola, Ohio Bicentennial, Miami-Erie Canal, 5 1/8 In.	7.00
Glass, Pepsi-Cola, You're In The Pepsi Generation, Oct. 1965, 4 7/8 In.	22.00
Glass, Pilsner, A-L, Red, Black, 5 1/4 In.	10.00
Glass, Ruhstaller's Gilt Edge Lager, Sacramento, Calif., Gold Rim, Waisted, 4 1/2 In.	45.00
Glass, Schmidt Beer, Red, 4 3/8 In.	12.00
Glass, Storz Beer, Red Enameled Shell, 1950s, 4 In.	5.00
Glass, Take One With Baily & Wicks, Purple	18.00
Glass, Wine, Garrett's Virginia Dare	16.50

Grenade Rack, Hanging, Imperial Trademark, Hand, Crown, Cast Iron, c.1890 .... 165.00
Gum, Coca-Cola Spearmint, Wrapper 3080.00
Hat, Beach, Coca-Cola, Cloth, 1960s 9.00
Hat, Dairy, Campbell's Dairy, Grove City, Pa., Paper 2.50
Jug, Beer, Kuehnrich, Los Angeles Brewing Co., Calif. 260.00
Knife, Anheuser-Busch, 2 Blades, Corkscrew, Eagle On Reverse, Engraved 100.00
Knife, Coca-Cola, Red & White, Drink Coca-Cola, 5 Cents, 1930-1940, 3 1/2 In. 13.00
Knob, Diamond State, Diamond State Brewing Co., Wilmington, Del 201.00
Knob, Eastside, Los Angeles Brewing Co., Los Angeles, Calif 70.00
Label, Atlantic Beer, Chicago., Ill 3.00
Label, Bohemian, Chicago, Ill. 8.00
Label, Brown Derby, Chicago, Ill 3.00
Label, Citizen's Pilsner Beer, Joliet, Ill 7.00
Label, Dad's Root Beer, Mama's Size, Blue, Orange & White, 1940s 2.00
Label, Dr Pepper, King Of Beverages 20.00
Label, Frostie Old-Fashioned Root Beer, Cameo Girl, 1947 .... 2.00
Label, Golden Creme Beer, Chicago, Ill 6.00
Label, Hapsburg Beer, Chicago, Ill. 5.00
Label, Keeley Lager Beer, Chicago, Ill. 6.00
Label, Koller Beer, Chicago, Ill 6.00
Label, Old Brew, Chicago, Ill 4.00
Label, Prager Beer, Chicago, Ill., Foil 8.00
Label, Prager Short Beer, Chicago, Ill., Foil 5.00
Label, Rheingold, Chicago, Ill., Foil 5.00
Label, Superb Beer, Chicago, Ill. 5.00
Label, Tavern Pale Draught, Chicago, Ill., Foil 3.00
Label, Whistle Co., Diamond, Girl Whistling Picture 76.00
Lamp, Busch, Figural, Quart Bottle, Can Pouring Into Glass, 20 In. 40.00
Lamp, Miller, Hanging, Plastic, Multicolored, 21 x 21 In. 20.00
Letter Opener, C.W. Abbott's Bitters, Ivory, 7 3/4 In. 35.00
Lid, Ball Ideal, Glass, Clear 20.00
Lighter, Budweiser, Bottle Shape, A-Eagle Logo On Label, 1930s, 2 5/8 In. 40.00
Lighter, Cigarette, Coca-Cola, Table Top, Box 478.00
Lighter, Cigarette, Smooth Mellow Jax, Red, Blue, Yellow 35.00
Lighter, Coca-Cola, Bottle Shape, 1954 .... 13.00
Magnet, Refrigerator, Coca-Cola, 1960s, 4 Piece 5.00
Marble, Coca-Cola 7.50
Match Holder-Ashtray, Green River Whiskey 100.00
Match Safe, Adam Scheidt Brewing Co., 2-Sided, Celluloid 110.00
Matchbook, A & W Root Beer, Arrow, 5 Cents 4.00
Matchbook, Coca-Cola, Complete, 1922 .... 187.00
Matchbook, Coca-Cola, Drink A Bottle, Full Pack, 1908 .... 250.00
Matchbook, Coca-Cola, Have A Coke, Hand & Open Bottle 7.00
Menu Board, Coca-Cola, Wooden, Late 1930s 750.00
Menu Board, Coca-Cola, Wooden, Metal Trim, 1940s 500.00
Menu Board, Orange Crush, Light-Up, 3 1/2 In. 200.00
Milk Bottle Cap, Drink More Milk .... *Illus*   3.00
Milk Bottle Cap, Eggnog .... *Illus*   2.00
Milk Bottle Cap, Haleakala Dairy, Grade A Raw Chocolate Milk 4.00
Milk Bottle Cap, Haleakala Dairy, Grade A Raw Orange Flavored 10.00
Milk Bottle Cap, Haleakala Dairy, Pure Buttermilk 10.00
Milk Bottle Cap, Higgins Bros. Dairy, Whole Guernsey, Medina, Oh., Blue, White. 50
Milk Bottle Cap, Merry Xmas .... *Illus*   5.00
Milk Bottle Cap, Shonk's Dairy, Millersburg, Oh., Red & Black 75
Milk Bottle Cap, Thompson Chocolate Milk, South Amherst, Oh., Maroon & Red 75
Milk Flag, Campbell's Dairy 5.00
Mirror, Coca-Cola, Pocket, 1907 .... 478.00
Mirror, Coors Extra Gold Draft, Diamond Shape, Wooden Frame, 24 In. 10.00
Mirror, Cunningham Whiskey, Paul Friedman, San Francisco, Calif., Barrel, Pocket 120.00
Mirror, Duff's Malt Whiskey, Pocket 40.00
Mirror, Genesee Cream Ale, Green, Red & Gold, Wooden Frame, 11 x 22 In 17.00
Mirror, Molson Beer, Ale, Red, Blue & Gold, Wooden Frame, 20 1/2 x 17 1/2 In. 2.00
Mirror, Pabst Blue Ribbon, Shield Shape, Red, White & Blue, 15 x 20 In 16.00

Mirror, Rainier, Seattle Brewing & Malting Co. 7.50
Mug, A & W Root Beer, Small.. 2.00
Mug, A-Eagle King Cobra Beer, Black 16.00
Mug, Anheuser-Busch, Bud Girl, Green Ground, Red A And Eagle 611.00
Mug, Anheuser-Busch, Metal Lid, A-Eagle... 40.00
Mug, Armour's Veribest, Stoneware 85.00
Mug, Buckeye Root Beer, In Black Circle, Pottery, 6 1/4 In. 55.00
Mug, Budweiser Champion Clydesdale, Wagon & Horses Decal, 4 3/4 In. 4.00
Mug, Budweiser, '79 Tribute To Ali 80.00
Mug, Budweiser, Bud Man, Hollow Head 280.00
Mug, Budweiser, Bud Man, Ye Olde Moustache Mug 127.00
Mug, Budweiser, Oktoberfest, Aurora Elks Lodge, No. 1921, Oct. 3, 1976, 5 3/4 In...... 9.00
Mug, Coca-Cola, Gold Lettering & Rim, Buff, Ceramic 8.00
Mug, Coca-Crush, Ceramic 347.00
Mug, Coors, Banquet Logo, Blue Split-Tail Lions, West Germany, 5 1/2 In.................. 16.00
Mug, Coors, Golden, Colo., White Ceramic, Red & Gray Enameled, 4 1/2 In. 10.00
Mug, Dad's, Don't Say Root Beer, Say Dad's, Red, Yellow, 5 In............................... 12.00
Mug, Genuine Hires Root Beer, White, Brown & Orange, 6 In.................................. 12.00
Mug, Greetings From Saratoga Springs, N.Y., Grand Union Hotel Picture, Germany 60.00
Mug, Heineken, Since 1592, Tan, Ceramarte, 6 1/2 In. 8.00
Mug, Jenner Brewing Co., Tan, Black Lettering, Pre-Prohibition 150.00
Mug, Leisy Brewing Co., Peoria, Ill., Green, Multicolored Top........................... 45.00 to 50.00
Mug, Nixon Restaurant, Cabin, Lake, Stoneware, 3 1/2 In... 88.00
Mug, Old Kentucky Root Beer, Ceramic 15.00
Mug, Richardson's Liberty Root Beer 25.00
Mug, Schlitz, Brown & Yellow Logo, Ceramarte, 2 3/8 In. 6.00
Mug, Schlitz, Move 'Em Out '71 .... 25.00
Mug, South Omaha Brewing Co., Multicolored Logo 435.00
Needle Holder, Coca-Cola, Cardboard, Needles... 816.00
Note Pad, Coca-Cola, Green Leatherette, 1905 .... 300.00
Paper Bag, Magoo Stag Beer, Carling Brewery, Belleville, Ill., Handle, 1958.............. 6.00
Pencil, 7-Up 2.00
Pencil, Pepsi-Cola, Mechanical, Double Dot, Metropolitan Bottling Co. 115.00
Pill Cutter, Apothecary, Handled Blade, Wooden Base, American, 1870, 12 1/2 In. 210.00
Pitcher, Bardwell's Root Beer, Stein, Gray, Pewter Lid, Geo.Washington Bust 1100.00
Pitcher, Borden's, Elsie In Black, McCoy, 4 In.. 43.00
Pitcher, Windsor Supreme Canadian, Head Shape, 8 3/8 In. 17.00
Plaque, Coors, 1 Can Picture & 1 Bottle Picture, Round, 14 In., Pair.......................... 42.00
Plate, Anheuser-Busch, Vienna Art, 10 In...*Illus*   55.00
Plate, Avon, Christmas Spirit, Sharing, 1981 .... 30.00
Plate, Avon, Christmas, 1973, Box 100.00
Plate, Avon, Christmas, 1975, Box 25.00
Plate, Avon, Christmas, 1982 .... 30.00
Plate, Avon, Christmas, 1989 .... 25.00
Plate, Avon, Mother's Day, 1981 .... 6.50
Plate, Avon, Mother's Day, 1985, Box 10.00
Plate, Avon, Mrs. Albee, Summer's Soft Whisper, 1990, Box 20.00
Plate, Avon, Queen Elizabeth II Anniversary.. 75.00

Go-Withs, Milk Bottle Cap, Eggnog; Go-Withs, Milk Bottle Cap,
Drink More Milk; Go-Withs, Milk Bottle Cap, Merry Xmas

Plate, Coca-Cola, Santa Claus, Plastic, 10 In. 6.00
Platter, Serving, Budweiser, Label, 15 1/2 x 11 1/2 In. 11.00
Pot, Brown's Cantharidine Horse Blister... 45.00
Pot Lid, Bazin's Unrivaled Premium Shaving Cream, Red Transfer, Base 93.50
Pot Lid, Bird, Trees & Bushes, Multicolored 75.00
Pot Lid, Calvert's Carbolic Toothpaste, White, Black Transfer, 2 1/4 In. Diam. 25.00
Pot Lid, Caswell, Massey & Co. Cold Cream, Cucumbers, Green Transfer, 2 1/2 In...... 176.00
Pot Lid, Dr. E.J. Coxes's Extract Of Copalla Sarsaparilla, Black Transfer, 3 1/4 In. 495.00
Pot Lid, James Atkinson Bears Grease, Bear Picture, 2/6 Size.. 80.00
Pot Lid, Jules Hauel Perfumer, Ben Franklin Center, Purple Transfer, 3 1/2 In. Diam. .. 300.00
Pot Lid, Pratt Type, Buck Deer, In Forest, Multicolored.. 80.00
Pot Lid, Pratt Type, Woman, Plumed Hat, Multicolored.. 55.00
Pot Lid, Taylor's Saponaceous Compound, Shaving Soap, Purple Transfer, Base.......... 154.00
Pot Lid, Trouchet's Corn Cure, White, Red Transfer, 2 1/8 In. Diam. 55.00
Pot Lid, X. Bazin, Philadelphia, Perfumed Bear's Grease, Black Transfer, 2 3/4 In. 1045.00
Print, Prof. Flint's Horse Cattle Powders, Dr. B.J. Kendall Co., Frame, 13 x 9 1/2 In.... 55.00
Purse, Coca-Cola, Change Slots, 1900s 300.00
Purse-Billfold, Coca-Cola Bottling Co., 1900s 250.00
Radio, Coca-Cola, Cooler, 1950 .... 575.00
Radio, Pepsi-Cola, Double Dot, 24 In. 850.00
Radio Set, Crystal, Coca-Cola, Miniature, 1950s... 500.00
Record, Pepsi-Cola, WWII, The Voice Of Your Soldier At Camp 42.00
Salt & Pepper, Busch Gardens, Tampa, Fla., Dark Continent, 2 3/4 In......................... 21.00
Salt & Pepper, Coors, Wooden Barrels 45.00
Salt & Pepper, Pepsi-Cola, Bottle Shape, Decals... 266.00
Scale, Druggist, Newark Scale Works, N.J., Iron & Brass, Glass, 7 In. 297.00
Sheet Music, Any Bonds Today, Cunningham Drug Store, Uncle Sam, 1941 .... 15.00
Sheet Music, Rum & Coca-Cola, Jeri Sullavan, 1940s....................................... 22.00
Sheet Music, When The Do-Do Bird Is Singing In The Coca-Cola Tree, 1912 .... 350.00
Shot Glass, A.M. Smith California Wine Depot, Minneapolis, Christmas, 1907-1908... 25.00
Shot Glass, Eclectic Medical Co., Richmond, Va.. 27.50
Shot Glass, Genuine Bitters, Clear, c.1910, 3 In.. 60.50
Shot Glass, Rooney's Malt Whiskey 66.00
Shot Glass, Thompson Straight Whiskey Co., Louisville, Ky., Etched 25.00
Sign, Boschee's Syrup & Greens, August Flower, Color, 13 x 7 In. 30.00
Sign, Budweiser, Clydesdales, Light-Up, 1950s, 13 x 18 In.................................. 115.00
Sign, Budweiser, Prohibition Sign, Anheuser-Busch Inc., Bottle On Box, 7 x 17 In. 260.00
Sign, Carvel Whiskey, Drink That Satisfies, Reverse Glass, 5 x 12 In........................ 90.00
Sign, Coca-Cola, 2 Couples At Home, TV & Popcorn, Cardboard, 1954, 20 x 36 In...... 425.00
Sign, Coca-Cola, Bottle, Die-Cut, Porcelain, 12 1/2 In.. 150.00
Sign, Coca-Cola, Button, White Tin, Bottle, 24 In. 550.00
Sign, Coca-Cola, Porcelain, White, Black Outline, Coca-Cola In Script, 6 x 19 In. 675.00
Sign, Coca-Cola, That Refreshing New Feeling, Wood, Metal, Plastic, 23 x 7 In........... 185.00
Sign, Coca-Cola, Waterfalls, Light-Up, Metal, Counter 1157.00
Sign, Coca-Cola, Yellow Dot, 1940s, 12 x 36 In.. 250.00
Sign, Dixon & Sons Chemist, High Class Mineral Water, Metal, 14 x 10 In. 132.00
Sign, Dr. Hail's Old Indian System Tonic For The Kidneys, Indian, Frame, 12 x 9 In. .. 250.00

Go-Withs, Plate, Anheuser-Busch,
Vienna Art, 10 In.

Go-Withs, Toy, Airplane, Made From
Pepsi-Cola Cans, 16 x 13 In.

Sign, Drink Hires In Bottles, Tin, 1920s, 5 x 14 In. 50.00
Sign, Green River Whiskey, Black Man, Horse, Tin, Frame, 1900s, 33 x 23 In............. 440.00
Sign, Green River Whiskey, Cardboard, Self-Framed, 17 x 24 In........................... 200.00
Sign, Green River, The Whiskey Without Regrets, Cardboard, 1935, 24 1/2 x 19 In....... 83.00
Sign, Hostetter's Celebrated Stomach Bitters, Grant & Generals, Paper, 10 x 8 In........ 253.00
Sign, Ice Cold Coca-Cola, Round, 1933 .... 567.00
Sign, Magnus Root Beer, From Barrel, Curved, 9 x 14 In. 295.00
Sign, Malt-Nutrine A Hurry Call, Tin, Anheuser-Busch Other Side, 7 3/4 x 13 In. 132.00
Sign, Moroney Army & Navy Whiskey, Glass, Leaf Fern Patterns, 1900, 15 In. Diam.. 154.00
Sign, Pepsi-Cola, Cardboard, Counter-Spy Pepsi Radio Thriller..., 1940s, 19 x 8 In. 28.00
Sign, Pepsi-Cola, Plastic, 6 Pack Carrier Shape, Light-Up........................... 605.00
Sign, Rack, Coca-Cola, 1930s, 11 x 15 1/2 In.. 165.00
Sign, Schlitz, Beer Made Milwaukee Famous, Paper, Metal Frame, 1900, 39 x 28 In. ... 743.00
Sign, Snaider Syrup's Root Beer Drink, 5 Cents, Cardboard, 11 x 13 In................ 30.00
Sign, Squirt, Tin, 1941, 18 1/2 x 11 In. 60.00
Sign, Valley Brew, El Dorado Brewing Co., Stockton, Calif., Tin, 9 x 13 In............. 80.00
Sign, Warner's Safe Cure, Stanley, Group Of Natives, Frame, c.1900, 15 x 19 In. 1155.00
Sign, Yuengling's Beer, Pottsville, Pa., Multicolored, Blue Ground, Tin, 19 x 17 In. 200.00
Slumber Bag, Coca-Cola, 1986 .... 30.00
Spoon, Coca-Cola, Large 110.00
Stand, Use Congress Record Ink, Iron, 2 Snail Inkwells, Brass Inserts, Pat. 1978 .... 375.00
Stein, Avon, Animals, Ceramarte, 1976, 9 1/4 In.. 9.00
Stein, Avon, Baseball, Ceramarte, 1984, 8 1/2 In. 12.00
Stein, Avon, Cars, Ceramarte, 1979, 8 3/4 In... 11.00
Stein, Avon, Football, Ceramarte, 1983, 9 In... 20.00
Stein, Bud Light, Spuds MacKenzie, Light Bulb Shape, Thumbholder, 7 1/2 In. 19.00
Stein, Budweiser, Endangered Species, Bald Eagle, 7 In................................. 150.00
Stein, Budweiser, German Olympia 95.00
Stein, Budweiser, Incised A-Eagle, Sales Convention, 1977, 10 3/4 In. 86.00
Stein, Budweiser, Twig Handle, 1876-1976, 5 In. 345.00
Stein, Old Heidelberg, Sun, Green, Yellow, 1930s, 5 1/8 In............................... 13.00
Stein, Pabst, Holiday, 1985, 6 1/4 In.. 10.00
Stereo View, Excelsior Spring Bottling House, Saratoga, N.Y., Writing On Back 75.00
Stopper, Hires Root Beer, Metal, Rubber 20.00
Tap Knob, All Star Lager Beer, Wooden, For 1994 All Star Game In Pittsburgh 40.00
Tap Knob, Atlantic Beer, Black Plastic, Gold & Blue Insert, Celluloid Cover.............. 275.00
Tap Knob, Coors Light, Plastic, Baseball Top, Blue, Red & White, 8 1/2 In. 11.00
Tap Knob, Coors Light, Silver & Red Plastic, 8 1/2 In.................................... 3.00
Tap Knob, Hampden Ale, Chrome, Red, Black, Celluloid Cover, 2 In. 65.00
Tap Knob, Harvard Ale, Chrome, White On Red, Celluloid Cover, 2 In. 75.00
Tap Knob, Heileman's Old Style Lager, Black Ball, White, Maroon, Black, Insert........ 55.00
Tap Knob, Hensler Light Beer, Chrome, Red, Gold, Blue White, Celluloid Cover, 2 In. 35.00
Tap Knob, Krueger Ale, Green & White Enamel, Gold Border, Red Plastic 35.00
Tap Knob, McSorley Lager Beer, Red Plastic, Enameled, Brown & Gold On Cream..... 171.00
Tap Knob, Old Milwaukee, Metal, Plastic, 1960s, 6 In.................................... 6.00
Tap Knob, Old Topper Ale, Black Ball, Black, Brown, Gold On Cream, Enamel Insert. 65.00
Tap Knob, Schlitz, Metal, Plastic, Woman On Globe, 12 In.............................. 11.00
Tap Knob, Stroh's Beer, Black Ball, Bohemian Beer............................... 100.00
Thermometer, Bubble-Up, Bottle Pictured, Red, Green, White, 16 x 6 1/2 In. 30.00
Thermometer, Carter Ink, 1915... 400.00
Thermometer, Coca-Cola, Tin Over Cardboard, 1920s.................................... 704.00
Thermometer, Coca-Cola, Tin, 1950s, 17 In.. 55.00
Thermometer, Hires, Tin, Red & Blue, 13 3/4 In.. 85.00
Thermometer, Orange Crush 225.00
Thermometer, Pepsi-Cola, Single Dot, Metal, Blue & White, Red Ground, 27 In. 90.00
Thermometer, Rolling Rock Beer, Tin, Bottle Shape, 7 1/2 x 29 In....................... 45.00
Thermometer, Royal Crown Cola, Red, White, Yellow, 1950s, 25 x 10 In................. 95.00
Thermometer, Taka-Kola, Tin Over Cardboard, Girl Holding Bottle 532.00
Thermometer, Thirsty Just Whistle, Elves Holding Bottle, Metal, Cream, Navy Orange.. 733.00
Thermos, Dr. Pepper, Tin, Chevron, Small... 85.00
Tip Tray, Clysmic King Of Table Waters, Partially Nude Woman, Stag, Oval 132.00
Tip Tray, Coca-Cola Girl, 1909 .... 770.00
Tip Tray, Coca-Cola, Betty, 1914... 250.00

Go-Withs, Toy, Bottle Cap
Figures, Erotica, Pair

Go-Withs, Toy, Car,
Pepsi-Cola, 3 In.

Go-Withs, Tray,
Pabst Blue Ribbon

Tip Tray, Coca-Cola, Garden Girl, 1920... 115.00
Tip Tray, Coca-Cola, Relieves Fatigue, 1907 .... 1200.00
Tip Tray, Coca-Cola, Smiling Girl, 1924.. 400.00
Tip Tray, Drink Lemon Kola, Roanoke, Va., 5 Cents, In Bottles & At Fountains 77.00
Tip Tray, Goebel, Multicolored Man With Red Vest... 100.00
Tip Tray, J. Chr. G. Hupfel Brewing Co., Embossed Trademark, 4 In........................... 30.00
Token, P.T. Cavanaugh, Good For 1 Drink, Nickel, Silver 35.00
Toy, Airplane, Made From Pepsi-Cola Cans, 16 x 13 In...*Illus* 25.00
Toy, Bottle Cap Figures, Erotica, Pair...*Illus* 20.00
Toy, Bubble Blower, Machine Gun, Coca-Cola, Repainted, 1930s................................. 266.00
Toy, Car, Pepsi-Cola, 3 In...*Illus* 10.00
Toy, Truck, Delivery, Coca-Cola, Smitty Toys, 16 Wooden Cases, 1940....................... 500.00
Tray, 14th Anniversary Beer Drivers Union, Philadelphia, 1920s, 13 In. 72.00
Tray, American Brewing Co., Carnation Girl, 1908, 13 In. 200.00
Tray, Bavarian Beer-Ale Porter, Mt. Carbon Brewery, Pa., Metal, 1950s, 13 In. 30.00
Tray, Bevo, Beverage All Year Round Soft Drink, Beer Wagon, Round, 1910, 13 In..... 104.00
Tray, Coca-Cola, Autumn Girl, 1922, Rectangular... 880.00
Tray, Coca-Cola, Bathing Beauty, 1930, Rectangular... 700.00
Tray, Coca-Cola, Elaine, 1917, Rectangular... 330.00
Tray, Coca-Cola, Farm Boy With Dog, Rockwell, 1931, Rectangular............................ 1936.00
Tray, Coca-Cola, Frances Dee, 1933, Rectangular 616.00
Tray, Coca-Cola, From The Pansy Garden Series, 1961, 11 x 13 In................................ 40.00
Tray, Coca-Cola, Girl With Wind In Her Hair, 1943, Rectangular................................. 525.00
Tray, Coca-Cola, Girl, With Glass, 1912, 10 1/2 x 13 In... 731.00
Tray, Coca-Cola, Golf Couple, 1926 .... 430.00
Tray, Coca-Cola, Sailor Girl, 1940 ....160.00 to 385.00
Tray, Coca-Cola, Soda Fountain Clerk, 1927, Rectangular 1126.00
Tray, Coca-Cola, Summer Girl, 1921, Rectangular 700.00
Tray, Dr Pepper, Girl, Bottle Each Hand, 1930s, Rectangular.. 385.00
Tray, Empire Bottling Works, Chrome, Denver.. 125.00
Tray, Encore Beer, Monarch Brewing Co., Chicago, Ill. 27.00
Tray, Enjoy Piel's Beer, Bert & Harry, 1957, Round, 13 In. 10.00
Tray, Fitzgerald's Ale & Beer, Red & Black, Yellow Ground, 1940s, Round, 13 In........ 11.00
Tray, Ginger Ale, Topless Girl, 1908, Round, 12 1/2 In.. 4207.00
Tray, Gold Standard Lager Record Brewing Co., Cream Ale, Mountain & Stag, 12 In... 28.00
Tray, Grain Belt, Mountain Grown Hops, Multicolored, Round, 13 In. 15.00
Tray, Muehlbach Beer, Red & White, 1950s, Round, 13 In. 18.00
Tray, Pabst Beer, Tan & White Ground, 1950s, Round, 13 In. 15.00
Tray, Pabst Blue Ribbon...*Illus* 75.00
Tray, Pepsi-Cola, Bottle Cap, Single Dot, 1950s, 12 In... 35.00
Tray, Pepsi-Cola, Girl At Fountain, Oval, 1909 .... 1650.00
Tray, Stegmaier's Quality Beers, Wilkes-Barre, Pa., Lithograph Design, 1950s, 13 In... 35.00
Tray, Tally-Ho Beer, Coach & 4 Horses, White Ground, 12 In. 40.00
Whistle, Coca-Cola, Tin, 1930s 194.00
Window, Dubuque Brewing & Malting Co.'s Banquet Export Beer, 24 x 135 In............ 2500.00

K O V E L S

SEND ORDERS & INQUIRIES TO: **Crown Publishers, Inc.,**
c/o Random House, 400 Hahn Road,
Westminster, MD 21157

SALES & TITLE INFORMATION
1-800-733-3000

ATT: ORDER DEPT. _____

NAME _____

ADDRESS _____

CITY & STATE _____ ZIP _____

PLEASE SEND ME THE FOLLOWING BOOKS:

ITEM NO.	QTY.	TITLE		PRICE	TOTAL
84623	____	Kovels' Antiques & Collectibles Price List, 28th Edition	PAPER	$14.95	_____
80128	____	Kovels' American Art Pottery	HARDCOVER	$60.00	_____
4668X	____	American Country Furniture 1780 –1875	PAPER	$16.95	_____
01375	____	Kovels' Dictionary of Marks—Pottery & Porcelain	HARDCOVER	$16.00	_____
59145	____	Kovels' New Dictionary of Marks	HARDCOVER	$19.00	_____
88829	____	Kovels' American Silver Marks	HARDCOVER	$40.00	_____
84356	____	Kovels' Bottles Price List, 10th Edition	PAPER	$16.00	_____
83821	____	Kovels' Depression Glass & American Dinnerware Price List, 5th Edition	PAPER	$16.00	_____
78069	____	Kovels' Know Your Antiques, Revised and Updated	PAPER	$16.00	_____
88404	____	Kovels' Know Your Collectibles, Updated	PAPER	$16.00	_____
83139	____	Kovels' Guide to Buying, Selling, and Fixing Your Antiques and Collectibles	PAPER	$18.00	_____
83813	____	Kovels' Quick Tips: 799 Helpful Hints on How to Care for Your Collectibles	PAPER	$12.00	_____
	_____	TOTAL ITEMS	TOTAL RETAIL VALUE		_____

CHECK OR MONEY ORDER ENCLOSED
MADE PAYABLE TO CROWN PUBLISHERS, INC.
or telephone 1-800-733-3000
(No cash or stamps, please)

Charge: ☐ Master Card ☐ Visa ☐ American Express
Account Number (include all digits)   Expires MO.   YR.

_____

_____

Signature_____

Shipping & Handling
Charge $2.00 for one book;
50¢ for each additional book.
Please add applicable
sales tax.   _____

TOTAL AMOUNT DUE _____

PRICES SUBJECT TO CHANGE
WITHOUT NOTICE. If a more
recent edition of a price list has been
published at the same price, it
will be sent instead of the old edition.

Thank you for your order.